Restructuring Capitalism

T0298669

The main theme of this book is that, within contemporary capitalist societies a materialist outlook informed by science has triumphed creating the lack of a spiritual dimension to give meaning and purpose to the activities that are necessary for a capitalist society to function effectively. Capitalist societies are in trouble and need to be restructured to provide for the material needs of all the people who work within the system, not just the 1 percent, but because of the lack of a spiritual connection with each other and with nature, this is not likely to happen.

It has been said that society and the organizations within treat one another as objects to be manipulated in the interests of promoting economic growth and treat nature as an object to be exploited for the same purpose. This way of treating each other, and nature, is consistent with the way a capitalist system has worked in the past and was supposed to enable it to function efficiently to provide a fulfilling and enriched life for all its adherents through growth of the economy.

However, as capitalist societies have become dysfunctional they will need a different kind of orientation to continue in existence. *Restructuring Capitalism: Materialism and Spiritualism in Business* argues that what is needed is a new sense of a spiritualization of the self and its relation to others and to the establishment of a spiritual connection with nature in order for capitalism to be restructured to work for everyone and for the society as a whole.

Rogene A. Buchholz is the Legendre-Soule Chair in Business Ethics Emeritus in the College of Business Administration at Loyola University New Orleans. He has published more than seventy-five articles and is the author or coauthor of twelve books in the areas of business and public policy, business ethics, and the environment.

Routledge Studies in Business Ethics

For a full list of titles in this series, please visit www.routledge.com

Originating from both normative and descriptive philosophical backgrounds, business ethics implicitly regulates areas of behaviour which influence decision making, judgment, behaviour and objectives of the leadership and employees of an organization. This series seeks to analyse current and leading edge issues in business ethics, and the titles within it examine and reflect on the philosophy of business, corporations and organizations pertaining to all aspects of business conduct. They are relevant to the conduct of both individuals and organizations as a whole.

Based in academic theory but relevant to current organizational policy, the series welcomes contributions addressing topics including: ethical strategy; sustainable policies and practices; finance and accountability; CSR; employee relations and workers' rights; law and regulation; economic and taxation systems.

Restructuring Capitalism

Materialism and Spiritualism in Business

Rogene A. Buchholz

Routledge
Taylor & Francis Group

LONDON AND NEW YORK

First published 2017 by Routledge

2 Park Square, Milton Park, Abingdon, Oxfordshire OX14 4RN
52 Vanderbilt Avenue, New York, NY 10017

Routledge is an imprint of the Taylor & Francis Group, an informa business

First issued in paperback 2019

Library of Congress Cataloging-in-Publication Data
A catalog record for this book has been requested

ISBN: 978-1-138-63668-2 (hbk)
ISBN: 978-0-367-24299-2 (pbk)

Typeset in Sabon
by Apex CoVantage, LLC

This book is dedicated to Stephen Rosenthal and Leslie Jacobs, my son and daughter by marriage, whose lifelong business and civic practices embody the highest moral ideals and the deepest meaning of community.

Contents

Acknowledgments

This book was made possible by many people, including William C. Frederick, who was my mentor while I was studying for my doctorate at the University of Pittsburgh and has been a continual source for new insights into the nature of corporate social responsibility and business ethics. Throughout my career I have also learned a great deal from my interactions with colleagues in the field many of whom have been the best friends one could hope for and from my many students at all the schools where I have taught. They have been the source of many ideas about capitalism and its impact on society some of which have found their way into this book

This book would also not have been possible were it not for my wife, Sandra B. Rosenthal, who introduced me to classical American pragmatism and has helped me to think more philosophically in general. We have had many inspirational discussions about philosophical issues in relation to capitalism and have collaborated on numerous papers and lectures which we have jointly presented both in the United States and abroad. She read most of the chapters for this book and had several important suggestions for improvement. For all of her contributions to my life I am eternally grateful.

Since I retired from teaching I have been auditing philosophy, sociology, and political science classes at the University of Colorado at Denver, which has broadened my horizons and introduced me to new ways of thinking, so I would like to thank all the instructors and students in these courses that gave me new ideas about capitalism and introduced me to books and articles that were relevant to this book. It has been great fun to audit these courses and have the privilege of interacting with these faculty and the students in the classes I audited. It is like going back to school without having to write papers or take exams, the best of all possible worlds.

The people I worked with at Routledge (David Varley, my editor, and Brianna Ascher and Megan Smith, both editorial assistants), as well as Kevin Kelsey, project manager at Apex CoVantage, have been a pleasure to work with and were very helpful in getting this book published. This is the third book I have had accepted by Routledge, and I am very grateful for their support of my work on capitalism. Finally, I would like to thank two anonymous reviewers who read the book and made several suggestions for improvements. Their efforts are greatly appreciated and their suggestions made for a much better book.

Finally I would like to thank Roman and Littlefield Publishing Group for permission to use and rewrite content from a book titled *America In Conflict: The Deepening Values Divide* that I had previously published with their subsidiary Hamilton Books, to Pearson Education Group for permission to use and rewrite content from the fifth edition of a book I had previously published with Prentice Hall titled *Business Environment and Public Policy: Implications for Management,* and to Taylor and Francis Group LLC Books for permission to use and rewrite content from a previous book I published with Routledge titled *Reforming Capitalism: The Scientific Worldview and Business.* Their generosity is greatly appreciated.

Introduction

In my previous books I tried to present different ways of thinking about capitalism that led to suggestions for reforming the present system. In the first book titled *Rethinking Capitalism: Community and Responsibility in Business* I argued that the philosophical foundations of capitalism were individualism and rights, that this perspective needed to be broadened to include a sense of community in both business organizations themselves and their role in the larger society, and that rights entailed corresponding responsibilities to each other and society.[1] In the second book titled *Reforming Capitalism: The Scientific Worldview and Business* I tried to make the case that the scientific worldview influenced how we think about business and its role in society, and I then presented a different way of thinking about science and how this would impact our view of business and its responsibilities.[2] In both books I ended up making the case for an ethics of service to provide a moral foundation for business and its role in society.

In this book I want to go further with regard to some of the philosophical foundations of capitalism and discuss the materialistic basis of capitalism and its lack of a spiritual dimension. This lack has contributed to the current crises facing Western capitalistic societies with regard to their economic performance and their relationship to the physical environment. These societies based on traditional free-market capitalism do not seem to be working very well; instead of creating wealth, which is what they are supposed to be about, they have created nothing but debt for the past several decades and are now in serious trouble with regard to finding the wherewithal to keep on functioning as viable societies that can provide job opportunities for their workers and the promise of a better life in the future for their citizens.

The main thesis of the book is that we have lost a spiritual connection with each other and with nature.[3] We treat each other by and large as objects to be manipulated in the interests of promoting economic growth and treat nature as an object to be exploited for the same purpose. This way of treating each other and nature, a despiritualization of the self and nature, if you will, is consistent with the way a capitalist system works and is supposed to enable it to function efficiently. But capitalist societies have become dysfunctional and need a different kind of orientation to continue in existence.

However, I have come to the conclusion that no amount of reconceptualization of human relations in terms of a social self as I have done in previous books or reconceptualizing our relation with nature will change anything. What is needed is some kind of a spiritualization of the self and its relation to others and the establishment of a spiritual connection with nature.

At the outset I want to make clear that I will not be advocating any form of socialism as I believe that capital is best left in private hands. Having worked in several corporations I know that they can be bureaucratic and involve collective decision making as modern technology has made it necessary to involve more people with technological expertise in the decision making process.[4] But the thought of any kind of social ownership of production that involves a collective decision-making process that most likely would be government and its politicians making decisions about the allocation of resources for the production of private goods and services in a timely and efficient manner is impossible to imagine. And I also believe that the market is the most efficient means to allocate resources for the production of private goods and services, or perhaps more fundamentally, the best way to determine the value of all the things that go into the production process and the things that come out of it and are available to consumers. There is no way that I am advocating centralized economic planning to replace the market as countries that tried this like the former Soviet Union with its five- and ten-year plans were not able to provide consumer goods and services on a large enough scale to satisfy the material needs of its citizens.

Societies that organized themselves completely around communist philosophy have collapsed, and while they may remain politically centralized as in China, they have had to decentralize their economies to some extent to encourage entrepreneurship and provide incentives for their citizens to do the work necessary to grow their economies. So I hope readers of this book will pay careful attention to these paragraphs because while I may be critical of capitalism in some instances, I do not want to be immediately branded as a socialist or, worse yet, a communist. These terms are thrown around all too loosely to brand something or someone that politicians or others don't happen to like or agree with and, rather than engage in rational argument or discussion, hope to dismiss them by branding them as socialistic or communist.

Obamacare, for example, has been branded by many politicians as socialistic, but it is nothing of the kind. Private insurance companies still exist to insure people, and Obamacare has expanded their market. Medical services are still provided by private hospitals and medical centers, and government in no way tells people what doctors they can see or can't see to get medical care. We do not have a single-payer system except for elderly people like myself that many experts think is more efficient than private insurance, but in any event I can choose which doctors I want to use and what hospitals I want to go to if necessary which unfortunately becomes more of a necessity as one gets older.

In the 2016 presidential campaign Bernie Sanders was branded a socialist, but he was also nothing of the kind. He never to my knowledge advocated government takeover of the means of production, which is what socialism means. He was a democratic socialist in that he wanted free medical care and free education for everybody like the democratic socialist Scandinavian countries provide for their citizens. Politicians and pundits ought to be more precise in their use of terms such as this; otherwise, they come to have no meaning at all and might as well be dropped from our vocabulary.

But I also want readers to take note that I mentioned private goods and services in the foregoing paragraphs. The market cannot provide for all of a society's needs and societies that organize themselves completely around market philosophy are also bound to collapse. There is something called the common good, I believe, and public goods and services that promote this common good. These goods and services will most likely be provided by the government so that the government does have a role to play in helping its citizens live full and prosperous lives. Public goods like clean air cannot be provided by the market, and this is not due to market failure, as it is often called, but simply due to the fact that market systems as they emerged in Western societies are not capable of responding to the demand for public goods and services. Government action is most often necessary to provide these goods and services and keep the market going as will be described in the first chapter. The most important decision a society often has to make is what goods and services are truly private and which are public in nature. Differences between the market system and the public policy process are further examined in a later chapter.

The first task in this book is to examine these crises capitalism faces and to look more closely at what is going on underneath the surface. This book thus attempts to go beyond the usual explanations for the problems capitalist societies are facing and looks for deeper philosophical problems that are of increasing importance. It is argued that Western societies, in general, and the United States, in particular, have become more and more materialistic in their outlook and lack a spiritual dimension that would enable their citizens to live better and more fulfilling lives. This materialistic outlook has resulted in the development of quantitative measures to determine how individuals, families, and country as a whole are doing. Success depends on these measures that are themselves materialistic in nature.

The first chapter thus contains an examination of what I call the materialistic crisis of capitalism, a crisis that stems from the problems that capitalism has posed for our society over the last century or so and how these problems have been addressed by public policy measures that have gotten the country into more and more debt such that we can no longer spend our way out of the troubles we experience. What happened in Greece during the second decade of the twenty-first century is perhaps only a harbinger of what capitalistic societies in general face at some time in the near future. The question is whether the capitalist system is affordable or whether it causes so many problems that have to be addressed that it is no longer a viable economic system as it currently exists and has to be drastically reformed or restructured in some fashion.

Then in the next chapter, what I call the spiritual crisis of capitalism is discussed by examining the philosophical writings of several scholars who have something to say about the spiritual dimension of our society and its relation to capitalism. In the third chapter I examine the state of politics and our relationship to nature in the United States, where the lack of a spiritual dimension most clearly manifests itself. The lack of a spiritual connection with each other has resulted in a dysfunctional government, and the lack of a spiritual relationship to nature has resulted in environmental problems that are unprecedented and have not been adequately addressed so that they continue to threaten the continued existence of the human race the world over. These three chapters constitute the first part of the book.

The second part of the book deals with various sources of spirituality that exist in American society. The spiritual dimension in this country has traditionally been left to religion, but religion has failed to provide for the spiritual needs its citizens. Science has relegated religion to focus on the supernatural, it is argued in the fourth chapter, and that has made religion less and less relevant to the everyday needs of people living in a natural world that is more and more explained and controlled by a materialistic science. In this chapter I also discuss the increasing involvement of the Christian religion in politics and how this has reduced religion to just another interest group competing for government favors, which has affected its ability to transcend materialistic concerns. The upshot of this discussion of religion is that the spiritual dimension of existence has atrophied in the United States and in Western societies, in general, and a more religious society is not the answer as it is becoming more and more irrelevant to contemporary economic, political, and social problems. This has left people with a spiritual void that they have attempted to fill with the material stuff produced by a capitalistic society. But this has not worked and has resulted in overuse of resources, environmental problems, and debt at unprecedented levels.

In the rest of this second part of the book I examine several other sources of spiritualism including what are called the New Atheists that have attacked traditional religions including both mainstream and evangelical religions and offer a different approach to life that does not involve the supernatural. In the next chapter several what I call secular paths to discovering the spiritual dimension in our existence are discussed that offer the promise of enhancing our lives and enabling us to live life to the fullest. Finally a movement that attempted to introduce spiritualism in the workplace will be examined as to the ability of this movement to make spiritualism relevant to the everyday working lives of people who work for capitalistic institutions.

Marxist thought will be discussed in the beginning chapter of the next part which deals with two major critiques of capitalism, as it sort of came back from the dead during the Great Recession of 2008. In this chapter

Marxism and its main tenants are examined along with a critique of its methods and relevance to today's world. The next chapter consists of a discussion of critical theory, which grew out of Marxism after the Second World War, and constitutes a different way of looking at capitalism and advocates certain changes to capitalism to overcome the dominance and instrumental thinking that constitutes the capitalist system. These critiques are examined as to whether they contain any kind of a spiritual dimension that would enable a spiritual connection with nature and each other.

The fourth part of the book deals with certain problems with spiritualism in American society including a chapter on science and the problems it poses for the existence of a spiritual dimension in society. Science has a particular worldview that is materialistic in outlook, and this approach provides a serious challenge to the reality of anything spiritualistic in nature. This leads into a discussion of the mind–body problem in the second chapter examining the question of whether the mind, particularly consciousness, can be fully explained with a materialistic approach by reducing the mind to the brain which can then be examined by scientific methods. Does this approach do away with any possibility of a spiritual dimension to reality? The next chapter in this section presents an alternative view of science based on a philosophical approach called classical American pragmatism that offers hope to overcome the problems that the traditional understanding of science poses for a vibrant spirituality. It is argued that science will have to be reconstituted to enable a spiritual connection with nature. Politics are also revisited in the final chapter of this section, where I argue that the ideology of radical individualism will have to be overcome to have a fully functional politics in the United States that is based on a spiritual connection with each other that will make the economy and democracy work for all its citizens.

The last section includes several chapters that discuss a new understanding of capitalism and the society in which it is embedded that is necessary for the spiritual dimension to be revived. The first chapter in this section deals with the use of numbers to represent wealth, where I argue that material wealth is a fiction and what financial numbers really represent is power over other people's lives. Thus, our society is currently experiencing vast inequalities of power and not wealth. This chapter also treats other uses of numbers in the economy and the power they have over management decision making in some instances. The next chapter examines how the market and public policy work and how they both are necessary to create a fully functional society. The third chapter in this section deals with the spirit of capitalism in both the traditional sense of the Protestant ethic and contemporary writings that advocate a new ethic for modern capitalism. Finally the book ends with a discussion of the future of capitalism by examining several writings that analyze what is wrong with capitalism and advocate solutions to make the system viable. This chapter ends with a rather radical proposal to restructure capitalism by broadening the understanding of capital and changing corporate governance to be consistent with this perspective.

At the outset terms such as *materialism* and *spiritualism* should be defined or at least some working definition spelled out for purposes of understanding what the book is about. Materialism is a metaphysical theory of reality that holds that the only thing that actually exists in the world we experience is matter, that physical matter is the only substance that exists and therefore the only fundamental reality. All the things we experience in the world are composed of matter, and all phenomena, including consciousness itself, are the result of interactions between different kinds of matter. In this view, mind or spirit is a product of matter acting upon matter. Matter is the primary or only reality and everything that we consider to be a spiritual dimension can ultimately be reduced to matter. According to Philip Clayton, who is a professor of religion and philosophy at the Claremont Graduate University in California, materialism has five essential components or central theses as he calls them.[5]

Five Central Theses of Materialism

1. Matter is the fundamental constituent of the natural world.
2. Forces act on matter.
3. The fundamental material particles or "atoms"—together with the fundamental physical forces, whatever they turn out to be—determine the motion of all objects in nature. Thus, materialism entails determinism.
4. All more complex objects that we encounter in the natural world are aggregates of these fundamental particles, and their motions and behaviors can ultimately be understood in terms of the fundamental physical forces acting on them. Nothing exists that is not the product of these same particles and forces. In particular, there are no uniquely biological forces (vitalism or "entelechies"), no conscious forces (dualism), and no divine forces (what came to be known as supernaturalism). Thus, materialism implied the exclusion of dualism, downward causation, and divine activity.
5. Materialism is an *ontological* position, as it specifies what kinds of things do and do not exist. But it can also become a thesis concerning what may and may not count as a scientific explanation. When combined with a commitment to scientific reduction, for example, it entails that all scientific explanations should ultimately be reducible to the explanations of fundamental physics. Any other science, say, biology or psychology, is incomplete until we uncover the laws that link its phenomena with physics. In its reductionist form—which historically has been its most typical form—materialism thus excludes interpretations of science that allow for "top-down" causation, also known as "strong emergence." Materialists may be divided on whether and if so how soon, these reductions will actually be accomplished. Still, it is an entailment of materialism in most of its modern forms that an omniscient knower would be able to reduce all higher-order phenomena to the locations and momentums of fundamental particles.[6]

There are two general principles of materialism: (1) its *monism*, which is an attempt to explain everything in the world according to a single principle, and (2) its *naturalism*, which means that everything in nature can be explained with natural laws without recourse to the supernatural.[7] Materialism involves a denial of the existence of spirit as it is considered to be something the lies outside the scope of its philosophy and the reductionstic claims of modern science. While materialism existed as a way of thinking about the nature of the world before the rise of modern science, it fits in well with the reductionistic scientific worldview. Materialists believe that the natural sciences will eventually be able to understand all human thought, including consciousness, in terms of neural structures, chemical composition, and electrodynamics of the brain and central nervous system. "When the knowledge of all things has been reduced to fundamental particles and universal physical laws . . . the victory of materialism will be complete."[8]

Before the rise of modern science, Christian thinkers presupposed the world to be composed of two parts, the material and the spiritual, existing alongside one another as independent yet interacting realms. With the emergence of classical materialism in the eighteenth and nineteenth centuries, however, the world of material particles was claimed to be the sole reality and all genuine knowledge about nature and humanity "must be reduced to the causal powers inherent in the interplay between basic physical constituents."[9] Thus, matter replaced God as the ultimate reality, and the realm of the mental was excluded as a genuine existing thing that had some kind of substance. As put by the two editors of a book titled *Information and the Nature of Reality*:

> For centuries, Isaac Newton's idea of matter as consisting of 'solid, massy, hard, impenetrable, and movable particles' reigned in combination with a strong view of laws of nature that were supposed to prescribe exactly, on the basis of the present physical situation, what was going to happen in the future. This complex of scientific materialism and mechanism was easily amalgamated with common-sense assumptions of solid matter as the bedrock of all reality. In the worldview of classical materialism, it was claimed that all physical systems are nothing but collections of inert particles slavishly complying with deterministic laws. Complex systems such as living organisms, societies, and human persons, could, according to this reductionistic world view, ultimately be explained in terms of material components and their chemical reactions.

Given this scientific emphasis on matter it is clear that materialism involves a preoccupation with material things as the most important things in life as opposed to that which is spiritual in nature. We live in a world surrounded by matter, and if science tells us that matter is the only thing that exists, it is easy to extrapolate from this philosophy, come to be distracted from spiritual pursuits by material possessions, become obsessed by the desire to obtain them, and go to great lengths to enhance the number of material things we possess. It is in the interests of the business community to perpetuate and enhance this philosophy so that people buy the material things business produces. It is what keeps a capitalistic system going, and it is necessary to keep creating new needs that these material possessions can fulfill. A satisfied consumer is anathema to the system, and business must continue to promote material goods as the way to the good life and continue to create dissatisfied consumers who will continue to purchase the material things business produces. Thus, the metaphysical concept of matter as being all that counts and the materialism that keeps capitalism going go hand in hand. This materialistic approach to reality, however, can be problematical. As stated by Iddo K. Wernick in an article titled "Living in a Material World,"

> [t]he materialistic approach influences not only how the United States sees itself, but how it sees other societies as well. The notion that aggregate wealth offers the best proxy for measuring social progress is not universal. Other cultures may aspire to a more equitable wealth distribution, greater national prominence, recognized technological prowess, or the exalted glory of God. These social goals remain important to societies around the globe and influence national-level decisionmaking in much of the world. The successes of neoliberalism notwithstanding, seeing the world through a strictly materialist lens may systematically underestimate the importance of the religious and cultural forces that motivate societies.[10]

Spirituality refers to a reality that transcends the material world and leads to the deepest values and meanings by which people live out their lives in the material world. Spiritual practices such as meditation, prayer, and contemplation can lead to an experience of connectedness with a larger reality that includes other individuals or the human community and can extend to nature or the universe as a whole. Spirituality can encompass beliefs in nonmaterial realities or experiences that transcend the material world. It can also involve a sense of the sacred, where some things are experienced as set apart from the ordinary and are worthy of special attention and veneration. Human consciousness is presumed to exist apart from and yet within the body, which is connected not only to the material world but to also to a spiritual world.

Many religions regard spirituality as an integral part of religious experience, and many people equate spirituality with religion. So successful has this materialist science been, however, it appears to have triumphed over religion. Astronomers have looked out into deep space, to the edges of the known universe; cosmologists have looked back into "deep time," to the beginning of creation; and physicists have looked into the "deep structures" of matter, to the fundamental constituents of the cosmos. From quarks to quasars, they find no evidence of God. Nor do they find any need for God. The universe seems to work perfectly well without any divine assistance.[11]

In doing away with the notion of some almighty supernatural being, Western science would appear to have done away with religion and, hence, with spirituality. Yet the real concern of spirituality is not with the realms of deep space, time, or matter but with the meaning and purpose of life and the kind of worldview we bring with us to interpret life's experiences. It is concerned with the development of consciousness and holds that this aspect of our being cannot be reduced to neurons firing in the brain, that there is more to consciousness than a material approach can begin to fathom. The growth of secularism in the Western world has resulted in a broader view of spirituality that can be considered separately from religion and that recognizes aspects of human experience that cannot be captured by a purely materialistic view of the world without accepting belief in the supernatural. There is no necessary connection between spirituality and religious belief. Spirituality can be sought through movements such as the environmental movement that can promote an ecological spirituality or through the effort of some scholars to introduce spirituality into the workplace.

Science is a way of describing our world, but as well as we have been served by science, there are times and places where our scientific knowledge is incomplete and in some cases absolutely wrong.[12] While science tells us how things work, spiritual traditions tell us how to apply such knowledge. Together each serves a part of a greater whole and gives us a greater understanding of our place in the universe and the wisdom needed to embrace the promise of our future and survive the greatest challenges that humans have ever faced.[13] Threats of war, disease, terrorism, dwindling resources, and climate change are all happening at the same time, and their sheer magnitude makes our current situation unprecedented. By overcoming the boundaries that separate materialistic science and a secular spirituality we can open the door to discoveries that will solve our deepest mysteries and perhaps even assure our survival into the future.[14]

Notes

1 Rogene A. Buchholz, *Rethinking Capitalism: Community and Responsibility in Business* (New York: Routledge, 2009).
2 Rogene A. Buchholz, *Reforming Capitalism: The Scientific Worldview and Business* (New York: Routledge, 2012).
3 Perhaps we never had a spiritual connection in the first place so there was nothing to lose, but I will leave that question for another time.
4 See John Kenneth Galbraith, *The New Industrial State* (New York: Houghton Mifflin, 1967).
5 Paul Davies and Niels Henrik Gregersen, "Introduction: Does Information Matter?" in Paul Davies and Niels Henrik Gregersen, eds., *Information and the Nature of Reality: From Physics to Metaphysics* (New York: Cambridge University Press, 2010), 1.

6 Philip Clayton, "Unsolved Dilemmas: The Concept of Matter in the History of Philosophy and in Contemporary Physics," in Paul Davies and Niels Henrik Gregersen, eds., *Information and the Nature of Reality: From Physics to Metaphysics* (New York: Cambridge University Press, 2010), 38–39.

7 Frederick C. Beiser, *After Hegel: German Philosophy 1840–1900* (Princeton, NJ: Princeton University Press, 2014), 81.

8 Clayton, "Unsolved Dilemmas," 53.

9 Niels Henrik Gregersen, "Introduction: Does Information Matter?," in Paul Davies and Niels Henrik Gregersen, eds., *Information and the Nature of Reality: From Physics to Metaphysics* (New York: Cambridge University Press, 2010), 1.

10 Iddo K. Wernick, "Living in a Material World," *Issues in Science and Technology* (Winter, 2014), 30.

11 Peter Russell, "Exploring Deep Mind," in Daniel Goleman, ed., *Measuring the Immeasurable: The Scientific Case for Spirituality* (Boulder, CO: Sounds True, 2008), 2.

12 Gregg Braden, "The Power and Promise of Spiritually Based Science," in Daniel Goleman, ed., *Measuring the Immeasurable: The Scientific Case for Spirituality* (Boulder, CO: Sounds True, 2008), 171.

13 Ibid., 174.

14 Ibid., 181–182.

Part I
The Crises of Capitalism

1 The Material Crisis of Capitalism

There is not much doubt that capitalistic economies have been more productive than any kind of socialism that has appeared in history. They have delivered an unprecedented array of material goods to those who have lived in such societies and have generated more so-called material wealth than any other kind of economic organization. Material incentives have proved to be effective in motivating people to work and take the risks involved in bringing a new product to market. The freedom to do what one wants and pursue one's self-interest within a system that minimizes bureaucratic interference leads to a high level of innovation and growth of the economy. Thus, even countries like Russia and China have adopted some form of capitalism to grow their economies and provide for the material needs of their citizens.

But capitalistic systems are not without problems. When a concept such as freedom is particularized in an economic system, all kinds of problems emerge over time that have to be addressed for the system to continue. In our society, those problems have been addressed by public policy measures designed to keep free-market capitalism functioning and providing benefits to the society as a whole. These benefits for society are not the result of unfettered capitalism working its way throughout history based on the inexorable laws of economics but are the result of conscious decisions by public policy makers to make the system work for all of society.

Concentration

One such problem that appeared in the late nineteenth century was the emergence of *concentration* in most major industries. Competition as a regulator of business behavior seemed to be disappearing during this period with the emergence of large-scale business enterprises that could exercise some degree of control over the economy. Free-market capitalism seemed to be destroying itself through such concentration and predatory competitive practices. Such developments awakened American's long-standing fear of concentrations of power whether political or economic. The concentration of economic power was unacceptable as it was believed that such power over markets would be used to ride roughshod over the public interest.

Indeed, it seems that common sense would lead one to understand how a concentrated system could happen. There are no scientific laws that assure that competition is going to continue in a completely unregulated system. Some companies are always going to be better than others in providing products people want to buy and being able to be more efficient and offer their products at a lower price. Some companies may be smarter than others or just plain lucky to be in the right place at the right time. Business managers don't like competition, and the goal of a business enterprise is to eliminate the competition in whatever way possible and to gain some control over their environment. What this means is that in a completely unregulated system some companies will emerge winners and gain a dominant market share even if they compete honestly. Others will engage in predatory practices such as price-fixing or price discrimination in order to gain a competitive advantage, meaning that other companies will have to do the same in order to remain in business and competitive behavior will sink to the lowest common denominator.

Government thus passed antitrust laws to prevent these things from happening and keep the system functioning. Antitrust laws focus on structure in making sure that competition continues to exist and industries do not become overly concentrated, and conduct in preventing companies from engaging in anticompetitive practices that would destroy the competitive process. The goals of antitrust policy are to maintain a workable competition, often defined as a system where there is reasonably free entry into most markets, no more than moderate concentration, an ample number of buyers and sellers, and the promotion of fair competition by not allowing competitors to engage in anticompetitive practices that would undermine the competitive process.

The Sherman Act of 1890 was the first piece of antitrust legislation. The most important parts of the Act are the first and second sections. The first section attacks the act of combining or conspiring to restrain trade and focuses on anticompetitive methods of competition or firm behavior. This section seems to make illegal every formal agreement among firms aimed at curbing independent action on the market. The second section enjoins market structures where seller concentration is so high that it approaches or attains a monopoly position.

The Clayton Act of 1914 attacked a series of business policies insofar as they could substantially lessen competition or tend toward creation of a monopoly position. The language of the Sherman Act was quite broad, leaving a good deal of uncertainty as to what specific practices were in restraint of trade and thus illegal. The Clayton Act was passed to correct this deficiency by being more specific and barring price discrimination (later supplemented by the Robinson–Patman Act), tying arrangements, and exclusive dealing arrangements. It also contained a section that was designed to slow down the merger movement by forbidding mergers that substantially lessened competition of tended to create a monopoly (later strengthened by the Cellar–Kefauver Amendments).

The Federal Trade Commission Act of 1914 created the Federal Trade Commission (FTC), which was empowered to protect consumers against all "unfair methods of competition in or affecting commerce." What methods of competition were unfair was left up to the commission itself to decide. In 1938 the Wheeler–Lea Act amended this language to include "unfair or deceptive acts of practices in commerce," thus giving the FTC authority to pursue deceptive advertising and other marketing practices that did not necessarily affect competition.

Subsequent developments included upgrading the penalties for violations of the Sherman Act in 1955, declaring that violations would be considered felonies rather than misdemeanors in 1974, and in 1990 upgrading the penalties again. The Hart–Scott–Rodino Antitrust Improvements Act of 1976 gave the Justice Department broadened authority to interview witnesses and gather other evidence in antitrust investigations. It also provided for premerger notification requiring large companies planning mergers to give federal antitrust authorities advance notice of their plans, which gives the agencies time to study the proposal and take action to block the merger before it is consummated if is deemed to be anticompetitive. The act also allowed state attorneys general to sue antitrust violators in federal court on behalf of overcharged consumers.

The application of these antitrust laws has been anything but consistent. The intentionally vague language of these laws allows each administration to interpret and enforce the laws in accordance with its economic philosophy. There are benefits to large-scale production, distribution, and organization such as economies of scale; more efficient coordination; and increased research and development expenditures. It is not clear that either a competitive or a concentrated system is superior in terms of pricing or innovations that are of importance to society. The antitrust laws thus maintain an allegiance to the ideals of competition and institutionalize the society's fear of large concentrations of power. Yet their application is flexible to allow the benefits of concentrated industries to be exploited when society deems appropriate.

Destructive Forms of Competition

A second problem resulted in industry regulation that proved to be an acceptable way to stabilize some industries that were believed to be inherently chaotic and where *destructive forms of competition* were likely to appear. Such was the case with the railroad industry in 1887 when the Interstate Commerce Commission (ICC) was established to provide continuous surveillance of private railroad activity across the country. Although some states had practiced such regulation before the federal government intervened, the inability of states to regulate railroads effectively led to passage of the act that created the ICC, which set the pattern for additional regulatory commissions of this type. The ICC was an innovation because it represented a new location of power in the federal system and served as a prototype for regulation by an independent commission as federal regulatory powers were extended into other areas of industry and commerce.

Other commissions such as the Federal Power Commission (FPC), the Civil Aeronautics Board (CAB), the Federal Communications Commission (FCC), and the Securities and Exchange Commission (SEC) soon followed. This type of regulation focuses on a specific industry and is concerned with its economic well-being as well as the way business is being conducted in the industry. The major concerns of the ICC, for example, are with rates, routes, and the obligation to serve. The FPC was created to regulate an industry such as utility companies, where natural monopolies exist such that one firm may be able to supply the market more cheaply and efficiently than several smaller firms. Since competition cannot serve as a regulator in these instances, government must perform this function to regulate these industries in the public interest. The CAB was created to prevent destructive competition in the airline industry and to see that service was provided to small towns and cities that would be ignored by the market. The FCC was created to allocate a limited space to broadcasters, among other things. And the SEC was created to prevent fraud and deception in the securities industry, something the industry cannot do for itself.

Over time many began to view these regulated industries as nothing more than government-supported cartels, where companies in the industry earned higher profits and charged higher prices than if competition prevailed. Thus, a deregulatory trend began to develop in 1978 when Congress passed a deregulation bill aimed at air passenger service. The bill allowed airlines to offer new services without CAB approval and granted them a great degree of freedom to raise and lower their fares. The CAB itself went out of existence with its remaining activities transferred to other agencies. Companies in the railroad industry were given the right to charge as little or as much as they pleased for hauling certain goods instead of following ICC-approved rates. Similar pressures mounted to deregulate some aspects of the trucking industry and to abolish some of the FCC's control over commercial radio and television broadcasting.

Instability

Another such problem appeared in the late 1920s when the Great Depression started. The system was seen to be *inherently unstable* due to over-investment and under-consumption and needed government action to try and stabilize things. While there had been boom and bust periods before this event, it was the Great Depression that brought the issue to a head so to speak. During this period the bottom dropped out of the economy, as the stock market crashed, banks closed their doors, people were thrown out of work, others lost their savings, and thousands of businesses went bankrupt.

The traditional approach to downturns of this nature was based upon a view of the economy as a self-correcting system. Unemployment would drive down the price of labor to the point where companies would find it profitable to hire people again. These workers would then buy more products so demand would begin to increase. Factories that were lain idle drove down the price of borrowing money to the point where entrepreneurs would find it feasible to take out loans and create new enterprises. Thus, an upward spiral would be set in motion that would eventually pull the economy out of a depression. Prosperity would thus be restored if people would just be patient and resist attempts to hasten this process with government intervention.

Roosevelt won the election of 1932 by promising a new deal for the American people. The depression was such a shock to the self-confidence of the nation and the distress it caused was so widespread that people came to fear that self-correction would not happen soon enough to do any good. They were not willing to sit in their Hoovervilles and starve to death while waiting for the market to correct itself. The traditional view of an inherently self-correcting market proved bankrupt to deal with the problems of the depression. The unregulated market was too unstable and too slow-moving to be trusted. People, including business leaders, wanted action, and they wanted it immediately. The Roosevelt administration promised action.

The New Deal consisted of a series of public policy measures that were unprecedented in American history. The federal government assumed responsibility for stimulating business activity to escape an economic depression. It sought to relieve the distresses that the adverse economic situation had placed on business, farmers, workers, homeowners, consumers, investors, and other groups. In the famous 100 days that followed Roosevelt's swearing in as president, the president asked for and Congress speedily granted an unprecedented amount of legislation that plunged the federal government deeply and unalterable into the affairs of the economy. This flow of legislation set the stage for the role that government would play generations later and dramatically increased the importance of public policy to society as a whole and to business, in particular.[1]

Many believed that Roosevelt, instead of being an enemy of free-market capitalism, actually saved the system and prevented a reformist movement from gaining much headway in moving the country along the road toward some form of socialism. Roosevelt himself saw the New Deal as a set of programs to save the free-enterprise system by fusing welfare benefits to a capitalist foundation to assure the system's long-term stability. For capitalism to survive he believed that reckless speculation and unregulated fluctuation would have to be eliminated and that, with government assistance, business could regulate itself for its own benefit and for the overall benefit of society.[2]

In any event, the public policy measures that came out of the early part of the New Deal were part of a social welfare program designed to help victims of the depression. The idea that public works programs, for example, should be designed to stimulate the economy through deficit spending had not yet taken root in the thinking of policy makers. The immediate problem was to relieve the widespread distress that the depression had caused. Only later did economic theories emerge to support the notion of ongoing government involvement to stabilize the system through countercyclical spending.[3]

These new theoretical developments came primarily from the thinking of John Maynard Keynes and his followers in the form of what has since come to be called Keynesian economics that provides a justification for large-scale public-works programs. Keynes believed that traditional economic theories based on a self-correcting system were wrong on two counts: (1) in the real world, prices and wages did not fall as expected because of rigidities built into the system and (2) a reduction in wages of sufficient magnitude to enable business to begin to hire workers again lowers a worker's income drastically and therefore reduces even further the total demand for goods and services in the economy.[4]

The fundamental problem, according to Keynes, was this deficiency in demand, especially the demand for investment goods by business, which kept the economy at low levels of output and employment. Because of this deficiency of demand, the economy could reach equilibrium at any level of activity, not only at full employment but also at the devastating low point of economic misery reached during the Depression.[5] Thus, if no one else could spend money, government should prime the pump, so to speak, by putting money back into the economy to stimulate the demand for goods and services. Because of the multiplier effect, government expenditures would be magnified throughout the economy.[6]

Eventually these notions took root and composed a new theoretical rationale for government policymakers, culminating in the Employment Act of 1946, which formally gave government the responsibility of managing the economy on an ongoing basis rather than just stimulating it in crisis situations like a depression. Government's role was to even out business cycles by pumping money into the economy when necessary through direct expenditures or by cutting taxes, dampening demand by raising taxes, stimulating investment by cutting interest rates, raising interest rates to control inflation when the economy appeared to be overheating, becoming the employer of last resort, and using other measures at its disposal to maintain a stable economic environment in which business and the society at large could prosper.

The idea that the market was self-regulating in this regard was rejected. It was believed that a completely unregulated market system was excessively prone to waves of overinvestment and excess capacity with deficient spending and underemployment of resources. Such boom-and-bust periods as had been experienced throughout much of capitalism's history were simply unacceptable. Management of the economy by government to promote stability of employment and purchasing power became a matter of public policy. Rather than trusting the market and succumbing to the ups and downs of normal cyclical behavior, government was given the responsibility for keeping inflation under control and creating the conditions for continuing economic prosperity.

Labor–Management Relations

Another area of public policy that came out of the depression to address a problem with the capitalistic system was in the way *labor–management relations* had developed in the system. The ordeal of the working class during the years of the Depression ignited a militancy that swept the country and revolutionized the industrial relations system. This militancy forced the federal government to intervene in labor–management relations and to adopt a national labor policy designed to protect the rights of workers to unionize. Out of this intervention came a revived labor movement, the development of collective bargaining, and an end to management's unilateral control of the workplace.[7]

Workers found that an unregulated market system, particularly during periods of recession and depression when there was what could be called a large reserve army of the unemployed, did not allow them to address problems they were experiencing with the workplace, including long hours, poor working conditions, low wages, and arbitrary hiring and firing practices. Individual workers had no bargaining power to correct these conditions in the face of the collective power of management. To deal with this situation they began to form collectives of their own called unions to counter this power of management. Before the Depression, however, management held an overwhelming advantage over unions. The courts upheld the right of employers to do almost anything to prevent workers from organizing. Companies could fire workers for joining unions, force them to sign a pledge not to join a union as a condition of employment, and require them to belong to company-controlled unions and to spy on them to stop unionization before it started. Attempts to form unions under these conditions were not very successful and before the Depression worker's interest in unionism was declining.[8]

The National Industrial Recovery Act (NIRA) rekindled interest in unionism. This act authorized businesses to form trade associations to regulate production of goods and services, and union leaders insisted that the bill also give employees the right to organize and bargain collectively with management. When the NIRA was found unconstitutional in 1935, a more comprehensive labor relations law called the Wagner Act was passed. The Wagner Act not only extended to workers the right to organize and bargain collectively; it also proscribed employer actions that interfered with that right and established the National Labor Relations Board as the enforcement mechanism to monitor employee actions in this regard.[9]

With this framework in place, unions grew in number and influence peaking in 1954 when they represented 35 percent of the workforce. Total union membership peaked in 1979 at 21 million. In 1980 they still represented

20.1 percent of the workforce, but with the election of the Reagan administration that same year, power began to shift back to management. The breaking of the air traffic controllers strike in 1981 was a critical event in weakening the strength of the unions. By 2010 union membership had declined to 11.9 percent of the private workforce, representing some 14.8 million workers. Increasingly unions turned to the public sector to gain membership. In 2011 unions represented 37 percent of public-sector employees, or 7.6 million people, compared with only 6.9 percent of private-sector employees, comprising 7.2 million people.[10]

The largest portion of public-sector employees that were unionized worked for local governments as teachers, police officers, or firefighters. In 2011 unions represented 43.2 percent of these employees.[11] Several states under Republican leadership engaged in union-busting efforts during the 2010–2012 conservative revolution. The Republican legislature in Wisconsin, along with the governor's support, passed a law that eviscerated collective bargaining rights for public-sector employees with the exception of police and firefighters. This resulted in mass protests of the part of public-sector employees and their supporters and a recall election of the governor in 2012 that returned him to office. A similar law in Ohio was struck down by a vote to repeal the legislation.

Entitlement Programs

Entitlement programs also grew out of the Depression. Many people were victims of circumstances beyond their control. They were willing and able to work, but there were simply no jobs available during the depression. Government accepted the responsibility to help who were not necessarily to blame for their situation. It was during these years that a philosophy of entitlements began to take hold in the society at large; people began to feel entitled to a good job, that they had a right to retire with dignity, that they were entitled to a minimum amount of food if they could not provide for themselves and their families, and that health care was a right for certain groups like the poor and elderly.[12]

The market left to its own devices was not perceived as taking care of these needs and respecting these rights, so the government stepped up by passing a number of entitlement programs to meet these needs. First was Social Security, which guaranteed that people would have at least some money to live on when they retired. Then came Aid to Families with Dependent Children (AFDC), which was a welfare program designed to aid poor families who could not provide adequate provisions for their children. Then came Medicaid to provide health care for the poor and Medicare to provide health care for senior citizens. The food stamp program was designed to provide food to those too poor to provide a basic level of nutrition for themselves.

The largest growth of these entitlement programs took place in the 1960s and 1970s as the nation mounted an effort to eliminate poverty and to assure every citizen some guaranteed minimum level of medical care, retirement income, food, and other amenities. The growth of these programs stemmed at least in part from an egalitarian movement in our society. These programs became a means of promoting equality instead of just a means to relieve the distresses of certain unfortunate groups in our society. Unfettered capitalism leads to gross inequalities as the capitalistic class receives the lion's share of the benefits from the system and the rest of society is left to fend for itself.

This egalitarian movement was primarily composed of blacks and other minorities who were left out of the system, women, welfare workers, and the leaders of new unions that organized government employees.[13] The goal of this movement was to promote an equality of result rather than of opportunity by transferring money from the upper-income levels of society to the lower levels through a series of cash income-assistance programs such as Social Security and in-kind assistance programs such as Medicare and Medicaid. These programs were meant to address the imbalances in income and wealth that resulted from unfettered capitalism and assure that every citizen in the country received some benefits from the system.

The growth of these entitlement programs sparked a lively debate. Critics were concerned about the further growth of government that these programs entailed. The drive for equality of results contributed to a strengthening of centralized bureaucratic power because government allocated outcomes.[14] Others raised questions about the trade-offs between equality and efficiency. In pursuing equality, so it was argued, society would forgo any opportunity to use material resources or rewards as incentives to production. Any insistence on carving the pie into equal slices would shrink the size of the pie for everyone. Egalitarians thus posed a threat to capitalism by reducing the motivation to be productive and to work hard to get ahead in the race for the system's goodies.[15] This debate continues today.

The growth of these entitlement programs slowed in 1981 with the election of the Reagan administration. Programs like AFDC and student loans were cut significantly, and eventually AFDC was eliminated under the Clinton administration, which revamped the welfare system entirely tying it more closely to productive activity. Social Security was revised to provide adequate funding for future retirees. These cuts in entitlement programs, which disproportionately affected lower-income groups coupled with the income tax cuts passed in the Reagan years reversed the egalitarian trend in our society. Throughout the 1980s the wealthier classes of our society received a larger share of income than they had previously, and trends were set in motion regarding the distribution of income and wealth that have continued into the present.

Entitlements were expanded, however, under the administration of George W. Bush and under the subsequent Obama administration. Under the Bush administration a revision to Medicare was passed that took the form of a prescription drug benefit for seniors that was the largest and most costly revision to Medicare since its inception. This entitlement was passed by a Republican-dominated Congress, a party that normally votes against the extension of such benefits. The Bush administration also tried to privatize Social Security by allowing social security money to be invested in the market but failed in this effort. The majority of people did not want to subject their retirement to the vagaries of the market.

Under the Obama administration, a new health care bill was passed that became known as Obamacare, the first such comprehensive health care law that was ever passed in this country. It sought to address the large number of people in the country who had no health insurance. Among other things, it prevented companies from denying insurance because of preexisting conditions and dropping people from coverage when they incurred medical expenses. The most controversial provision was that it required everyone to buy health insurance subject to a penalty if they refused. This was necessary in order for health insurance to be affordable for everyone. Otherwise, the young and healthy would go without insurance, driving up the cost of insurance for everyone else who needed it because of medical problems.

The constitutionality of this mandate was challenged by the attorneys general of several states and due to conflicting rulings of lower courts eventually wound up in the Supreme Court. In June 2012 the court upheld the mandate as constitutional by a 5–4 vote, arguing that the penalty was actually a tax and within the taxing authority of the federal government. The Obama administration did not want to call it a tax and had argued that such a mandate was within the constitutional authority of the federal government on the basis of regulation of interstate commerce. The Supreme Court explicitly denied this rationale. This decision was not the end of the story, however, as the Republicans promised to repeal the law if they took control of Congress and the presidency in subsequent elections.

Social Problems

Other problems appeared in the 1960s and 1970s that were addressed by a new area of regulatory activities called *social regulation*. The social movements of the 1960s including the civil rights and equal rights movements and concern about environmental problems raised some serious problems such as discrimination and pollution were not being adequately addressed. Minorities and women were not being treated equally in the workplace, and discrimination was not being eliminated by the unregulated market as something called "systemic discrimination" was built into the personnel practices of our economic institutions. The market system provided no means of controlling pollution as it provided no incentives to reduce pollution or to dispose of toxic wastes properly to mitigate the environmental effects of new technology. These problems demanded more direct attention to improve the quality of life for all citizens.

Thus, a new area of public policy was created to deal with these problems with the passage of new legislation directed at these problems and the creation of a new form of regulation called social regulation. Congress passed many types of social legislation in the 1960s and 1970s related to environmental cleanup, consumer concerns, equal opportunity in the workplace, workplace safety and health, and other such social issues. It also created new regulatory agencies to implement this legislation, such as the Environmental Protection Agency (EPA), the Equal Employment Opportunity Commission (EEOC), the Consumer Product Safety Commission (CPSC), the Occupational Safety and Health Administration (OSHA), and the National Highway Traffic Safety Administration (NHTSA), and gave expanded power to existing agencies, such as the Food and Drug Administration (FDA) and the Federal Trade Commission (FTC).

This new type of regulation affected every industry in the country rather than just a particular industry as was the old style of regulation patterned after the ICC model. For example, in some cases these agencies set and enforced standards that all companies, regardless of industry, were expected to meet. In this manner business was forced to internalize the so-called social costs of production and was required to mitigate the social effects of its economic decisions. This new type of regulation was concerned with the conditions under which goods and services were produced and the physical characteristics of products rather than rates, routes, and the obligation to serve. Social regulatory agencies became involved with many detailed facets of the production process interfering with the traditional prerogatives of management. For example, OSHA sometimes specified precise engineering controls that had to be adopted and the CPSC mandated specific product characteristics that it believed would protect consumers from injury.[16]

The purpose of OSHA is to set and enforce safety and health regulations in the workplace to reduce workplace injuries and fatalities. The EEOC enforces the antidiscriminatory provisions of the Civil Rights Act and other related laws such as the Equal Pay Act that came under its jurisdiction. The CPSC was created to protect the public from unreasonable risks of injury and death associated with consumer products. Protection and enhancement of the physical environment are the responsibility of the EPA. The Bureau of Consumer Protection in the FTC deals with false or deceptive advertising of consumer products. The FDA protects the public against impure and unsafe food, drugs, and cosmetics, and to regulate hazards associated with medical devices and radiation. Finally, NHTSA set standards for motor vehicle safety and fuel economy.

These goals became important as the society matured and became more concerned with the quality of life that was being created rather than with the production of more goods and services. The relentless drive for profits did not provide any incentives for attention to these social concerns so government had to step in and pass laws related to these concerns and create new regulatory agencies to set and enforce standards across all of industry. This left all businesses in the same competitive position as they all had to spend money to meet these laws and standards. At the same time, these social goods and services were thus provided for society to enhance its quality of life.

Bailouts

Another major problem with capitalism that the government addresses concerns those enterprises whose bankruptcy would have too large an impact on the economy. The market system disciplines those companies that are not managed effectively or that are no longer producing products the public wants to buy because they have been rendered obsolete by new technologies. In these cases, if the company cannot recover on its own it has to eventually file for bankruptcy. There are laws related to bankruptcy and different ways for the company to declare bankruptcy that have implications for its reorganization among other things. But in some cases there are companies that are considered "*too big to fail*," companies whose failure would be too severe an impact for the economy to absorb. In this case, the market is not allowed to work its discipline and the government steps in with some kind of *bailout*.

In the late 1960s and early 1970s Lockheed Corporation faced serious financial problems and needed help to keep it from going bankrupt. The risk was too great for banks and other creditors to extend any more money to Lockheed under normal guarantees. Enough politicians became convinced that Lockheed could not be allowed to fail and passed Emergency Loan Guarantee Legislation that guaranteed loans up to $250 million specifically for Lockheed. With the federal government standing behind the loans to pick up the tab in case of default, banks and other creditors were then willing to give the Lockheed the cash it needed to continue operations.[17]

Chrysler Corporation faced a similar situation in the early 1980s and was faced with imminent shutdown unless someone helped. A Chrysler bankruptcy would have been the largest in the United States up to that time. Some 260,000 jobs were at stake, taxes would be lost to the government, and many workers would be eligible for unemployment insurance. A Chrysler shutdown would have cost about $1.5 billion a year in unemployment benefits, and the government would have been out about $500 million in federal income taxes. In addition the Federal Pension Guarantee Corporation would have been swamped by the $800 billion of unfunded liabilities washing around in Chrysler's enormous pension funds.[18]

Opponents of the guarantee blamed Chrysler's problems on bad management that had made a series of wrong decisions and should not be helped out in a state of emergency. Subsidizing a failing company, they argued, would undermine the very purpose of a competitive economy that ensures that the resources of society are used efficiently. The management of Chrysler was inefficient, it was charged, and to save the company from bankruptcy would be rewarding poor management. If government played the role of guaranteeing the survival of inefficient companies the incentives for big business to be efficient would be removed.

Nonetheless, in December 1979 Congress passed the Chrysler Corporation Loan Guarantee Act that authorized up to $1.5 billion in loan guarantees to the company. As a condition of this financing, Chrysler had to obtain at least $1.43 billion in nonfederally guaranteed financing, and the union had to make concessions to keep the company going. Chrysler had to submit its financing and operating plans to the Chrysler Corporation Loan Guarantee Board that was composed of government officials. This board had considerable authority over the company's operations during the time the loan guarantee was in effect.[19]

Other bailouts followed including banks such as Continental Illinois National Bank of Chicago, which received a complicated rescue package from the federal government. The Federal Deposit Insurance Corporation (FDIC) agreed to buy $4.5 million in bad loans from Continental for $3.5 billion with the bank writing off the remaining $1 billion. An additional $1 billion was given to the bank in return for an issue of preferred stock in the bank's parent company, the Continental Illinois Corporation. These preferred shares were eventually to be converted into 80 percent of the parent company's common stock. The government, in effect, owned the company, although it eventually sold its shares to the public. The total bailout package for Continental cost the government $10 billion.[20]

In 1987, the FDIC put $970 million into Houston's First City Bancorporation to keep it from failing.[21] In the summer of 1988, the FDIC turned over management of First Republic Bancorporation of Dallas to North Carolina National Bank, which agreed to jointly own the bank with the FDIC for five years.[22] From 1982 to 1987, the FDIC shut down or bailed out 600 banks at a cost of $9.9 billion. By the end of 1991, the fund that insures bank deposits was virtually broke. Nearly 900 banks with assets of $162 billion had failed since 1987 because of bad loans to real estate developers, takeover artists, and third-world countries. To deal with these failures, the FDIC had paid out $56 billion, of which it expected to recoup no more than a third. Some experts predicted that the final tab for reviving the banking industry could top $180 billion, $52 billion of which would go to pay depositors and sell the assets of failed banks.[23]

While more and more banks were being bailed out, the situation in the savings and loan industry was becoming a major disaster. By the middle of 1988, at least 500 of the more than 3,000 savings and loans across the nation were insolvent. The Federal Savings and Loan Insurance Corporation (FSLIC), the counterpart for the FDIC for the savings and loan industry, sold 205 savings and loans in a series of deals that offered buyers guaranteed returns on thrift assets and deposits. Such actions eventually overwhelmed the agency, and Congress had to mount a rescue plan for the entire industry by establishing another agency called the Resolution Trust

Corporation (RTC), whose mission was to peddle insolvent saving and loan institutions and distressed real estate.[24]

On January 23, 1991, the Congressional Budget Office (CBO) announced that the savings and loan bailout could involve as many as 1,600 thrift institutions and could cost as much as $155 billion. Adding interest on debt incurred to pay for the bailout increased the cost to nearly $500 billion.[25] The RTC was criticized for wasting money through giveaway deals with private investors, for exacerbating the real estate depression, and for general mismanagement. It was given credit, however, for recouping a respectable 95 percent of the value of liquid assets and gaining an average of 70 cents on the dollar for real estate sales.[26]

The mother of all bailouts stemmed from the financial crisis of 2008–2009 when banks were again in trouble. The financial sector channeled too much money into real estate and, in particular, to people who could not repay their debt as they were encouraged to take out subprime loans with adjustable rates and, in some cases, did not even require proof of income. The financial industry failed to allocate money where the returns to society were greatest but was most concerned about profits for itself and had come to see their business as an end in itself rather than a means to the end of prosperity and efficiency for the society as a whole.[27] A new class of superrich had been created in America who, according to one author, "had invented nothing and built nothing, except intricate chains of paper claims that duller people mistook for wealth."[28]

This financial crisis brought economic adversity to millions of people in our society who were forced out of houses they recently bought, who lost their jobs and couldn't find new ones, for workers who lost their pensions in companies that went bankrupt, for people who couldn't get credit to continue their business or start a new one, and for people who lost money in a declining stock market. The financial crisis resulted in a massive increase in the federal debt because of government efforts to bail out failed or failing banks and stimulate the economy to promote growth.

The ordinary mind cannot begin to fathom the losses that occurred during this financial meltdown. During the 2008 stock market crash it is estimated that $7 trillion of shareholder wealth disappeared. An additional $3.3 trillion was lost in the value of homes as real estate prices fell. Globally, financial losses amounted to a staggering $50 trillion, which included a $25 trillion loss in stock values. The International Monetary Fund (IMF) estimated in April 2009 that financial institutions around the world would have to write off a total of $4.1 trillion in losses through 2010.[29] Such losses are difficult for most people to begin to comprehend.

The economy went into a nosedive as consumers and businesses cut their expenditures in response to the meltdown on Wall Street because of interruptions in the flow of credit from major financial institutions which had an impact on spending decisions and employment prospects. Consumer spending on durable goods fell 22 percent on an annualized basis in the last three months of 2008 while total private investment fell 23 percent and exports, 24 percent. In the first quarter of 2009 investment fell at an annual rate of 31 percent and gross domestic product (GDP) fell at an annualized rate of more than 6 percent. The unemployment rate shot up from 6.2 percent in September 2008 to 9.5 percent in June 2009, as more than 5 million jobs were eliminated, and remained at close to 10 percent for some time is spite of the government's efforts to stimulate the economy.[30]

Banks had to hoard cash rather than lend it out to others in anticipation of the losses on the mortgage bonds that they had warehoused. Bear-Stearns alone, for example, had billions of dollars of mortgage debt on its books that was losing value every day and eventually led to a takeover of the company. The amount of illiquid mortgage debt held by these firms was so large that no amount of interest rate easing by the Federal Reserve could restore the mortgage market to health and in the late summer and early fall of 2007 it shut down completely. In past crises, the injection of massive amounts of liquidity had been able to repair the financial system as borrowing became cheaper, and firms were able to make money on trades and restore their profitability. But this time the problem was too large and too widespread. Everyone learned just how important credit was to the economy because when it dried up, the economy tanked.[31]

Capitalism cannot exist without capital, yet during the financial crisis the credit markets seized up, credit was not available, and banks were afraid to lend to anyone or any other institution. Trust is important for an economy to operate. People have to have trust that the products they are buying are safe to use as directed. Creditors have to trust that the company they are lending money to is a viable institution that will be able to pay off its debts at some time in the future. During the financial crisis of 2008–2009, trust was lacking, and the banks and other financial institutions would not lend any more money because they did not believe debt would be paid. The government had to restore that trust with a bailout package to get credit moving again and to restore the economy.

The bailout package was called the Troubled Asset Relief Program (TARP), and while very unpopular in the country as a whole and ended the careers of several politicians, it proved to be successful in preventing a total collapse of the financial system. Originally set at $700 billion and eventually lowered to $475 billion, most of the money was repaid, and the final cost to taxpayers was estimated to be around $50 billion. Even American Insurance Group (AIG), which was given $70 billion, was expected by some to make money in the final analysis, although that was speculative, at best, and a loss of around $10 billion was thought to be more realistic.[32] Banks were given $250 billion, but the bulk of these funds had been repaid and the government expected to make a profit from these payments.[33]

However, even the $700 billion TARP bailout program was insufficient to deal with the troubled assets that had been created and acquired by Wall Street firms. The Federal Reserve had to step in and buy bad subprime mortgage bonds directly from the banks. By early 2009 losses associated with more than a trillion dollars of bad investments had been transferred from Wall Street to the American taxpayer.[34] Even as the government (taxpayers) provided banks with money to recapitalize and ensure a flow of credit, some of this money was used to pay themselves record bonuses. According to Joseph E. Stiglitz, a Nobel Prize–winning economist who teaches at Columbia University, nine lenders that together had nearly $100 billion in losses received $175 billion in bailout money from the government and paid out nearly $33 billion in bonuses. They also used some of this money to pay dividends, which, in this case, came from government handouts rather than from profits.[35]

Such a bailout sends a signal to the banks that they do not have to worry about lending practices that get them in trouble. The government will always pick up the pieces and will not let them fail because such failure would be too damaging to the economy as a whole. They can do whatever they want with this bailout money. This practice does the exact opposite of what the market should do in enforcing discipline on the banks by rewarding those that had been prudent and letting fail those that had been foolish and taken on more risk than they could handle. The bailout gave the banks that did the worst in risk management the biggest gifts from the government.[36] This is not the way the system is supposed to work to benefit the entire society. As Michaelson, a former executive with Countrywide Financial says,

> [w]hen government rescues, bails out, helps—whatever you call it—those who acted financially *irresponsibly*, engaged in reckless speculation, or otherwise made their own mess, government potentially rewards that behavior, ensuring its perpetuation, enabling its proliferation into greater levels of nuttiness, and motivating even greater levels of risk-taking . . . There is extreme danger for the future in rewarding bad decisions, yes, but a foreclosed home also does not pay property taxes, which is already beginning to cripple state and local government budgets. It is arguable, but it may actually be *less* expensive overall to bail people out than to let the system self-correct. Whether or not the math favors either action may come down to the final scale of the damage, which is, as yet, frighteningly undetermined. But the point is, the moral issue is very complex.[37]

According to Stiglitz again, these actions of the government only strengthened the too-big-to-fail banks and worsened the problems of moral hazard. Future generations of Americans were saddled with a legacy of debt that increased the possibility of inflation in the future and put the U.S. dollar at risk on world markets. These actions also strengthened many Americans' doubt about the fundamental fairness of the system. If you were big enough such that failure would threaten to bring the entire financial system down, you did not have to worry about taking on risky investments. But if you are unlucky enough to be an average citizen, the government would not necessarily come to your aid with a big enough aid package to make a real difference.[38]

Greed is a given on Wall Street. The problem was the system of incentives that had channeled greed in a self-destructive manner and allowed a huge bubble to occur that no one wanted to burst. As one author points out, the problem wasn't that Lehman Brothers had been allowed to fail. The problem was that it had been allowed to succeed based on such risky investments. Without government intervention, every one of these investment banks would have failed, and the world's most highly paid financiers would have been entirely discredited.[39] Yet no one wanted the music to stop; it kept going until the entire system collapsed, and when it did, the government had to step in to save the system.

Creating a financial system that actually works and fulfills the functions that a financial system is supposed to perform is the first priority of reform. A better-regulated financial system would actually be more innovative, according to Stiglitz, and direct the creative energy of financial markets to develop products that enhance the well-being of society rather than line the pockets of financiers.[40] Any institution that has to be rescued during a crisis situation because it plays such an essential role in the financial system, should be regulated when there is no crisis to be sure it does not take on excessive risks that jeopardize its integrity and ability to continue in business.[41]

Since the early 1980s, then, state power has been used to bailout companies and stabilize market outcomes for players that have floundered for one reason or another. It has provided loan guarantees for Lockheed and Chrysler, it set up a Resolution Trust Corporation to take over failed saving and loan institutions and stabilize that industry, it dealt with the failure of Long Term Capital Management, and now it has bailed out the entire financial industry. The state has stepped in on numerous occasions to maintain confidence in the economy, to ensure that companies will continue in existence rather than go bankrupt, and to guarantee market results.[42] We do not have a free-enterprise system that operates according to its own dictates but a system where failure is not an option for certain firms that are deemed too big to fail. What this kind of a system amounts to is private gains for these firms and socialized losses that are picked up by the taxpayers.[43] It is crony capitalism at its worst.

Inequality

The last problem that will be mentioned concerns the growing *inequality* in American society. As mentioned before there was a movement toward more equality in society as a whole during the postwar years that was reversed with the election of the Reagan administration in 1980, which revised the tax code to favor the wealthy, reduced the power of unions, and began to attack what was perceived as an overregulated economy. For thirty years after World War II the country experienced growth of income in every segment of the population, with those at the bottom of the income distribution growing faster than those at the top.[44] The country was enjoying levels of prosperity that were somewhat unprecedented. Typically during this period the top 1 percent of income earners received only 12 percent of the nation's income due mainly to government policies that redistributed income downward.[45] According to Michael Lind, cofounder of the New America Foundation and policy director of its Economic Growth Program,

> [t]he New Deal system of trickle-up, demand-side economics succeeded in creating a mass middle-class that was also a mass market for the products of American factories and farms. Thanks to the New Deal, working Americans were guaranteed a minimum income by minimum wage laws and unemployment insurance, while retirees were guaranteed a minimum income in old age by Social Security. Union membership added an additional wage premium for Americans in organized industries. These income guarantees benefited American businesses in two ways. By removing the possibility that competitors would use starvation wages to their advantage, they permitted all businesses to compete on the basis of price and quality rather than success in exploiting labor. And they solved the pre—New Deal problem of the misdistribution of income and underconsumption by enabling sufficient levels of mass consumption by adequately paid workers and retirees.[46]

But in the past three decades, those in the bottom 90 percent have seen a growth of only about 15 percent in their wages while those in the top 1 percent enjoyed an increase of almost 150 percent and the top 0.1 percent an increase of more than 300 percent.[47] Other figures show that in 1979 the top 10 percent received 67 percent of the income from capital while 33 percent went to the bottom 90 percent. In 2006, the share of income going to the top 10 percent had increased to 81.3 percent while that of the bottom 90 percent had declined to 18.7 percent.[48] From 1983 to 2009, 82 percent of all gains in wealth went to the richest 5 percent of American households.[49]

The financial crisis of 2008 made these inequalities even worse, and the gains since the so-called recovery have gone mainly to the wealthy. The upshot of these figures, according to Joseph E. Stiglitz again, "the rich are getting richer, the richest of the rich are getting still richer, the poor are becoming poorer and more numerous, and the middle class is being hollowed out. The incomes of the middle class are stagnating or falling, and the difference between them and the truly rich is increasing."[50] According to Michael Lind, this maldistribution of income and wealth should come as no surprise: "What else could one expect to happen once unions were crushed, the minimum wage was reduced by inflation, labor markets were flooded with low-wage immigrants, taxes on the rich were dramatically lowered, and salaries and stock options for corporate executives were raised to obscene levels."[51]

Because of growing inequalities, the middle class has not seen its income increase in several years while the very rich have gotten significantly richer. Inequality in our society is at a level not seen since before the Great Depression.[52] This is an imbalance that needs to be corrected. Quite apart from moral considerations, the economy simply cannot function unless income is distributed more equally across the society so that people have money to spend on the products capitalism produces. As more and more chips, to use a poker analogy, have gone to the rich in our society, many people, particularly in the middle class, have been driven out of the game. People must have buying power equal to the amount of goods and services that are produced by capitalism. To quote from Michael Lind again:

> When too much of the wealth of a nation is channeled to too few people, industries are starved of the mass demand they need to keep running or to expand. At the same time, the economy can be destabilized, when the rich try to become even richer by speculating with the money they do not consume or save. The series of asset bubbles the world has experienced in recent years—in housing, in stocks, and in commodities such as gold and energy—is a telltale sign that too much money is going to the rich, who use it to gamble on assets, rather than the middle class and poor, who would have spent the money on goods and services generated in the productive economy.[53]

One of the best books on this subject was written by Robert B. Reich, secretary of labor in the Clinton administration and now a professor at the University of California at Berkeley. Reich declares that the stagnant incomes of the middle class have been a drag on growth. "The fundamental problem," he says, "is that Americans no longer have the purchasing power to buy what the U.S. economy is producing." This describes the American experience from the 1990s leading up to the financial crisis of 2008–2009. Reich does not focus as much on the moral argument of unfairness, as more and more income and wealth to go to the top 1 percent, but instead argues that redistribution is a prerequisite for economic growth.[54]

Caught between rising aspirations and stagnant wages, Reich describes several coping mechanisms that the middle class has gone through in the past decades. First, many married women joined the workforce giving families a second income. If the couple had children, they had to pay for child care while the mother worked. Next both husbands and wives worked longer hours to increase their income. Finally, they went into debt to keep up their lifestyle and helped stroke the credit bubble if they took on a subprime mortgage. When that bubble burst in the financial crisis these coping mechanisms were exhausted. Middle-class Americans are now faced with the prospect of doing more with less, but such belt tightening will only further depress the economy.[55]

Reich recommends a series or reforms that might revive the economy and head off any political convulsions that result from such gross inequalities in our society. He argues for a more progressive income tax, which includes a negative tax for anyone earning below $50,000 a year. The top income tax rate should be raised to 55 percent with income from capital gains, now taxed at 15 percent, treated the same as income from wages and salaries. Temporary compensation in the form of wage insurance should be made available to workers who take big pay cuts when they shift jobs as well as investment in infrastructure to make public transportation more available. And Medicare should be made available for all citizens with subsidies for middle-class and lower-income families.[56]

None of these recommendations are even remotely political feasible given the current political situation in Washington. The Republicans will not budge on tax increases for the wealthy arguing that the job creators should not be saddled with additional taxes, failing to realize that jobs will not be created unless people have money to buy the products the jobs will create. Focusing on the investment or supply side is all well and good, but demand, as Keynes pointed out long ago, cannot be ignored. The Republicans would only make the situation worse by giving more money to the already wealthy, cutting jobs and programs that benefit the middle class, and reducing their ability to spend money to keep the economy growing.

In response, the Democrats dig in their heels regarding reform of entitlement programs. The two parties can't even agree on a simple solution to Social Security, like raising the age at which people can start receiving benefits. They can't entertain a means test for Medicare benefits. But entitlement programs have to be reformed in some fashion. There is simply no way that current levels of benefits can be paid to increasing numbers of retirees. We cannot borrow our way out of this mess as there isn't enough money in the world to continue our extravagant expenditures on entitlement programs. Gar Alperovitz writing in *Dissent* says,

> One thing is certain: traditional liberalism dependent on expensive federal policies and strong labor unions, is moribund. The government no longer has much capacity to use progressive taxation to achieve the goal of equity or to regulate corporations effectively. At the same time, ongoing economic stagnation or mild upturns followed by further decay, and "real" unemployment rates in the 15 percent to 16 percent range appear more likely than a return to booming economic times.[57]

An article in *Newsweek* paints a pretty bleak picture for most people in the country. People nearing retirement have questions regarding their ability to retire and whether Medicare and Social Security will be available for them when they retire. Getting old is expensive, particularly as medical costs mount and the ability to pay for medical care shrinks. Those nearing retirement had counted on gains from stocks in their 401K accounts and increases in housing prices to help along with their Social Security benefits. These expected gains have turned into losses, and Social Security in its present form is unstainable as the baby boomers retire in ever-increasing numbers.[58]

The article points out that it is the young and the poor who have the most to worry about. Families that are headed by people younger than thirty-five are about 70 percent poorer that they were in 1984 because of lower wages, more expensive housing, and student debt. The chances that a male offspring will rise to a higher social standing than his father have dropped by nearly half since 1980. The poor are mired in poverty, and the chances that children born into this situation will escape it are becoming less and less. The article of faith that tomorrow would be better than today, that the young generation would be better off than their parents is fading. Only the fortunate few will find opportunities to get ahead while most will experience a decline in living standards and life chances. The promise of a better economic future for all citizens may no longer be viable.[59]

This pessimistic conclusion is supported in a widely acclaimed book by Thomas Piketty, a professor at the Paris School of Economics that was more extensively reviewed when it first came out than any book I know of in modern history.[60] Piketty's general conclusion is that in the twenty-first century the rate of return on capital is quite likely to exceed the rate of growth of output and income generating "unsustainable inequalities that radically undermine the meritocratic values on which democratic societies are based."[61] While he does issue a disclaimer that the answers in his book are imperfect and incomplete, Piketty also makes the claim that his conclusions are based on more extensive historical and comparative data than previous researchers on the topic of income and wealth distribution had available. His data cover three centuries and more than twenty countries and is based on a new theoretical framework that he claims gives him a deeper understanding of the underlying mechanisms regarding income and wealth distribution in capitalistic countries.[62]

Based on his sources, Piketty claims that[63] from 1910 to 1920 the top decile in the United States claimed as much as 45 to 50 percent of national income before it dropped to 30 to 35 percent by the end of the 1940s, stabilizing at that level through the 1970s. Then in the 1980s and continuing into the 2000s, the top decile returned to a level on the order of 45 to 50 percent of national income, a change that Piketty calls impressive and bears asking how long this trend might continue. Looking at the dynamics of wealth distribution shows that there are powerful mechanisms pushing alternately toward convergence and divergence. And a powerful conclusion he makes is that "there is no natural, spontaneous process to prevent destabilizing, inegalitarian forces from prevailing permanently."[64]

The main forces for convergence, according to Piketty, are the diffusion of knowledge and investment in training and skills that are the key to productivity growth and also the reduction of inequality both within and between countries. Despite these forces, however, there is little evidence, according to Piketty, that labor's share of national income has increased significantly in a very long time, meaning the forces of divergence have prevailed for several decades.[65] Interestingly, Piketty mentions the explosion of income going to top managers of large firms who have become separated from the rest of the population as a major force behind the increase in inequality. While the skills and productivity of these managers could have risen in relation to other workers, he thinks a more plausible explanation is that these managers have been able to set their own remuneration without limit, in some cases, and without any relation to their individual productivity, in many cases.[66]

However, the most fundamental force for divergence, according to Piketty, is the relation between economic growth and the return on capital. When the rate of return on capital significantly exceeds the growth rate for the economy as a whole for an extended period, then a divergence in the distribution of wealth in very likely. This was true for much of history until the nineteenth century and is likely to be the case again for the twenty-first century as the rate of growth in both the population and the economy is most likely to decrease.[67]

However, Piketty warns us not to interpret these trends in the distribution of wealth and income as some kind of economic determinism. On the contrary, he argues that the distribution of wealth has always been deeply political and cannot be reduced to purely economic mechanisms. The reduction of inequality that took place in the first half of the twentieth century was largely the result of two World Wars and the policies adopted to cope with the aftermath of these wars. Similarly, the increase of inequality after 1980 is due largely to the conservative revolution of the past several decades when new policies were adopted with regard to taxation and finance that favored capital over labor.[68]

Piketty argues that the history of inequality is shaped by the view of actors in the economic, social, and political realms as to what is a just distribution and what is not and their relative power in influencing the collective choices that are made with regard to financial and taxation matters. He is highly critical of the discipline of economics in this regard, accusing it of having a passion for mathematics and purely theoretical and ideological speculation that ignores historical research and collaboration with the other social sciences. "Economists are all too often preoccupied with petty mathematical problems of interest only to themselves . . . they must set aside their contempt for other disciplines and their absurd claim to greater scientific legitimacy, despite the fact that they know almost nothing about anything . . . If we are to progress in our understanding of the historical dynamics of the wealth distribution and the structure of social classes, we must obviously take a pragmatic approach and avail ourselves of the methods of historians, sociologists, and political scientists as well as economists."[69] These are strong words indeed.

While modernizing of the social state that provides educational, health, and retirement benefits to its population rather than dismantling it and rethinking the progressive income tax have an important role to play in the future of income and wealth distribution, they are not enough to regain control over the globalized financial capitalism of this century. In addition, Piketty recommends a progressive global tax on capital coupled with a very high level of international financial transparency. Those with the greatest wealth are to be taxed more heavily, and all types of assets are to be included as taxable assets. While Piketty admits that such a global tax "would require a very high and no doubt unrealistic level of international cooperation," countries wishing to move in this direction could do so incrementally. But to reduce inequality in this manner there must also be financial transparency as there has to be clarity about who owns what assets in the world. Rather than rely on taxpayers to declare their own asset holdings, Piketty suggests that banks should automatically supply information about asset ownership and share this information internationally.[70]

In another book titled *The Great Divide: Unequal Societies and What We Can Do about Them*, Joseph Stiglitz quotes some figures from an organization called Oxfam which found that in 2014, a bus with eighty-five of the world's billionaires on it would have as much wealth as the bottom half of the world's population. A year later the bus would need to hold only eighty people to achieve the same result. The organization also found that the top 1 percent of the world's population owned nearly half of the world's wealth and by 2016 would own as much as the rest of the 99 percent combined if present trends continued.[71]

In the United States the typical family was worse off than it was a quarter century ago when adjusted for inflation. Among advanced countries in the world, the United States had the highest level of inequality and also had one of the lowest levels of equality of opportunity, making it difficult for people to better their financial situation. Differing from Piketty, Stiglitz states that these inequalities were not inevitable, due to the workings of the laws of economics, but were the result of our politics and policies. Economic inequality gets translated into political inequality so that the rich can influence the political system to respond to their needs and make it easier to get ever more wealthy, leaving the rest of the country behind.[72]

Inequality in the United States is not so much a function of *capitalism*, says Stiglitz, but is more a function of *democracy in* the twentieth century.[73] Our political system is closer to a matter of one dollar one vote than it is of one person one vote. With cuts in capital gains and other taxes that favor the rich, they have increased their share of the pie, and when they get in trouble they are bailed out by the government resulting in privatized gains and socialized losses. Stiglitz call this "rent seeking," which is simply nothing more than redistribution from one part of society to another, namely, from the bottom to the top rungs of society. Rent seeking does not help grow the economy because it involves getting a larger size of an already-existing pie and distorts allocation of resources and makes the economy weaker.[74] Stiglitz describes rent seeking in our society as follows:

> In a broad sense, "rent seeking" defines many of the ways by which our current political process helps the rich at the expense of everyone else, including transfers and subsidies from the government, laws that make the marketplace less competitive, laws that allow CEOs to take a disproportionate share of corporate revenue, and laws that permit corporations to make profits as they degrade the environment.[75]

Too much of the wealth of those at the top of the economic ladder arises from exploitation of others resulting in contradictions that make the American dream something of a myth. We are a rich country with many billionaires and yet have millions of poor people who live below the poverty level. We pride ourselves on being the land of opportunity, but a child's prospects of living the American dream depend more on the income and education of his or her parents than on their own efforts to get ahead. We say we believe in fair play yet the richest often pay a smaller percentage of their income in taxes than those who make much less. We pledge allegiance to the flag and assert there is "justice for all," but increasingly "there is only justice for those who can afford it."[76]

Ninety-five percent of all income gains since 2009, according to Stiglitz, have gone to the top 1 percent, while the median income in the United States hasn't budged in almost a quarter century. The typical American makes less than he or she did forty-five years ago after taking inflation into account.[77] The even higher levels of inequality that Piketty forecasts, however, are not the result of the inexorable laws of economics, says Stiglitz. "Simple changes—including higher capital gains taxes, greater spending to broaden access to education, rigorous enforcement of antitrust laws, corporate-governance reforms that circumscribe executive pay, and financial regulations that rein in bank's ability to exploit the rest of society—would reduce inequality and increase equality of opportunity markedly."[78]

Trickle-down economics, the notion that if government keeps its hands off the economy, the rich may indeed get richer but they will use their talents and resources to create jobs so that everyone will benefit, doesn't work according to Stiglitz, and he claims that the historical data prove his case.[79] Since those who are less wealthy spend a greater share of their income than do the rich, demand is expanded and jobs are created. Thus, it is ordinary Americans who are the real job creators, and if the rich get richer and inequality gets worse this only weakens the economy and results in lower growth and more instability.[80] It also creates a vicious circle as economic inequality leads to political inequality, which then leads to a rewriting of the rules to increase the level of economic inequality even further.[81]

According to Stiglitz, about 14.5 percent of the American population lives below the poverty line, but 19.9 percent of children, which amounts to some

15 million children, live in poverty. Among developed countries, he claims, only Romania has a higher rate of child poverty. Such poverty among children amounts to poor health care, diminished access to a good education, and exposure to environmental hazards. These children bare a greater burden in life than other segments of the population that are better off economically. The country is thus wasting some of its most valuable assets as young people with no skills turn to dysfunctional activities. The result is that some states spend as much on prisons as they do on higher education.[82]

America has expanded its corporate safety net to cover not only commercial banks but also investment banks, insurance, and also automobiles, all of which were bailed out during the Great Recession under the too-big-too-fail philosophy. But Stiglitz claims that it has long been recognized that if banks are indeed too big to fail, they are also too big to manage. A system in which profits are privatized and losses socialized is doomed to failure as market discipline disappears and incentives are distorted. This is not socialism, he says, but simply an extension of corporate welfare. The rich and powerful turn to government to help them when they get in trouble while needy individuals are given little social protection.[83]

Our tax system is much less progressive than it was for much of the past century as the top marginal income tax rate, which was at 70 percent during the 1960s and 1970s, is now at 39.6 percent. Coupled with a capital gains rate at 20 percent, it should not be surprising that the share of income going to the top 1 percent doubled since 1979 and that the share going to the top 0.1 percent has almost tripled during that same period. Our tax system, Stiglitz claims, has helped us become a rent-seeking society, in which more efforts go into increasing the size of the pie going to the wealthy than in trying to grow the pie larger so that everyone can benefit. If Americans come to believe that government is unfair and has become captured by the wealthy, then faith in democracy is in peril.[84]

This kind of unfairness results in a loss of trust without which no society can function. Trust makes the world go around, says Stiglitz; it is what makes contracts, plans, and everyday transactions possible. It facilitates the democratic process and is necessary for social stability. But as the gap between American widens people lose faith in a system that seems to be stacked against them as the 1 percent rise to ever-more distant heights of income and wealth. The bankers who got us into a severe financial mess resulting in the Great Recession go unpunished and, in fact, get bailed out while the average homeowner whose mortgage was underwater got little if any help from government. This kind of favoritism erodes trust, and without trust there can be no harmony in society.[85]

In sum, Stiglitz believes that the inequality in our society is mainly caused by a redistribution of income and wealth from the bottom to the top that has taken place through the political system and is not just the result of underlying economic forces. Tax and expenditure policies have favored the rich ever since the Reagan administration but took a marked acceleration during the second Bush administration with two rounds of tax cuts that favored the wealthy. This inequality has produced a rent-seeking society that has resulted in slower growth of the economy that has made the American dream impossible for more and more people.

Reducing this inequality has clear economic and social benefits as people's sense that society is fair improves social cohesion and mobility, as well as providing support for growth initiatives. The country must invest in policies that boost the growth and development of human capital, which modern economies increasingly need as well as invest in infrastructure to facilitate a dynamic economy. Finally, the financial system must be fixed so that we get a banking system that serves society rather than the other way around. Banks need to get out of the business of speculating with other people's money and get back to the boring business of lending.

Ronald Inglehart, a professor of political science at the University of Michigan writing in *Foreign Affairs*, agrees with Stiglitz that economic inequality is not an inherent feature of capitalism as Piketty argued but instead is a political question. What most analyses of inequality miss, he says, "is the extent to which both the initial fall and the subsequent rise of inequality over the past century have been related to shifts in the balance of power between elites and the masses, driven by the ongoing process of modernization."[86] The conflict in today's economy is no longer between the working class and the middle class but instead is between a tiny elite and the great majority of citizens, in other words, between the 1 percent and the 99 percent. These rich elite have used their privileged position to shape policies of the government to further increase their wealth often going against the wishes of the middle and lower classes.[87]

Because of the advantages those born into wealthy families have over other people in society there is an enduring tendency in society for the rich to get even richer and the poor to be left further and further behind. Inglehart argues that market forces show no signs of reversing these trends, but politics might do so particularly as growing insecurity and relative immiseration gradually change the attitudes of citizens and create greater support for government policies designed to alter these trends. Since a large share of the population is already highly educated, well-informed, and has political skills, "all it needs to become politically effective is the development of an awareness of common interest." Democracies have the vitality to successfully adapt to changing conditions and pressures despite current signs of paralysis.[88]

Writing in that same issue of *Foreign Affairs*, Danielle Allen, a professor in Harvard's Department of Government and Graduate School of Education, argues that during the early years of the republic, liberty and equality were understood to reinforce each other. By the middle of the twentieth century, however, these two values were seen to be in conflict such that any attempt to promote economic equality was described as making "despotic inroads" on individual liberties such as the right to property. This conflict became embedded in the country during the Cold War where free-market capitalism became the defining feature of the United States and totalitarian equalization as the defining feature of the Soviet Union.[89]

This resulted in a broad consensus, claims Allen, that straight equalization of economic resources will produce extreme, unjust, and counterproductive restrictions on personal liberty and a significant reduction of economic growth. However, there is also consensus that there is no such thing as a totally free market and that markets depend on rules, norms, and regulations backed by law and the power of the state. Politics trumps economics as the political system determines what these rules, norms, and regulations will be or, in other words, sets the terms as to how the economic game is played. The focus of reformers should be on restoring political equality in our society and creating "a virtuous circle in which political equality supports institutions that, in turn, support social and economic equality."[90] As stated by Allen,

> [b]olstering political equality throughout the lower and middle layers of the U.S. federalized political system is not an easy or sexy task, but that is what is required to redress the outsize power of money in national life that has been both the consequence and the enabler of rising economic inequality. Liberty and equality can be mutually reinforcing, just as the founders believed. But to make that happen, political equality will need to be secured first and then used to maintain, and be maintained by, egalitarianism in the social and economic spheres as well.[91]

Peter Georgescu, former chairman of Young and Rubicam, argues if this issue of inequality is not addressed by our society it will most likely be resolved in one of two ways: by major social unrest that will disrupt the economy and society, or through oppressive taxes that the wealthy will find intolerable. A caste system is being created in this country that few will be able to escape. Business itself needs to deal with this situation, says Georgescu who believes business has the most to gain from a healthy society, by investing more in its employees and by compensating them fairly by allowing them to share in productivity increases and creative innovations. He points out that while wages have been flat for decades, productivity has increased by 80 percent. Most of these gains have gone to shareholders rather than to employees. Business must also invest more in its own operations to increase productivity and innovation to boost its own performance.[92]

James K. Galbraith, holder of the Lloyd M. Bentsen Chair in Government/Business Relations at the University of Texas at Austin, is concerned with the instability associated with inequality. Since the 1980s, he states, the business cycle in the United States has been based on financial and credit bubbles and on the enrichment of a very small number of people through the capital markets. Recent business cycles, he says, have been more like waves where certain sectors and areas ride the peaks and then crash on the shore: "That which rises like a rocket above the plain also eventually falls back to earth." Generating prosperity through inequality cannot be continually repeated and bubbles are no longer, he believes, a plausible way to generate economic growth. Bubbled economies are unstable and are closely associated with inequality of income, wealth, and power, an instability "for which we pay a fearsome price."[93]

There is thus no end of analysis and proposals to deal with the issue of inequality, but any proposal to redistribute income and wealth will have to take into account the economic impact that egalitarianism could involve.[94] Some economists see any attempt at redistribution as posing a serious threat to business and the economy. Arthur Okun, for example, who is a former chairman of the Council of Economic Advisors, sees the issue as one of equality versus efficiency and states that this is the big trade-off that society faces as it makes attempts to deal with inequality. The American economy is based on private property and for the most part relies on the market to determine rewards and allocate resources. Differences in wages and profits are essential, Okun argues, to keep the economic mechanism running. Public efforts to promote equality represent a deliberate interference with the results generate by the market. In pursuing equality, Okun states, society would forgo any opportunity to use material resources or rewards as incentives to production. This would lead to inefficiencies which would be harmful to the welfare of the majority.[95]

Curiously enough, Okun supports the notion of egalitarianism on ethical grounds. He states that "equality in the distribution of incomes as well as the distribution of rights would be my ethical preference . . . [To] extend the domain of rights and give every citizen an equal share of the national income would give added recognition to the moral worth of every citizen, to the mutual respect of citizens for one another, and to the equivalent value of membership in the society for all." Okun rests his case, however, on the effects such an ethical ideal would have on economic efficiency. "Any insistence on carving the pie into equal slices" he says, "would shrink the size of the pie. That fact poses the tradeoff between economic equality and economic efficiency . . . Although the ethical case for capitalism is totally unpersuasive, the efficiency case is thoroughly compelling to me."[96] This sounds like something like an ethical cop-out as it is clear that for Okun economics trumps ethics as he argues that material incentives are absolutely necessary to keep the system going.

Economists like Okun, however, need not worry that this issue is going to be faced in the immediate future. Given the current partisan climate in Washington there seems to no hope that the parties can work together to deal with the inequalities of income and wealth that exist in our society. While the democrats made it something of a campaign issue in the 2016 presidential election, the prospects for actually taking some action to reduce these inequalities remains bleak. The Occupy Wall Street and other Occupy movements around the country in response to this issue perhaps increased the consciousness of the public about the 1 percent versus the 99 percent, but this movement had no leadership or political program that could be implemented as did the civil rights movement in the 1980s. It fizzled out after a while, and there has been no concerted movement since to continue this effort. The vast majority of the population seems passive on this issue and appears to accept that such inequalities are an inevitable result of the capitalistic system and can't be changed through our dysfunctional political system.[97]

Indeed, the problem with inequality, according to Simon Reid-Henry, an associate professor in the School of Geography at Queen Mary University in London and senior researcher at the Peace Research Institute at Oslo, is that it cannot be resolved by the usual arguments of left versus right, as the level of inequality that exists today is indicative of a more general crisis in political thought. There is no place for public reason or the common good in today's political discourse. Dealing with inequality would take compromises on both sides of the political spectrum in the interests of a common good. The right will need to get over its dislike of socially determined objectives and revisit their blind faith in the market to solve all the problems of society. They must acknowledge the role the state often plays when the market triumphs and deals with an issue effectively. The left, in turn, must overcome its opposition to the private sector and cannot put all its faith in civil society. Creating alternative spaces challenging hegemonic norms is an important goal, but not the only one worth attaining. While we are all different and have different needs, in the final analysis we can fulfill our individual needs best when we work with others and protect ourselves from both states and markets.[98]

The Future of Public Policy

Thus, there were many issues that capitalism posed for the society that were addressed by public policy measures. Both the public policy process and the market mechanism are processes through which members of society make decisions about the allocation of resources for the provision of goods and services. Through the public policy process public goods and services are provided to people as distinguished from the private goods and services provided through the market. Levels of abstraction are often confounded when dealing with public policy and government. Government is seen as interfering with the free market when the appropriate level of abstraction is to think of government in relation to business organizations. These are two institutions in society that provide different kinds of goods and services to fulfill the needs of society, while public policy and the market are two decision-making processes in society that that represent two means of keeping a proper balance between community needs for public goods and services and individual needs for private goods and services. Such a balance must be maintained for ongoing economic growth.

The issue is not government interfering with the free market but whether the good or service in question is a public good or service and then whether the government or business is the best institution to provide this good or service. Once a decision is made that a good or service is public, then the public policy process is the appropriate means to allocate resources to provide this good or service and government will most likely be the representative institution to provide this good or service through legislation or administrative decisions. Private organizations can be used to actually make the good or provide the service, but it is government that makes the decisions about allocation of resources.

The health care debate that took place in 2009–2010 reflects this problem. The bill that eventually emerged is a hodgepodge of special interests, in which compromises had to be reached to get the bill passed. The public option along with other provisions in the original bill that may have been beneficial were dropped because of opposition of the health insurance industry and other factions in society. The basic question about health care was never asked or answered, that question being whether health care is a private or public good. However, that question is answered the rest follows. What the country ended up with is a bill that tries to have it both ways. People have been given new rights not to be denied coverage because of preexisting conditions and have confidence that their insurance will not be dropped when they get ill. But everyone is also required to have health insurance in order for the system to work. The private health insurance industry will provide this coverage and will be given a larger cliental to serve with the opportunity of making more money so the bill may end up serving private interests to a greater extent than the public interest.[99]

Most people were not happy with this bill and with the way it was passed. Protests were held all over the country and the Republicans, none of whom voted for the bill, promised to repeal it if they were able to take over Congress and wield enough power. The attorneys general of several states also challenged the bill alleging that it was unconstitutional because it encroached on individual freedom of choice by requiring all citizens to have health insurance subject to fines if they refused. This issue reached the Supreme Court, which upheld the mandate under the taxing authority of the federal government. The process by which the bill was finally passed was seen to be corrupt, and many people were disgusted with government because of all the deals that had to be cut to get it passed. The bill that finally passed did not seem to reflect a common interest in improving our health care system but was an amalgam of private interests that did not please anyone.[100]

Jeffrey Sachs, director of the Earth Institute at Columbia University and a Nobel Prize winner, has stated that the actual health consequences of the bill were never reviewed or debated coherently. The legislative process was driven by political and lobbying considerations without the input of experts who were never invited to comment or debate about the legislation, which would have helped the public and politicians understand the issues, and without the informed participation of the American people, leaving the public at large with "little basis for reaction other than the gut instincts and fearful sentiments fanned by talk-show hosts." Commenting on the public policy process in general, he further states that "a systematic vetting of policy options, with recognized experts and the public commenting and debating, will vastly improve on our current policy performance, in which we often fly blind or hand the controls over to narrow interests and viewpoints."[101]

As should be obvious, government had to grow and spend money to mitigate these contradictions in the capitalistic system. Capitalism would not have continued to exist if these problems had not been addressed. Government committed itself to protecting its citizens from the worst excesses of capitalism and reining in market forces in a wide variety of ways as described in this chapter so that the country could continue to enjoy capitalism's benefits. The political and economic order that emerged after 1945 generated levels of sustained growth, prosperity, and social equity that lasted for several decades. This social democratic order succeeded, in large measure, in reconciling the two halves of capitalism that are inextricably intertwined. These have been called its productive and destructive tendencies and sensible political activism can keep the productive aspects going and prevent the destructive aspects from getting out of hand.[102]

This order has frayed in recent decades and the question is whether public policy can be counted on to continue this mitigation of contradictions and make capitalism benefit the public at large. Because of the Bush tax cuts, which went mainly to the wealthy, and the wars in Afghanistan and Iraq we are now in a situation where the national debt has to be addressed. In the past several decades, Western societies have not been creating wealth so much as they have been creating debt to deal with problems of capitalism. But we simply cannot continue to run up trillion-dollar deficits year after year and have a viable economy. We cannot continue social security and Medicare and Medicaid as they are currently structured in the face of the baby boomer's retirement. The piper has to be paid at some point, and that point seems to be now. Yet we seem to be out of ideas that have any chance of dealing with current economic and social issues and certainly out of money to spend our way out of the current crisis.

We may be in such a mess that we cannot dig ourselves out of the hole that has been created with more government expenditures. Many have argued that the stimulus program of the Obama administration was not nearly big enough, and they may be right. We did not really get out of the hole the Great Depression created until World War II necessitated increased military expenditures and put people to work. While a new war is certainly not the way out, can anybody envision such a massive expenditure that would put people to work and grow our economy? And can we afford such a massive expenditure at this point? While the unemployment rate has gone down and is approaching "normal" levels, the jobs many people have do not pay enough so they can live decent lives. And there seems to be no way for many of these people to improve their standard of living. One could argue that capitalism is working extremely well for the 1 percent, but the 99 percent are struggling, and if the Republicans have their way, the 99 percent would be left to fend for themselves, creating an even greater maerial crisis for capitalism.

Notes

1 See "Interventionist Government Came to Stay," *Business Week*, September 3, 1979, 39. See also Michael Hiltzik, *The New Deal: A Modern History* (New York: Free Press, 2011).
2 Edward S. Greenberg, *Capitalism and the American Political Ideal* (New York: M.E. Sharpe, 1985), 95.
3 "The Scars Still Mark Economic Policy," *Business Week*, September 3, 1979, 22.
4 Ibid. See also Melville J. Ulmer, "Fifty Years of Keynes," *The Public Interest*, No. 87 (Spring 1987), 114.
5 "What made the *General Theory* so radical was Keynes's proof that it was *possible* for a free market economy to settle into states in which workers and machines remained idle for prolonged periods of time." Sylvia Nasar, *Grand Pursuit: The Story of Economic Genius* (New York: Simon & Schuster, 2011), 330.
6 "Scars," 23. See also John Cassidy, "The Demand Doctor," *The New Yorker*, October 10, 2011, 46–57.
7 "The Ruins Gave Rise to Big Labor," *Business Week*, September 3, 1979, 26.
8 Ibid.
9 Ibid., 27–28.
10 "Bureau of Labor Statistics, News Release," *Union Members-2011*, January 27, 2012, 1–3.
11 Ibid.
12 "A Watershed in American Attitudes," *Business Week*, September 3, 1979, 46–50.
13 John Cobbs, "Egalitarianism: Threat to a Free Market," *Business Week*, December 1, 1975, 62–65; John Cobbs, "Egalitarianism: Mechanisms for Redistributing Income," *Business Week*, December 8, 1975, 86–90; and John Cobbs, "Egalitarianism: The Corporation as Villain," *Business Week*, December 15, 1975, 86–88.
14 See Dow Votaw, "The New Equality: Democracy's Trojan Horse," *California Management Review*, Vol. XX, No. 4 (Summer, 1978), 5–17.
15 Arthur M. Okun, *Equality and Efficiency: The Big Tradeoff* (Washington, DC: The Brooking Institution, 1975).
16 William Lilley III and James C. Miller III, "The New Social Regulation," *The Public Interest*, No. 47 (Spring 1977), 53.
17 See George A. Steiner, *Casebook in Business and Society* (New York: Random House, 1975), 165–173.
18 "Should We Bail Out Chrysler," *Commonweal*, November 9, 1979, 613.
19 Chrysler Corporation, *Annual Report*, 1982, 30.
20 "Chicago Bank," *Dallas Times Herald*, July 27, 1984, 1.
21 Todd Vogel, "Bob Abboud Is Back in Banking—But What a Bank," *Business Week*, September 1, 1987, 30.
22 Leonard M. Apcar, "First Republic Bank Bailout May Damage Capital-Raising Efforts by Other Banks," *Wall Street Journal*, August 1, 1988, A-3.

23 Christine Gorman, "Cracks in the System," *Time*, August 29, 1988, 54–55.

24 Catherine Yang, "The Thrift Mop-Up Is Already a Mess," *Business Week*, February 5, 1990, 70–72.

25 John Meehan, "Is There Any Bottom to the Thrift Quagmire?" *Business Week*, March 4, 1991, 62–63.

26 Tim Smart, "Resolved: Resolution Trust Corp. Is Doing a Credible Job," *Business Week*, April 20, 1992, 100–103.

27 Joseph E. Stiglitz, *Free Fall: America, Free Markets, and the Shrinking of the World Economy* (New York: W.W. Norton, 2010), 36.

28 Charles R. Morris, *The Two Trillion Dollar Meltdown: Easy Money, High Rollers, and the Great Credit Crash* (New York: Public Affairs), x. An interesting question is why this financial meltdown was not foreseen by economists and public officials. See Jeff Madrick, "Why the Experts Missed the Recession," *The New York Review*, September 14, 2014, 66–68; and Paul Krugman, "Why Weren't Alarm Bells Ringing," *The New York Review*, October 23, 2014, 41–42.

29 John Gillespie and David Zweig, *Money for Nothing: How the Failure of Corporate Boards Is Ruining American Business and Costing Us Trillions* (New York: Free Press, 2010), 44. Other estimates put the total loss of household wealth at more than $13 trillion. See Charles Gasparino, *The Sellout: How Three Decades of Wall Street Greed and Government Mismanagement Destroyed the Global Financial System* (New York: Harper Business, 2009), 492.

30 John Cassidy, *How Markets Fail: The Logic of Economic Calamities* (New York: Farrar, Straus and Giroux, 2009), 332.

31 Gasparino, *The Sellout*, 280.

32 See James Sterngold and Hugh Son, "AIG's Declaration of Independence," *Bloomberg Businessweek*, June 7–13, 2010, 73–76.

33 Amy Schoenfeld, "Rolling Up TARP, Though the Cleanup Isn't Over," *New York Times*, October 3, 2010, BU8; Rebecca Christie with Hugh Son and James Sterngold, "Love It or Hate It (Most Do), TARP Didn't Bust the Bank," *Bloomberg Businessweek*, October 4–10, 2010, 29–30.

34 Michael Lewis, *The Big Short: Inside the Doomsday Machine* (New York: W.W. Norton, 2010), 261. The $700 billion TARP package amounted to only 3 percent of the total amount government and the Federal Reserve provided to the financial industry. More than $19 trillion in bailouts and subsidies was provided at the height of the crisis to bolster the industry and absorb its toxic assets. The New York Fed and the Federal Reserve provided $8.2 trillion in loans and asset guarantees while the U.S. Treasury provided another $6.8 trillion in subsidies and bailouts. In addition, the FDIC instituted a $2.3 trillion liquidity guarantee program to keep capital flowing. See Nomi Prins, *All the Presidents' Bankers: The Hidden Alliances that Drive American Power* (New York: Nation Books, 2014), 414.

35 Stiglitz, *Free Fall*, 80.

36 Ibid., 135. Wall Street was never punished for its wrongdoing as no bankers went to jail and no one was held accountable. As stated by William D. Cohan in "How the Bankers Stayed Out of Jail," *The Atlantic*, September 2015, 20–21, "But without holding real people accountable for their wrongdoing in the years leading up to the financial crisis, the message that their behavior was unacceptable goes undelivered. Instead a very different message is being sent: for financiers, justice is just a check someone else has to write."

37 Adam Michaelson, *Foreclosure of America: Inside Country Wide Home Loan and the Selling of the American Dream* (New York: Berkley Books, 2010), 310–311.

38 Stiglitz, *Free Fall*, 145.

39 Lewis, *The Big Short*, 262.

40 Stiglitz, *Free Fall*, 182.

41 Some think that the banking reforms that were adopted did not go far enough
    and will not necessarily prevent another financial meltdown. See William D.
    Cohan, "Can Bankers Behave," *The Atlantic*, May 2015, 75–80; Sheila Blair,
    "Looking Forward to the Sequel," *The American Prospect*, Winter 2015, 93–95;
    William D. Cohan, "How We Got the Crash Wrong," *The Atlantic*, June, 2012,
    36–39; Rana Foroohar, "The Case for Banking Regulation," *Time*, June 4,
    2012, 22; "Issue of the Week: Wall Street's Unfinished Reform, " *The Week*,
    July 31, 2015, 34; and Roger Alcaly, "The Right Way to Control the Banks,"
    The New York Review, June 5, 2014, 58–60. "Since 2009, the U.S. has brought
    156 criminal and civil cases against 10 of the largest Wall Street Banks, resulting
    in charges against 47 people, but only one boardroom-level executive. In 81 per-
    cent of the cases, individual employees were neither identified nor charged."
    "The Bottom Line," *The Week*, June 10, 2016, 36.

42 Mark A. Martinez, *The Myth of the Free Market: The Role of the State in a
    Capitalist Economy* (Sterling, VA: Kumarian Press, 2009), 243–245.

43 The auto industry also received some TARP money but the amounts are minis-
    cule compared to the financial bailout. Chrysler was extended a $12.5 billion
    bailout package and General Motors $49.5 billion. These bailouts enabled the
    companies to survive by restructuring and installing new management. In Octo-
    ber 2011, Chrysler posted a quarterly profit of $212 million as compared with
    a loss of $84 million the year before. The government recovered $11.3 billion of
    its loan to Chrysler but was expected to lose more than $13 billion on its bailout
    of General Motors. See David Shepardson, "Rattner Applauds Auto Bailouts'
    Happy Ending'," *The Detroit News*, November 1, 2011, 1.

44 "During the thirty glorious years, the Western democracies experienced similar
    combinations of high growth and rapid expansion of the middle classes, under-
    pinned by high labor-union membership, middle-class welfare states, and highly
    regulated economies. By the 1950s, all democratic societies of the North Atlantic
    world had 'settlements' or 'new deals' that were similar in combining various
    forms of social insurance with increased government regulation of or ownership
    of banking and industry. The term "mixed economy" was sometimes used for an
    economy that blended private enterprise with public regulation, redistribution,
    and in some cases public ownership." See Michael Lind, *Land of Promise: An
    Economic History of the United States* (New York: Harper-Collins Publishers,
    2012), 330.

45 Joseph E. Stiglitz, *The Price of Inequality: How Today's Divided Society Endan-
    gers Our Future* (New York: Norton, 2012), 4.

46 Lind, *Land of Promise*, 360–361.

47 Stiglitz, *The Price of Inequality*, 8.

48 Lind, *Land of Promise*, 443.

49 Ibid., 450.

50 Stiglitz, *The Price of Inequality*, 7.

51 Lind, *Land of Promise*, 470. See Kim Phillips, "Why Workers Won't Unite," *The
    Atlantic*, April 2015, 88–98, for an analysis of the plight of unionism in the United
    States and a plea for people to find ways of speaking about their aspirations "in
    a political language that lays claim to democratic principles and counters the illu-
    sion that the world must be divided between a superelite and those whole mission
    is to serve it." Phillips also says that whatever form of labor organizing comes
    next will have to start from scratch and be something entirely new.

52 "Between 1923 and 1929, labor's share of income in manufacturing, mining,
    transportation and utilities declined from 77.9 percent to 72.9 percent, while the
    share going to capital rose from 19.6 percent to 25.5 percent. In the same period,

the share received by the top 1 percent grew by 35 percent, from 13 percent of the total in 1923 to 19 percent in 1929; profits increased by 62 percent but wages increased only 11 percent. The wages of unskilled workers underwent absolute decline." Lind, *Land of Promise*, 262.

53 Ibid., 470.

54 Robert B. Reich, *Aftershock: The Next Economy and America's Future* (New York: Alfred A. Knopf, 2010), 75–76.

55 Ibid., 60–64.

56 Ibid., 127–140. At least one of these provisions was proposed by President Obama in his 2016 budget proposal that included a new wage insurance program that would provide supplementary income to workers who lost their jobs and end up taking new jobs at lower salaries. The plan would replace half of a worker's lost wages up to $10,000 for two years for those earning less than $50,000 who were with their previous employer for at least three years. See "Obama Will Propose New Wage Insurance Program Next Month," *Denver Post*, January 17, 2016, 2A.

57 Gar Alperovitz, "Neither Revolution nor Reform: A New Strategy for the Left," *Dissent*, Fall 2011, 63.

58 David Frum, "America the Anxious," *Newsweek*, August 13 & 20, 2012, 38–42.

59 Ibid.

60 See Paul Krugman, "Why We're in a New Gilded Age," *The New York Review*, May 8, 2014, 15–18; "Piketty: Will His 'Soft Marxism' Change the Political Debate?" *The Week*, May 5, 2014, 4; Ross Douthat, "Marx Rises Again," *The New York Times*, April 20, 2014, SR9; Steven Erlanger, "Taking on Adam Smith (and Karl Marx)," *The New York Times*, April 20, 2014, BU1; John Cassidy, "Forces of Divergence," *The New Yorker*, March 31, 2014, 69–72; and Rana Foroohar, "Marx 2.0," *Time*, May 14, 2014, 46–49. As some of these titles suggest, Piketty has been called a French Marxist, particularly by the American right-wing, but he is really a Social Democrat. About a year after the book was published, Piketty backtracked a bit on his central proposition about inequality and growth, calling his book primarily a book of history rather than an analysis of the causes of inequality in today's world. See Robert Rosenkranz, "A Critic of Inequality Backtracks," *The Week*, March 20, 2015, 34.

61 Thomas Piketty, *Capital in the Twenty-First Century* (Cambridge, MA: The Belknap Press of Harvard University Press, 2014), 1.

62 Ibid. See 16–20 for the sources used in this book.

63 Ibid., 23.

64 Ibid., 21.

65 Ibid., 21–22.

66 Ibid., 24.

67 Ibid., 25–27.

68 Ibid., 20.

69 Ibid., 32–33.

70 See chapters 13 and 14 (471–514) for Piketty's thoughts on the progressive income tax and chapter 15 (515–539) for more information on his proposal for a global tax on capital.

71 Joseph E. Stiglitz, *The Great Divide: Unequal Societies and What We Can Do about Them* (New York: W.W. Norton, 2015), xii. Figures released by Oxfam in 2016 showed that the wealthiest sixty-two people owned as much wealth as the 3.6 billion people who make up the poorer half of the world's population. The wealth of these sixty-two people rose 44 percent, or $542 billion, since 2010 while the wealth of the poorest half fell 41 percent during that same period. See "Inequality," *Time*, February 1, 2016, 13 and "Talking Points," *The Week*, January 29, 2016, 16.

72 Ibid., xvi–xviii. See Robert Kuttner, "The New Inequality Debate," *The American Prospect*, Winter 2016, 56–61 for a persuasive argument that inequality in America reflects the political sway of elites rather than economic imperatives.

73 See also Joseph Stiglitz, "Inequality Is not Inevitable," *The New York Times*, July 29, 2014, SR1. For a comprehensive review of three books by Stiglitz see James Surowiecki, "Why the Rich Are So Much Richer," *The New York Review*, September 24, 2015, 32–36.

74 Stiglitz, *The Great Divide*, 86, 98–99.

75 Ibid., 98.

76 Ibid., 105.

77 Ibid., 120.

78 Ibid., 120, 125.

79 Ibid., 145.

80 Ibid., 146.

81 Ibid., 149.

82 Ibid., 178–180.

83 Ibid., 192–194.

84 Ibid., 196–202.

85 Ibid., 223–229.

86 Ronald Inglehart, "Inequality and Modernization: Why Inequality Is Likely to Make a Comeback," *Foreign Affairs*, Vol. 95, No. 1 (January/February, 2016), 2.

87 Ibid., 3–4. In the spring of 2016, something of a scandal erupted when a leak from the Panamanian law firm Massack Fonseca revealed how a global elite hid billions in offshore tax havens and how the firm helped heads of state, oligarchs, and celebrities launder money, avoid taxes, and dodge sanctions. Some called it another blow to capitalism at a time of global economic instability and frequent corporate scandals. See Rana Foroohar and Matt Vella, "The Panama Papers Expose the Secret World of the 1%," *Time*, April 18, 2016, 11–12; "Panama Papers: The Dark Side of Capitalism," *The Week*, April 22, 2016, 18; and Megan McCardle, "Panama Paper's Lessons," *The Denver Post*, April 10, 2016, 5D.

88 Ibid., 3–10.

89 Danielle Allen, "Equality and American Democracy: Why Politics Trumps Economics," *Foreign Affairs*, Vol. 95, No. 1 (January/February, 2016), 24.

90 Ibid., 26–28.

91 Ibid., 28.

92 Peter Georgescu, "Capitalists, Arise," *The New York Times*, August 9, 2015, SR6. Some think that business is hampered in its ability to consider its long-term impact on issues like inequality because of its focus on quarterly earnings. See "Issue of the Week: The Tyranny of 'Quarterly Capitalism,'" *The Week*, August 14, 2015, 34.

93 James K. Galbraith, *Inequality and Instability* (New York: Oxford University Press, 2012), 148–149.

94 For a thorough analysis of inequality that is somewhat dated at this point see a special section in *Science*, Vol. 344, No. 6186 (May 25, 2014), 819–867. See also a special section in *The American Prospect*, Spring 2015, 26–55.

95 Arthur M. Okun, *Equality and Efficiency: The Big Tradeoff* (Washington, DC: The Brookings Institution, 1975), 48.

96 Ibid., 47, 64.

97 Some commentators think that consumerism explains why people are not angrier about inequality. Consumer choice goes a long way to keep most Americans reasonably content. See Steven Quartz and Anette Asp, "Unequal, Yet Happy, *The New York Times*, April 12, 2015, SR4.

98 Simon Reid-Henry, *The Political Origins of Inequality: Why a More Equal World Is Better for Us All* (Chicago: The University of Chicago Press, 2015), 183–184. See also Pierre Rosanvallon, *The Society of Equals* (Cambridge, MA: Harvard University Press, 2013).
99 See Joe Klein, "Democracy's Discontent: The Debate Over Health Reform Is a Case Study of How Special Interests Trump the Common Good," *Time*, August 10, 2009, 34–35.
100 Jeffrey D. Sachs, "Flying Blind in Policy Reforms: Health Care, Climate Change, and Other Complex Topics Demand More Expert and Public Debate," *Scientific American*, May 2010, 32.
101 Ibid.
102 Sheri Berman, "What Marx Forgot," *Dissent*, Fall 2011, 99.

2   The Spiritual Crisis of Capitalism

In the first chapter I tried to show that there is a material crisis in capitalistic countries in that Western societies like the United States have had to take on more and more debt to keep capitalism going. Public policy measures have been adopted to keep competition alive, provide some stability to the system through measures designed to stimulate the economy when necessary, take steps to deal with poverty in the midst of plenty, pass measures to assure people will have something on which to retire, provide health care to the elderly and those in poverty and more recently extend medical insurance to the uninsured, bail out companies and whole industries when necessary, and now to deal with inequality. This material crisis is part and parcel of another crisis that I call the spiritual crisis of capitalism.

Capitalism has created a spiritual void which is related to the seeming inability of capitalistic societies to come to grips with the material problems they are creating. This chapter will present several philosophical critiques of capitalism that examine this spiritual crisis from various perspectives. This discussion sort of sets the stage for the following chapter, which looks at the political problems facing the United States, where we seem to have lost a spiritual connection with each other, and then a discussion of environmental problems, where we have lost a spiritual connection with nature. We seem to have lost any sense of community in our political discourse and view nature in largely instrumental terms as something to be exploited in the interests of capitalistic growth.

Philosophical Critiques

In his book *Critique of Western Philosophy and Social Theory*, David Sprintzen, professor emeritus of philosophy at Long Island University, believes that we are currently in the midst of a global cultural and metaphysical transformation that is at least equal in scope to that which transformed culture some four centuries earlier. The Industrial Revolution and the Protestant Reformation undermined feudalism in the sixteenth and seventeenth centuries, and likewise the globalization of information, communication, production, and investment have undermined traditional conceptions of national and local sovereignty beginning in the late twentieth century. Breakthroughs in science have forced revisions in our understanding of time, space, matter, energy; of society, self, consciousness; and of life.[1] As he puts it,

> [o]ur fundamental modes of thought and action, institutional structure, personal identity, economic development, and relation to nature, all require radical revision if human life on this planet (and beyond) is to survive and prosper.[2]

There is a crisis of belief in modern civilization that becomes, as Sprintzen states, a crisis of purpose and values. People need to believe in something; they need a direction for their lives, a purpose for it all, and a set of values by which to live and organize their relations with others in a meaningful fashion. But we no longer have these values, according to the author, with the kind of assurance that is needed to sustain a direction for our lives and give them meaning and purpose. Religion has been the source for many of these values and gives purpose and meaning to life for many people:[3]

> Religions across the world have built up, on, and around these mythic stories, giving personal meaning, institutional sustenance, and salvific promise to our lives. They have provided us with the dramatic sense of being on a cosmic journey, a divinely ordained providential mission that grounds moral values and social institutions, orients our individual and collective lives, gives direction to human undertakings, and offers the vision and holds out the promise of eternal felicity.[4]

Yet religion is increasingly being confronted by a scientific worldview that is composed of matter that operates in accord with mechanical and purpose-less natural laws that govern the universe. Religion, however, sees a spiritual world that was created by God that is ruled by moral values rather than natural laws, where humans are generally free and responsible agents serv-ing some divine purpose.[5] Scientific hypotheses can be tested by empirical methods that verify the truth or falsity of scientific claims. Religion, on the other hand, relies on revealed truth and, when challenged, has no procedure by which its claims can be verified.[6] This scientific worldview has provided a challenge for the religious worldview that poses a dilemma for people in modern society:

> Increasingly, the practical world of the everyday operates independently of, if not at odds with, the mythic frame of traditional religions. More and more, individuals find themselves living in two incompatible worlds, "earning a living" in a world dominated by the institutions and thought patterns of modern science, business, and technology, while interpret-ing and celebrating our life in the ceremonial world of traditional moral and religions observance . . . Modern civilization is thus confronted

with an increasingly agonizing contradiction: between the science (and technology) upon which its survival and development depends and the mythology and religion without which humans seem to feel totally lost.[7]

This is a spiritual crisis as the traditional source of spirituality is not longer plausible in a scientific and technological culture. While religion provides a spiritual foundation for many people who are concerned about freedom, dignity, purpose, quality, and value, the growing practical theoretical ascendancy of the scientific worldview has put this religious perspective on the defensive and spawned an uncompromising fundamentalist reaction.[8]

This reaction can get quite extreme and involve the teaching of creationism (or as it is now called intelligent design), the rewriting of history to make America seem a Christian nation from its founding, a rejection of scientific findings on global warming, and other such flights from reality.

But science has its own problems as the Newtonian view of the universe is reductionistic, mechanistic, atomistic, deterministic, and entirely material in its outlook.[9] In principle, everything is entirely predictable if one knows the initial conditions, as atomic elements follow the deterministic laws of nature.[10] Such a world has no place for spirituality or for consciousness, mind, choice, freedom, or value. These things are held to be the product of our subjective fantasy or imagination; they are but subjective illusions created by the objective working of material nature. The only thing that is real, according to the scientific worldview, is that which can be completely described by mathematics.[11]

As Galileo is reported to have said, mathematics is "the language of nature." The power of science to explain the world and to produce technology that has transformed our world cannot be denied, according to Sprinzen. Yet who among us can live in a world without values, that is predetermined and apparently without values, and that has no spiritual dimension.[12] Science has undermined values as scientific method cannot be used to verify which values are the right ones that will lead to human fulfillment. Thus, values are considered to be matters of opinion or personal preference. There is no way to establish, apart from an appeal to some secular or religious authority, the values one should live by and society should follow. Confusion about values abounds, which results in something of an amoral society where scientific method dominates the search for truth. A scientific worldview holds that education can and should be value-free, and scientists can and should conduct value-free research that is completely objective in nature. Thus, values are highly problematic in a scientific and technological world.

The great American philosopher John Dewey states the problem in the following manner:

> It is more of less commonplace to speak of the crisis which has been caused by the progress of the natural sciences in the last few centuries. The crisis is due, it is asserted, to the incompatibility between the

conclusions of natural science about the world in which we live and the realm of higher values, of ideal and spiritual qualities, which get no support from natural science. The new science, it is said, has stripped the world of the qualities which made it beautiful and congenial to men; has deprived nature of all aspiration toward ends, all preference for accomplishing the good, and presented nature to us as a scene of indifferent particles acting according to mathematical and mechanical laws . . . philosophers have been troubled by the gap in kind which exists between the fundamental principles of the natural world and the reality of the values according to which mankind is to regulate its life.[13]

When the subject matter of science became exclusively physical and mechanistic and science took over the domain of the natural world, according to Dewey, the dualistic opposition of matter and spirit arose, the split of nature from ultimate ends and goods and values worth pursuing. Concerns about qualities and purposes of life were excluded from nature by science and had to become rooted in the realm of the spiritual, which was considered to be above nature but yet was its source and foundation. The tension created by these oppositions gave rise to all the characteristic problems of modern philosophy. There was a necessary connection between nature and spirit, yet philosophy could be neither frankly naturalistic and give up the spiritual realm nor fully spiritual and disregard the conclusions of modern science. Since human beings were, on one hand, a part of nature and, on the other hand, a member of the realm of the spirit, all problems of philosophy came to focus on this double nature.[14] Again according to Dewey,

> [t]hus, either we find the world divided between two completely incompatible metaphysical orientations, each of which is essentially monistic and reductive, or we are left with a completely implausible dualistic amalgam. The vast majority of the world's people believe in a religio-idealist interpretation that is fundamentally inconsistent with the scientific worldview that provides the foundation for technological developments by which we all increasingly live. But it is this very spiritualistic approach that ground's the world's ethical systems, and sustains human beings' sense of the meaning and dignity of their lives and the possibility of their having some effective control over their daily life.[15]

Sprintzen argues that we need to find a way to celebrate our life recognizing that we are part of a collective rather than a lonely individual. We need to find purpose and meaning in life and affirm values that lead to human fulfillment without appealing to a divine being to justify our lives and given them meaning.[16] We need a spiritual rebirth as social change depends upon such a spiritual transformation. Social policy cannot produce moral development and social improvement without such a spiritual transformation that will lead to a change in values and attitudes on the part of individuals and families.[17] Such a transformation involves a "secular vision of a religious ideal that can inspire human activity and sustain communal life." Ethical reflection must be grounded in scientific intelligence, without an appeal to the supernatural, that offers a moral vision and undergirds social institutions that can truly sustain and nurture community life and fulfill urgent human needs:[18]

> [W]e need to feel we are a meaningful center of activity and value in a socially rooted cosmic drama. We need to construct a social order that gives us a sense of place and that sustains a sense of the meaningfulness of our personal effort. Without sustaining communities, we are cut loose; without soil, we cannot take root and grow . . . Such communities themselves need a habitat . . . Such communities must thus remain both open to diversity and supportive of the individuality of their members and yet sufficiently cohesive so as to be effective forces for humanization in the wider society. Only by providing both emotional and social sustenance for their members with the opportunity to participate in a common effort with self-transcending human significance can they begin to effectively address the pervasive spiritual hunger of our "postreligious" world.[19]

Instead of success being rooted in the "competitive accumulation of material wealth" it must be transformed into a more modest attitude that supports communal life. Torn between individual and community, Americans need to find a way to collectively celebrate their shared destiny.[20] Otherwise, says Sprintzen, we will not be able to control the growing hostilities that are tearing at the fabric of the country's personal and institutional life. If these forces are not controlled it will lead to the imposition of an increasingly repressive techno-bureaucratic order by the "established bureaucracies of power and wealth."[21] Unless the country combats executive supremacy, capitalist audacity, and imperialist penetration (almost always in the name of promoting freedom and democracy), America will be unable to "avoid the disaster of benign fascism toward which it has been creeping."[22]

In a book titled *Plato's Revenge: Politics In The Age Of Ecology*, award-winning author William Ophuls, attempts to sketch the basic outline of a new public philosophy based on political as well as ecological grounds. He argues that the old political paradigm based on the concepts and beliefs that came from Thomas Hobbs and his successors is no longer viable because it abandons virtue and rejects community. It was bound to self-destruct even before ecological scarcity emerged as a major problem for modern societies. The moral decay, social breakdown, economic excess, and administrative despotism that are evident everywhere in the developed world are not, according to Ophuls, the result of defective public *policies* but rather are the result of a defective public *philosophy*.[23]

Hobbs deserves much of the blame for this defective philosophy says Ophuls. Hobbes rejected the idea that the state has a duty to make its citizens virtuous in accordance with some common ideal of the good life and, instead, let individual citizens pursue their own ends and follow their own ideals with the state merely keeping the peace and refereeing the actions of its citizens to prevent harm to others. Morality was relegated to the private sphere, where rationality was supposed to guide individual behavior into beneficial social outcomes.[24] Freed of the obligation to promote virtuous outcomes, the state dedicated itself to provide material gratification for its citizens.[25]

Limited government that promotes a wide space for personal liberty requires a virtuous people. However, while rationality may liberate us from superstition and dispose of myth and religion as well, it ruthlessly deconstructs every form of meaning and authority.[26] A politics that is purely rational and material, that has no moral code or a vision of what constitutes the good life and no sense of the sacred, is a contradiction in terms according to Ophuls. As a result, "polity today is more and more a mere alliance of self-interested individuals who pursue their own private ends and who accept only minimal restraints on their actions. Liberty has become license, and the social basis of the modern, liberal state has eroded away."[27]

When Hobbs separated politics from virtue, it led to a moral decay in the society at large. As a result, "the legal and bureaucratic machinery of government has grown larger and more oppressive in a vain attempt to make up for the social decline."[28] Anarchy must be avoided by an increase in outer compulsion to make up for the decline in inner lawfulness in society at large. The modern state has had to step in to replace a civil society that has had its vigor sapped by moral entropy. Hobbes himself maintained that a Leviathan would have to arise to keep order in a society based on liberal but amoral principles. In our day that means an increasingly heavy-handed legal and administrative tyranny. The lack of virtue in society means a government of force rather than consent where the behavior of people is shaped by laws rather than morality.[29]

The only possible source for a new moral code, says Ophuls, is natural law—a law that is in agreement with the natural world. He recognizes that the idea of a natural law has lost all philosophical respectability in modern times. The application of science to human affairs has undercut any epistemological stance from which to derive natural law. Rather than a sentient universe charged with moral meaning, science discovered a machine—dead matter—that is governed by mathematical laws that teach us nothing about how we should live our lives. The way out is to rediscover the relevance of natural law:[30]

> By discovering and appreciating the moral order implicit in the natural world, we can derive ethical principles that will serve as a basis for polity and society in the twenty-first century and beyond . . . Ecology, physics, and psychology—that is, biological nature, physical nature, and human nature—reveal fundamental and eternally valid moral principles with which to reconstitute our polity.[31]

On this foundation, Ophuls attempts to construct a rule of life at the core of which is a politics of consciousness grounded in ecology and dedicated to the notion that ennobling human beings is more important than accumulating dead matter. The dominance of material values must be rejected in favor of a quest for wisdom and virtue. In no other way can the passions of modern humans be tamed so that they are fit for civilization and in turn can remake civilization so that it is fit for them and in which they can live a fulfilling and meaningful life.[32] The root problem of society, he states, "is that we are approaching, if we have not already exceeded, the limits of material development." Thus, we must shift our focus from quantity to quality, from matter to spirit, from outer expansion to inner cultivation.[33]

To enable this shift Ophuls recommends that more attention must be given to an aesthetic education that goes beyond mere music or art appreciation. Education must include an expanded more Platonic version of the classical liberal arts curriculum including music, gymnastics, and poetry in addition to logic, mathematics, and other rational disciplines. This emphasis on aesthetics must be balanced against the need for scientific and technical education to enrich us physically, psychologically, emotionally, and intellectually.[34]

Science has not eliminated the need for humans to make sense of their world nor has it abolished the human desire for satisfactory answers to the suffering people experience. Beyond rational explanation lies a vast realm of silence, as he puts it, that contains everything that is most important to human beings "without an emotionally satisfying story, the average man or woman simply has no answer to the riddle of life and death and is therefore liable to lapse into a state of spiritual vertigo."[35]

Lacking such a story humans have cast about for a substitute, which is most often an ideology that provides the answer to life's complexity by focusing on the *one* right way to do things. It purports to explain everything that is wrong with the world and provides a simple solution to these wrongs whether it be overthrowing of the bourgeois, leaving it to the market, getting government out of the way, abolishing sexual repression, or whatever. Ideology simplifies things and makes it possible for people to think they understand how the world works and what they should do to make things better.[36]

The attempt to live scientifically, which Ophuls describes as relying on reason that is unalloyed by myth, has failed miserably. The myths that informed Western civilization in former times have been transformed into instrumental rationality, where it is believed that humans can control organic and human nature and use the power that this rationality provides for mostly benign or utopian ends. But humans cannot exist without some kind of story that gives them meaning and coherence and provides the moral and intellectual basis for political community:[37]

> We need to rediscover a sacred truth that neither conflicts with reason nor oppresses the individual and then to make that understanding the

basis of a spiritualized politics. In other words, we need a nonsacerdotal, nonsectarian, nontheological, nontribal religious worldview that is compatible with science and that provides personal orientation, moral guidance, and a framework for public order without imposing dogmas that must be believed or priests who must be obeyed.[38]

Modern societies live on depleting energy and borrowed time, says Ophuls, but a day of reckoning approaches. For civilization to survive it must be inspired and guided by a different ideal that renounces endless material acquisition and "makes a virtue out of the necessity of living within our ecological means."[39] Material simplicity, as Thoreau said, is the prerequisite for spiritual abundance. Nature imposes intrinsic limits on human greed and selfishness, but the scientific and industrial revolutions removed those limits leaving humans "free" to pursue wealth and power without constraint. We must recover those limits and ground human life on the natural values of humility, moderation, and connection:[40]

> We have carried the drive for material wealth and power to an extreme beyond which it cannot advance much further. It becomes daily more apparent that modern civilization confronts deep structural problems that have no plausible solution—if by solution is meant more tinkering with our current social and political arrangements.[41]

> The essential lesson of systems ecology is that our fate is linked to everything else in the biosphere and that we do not and cannot exist apart from the rest of nature . . . A race that has overrun the planet materially has nowhere to turn but the *spiritual* realm. Now that we can no longer live at the expense of the rest of creation, we must learn to live in harmony with it, and such a state of harmonious interdependence will require a mature culture that fosters inner satisfaction and intrinsic meaning.[42]

According to Ophuls there are five great ills that have plagued civilization since its beginning. These are ecological exploitation, military aggression, economic inequality, political oppression, and spiritual malaise.[43] These five ills have become evils in modern times that threaten the continued existence of human society. We ruthlessly exploit and abuse nature degrading our natural habitat. Military aggression has escalated into a potential holocaust. Our economic system has resulted in greater and greater inequality. Political oppression has hardly vanished and is evident even in states that value liberty. Even democracies have become a sham as powerful economic interests have come to make all the important decisions. And finally, he says, spiritual malaise is pandemic.[44]

The Enlightenment philosophy that informs modern society has tried to cure these ills with more power, more aggression, more exploitation, more abstraction, and more alienation. The result is a state in which civilization's flaws are amplified and intensified so that it becomes an engine of destruction. The solution cannot possibly be more of the same but must involve the creation of a civilization that does not repeat past errors but yet incorporates the wisdom of past civilizations. We have tried to escape from the constraints of nature by overpowering them and from social and moral constraints by discarding them. "This is a mistaken strategy for achieving either individual happiness or collective well-being."[45]

The greatest weapon of mass destruction on the planet, according to Ophuls, is the collective ego. History teaches us that the human capacity for evil is virtually unlimited and unless wisdom and virtue are employed to counteract the ego's potential for destruction actual destruction is inevitable.[46] Only a politics of consciousness that is rooted in the moral vision of ecology can save humankind and create a civilization that is worthy of the name. This must be an ecological civilization that lives in harmony with nature, where wealth is measured in spirit and not in property, and a political civilization where liberty, equality, and fraternity can flourish.[47]

For many, science's disenchantment of the world is seen as a liberation as science empowers us and gives us control over nature manipulate it in our interests. Science removes technical obstacles through technology, which constructs machines that provide the means for us to reach our goals. Science also conquers superstitions and gives us an understanding of how the world works, but in the process it also *disenchants* the world by eliminating all sorts of imaginary beings, forces, and powers that used to constrain us from doing certain things. Once these are done away with, we can take full advantage of the technology that stems from scientific discoveries. In empowering us and giving us control over nature, science drains the world of meaning and purpose which threatens to undermine its capacity to empower us further.[48]

According to David Owens, who teaches at the University of Sheffield in the United Kingdom, science enables us to manipulate the world and bend it to our will: "In the last four hundred years, a comprehensive theory of the physical world has been devised." This theory was applied to all aspects of human life during the Industrial Revolution, which could not have occurred without the technology that was science's most tangible product. Science acknowledges that humans have purposes and that we try to impose those purposes on the world in fixing our environment to suit ourselves. By itself technical know-how was useless until science disenchanted the world by stripping it of any purpose that might conflict with our aims. Once this happened, according to Owens, we felt entitled to apply technology everywhere:[49]

> The Industrial Revolution required us to exploit the natural world, to interfere with its workings on a scale never before imagined: we had to

dig up fossil fuels, create canals, divert rivers, build factories and cities on virgin land, and that was only the beginning. Those who did all this viewed nature as a resource, there to be used by humanity for its own ends and, with the aid of genetic technology, these people are now redesigning our crops and livestock. For them, nature has no purpose of its own, it is dumb material waiting to be made into some useful.[50]

Disenchantment of the world, for Owens, refers to science's removal of natural purpose and meaning from the world. For many people this disenchantment is liberating as it enables us to shape our natural environment to suit ourselves. But regardless of whether this disenchantment is seen as a good or bad thing who among us can live without modern technology? And who would forgo the benefits of industrialization? The scientific attitude may be the right attitude toward the natural world or at least the only feasible one for us to adopt, says Owens. But the disenchantment of nature also affects the understanding we have of ourselves and leads to the disenchantment of human beings themselves.[51]

Science considers human beings to be part of the natural world and material in nature so that we can discover how we function and find ways to make the body and mind more pleasing to ourselves. The human body is under our control, and we can cure diseases, overcome handicaps, and remove physical deformities. We can shape the body to our liking with breast implants, face lifts, and even change our gender. The body is a machine that exists to serve our purposes. This image of the body as a machine is meant to be liberating as nothing about the body can be taken as a given to limit us in certain ways. We have the ability to overcome those limits by making changes to the body through surgeries or through other means like exercise to build muscles.[52]

While we are still subject to mental illness and mental defects, we can through therapy and medication overcome mental illness to some degree and change our moods and attitudes toward life in general. Once we understand what causes our behavior, the physical basis of our desires, for example, we can manipulate its causes in the brain and predict even our own behavior. Science leads to a technology of the mind that eliminates purpose and meaning and disenchants human beings. Once we can alter our desires and moods in any way we please, how shall we decide what to do in this regard? Far from expanding our powers of self-control, mind-altering drugs threaten to undermine any grounds we have for make such a choice.[53]

For Owens, a scientific understanding of humans threatens their freedom because it undermines the capacity for self-governing by making decisions. If we are just a bunch of chemicals interacting with each other, once we know what these chemicals are, the Pharmacy of the Future gives us the ability to remix them at will so that we can choose whatever character we happen to prefer. What Owens is worried about is that science threatens to remove the fixed points that are needed to make decisions making possible. Science confronts us with the possibility of an indefinite of both the self and its environment. But science also tells us that there is nothing normative about these decisions so that they are more or less arbitrary and random and have no grounding in a normative framework. Owens concludes that "[s]hould science be the whole truth about human beings, that truth will not set us free."[54]

Theodore Adorno, a critical theorist who helped found the so-called Frankfurt School (see Chapter 9), believes that modern science possesses an undeniable authority in modern society because of the success of its technological applications. But he also thinks that science empties the world of an objective meaning and that modern science and bureaucratic rationality lead to a disenchantment of the world and increase a sense of metaphysical despair.[55] His main concern is the fact that the progress of scientific rationality is too rarely adequately matched by advances in the social forms of organization in which that progress is located.[56] Contradictions between the individual and the social are the product of the split between the individual and the social that resulted from the demise of the idea of a natural social order that is constitutive of modernity and a condition of modern conceptions of freedom. The individual stands over against the social order rather than being a part of it and is in constant tension with the demands of social institutions that need order in order to function effectively.[57] According to Andres Bowie in a book about Adorno,

> Adorno is quite happy to accept the truth of well-confirmed scientific theories; his philosophical concern is rather with how those truths affect human culture in the face of the failures of societies in modernity to achieve just social arrangements . . . Adorno is clear that so much of what happens in the social world is the product of competing forces, where individual actors will find it very hard to judge what the implications and consequences of their ideas and actions are. Precisely because it is so hard to judge such matters, a narrow analytical focus can, though, become a problem.[58]

Adorno questions the cognitivist assumption that our essential relationship to the world is that of a subject seeking objective knowledge, including knowledge of itself, and that philosophy's task is to find a way of legitimatizing that knowledge. Modern philosophy that is oriented toward what he calls the scheme of subject and object produces contradictions precisely it seeks to ground our relationship to the world in a derivative mode of access in which the subject takes a neutral stance toward the object. Adorno argues that we have to "understand" the world in order to cope with it in a practical manner, and this depends on it making sense to us before we can abstract from that understanding in the form of objective explanation.[59] "The objectifications of the sciences are both an achievement of subjectivity and yet can also take on the objective power of the nature which the subject sought to control by these objectifications."[60] Again according to Bowie,

> [s]ince Kant much Western philosophy has . . . tended to regard nature predominately as the object of the natural sciences, and this has led to the sense that questions of subjectivity are somehow radically different from questions in the physical sciences, of will eventually be reduced to physicalist forms of explanation. Neither position, though, is satisfactory . . . He [Adorno] is, then, concerned not with an attempt so see truth claims in the natural sciences as inherently infected by ideology, but rather with the over-extension of scientific claims into what is in fact the realm of obsolete metaphysics.[61]

Discussion of "nature" in metaphysical terms, according to Adorno, became an increasing problem in the twentieth century as the world was explained ever more successfully by the natural sciences. Many philosophical accounts of nature were rendered redundant by this scientific approach because they lacked empirical confirmation and either overtly or covertly sought to restore teleological assumptions that were contradicted by nonteleological forms of scientific explanation. However, philosophical concern with "nature" and our place in it has been revived because of a contemporary sense that the relationship of humans to the nonhuman world is in crisis. The assumption that scientific discovery of nature's laws should be the main focus of philosophical attention has given way to questions about the relationship of science to the rest of human culture. The obvious problem for Adorno is all this is what is actually meant by "nature":[62]

> What emerges here is a conflict over how nature is understood which is not just a philosophical dispute about a contested concept. Wellmer makes the decisive point: 'The nature which we, as acting and deliberating creatures, are *aware of* as our own nature—the nature Adorno speaks of—is not the nature of scientific objectified brain processes, but the living nature of our body with its neediness, its impulses, its potentials and its vulnerability'. Nature is both the 'the lawfulness of appearances in space and time' of natural science, and what, even from a post-metaphysical, Darwin-informed point of view, we know or feel ourselves to be, independently of however much science we also happen to know. I may think my depression has to do with serotonin levels, but that is not how I experience it: depression can only be properly understood *as* depression via its phenomenology, not by putative physical causes and states whose alteration may alleviate it.[63]

Adorno wants to avoid making nature into a kind of foundational concept that is defined by what it is not thus contrasting it to mind in whatever sense it gets in philosophy. This approach avoids the need to define nature or mind in a true philosophical sense and makes the very idea that one should define these concepts a mistake, which is why nature and history are inextricably linked.[64] While Hegel made the end result of mediation of subject and object the foundation of his philosophy, Adorno argues against such a foundational given and maintains that there is no such last thing that is a given and is purified of all mediations whether it be pure consciousness or pure sense data.[65] At the same time, however, Adorno adopts much of the dialectical manner of Hegel's thinking and his insights into the nature of contradictions, which Adorno sees as arising through social interaction.[66]

Adorno also sees a deficit in Hegelian rationalism as it fails to take sufficient account of the dialectical nature of instrumental rationality which can mutilate the human and natural worlds as it shapes them according to human purposes: "The success of the natural sciences seems, though, to bring more and more of what the subject is onto the side of nature by bringing it under natural laws." This success is a cultural achievement and in this sense an achievement of subjectivity.[67] While Hegel attempts to see the rational element even in the most appalling circumstances and deals with human suffering with a rational understanding of its necessity to advance reason in history, Adorno sees this as a repression of suffering in the name of "optimism about history":[68]

> The Holocaust employed the rationalized means of technologically developed societies to enable what would otherwise have been impossible. On aspect of this was precisely the fact that these rationalized means allowed many of those contributing to the horror to exclude the kind of thoughts and feelings that would have prevented them from contributing. They did so by reducing the victims to ways of thinking which wholly objectified them, by abstracting from their nature as individual sufferers.[69]

Hegel criticizes Kant's categorical imperative for being empty and formalistic because it offers only an abstract criterion for how to act in any given situation and fails to recognize that individual action is always situated and always informed by the historically developed ethical life of a community. But by adhering to the norms of a community something which leads to gross inhumanity may well be produced.[70] "If one lacks the insight into what can be evil, and simply follows desires and urges, there is no good or evil, just the functioning of the natural ground."[71] Such scientific reductionism means that there is no moral basis for sanctioning human behavior and that we should instead rely on present or future forms of chemical or other intervention to correct deviations that threaten society. But where would the authority for such interventions come from? According to Adorno, "any answer to this question presupposes more than can be legitimated in terms of a scientific explanation based on the assumption of the solidity of facts as opposed to the arbitrariness of values."[72]

> Much of the contemporary debate over naturalism seeks . . . to reduce the mental to being part of nature in the formal sense. This kind of identity of mind and nature leaves no role for freedom, and tends to lead to ineffectual appeals to compatibilism. The problem is that if the world is to be fully explained in deterministic terms, it becomes hard to understand why there are moral issues in any meaningful sense at all. The power of such reductionist positions derives from the fact that natural scientific research reveals the extent of our causal dependence, and social and historical research reveals the ways in which we are influenced by social and historical circumstances. The position suffers, though, from a metaphysical assumption which is not based on such research, or is invalidly extrapolated from it.[73]

According to Adorno, however much we gain from the insights of neuroscience and other scientific discoveries about the human organism, "one of the key tasks of contemporary philosophy is to break the link between such insights and a reductive metaphysics which easily becomes a form of manipulative ideology."[74] Adorno thinks that the potential dangers of such an atomistic approach have not been the least bit obvious in key areas of modern thought. The method of reducing what is at issue to objects of specific and often mathematical analysis has regularly led to serious problems. Adorno's point is "not just that any intellectual tool can, in the wrong circumstances produce disaster, but that the reason for the disaster is that the tool is employed to the exclusion of what lies outside its frame of reference":[75]

> The whole trend of much modern economic theory, in which mathematical models are built which eliminate consideration of what people are actually know to do in real contexts, had now, in the light of such effects, led to a crisis in the subject . . . Models of the kind used in 'thought experiments' may play a useful role in the physical sciences, but the kind of debate engendered in the human sciences by such models is more of an obstacle to insight than an illumination, because it fakes a conceptual clarity which the complexity of real circumstances precludes. History tells us we often don't know what ultimately motivates people to do morally praiseworthy things, but it tells us a lot about what makes them do appalling things[76]

Morris Berman, assistant professor in the Programme in Science and Human Affairs at Concordia University in Montreal, Canada, writing in *The Reenchantment of the World*, argues that the most fundamental issues civilization confronts at any time in its history are issues of meaning. This holds true for individuals as well. And the loss of meaning experienced in the contemporary world stems from the Scientific Revolution of the sixteenth and seventeenth centuries. The dominant mode of thinking that comes from this revolution includes disenchantment as it involves a total separation from nature. Science is based on a mechanical worldview and insists on a rigid distinction between observer and observed; "subject and object are always seen in opposition to each other." People do not feel a part of the world around them, they are alienated from it and do not really feel a sense of belonging. This alienation results in the various ills society is experiencing.[77]

For the great majority of human history, the world was an enchanting place and humans felt they belonged. The disenchantment that has taken place in the last 400 years or so has destroyed the continuity of human experience and the integrity of the human psyche and has nearly wrecked the planet, according to Berman. The only hope lies in a re-enchantment of the world.[78]

The scientific worldview sees the world as something to be acted upon rather than merely contemplated. This was a departure from Greek thought which was more static than dynamic. The question of "how" became more important than the "why," which became increasingly irrelevant.[79] Disturb nature, alter it, do anything to it, but do not leave it alone. It is to be manipulated to our advantage. The world we confront is a separate object that can be broken down into its components. Knowledge consists of subdividing a thing into its smallest components so they can be manipulated. The world consists of matter and motion, and the realm of the spiritual plays no part in its operation. As Berman says, the scientific worldview treated all nonmaterial phenomena as ultimately having a material basis.[80]

Descartes did not want to subject the mind to this mechanical and reductionistic worldview, so he located it outside of nature where it became a radically disparate entity from the body. The mind was located in a totally different category from the body and resulted in the mind–body duality that plagues philosophy and science even today. For Descartes this mind–body split meant that in the act of thinking one was perceived as a separate entity, the "in here," that confronted things "out there." This mind-body duality formed the heart of the Cartesian paradigm.[81]

Newton validated the Cartesian outlook that the world is a vast machine of matter and motion that obey mathematical laws that can be discovered by the power of scientific thinking. The universe that may once have been seen as alive in some sense having its own goals and purposes became a collection of inert matter having no particular purpose or meaning. What could not be quantified was not real, and truth became equated with utility, which involved the purposive manipulation of the environment. The holistic view of humans as a part of nature and as being at home in the universe became a romantic notion that had no validity in a scientific understanding of the world.[82]

Reason became instrumental. The question, "Is this good?" was no longer asked. The only relevant question became, "Does this work?" a question that reflected the growing emphasis on production, prediction, and control.[83] Science is integrally related to the rise of capitalism as instrumental reason led to the exploitation and manipulation of the environment to served human interests in economic growth and increasing production for profit. Modern science and technology are based on a hostile attitude toward the environment and see the environment as only a source for raw materials for use by the industrial facilities of capitalism and as a gigantic dumping ground for the waste material that results from capitalistic production.

To deal with the problems modern science poses for the world, Berman argues that we must restore a participating consciousness that is scientifically or at least rationally credible. If this can't be done what it means to be human will be lost forever.[84] An understanding of what he calls the "stubborn persistence" of participating consciousness can help solve the problem of radical relativism and suggest some theoretical underpinnings for a post-Cartesian science.[85] Yet the denial of participation lies at the heart of modern science, as modern textbooks describe a formally applied "scientific method" in which any notion of participating consciousness would be tantamount to heresy. But the disparity between the official image of science and its actual practice is enormous as the scientist participates in nature even if it is described as mechanical and materialistic.[86]

The emergence of quantum mechanics involves a break with this classical image of science, as it implies that there is no such thing as an independent observer. Human behavior itself becomes part of the experiments physicists do as it alters the outcomes. There is no clear boundary between subject and object as humans are participants in the world they are describing. As Heisenberg put it, "[w]hat we observe is not nature in itself but nature exposed to our line of questioning." Thus, subjectivity cannot be ruled out in our perceptions of reality which is more indeterminate than we would like to think. Instead of certainty we have to deal with probabilities that enter into our measurement systems.[87]

There is something material out there that does exist independently of us, but we are in a systemic relationship with that reality and unknowingly alter it in the course of our investigations and end up finding what we seek because of the way we structure our experiments. The subject/object merger is intrinsic to quantum mechanics, according to Berman, and is part of a very different scientific paradigm that involves a new relationship between mind and body and the conscious and unconscious mind.[88] We need to deny that such distinctions exist and formulate a new set of scientific questions based on something other than the traditional Cartesian paradigm. What is at issue, according to Berman, "is the notion that observation makes no difference for what we learn about the thing being investigated."[89]

Mastery over nature and economic rationality that stem from the Cartesian paradigm have resulted in the most unecological and self-destructive culture ever created. This can be overcome, says Berman, by creating a holistic science which he sees as the great project and the great drama of the late twentieth century.[90] The work of Gregory Bateman, according to Berman, who is a little-known cultural anthropologist, represents the only fully articulated holistic science available. It is both scientific and based on an unconscious knowing. It situates us in the world and recognizes humanity's embeddedness in a complex and natural system.[91]

Bateman offers a non-Cartesian mode of *scientific* reasoning, according to Berman, that is holistic and as much intuitive as it is analytic. He describes it as a stance toward life and knowledge that is more of a commitment than a formula. Realities lay in wholes rather than parts, and immersion rather than analytic dissections is the way to wisdom.[92] Mind is imminent in the arrangement of phenomena rather than inherent in matter itself. Bateman understands participation as meaning that we are not separate from the things around us. The differences between the Cartesian paradigm and the paradigm of Bateman are shown in the chart that follows.

Comparison of Cartesian and Batesonian World Views

World view of modern science	World view of Batesonian holism
No relationship between fact and value	Fact and value inseparable
Nature is known from the outside, and phenomena are examined in abstraction from their context (the experiment).	Nature is revealed in our relations with it, and phenomena can be known only in context (participant observation).
Goal is conscious, empirical control over nature	Unconscious mind is primary, goal is wisdom, beauty, grace
Descriptions are abstract, mathematical; only that which can be measured is real.	Descriptions are a mixture of the abstract and the concrete; quality takes precedence over quantity.
Mind is separate from body, subject is separate from the object, linear time, infinite progress; we can in principle know all of reality.	Mind/body and subject/object are each two aspects of the same process, circuitry (single variables in the system cannot be maximized); we cannot in principle know more than a fraction of reality.
Logic is either/or; emotions are epiphenomenal.	Logic is both/and (dialectical); the heart as precise algorithms
Atomism	Holism
1. Only matter and motion are real.	1. Process, form, and relationship are primary.
2. The whole is nothing more than the sum of its parts.	2. The whole has properties that parts do not have.
3. Living systems are in principle reducible to inorganic matter; matter is ultimately dead.	3. Living systems, or minds, are not reducible to their components; nature is alive.

Source: From Morris Berman, *The Reenachment of the World* (Ithaca, NY: Cornell University Press, 1981), 238.

Batesonian ethics is based on relationship, recognition of the complex network pathways in which the individual is involved. The unit of survival is the entire ecosystem in which the creature lives, not the individual organism or species itself. If a creature destroys its environment, it destroys itself. In pitting individual survival against the survival of the ecosystem, in pitting man against nature, Western thought has managed to throw individual survival into question. There are limits to how many times nature can be exploited in the interests of humans before the planet decides to render humans extinct in order to save itself. As Berman puts it, "[t]he Judeo-Christian tradition sees us as masters of the household. Batesonian holism see us as guests in nature's home."[93]

We are addicted, according to Bateman, to maximizing variables that are destroying our natural ecosystem. Variation is seen as a threat, and we tend to strive for homogeneity, for unity of thought and behavior. We wipe out native cultures, individual ways of life and diverse ideas in order to substitute a global and homogeneous way of life that is more profitable for capitalism and more controllable for Western political systems. The natural world, however, avoids homogenous types because they create weakness, cannot produce anything new, have little flexibility, and are easily destroyed. Without diversity there cannot be emergence of new behaviors, genes, or organs for natural selection to operate upon. The streamlining of life has destroyed this diversity, and systems that are reduced in complexity become unstable and vulnerable.[94]

By way of contrast to Western civilization based on eliminating variation, a holistic civilization would cherish diversity and "see it as a gift, a form of wealth and property."[95] It will have a greater tolerance for the strange, the nonhuman, and diversity of all kinds. This civilization will also emphasize community over competition and individuation rather than individualism. Power will stem from an inner authority rather than from a particular position in an organization and will be used to influence others without pressure of coercion. Education will take the form of life-long learning that follows one's changing interests as people will not have careers but a life. And finally, "[t]he posture towards others, and toward natural resources, will be one of harmony rather than of exploitation or acquisition."[96]

These are idealistic ideas to be sure, but Berman is attempting to describe the mental framework of an emerging civilization that will create a new species and a new human being. Getting there will require that we get beyond the scientific worldview with its reductionistic approach: "we must try to see science as a thought system adequate to a certain historical epoch and attempt to separate ourselves from the common impression that it is some sort of absolute, transcultural truth."[97] This will be difficult for the Western world because science and technology have been so successful in improving our lives and making them easier in some sense. But, as Berman says, "we are living on a dying planet, and that without some radical shift in our politics and consciousness, our children's generation is probably going to witness the planet's last days."[98]

All of these authors in one way or another make the case for a spiritual crisis in our society that needs to be addressed. Sprintzen thinks there is a cultural and metaphysical transformation taking place that has produced a crisis of purpose and values. Religion, which has been a traditional source for meaning and purpose, has been undermined by science, which has no need for a supernatural dimension. Yet science is totally materialistic and does not deal with spiritual matters. Humans are part of a nature but are also members of the realm of the spirit. Humans cannot live without values to guide their life, yet science denigrates values to mere opinion or preference. Confusion abounds as to which values to live by necessitating a spiritual rebirth as meaningful social change depends upon such a spiritual transformation. What society needs is a spiritual revival that does not appeal to the supernatural.

Ophuls argues for a new public philosophy based on both political and ecological grounds. The problems the world is experiencing points to a defective public philosophy, not just specific public policies as such. Politics has become separated from virtue and has led to a government of force rather than consent, where behavior is shaped by laws rather than morality. Public philosophy must be based on a new foundation that Ophuls thinks should be founded on natural law despite the problems with a natural law approach that currently exist in philosophical thought. We must revive the idea that there is a moral order implicit in the natural world. We are nearing the limits of material development necessitating a shift in our approach to life from matter to spirit. A new politics of consciousness must be rooted in ecology, and we must learn to make a virtue out of limits to live within our ecological means implying that wealth should be measured in spirit rather than property.

Owens argues that science disenchants the world by eliminating all sorts of imaginary beings, forces, and powers that used to provides constraints, but once these are done away with, we can take full advantage of the technology that stems from scientific discoveries. Disenchantment means removal of purpose and meaning from the world, which for many people is liberating as it enables us to mold our natural environment to suit ourselves. As science discovers more about human beings themselves, it gives us ways to make the body and mind more pleasing to ourselves. But science also removes any normative grounding to make these kinds of decisions, thus undermining our capacity to make such decisions and threatening our freedom.

Adorno thinks that despite the success of modern science and its undeniable authority in Western societies, science has also emptied the world of an objective meaning that along with its bureaucratic rationality leads to a disenchantment of the world and increases a sense of metaphysical despair. His main concern is the fact that scientific progress is rarely matched by advances in the social forms of organization in which that progress is located. Adorno is concerned with the impacts of scientific truth on human culture given the failures of modern societies to achieve just social arrangements. The assumption that scientific discovery of nature's laws should be the main focus of philosophical attention has given way to questions about the relationship of science to the rest of human culture. The scientific method of reducing what is at issue to objects of specific and often mathematical analysis has led to serious problems in society.

Finally, Berman focuses on issues of meaning and argues that people do not feel a part of the world around them and are alienated from it and have no sense of belonging. Our society has lost a sense of meaning to life and has experienced a separation from nature that we manipulate to our advantage. A holistic view of humans as a part of nature has become a romantic notion in a scientific understanding of the world. The only hope for humans, he says, is a re-enchantment of the world that involves restoration of what Berman calls a participating consciousness that is credible in a scientific world. We must develop a holistic science that recognizes humanity's embeddedness in a complex natural system. The unit of survival is the entire ecosystem, not the individual organism or the species itself. A holistic civilization would cherish diversity and involve a radical shift in politics and consciousness, where diversity is cherished and community is emphasized over competition.

Notes

1 David Sprintzen, *Critique of Western Philosophy and Social Theory* (New York: Palgrave Macmillan, 2009), 9.
2 Ibid.
3 Ibid., 17.
4 Ibid., 5.
5 Ibid., 36.
6 Ibid., 18.
7 Ibid., 6, 7. "When you think about the incongruity of Christian or Muslim fundamentalists employing the most up-to-date communications technology to propagate a doctrine that rejects the scientific truths that make that technology possible, you can only marvel at the capacity of the human mind for self-deception—as well as the extent to which human beings will go in their desperate need to believe." Ibid., 17.
8 Ibid., 47.
9 Sprintzen refers to scientific reductionism when he discusses the mind, which contemporary science reduces to the brain, which is then understood as nothing but another organ in the body operating according to causally determined chemical principles. Thus, the possibility of human freedom is nothing but an illusion. Ibid., 151. "The tendency of many to assume that if they have found a physical process that is correlated with a specific mental activity they have thus explained that activity is but another expression of the implicit dualism that tends to infect so much of contemporary thought, thus providing the framework for the 'scientific' reduction of the mental to the material." Ibid., 252, n 26.

Instead of reductionism Sprintzen proposes that we think in terms of emergence: "Emergent phenomena are ones whose nature and operation cannot be completely explained by a description of the behavior of their constituent parts. They are systems of structured networks of relationships that have properties quite different from those of their 'constituent elements.' This means that the emergent has properties, powers, and modes of operation that: (a) are not possessed by the elements that make it up and (b) cannot be completely explained by, or reduced to, the properties and causal powers of those elements alone. Rather the properties and causal powers of the emergent are systemic. They are properties of the structure of the system. They operate with accordance with a causal logic that is particular to the emergent structures, and that requires the use of concepts and principles that cannot be completely replaced by those that describe the behavior of its constituent elements. Furthermore, the emergent's systemic properties and causal powers will usually have consequences that can actually determine the behavior of the very elements that compose it." Ibid., 68.

10 Ibid., 31. "Thus, if one could but know the initial position of each particle in the system, along with the natural laws of association, one could theoretically explain and predict all subsequent behavior. That also meant that one could explain more complicated things with the laws drawn from the simple since the more complicated were nothing but the result of the interactions of the simpler particles." Ibid., 34.

11 Ibid., 33.

12 Ibid., 35.

13 John Dewey, *The Quest for Certainty: A Study of the Relation between Knowledge and Action* (New York: Capricorn Books, 1960), 40–41.

14 Ibid., 53.

15 Ibid., 52, 53.

16 Sprintzen, *Critique of Western Philosophy*, 25.

17 Ibid., 156.

18 Ibid., 209.

19 Ibid., 26.

20 Ibid., 27.

21 Ibid., 186.

22 Ibid.

23 William Ophuls, *Plato's Revenge: Politics in the Age of Ecology* (Cambridge, MA: MIT Press, 2011), x.

24 Ibid., 16, 17.

25 Ibid., 19.

26 Ibid., 17.

27 Ibid., 6–7.

28 Ibid., 7.

29 Ibid., 18.

30 Ibid., 21–22.

31 Ibid., 22.

32 Ibid., 94.

33 Ibid., 107. Ophuls states that to create a rich, vibrant, and successful culture going forward, we will need the qualities of appreciation, intuition, discernment, imagination, vision, creativity, and other such qualities.

34 Ibid., 108.

35 Ibid., 80.

36 Ibid., 79–80.

37 Ibid., 122.

38 Ibid., 158.

39 Ibid., 167.
40 Ibid., 168, 170.
41 Ibid., 161.
42 Ibid., 176, 178. Italics mine.
43 Ibid., 1.
44 Ibid., 3–5.
45 Ibid., 195–196.
46 Ibid., 73.
47 Ibid., 196–197.
48 David Owens, "Disenchantment," in Louise M. Antony, ed., *Philosophers without Gods: Meditations on Atheism and the Secular Life* (New York: Oxford University Press, 2007), 165.
49 Ibid., 166–168.
50 Ibid., 168.
51 Ibid.
52 Ibid., 169.
53 Ibid., 172–174.
54 Ibid., 177–178.
55 Andres Bowie, "Introduction: Contemporary Alternatives," in Andrew Bowie, ed., *Adorno and the Ends of Philosophy* (Cambridge, UK: Polity Press, 2013), 46.
56 Ibid., 73.
57 Ibid., 126.
58 Ibid., 18–19.
59 Ibid., 51–52.
60 Ibid., 73.
61 Ibid., 92–93.
62 Ibid., 75.
63 Ibid., 79.
64 Ibid., 93.
65 Ibid., 57.
66 Ibid., 55.
67 Ibid., 72.
68 Ibid., 59.
69 Ibid., 19.
70 Ibid., 98–99.
71 Ibid., 116.
72 Ibid., 98.
73 Ibid., 114.
74 Ibid., 134.
75 Ibid., 27–28.
76 Ibid.
77 Morris Berman, *The Reenchantment of the World* (Ithaca, NY: Cornell University Press, 1981), 16–17. These ills include the collapse of capitalism, the general dysfunction of institutions, the revulsion against ecological spoliation, the increasing inability of scientific worldview to explain the things that really matter, the loss of interest in work, and the statistical rise in depression, anxiety, and outright psychosis. Ibid., 23. While new developments such as quantum mechanics have thrown the traditional mechanical worldview into question, they have not made a significant dent in the dominant mode of thinking according to Berman. Ibid., 16.
78 Ibid., 23.
79 Ibid., 28–29.

80 Ibid., 34.
81 Ibid., 34–35.
82 Ibid., 45–46.
83 Ibid., 54.
84 Ibid., 132.
85 Ibid., 136.
86 Ibid., 142–143.
87 Ibid., 144–145.
88 Ibid., 148–149.
89 Ibid., 184.
90 Ibid., 189.
91 Ibid., 196.
92 Ibid., 233, 234.
93 Ibid., 259.
94 Ibid., 262–263.
95 Ibid., 263.
96 Ibid., 275–277.
97 Ibid., 150. Berman's view of particle physics is worth repeating here. He says, "This attempt to find the ultimate material entity is still, foolishly, going on. Of the two hundred or so nuclear particles now recognized as existing, 90 percent of these have been discovered in the postwar era, suggesting that reality is more a function of the national budget than anything else. Since 1964, atomic physicists have posited the existence of 'quarks' (a word taken from *Finnegan's Wake*) to explain these particles, but their number has multiplied to the point that we may soon have a quark to explain each particle. Nor is this the end: to explain quarks, hidden variables have now been suggested. In fact, there is no end to the process. As Geoffrey Chew has pointed out, we detect particles because they interact with the observer, but in order to do so they must have some internal structure. This means that we can in principle never get to some object that has no internal structure, for a truly elementary particle could not be subject to any forces that would allow us to detect its existence (if we find it by its weight, for example, then it must contain something within it producing a gravitational field). On the Cartesian model we shall be chasing 'hidden variables' to the end of time. The disarray in modern physics became embarrassingly clear at the 1978 meeting of the American Physical Society in San Francisco, at which an appeal was made for a new Einstein to sort things out. The cul-de-sac of Cartesianism came out in a remark made by one Berkeley physicist that although no one knew what the proliferation of particles meant, at least we could measure them with great precision (!). On a more intelligent level, Werner Heisenberg called for a end to the concept of the elementary particle in 1975. William Irwin Thompson's remark that an 'elementary particle is what happens when you build an accelerator is not without some relevance here." Ibid., 319–320.
98 Ibid., 269.

3 The Crises of Politics and Nature

The materialistic and spiritualistic crises manifest themselves in our politics in and our treatment of nature. While the economy has seemingly recovered from the Great Recession of 2008 in that unemployment is down to reasonable levels and we have had some degree of growth in the economy in recent years, many people are struggling, can barely make it in our society, and have largely given up on the American dream. Many have jobs that barely pay enough for them to survive, and they see no hope of bettering themselves as good job opportunities are just not available. Those young people who see education as the way out are saddled with student debt at unprecedented levels that will take them years to pay off once they graduate. Meanwhile the rich are getting richer, and the really rich are getting ever-more richer, giving many people cause to wonder if the deck is not staked against them and the capitalistic society they live in is not fair in giving them a reasonable chance to get ahead.

Our political system seems unable to deal with this situation as the Republicans and Democrats are hopelessly divided in their view of the role of government in society. Republicans want to reduce the role of government in the economy and society and rely more on the market to do its magic and restore our country to its previous greatness. Many of their proposals would make the rich, who they consider to be the job creators, even richer while cutting support programs for the poor and letting them fend for themselves. Democrats, meanwhile, see a much more positive role for government to play in dealing with social and economic issues but have difficulty in getting their programs through Congress in the face of Republican intransigence. These political polarizations reflect the divisions in society as a whole and grow out of the lack of a spiritual connection with each other that would enable us to overcome these divisions in the interests of the society as a whole.

Meanwhile, our environmental problems continue to mount and increasingly demand more and more and money and attention. There are many climate change deniers in politics and in society as a whole despite all the evidence around them. The temperature of the earth continues to increase as 2015 was the warmest year ever recorded on earth by the largest margin on record and is the fourth year in the current century that a new global record has been set, yet it only deserved a short paragraph in some of our news media.[1] We continue to experience record heat, record droughts, record rain, and record snowfall in many parts of our own country, let alone the entire world, yet continue to deny that the climate in changing in ways that threaten our very existence. We have lost any spiritual connection with nature and continue to believe nature is something apart from ourselves that we can continue to treat as a garbage dump for our carbon emissions and other pollutants.

This chapter looks at our dysfunctional political system in some detail and examines the ways in which the environment is being affected by our activities to the detriment of our quality of life, if not our existence. The political difficulties we are experiencing goes way back to the founding of the country in some sense, as does our treatment of the natural world. Our country was rich in natural resources that could be exploited by a capitalistic system in the interests of making money and expanding corporate interests throughout the entire country. Our political system was founded on liberty and freedom (except for slaves) for people to pursue their own interests with little or no government interference. These values served us well for several centuries, but we are now in a situation where we have to examine these values and the political and economic systems we live in and determine if they can be perpetuated for coming generations.

The Political Crisis

A radical shift in our politics certainly seems necessary given the state of politics in the early years of the twenty-first century. Republicans and Democrats have had difficulty reaching an agreement on most everything brought before Congress, including immigration reform, gun control, and a host of other issues. In order to bypass Congress, President Obama issued various executive orders to address some of these issues like immigration, but these orders were opposed by Republicans, who claimed that the president had exceeded his executive authority, and some of these challenges ended up in the Supreme Court. There does not seem to be any willingness in Congress to work together in the interest of the country as a whole as Congress is polarized, reflecting the divisions in the country at large.[2]

Republicans have held the country hostage on several occasions over budget resolutions threatening to shut down the government or default on our national debt. They have carried out this threat on at least two occasions when Congress failed to reach agreement on the budget and the government had to shut down for some time because it ran out of money. In 2105, for example, the most conservative Republicans threatened to oppose any funding bill that did not defund Planned Parenthood because of the controversy over its abortion procedures. There were other controversies over the Iran nuclear deal made by the Obama administration without Congressional approval: reauthorization of the Export-Import Bank, increasing the debt limit, changing the defense and nondefense caps that had been imposed because of failure to reach an agreement on debt reduction in an earlier Congress, and keeping the Highway Trust Fund from running out of money.

At almost the last minute, just before midnight on October 26, 2015, Republicans and Democrats reached an agreement to increase the budget caps for fiscal years 2106 and 2017 and temporarily suspend the debt limit until March 15, 2107. The agreement authorized $80 billion in increased spending over two years which is to be offset by changes to Medicare, Social Security disability insurance, and other changes. It also repealed a provision of the Affordable Care Act (Obamacare) that would have required businesses that offered one or more health plans and have more than 200 employees to automatically enroll new full-time employees in a health plan. This provision had not yet taken effect. In order to achieve this agreement, however, the Speaker of the House, John Boehner, had to resign in order to install Paul Ryan, who was more acceptable to the most conservative Republicans and could convince them to give up on some of their more controversial demands, as Speaker.

Even so just over two-thirds of Republicans in the House and thirty-five Republicans in the Senate voted against the bill, which was called the Bipartisan Budget Act of 2015, making the title of the bill something of a misnomer. The deal also continues a trend beginning in 2010 with more emphasis placed on spending cuts rather than revenue increases. Ignoring the revenue side of the budget means that the wealthy will continue to benefit from tax breaks enacted over the last decade while spending cuts to education, affordable housing, and other such programs will hit families that are already struggling to keep their heads above water. Thus, the bill does nothing to address the inequality issue in our society. Nor does it address the needs of Social Security and Medicare for more resources due to the aging of the population.

What we have is fragmented government as the above example illustrates where the various interests on most issues find it impossible to compromise and get anything done at the federal level. The public's view of Congress is at an all-time low and does not seem likely to improve in the near future. Each party digs in its heels and will not deviate from what its ideology dictates. The Republicans will not agree to any tax increases even on the very rich, and correspondingly, the Democrats will not agree on any significant changes to entitlement programs. The public interest seems to get lost in the process as each faction is out to protect and promote its particular interests. The behavior of the two parties seems to reflect a view of government that denies there is anything like the public interest and sees government as just a competition of individual interests.

This view of government was described very clearly in a book published at the turn of the century. In 1908 to be exact, the University of Chicago Press published a book titled *The Process of Government* written by Arthur Bentley, a newspaperman who worked mostly at the Chicago *Times-Herald*.[3]

In this book, which received almost no attention at the time, Bentley maintained that all politics and all government are the result of group activities and that any other attempts to explain how politics and government works are doomed to failure. In its time this was a wildly contrarian position according to Nicholas Lemann writing in *The New Yorker*, as many people believed in a more idealistic vision of government and saw interest groups as subverting good government. For Bentley, there was no such thing as the public interest; it was a useless concept, he said, because there was nothing that was best for the society as a whole. Politics involved deal making, and morality is not a force in politics because such talk is almost always a cover for somebody's interests. While we would like to think that procedural reforms will eventually lead to something we can call "good government," the truth is that the only way to defeat one set of interests is with another set of interests.

Bentley's view of government, many would argue, accurately describes the way government operates where competitive interests clash in a political marketplace. The political marketplace is no different from the economic marketplace, where competition results in goods and services being produced and distributed. Various interests compete in the political marketplace for the goods and services government has to offer. The problem with such a view, which is often called interest group pluralism, is that there is anything but fair and balanced competition in the political marketplace, as corporations and their representatives, along with wealthy individuals, have an advantage when it comes to lobbying and other forms of political influence.[4] Corporations and the wealthy have vast sums of money to tap into for such influence that most other groups and interests in society do not have, and money seems to be what counts when it comes to political influence. Rather than one person one vote, the prevailing principle seems to be one dollar, one vote.

Many lobbyists, for example, have had previous experience in government and thus have access and expertise in a particular area that others in the political arena do not that gives the firms that hire them an unfair competitive advantage. Politicians gain experience in government and then when they either lose an election or just quit government for other reasons can get lucrative positions as lobbyists for companies that value their expertise and access to the political system. They can sell their influence for big money as their salaries can go from $162,500 a year if they are in Congress or $95,000 if they are staff to $300,000 a year or more overnight.[5] There were approximately 2,000 lobbyists involved in the financial reform bill that Congress passed in 2010, and more than 1,400 of these had been in government working as congressional staffers or in some position in the Executive Branch itself. Some seventy-three of these lobbyists previously had been in Congress and moved into a lucrative lobbying position upon leaving government. These lobbyists were able to exercise a great deal of influence over the bill that finally emerged.[6]

The influence of money in the political process was extended in a 2010 Supreme Court ruling. In *Citizens United v. Federal Election Commission*, the court ruled that First Amendment rights of free speech applied to corporations and unions as well as individuals, and thus, these collective entities could make unlimited expenditures supporting the election or defeat of specific federal candidates. Before this ruling, corporations and unions could run ads as long as they did not explicitly endorse or oppose specific candidates. This ruling overruled two prior Supreme Court opinions and struck down part of the McCain–Feingold election law passed in 2002 that, among other things, banned the use of corporate treasury funds to back or oppose candidates in elections.[7]

This ruling contributed to the development of what are called "super PACs" that was one of the first effects that became apparent. These PACs were seen as a new potent political weapon as they spent more than $8 million on TV advertising and other expenditures mostly within one month alone during the 2010 elections and proved to be an easy way for corporations to spend unlimited funds on an election. They are free of most constraints that apply to other types of corporate PACs that must comply with strict limits on donations. The only thing they are not allowed to do is coordinate their ads directly with candidates or political parties, a restriction that is undoubtedly circumvented in ways that are difficult to uncover. Corporations can now donate unlimited funds to these PACs because of the ruling that overturned the ban on corporate expenditures for specific election campaigns.[8]

So what we have is a government that is for sale to the highest bidder, which is quite often corporations and particular wealthy individuals.[9] In the 2016 campaign, 158 wealthy families contributed $176 million which mostly went to Republican candidates and constituted half of the money donated to the campaign.[10] This does not sound like a government of the people, by the people, and for the people.[11] It sounds more like a government that is beholden to corporate and private interests who have the money to wield undue influence in the political process and can shape public policy to enhance or protect those interests. It is a government by the rich, for the rich, and of the rich.[12] Inequality is perpetuated as the rich can get tax breaks and other favors from the government to allocate more money to themselves. According to Jeffrey D. Sachs, director of the Earth Institute at Columbia University,

> [w]e can consider America's political system today to be not so much a true democracy as a stable *duopoly* of two ruling parties, whose members shout at each other from time to time but which both basically stand for many of the same things when it comes to issues touching the interests of business, the rich, and the military. Both parties are instruments of powerful businesses and the rich. Rather than aiming for the median voter, as in the textbook two-party election theory, both parties

actually aim to the *right* of center to attract high-income contributors. For the Republican Party, this is easy and natural. For the Democrats, who ostensibly represent the needs of the poor, it means party leaders such as Presidents Clinton and Obama, who relentlessly side with Wall Street and the rich and just as relentlessly apologize to their base.[13]

David Marcus, a coeditor of *Dissent*, reviews the work of Sheldon Wolin, a former professor at the University of California at Berkeley. Quoting from Wolin's later work entitled *Democracy Incorporated*: "It is not morning in America . . . the changes of the past half-century . . . have distorted the cultural supports of democracy and eroded its political practices while preparing the way for a politics and culture favorable to inverted totalitarianism." Marcus goes on to say in the spirit of Wolin:

> that the work of political renewal was not much more than an uphill battle; it seemed next to impossible . . . Inverting the way authoritarian regimes have come to economize those public domains that had once given us a collective sense of meaning; it now often rules them. The Greeks believed public life was corrupted when the demands of one sphere—the family, the market—intruded on the commonweal of the political domain. Today, capitalism intrudes into virtually every sphere of life. Politics has revealed itself more clearly than ever to be the domain not only of the interests but of *elite* interest. 'Democracy incorporated' is pretty close to the mark.[14]

Reforms to this process to open it up to more public participation are not going to work until we get a new philosophy of government, one that undercuts the notions of isolatable individuals with absolute rights in favor of inherently social persons that are an integral part of a larger community. Some sense of community is important for a society in order for people to agree on common courses of action to deal with problems that can't be handled on an individual basis through the market. People have to agree on things that are good for all members of the community or the community as a whole, things like clean air and water, for example, or national defense. When individuals bump into each other, or in other words when the interests of individuals clash such that not everyone can get what they want, compromises have to be reached that are going to affect these individual interests. There has to be some sense of the common good of the whole community for common problems to be addressed.

Political systems exist to help people reach these compromises and adjudicate differences in the interests of preserving order and preventing people from going to war with each other to preserve their interests. Some people may have to sacrifice their individual desires for this to happen; thus, any institution that represents the whole society such as government is seen as a necessary activity that has to encroach on individual interests to keep the whole society together. The state, as Aristotle said centuries ago, aims at the highest good to a greater degree than any other institution in society:

> Every state is a community of some kind, and every community is established with a view to some good; for mankind always acts in order to obtain that which they think good. But, if all communities aim at some good, the state or political community, which is the highest of all, and which embraces all the rest, aims at good in a greater degree than any other, and at the highest good.[15]

An individualistic worldview, however, undermines these notions of a common good and a sense of the whole that the notion of community involves. When atomic individualism is taken as a basic assumption regarding beliefs about the individual in the sense that the individual is believed to be the basic building block of society in a reductionistic sense, a true community can never be reached. When individuals are seen as the basic building block of society, society is comprised of nothing more than individual egos clashing with each other. Whatever sense of community that may develop is nothing more than the sum of these individuals and their interests, these egoistic desires and drives that are rooted in the individual.

Alasdair MacIntyre, professor of philosophy at Vanderbilt University, believes that the United States may well be founded on incompatible moral and social ideals: on one hand, a communitarian vision of a common "telos" and, on the other hand, an ideal of individualism and pluralism. Thus, he holds that "[w]e inhabit a kind of polity whose moral order requires systematic incoherence in the form of public allegiance to mutually inconsistent sets of principles."[16] Thus, it is difficult for Americans to see both individual responsibility and responsibility to the community as part of the same moral matrix. We tend to focus on one of the other of these poles, and all too often community interests or the common good is pitted against the rights and freedoms of the individual. Anything the government does in the interests of promoting the good of the whole society is seen as an encroachment on the sacred right of individuals to be free to do as they please.

What this extreme individualism really means is that we do not have a spiritual connection to each other. While theories of the social self are necessary to provide a theoretical understanding of how the self develops in society to counter an individualistic view, they are not enough. We need to develop some kind of a spiritual connection with each other in order to counter the notion of an isolated individual. Even though Americans are very generous in their response to tragedies like hurricanes and tornadoes, we need to care more about each other in our daily existence. We need to care more deeply about the public sphere and the social environment in which we live and be less concerned about the preservation of our freedom to acquire more and more material wealth. Americans generally do not want to be bothered or constrained by others, but others are a part of ourselves and are not alien beings that constitute a threat to our existence.[17]

The result of this demise of the common or public good and the increasing emphasis on individual freedom is what Jacob S. Hacker and Paul Pierson have described as winner-take-all politics. Jacob S. Hacker is the Stanley B. Rose Professor of Political Science at Yale University while Paul Pierson is the John Gross Professor of Political Science at the University of California at Berkeley. They argue that step by step, over the past three decades, public officials have rewritten the rules of the game in both our political and economic systems in "ways that have benefited the few at the expense of the many." They see a transformation in American government that has taken place over the last generation that has fundamentally changed what government does and for whom it is done.[18]

This trend, according to the authors, began around 1980 when the share of national income going to the richest Americans began to increase eventually resulting in a hyperconcentration of income at the very top of the income ladder. During the same time, most Americans experienced only modest gains in income as the economy stopped working to provide security and prosperity for the broad middle class.[19] Instead of a trickle-down economy we have experienced a trickle-up economy, where the gains of the rich have come at the expense of those who were lower on the economic ladder. As inequality has grown, social mobility has not increased as people on the bottom of the income ladder find it more and more difficult to move up the ladder. This hyperconcentration of income set the United States apart from other rich countries as they have not experienced such a dramatic rise in inequality.[20]

The growth of this winner-take-all economy was not the result of changes in technology or a lack of education, say the authors, but was the result of government actions that favored the rich or government inaction that failed to reign in excesses that appeared. Beginning with the Reagan administration but accelerating with the second Bush administration, tax rates on the rich have fallen dramatically where wealthy people in some cases pay a lower tax rate overall than those on the bottom rungs of the income ladder. Other factors accelerating the trend toward this kind of economy include the collapse of unions which used to provide a countervailing power to corporations and government. This collapsed was facilitated by antiunion actions the government adopted which undermined union strength. Regarding failures, the government took little or no action to reign in the excessive pay of corporate management, actually took steps to allow the financial industry more freedom in repealing the separation of commercial and investment banking, and took no action to regulate financial derivatives. The real story, according to the authors, is not what has been done or not done for those at the bottom but what the government has done and not done regarding those at the top of the income ladder.[21]

Beginning in the 1980s, according to the authors, the Democratic Party shifted its concerns from the poorest people in society to the middle class and, in the process, lost the capacity to create an effective economic message and develop viable legislative coalitions to support a populist agenda. They were also receptive to a deregulatory agenda that began with deregulation of the airlines in the waning years of the Carter administration and spread to other areas like trucking and railroads. The Republicans, meanwhile, under the Reagan administration placed tax cuts at the heart of the GOP agenda to be pursued at every opportunity. These tax cuts, which favored the wealthy, replaced the traditional Republican agenda of fiscal conservatism and balanced budgets.[22]

The Republicans became the party of no: no progressive tax system, no effective minimum wage, no Social Security, no support for employer-provided health care, and almost no financial regulation. They sought to reestablish the policies of the Gilded Age, in other words, as the authors describe it in the title of a chapter, to build a bridge back to the nineteenth century.[23] Their top priority became tax cuts for those at the top of the income ladder consummating a marriage of the winner-take-all economy with a winner-take-all politics. The Democrats eventually climbed aboard this effort and its populist tradition, according to the authors, became more like a costume to be donned from time to time in campaigning rather than being a basis for governing. They became increasingly reliant on donations from the financial industry, reflecting the industry's growing clout in the economy and in the political system.[24] Nothing they have done such as passage of health care reform has done anything to shake their commitment to the restoration of the Gilded Age of the nineteenth century.[25]

To reverse this trend toward a winner-take-all politics will take more than just an improvement of the economic standing of the middle class but will also require diminishing the advantages of the privileged. The aim of political reform should include the following three goals: (1) to reduce the capacity of entrenched elites to block needed reform, (2) to facilitate broader participation among those while voices are currently drowned out, and (3) to encourage the development of groups that can provide a continuing, organized capacity to mobilize middle-class voters and monitor government and politics on their behalf. The authors consider the last of these goals the most important and the most difficult to realize. Yet "reform will rest on the creation of organized, sustained pressure on legislators to make American politics more responsive and open to citizen engagement."[26]

Bruce Judson, a senior fellow at the Yale School of Management, writing in a book titled *It Could Happen Here: America on the Brink*, believes that a revolution is possible in this country on a par with the revolution against the rule of the British. He states that "as extreme economic inequality increasingly divides the country, the nation become far more vulnerable to the disruptive forces that could be unleashed by a single, highly divisive event." There are any number of scenarios that are possible based on activities of the extreme right or extreme left or perhaps a natural disaster that could kick off a revolution. Judson believes that "history teaches us that there are limits to the extent of acceptable economic inequality in any society."[27]

Judson states that when the middle class loses faith in the system of governance, revolutions are most likely to occur. In our country the middle class is suffering and sees the American dream, which includes "a vision of economic security through steady employment, home ownership, modern medicine, retirement without worry, and the ability to send the kids to college" as steadily eroding. This dream is essentially a middle-class dream, yet this vision is only possible for a smaller and smaller segment of the population. More and more Americans are coming to the conclusion that their children will not necessarily be better off than themselves. As the middle class disappears, says Judson, our society will be further polarized with the rich or the 1 percent on one side and everybody else on the other.[28]

The potential for revolution in the United States depends upon five risk factors that he claims have received major attention from Aristotle to modern historians: "(1) the distribution of wealth and the health of the middle class, (2) the impact of recent economic or political shocks, (3) the lack of satisfaction of rising expectations, (4) the perception of unfairness in the in the distribution of wealth, and (5) the history and efficacy of institutions in the society." The greater these risk factors are present in any society, the exponentially greater is the risk of revolution.[29]

Regarding the first factor, as inequality rises the wealthy tend to insulate themselves from the rest of society by living in gated communities, sending their children to private schools, socializing with each other, and so on, such that they become less dependent on public services and increasingly less connected to the rest of society. Inevitably, says Judson, this leads them to oppose tax increases to fund public amenities and, instead, use their wealth to obtain political influence to solidify their privileged position. This leads to more and more inequality and a further hollowing out of the middle class and with it the disappearance of the American dream, leading eventually to revolution. As Judson states, "America cannot exist principally as a nation of haves and have nots without the broad middle. In such a world, all types of previously unimaginable scenarios become possible."[30]

As for recent economic or political shocks, the extent to which an economic shock can lead to political instability, according to Judson, depends on the extent of suffering, the trust of people in their government, and the degree to which the tragedy had been anticipated. The Great Recession of 2008 caused widespread suffering, thousands went underwater on their mortgages, destroyed trust in government as Wall Street was bailed out but little was done for the average homeowner, and was not anticipated by most economist and government officials. Regarding the third factor, when rising expectations are not fulfilled, the resulting dissatisfaction can result in radical change. America has always been known as the land of opportunity, that each generation would be better off than its predecessor. But mobility in the United Sates has decreased along with rising inequality such that the next generation can no longer expect that they will be better off than their parents. If these expectations continue to be unfulfilled and people give up on bettering themselves, the resulting anger and frustration can lead to revolution.[31]

Deprivation is always relative to expectations. If one doesn't expect much out of life than deprivation will not necessarily lead to a great deal of dissatisfaction. But Americans are encouraged to emulate the life of the well-off and work hard to attain more consumer goods and financial independence. The media are fixated with celebrity and wealth so that average people are bombarded with the way in which the rich and famous are living. This can create a sense of unfairness as most people begin to realize that they can never attain this kind of lifestyle no matter how many jobs they hold.[32]

Finally the history and competence of political institutions, says Judson, breaks down into four central questions: (1) what is the political history of the society, (2) to what extent is government willing to use violence and repression against its own population to stay in power, (3) how well is government functioning, and (4) are political institutions able to adapt sufficiently to changing realities.[33] These are the important questions to ask in regard to assessing the viability of governmental institutions. Our governmental system has been around for more than two centuries, so it is quite stable in that regard, but nonetheless it has become dysfunctional and has not adapted very well to changing economic and environmental circumstances.

In conclusion, Judson lists three factors that he claims are the most common preconditions that precede political instability: (1) extreme economic inequality, (2) an unexpected and significant major economic or political shock, and (3) a long-suffering middle class.[34] At the present time our society has all three of these preconditions leading Judson to conclude that in the more than 200 years since the American Revolution we have had three existential crises: the Civil War, the Great Depression, and now.[35] Our society is permeated by a lack of trust, Judson claims, as trust has been decreasing as economic inequality has been increasing. We lack trust of each other and have little or no trust in our institutions, witness the extremely low approval ratings of Congress. Anger in America is increasing as people work harder and longer just to keep their heads above water, while the rich bask in their wealth. The country is vulnerable and at a point where it will only take some untoward event to act as a trigger point to precipitate the beginning of a revolution.[36]

The revolution Judson talks about may already be underway. At the time this chapter was written the campaign for the Republican and Democratic presidential nominations was well underway, and, in fact, the Iowa causes were held the day these last few paragraphs of this section were written. One commentator asks the question whether Western democracies are facing an existential crisis. Anger and frustration, he claims, are fueling what may be another historic challenge to the party establishment as voter discontent is giving traction to marginalized parties and candidates. Nowhere is this more evident than in the United States, where political outsiders are being swept along by a wave of voter discontent. Donald Trump and Bernie Sanders might in a more normal year be considered unelectable and thus not receive much support. But Trump surprisingly won the Republican primary and the general election and is the 45th President of the United States, and Bernie Sanders gave Hillary Clinton a run for her money in the Democratic primary.[37]

Candidates with little or no experience in politics had the advantage in this election, where voters did not favor the establishment candidates. This is most evident in the Republican Party, where Jeb Bush, who was initially the establishment candidate, did not enjoy that status for long as Trump tapped into voter anger by attacking Mexico for sending people to this country with "lots of problems" and promising to build a wall clear across our southern border and getting Mexico to pay for it. He went on to attack John McCain, an American hero, and then went on to say he would ban all Muslims from entering the country. Every time he made such an outrageous statement his poll numbers went up as he provided a way for Americans to vent their anger. Interviews showed that the many people thought the American dream was dying, and the deck was stacked against them in that the wealthy were winning and the middle class was faltering.[38] They wanted their elected leaders to feel their pain and reflect their fury which both Trump and Sanders were doing by promising to remake the nation with a populist revolution.[39]

This political crisis in our society has basic philosophical underpinnings that relate to our excessive individualism. If we see government as nothing more than a set of interests competing for the things government can provide and there no sense of the public interest or common good that government should be promoting, then those interests that are the strongest will exercise the most influence in government. Since the Supreme Court has ruled that money is speech, those with the most money can speak the loudest, get government to hear them, and pay attention to their interests. Thus, the wealthy have been able to get government to favor them with tax cuts and other measures that increase inequality and destroy the middle class We become a nation of have-nots, the 99 percent, against the haves, the 1 percent, which leads to a loss of trust in both the economic and political systems and a breakdown of faith in the future of the country. While there are all kinds of measures that have been proposed to rectify this situation, it is this philosophy of individualism that must change for there to be any kind of long-lasting resolution of the problems facing the nation.

The Environmental Crisis

The natural environment poses a profound challenge to a culture which is hooked on economic growth and an ever-increasing material standard of living. The American dream is one of unlimited economic opportunity in a land of abundant resources, of opportunity for people to better themselves economically, limited only by the lack of good jobs or their own lack of ambition or vision. It is a dream of unending economic prosperity, that every new generation should be better off than the next, that gross national or domestic product should ever increase, that we should be able to produce more cars, more houses, more consumer goods, more of everything. This is a dream that has informed the American psyche for generations and has become the nation's primary purpose.

Yet the pursuit of this dream has resulted in environmental problems that threaten to overwhelm our ability to deal with them. We seem unable to come to grips with global warming or climate change, for example, as Congress has stalled again and again in coming up with a cap and trade system or some other means of limiting carbon emissions.[40] Yet the earth keeps getting hotter and hotter as March 2016 was the hottest on record, making it the eleventh month in a row to break the global high-temperature record. It was 2.3 degrees F over the 1951–1980 average for the month and an even more drastic departure for the norm than February's record breaking heat.[41] Weather patterns are changing all over the world as freak storms, such as Hurricane Sandy, wreak their devastation on various regions. Efforts to link climate change to this kind of severe weather are beginning to gain some ground.[42] Climate change is also said to be responsible for deterioration of coral reefs including the Great Barrier Reef off the Australian coast.[43]

Meanwhile, the Arctic ice pack is disappearing faster than scientists had predicted, and the Greenland ice sheet is melting at a faster rate than anyone expected.[44] Because of this melting oceans are rising faster than they have in almost 3,000 years and could rise as much as 4 feet by 2100, forcing many coastal communities to be abandoned.[45] Deforestation continues at an alarming rate as the rainforest is cut down or burned for various reasons, all of which makes sense to the parties involved who are seeking to make a profit but which causes serious environmental problems. Fisheries are depleted in various parts of the world and are not likely to recover. Oceans are polluted and warming because of absorption of carbon dioxide, which also makes them more acidic, affecting coral reefs in particular.[46] Air pollution continues to be a major problem in many parts of the world.[47] The list could go on and on as environmental problems continue to worsen and raise serious questions about survival of people in various parts of the world that face starvation and depletion of necessary resources.[48]

Physicist Stephen Hawking, never one to avoid a dramatic headline, has suggested that we have a shorter-term imperative to get out into space if we want to continue surviving as a species. "We are entering an increasingly dangerous period of our history," Hawking commented in an interview. "Our population and our use of the finite resources of planet Earth are growing exponentially, along with our technical ability to change the environment for good or ill. But our genetic code still carries the selfish and aggressive instincts that were of survival advantage in the past. It will be difficult enough to avoid disaster in the next hundred years, let alone the next thousand or million." The scientist believes that we will soon render the Earth uninhabitable, making manned space exploration essential.[49]

Most countries around the world remain committed to economic growth as their main purpose and do everything they can to promote such growth. Countries such as China and India with huge populations are now trying to emulate the Western world and grow their economies as fast as possible. People in China who once used to ride bikes are now driving cars making congestion a problem in many cities helping China to become the world's major emitter of carbon dioxide into the atmosphere contributing to global warming. Some of its cities are so polluted that people have to wear masks to go outside and have respiratory diseases at a much higher rate than normal.[50] These countries cannot be blamed for improving the lot of their citizens, and yet this emphasis on economic growth puts added stress on the environment and uses up more and more natural resources. Developed countries continue to pursue economic growth as their major objective and adopt policies to promote growth often at the expense of the environment.

According to some estimates, since 1900, the number of people inhabiting the earth has multiplied more than three times, and the world economy has expanded more than twenty times during the same period. The consumption of fossil fuels has grown by a factor of thirty, and industrial production has increased by a factor of fifty, with four-fifths of that increase occurring since 1950 alone.[51] And these figures do not even take into account the recent growth of China and India. While there have been great gains in human welfare because of these developments and the potential for future gains is even more promising, development at this pace has also produced environmental destruction on a scale never before imagined and is undermining prospects for future economic development as well as threatening the very survival of the earth's inhabitants.

Other estimates show that consumption expenditures per person almost tripled between 1996 and 2010, resulting in increased use of fossil fuels, more mining of minerals and metals, increased deforestation, and more land used for agricultural purposes to feed an ever-growing population. An indicator called the Ecological Footprint Indicator which shows the world's biological capacity that is sustainable shows that in 2005, people were using the resources and services of 1.3 earths, meaning that we were using about a third more of the earth's capacity than was available on a sustainable basis. This kind of usage puts increasing pressure on the earth's ecosystems and disrupts these systems on which human beings, animal, and plant species depend.[52]

A fivefold to tenfold increase in economic activity translates into a greatly increased burden on the ecosphere. Such an increase is not unrealistic as it represents annual growth rates of only between 3.2 and 4.7 percent, well within the aspiration levels of many countries. Such growth has severe implications for investment in housing, transportation, agriculture, and industry.

Energy use would have to increase by a factor of five just to bring developing countries, given their present populations, up to the levels of consumption now existing in the industrialized world. Similar increases could be projected for food, water, shelter, and other things that are essential to human existence.[53]

These projections indicate the kind of impact human activity has on the Earth motivating an international team of scientists to suggest that we may have entered a new geological epoch called the Anthropocene or human epoch. This would mark the end of the present epoch called the Holocene, which began some 12,000 years ago when the planet had thawed enough to move out of the Ice Age. These scientists argue that "[w]e are becoming a geological agent in ourselves," as technological advancements and population growth, which date back to the mid-twentieth-century mark a new geological age. Increases in the use of certain materials such as plastic, aluminum, and concrete are changing the face of the planet as human infrastructure covers half the Earth's surface. Among other things, the "burning of fossil fuels has doubled the amount of carbon dioxide in the atmosphere and warmed the globe." These scientists were expected to recommend that his new epoch be adopted later in the year.[54]

The question being asked ever more frequently by commissions and policy makers all over the world is whether growth on the scale projected over the next one to five decades can be managed on a basis that is sustainable both economically and ecologically. Continued growth in consumption of goods and services and the expansion and growth of a materialistic lifestyle may not be possible under conditions of sustainable growth.[55] The world is already overconsuming many resources, as is evident in the depletion of fish stocks around the world, and cannot continue on the path of more and more production. Thus, the challenge the environment poses to continued economic growth is an important one, and whether overconsumption is a legitimate problem, and changing patterns of consumption are necessary are questions that need consideration.

If we have not attained sustainability within the next forty years, say some experts, environmental deterioration and economic decline are likely to be feeding on each other pulling us into a downward spiral of social and economic disintegration.[56] The foundations for further economic growth will be eroded, and social upheaval will take place throughout the world on an unprecedented scale. But sustainable growth has implications for the distribution of economic wealth and income throughout the world and raises questions about intergenerational equity, as well as equity among peoples of the world as developing nations strive to better themselves with shrinking resources.[57] Greater equity must also be achieved between the industrialized world and developing countries, as the latter consume about 80 percent of the world's goods and have only one-quarter of the world's population. With three-quarters of the world's population, developing countries command less than one-quarter of the world's wealth. This imbalance is getting worse and cannot be continued if sustainable growth is to become a reality throughout the world.[58]

Many developing countries, as well as large parts of many developed countries, are resource based in the sense that their economic capital consists of stocks of environmental resources such as soil, forests, fisheries, and other such natural resources. Their continued development depends on maintaining and perhaps increasing these stocks of resources to support agriculture, fishing, and mining for local use and export purposes. But during the past several decades, the poorer countries of the developing world have experienced a massive depletion of this capital. Environmental and renewable resources are being used up faster than they can be restored or replaced, and some developing countries have depleted virtually all of their ecological capital and are on the brink of environmental bankruptcy.[59]

According to the World Commission on Environment and Development, sustainable growth is based on forms and processes of development that do not undermine the integrity of the environment on which they depend. But modern civilizations have been characterized by unsustainable development utilizing forms of decision making that do not take the future into account. They have ignored the long-term ecological costs of development and these costs are now coming due in economies all over the world. Yet many governments refuse to change their policies to correspond with an emerging reality and continue to act as if environmental conditions can be ignored and that nature will take care of itself.[60]

Ignoring the environmental implications of policy making means that the costs of environmental degradation are borne by the larger community in the forms of air, water, land, and noise pollution and of resource depletion and climate change. Or these costs are transferred to future generations who are stuck with degraded environment that will no longer support growth rates that have been attained in the past. Internalizing these costs requires some acceptable means of determining the costs of this degradation and then finding the political will to impose these costs on marketplace transactions, so the cost of goods and services will reflect the environmental impacts of production and consumption activities. Environmental degradation should also be integrated into resource accounts in national economic systems, so policy makers will have a more accurate picture of the way certain economic policies will affect ecological systems and stocks of resources.[61]

Science contributes to these environmental problems as it *dehumanizes* nature by treating nature objectively in the interests of manipulating it to suit human interests. In doing so it abstracts nature from the relational context in which humans exist and flourish. It treats nature as something external to humans that can be exploited for self-interested purposes and views nature in instrumental terms as existing only to serve human needs and interests. The traditional view of humans and their relationship to nature has been dualistic: the idea that humans stand over against nature and are somehow seen apart from nature. The task of humans has been to conquer nature, to take dominion over the animals and the natural world as some religious doctrines have emphasized, to gain more and more power over nature, and to shape it according to our visions and our interests. This dualistic view leads to an objectification of nature and allows us to manipulate it to our advantage and exploit it for our own purposes. Such a dualism leads to a disconnect between humans and nature.

We are victimized by all the dichotomies we live with such as mind and body and subjective and objective that tend to separate us from the natural world on which we depend for our existence. This is a philosophical problem that involves a certain way of thinking about nature that has hindered thinking of ourselves as being connected with nature. We do not think of ourselves as being embedded in nature but tend to see nature in objective terms that is something apart from us and can be shaped to serve our interests. We are the subject that has dominion over nature and can use it for various self-interested purposes.

The idea that nature exists to serve human interests has been called an anthropomorphic view of nature. This term simply refers to the human-centered way we have traditionally approached nature. We manipulate it to serve our own visions of the good life and our own sense of progress. Nature must be "developed" to fit this vision and has no value in its natural state. It only has value as it is shaped to serve some human purpose. Resources in the ground have no utility until they are extracted and processed by some industrial system to make something useful that can be sold to consumers. Only then does nature have any use or value and become part of the system that measures economic wealth. This kind of exploitation has resulted in serious environmental problems that call for new approaches and strategies.

Science objectifies nature and considers it to be something apart from humans and their activities. Nature operates according to its own laws that govern its comings and goings, and humans seek to understand and increase their knowledge of nature so that they can manipulate it and exploit it to serve their interests. But nature is by and large left to take care of itself, and humans pay minimal attention to what impacts their activities make on nature and its workings. They tend to think that nature will go its own way and continue to provide humans with a nurturing environment that will support their growth and development.

Taking responsibility for nature involves making conscious and responsible value judgments regarding the kind of planet we want. These value judgments include the answers to such questions as "How much species diversity should be maintained?" "How much of nature should be preserved and placed off-limits to industrial development?" "What natural resources do we wish to leave for our children?" "How much climate change is acceptable?" and "Does population growth need to be limited in some fashion?" Science can tell us something about the broad patterns of global transformation taking place, but value questions about the pace and directions of those patterns have to be answered through political and economic systems.

It is not a matter of saving planet earth as it is often put in the literature. The planet will be here billions of years until the sun burns up its hydrogen fuel and becomes a red giant that swallows the earth. During this time it will have some kind of a natural environment. The real question is whether that environment is such that it can continue to sustain human life and provide an enriching experience for human existence; thus, we should be talking about saving ourselves. Creating such an environment involves a new approach that emphasizes responsibility and community, taking responsibility for enhancing the environment to promote a human community that can thrive and experience continued enrichment of its existence. A continued emphasis on the right to use one's property in one's own individual interests will not get us where we need to go and will only continue down the path of self-destructiveness.

It seems that the consumer culture that has emerged over the past several decades cannot continue on its current path. Consumer culture is built on two assumptions: (1) that the world contains an inexhaustible supply of raw materials and (2) that there are bottomless sinks in which to continue to dispose of waste material. Both of these assumptions have been questioned in the past several decades causing many to take a look at the sustainability of consumer culture into the future. These concerns have profound implications for corporate activity that is based on the never-ending quest for profits through the promotion of consumption and an ever-increasing material standard of living throughout the world.

Concerns for the environment as embodied in sustainable growth and other such concepts provide ample evidence for the emergence of an environmental ethic. Many are beginning to recognize that nature provides an enriching experience in itself and that harming nature is ultimately destructive of the search for meaningfulness and self-fulfillment. Environmental concerns about pollution, climate change, resource usage, and the enjoyment of nature obviously run headlong into cultural values related to increased production and consumption and immediate gratification. Production, consumption, and continued economic growth with their own self-justifying ends seem on a collision path with a concern for the environment and the self-fulfillment it provides.

What some see as necessary to adequately account for the natural environment in our decision making is the development of an environmental ethic as a comprehensive ethic that can place production and consumption activities in a moral context. An environmental ethic of some kind is the best candidate for a comprehensive ethic, it is believed, because of the persistence and pervasiveness of environmental problems. Such an ethic is necessary to guide the direction of production and consumption in a manner that nourishes the desire of humans for opportunities to live a meaningful life and for self-development that enriches their existence. This entails the growth and flourishing of the multiple environments in which they are embedded and that contribute to the fullness of human existence in all its richness and complexity. An answer to environmental problems is not to be found in a forced choice between artificially created alternatives such as the conflict between economics and the environment. These alternatives distort the nature of the reality they must ultimately serve, that of enriching the life of humans in all the multiple dimensions in which they work out a meaningful and fulfilling life for themselves.

The theories that are part of business ethics such as utilitarianism and the like are not congenial to the needs of an environmental ethic because they have no philosophical structure to provide an inherent relatedness of the individual and the broader natural environment. For all of these positions, the source of ethical action lies either in the application of abstract rules to cases or in the inculcation of tradition. Neither approach incorporates the type of attunement to nature that is required for an environmental consciousness. They are by and large anthropocentric in nature and view the environment as something separate or external to humans. They reflect the individualism and dualism of the modern worldview, where the environment has merely instrumental value. Thus, in the environmental literature one finds little application of these theories to the natural environment.

This problem has given rise to a separate area of ethics called environmental ethics that has developed its own approaches and theories. One such approach is called *moral extensionism and eligibility*, which has to do with the extension of rights to the natural world. In the past several decades, rights have been extended to blacks and other minorities in civil rights legislation, rights given to women under equal rights legislation, rights extended to workers regarding safety and health in the workplace, rights provided to consumers for safe products and other aspects of the marketplace, and, more recently, rights to marry extended to gay couples. The questions are whether rights can also be extended to the natural world or at least some aspects of it and whether this approach can help deal with environmental problems in an effective manner. Where does the ethical cutoff fall with regard to moral eligibility? What aspects of nature can be justifiably brought into the moral realm in this manner?

Many philosophers extend such rights only to animals on the grounds that animals are sentient beings in that they are able to suffer and feel pain. But more radical thinkers widen the circle to include all natural organisms, including plants. Still others see no reason to draw a moral boundary at the edge of organic life and argue for ethical consideration for rocks, soil, water, air, and biophysical processes that constitute ecosystems. Some are even led to the conclusion that even the universe has rights superior to those of its most precocious life-form.[62]

The attempt to extend rights in this manner represents an effort to build a wider moral community that includes all or parts of the natural world and to overcome the anthropocentrism, which separates humans from nature. But while moral extensionism and eligibility in environmental ethics attempt to bring animals and even other aspects of nature into the moral community by extending rights to them, these arguments are subject to strong theoretical attack. Rights are bestowed on animals and other aspects of nature by humans, thereby making the moral standing of nonhuman aspects of nature dependent on humans. Animals cannot pursue their own interests through the courts but need someone to take up their cause for them. While rights theory in environmental ethics thus tries to overcome traditional limitations on rights by extending them to animals and other aspects of nature, it is caught up in the theoretical web of anthropocentrism and atomic individualism, which are found in the tradition of rights theory.

Partly as a result of the problems with moral extensionism and eligibility, a *biocentric ethics* or *deep ecology* developed as an alternative approach to the environment. Deep ecology leads to a devaluation of individual life relative to the integrity, diversity, and continuation of the ecosystem as a whole. This perspective on environmental ethics created entirely new definitions of what liberty and justice mean on planet Earth and involved an evolution of ethics to be ever more inclusive. This approach recognized that there can be no individual welfare or liberty apart from the ecological matrix in which individual life exists. "A biocentric ethical philosophy could be interpreted as extending the esteem in which individual lives were traditionally held to the biophysical matrix that created and sustained those lives."[63]

This approach holds that some natural objects and ecosystems have intrinsic value and are morally considerable in their own right apart from human interests. Nature has value in and of itself apart from human interests. This ethic respects each life form and sees it as part of a larger whole. All life is sacred, and we must not be careless about species that are irreplaceable. Particular individuals come and go, but nature continues indefinitely, and humans must come to understand their place in nature. Each life-form is constrained to flourish in a larger community according to this view, and moral concern for the whole biological community is the only kind of an environmental ethics that makes sense and preserves the integrity of the entire ecosystem.[64]

Nature itself is a source of values, it is argued, including the value we have as humans, since we are a part of nature. The concept of value, according to this position, includes far more than a simplistic human-interest satisfaction. Value is a multifaceted idea with structures that are rooted in natural sources.[65] Value is not just a human product. When humans recognize values outside themselves, this does not result in a dehumanizing of the self or a reversion to beastly levels of existence. On the contrary, it is argued, human consciousness is increased when we praise and respect the values found in the natural world and this recognition results in a further spiritualizing of humans.[66] Thus, this school of thought holds that there are natural values that are intrinsic to the natural object itself apart from humans and their particular valuing activities. Values are found in nature as well as humans. Humans do not simply bestow value on nature as nature also conveys value to humans.[67]

The world of nature is not to be defined in terms of commodities that are capable of producing wealth for humans who manage them in their own interests. All things in the biosphere are believed to have an equal right to live and reach their own individual forms of self-realization. Instead of a hierarchical ordering of entities in descending order from God through humans to animals, plants, and rocks, where the lower creatures are under the higher ones and are ruled by them, nature is seen as a web of interactive and interdependent life that is ruled by its own natural processes. These processes must be understood if are to work in harmony with nature and preserve the conditions for our own continued existence.[68]

Deep ecology thus accords nature ethical status that is at least equal to that of human beings. From the perspective of the ecosystem, the difference is between thinking that people have a right to a healthy ecosystem or thinking that the ecosystem itself possesses intrinsic or inherent value.[69] Deep ecologists argue for a biocentric perspective and a holistic environmental ethic regarding nature. Human beings are to step back into the natural community as a member and not the master. The philosophy of conservation for Holmes Ralston was comparable to arguing for better care for slaves on plantations. The whole system was unethical, not just how people operated within the system. In Ralston's view, nothing matters except the liberation of nature from the system of human dominance and exploitation. This process involves a reconstruction of the entire human relationship with the natural world.[70]

Both of these approaches are useful in understanding the relationship between humans and nature, but these approaches treat the environment differently and make different assumptions about the locus of moral consideration. Moral extensionism and eligibility use the vehicle of rights to extent moral concern to various aspects of nature, but these rights are bestowed by humans and are not intrinsic to nature itself. Deep ecology assumes nature already has intrinsic value that needs to be recognized by liberating nature from the system in which it is currently trapped. By recognizing this intrinsic value of nature, the last remnants of anthropocentrism, still operative in moral extensionism and eligibility, is supposedly excised. Furthermore, while moral extensionism and eligibility stress the individual to the exclusion of the whole, deep ecology subordinates the individual to the good of the whole.

The biological egalitarianism of deep ecology provides no means to make distinctions between which parts of nature to preserve and which to use for the promotion of human welfare. The debate over systems versus individuals is still rooted in an individualistic worldview and deep ecology does not provide an adequate framework for understanding the relation of humans and nature in all its richness. Each of these alternatives may provide a sense of moral concern for nature but neither offers a useful framework for understanding the moral dimensions of economic activity in relation to the natural environment. They do not provide an adequate understanding of the relationship of humans and nature that can challenge the scientific world-view, which objectifies nature and seeks to manipulate it to serve human interests.

Capitalism leads to a despiritualization of nature as it becomes objectified and is treated as solely a source of raw material and a depository of waste material. But it cannot continue to be treated in this manner, according to Sprintzen, writing in *Critique of Western Philosophy*, as the earth is the stuff of which we are made. He means this not just in a material sense but also socially, morally, aesthetically, and spiritually. Our material and spiritual roots in the earth must be addressed, and we cannot continue to assume that the earth will provide an unending supply of raw materials that fuel and ever-growing economy with increasing consumption and an expanding population. We must be concerned about the earth's "carrying capacity," however difficult that may be to determine.[71] As he says,

> [t]he ecological movement at its best is not a celebration of primitivism but a recognition that we are beings of the Earth. We need viscerally to feel out earthly rooting. We need to build our human habitat in consonance with a new "ecosense." That means that the Earth can no longer be viewed as "our dominion," nor as simply "natural resources" or "raw materials" in need of development. The quantitative ideal of material growth must give way to a cosmic vision that treasures qualitative development and the aesthetic.[72]

According to Ophuls writing in *Plato's Revenge*, the followers of Hobbs, which he names as John Locke and Adam Smith, made a shift in the orientation of society from the sacred to the secular explicit. Politics focused on facilitating the acquisition of private property and an increase in national wealth. This unleashing of human appetites resulted in the destruction of nature. Because there were no mores to promote self-restraint and respect for nature, the long-term effect of these unleashed passions has been a violation of nature's laws and limits and the creation of an ecological crisis. Dealing with crisis demands a radical shift in consciousness, says Ophuls, the creation of a new moral order that involves the pursuit of some higher end than continued material gratification.[73]

The Scientific Revolution inspired by Descartes, Newton, and others viewed the world as a kind of mechanism that obeyed the laws of physics. It created the modern world as we know it with its characteristics of reductionism, determinism, materialism, and individualism. It was believed that there was an objective reality "out there" that was accessible to scientific investigation and that it should be possible, in principle, to discover the whole truth about that external reality and thereby achieve a Godlike position above nature, allowing us to become it master and possessor.[74]

We tend to believe that scientific discovery of how nature works leads to technological developments that can enable us to deal with environmental problems, that there is a technological fix to global warming, for example. But Ophuls further states that technology has neither abolished natural scarcity nor transcended natural limits. All the technological man has done, he states, is arranged matters so that the effects of his continued exploitation of nature are felt by others. Other species, other places, other generations suffer the consequences of the intensified ecological imperialism of modern society[75] He argues that humility is the essence of ecological wisdom that will allow to us to come to moral terms with the web of life and to find a place in nature instead of thinking of ourselves apart from nature. Once we abandon this anthropocentric point of view, natural limitations can be seen as a creative force that fosters quality instead of quantity:[76]

> The corollary of natural limits is natural balance. The organic world is a complex, interconnected living system that has its own autonomy, integrity, and value. To treat it as though it were simple, divisible, and dead—that is, as though it were a machine to be manipulated at will—shows a fatal lack of understanding . . . It follows that humanity's attempt to maximize its wealth and power at the expense of the rest of creation is fundamentally antibiological and self-destructive.[77] Nature is not a machine. Nor does humanity stand apart from nature entitled by evolutionary right to lord it over the earth. In consequence, the modern way of life and politics based on the mechanical worldview is rendered obsolete, both philosophically and practically.[78]

Ophuls believes that ecology will have to be the master science and guiding metaphor of any future civilization. Humans and nature must be reconciled in an ecological way of thought and life, he says, which would restore the meaning that was lost when nature was made into an enemy. Thus, humans would no longer be orphaned and would once again by at home in the universe.[79] He argues that even physics is fundamentally ecological: "Everything is connected to everything else, and nothing exists in isolation because all phenomena are part of a larger, unified whole whose texture is determined not by the objects it contains but by the complex tissue of interrelationships that create the contents. Thus the wisdom and ethic of ecology emerge equally from physics."[80]

> Like the biosphere, the physical world is characterized by inescapable limits on human action and understanding. Ignoring these limits upsets preexisting natural balances and ultimately menaces the sustenance and survival of the human race. Humanity does not stand apart from the whole system. We exist because of the system, and our continued existence requires understanding and respecting the mutual interrelationship that binds man's fate to the rest of nature, living and nonliving alike. From this follows the same rebuke to human hubris and the same set of natural laws enjoined by ecology. Indeed, the case for humility,

moderation, and connection becomes even more compelling.[81] A natural world conceived of as dead and treated as such eventually becomes dead in fact. Similarly, when nature is taken to be essentially atomic, the result is political and economic doctrines that grind men and women into social atoms. And if material reality is all that exists, then spirit and instinct are meaningless categories slated for the dustbin of history.[82]

The fundamental problem with the environment, then, is that humans have lost a spiritual connection with nature. There are many reasons for this including scientific objectivity, capitalist exploitation, and religious supernaturalism. Attempting to bridge a so-called disconnect or divide between humans and nature will not work in developing an environmental consciousness that can transform our industrial economy into a sustainable society. Rather, we must come to recognize that there is no disconnect or divide to overcome. There is no separation of humans from nature such that humans are subjective beings that manipulate an objective nature for purposes of enhancing their material well-being. This realization involves the inculcation of a different philosophy from that which forms the foundations of a scientific worldview that separates mind and body, subjective and objective, and other such dichotomies that separate us from nature and a religious worldview that emphasizes the supernatural as the locus of meaning and purpose for human life.

Nature cannot be dehumanized, nor can humans be denaturalized. Neither human activity in general nor human knowledge can be separated from the fact that humans are natural organisms embedded in and dependent upon a natural environment with which they are continuous. Human development is connected with its biological world, and the self is not something that can be viewed apart from its rootedness in nature. The human being is located in nature and emerges from and opens onto the natural world in which humans function. We are not only part of a human community but also part of a broader community that includes the natural environment and have a responsibility to and for that larger community. Humans and nature must be seen in a relational context to overcome the separation between humans and nature that exists in Western culture.

Our Western tradition works against this relational understanding of nature, not just in the economic realm but in all areas of Western culture as well. Science *dehumanizes* nature by treating nature objectively in the interests of manipulating nature to suit human interests. In doing so it abstracts nature from the relational context in which humans exist and flourish. It treats nature as something external to humans that can be exploited for self-interested purposes and views nature in instrumental terms as existing only to serve human needs and interests. The Christian religion *denaturalizes* humans by taking them out of nature with belief in the supernatural and in doing so abstracts humans from the natural world in which they live, move, and have their being. Meaning and purpose are found outside of nature and not in the natural world itself. Human origins, as well as their final destiny, are located outside of the natural world. Neither approach does justice to the natural world and the context in which humans and nature interact.

Neither of these two worldviews is adequate to deal with our environmental problems and overcome the separation between humans and nature. Science dehumanizes nature, Christianity denaturalizes humans, and neither worldview can change to incorporate humans and nature into an inseparable whole and remain what they are as worldviews. What is needed is a revolution in the way we understand our relationship to nature, a new consciousness that will allow us to see and relate to nature in a different manner and allow us to develop a spiritual connection to nature where we feel nature as a part of ourselves and not something separable.[83] Only by some revolutionary change of this nature can the human race survive and come to live in harmony with the natural environment in which we are embedded.

In sum, the spiritual crisis of Western societies has resulted in an extreme individualism where we have lost connection with each other and with it any sense of community and the common good and an objectification of the environment that has severed a connection between humans and nature that allows nature to be exploited in the interest of economic growth. Our political system is dysfunctional as compromises cannot be worked out between parties to deal with problems like immigration, entitlement reform, tax overhaul, climate change, inequality, and many other such problems, and the environment is being destroyed on which we depend for our very existence. A spiritual renewal is indeed crucial to the survival of our country and our world to establish a connection with each other and with nature that goes beyond science and capitalism into a different way of acting toward each other and with nature.[84]

Notes

1 See "Environment," *Time*, February 1, 2016, 16. See also "Climate Change: Does 2015 Prove It's Real?" *The Week*, February 5, 2016, 19.

2 Some commentators think that we have two ideological based societies in this country and the differences between them are growing. See Paul Starr, "The American Situation," *The American Prospect*, Fall 2014, 5–7. See also Ryan Lizza, "A House Divided," December 14, 2015, 30–37.

3 Nicholas Lemann, "Conflict of Interests," *The New Yorker*, August 11 & 18, 2008, 86–92.

4 Barack Obama focused on lobbying on his first day in office by issuing an executive order to restrain lobbyists after the scandals of the Bush administration. This order stated that if you had been a registered lobbyist in the past two years you could not work for the administration on any issue in which you were involved. Also after you left government you couldn't lobby the administration at all unless a special waiver was obtained from the White House budget director. These rules, however, created problems of their own by placing limits on legitimate advocacy. See Jacob Weisberg, "All Lobbyists Are not Created Equal," *Newsweek*, April 27, 2009, 35.

5 Michael Tomasky, "Washington: Will the Lobbyists Win?" *The New York Review*, April 9, 2009, 20. See also Jeff Madrick, "How the Lobbyists Win in Washington," *The New York Review*, April 7, 2016, 50–52.

6 Steven Brill, "On Sale: You're Government. Why Lobbying Is Washington's Best Bargain," *Time*, July 12, 2010, 29–35. Goldman Sachs alone, which was charged with civil fraud for some of its practices during the financial meltdown, spent $1.2 million on lobbying during the first three months of 2010, which amounted to a 72 percent increase over the same period the previous year. The firm also hired two former influential senators to lobby Congress on its behalf. "Noted," *The Week*, May 7, 2010, 18.

7 Ciara Torres-Spelliscy, "Spending on Politics? Tell Shareholders," *Business Week*, November 2, 2009, 80. See also Garrett Epps, "Money Changes Everything," *The American Prospect*, May 2012, 32–37.

8 Dan Eggen, "PACs Gone Wild: New Groups Ups Ante," *The Denver Post*, September 28, 2010, 9A. The article points out that one such PAC, American Crossroads, which was founded with the help of Karl Rove, who was an influential adviser in the George W. Bush administration, spent more than half of this money. American Financial Group, a publicly held company, donated $400,000 to this group. Another source claims that these PACs spent $98 million between September 1 and October 17, 2010, on House and Senate races. The great majority of this money was spent supporting Republican candidates. See Jonathan D. Salant and Kristin Jensen, "The Many Ties That Bind GOP Fundraisers," *Bloomberg Businessweek*, October 25–October 31, 2010, 34–38. According to some reports these outside groups are playing roles in political campaigns that were hard to imagine just a few years ago. See Zeke J. Miller and Michael Scherer, "The Bucks Start Here," *Time*, April 6, 2015, 20–21.

9 See Jane Mayer, *Dark Money: The Hidden History of the Billionaires behind the Rise of the Radical Right* (New York: Doubleday, 2016), for the story about how certain wealthy people, particular the Koch brothers, exercise influence over society and the political system. See also Michael Tomasky, "The Billionaire Bothers Take on the US," *The New York Review*, June 19, 2014, 22–24; "The Koch Brothers' Agenda," *The Week*, March 13, 2015, 11; David Cole, "Free Speech, Big Money, Bad Elections," *The New York Review*, November 5, 2015, 24–26; Phillip Elliott, "Power Brokers Recharge," *Time*, August 17, 2015, 28–32; Zachary Mider, "The Koch Brothers Say Don't Be Shy," *Blomberg Business Week*, February 8–14, 2016, 27; Bill McKibben, "The Koch Brothers' New Brand, *The New York Review*, March 10, 2016, 16–18; and John H. Richardson, "Billionaires, Unleashed," *Esquire*, December/January, 2016, 162–168. In the 2016 election cycle the Koch brothers alone vowed to spend almost $1 billion to influence the outcome of the election.

10 Eric Lichtblau and Kitty Bennett, "From Only 158 Families, Half the Cash for '16 Race," *The New York Times*, October 11, 2015, Y1. As the 2016 campaign wore on, however, there was some question as to whether all this money was having an effect on the outcome. Despite being backed by $100 million, for example, Jeb Bush dropped out of the race early. But many think that despite this kind of evidence big money still skews elections. See Megan McArdle, "Big Donations Can't Buy a Victory," *The Denver Post*, October 25, 2015, 1D and "Citizens United: Has Big Money Lost Its Power?" *The Week*, January 29, 2016, 17.

11 See Robert G. Kaiser, *So Damm Much Money: The Triumph of Lobbying and the Corrosion of American Government* (New York: Knopf, 2010).

12 See Robert Kuttner, "An Embarrassment of Riches," *The American Prospect*, Summer 2015, 96.

13 Jeffrey D. Sachs, *The Price of Civilization: Reawakening American Virtue and Prosperity* (New York: Random House, 2011), 114.

14 David Marcus, "Into the Cave: Sheldon Wolin's Search for Democracy," *Dissent*, Winter 2016, 107.

15 Richard McKeon, ed., *The Basic Works of Aristotle* (New York: The Modern Library, 2001), 1127.

16 Alasdair MacIntyre, *"Is Patriotism a Virtue?" Lindley Lecture* (Lawrence, KS: University of Kansas, 1984), 19–20.

17 David Sprintzen, *Critique of Western Philosophy and Social Theory* (New York: Palgrave Macmillan, 2009), 174.

18 Jacob S. Hacker and Paul Pierson, *Winner-Take-All Politics: How Washington Made the Rich Richer—and Turned Its Back on the Middle Class* (New York: Simon & Schuster, 2010), 6–7.

19 According to some estimates, nearly half of American citizens would have difficulty raising $400 to deal with an emergency. See Neal Gabler, "My Secret Shame," *The Atlantic*, May 2016, 52–63. The author is one of these people.

20 Hacker and Pierson, *Winner-Take-All Politics*, 11–40.

21 Ibid., 41–72.

22 Ibid., 184–193.

23 Ibid., 200.

24 Ibid., 224–227.

25 Ibid., 293.

26 Ibid., 302–303.

27 Bruce Judson, *It Could Happen Here: America on the Brink* (New York: HarperCollins, 2009), 45–46.

28 Ibid., 50–51.

29 Ibid., 74.

30 Ibid., 75–80.

31 Ibid., 81–88.

32 Ibid., 89–90.

33 Ibid., 91–93.

34 Ibid., 160.

35 Ibid., 162.

36 Ibid., 171–182.

37 Floyd Ciruli, "The Year of the Outsider," *The Denver Post*, January 31, 2016, 1D.

38 See Steve Peoples and Emily Swanson, "Voters Feel Disconnected, Helpless about Candidates," *The Denver Post*, May 31, 2016, 12A.

39 Phillip Eliott, "How Trump and Sanders Voters Are Upending U.S. Politics," *Time*, February 1, 2016, 32–36. See also Joshua Green, "The Great GOP Realignment," *Bloomberg Business Week*, February 8–14, 2016, 6–8; Ross Douthat, "The Revolt against Decadence," *The New York Times*, January 31, 2016, SR11; John Leland, "They're Mad and Sure Their Guy Is the One to Lead the Fight," *The New York Times*, January 31, 2016, Y1; Michael Tomasky, "The Dangerous Election," *The New York Review*, March 24, 2016, 4–6; and "A Bitterly Divided GOP Heads for a Crackup," *The Week*, March 18, 2016, 6.

40 The pope weighed in on climate change in 2015 in the first papal encyclical focused solely on the issue. He proclaimed that climate change is real and that humans are largely responsible for the "unprecedented destruction of eh ecosystem." Addicted to fossil fuel consumption, the richest countries have exploited the land leaving the poor to deal with the consequences which include drought, famine, and floods. See "Pope Francis: The Vatican's Crusade against Climate Change," *The Week*, July 3, 2015, 16; Bill McKibben, "The Pope and the

Planet," *The New York Review*, August 13, 2015, 40–42; Ross Douthat, "More Than a Plea for the Planet," *The New York Times*, June 21, 2015, SR11; and Chris Mooney, "Papal Challenge to U.S. Preconceptions," *The Denver Post*, June 21, 2015, 12A. See also Elizabeth Shogren, "The Campaign against Coal," *High Country News*, November 9, 2015, 13–18; and Naomi Oreskes, "How to Break the Climate Deadlock," *Scientific American*, December 2015, 74–79.

41 "Noted," *The Week*, April 29, 2016, 16. See also the November 2015 issue of *National Geographic* entitled "Cool it: The Climate Issue," as the entire issue is devoted to climate change.

42 See "Climate Science: Efforts to Link Climate Change to Severe Weather Gain Ground," *Science*, Vol. 351, No. 6279 (March 18, 2016), 1249–1250.

43 See Justin Worland, "The Great Barrier Reef Is under Attack from El Nino and Climate Change," *Time*, April 25, 2016, 14. Also see Kristen Gelineau, "Bleaching Kills Third of Coral in Parts of the Reef," *The Denver Post*, May 31, 2016, 14A.

44 See Andy Isaacson, "Into Thin Ice," *National Geographic*, January 2016, 99–117; and Chris Mooney, "North of Normal," *The Denver Post*, February 19, 2016, 14A. Because of melting ice, the Intergovernmental Panel on Climate Change projects that sea levels could rise by as much as three feet by the end of the century. Cities like Miami have already spent some hundred million dollars to deal with flooding problems and plan on spending several hundred million more. See Elizabeth Kolbert, "The Siege of Miami," *The New Yorker*, December 21 & 28, 2015, 42–50.

45 See "Health & Science: Oceans Rising Faster Than Ever," *The Week*, March 11, 2016, 19. See also Peter Brannen, "Lessons from Underwater Miami," *The New York Times*, April 24, 2016, SR4.

46 See a special section by several authors titled "Oceans of Change," *Science*, Vol. 350, No. 6262 (November 18, 2015), 750–782. See also "Ruining the Oceans," *The Week*, February 26, 2015, 13.

47 Air pollution is one of the world's leading causes of death and disease claiming some 5 million lives a year. More than half of these deaths occur because of poor air quality in India and China. More than 85 percent of people worldwide live in places that do not meet the air-quality standards set by the World Health Organization. See "Air Pollution: A Mass Killer," *The Week*, March 4, 2016, 21.

48 "Weather patterns are changing all over the world as freak storms, such as Hurricane Sandy, wreak their devastation on various regions." See Marcia Angell, "Our Beleaguered Planet," *The American Prospect*, Spring 2016, 90–94. Proposals have been made to designate a new geological age called the Anthropocene, which is defined by the dominance of humans that are capable of altering the planet on a geological scale. See Beth Lord, ed. *Spinoza Beyond Philosophy* (Edinburgh: Edinburgh University Press, 2015), 33.

49 Brian Clegg, *Final Frontier: The Pioneering Science and Technology of Exploring the Universe* (New York: St. Martin's Press, 2014), 7–8.

50 In December 2015, authorities in Beijing issued their first-ever "red alert" because of thick smog that blanketed the city. This was the highest possible warning resulting in the closure of schools, the halting of construction projects, the closure of heavily polluting factories, and the ordering of half of privately owned cars off the road based on license plate numbers. "The World at a Glance: Beijing," *The Week*, December 18, 2015, 9.

51 Jim McNeill, "Strategies for Sustainable Economic Development," *Scientific American*, September 1990, 155.

52 Erik Assadourian, "The Rise and Fall of Consumer Cultures," in Linda Stark, ed., *The State of the World 2010: Transforming Cultures* (New York: W.W. Norton, 2010), 4.

53 McNeill, "Strategies for Sustainable Development," 156. "If the global economy grows at 3 percent a year, it will expand from an output of $29 trillion in 1997 to $57 trillion in 2020, nearly doubling. It will then more than double again by the year 2050, reaching $138 trillion. Yet even in reaching $29 trillion, the economy has already overrun many or the Earth's natural capacities." Lester R. Brown and Jennifer Mitchell, "Building a New Economy," in Lester R. Brown, Christopher Flavin, and Hilary French, eds., *State of the World 1998* (New York: W.W. Norton & Company, 1998), 168.

54 "Humanity's Profound Impact on the Earth," *The Week*, January 29, 2016, 20.

55 McNeill, "Strategies for Sustainable Development," 155–156.

56 Lester R. Brown, Christopher Flavin, and Sandra Postel, "Outlining a Global Action Plan," in Lester R. Brown, ed., *State of the World 1990* (New York: W.W. Norton & Company, 1990), 173–174.

57 Ibid., 174–175.

58 McNeill, "Strategies for Sustainable Development," 156. See also Paul F. Steinberg, *Who Rules the Earth? How Social Rules Shape Our Planet and Our Lives* (New York: Oxford University Press, 2015), who argues that the shift toward a sustainable world requires modifying the rules that guide human behavior and shape the way we interact with the natural world. See also Andrew Holland, "Preventing Tomorrow's Climate Wars," *Scientific American*, June, 2016, 61–65.

59 Ibid., 157.

60 Ibid.

61 Ibid., 158–163.

62 Roderick Frazier Nash, *The Rights of Nature: A History of Environmental Ethics* (Madison, WI: University of Wisconsin Press, 1989), 125.

63 Ibid., 160.

64 Holmes Ralston III, "Just Environmental Business," in Tom Regan, ed. *Just Business: New Introductory Essays in Business Ethics* (New York: Random House, 1984), 325–343.

65 Holmes Ralston III, *Philosophy Gone Wild: Essays in Environmental Ethics* (Buffalo, NY: Prometheus Books, 1987), 121.

66 Ibid., 141.

67 Ibid., 103–104.

68 Sara Ebenreck, "An Earth Care Ethics," *The Catholic World: Caring for the Endangered Earth*, Vol. 233 (July/August 1990), 156.

69 Nash, *The Rights of Nature*, 10.

70 Ibid., 150.

71 Sprintzen, *Critique of Western Philosophy*, 42.

72 Ibid., 26.

73 William Ophuls, *Plato's Revenge: Politics in the Age of Ecology* (Cambridge, MA: MIT Press, 2011), 19–20.

74 Ibid., 45–46.

75 Ibid., 30.

76 Ibid., 31.

77 Ibid., 32–33.

78 Ibid., 39.

79 Ibid., 43.

80 Ibid., 60.

81 Ibid., 67.

82 Ibid., 47.

83 See Llewellyn Vaughan-Lee, ed., *Spiritual Ecology: The Cry of the Earth* (Point Reyes, CA: The Golden Sufi Center, 2013).

84 Fred Magoff, professor emeritus of plant and soil science at the University of Vermont, and John Bellamy Foster, professor of sociology at the University of

Oregon, say the following: "The reality is that that major environmental problems we face today—of which climate change is only one—cannot be solved by means of technological or market-based solutions while keeping existing social relations intact. Rather, what is needed most is a transformation in social relations: in community, culture, and economy, in how we relate to each other as human beings, and how we relate to the planet. What is needed, in other words, is an ecological revolution." Fred Magdoff and John Bellamy Foster, *What Every Environmentalist Needs to Know about Capitalism* (New York: Monthly Review Press, 2011), 122.

Part II
Sources of Spirituality

4 Religion

In the previous chapter the breakdown in contemporary politics was discussed along with a radical individualism in contemporary American life that contributes to a dysfunctional political system. It was argued that this individualism leads to an atomized society of disengaged individuals who feel demoralized and socially powerless to do anything about the problems they face. The net result is that we have lost a spiritual connection with each other are only left with individual interests that the political system can't handle very well without some sense of the public good and a holistic community. The environmental crisis likewise has left us feeling powerless to do anything about issues like global warming, leaving us to cope with the effects as best as possible. While reformulations of the relationship between humans and nature are useful, they are not enough as again the fundamental problem is that we have lost a spiritual connection with nature and not only see it but also feel it as something apart from ourselves. Thus, we need to establish a spiritual connection with ourselves and nature that leads to the question of where we look to find this spirituality.

Religion is the traditional source of spirituality in many societies as people look to religion to fulfill their spiritual needs. While religious influence has waned in many, if not most European societies, it remained strong in the United States and continued to be an important part of American society for many decades. While mainstream religions lost some of their authority and influence in a society that became increasingly secular over the past several decades, this loss was more than made up by the growth of the evangelistic or fundamentalist churches that continued to exercise an increasing influence in all aspects of American society. However, there is some evidence that even evangelical religions are experiencing a decline in membership and influence in recent years, leading some authors to proclaim the end of white Christian America in light of the increasing secularization of American society.[1]

There are many different religions in the world, of course, and each of them has a perspective that is different from the others, but it is, of course, the Christian religion that has been the main source of spiritual values for the American people over the years. Every religion has a story to tell that attempts to address some, if not all, of the deepest mysteries of life, such as how the earth was created, what is the meaning of life, and where do we go, if anywhere, after death. The Christian religion has a particular story about the origins of life, the end of times, and everything between spelled out in a book called the Bible. To many Christians, particularly fundamentalists, this book is the ultimate authority and contains the absolute truth about all these questions. It is looked to for answers to all life's problems and for rules as to how to live one's life. But even for so-called mainstream religions some of whom do not necessarily believe in a literal interpretation of the Bible, it still serves as the foundation for faith and is where one goes to find the essential elements of the Christian worldview.

Religion and Science

Science has its own story to tell about the origin of the universe in the big bang and how our solar system is going to end when the sun burns up all its hydrogen fuel and become a red giant. It is a worldview very different form religion in explaining how the world works and has no need for the supernatural as it a naturalistic endeavor that explains everything through the laws of nature that are discoverable through the scientific method. Obviously, it is a worldview that is in competition with the religious worldview so the question of how science and religion relate to each other is important and constitutes an ongoing debate. Modern science arose during what is called the Enlightenment, a historical period in Western thought and culture that stretched roughly from 1685 to 1815 and saw revolutions in science, philosophy, society, and politics that swept away the worldview of the medieval period and ushered in the modern Western world that we live in today. The primary goal of the Enlightenment was the development of a better and more secular world for humankind as a whole.[2] The rise of modern science was perhaps the most impressive achievement of the Enlightenment as it changed the perception of the world toward a more naturalistic view of the universe and a more secular view of human society.[3] According to Stuart Jordan, president and board member of the Institute for Science and Human Values,

> [t]he Enlightenment was primarily an ethically motivated humanistic movement to improve the secular lives of people everywhere. To do so, it advocated science and reason as the means to realize that goal . . . The Enlightenment was the culmination of ideas that developed first in Italian city-states and eventually became widespread among educated Western Europeans during the Renaissance . . . *The Age of Reason* is the term frequently used to describe this historical period; and the scientific approach required that empirical evidence, not faith, must be combined with reason to better understand the secular world.[4]

Because major societal progress was virtually nonexistent in the medieval world the idea of progress was central to the Enlightenment movement. This movement involved an enlightened approach to life and holds that by overcoming ignorance and superstition and applying knowledge to life-enhancing skills, secular life can be made better for more people and become more fulfilling so that the human race can move forward.[5] From the original Enlightenment came a vision in which the opportunity for a fulfilling life would be made available to people all over the world. The means to attain this vision involved the use of science and reason as science was considered to be the best way to learn about the natural world and this knowledge would enable people of all nationalities to better their lives.[6] Jordan believes this enlightenment vision is valid and is relevant to the present world and its problems He thinks that

> junk thought seems to be growing in many other parts of the world today. It is a major issue in many contemporary Islamic countries, where creationism has become popular among some of the more radical Islamic clergy. There could be few better examples of competing reactionary religions than aggressive Protestant fundamentalism in the United States and equally aggressive Islamic fundamentalism in these other countries. Yet the two have much in common, psychologically, and share a rigid close-mindedness to science when it conflicts with their ancient texts.[7]

Efforts to politicize science and distort public perceptions of scientific findings have stemmed, according to Jordan, from the success of science to uncover and, in many cases, resolve social and environmental problems. The results of scientific research often conflict with religious dogmas and economic interests, and this leads to conflicts between scientists and religious or political authorities. Jordan believes that scientists themselves are best qualified to evaluate the results of scientific research and its implications for society rather than nonscientists who have an ideological position or economic interest to defend.[8] Yet religion remains of importance to a vast number of people around the world who do not find the humanistic vision of the Enlightenment that focuses on the welfare of human beings in a secular world very attractive. Jordan says that

> [i]It has long been one of the functions of religion to provide an inspiring vision to compensate for life's many hardships and inevitable personal morality. It is easy to understand why so many people living impoverished lives cling to religious superstitions, even in the absence of reliable evidence for the claims of their faith. Once more we note the need for a vibrant secular vision, if nontheists expect to compete with, much less replace, a supernatural religion in the minds of people ill prepared to confront life's challenges with stoic acceptance.[9]

Jordan believes that science is ethical because it gives us reliable knowledge that can help solve many of the world's most pressing problems and will likely matter even more in the future.[10] Scientists do not claim that science has replaced ethics as the field of ethics provides a foundation for prescriptions that guide personal actions as well as formulations of the laws that society passes.[11] But the primary ethical vision of the Enlightenment is a better world for people everywhere, and if this vision is to be realized it is hard to argue that there is any other factor other than science, according to Jordan, that can fulfill this promise.[12]

Stewart Shapiro, O'Donnell Professor of Philosophy at The Ohio State University, believes that there are three stances that can be taken on the interaction between religion and science or between faith and reason. The first stance is that they are at war with each other and that religion argues that reason has its limits with regard to knowledge of the truth about the world and human life whereas revelation is the method by which we know the ultimate truth about these things, while the opposite camp believes that religious faith is inherently irrational and that its propositions are held on faith alone with no evidence to support them. Faith and reason thus stand in the way of each other, and neither can give ground to accept the legitimacy of the other, which must be vanquished in order for its truth to prevail.[13]

The second stance holds that religion, properly understood and, rationality, properly applied, pull in the same direction. The rational mind that comes as standard equipment with the human body is a gift from God and God would not or could not give us tools that would lead us astray when they are used properly. Every statement in the Bible, for example, is not to be taken literally, and we are to use our rational minds to help tell us which are literal truths and which are to be taken metaphorically. This rational approach has occupied some of the best minds throughout history in the search for a way to reconcile the differences between faith and reason.[14]

In the third stance, faith and reason are incommensurable; they have nothing to do with each other. Science is at cross purposes with religion. Science is concerned with facts about how the universe operates and how planet Earth developed and other such scientific questions, while religion is normative and concerned with how we should live our lives.[15] Science is about what can be observed while religion is about salvation. The two deal in different realms, and there is no serious conflict between science and religion as long as they stay within their appropriate realms of knowledge. As stated by Marvin Belzer, associate professor of philosophy at Bowling Green State University, "[i]t is not difficult to find ways to reconcile any scientific theory with speculative beliefs about what is beyond direct observation just so long as one does not claim that religious speculation is based on science or assume that science is the only source of knowledge or insight about things."[16]

Shapiro himself does not agree with this last stance and questions whether all the world's religions can withdraw completely from factual claims. And it also seems to him that moral concerns are susceptible to rational appraisal, which is to say that he believes that rationality has something to say about the best way to live in the world and that arena should not be entirely abandoned to the world's religions. Incommensurability is unacceptable to him as faith is continually at war with reason and one has to choose sides. The best that can be hoped for is a mutual respect between faith and reason—that both sides agree to disagree and keep the dispute from getting violent.[17]

Religion has been shaped and influenced by the scientific and technological culture in which we all live, making it appropriate and necessary to inquire into the impact the scientific worldview has had on religious life and thought in America. As science took over the world, so to speak, in the sense of being the primary way we understand and manipulate the natural world in which we live, religion was forced to find its foundation in the supernatural realm. Science emptied the world of purpose and meaning, of any sacred or spiritual dimension, and of ethics and values with its mechanistic and reductionistic understanding of humans and nature. The world grinds on according to the laws of nature that have no purpose and no value dimension. These qualities, then, according to many religious people, can only be retained by a turn to the supernatural.

Religion involves myths that explain the world and provide an understanding of how the world came about and where it is going. Christianity has its creation myth, for example, that describes how the world came into being, and its eschatological myth that describes a catastrophic end to the present world order. These myths are at odds with the scientific worldview that holds that the universe came into existence with the big bang, which is the most accepted theory at this time, and that the earth will cease to exist in its present form when the sun exhausts its fuel and expands into a red giant that will incinerate the earth. Many people in our present world believe in myths and their supernatural basis rather than the scientific explanation, and so mythology still has a hold on people and describes a different reality that science cannot prove or disprove. Many religious people do not even consider religious stories as myths but accept them as the truth about the world and human beings.

By pitting itself against science religion loses hold of the natural world and is forced more and more into the supernatural realm. God is used to fill in the gaps in our knowledge and explain the unexplainable, but as science discovers more and more about our world, God gets pushed further and further away from our daily existence in the material world. The Catholic Church supposedly can live with the big bang theory but it had trouble accepting Einstein's theory about a static universe.[18] The big bang theory at least has a point of creation from which the universe started, and science cannot explain where the small point of matter that started the universe came from in the first place. This theory still leaves a place for God and the idea of creation out of nothing so that God can still be believed to be the first cause of everything. But God gets pushed further and further back in time as gaps in our knowledge of the physical world are filled in by science.

Religion has been affected by the scientific worldview in many ways, but this does not mean that religion has been replaced by science or that religion is of no importance. That mythology has not been completely replaced by science is quite evident in the religious beliefs held by people all over the world. Thus, a religious worldview is different from the scientific worldview and the two are not reconcilable. Science is rooted in the natural world and has a specific kind of methodology to get at truths related to how the world works. Religion, on the other hand, is rooted in the supernatural for the source of its truths and relies on revelation as a method to uncover these truths. Science cannot prove or disprove the truths of religion, and religion cannot prove or disprove the findings of science. They are two incompatible worldviews that involve different kinds of truth claims and different methods of discovering what the world is about.

Perhaps a contemporary example will help to clarify this difference. In 2007, the governor of Georgia asked the citizens of the state to pray for rain to alleviate the state's drought. For those with a scientific worldview, the rain that eventually fell was seen as the result of changing weather patterns. The committed religious person, however, would hold that the rain was the result of God's action in response to prayer. The way the world works is relative to one's worldview, and no amount of evidence or argument is going to convince either the religious person or the scientific person that they are wrong and ought to adhere to the other's point of view.[19] One has to choose between one or the other worldview in these kinds of situations. As David Sprintzen puts the matter,

> [i]t [religion] is a total worldview, always with its own particular texts and/or stories that dramatically undergird its particular values, practices, and programs. To use its language is to invoke its worldview. It is usually to operate within a mythological and associative-emotive frame of reference, and thus to become more of less a prisoner of that discourse, addressing issues on its terms, and arguing about its problems. That is a devil's bargain. And it is not necessary. We can seek to find common ground on values, positions, and programs in our terms and for our reasons. If we cannot find common values and make common cause around shared programs, then we are truly in different worlds, and there is very little cooperatively that can be done about that. There is no guarantee that all people are reachable through rational dialogue, scientific attention to reality, and a common concern for human dignity.[20]

There are many people, including some scientists, who believe that science and religion are not in conflict and that one can accommodate both worldviews as they deal with different kinds of truth and have different methods of determining the nature of reality and are simply complementary ways of knowing and are not in competition with each other. However, Jerry A. Coyne, a professor in the Department of Ecology and Evolution at the University of Chicago, argues that science and religion are incompatible because they use different methods of obtaining knowledge of reality, establish the reliability of that knowledge in a different manner, and reach different conclusions about the nature of the universe. Science relies on reason, observation, testing, and experiment while religion relies on faith, which Coyne describes as belief in things for which there is no evidence, insufficient evidence, or even counterevidence. Such faith involves dogma and an authoritarian mindset to establish the truth of the claims that faith makes about the world.[21]

Science and religion, according to Coyne, are competitors in discovering truths about nature. Coyne believes that science can disprove the truth claims of religion and has done so in many instances while religion has no way of overturning the truth claims of science. As an example of the former, science eventually overturned the claim of the Catholic Church that the earth was the center of the universe and everything revolved around the earth. There are many other examples of science challenging the truth claims of religion. Coyne is critical of accommodationism and argues that faith is not fact and personal or public decisions should not be based on faith. Faith is a danger to both science and society, and those faiths that do not believe in modern medicine expose their children to death and disease. They have been involved in the vaccination controversy, opposition to assisted dying, and the denial of global warming. These are areas where faith has opposed the findings of science and affected the resulting outcome.[22]

In a book titled *In Praise of Reason*, Michael P. Lynch, professor of philosophy at the University of Connecticut and director of the Humanities Institute, sets out "to defend both the value of giving reasons in public discourse and the value of certain principles over others—in particular the principles that constitute a scientific approach to the world." According to Lynch, the value of reason is one of the oldest philosophical problems in existence. Skepticism is most often associated with the idea that we lack knowledge of certain things and poses a challenge to the importance of reasoning and the practice of exchanging reasons on any given issue. What matters most to Lynch is not knowledge itself but the ability to defend and articulate whatever knowledge is under consideration.[23]

Lynch believes that many people are skeptical about *reason* and end up thinking that all "rational" explanations are arbitrary and that in the final analysis, it all boils down to what a person happens to believe—what people feel in their gut so to speak or what they have faith in. Just go with what you believe in even if it does not square with the evidence. This thought that everything is arbitrary undermines our commitment to civil society, according to Lynch, in that we owe our fellow citizens an explanation for what we do in the public realm. Civil societies value reason giving, questioning assumptions, and discussing differences with others. They embrace the idea that there are better or worse ways of doing things and that reason can ascertain these differences.[24]

Reason matters and *appeals* to reason matter in the everyday world and not just on an academic or abstract level. Lynch defines reason as "the ability to explain and justify our beliefs and commitments."[25] Reason plays a role in any healthy public culture. Democracies, in particular, should be spaces for reason as they are established to allow for mutual deliberation of the issues that are important to that democracy. What is needed is a common background of standards against which to determine what counts as a reliable source of information or a reliable method in inquiry. Otherwise, people in a democracy won't be able *to agree on the facts*, let alone values. And if people can't agree on the facts, they can hardly agree on what to do about any given issue.[26]

Lynch believes the United States has headed in this direction as we tend to live in our own isolated bubbles of information that comes from sources that only reinforce our prejudices and never challenge the basic assumptions we make about the history of our nation as well as the physical structure of the world.[27] Thus, we can't come to an agreement about how to deal with an issue like global warming because we can't come to an agreement on the facts about whether the earth is actually warming and whether the cause is due to human activities or natural processes. The same could be said for an issue like immigration where some solutions ignore facts on the ground. How in the world is the government going to round up 11 million people and deport them back to Mexico? Such a proposal is utter nonsense.

A separation between reason and emotion goes all the way back to the ancient Greeks and has dominated Western philosophical thought for centuries. Reason and emotion are considered to be warring components of the human mind, and reason wins, or at least should win, in successful and happy people. Humans either are or *ought* to be rational animals. Lynch finds these key elements of reason and emotion in some of the basic assumptions of traditional economic theory which assumes that our actions in the economic realm are the result of a detached and so-called objective analysis of our preferences using a cost–benefit framework to make these determinations. Standard economic theory assumes that we are rational creatures making economic decisions that reflect our calculated self-interest that is unaffected by emotions and other noncognitive factors.[28]

Lynch challenges this view of the dispassionate rational actor and argues that we are not dispassionate reasoners; we are not built like that and do not make decisions like that. We are in many cases irrational and this seems to be deeply rooted in the human psyche so that commands to be a dispassionate reasoner will not have an effect on human behavior. Even more problematic is the argument that it would be bad for us if we were able to be such detached reasoners. Completely dispassionate people are often considered to be cold and lonely people and perhaps unhealthy to boot. Some have argued that people who lack the capacity for certain types of emotions are severely impaired reasoners. Feelings connect us with the circumstances in which we exist and play an important part in our ability to reason.[29]

David Hume took an extreme position on this issue and held that humans are not ruled by reason but by what he called "passions" and "sentiment." Reason can give us information but not motivate us to do something. For that we need a desire or a feeling to want to do something. Hume thus turns the Platonic conception upside down in that the emotional aspects of our lives cause us to act and is immune to rational assessment. Lynch adopts a more balanced approach and agrees that while all motivation may have an emotional component, that doesn't leave rationality without an important role to play. As he states, "neither reason nor emotion is master or slave; they intertwine more intimately and equally than that."[30]

Likewise with intuition, which generally means to know something and find it believable without exactly knowing the reasons behind this belief. Some people seem to know what to do in a given situation without appearing to think about it or engage in any rational reflection or analysis. Rather than think things through, they make intuitive or unreflective judgments. However, Lynch thinks that while intuition may appear to be entirely independent of reason, intuition itself may be the product of some sort of rational belief, and intuitions themselves can be assessed as to their rational coherence. Thus, while reason plays a significant role in judgment it shares the stage with intuition as well as emotion.[31]

Reason also plays a role in value judgments even though many believe that when it comes to our most deeply held values and commitments reasons are not causally efficacious. When challenges come along to our core commitments our first reaction is to question the experience or information that provides this challenge rather than give up our core commitment. It takes a good deal of counter information to make us change our mind about such commitments and make us alter our worldview. But this doesn't mean that reason doesn't matter in these situations, only that it oftentimes works very slowly. People do change their minds on issues in the light of new scientific and other evidence and in light of their own experience. Many Americans' attitudes toward the Iraq war, for example, changed over time as new evidence became available.[32]

In a democracy, Lynch believes that disagreements between citizens must be handled by reasons alone and uses of political power by either citizens or the state must be supported by reasons. These reasons cannot be based on force or manipulation as these are considered to be illegitimate in a democracy. Persuasion must be relied on to change people's minds and win support for a particular course of action. Only then are people treated with respect as autonomous rational beings that are capable of judging on their own what they decide to believe as true and beneficial for themselves and society. Power alone is not a legitimate means of effecting change in a democracy, which is why the events in Egypt that took place in 2013 to remove from office a president who had been elected by the people did not bode well for democracy in that nation.[33]

Conservative intellectuals going all the way back to Edmund Burke have stressed the importance of tradition for centuries, that beliefs are embedded within traditions, certain practices that are woven into a community that are the accepted way of doing things. Change is not easily tolerated and tradition poses severe limits to the use of reason in politics. Tradition is often placed outside of rational examination and is just accepted as the right way to go on living. But this gives us no way to resolve disagreements over whose traditions are better as there are obviously many different traditions in any given society. Some traditions are better than others but holding tradition above rational discussion seems to say that no worldview is better than any other.[34] Yet in practice this view is never acceptable as was evidenced in this country by the failure to accept the Mormon point of view with regard to marriage or the Southern worldview with respect to slavery.[35]

According to Lynch commitment is not the same as belief because one can commit to a principle without necessarily believing. An example is a scientist who commits to a theory while retaining some doubt about its ultimate truth or a person who feels something is true without acting on that feeling. Commitment to a principle means commitment to its truth and further inquiry into the matter is no longer necessary. The issue is closed unless further events force reconsideration. Lynch believes it is crucial for the good of civil society to commit itself to the ideal of reason. Having faith in reason is to commit to certain fundamental epistemic principles that include logical inference and observation as well as the use of evidence to support one's positions.[36]

Science occupies a privileged position in a democratic society. It is, first of all, a group enterprise and, in this sense, is *intersubjective*. Scientific studies are subject to critical review by one's peers in order to be published. Second, scientific practice is relatively *transparent* in that the data on which a study is based are open to question and possible refutation. This transparency is part of the public character of science. Science is also *repeatable* in that like cases should give like results if the experiment or study is performed again. Results should be able to be confirmed by this process. The methods of science such as observation, deduction, and induction also come *naturally* to people and most of us can employ them to some degree. And finally, these basic methods are highly *adaptable* and can be used to address a variety of questions. These five features give science its open character where the application of its methods can be judged publicly and independently.[37] These features also make science a self-correcting endeavor that is somewhat unique in society as Lynch describes:

> Nonetheless, the idea that science is self-correcting gets at something about the principles that underlie scientific methods and sets them apart from others. Scientific principles of inquiry have certain features that lend them a distinctively open character. That is reasons generated by

such principles are public reasons—reasons that can be appreciated from the common point of view. I don't take it to be particularly controversial that science has these features, even for skeptics about reason.[38]

The force of objective reasons does not depend on any one person's point of view, as they are impartial and can be judged from a common point of view. This does not make them value-free, however, as epistemic principles *are* values in that they tell us what sources and methods of belief to trust. What matters is not that they comprise a "view from nowhere" but that they can be assessed from *many* different points of view. Their truth or falsity can be *"judged from diverse perspectives."* This is what Lynch means by a common point of view. Thus, for "objective reasons" it is not just truth or falsity that matters but also *"the manner in which that reason can be judged."* Objectivity is thus a "matter of openness to evaluation from a common point of view."[39]

Those principles that allow us to have a common point of view must also be justifiable from a common point of view. To accomplish this Lynch first argues that *"the fundamental principles we should be committed to are those that persons concerned to advance their interests would endorse in a position of epistemic and social equality."* This stance is similar to Rawl's veil of ignorance, from which he derives his principles of justice.[40] The principles that would be acceptable in this kind of position are open and objective, making it rational to commit to such principles. Second, principles should be privileged that have the virtues he discussed earlier, namely, principles that support methods and practices that are *repeatable, adaptable, intersubjective, and transparent.* Thus, it will be rational to privilege principles because they are open and the methods they recommend can be used to generate objective, public reasons.[41]

Lynch concludes his book by reiterating his argument that we can and must defend our fundamental epistemic commitments with reason that are objective in the sense defined earlier and practical. We should not give up on the value of reason and conclude that everything is arbitrary. Skepticism about reason encourages us to give up on the Enlightenment idea that "we share a common currency of reason with our fellow human beings." Once we give up on the idea that there is something like a common point of view that involves a commitment to shared principles that help us distinguish what is rational from its opposite then we also give up on the idea of civil society. Conservatives and liberals stop debating with each other and come to regard each other as lunatics and idiots and the political climate becomes poisoned. Lynch hopes to live in a society that is passionately committed to reason and puts its principles into action.[42]

In conclusion, then, the scientific worldview poses many problems for religion in modern society and undermines many of the foundations upon which religion depends. It questions the existence of a supernatural realm and has no need for a belief in a God that controls the world and everything in it and has a plan for everyone's life. The world operates according to natural laws that are immutable and intervention by an outside force that would suspend these laws to make the sun stand still, for example, is not possible. Many believe that science has rendered religion irrelevant in the contemporary world and as one famous scientist is reported to have said, "I have no need for that hypothesis."[43] Yet the spiritual dimension is necessary to life and while the Christian religion may not be a source of spirituality for many people anymore they must find other sources that can provide this dimension. As stated by Arthur Peacocke, who was a biochemist and theologian from Oxford University,

> [a] host of surveys indicate that what Christians, and indeed other religions believers, today affirm as 'real' fails to generate any conviction among many of those who seek spiritual insight and who continue as wistful agnostics in relation to the formulations of traditional religions—notably Christianity in Europe, and in intellectual circles in the USA. Many factors contribute to this state of affairs, but one of these, I would suggest, is that the traditional language in which much Christian theology, certainly its Western form, has been and is cast is so saturated with terms that have a super-natural reference and colour that a culture accustomed to think in naturalistic terms, conditioned by the power and prestige of the natural sciences, finds it increasingly difficult to attribute any plausibility to it. Be that as it may, there is clearly a pressing need to describe the realities that Christian belief wishes to articulate in terms that can make sense to that culture without reducing its content to insignificance. Correspondingly, there is also a perennial pressure, even among those not given to any form of traditional religiosity, to integrate the understandings of the natural world afforded by the sciences with very real 'spiritual' experiences, which include interactions with other people and awareness of the transcendent.[44]

There is a need for a spiritual dimension to life, but Christianity may not be the source of that spirituality for increasing numbers of people. Its truth claims are suspect to those who have a scientific orientation while the truth claims of science are accepted because science works. Science continues to discover new things about our world are often translated into technology that enhances our lives and makes it possible to live a more fulfilling and enriched life. The success of science and its worldview has made us a more secular society, where we rely on evidence and experiment to establish truths about the world and have less and less need for supernatural explanations of phenomena we experience in our everyday lives. Many turn to science for answers rather than religion.[45]

Religion and Society

The founders of the United States were well aware of the dangers religion posed for a free society. Many of them had watched Europe destroy itself over religious wars of one kind or another. Colonial America also had its share of religious controversy like the one over antinomianism in Massachusetts where the Puritans were banished and had to establish a new colony in Rhode Island. As Thomas Jefferson put it, "[m]illions of innocent men, women, and children, since the introduction of Christianity, have been burnt, tortured, fined, imprisoned; yet we have not advanced one inch towards uniformity. What have been the effects of coercion? To make one half of the world fools, and the other half hypocrites."[46]

Contrary to popular opinion among the religious right, the founders did not create a Christian nation based on Christian principles. They were products of the Enlightenment whose philosophers had laid the groundwork for a secular political system as free as possible from religious influences. There was to be no established church in the country. The rights and values this country held dear—the right to life, liberty, and the pursuit of happiness—were not grounded in religion or some supernatural force; they were rather part of the natural order of things. They were derived from nature and secured by the consent of the governed, not by the dictates or dogmas of any particular religion.[47]

The only direct reference to God in the Declaration of Independence appears in the very first paragraph, where it invokes the "laws of nature and of nature's god." Even though the final copy capitalizes all four nouns, Jefferson wrote these words without capitalization. This phrase, "nature's god," is said to reflect Jefferson's deism, a belief that he shared with Franklin, in a creator whose divine handiwork is evident in the wonders of nature, a naturalistic conception. They did not believe in a personal God who interceded directly in the daily affairs of humankind.[48]

The Constitution does not even mention God and, in that sense, is a godless document. Religion is mentioned only twice, once in the First Amendment's separation of religion and government, and second in Article VI's prohibition of religious tests for public office. There were attempts during the Constitutional Convention to favor recognition of Christianity in the Constitution, but these were rejected.[49] Fundamentalists themselves favored the separation of church and state as they rightly feared that if the United States were declared to be a Christian nation, the denominations in the majority at that time would gain effective control at their expense, and they remained separationists for some 200 years. It was only in the 1980s when Ronald Reagan brought them into the Republican tent that they began to get involved in politics and threaten such a separation.

Christian fundamentalists now contend that the United States was meant to be a Christian nation that has lost touch with its Christian origins. However, nothing could be clearer than that the Founding Fathers intended to create a constitutional separation of church and state after careful deliberation and extensive, documented debate.[50] The perpetuation of the Christian myth, however, allows for the promotion and insertion of fundamentalist beliefs into all aspect of our public life on the basis that all contemporary social ills are the result of the removal of God and religion from the public sphere.[51] The so-called culture wars have been going on in this country for several decades, and the separation between church and state is one of the things that is always under threat by religious fundamentalists. According to Stuart Jordan again writing in the *Enlightenment Vision*,

> [t]he primary antagonists in the contemporary religious culture war are those who insist on literal interpretations of ancient religious texts on [the] one hand, and an increasingly concerned population of scientifically literate nonbelieving and other open-minded people on the other. The latter group in America had previously adopted a live-and-let-live approach throughout much of the twentieth century, fortified by a reasonable degree of institutional church-state separation. These nontheists and many religions liberals have since become disturbed by the increasingly aggressive approach of religious fundamentalists to break down this separation and move American society in a more theocratic direction . . . Notwithstanding the false claim that secular humanism is a religion, the fundamentalists assert that liberals have tried to impose "the religion of secular humanism" on America. The nontheists and religious liberals have responded that the struggle began in earnest only when transparent attempts to break down the wall of separation of church and state started to score some executive and judicial successes within the federal government . . . it may not be an exaggeration to say that battle lines have been drawn between uncompromising religious extremists and those who detest the idea of any kind of theocratic republic.[52]

Religious freedom is protected in this country, and the counterpart to the prohibition of a state religion is the prohibition against government interference in how people in this country freely exercise their beliefs.[53] People are free to believe what they want, but this can only be exercised if religion is separated from government. History is replete with examples showing that where church and state are wedded, individual liberty suffers, especially religious liberty. But it is not only liberty that suffers; it may also be prosperity. Bernard Lewis, a historian of the Middle East, alleges that the secularization of Western cultures is on of the strongest reasons for their prosperity and progress in science, technology, and culture. It is the lack of separation of church and state in Muslim countries that has driven the Arab world from its medieval apex of human achievement to its current status as a cultural backwater.[54]

According to Michael Shermer writing in the *Science of Good & Evil*, in order to generate liberty for more people we must maintain the separation of church and state and foster the greater secularization of society. Public morality must be legislated only by secular bodies. Private morality can be as religious as the individual prefers, and the members of secular bodies may be as religious as they prefer, but the body itself must remain religiously neutral.[55] In other words, people elected to public office have religious freedom to believe whatever they want, but they should be religiously neutral as to how they vote on particular issues, how they decide cases as judges, and how they see their role in government. Such neutrality is difficult to maintain, however, and in recent decades has not been closely followed by politicians on many issues.

People who are more fundamentalist in their approach to religion do not value liberty this highly and have to be hostile to democracy because it involves the ability to compromise. Those who are imbued with the absolute certainty of their positions because they come from God can never compromise these beliefs nor be persuaded of the importance of liberty. They would like to see everyone adhere to the same beliefs as they and their goal is to establish a theocracy in this country. In a democracy the government derives its legitimacy from the consent of the governed; in a theocracy the government derives its legitimacy from God, and those who claim to speak for God have the ultimate authority in government. The words of Pat Robertson as a presidential candidate in 1988 are instructive:

> When the Christian majority takes over this country, there will be no satanic churches, no more free distribution of pornography, no more abortion on demand, and no more talk of rights for homosexuals. After the Christian majority takes control, pluralism will be seen as immoral and evil and the state will not permit anybody to practice it.[56]

For much of the nation's history, fundamentalist Christians concentrated on saving souls rather than on electing politicians to represent their beliefs in the political system. This began to change in the 1970s, and the turning point may well have been the Supreme Court's decision on abortion.[57] *Roe v Wade* was decided in 1973, and in 1979 Jerry Falwell formed the Moral Majority, an organization of the religious right that urged Christians to endorse political candidates with conservative religious beliefs. Falwell believed that America had lost its way and mentioned abortion, pornography homosexuality, divorce, and secular humanism as major evils threatening the country:[58]

> I never thought the government would go so far afield, I never thought the politicians would become so untrustworthy, I never thought the courts would go so nuts on the left. We have defaulted by failing to show up for the fight.[59]

The Moral Majority came to an end in 1989 as a result of a flawed strategy. Some have pointed out that Falwell thought he could change America from the top down, and after helping Ronald Reagan win the presidency in 1980, believed the Reagan administration would vigorously pursue the agenda of the organization. This did not happen, but the Moral Majority did play a major role in politicizing religious conservatives and giving them a taste of political power that they apparently found appealing. After the demise of the Moral Majority, the Christian Coalition led by Pat Robertson was formed, an organization that recognized that real change comes from the grass roots and focused on local politics, as well as politics at the state and federal levels.[60]

The Christian Coalition became a dominant force in the Republican Party, and Robertson did not hide his goal of wanting to take over the party 100 percent.[61] Fundamentalist Christians have been enormously successful in getting the party to respond to their issues by getting voters registered, platforms adopted, and candidates elected. They changed the terms of the political debate in the country, as every candidate, Republican or Democrat, has to pay homage to his or her religious beliefs at some point in their campaign. Religion has taken on an importance in public life that is unprecedented. Herb Silverman, a national board member of the American Humanist Association, made the following comment regarding the effectiveness of the religious right:[62]

> What gives the religious right its power is a clear vision of the kind of society it wishes to create. In part, because of their effectiveness with the media, the religious right is currently much more organized than the political left. They vote in greater proportion to their numbers and they communicate with their elected representatives . . . fundamentalist leaders often manipulate religion to meet their political ends. They are well versed in political processes and marketing techniques. They seem to thrive because secular modernity seems exhausted of solutions to social problems.[63]

With respect to the Republican Party and what it used to stand for, the influence of the religious right changed its priorities for several decades as social issues became more predominant. The Republicans traditionally stood for fiscal conservatism which meant a balanced budget or semblance thereof and fiscal restraint regarding government expenditures. While Republican leaders gave lip service to a balanced budget, since the Reagan administration the Republicans have presided over the largest deficits in the history of the nation. It is only in the twenty-first century that the party has again turned its attention to fiscal responsibility by attacking the deficit and entitlement programs.

Christian fundamentalists apparently find political power so attractive that they feel it necessary to abandon the teachings and the examples set by Jesus Christ, their Lord and Savior. Jesus continually refused any political office or title that the Jews wanted him to take, reminding them that his kingdom was not of this world. Render unto Caesar the things that are Caesar's and unto God the things that are God's, he is reported to have said. He spent the majority of his time with the sinners and outcasts of Jewish society, not with the political leaders plotting how to take over the leadership of society. One wishes the fundamentalists would follow his example and get out of politics and respect the wisdom of the Founding Fathers to keep religion and politics separate.

Yet the opposite seems to be happening as the Catholic Church got into the act in recent years. During the presidential campaign of 2004 some Catholic bishops announced that they would refuse communion to candidates running for political office who supported abortion. This put the Democratic candidate, John Kerry, in something of a bind as he was a practicing Catholic who supported a woman's right to choose. The bishop of Colorado Springs, Colorado, went even further by suggesting that communion ought to be denied any parishioner who did not adhere to the position of the church on the issues of abortion, gay marriage, and stem cell research. No mention was made about the war in Iraq, the poor, crime, or other social problems.[64]

One can understand the frustration some church leaders must feel about the things going on in the country that run counter to their values. Perhaps the fundamentalists have become tired of waiting for Jesus to return and have decided to take things into their own hands. There have been numerous predictions throughout history regarding the Second Coming of Christ none of which has ever proven to be true. This must be terribly frustrating to fundamentalists so perhaps they have decided to take action and build the Kingdom themselves. And the Catholic Church must be frustrated about issues like abortion and perhaps has decided to get politically involved to change society. Apparently, these religious groups have found the love of Christ to be a weak force for change in society and have decided to try to force their beliefs on others through the use of political power.[65] According to Edward Frederick Kagin, an attorney who is an outspoken critic of violations of the separation of church and state, writing in an article titled "The Gathering Storm":

> To be sure, Christian fundamentalism is not unique in its "we are right and you are wrong" mentality and its insistence upon a literal reading of invented histories framed in legend and allegory. There is little difference in essence between Christian fundamentalism and Islamic fundamentalism. Nor is there much difference in any other system that believes the entire body of an ancient mythical system, frozen in time, is rendered holy by antiquity, and is made more worthy of belief by faith and hope than by merit and proof. All religious fundamentalists, however called, are much the same under the skin. They may be highly dissimilar in methods and goals, and their words may be different, but their tune is the same. God is on their side, and therefore their beliefs are true and should be involuntary enforced on all members of a society.[66]

Leaders of mainstream churches have been strangely silent on these issues. One church member has argued that mainstream Christians have let the religious right get away with peddling distortions and fantasies and with defining the election of George W. Bush to a second term as a vote for Bush being a vote for Jesus. They should be asking such questions as "Was it God that put Bush in the White House or was it the work of his powerful father?" Or "Where in the Bible does Jesus teach that thou shall kill to spread my love?" The member then goes on to say that it is going to take some real noise to keep democracy and religion on course and in balance and that we must not become a nation of sheep.[67]

Yet religion was everywhere in the 2004 election. The candidates themselves had to interject religion into their campaigns leading one pastor to remind voters that we are not electing a religious leader and that people should focus on how well candidates might serve the nation's common good as civil leaders.[68] Voter registration drives were held in some churches, leading to criticism from people concerned about church–state issues. And there was pressure on lawmakers to change a fifty-year-old tax policy, which says that churches can lose their tax-exempt status if they participate in political speech. Speaker of the House Dennis Hastert and Majority Leader Tom DeLay, among others, believed that clergymen should be allowed to speak from the pulpit freely on political issues and even be allowed to go so far as to endorse candidates.[69]

This involvement of religion in political campaigns has continued as candidates have had to bring religion into the discussion and confess their personal commitment to their religious faith. President Obama had to deal with the negative comments his pastor in Chicago, Jeremiah Wright, made about the United States and reaffirm his own religious faith. More recently, Donald Trump visited Liberty University, a nonprofit Christian University founded by Jerry Falwell, to make an appeal to the religious right. He promised to protect Christianity and then quoted a verse from scripture about the spirit of the Lord and liberty but referred to it as being from Two Corinthians rather than Second Corinthians, which anyone familiar with Christianity knows is the correct reference. In any event, the point is that in spite of the Constitution we do, in fact, have a religious test for public office, as I seriously doubt an atheist would get very far if he or she ran for president of the United States.[70]

Church and state issues in which religious neutrality has been a concern have taken many forms in public policies throughout the nation's history. Many issues have emerged over the use of tax money to support religious activities or institutions. One relatively recent example was the faith-based initiative program of the George W. Bush administration. Church and state issues are also part of the battle over the teaching of evolution versus creationism in our public schools.[71] Church–state issues are also involved in the posting of the Ten Commandments in public buildings, prayer in public schools, the words "Under God" in the Pledge of Allegiance, and the debate about school vouchers.

Over the past several years, the Supreme Court reversed course in allowing a variety of public subsidies for religious instruction and permitting religious displays in public places. In 2002, the Court struck down limitations on state subsidy of educational materials in sectarian schools (*Mitchell v. Helms*). Also in 2002, the Court upheld an Ohio school-voucher program even though 96 percent of the students receiving the vouchers were attending church-affiliated schools. In addition the court allowed religious groups to operate government-subsidized social services as long as there was no explicit proselytizing in the programs.[72],[73]

In his first term, George W. Bush moved ahead with his plan to fund faith-based groups. One of the first acts of his presidency was to create a White House Office of Faith-Based and Community Initiatives. Such offices were also established in seven executive agencies including the Department of Justice, the Department of Labor, the Department of Agriculture, and the Department of Health and Human Services. These departments were to give equal treatment to faith-based programs when providing grants and not hold these organizations to a different standard or deny them grants because they were faith-based. In 2003, more than $1 billion of federal government money was sent to religious organizations for charitable purposes.[74]

The argument the Bush administration used to support these actions is that religious faith plays an important role in healing and restoration, and therefore, faith-based programs can be more effective in dealing with prison populations, the homeless, drug abuse, and other social problems. Bush had to make the case that his administration was not funding these organizations so they could spread their religious beliefs. These groups must use the government funds they received to assist the needy and not try to convert them to a particular religious faith. But this distinction may not hold up in practice, as the very phrase "faith-based" implies that some kind of faith commitment is integral to the healing process.[75] The president himself asserted that faith-based programs are effective only because they are based in a particular faith. He also described the Bible as the "handbook" for federally funded child-care programs.[76]

President Bush said that faith-based initiatives can start with any group "from Muslims, Mormons, and good people with no faith at all." Yet as one author suggests, "[i]magine an atheist applying to the Office of Faith-Based Services." The point is that there is no practical way of promoting faith, in general, without promoting particular faiths.[77] While the fundamentalists may have had the upper hand in these efforts during the Bush administration, some believe there is an iron law of religious zealotry: "Breach the church-state wall and a zealot whose beliefs are more dogmatic and dangerous than yours will seize the opening."[78]

The influence that religion has on public policy is apparent not only in these kinds of issues but show up in many different kinds of ways where it is not usually expected. Elected officials who adhere to fundamentalist beliefs see themselves as having a mission to implement those beliefs in their role as government officials whether as legislators voting on bills, as court judges making decisions about cases before their court, or as members of the executive branch making decisions and implementing policy. They have abandoned a secularist or neutral position regarding religion and, in many cases, have been quite honest about their avowed mission in government. While this characteristic has most often been called ideology in the popular press, religion is the fuel that keeps ideology burning so intensely.

During the George W. Bush administration, we had a president who attempted to integrate the Christian faith into American policy at the most practical level by using faith-based institutions to solve that nation's social problems and transform American social policy.[79] We had an attorney general as part of the same administration who received a 100 percent rating on every Christian Coalition scorecard from the time he entered the U.S. Senate. The American Civil Liberties Union (ACLU) stated that John Ashcroft had steered his "entire political career" in one direction. He has been trying to institute sectarian religious practices and beliefs into the laws of the United States.[80]

Tom DeLay, House Majority Leader during part of that administration, said that "Christianity offers a way to live in response to the realities we find in this world—only Christianity." Furthermore, he suggested that the tragic shootings at Columbine High School in Littleton, Colorado, occurred "because our school systems teach our children that they are nothing but glorified apes who have evolutionized out of some primordial mud." Peter Singer states that "DeLay apparently believes that God is using him to promote a biblical worldview in American politics."[81] Rod Paige, secretary of education during Bush's first term, was quoted as saying "that he would prefer to have a child in a Christian school partly because there were too many different values in the public schools to easily arrive at a value consensus."[82] God forbid that kids should be exposed to different points of view and have to think for themselves. And finally, late Supreme Court Justice Antonin Scalia made the following remarks on the subject of the death penalty at the University of Chicago Divinity School:

> This is not the Old Testament, I emphasize, but St. Paul . . . [T]he core of his message is that government—however you want to limit that concept—derives its moral authority from God . . . Indeed, it seems to me that the more Christian a country is the less likely if is to regard the death penalty as immoral . . . I attribute that to the fact that, for the believing Christian, death is no big deal. Intentionally killing an innocent person is a big deal: it is a grave sin, which causes one to lose his soul. But losing this life, in exchange for the next? . . . For the nonbeliever, on the other hand, to deprive a man of his life is to end his existence. What a horrible act? . . . The reaction of people of faith to this tendency of democracy to obscure the divine authority behind government should not be resignation to it, but the resolution to combat it as effectively as possible. We have done that in this country (and continental Europe has not) by preserving in our public life many visible reminders that—in the words of a Supreme Court opinion from the

1940s—"we are a religious people, whose institutions pre-suppose a Supreme Being," . . . All this, as I say, is most un-European, and helps explain why our people are more inclined to understand, as St. Paul did, that government carries the sword as "the minister of God," to "execute Wrath" upon the evildoer.[83]

Thus, we had in this country government officials in positions of great power, including the president himself, who had no trouble seeing God as guiding the affairs of this nation and letting the Christian religion be the determining factor in their public decisions. They saw themselves as promoting religion, not religion in general but a particular kind of religion favored by the president and leaders of his party. This meant that non-Christians and those who may be Christians but believe religion should stay out of politics had no standing and were not equal participants in the public policy process to say the least. Thus far, this period seems to have been the nadir of religious involvement in public policy, but it is something we always need to be aware of and guard against as there is no end of attempts to introduce narrow religious views into public policy.

The ultimate goal of fundamentalist Christianity is to reverse the restructuring of culture that has taken place in American society based on Enlightenment philosophy that focuses on reason rather than revelation as the source of truth about the world. According to some authors, "religious fundamentalists want to restore religion to the controlling position is enjoyed in Puritan New England and restore what they see as "traditional God-given values." After conducting a series of interviews with leaders of the religious right, Conway and Siegelman came to the conclusion that the fundamentalist's goals are

[t]o Christianize America, to fill all government position with Bible believing Christians, to gain ascendancy over the national media, to have fundamentalist beliefs taught as science in public schools, to dictate the meaning of human life and ultimately to convert every person on earth.[84]

Some argued that the Bush administration framed the 2004 election as a referendum on God and assembled an army of religious warriors to keep the president in office. In a speech to the White House Conference on Faith-Based and Community Initiatives, the president gave a sermon about the Good Book and the need to surrender one's life to a higher being. His faith-based czar, Jim Towey, told the crowd that a Kerry victory "could almost wind up creating a godless orthodoxy."[85] In the same article, another commentator stated that for three years, the Bush administration has been waging a concerted campaign to tear down the wall between church and state:

This campaign goes far beyond Bush's frequent use of evangelical code words and his loyalists shocking suggestion that he was chosen for his position by God himself. Bush has used the power of the presidency to fill federal judgeships with right-wing Christian ideologues, to block stem-cell and other scientific research that doesn't mesh with fundamentalism, and to withhold billions in federal funds from family planning programs that offer such forbidden options as contraception and abortion. Those taxpayer dollars are being funneled to faith-based groups whole primary mission is religious proselytization. Under this president, the secular state is under siege.[86]

Having religion assume such a dominant position within society ensures that conflicts will then assume a religious character and be more destructive to democracy and society than ever, as history has proved over and over again. There is no such thing as a religious democracy. There is a great diversity of religious beliefs all over the world, and particularly in this country where religious diversity has been encouraged and protected by the Constitution. Religions differ on all sorts of issues and this diversity should be respected. But the Bush administration was based on a particular fundamentalist faith that did not reflect the beliefs of many people in the country. A faith-based presidency has to favor a particular brand of religion; all religions cannot be amalgamated into some kind of general religious approach. When public policy reflects a particular religious worldview that is not shared by the entire country, we are going down the road toward a theocracy, and democracy suffers.

Religion also loses credibility by becoming politically involved as it becomes just another interest group seeking favors from the government rather than an institution that can transcend political and economic differences and offer a path to a meaningful and purpose-driven life for its adherents. It loses the ability to provide a spiritual dimension to society as a whole when it becomes solely identified with a particular set of political beliefs and wants to influence policy making to be consistent with its worldview rather than might be good for society as a whole.

Public policy needs to be based on scientific findings, not on religious convictions. We are not going to progress as a nation if we teach intelligent design in our public schools. We need to teach our children to question scientific findings to be sure, but science should not be replaced by religious dogma. Critical thinking is a skill needed to question both religion and science. Our children should be brought up to think for themselves and not accept the conventional wisdom in either religion or science. This is the path to progress—openness to the future and a willingness to explore one's own mind and develop new ideas and new ways of thinking. No progress is possible if people have closed minds and are brought up to accept religious beliefs of whatever faith unthinkingly without examining them and the assumptions built into a belief system. The same holds for science.

Religious fundamentalism needs to be seen for what it is—an authority system that needs no evidence to justify its claims but rests on the authority of a book called the Bible and religious leaders and followers who buy into this system of beliefs for whatever reason. The need for security and certainty plagues all of us but we need not sacrifice our intelligence and humanness in the process. It is hoped that people who need religion will at least get a religion that is compatible with twenty-first-century science and technology and is not rooted in ancient mythology. We cannot afford to carry around such primitive beliefs any more as they threaten our very existence.

Some have said that we ought to keep all this talk about religion in the public sphere where it belongs—in the churches. "It is one of the saddest ironies of our time that as America tries to calm the fires of theocracy abroad, it should be stoking milder versions on the same at home."[87] If religion becomes more involved in political life this only deepens the conflicts in society. If the Mormons in this country, whose numbers are growing; the Amish; and other religious movements, including Muslims, should become more involved politically, we would have conflict on a larger scale. The debate would then be over religious dogma and beliefs, a debate that has no resolution. Scientific findings would not help in resolving these debates as no amount of data is going to change one's religious beliefs. Nor are changing circumstances going to matter for someone who believes in absolutes. Thus, we would have such factionalism that democracy would be unworkable, and we would see the end of democracy. As stated by Stuart Jordan writing in *The Enlightenment Vision*,

> [g]ranting many cultural variations, it is still hard to imagine a democratic theocracy, since the ultimate authority in a theocracy rests with a minority who presume to know a divine law that arose independent of empirical evidence. Or so it is claimed in a theocracy. The writers of the American Constitution were deeply influenced by the Enlightenment goal of removing political authority from any priesthood. Contrary to claims of certain contemporary American writers of the religious and political Right, the founders, while often non-dogmatically religious, were determined to minimize the role of organized religious institutions in the new American government . . . [However] lack of confidence in a people opens the political field to authoritarian leadership that often associates itself with religious reactionaries. When this happens, progressive political leaders may need to make concessions to the churches if the body politic demands it, even if the legal grounds seem shaky. Despite America's strong global position entering the twenty-first century, the recent movement toward greater church-state entanglement seems to have had broad popular support, suggesting widespread personal insecurity, ignorance, and fear of the modern world, or all these together.[88]

According to Jordan religion remains inextricably involved with government both on the level of personal conviction and on the institutional level. Humanity, in general, while still struggling toward Enlightenment goals, remains too threatened by crises that are real or imagined to achieve these goals. Thus, we can expect religion to be with us for the foreseeable future since large numbers of people have shown that is what they want especially when going through a difficult period.[89] As Jordan says,

> [m]edieval history suggests that when secular conditions of life are harsh, people may turn to religion, even authoritarian religion, if it offers personal hope and some semblance of social order . . . [However,] authoritarianism in religion creates a mind-set hardly conducive to democracy in politics. The struggle toward political democracy demands that certain minimum conditions exist in any coherent society. Should these conditions fail to emerge or cease to exist, democracy becomes far more difficult to establish or maintain. We are learning, arguably the hard way that American-style democracy may not work without significant modifications in certain Islamic countries today.[90]

Critics of religion often overlook the fact that many of the more offensive passages in religious texts are discounted by most modern theologians and educated laypeople. These critics also blame religion for every crime committed in religion's name ignoring how often religion is used by secular powers to achieve their own agendas.[91] And those who would eliminate religion entirely if they could have failed to show how a completely secular society can satisfy those basic human needs that make religion attractive to many people today.[92]

Thus, religion will always be a factor in a democracy, and religious extremists will want to inject their religious beliefs into the public policies that government formulates. But as it does so, the Christian religion, in particular, has become more and more irrelevant as a source of spirituality. Its supernatural basis has been undermined by science that has forced Christianity as an explanation of the natural world further and further into obscurity. It no longer provides meaning and purpose to many people in society. And as Christianity has become politicized and sought political power it has lost its ability to transcend political and economic systems and has become identified with a particular political and economic viewpoint. As such it has become just another interest group in our society trying to get government to pursue its interests over others and has lost the respect and commitment of many people who must search elsewhere for a spiritual dimension to inform their lives and to give them purpose and meaning.[93]

Notes

1 See Robert P. Jones, *The End of White Christian America* (New York: Simon & Schuster, 2016).
2 Stuart Jordan, *The Enlightenment Vision* (Amherst, NY: Prometheus Books, 2012), 204.

3 Ibid., 205.
4 Ibid., 11, 18–19. "The Enlightenment is also called the Age of Reason because its basic idea was that only the critical use of reason should direct society and politics. In the same way that truths in science could be discovered, demonstrated and agreed upon by all rational thinkers, so a rational and just political order could similarly be established. Prejudices and fears, disagreements and conflicts, illusions and myth were all consequences of ignorance and irrationality, and these could be dissipated by the light of reason." Johanna Oksala, *Political Philosophy: All that Matters* (New York: McGraw-Hill, 2013), 71.
5 Ibid., 209.
6 Ibid., 71–72.
7 Ibid., 180.
8 Ibid., 208.
9 Ibid., 166.
10 Ibid., 83.
11 Ibid., 218.
12 Ibid., 101.
13 Stewart Shapiro, "Faith and Reason, the Perpetual War: Ruminations of a Fool," in Louise M. Antony, ed. *Philosophers without Gods: Meditations on Atheism and the Secular Life* (New York: Oxford University Press, 2007), 7.
14 Ibid., 9–14.
15 Ibid., 14.
16 Marvin Belzer, "Mere Stranger," in Louise M. Antony, ed. *Philosophers without Gods: Meditations on Atheism and the Secular Life* (New York: Oxford University Press, 2007), 92.
17 Shapiro, "Faith and Reason," 14–17.
18 David Filkin, *Stephen Hawking's Universe: The Cosmos Explained* (New York: Basic Books, 1997), 77–86.
19 "Facing a need for $743 million worth of repairs to crumbling infrastructure, the mayor of Jackson, Miss., has told residents the city can fix its many potholes through the power of prayer. Yes, I believe we can pray potholes away, said Mayor Tony Yarber, who is also a church pastor. Moses prayed, he said, and a sea opened." See "Only in America," *The Week*, September 4, 2015, 6.
20 David Sprintzen, *Critique of Western Philosophy and Social Theory* (New York: Palgrave Macmillan, 2009), 208–209.
21 Jerry A. Coyne, *Faith vs Fact: Why Science and Religion Are Incompatible* (New York: Viking, 2015).
22 Ibid.
23 Michael P. Lynch, *In Praise of Reason* (Cambridge, MA: MIT Press, 2102), x.
24 Ibid., 2.
25 Ibid., 3.
26 Ibid., 8–9.
27 Ibid., 9.
28 Ibid., 15–16.
29 Ibid., 16–19.
30 Ibid., 20–25.
31 Ibid., 25–30.
32 Ibid., 31–39.
33 Ibid., 39–40.
34 Ibid., 61–71. An interesting variation of this view is provided by Richard Rorty, who argues that neither tradition nor reason gives us a route to objective knowledge. We can be cut off from such knowledge and are more or less trapped in our traditions. But we cannot claim to lay hold on truth and inquiry is an evolving

conversation. In order to live together we must find a way to keep this conversation going. Ibid., 67.

35 Reason does seem to have its limits in these examples as no amount of reasoning was going to persuade the Mormons to change their practices or the South to give up its way of life. It took the force of law and a bloody war in the latter case to bring about change that even now is resisted in some instances.

36 Ibid., 83–84.

37 Ibid., 90–93.

38 Ibid., 90.

39 Ibid., 94–95.

40 See John Rawls, *A Theory of Justice* (Cambridge, MA: Harvard University Press, 1971).

41 Lynch, *In Praise of Reason*, 96–103.

42 Ibid., 137–139.

43 The scientist was Pierre-Simon Laplace, who made the statement allegedly as a reply to Napoleon, who asked why he had not mentioned God in his new book on astronomy.

44 Arthur Peacocke, "The Sciences of Complexity: A New Theological Resource," in Paul Davies and Niels Henrik Gregersen, eds., *Information and the Nature of Reality: From Physics to Metaphysics* (New York: Cambridge University Press, 2010), 249.

45 See Adam Kirsch, "Is Reason Enough?" *The New York Review*, April 23, 2015, 42–43 for a review of a book by Philip Kitcher titled *Life after Faith* that makes a strong case for secular humanism. Also see Jack Miles, "Why God Will not Die," *The Atlantic*, December 14, 2014, 96–107, who argues that science keeps revealing things that we don't and perhaps can't know, making religion important for helping humans to seek closure.

46 Robert Kuttner, "What Would Jefferson Do?" *The American Prospect*, November, 2004, 31–32. "In 1804, Thomas Jefferson used a razor to remove all passages of the King James Version of the New Testament that had supernatural content—such as the virgin birth, resurrection, or turning water into wine. About one-tenth of the bible remained, which he pasted together and published as *The Philosophy of Jesus of Nazareth*. Apparently, Jefferson admired Jesus as a teacher and prophet but was not always interested in the cloak of divinity." Clifford A. Pickover, *Archimedes to Hawking: Laws of Science and the Great Minds Behind Them* (New York: Oxford University Press, 2008), 106.

47 See Matthew Stewart, *Nature's God: The Heretical Origins of the American Republic* (New York: W.W. Norton, 2014). See also Simon Brown, "Founded on Faith," *Church & State*, July/August, 2015, 4–6; Steven K. Green, "The Invention of a Christian America," *Church & State*, July/August, 2015, 9–10; Rob Boston, "Myths Debunked," *Church & State*, February 2015, 9–13. For a different view of the role American Protestantism played in the development of American nationalism, see a review of Sam Haselby's, *The Origins of Religious Nationalism* by Gordon S. Wood, "A Different Story of What Shaped America," *The New York Review*, July 9, 2015, 27–29. For an interesting discussion of the effect the Bible had on early American history, see Mark A. Noll, *In the Beginning Was the Word: The Bible in American Public Life 1492–1783* (New York: Oxford University Press, 2016).

48 Walter Issacson, "God of Our Fathers," *Time*, July 5, 2004, 62. See also Jon Meacham, "God and the Founders," *Newsweek*, April 10, 2006, 52–55; and "The Faith of the Framers," *The Week*, June 10, 2005, 15.

49 Robert Boston, *Why the Religious Right Is Wrong* (Buffalo: Prometheus Books, 1993), 223.

50 See John Ragosta, *Religious Freedom: Jefferson's Legacy America's Creed* (Charlottesville, VA: University of Virginia Press, 2013) for an in-depth perspective on Jefferson, the First Amendment, and religious liberty in the United States.

51 John M. Suarez, "The Path to Theocracy: The Purgation of the First Amendment," in Kimberly Blaker, ed., *The Fundamentals of Extremism: The Christian Right in America* (New Boston, MI: New Boston Books, 2003), 159.

52 Jordan, *The Enlightenment Vision*, 139.

53 There are lines that can be crossed, however, as the Mormons discovered when they had to move to the desert of Salt Lake City to practice their beliefs. Even there the laws of the country eventually forced them to modify some of their practices with regard to marriage.

54 Michael Shermer, *The Science of Good & Evil* (New York: Times Books, 2004), 261.

55 Ibid.

56 Richard Swift, "Fundamentalism Reaching for Certainty," *New Internationalist*, August 1990, as quoted in Herb Silverman, "Inerrancy Turned Political," in Blaker, ed., *The Fundamentals of Extremism: The Christian Right in America* (New Boston, MI: Boston Books Inc., 2003), 179.

57 Ibid., 177.

58 There is also a theory that the rise of the religious right was a reaction to the New Deal when business executives mounted a public relations offensive that cast capitalism as the handmaiden of Christianity. In this campaign business and religion were wedded in opposition to the creeping "socialism" of the New Deal and its growing influence in American society. See Kevin M. Kruse, *One Nation Under God: How Corporate America Invented Christian America* (New York: Basic Books, 2015). See also Sarah E. Jones, "One Nation under God," *Church & State*, July/August, 2015, 21–21, and Kevin M. Kruse, "How Business Made Us Christian," *The New York Times*, March 15, 2015, SR1.

59 Jerry Falwell, *Listen America* (New York: Doubleday-Galilee, 1980), 202 as quoted in Silverman, "Inerrancy Turned Political," 178.

60 Ibid., 178–179.

61 Joseph L. Conn, "Power Trip," *Church & State*, October 1995, as quoted in Silverman, "Inerrancy Turned Political," 181.

62 The religious right received a shot in the arm in 2013 from a growing Latino population that was increasingly becoming born-again, Bible-believing, evangelical Protestants. They represented one of the fastest-growing segments among the country's churchgoing population. They see this move as a break from the past which was associated with Catholicism representing upward mobility and a quicker assimilation into the middle class. See Elizabeth Dias, "Evangelicos!" *Time*, April 15, 2003, 21–28.

63 Silverman, "Inerrancy Turned Political," 206.

64 Anna Quindlen, "Casting the First Stone," *Newsweek*, May 31, 2004, 82. Starting in 2015 Pope Francis attempted to change the focus of concern back to the poor and those left behind by modern society.

65 Cal Thomas has argued that government can't be used to advance a moral and spiritual agenda because it is the church and not the state that is commissioned to preach and observe God's message of love that alone can change human hearts. If the church seeks to attach God to political parties and earthly agendas, it is doomed to futility. See Cal Thomas, "There Are Places That Government Can't Go," *Denver Post*, June 22, 7(B).

66 Edwin Frederick Kagin, "The Gathering Storm," in Blaker, ed., *The Fundamentals of Extremism: The Christian Right in America* (New Boston, MI: Boston Books Inc., 2003), 27.

67 Barrie Hartman, "Raising a Red Flag in Christendom," *Denver Post*, October 3, 2004, 5(E).

68 The Interfaith Alliance, Roundup, *September* 10, 2004. http://141.164.133/3/exchange/forms/IPM/NOTE.read.asp?command=open&obj=000000. (September 11, 2004).

69 Ibid.

70 There is, in fact, a religious test for public office as all candidates for president has to tout their religious beliefs at some point to convince voters that they are upstanding citizens fit for public office. An atheist would never stand a chance running for president because atheists are believed to lack morals and are not fit for the office. See Simon Brown, "The Last Political Taboo?" *Church & State*, February 2016, 4–5.

71 See an article by Evan Ratliff, who describes how the creationists use the argument for intelligent design as a sort of Trojan Horse to sneak the teaching of creationism into the curriculum of public schools. Evan Ratliff, "The Crusade against Evolution," *Wired*, October 2004, 157–205. In 2004, eight families from a school district in Pennsylvania filed a lawsuit against the district for voting to include the teaching of intelligent design in the ninth-grade science curriculum, claiming that this theory is a more secular form of creationism that may violate the constitutional separation of church and state. Martha Raffaele, "Lawsuit Challenges Teaching of Alternative to Evolution," *Denver Post*, December 15, 2004, 4(A). In 2006, another church–state issue appeared in the news when Colorado Christian University in Lakewood, Colorado, wanted its students to be eligible for state-funded scholarships to pursue a "Christ-centered" education. Colorado education officials turned them down, citing a violation of the principle of separation of church and state, which prompted a federal lawsuit and national attention. Subsequently the U.S. Justice Department filed a friend-of-the-court brief siding with the university. Alicia Caldwell, "Money, State, Church Collide," *Denver Post*, February 6, 2006, 1(A).

72 Kuttner, "What Would Jefferson Do," 37.

73 Arthur Schlesinger, Jr. "Holy War," *Playboy*, November 2004, 42. In 2005, $2.15 billion in tax aid was directed to faith-based groups according to an administration report. In view of the tax cuts in social service spending by the Bush administration, critics used these figures to argue that faith-based initiatives were being used as a cover for these cuts in social services for the needy. See "Bush Resumes Push For 'Faith-Based' Initiative at Washington Gathering," *Church & State*, Vol. 59, No. 4 (April 2006), 15.

74 These faith-based programs were continued under the Obama administration. See Sarah Posner, "Obama's Faith-Based Failure," *Salon.com*, May 4, 2012. www.salon.com/2012/05/04/obamas_faith_based_failure/print, accessed April 13, 2013.

75 In June 2004, a lawsuit was filed by a group in Wisconsin called the Freedom from Religion Foundation, alleging that the faith-based initiative program favors religious organizations in the awarding of federal contracts. Such favoritism, they claimed, violates the First Amendment's concern with separation of church and state. The defendants in the case were several cabinet secretaries who oversaw agencies with offices that were set up to help religious groups apply for the grants these agencies were offering. They were alleged to have cajoled religious organizations to come to them, showed them how to fill out forms, and gave untried groups money. The suit asks that the use of taxpayer money for faith-based endeavors be barred and that new rules be established to ensure that future appropriations do not go to social service providers that include religion as an integral component of their services. See J. R Ross, "Group Sues over Bush's Faith-based Initiative," *Denver Post*, June 18, 2004, 4(A).

76 Correspondence from the Interfaith Alliance, undated, 2.

77 Kuttner, "What Would Jefferson Do," 37.

78 Ibid., 36.

79 Stephen Mansfield, *The Faith of George W. Bush* (New York: Tarcher/Penguin, 2003), xiv–xv. Nicholas Kristof writing in the *New York Times* pointed out that there was a real "sex scandal" in the White House that involved millions of taxpayer dollars going to support "abstinence-only" sex education programs that cannot mention condoms or other birth control methods. He argues that that the real agenda of these programs was not to educate teens about sex but to stamp out premarital sex altogether on the grounds that it is sinful. According to Kristol, this is religion rather than sane public policy. These policies, in his opinion, were likely to lead to thousands of more deaths from AIDS and tens of thousands of abortions, what he called a real sex-scandal. See Nicholas Kristof, "A Sex Scandal That Really Matters," *The Week*, March 4, 2005, 12.

80 Silverman, "Inerrancy Turned Political," 197.

81 Peter Singer, *The President of Good & Evil: The Ethics of George W. Bush* (New York: Dutton, 2004), 110–111.

82 Ibid., 111.

83 A. Scalia, "God's Justice and Ours," *First Things*, Vol. 123 (May 2002), 17–21, as quoted in Sam Harris, *The End of Faith* (New York: W.W. Norton, 2004), 156–157. Scalia also weighed in on the subject of the Ten Commandments. At one point he disagreed that the Ten Commandments were mostly a secular statement. They have, he argued, a religious meaning and to state otherwise is to water them down. With this interpretation, many would have no argument, but then he went on to say that not only did he find the Ten Commandments to be religious, but they were also "a symbol of the fact that government derives its authority from God." The founders of the country might disagree with this statement as they believed government derived its powers from the consent of the governed. See Richard Cohen, "The Miracle of Antonin Scalia," *Denver Post*, March 13, 2005, 5(E). Also see Simon Brown, "The Wall Banger," *Church & State*, April 2016, 10–13, for a review of Scalia's attempts to overcome the separation of church and state.

84 Edward M. Bruckner, "Winning the 'Battle Royal': Parallels and Solutions to the Growing Danger," in Blaker, ed., *The Fundamentals of Extremism: The Christian Right in America* (New Boston, MI: Boston Books Inc., 2003), 204.

85 "The Election: A Question of Faith," *The Week*, June 14, 2004, 19.

86 Ibid. See also Richard Cohen, "President Bush Mixing Religion and Politics," *Denver Post*, May 26, 2005, 7(B).

87 "Religion and Politics: When God Is Your Running Mate," *The Week*, November 5, 2004, 8.

88 Jordan, *The Enlightenment Vision*, 144–146.

89 Ibid., 148.

90 Ibid., 144.

91 Jordan defines religion "as belief in a supernatural realm that has a substantive existence independent of what human imagination alone conceives. Religion so defined contrasts to the view of the nontheist that, however real they may seem to the imagination, it has no substantive reality outside of the human mind . . . Suffice to say, to the nontheist, all experiences of gods, demons, or other thrilling or terrifying spiritual manifestations are entirely a product of the human mind . . . Thus in agreement with common practice, I will consign all gods, demons, ghosts, immortal souls, and other postulated inhabitants of the spirit world to this supernatural world . . . several generations of Western nontheists have attacked religion on grounds ranging from lack of evidence for religious beliefs to outrage over crimes committed in religion's name." Ibid., 127–128.

92 Ibid., 134.

93 For a viewpoint that makes the claim that secular idealists have failed to create a powerful and convincing political culture that would offer a spiritual home to those who still seek spirituality in religion, see a review of Michael Walzer's book titled *The Paradox of Liberation: Secular Revolutions and Religious Counter-revolutions*, by Michael Ignatieff, "The Religious Specter Haunting Revolution," *The New York Review*, June 4, 2015, 66–68. Walzer holds that when secular revolutions fail, they leave nothing behind to restrain fundamentalist impulses that lead to religious extremism.

5   The New Atheism

If traditional religion cannot provide a spiritual dimension to life because of challenges the scientific approach has raised about some of its fundamental assumptions and because of its political involvement that has made it into just another interest group competing for government favors, then what about atheism as a source for spiritualism. According to Michel Onfray writing in a book titled *Atheist Manifesto*, the word *atheist* did not enter the French and English language until the sixteenth century. But the idea itself goes back much further in history; in fact, the Bible itself alludes to atheists in various places.[1]

Atheism is characterized by its rejection of the existence of God, which, of course, is the foundation of the three religions he critiques. The belief in God is considered to be a fiction invented by people who need meaning and purpose in their lives and a belief that someone is in control of what was perceived to be a chaotic and purposeless universe. The belief in God gives comfort to people and helps them deal with the inevitability of death. The word *atheist* is an insult to conventional thinking in religious societies, and an atheist is considered to be immoral or, at best, amoral and is treated as sort of an outcast. Atheism involves the denial of transcendence and the supernatural and rejects any belief in an afterlife and miracles such as the resurrection. As summarized by Louise M. Anthony, professor of philosophy at the University of Massachusetts at Amherst, in her edited book on atheism,

> [l]ike theists, we [atheists] affirm the limitations and fallibility of the human mind; like them, we acknowledge, with awe, the vastness and complexity of the natural world. Unlike them, however, we have no master story to tell about the origins or the ultimate future of the world . . . We have no sacred texts, no authorities with definitive answers to our questions about the nature of morality or the purpose of life, no list of commandments that cover every contingency and dilemma. We can have no confidence, the evidence of history being what it is, that the truth will win out, or that goodness will triumph in the end. We have no fear of eternal punishment, but no hope, either, of eternal reward.

We have only our ideals and our goals to motivate us, only our sympathy and our intelligence to make us good, and only our fellow human beings to help us in time of need. When we speak, we speak only for ourselves—we cannot claim inspiration or sanction from the Creator and Lord of the universe.[2]

While atheism has thus been around for several centuries, it never constituted a major threat to religious societies and was more of less limited to the more intellectual classes of those societies. However, in contemporary times there has been more attention given to atheism and more books on the subject. There has emerged a new antireligious movement led by several writers on the subject. According to Victor J. Stenger, an adjunct professor of philosophy at the University of Colorado and an emeritus professor of physics and astronomy at the University of Hawaii, a publication by Sam Harris, an American author, philosopher, and neuroscientist, in 2004 marked the first of several best-selling books that "took a harder line against religion than had been the custom among secularists." These books constituted a movement Stenger called the New Atheism.[3]

Review of the Seminal Books

The title of Harris's book is *The End of Faith: Terror and the Future of Reason*, a book that is largely concerned about the harm religion does in the world and its link with violence. For example, he argues that Islam has all the makings of a thoroughgoing cult of death, more so in his opinion than any other religion human beings have devised throughout history. On almost every page of the Koran, he states, there are instructions for observant Muslims to despise non-believers laying the ground for religious conflict. His book includes five pages of quotes from the Koran to support this conclusion and he then states that anyone who reads these passages and still does not see a link between Muslim faith and Muslim violence has a serious problem.[4]

Christianity and Judaism also have the same problem as the God of the Old Testament is a God of wrath. There are ample biblical passages that are violent to the extreme. Consider the following passage from Deuteronomy 20:10–18:

When you draw near to a city to fight against it, offer terms of peace to it. And if its answer to you is peace and it opens to you, then all the people who are found in it shall do forced labor for you and shall serve you. But if it makes no peace with you, but makes war against you, then you shall besiege it; and when the LORD your God gives it into your hand you shall put all its males to the sword, but the women and little ones, the cattle and everything else in the city, all its spoil, you shall take as booty for yourselves; and you shall enjoy the spoil of your enemies, which the LORD your God has given to you. This you shall do to the cities which are very far from you, which are not cities of the nations here. But in the cities of these peoples that the LORD your God gives you for an inheritance you shall save alive nothing that breathes, but you shall utterly destroy them, the Hittites and the Amorites, the Cannaanites and the Hivites and Jebsuites, as the LORD your God has commanded; that they may not teach you to do according to all their abominable practices which they have done in the service of their Gods and so to sin against the LORD your God.[5]

Not much compassion and forgiveness appears here as this kind of God is extremely jealous and will stop at nothing to eliminate the competition. As another example, those people who are so concerned about posting the Ten Commandments in public places conveniently ignore the punishment for breaking those commandments.[6] The punishment for taking the Lord's name in vain is death (Leviticus 24:16). Working on the Sabbath is also punishable by death (Exodus 31:15) as is punishment for cursing one's father or mother (Exodus 21:17) and adultery (Leviticus 20:10). Should these punishments also be posted in our courts so that judges can take them into account when it comes to sentencing? Fortunately, we have become more civilized over the years and do not take these directives seriously as do some religions.

The point is that the Bible is full of violence and incites people to violence in defense of the faith.[7] This leads Harris to conclude that all reasonable men and women throughout the world have a common enemy that threatens to destroy the very possibility of human happiness and of human life itself. That enemy is nothing other than religious faith itself.[8] Respect for other faiths and, in particular, the view of unbelievers is not an attitude that a god of any stripe endorses. Intolerance is intrinsic to every religious creed, says Harris, and true believers cannot tolerate the possibility that other religions or no religion at all holds some truth about human life and happiness. Beliefs define one's vision of the world and dictate behavior and one's emotional response to other human beings.[9]

Religion is a curious facet of human existence. We live our daily lives using our reason to figure things out based on things our experiences with what the world teaches us, and the use of evidence is important in our choice of activities. For example, children eventually learn by gathering enough evidence that touching a hot stove is a painful thing to be avoided. But when it comes to religion, according to Harris, our beliefs about the world and its meaning and purpose can float entirely free of reason and evidence.[10] Even fundamentalists live by using reason to get through the day and need evidence to support most truth claims they encounter, yet when it comes to beliefs about the Bible as the literal word of God and the incredible claims it makes about the creation of the universe and the existence of the supernatural realm, they require no evidence whatsoever beyond what is contained in the Bible.[11]

Every religion, according to Harris, preaches the truth of certain propositions for which no evidence is even conceivable.[12] Thus, religion requires a leap of faith to believe in certain propositions, a leap into a realm where rational discourse is impossible. It seems that most people need a belief in something beyond this world that gives them certainty in a highly uncertain world, that provides purpose in a purposeless world, and that gives them meaning when so much of their life is meaningless. But when challenges to faith arise one cannot engage in rational discussion and will end up using violent means, if necessary, to defend the faith. Thus, religion has been one on the most pervasive sources of violence throughout history according to Harris. Far from religion being the solution to human hatred and violence, the practice of religion is the source for much of that hatred and violence. Far from being the source of morality, it is the source for some of the most immoral acts humankind has ever committed.

It would seem that a moderate approach to religion would put a damper on religious fanaticism that can lead to violence. In a moderate approach, religion is just one part of life, where religion has a place but is not pervasive through all of one's life. There are other sources of truth than the Bible or the Koran and science has a legitimate place in the determination of the truth about the world we live in. The moderate has a tolerance of other religious approaches and does not need to believe that he or she has the absolute truth that needs to be defended at any cost. This would seem to be a reasonable approach to religion that should be cultivated and might help to stem the tide of religious fanaticism.

But according to Harris, religious moderation will do nothing to lead people out of the wilderness. Moderation does not permit anything very critical to be said about religious literalism and does not call into question the core dogmas of religious faith. Religious moderates betray both faith and reason, according to Harris, and are the product of secular knowledge and scriptural ignorance. Religious moderates have no credibility to attack fundamentalism and thus offer no bulwark against religious extremism and religious violence.[13] Their beliefs provide a context in which scriptural literalism and religious violence can flourish without effective opposition and thus are in large part responsible for religious conflict in the world. The greatest problem, according to Harris, is not only religious extremism, but the cultural and intellectual accommodation we have made to faith itself as well.[14]

The solution Harris advocates is for people to give up faith itself and find a way where faith without evidence disgraces anyone who makes outrageous claims and expects to be taken seriously. In an age where a single person or small group of terrorists can cause millions of deaths, humankind has simply lost the right to live out our myths and hang on to our mythic identities. Beliefs people have must be open to evidence and argument, and we must have a willingness to modify those beliefs in the light of new evidence. Such openness and a spirit of mutual inquiry will help secure a common future for humankind. Religious dogma that has to be defended at whatever cost has to be given up in the interests of self-preservation.[15]

In *The God Delusion*, Richard Dawkins, the Charles Simonyi Professor of the Public Understanding of Science at Oxford University, quotes a little-known author by the name of Robert M. Pirsig that is relevant to the title of his book: "When one person suffers a delusion, it is called insanity. When many people suffer from a delusion it is called Religion."[16] In his book, Dawkins attacks the God Hypothesis which he defines as *"there exists a superhuman, supernatural intelligence who deliberately designed and created the universe and everything in it, including us."* His alternative hypothesis is that *"any creative intelligence, of sufficient complexity to design anything, comes into existence only as the end product of an extended process of gradual evolution."*[17]

Dawkins proceeds to discuss various arguments that have been advanced over the years to prove God's existence. He first looks at the proofs of Thomas Aquinas, a Catholic theologian of the thirteenth century, who argued for an unmoved mover and the uncaused cause. These arguments, says Dawkins, are based upon the idea of a regress that makes an unwarranted assumption that God lies at the end of the regress and is not subject to the regress itself. Dawkins then looks at the ontological argument and other a priori arguments. With regard to the argument from experience, which refers to people who claim to have experienced God directly in some fashion, Dawkins quotes Sam Harris in the *End of Faith*:

> We have names for people who have many beliefs for which there is no rational justification. When their beliefs are extremely common we call them 'religious'; otherwise, they are likely to be called 'mad,' or 'psychotic' or 'delusional' . . . Clearly there is sanity in numbers. And yet, it is merely an accident of history that it is considered normal in our society to believe that the Creator of the universe can hear your thoughts, while it is demonstrative of mental illness to believe that he is communicating with you by having the rain tap in Morse code on your bedroom window. And so, while religious people are not generally mad, their core beliefs absolutely are.[18]

Dawkins then proceeds to discuss the argument from design, which he characterizes as an illusion. He also criticizes the God of the Gaps, where God is used to fill in the void where there are so far unexplainable phenomena. The problem with this approach is that as sciences advances and the gaps in our knowledge shrink, God eventually has nothing to do and nowhere to hide.[19] With regard to morality, Dawkins believes, along with many others, that God is not necessary in order for people to be good or evil. While he suspects that many religious people think religion is what motivates them to be good, especially if they adhere to a faith that systematically exploits personal guilt, it requires "quite a low self-regard to think that should belief in God suddenly vanish from the world, we would all become callous and selfish hedonists, with no kindness, no charity, no generosity, nothing that would deserve the name of goodness."[20]

Dawkins contrasts fundamentalism with science and states that the truth of a holy book such as the Bible is not the end product of a process of reasoning but is accepted as the truth as a matter of faith, and if evidence seems to contradict some part of it, the evidence is discarded or ignored, not what the book says. By way of contrast, science is self-correcting in that when new evidence is discovered that contradicts the accepted truth of some phenomena, the theory regarding that truth is either discarded of revised because of the evidence, the opposite of religion. Evolution is accepted as true because the evidence supports it, but if new evidence were discovered that convincingly disproves the theory of evolution, it would be discarded overnight.[21]

Fundamentalist religion ruins the education of countless thousands of innocent young minds, according to Dawkins, by teaching children from their earliest years that unquestioning faith is a virtue. Such absolutions have a dark side, as Dawkins makes the case that belief in God is not only just plain wrong but can be potentially deadly as well. He shows how religion fuels war, foments bigotry, and abuses children, who should be taught not so much *what* to think but *how* to think.[22] Teaching children that unquestioned faith is a virtue sets them up to become potentially lethal weapons in future jihads or crusades against other religions or peoples. Unquestioned faith can be very dangerous, and to implant it into the vulnerable mind of an innocent child is a grievous wrong, according to Dawkins.[23]

Religion has been used to fulfill four main roles in life, explanation, exhortation, consolation, and inspiration. Religion has tried to explain our existence and the nature of the universe, a role which has been completely superseded by science. Exhortation means moral instruction on how we ought to behave a role in which an absolute approach to morality can lead to all sorts of horrific outcomes. Science can give consolation of a nonmaterial kind and inspire people by opening people unto a rich and meaningful universe full of possibilities.[24] Dawkins shows us that we can live a meaningful and fulfilling life without the God hypothesis and that it is a delusion to think otherwise.

Daniel C. Dennett, an American author, philosopher, and cognitive scientist, is another of the new atheists. In his book *Breaking the Spell*, he explores the role that religion plays in our lives, in interactions with other people, and in our country.[25] He defines religions as "social systems whose participants avow belief in a supernatural agent or agents whose approval is to be sought."[26] This supernatural agent is, of course, most often referred to as God, which Dennett holds to be the core phenomenon of religion: gods who act in real time and play a central role in what adherents think about and what they ought to do with regard to ethical behavior. Religions are granted respect in the world because religious people are generally believed to be well intentioned, attempting to lead morally good lives and avoid evil and to make amends for their transgressions.[27]

For many people, and perhaps for a majority of people, nothing matters more in their lives than religion. For this reason alone, it is important that we learn as much about religion as is possible. The spell that must be broken "is the taboo against a forthright, scientific, no-holds-barred investigation of religion as one natural phenomenon among many."[28] Dennett believes there has been a largely unexamined mutual agreement among scientists and other researchers to leave religion alone because so many people get upset merely thinking about an intensive inquiry into religion. Dennett proposes to break this spell by treating religion as a natural phenomenon, by which he means that religion is natural instead of supernatural and is a human endeavor that is composed of events, organisms, objects, structures, and patterns that obey the laws of physics or biology and do not involve miracles.[29] The main question he addresses is how and why this phenomenon of religion commands the allegiance of so many people and shapes their lives so thoroughly.

There are some who believe that religion and science are two separate domains that can coexist peacefully as long as they respect each other's boundaries. But Dennett believes that science can and should study religion even though there may be some domain that is religion's alone to command. He does not think that science should do what religion does and try to replace it but that it should study religion scientifically and add to our knowledge of what religion does in the world and what needs it fulfills. There is an absence of information about religion, according to Bennett, and we should not remain ignorant about something of such great importance.[30]

We value things for reasons, many of which are hidden to our conscious minds and are evolutionary in nature, sort of free-floating rationales, as Dennett calls them, that have been endorsed by natural selection. Religion is not exempt from this kind of evolutionary process as it evolved to deal with certain kinds of problems humans were experiencing. Folk religions emerged as did language without conscious and deliberate design by interdependent processes of biological and cultural evolution. These religions emerged because of three major reasons according to Dennett: (1) to *comfort* us in our suffering and allay our fear of death, (2) to *explain* things we can't otherwise explain, and to (3) encourage group *cooperation* in the face of trials and enemies.[31]

As human cultures grew in size and sophistication and people became more reflective, folk religion grew into organized religion and became domesticated in some sense. Those who practiced folk religion didn't think of themselves as practicing religion at all as their religious practices were a seamless part of their practical lives alongside hunting and other activities necessary for survival.[32] Organized religion, on the other hand, became a designed system of competing entities in a dynamic marketplace for adherents with different needs and tastes.[33] Religion concerned itself with people's spiritual needs, as opposed to material needs, and practiced a stewardship of religious ideas and beliefs that became difficult if not impossible to rationally investigate.[34]

The belief in God, for example, is so central to organized religion that it must not be subjected to serious criticism. Beliefs such as this were made so incomprehensible that proving or disproving God's existence is what Dennett calls a "quixotic quest," and for that reason not very important. The important question for Dennett is whether religions deserve the continued allegiance and protection of their adherents. Many people love their religions more than they love anything else in life, but the question is whether their religions deserve this kind of adoration and commitment.[35]

Many people believe in God because they want to be good and live meaningful lives that have a purpose, and they can find no better way to do this than to put themselves in the service of God and seek to do his will in the world. For them God is the foundation of morality, and if God did not exist, there would be no reason to be moral and seek to do good in the world. But do we get the content of morality from religion? Is it an irreplaceable infrastructure of organizing moral action asks Dennett? Does religion provide moral or spiritual strength? For many the answers to these questions are obviously positive, but Dennett wants to reexamine them in the light of what has been learned about religion thus far in his book.[36]

Religion supports morality by giving people an unbeatable reason to do good: the promise of an infinite reward in heaven or being condemned to an infinite punishment in a fiery hell. Religion is sort of an insurance policy to keep from going to hell and suffering eternal damnation. But Dennett believes that this idea of a heavenly reward that motivates people to be good is demeaning and unnecessary. He states that "the idea that religious authority grounds our moral judgments is useless in genuine ecumenical exploration; and the presumed relation between spirituality and moral goodness is an illusion."[37]

Dennett concludes that more research needs to be done into the evolution of religions and religious convictions. A research topic that he believes is of particular urgency is the effect of religious upbringing and education on young children. There are ethical issues involved in the teaching of a belief system to young minds, as some children are raised in such an ideological prison that they cannot consider any ideas that might change their minds.[38] Children do not have a right to be free from indoctrination by their parents or their church and often grow up with closed minds. Religion can be dangerous if people cannot question their religious commitments and be free to accept or reject them. In the final analysis, Dennett's central policy recommendation "is that we gently, firmly educate the people of the world, so that they can make truly informed choices about their lives."[39]

The last of the so-called New Atheists is Christopher Hitchens, who was an English author, literary critic, and journalist. He was a severe critic of religion and promoted the term *antitheist*, which he defined as someone who is relieved that there is no evidence for the assertion that God exists.

Belief in a supreme being, according to Hitchens, destroys individual freedom, and organized religion is "the main source of hatred in the world. It is violent, irrational, intolerant, allied to racism, tribalism, and bigotry, invested in ignorance and hostile to free inquiry, contemptuous of women and coercive toward children."[40] He became known for a statement that was called Hitchens's razor: "What can be asserted without evidence can be dismissed without evidence."[41]

His book *God Is Not Great: How Religion Poisons Everything* focuses mainly on the Abrahamic religions of Judaism, Islam, and Christianity.[42] Consistent with this title, he describes how some religions can be hostile toward the treatment of diseases and presents the example of Muslims who thought the polio vaccine was a conspiracy and thus allowed the virus to spread.[43] The Catholic Church supposedly told people in Africa that condoms were ineffective, which contributed to the death toll from HIV.[44] He points out that some Catholic and Muslim believers held that HIV and HPV were punishment for sexual sin, in particular, homosexuality.[45] He described religious leaders as "faith healers" and believed that they were hostile to modern medicine because it threatened their position of power.[46]

Hitchens argues that we do not need God to explain things and religious faith cannot stand up to any kind of reason and becomes obsolete when it becomes optional. He writes that the Abrahamic religions encourage low self-esteem by making people feel like lowly sinners that are not worthy of God's grace but then leads them to believe that God cares for them anyhow despite their sinful character. The Old Testament is a nightmare full of inconsistencies and anachronisms, but the New Testament is in some ways even worse. The multiple authors of the Gospels could not agree on anything and are certainly not to be taken literally. The Gospels were written many decades after the Crucifixion and provide little evidence for the life of Jesus.[47] Hitchens contends that the Bible is, on the whole, a "feeble" publication but that until recently, Christians who were faced with arguments that questioned the logic or factualness of the Bible "could simply burn or silence anybody who asked any inconvenient questions."[48]

As for miracles, Hitchens argues that no such supernatural events have ever occurred in history. The evidence for such miracles is fabricated or based on the unreliable testimony of people who were mistaken or biased. He goes on to claim that most religions are founded by corrupt and immoral individuals and cites the founder of Mormonism, who was accused of being a "disorderly person and imposter," as an example.[49] In conclusion, Hitchens argues that the human race no longer needs religion and that the time has come for science and reason to take a more prominent role in the life of individuals and in the larger society. A de-emphasis of religion will improve the quality of life for individuals and assist in progressing toward civilized societies. However, religion will remain entrenched in some in some societies as long as people cannot overcome their primitive fears, in particular that of their own mortality.[50]

In his own book titled *God: The Failed Hypothesis. How Science Shows that God Does not Exist*, Stenger argues against the notion that science has nothing to say about a supreme being and that religion constitutes a spiritual realm that is beyond scientific examination. He claims that religions make basic pronouncements about nature that science can evaluate, that religions make factual claims that can be subjected to scientific reason and objective observation. He states that "[w]e now have considerable empirical data and highly successful scientific models that bear on the question of God's existence. The time has come to examine what those data and models tell us about the validity of the God hypothesis."[51]

Stenger's analysis assumes that God should be detectable by scientific means simply because the Judeo–Christian–Islamic God plays such a central and crucial role in the creation and operation of the universe and is active in the lives of human beings. He claims that he will consider the existence of God as he would any scientific hypothesis and look for empirical evidence to test specific attributes that God is assumed to possess. If no evidence can be found and there is no other reason for believing in God, then we can be pretty sure he does not exist. Absence of evidence becomes evidence of absence.[52] The thesis of Stenger's book "is that the supernatural hypothesis of God is testable, verifiable, and falsifiable by the established methods of science."[53] The scientific argument against the existence of God includes the following steps:

1. Hypothesize a God who plays an important role in the universe.
2. Assume that God has specific attributes that should provide objective evidence for his existence.
3. Look for such evidence with an open mind.
4. If such evidence is found, conclude that God *may* exist.
5. If such evidence is not found, conclude beyond a reasonable doubt that a God with these properties does *not* exist.[54]

Since the argument from design is used quite frequently to argue for the existence of God, Stenger first examines this claim, which used to go by the name of creationism. The modern movement is called intelligent design, which argues that many biological systems are too complex to have emerged naturally and that living organisms are simply too complicated to have arisen by any conceivable natural mechanism. The issue is whether some intelligent agent designed biological organisms for some purpose or whether these organisms evolved by a combination of pure accident in the process of natural selection. In examining evidence for or against design, Stenger wants to look for any sign of preexisting purpose or plan, and if there is none, one can safely conclude that the organism evolved mindlessly by natural selection.[55]

Without going into all the details, Stenger does state that evolution, while not explaining the origin of life, does not need God to explain the development of life from the simplest organisms to the complexity of human life.

Darwin's theory of natural selection is a well-established theory that is supported by a great deal of evidence over the years and has been accepted "as an observed fact by the great majority of biologists and scientists in related fields, and is utilized in every aspect of modern life including medicine."[56] After refuting the idea of irreducible complexity and other claims of intelligent design, Stegner concludes that earth and life appear just as expected if there is no designer. There is no need for God as natural selection is purposeless and is indifferent as to outcomes of the process.[57]

As for the existence of a world beyond matter, or more specifically whether there exists an immaterial soul that is responsible for thinking, consciousness, abstraction, and understanding, Stenger finds no evidence for its existence and states that a wealth of empirical data suggest that no spiritual element is required for existence and that "matter alone appears to be able to carry out all the activities that have been traditionally associated with the soul."[58] Modern neuroscience has shown that our bodies and brains are made up of nothing more than atoms and that there is nothing supernatural taking place as well-understood physical and chemical processes are sufficient to explain all the interactions between various parts of living organisms.[59] Our bodies and brains do not survive death, and there is no convincing evidence of an immaterial soul that survives in a world beyond matter. Again God is an unnecessary ingredient to explain human activities, such as consciousness, and thinking as such activities can be reduced to nothing more than material properties.[60]

Regarding cosmic evidence for the existence of God, Stenger states that there is neither empirical data nor are there theories based on those data that suggest the universe came about because of a purposeful creation. Based on the best current scientific data available, if follows that there is no creator called God or whatever who left some "cosmological imprint of a purposeful creation."[61] As for divine intervention and miracles, there is no event in history that cannot be accounted for in terms of natural causes. There is no need for a supernatural element to be added to describe those events.[62] The laws of physics that govern the operation of the universe came from nothing; they were not handed down from above.[63]

Another argument for the existence of God has to do with the congeniality of earth for the creation of life, that the universe must have been created with this in mind. The earth is sort of fine-tuned for life, and if the physical constitution of earth had been just a tiny bit different in some instances, life could never have existed. Yet Stenger will have none of this and argues that it is difficult to conclude based on the evidence that the universe was created with some kind of a cosmic purpose for the creation of humanity. It seems inconceivable to him "that a creator exists who has a special love for humanity, and then just relegated it to a tiny point in space and time. The data strongly suggest otherwise."[64]

Revelation also fails a scientific test as any records we have of such supernatural events can be accounted for without recourse to some kind of special revelation. Similarly, no reports of some kind of special religious experience in which God has provided humans with important knowledge obtained by nonmaterial means has passed the test of scientific scrutiny. And as far as any revelatory knowledge in the Bible is concerned, Stenger treats the Bible as an assembly of mythological stories by ancient authors who were not concerned to give us a historically and scientifically accurate accounts of events. They wrote out of the mythological worldview in which they lived, and their writing reflects this worldview.[65]

Many religions claim that moral standards come from only one source, the particular God they believe in and constitute the foundation of their faith. Otherwise, moral standards would be relative depending on the culture, and without authoritative moral standards that have an absolute character, everything is permissible, and society would become morally degenerate. Yet Stenger argues that empirical evidence shows that a common set of moral standards is agreed on by the majority of people from many different cultures. While there are differences between cultures with respect to some moral standards, a set of universal standards does seem to emerge.[66]

People have to learn to live together in some degree of harmony in order to have a functional society. As they become more civilized these standards become more sophisticated and widespread. They become embedded in customs and laws that guide people's behavior. In this manner, a natural morality emerges that has nothing to do with God or standards handed down from on high like the Ten Commandments. Those standards that work to provide harmony and enrich the life of the community are kept and become more of less embedded in people's behavior. Those who deviate from these standards are punished and often removed from society in some manner. Humans learn their sense of right and wrong from experience, not from some authority. Stenger claims to have turned the argument that God is necessary for a moral conscience on its head: "The very fact the humans have a common moral conscience can be taken as evidence against the existence of God."[67]

Stenger next tackles the problem of evil which is one of the most powerful arguments against the existence of God. The traditional notion of God is that he has the attributes of omnibenevolence, omnipotence, and omniscience. So the problem is one of reconciling a God of infinite goodness, power, and wisdom, with the undeniable existence of so much pain and suffering in the world. If God has the power to intervene in history and knows how much people are in pain, and if he is a loving God and not some kind of monster who enjoys seeing his people suffer, why doesn't he intervene to stop such suffering?

Why does evil even exist in light of the power of God to stop bad things from occurring to good and faithful people? This is a logical difficulty that has plagued theologians for years and they have not had much success in dealing with this problem.[68] While there has been a large literature dealing with the problem of evil, Stenger concludes that from the standpoint of science, the empirical fact of suffering in the world is inconsistent with a God that has the attributes listed above and therefore such a God does not exist.[69]

In his concluding chapter, Stenger deals with the issue of living in a godless universe. He argues that while we might think that faith in a beneficent and all-loving God that is widely worshiped would lead to a better world, the exact opposite is the case. The world seems worse off as a result of faith in God as there are differences between religions, particularly the major religions of Christianity, Judaism, and Islam, as well as Buddhism and Hinduism, that are major sources of conflict. These conflicts have led to wars in which tens of thousands of people have been killed in the name of a particular religion.[70]

As far as meaning is concerned, many people think their life is pointless unless they have a belief that they fit into some grand cosmic scheme that has been assigned or created by some external higher authority. But Stenger asks the question of why we can't find meaning internally by devoting ourselves to some goal in life that we find meaningful. As he says, "God is not necessary for someone to find fulfillment in contemplation or social activity." As Peter Singer emphasizes, "we can live a meaningful life by working toward goals that are objectively worthwhile."[71]

Stenger believes that science can help us to live a better life in the years we have left. Science and technology have made out lives easier and have enabled us to more interesting things and travel to other parts of the world and learn how other people live their lives and find fulfillment. Science is not cold and impersonal but can fill us with a sense of awe and wonder as we learn about the earth of which we live and the universe in which we are embedded. The beauty and majesty of nature can give us great pleasure and inspiration. It can give us more comfort and meaning that religion ever can because religion more often than not creates fear and anxiety. Thus, living without God, because it is a failed hypothesis can lead to a fulfilling and meaningful life if we will but embrace it free of the restrictions and fantasies that religion involves.[72]

Summary of the New Atheism

The new atheists write mainly from a scientific perspective and take a hard line with respect to religion. They see a great danger in the irrational thinking that they see associated with religion. They do not take a benign view of even moderate religion and have been criticized for this hard line position. They do not see religion and science as separate realms of reality that have nothing to say to each other and, in this respect, differ with the National Academy of Sciences and many other scientists who hold that science has nothing to say about God or the supernatural. Since the gods most people worship are believed to play an active role in history, this activity should be observable and subject to scientific investigation.[73] As Stenger says,

> [p]erhaps the most unique position of New Atheism is that faith, which is belief without supportive evidence, should not be given the respect, even deference, it obtains in modern society. The theist argument that science and reason are also based in faith is specious. Faith is belief in the absence of supportive evidence. Science is belief in the presence of supportive evidence. And reason is just the procedure by which humans ensure that their conclusions are consistent with the theory that produced them and with he data that test those conclusions.[74]

The New Atheists believe that all the evidence supports the notion of a purely material universe, including the bodies and brains of humans, that does not need to consider any thing like soul or spirit or anything else immaterial. Morality does not come from on high handed down by some God but is the result of human's own social development as societies mature and become more civilized and sophisticated. Religion is not necessary for happiness and contentment, and the New Atheists believe that life is much more meaningful and comfortable without religion.[75]

Science is the best means that humans have for understanding the world they live in, and humans should use the findings of science to make a better world for themselves. And as far as science is concerned, the universe is matter and nothing more. The theist thinks that revelation is the ultimate source of truth about the universe and that he or she has some kind of superior access to this reality. The atheist argues, on the other hand, that empirical science and the use of reason give us the best access to the truth about how the world works. Science and reason have worked, so it is claimed, to make the world a better place for humans to flourish and find fulfillment for their lives, while religion leads universally to dismal failure and untold human suffering.[76]

A book by Alex Rosenberg titled *The Atheist's Guide to Reality: Enjoying Life without Illusions* makes the case for a scientific based reality better than many other books. Rosenberg, who is the R. Taylor Cole Professor, chair of the philosophy department at Duke University, and co-director of the Duke Center for Philosophy of Biology, makes clear in the beginning of the book that he is not out to, as he puts it, hammer another nail into the intellectual coffin of theism. Thus, he wants to make his book different from those reviewed previously and thinks the effort to argue people out of their religious belief is futile. There is little point, in his opinion, in preaching to either the unconverted or the converted. He wants to lay out what atheists should believe about reality and our place in that reality. He is disturbed by those who argue that there is no incompatibility between religion and science and agrees with Hume that there is no more to reality than the laws of nature that science discovers. All the rest are just stories of one kind or another.[77]

The worldview that all atheists share Rosenberg calls "scientism," which is the "conviction that the methods of science are the only reliable way to secure knowledge of anything; that science's description of the world is correct in it fundamentals and that when complete what science tells us will not be surprisingly different from what it tells us today . . . Science provides all the significant truths about reality, and to know such truths is what real understanding is all about."[78] Being scientistic means accepting science as the exclusive guide to reality regarding nature, including our own nature and everything else's nature.[79] According to Rosenberg,

> [s]cience has three things going for it that religion doesn't have. First, that facts that make any story true, when it is true, are to be found in equations, theories, models, and laws. Second, most of religion's best stories are false. Third, and most important, science shows that the stories we tell one another to explain our own and other people's actions and to answer the persistent questions are all based on a series of illusions. That should be enough to forestall our innate penchant for stories.[80]

The human need for stories is the greatest barrier, according to Rosenberg, to understanding what science is trying to tell us about the nature of reality. It is also the slippery slope down which people can slide into superstition. When it comes to science and its understanding of reality, these stories have to give way to equations, models, laws, and theories. If we are going to be scientistic, then we will have to embrace physics as *the whole truth about reality*. Stories upon which religion relies have to be seen as just stories that may express some human need for understanding themselves and the world but have nothing to say about the fundamental nature of reality.[81]

There are three reasons to believe that physics tells us the whole truth about reality: (1) the phenomenal accuracy of its prediction, (2) the unimaginable power of its technological applications, and (3) the breathtaking extent and detail of its explanations. Physics is both *causally closed* and *causally complete*: "The only causes in the entire universe are physical, and everything in the universe that has a cause has a physical cause." Rosenberg goes even further to assert that the physical facts *fix* all the facts. By this he means "that the physical facts constitute or determine or bring about all the rest of the facts." This includes the chemical, biological, psychological, social, economic, political, and other human facts. In other words, everything that other sciences deal with can be ultimately be reduced to the particles of physics and the laws that govern their interaction.[82]

Rosenberg obviously rejects any notion of design or purpose to the universe. Purpose can be banished in the biological realm by recognizing that the process of natural selection discovered by Darwin is simply physics at work among the organic molecules. Any notion of purpose in the universe must be treated as an illusion. Newton expunged purpose from the physical world, and Darwin did the same thing for the biological world. There is no rhyme or reason to the universe. It is more of less on damn thing after another. Whatever happens in the universe is without purpose or design. Things just happen for no reason and for no particular purpose.[83]

With regard to morality, Rosenberg makes a case for nihilism to counter the theistic view that without God life would have no value, and there would be no reason to be decent people. Moral disputes can be resolved in many different ways, but they can never be resolved by finding something that is considered to be the right answer as there are none. According to Rosenberg, nihilism is not moral relativism, nor is it moral skepticism, but it does hold that the idea of the "morally permissible" is nonsense but equally nonsensical is the idea that "everything is morally permissible." Nihilism denies the idea that there is anything that is good in itself or anything that is bad in itself.[84]

All is not lost, however, as almost all of humanity, including those with different scientific, or theological beliefs are committed to the same basic morality and values. There is long-standing evidence that there exists a core morality that the world's major religions agree on in their ethical arguments. Neuroscience increasingly shows that the human brain reacts in roughly the same way to ethical problems across cultures. This core morality has important consequences for survival and reproduction and must have been heavily influenced by natural selection. People had to agree on certain moral norms to stay alive and reproduce themselves. But this core morality is not true in any sense; it is an adaptation to a specific environment. If the environment had been different, a different core morality would have evolved.[85]

Science gives us reason to be suspicious about introspection, what we think we know about the mind, the self, and the person from the inside, so to speak. Thinking about what goes on in the conscious self is completely untrustworthy as a source of knowledge about the mind. We can't trust it to tell us anything about ourselves. It can't tell us anything about the mind, the self, or what makes us the kind of person we think ourselves to be. Introspection into our consciousness is not a reliable guide to any of the questions we have about the nature of the self.[86] As Rosenberg says.

> [s]cience provides clear-cut answers to all of the questions on the list; there is no free will, there is no mind distinct from the brain, there is no soul, no self, no person that supposedly inhabits your body, that endures over its life span, and that might even outlast it. So introspection must be wrong.[87]

Thinking itself is nothing like what conscious introspection suggests. Thinking about things doesn't happen, according to Rosenberg, and when conscious introspection says your brain has thoughts, it is wrong. The brain deals with information in a totally different way from what introspection implies. Knowing what something looks like is no more than having a set of neurons wired up in a certain manner. These neural activities give us the illusion that the thoughts in the brain are really about the world. But it is all just a physical process as consciousness itself is just another physical process.[88]

Introspection provides us with two other illusions that have persisted throughout the ages. One is that humans have purposes that give our actions and our lives meaning. The other is that there is a person "in there" who guides our activities. Scientism compels us to give up any answers we think we may have to question about free will, the self, the soul, and the meaning of life. The mind is the brain, and it can't be anything else since thinking, feeling, and perceiving are physical processes going on in the brain.[89] "Since are no thoughts about things, notions of purpose, plan, or design in the mind are illusory."[90]

Since science can never capture the subjective point of view of the person inside the body, the conclusion of scientism is that there is no such point of view and the person or the self is an illusion. Since the physical facts fix all the facts there can be no subjective point of view that belongs to the self. There can't be a me or you inside the bodies we have that has a special point of view.[91] The existence of the self as distinct from the body has existed practically forever and in every culture and it was always a challenge to explain how a nonphysical self could control the physical body. But this is a false challenge as scientism holds that all these beliefs in a nonspatial, nonphysical self, person, or soul is just wishful thinking.[92]

Rosenberg concludes that these views of scientism are intellectually respectable. The evidence for the truth of physics as a complete theory or reality is much stronger than any evidence we have for the truth that relies on introspection, which has been wrong about so many things that it doesn't carry any weight against science. If one is going to allow for real purposes and designs to suddenly pop up out of nowhere in a world where physics had previously fixed all the facts, then, Rosenberg says, one might as well put God into the universe at the outset.[93]

Scientism treats history as blind; there is no purpose to history and no design any more than there is in the biological realm. Christianity as well as many philosophies such as Hegelianism and Marxism have an end point to make sense out of history, but according to Rosenberg, these hopes are in vain. History is not a source of knowledge but is more like an entertaining activity. It is a source of enjoyable stories or polemics that moves readers to action, to tears, or nostalgia. But history provides no source of knowledge about the future of humanity.[94] Rosenberg goes on to say that

> [u]nfortunately for historians, history—the actual events of the human past—shows no pattern, cycle, or regularity that can provide predictive knowledge about the human future. Scientism has strong proof that it can't. That is why, when it comes to providing the foresight required to certify something as knowledge, history is bunk. The past is not just bereft of meaning. The only patterns it may have had in the past cannot be exploited to provide foreknowledge.[95]

Rosenberg is equally as hard on the human sciences, stating that they are, at best, myopic. Like the natural sciences the purpose of the human sciences is to discover reliable regularities, generalizations, laws, models, and theories that can be used to predict human behavior in the future. But anything like a law discovered by the social or behavioral sciences is nothing more than a temporary equilibrium that will eventually be broken up into something different. Some of these equilibria will last longer than others, but all will eventually be taken over by events. There are patterns of human behavior to be discovered but they will hold for shorter and shorter periods of time before they unravel. At best the human sciences will only be able to see a little way into the future. If history is blind, social science must be myopic.[96]

Most people who embrace atheism don't need secular humanism to be nice or to go on living. It won't work as a substitute for religion. The idea that we need something to make life meaningful and to give us a reason to keep on living, according to Rosenberg, is another one of those illusions fostered by introspection. Most of us will turn out to be reasonably well-adjusted, happy people somewhere between within two standard deviations from the mean between severe depression and hopeless euphoria. But here are always going to be people at the extremes who are both hopelessly depressed and maladjusted or who sail through life without a care in the world.[97]

Since science concludes that no one acts with free will, no wrongdoer ever earns punishment. This is probably one of the most controversial conclusions Rosenberg states as it means that we have to rethink the moral justification of punishment. It will have to be based on something else than the accepted principle that freely committed wrongdoing earns punishment. Prisons are for rehabilitation and the protection of society but not for punishment. Nothing is earned and nothing is deserved, including the wealth that some people are able to accumulate. We didn't earn our inborn talents and abilities, and we had no choice about the circumstance into which we were born that could either nurture or destroy those talents and abilities. Thus, science, according to Rosenberg, turns out to be redistributionist and egalitarian even when coupled with free-market economics.[98]

These are the main tenants of Rosenberg's book. His views are the most explicit of any of the books on the new atheism that I have read. He believes in scientific reductionism through and through in that science explains all of reality and leaves no room for religion or any other approach that relies on some form of supernaturalism or nonmaterial substance to explain human behavior. The dualism of Descartes is done away with as the mind is reduced to nothing more than the brain, which functions more or less mechanically with a neuronal basis. There is no room for morality of any kind, and no one is to be blamed for wrongdoing or praised for making a success of life. These things just happen because of the characteristics we are born with and the circumstances into which we are born, neither of which are under our control.

Faith is believed to be absurd by the New Atheists and is not a benign force that can be tolerated as the opium of the masses, as Marx held, because it is the source of much of the violence and conflict in the world. Religious faith does not promote an objective investigation of situations and a willingness to confront empirical facts that are needed to deal with the various problems the nation and the world faces. There is no better example of the disaster that faith-based decisions can cause than that of the George W. Bush administration, where scientific and historical evidence was ignored and decisions were based on "an irrational mode of thought founded on faith and suspicious of any reasoned argument that contradicted that faith."[99]

The world faces many catastrophic problems such as global warning; overpopulation; flooded coastal areas; worldwide epidemics; starvation for much of the world; severe water shortages in parts of the world, including the United States; and other such problems. Such disasters will cause worldwide conflicts on a scale that has not thus far ever been experienced. To constructively deal with such problems will require the best scientific thinking, new technologies, and creative thinking along with unselfish politicians who can work out bipartisan solutions. God will not solve these problems; only humans who are dedicated to secular approaches rather than hoping for the return of Jesus and the establishment of heaven on earth can.[100] As Stenger says, faith is not the answer to the resolution of such conflicts:

> Faith has no checks and balances, no follow-up investigations to see if an intuition works. Science does. As documented fully in the new atheist and other recent literature, it is precisely the certainty, indeed the madness of faith—the unbridled conviction that one is doing God's work—that has over the centuries and down to the present day enabled otherwise normal human beings to commit the most cruel atrocities against their fellow humans.[101]

The strongest case against religion, according to Stenger, is its unbroken history as a source for some of the major atrocities the world has ever seen. According to one source cited by Stenger, polytheism did not have holy wars where both antagonists believed God as on their side, it did not have inquisitions where people who questioned the faith were burned at the stake, and it did not have crusades whose purpose was to kill the "infidels" who had occupied the holy lands and take them back in the name of Christianity. Such atrocities were all the products of monotheism as the core values of polytheism were religious liberty and diversity. *Monotheism* means one God, and that God has to be the supreme being over all the world, and his reign must be enforced by whatever means necessary.[102]

Christian morality has not led to a fulfilling life for much of humanity and has not led to the eliminating of suffering in the world but, in many cases, has caused more suffering thought discrimination against certain people and groups such as gays because they were not acceptable by the community of believers. Morality does not come from God, according to the New Atheists, but is a product of natural selection as people learned to live together and cooperate in order to survive. Codes of conduct were necessary as population increased and the consequences of everyone's behavior affected other people. These codes were necessary to create some kind of functional society.[103]

While the New Atheism has science at its base, science does not have its mind closed to the supernatural, according to Stenger, but simply finds no empirical or theoretical reason to consider anything other than natural causes for all events in the world. There is nothing but nature, and nature is composed of matter and nothing else. Thus, reality is materialistic, and humans are composed of 100 percent matter without a connection to some supernatural agency or force. There is no substance we could call spirit, soul, or living force that influences our behavior. The mind, which Descartes tried to preserve in a nonmaterial realm, is reduced to the brain, and "human consciousness and self-awareness reside in a purely material brain and nervous system."[104]

As far as the future of atheism is concerned, Stenger presents data to show that secularism is the fastest-growing belief system in the world. From 1900 to 2000 the number of people classified as nonreligionists grew from 3.2 million to 918 million. During that period, the rate of agnostics and atheists added 8.5 million converts per year and grew from 0.2 percent of the population to 15 percent of the population. This growth is contrasted with the trend in religion, which in the United States is trending slowly but surely downward.[105]

There are any number of societies, according to Stenger, where the majority of people are nonbelievers, and far from being dens of iniquity, they are the happiest, safest, and most successful places in the world.[106] Without some supernatural force determining meaning in life, humans must make their own meaning and recognize that meaning, value, and purpose are human ideas and that humans are responsible for the content of those ideas in their own existence and the existence of the society in which they function.[107] They must work out their own morality on the basis of what works to promote human community and human flourishing. "Religion is an intellectual and moral sickness that cannot endure forever if we believe at all in human progress. Science sees no limit in the human capacity to comprehend the universe and ourselves. God does not exist. Life without God means that we are the governors of our own destinies."[108]

It is abundantly clear that the New Atheism is based on a scientific, materialistic worldview. There is no room for any kind of spiritual dimension as the New Atheism does not believe anything exists beyond the material world that science examines. Thus, it cannot serve as a source for a new approach or understanding of spiritualism that is relevant to the scientific and technological world in which we live. We are left with nothing but a cold, materialistic approach to the world in which science provides all the answers that we will ever need to live a fulfilled life and find meaning in who we are and what we do in the world.

While the New Atheism contains many valid criticisms of conventional religion, it is equally dogmatic about its worldview as is the most die-hard fundamentalist. It leaves no room for anything but science and a materialistic approach to the world. It is reductionistic in its outlook as the universe, and everything in it is ultimately reducible to the fundamental particles of physics. The mind, for example, is reduced to the brain, which is subject to scientific analysis. Human consciousness resides in the brain and is ultimately a function of physical particles interacting with each other. There is no other reality other than that which can be examined by the scientific method.

Thus, we are cut off from any kind of spiritual reality and left with nothing but a meaningless and purposeless universe that operates according to the laws of physics that are indifferent to human concerns. The scientific worldview is the only reality for the New Atheists; everything can be subject to examination by science, and if it does not pass the test that science applies to the things it examines, then it does not exist in any real sense. Science is the ultimate authority in matters of morality and in deciding what is real and what is fantasy. This is as dogmatic a position as a fundamentalist position, where the Bible is the final authority in matters of morality and human behavior and where revelation is the final source of truth about the world and humans place in the grand scheme that God has in mind.

That science is the final authority in matters of truth and reality is an unproven assumption. Science cannot be used to prove itself as the ultimate authority. The New Atheism simply assumes the scientific worldview is the only one worth considering and rejects the religious worldview as being unproved and unable to pass scientific scrutiny. But science is an authority only for what it can examine and that can be subjected to its reductionistic and quantitative approach to reality. Everything else such as mind, subjectivity, feelings, and spirituality are left out because they are not subject to examination by the scientific method. But this does not make them any less real if one does not limit his or her approach to reality to the scientific method.

There are new ways of understanding science itself that are nontraditional in nature and that are open to considering the so-called subjective dimension as a part of the reality that humans experience. Spirituality is a part of this dimension and interacts with the so-called objective reality that science discovers to produce a complete picture of the depth and breadth of the real world in which we live and breathe. But the New Atheism does not help us to grasp that reality but remains rooted in a traditional scientific worldview that leaves no room for spirituality.

Notes

1 Michel Onfray, *Atheist Manifesto: The Case against Christianity, Judaism, and Islam* (New York: Arcade Publishing, 2011), 15.

2 Louise M. Antony, "Introduction," in Louise M. Antony, ed. *Philosophers without Gods: Meditations on Atheism and the Secular Life* (New York: Oxford University Press, 2007), xiii.

3 Victor J. Stenger, *The New Atheism: Taking a Stand for Science and Reason* (Amherst, NY: Prometheus Books, 2009), 11.

4 Sam Harris, *The End of Faith: Religion, Terror, and the Future of Reason* (New York: W.W. Norton, 2004), 117–123. Onfray makes the same point: "Nearly two hundred and fifty verses—of the six thousand two hundred and thirty-four of the book [the Koran]—justify and legitimize holy war, jihad, enough to drown the handful of very inoffensive phrases recommending tolerance and respect for one's neighbor, magnanimity or nonrecourse to violence in questions of religion (!). In such an ocean of blood, who can still take the trouble to linger over two or three sentences that recommend tolerance over barbarity? Particularly since the Prophet's biography bears eloquent witness: murder, crime, the sword, and the punitive expedition constantly recur. Too many pages encourage anti-Semitism, hatred of Jews, despoiling and exterminating them, for a Muslim fighter not to feel justified in putting them to the sword." Onfray, *Atheist Manifesto*, 200.

5 As quoted in Michael Shermer, *The Science of Good & Evil* (New York: Henry Holt and Company, 2004), 37–38.

6 Harris, *The End of Faith*, 155.

7 "History bears witness: millions of dead in the name of God, millions on every continent and in every century. Bible in one hand, sword in the other: Inquisition, torture, the rack; the Crusades, massacres, pillage, rape, hangings, exterminations, the African slave trade, humiliation, exploitation, serfdom, the trade in men, women, and children; genocides, the ethnocides of the most Christian conquistadors, of course." Onfray, *Atheist Manifesto*, 182. In another part of the book Onfray claims that "monotheism is fatally fixated on death. It loves death, cherishes death, is fascinated by death. It gives death, doles it out in massive doses; it threatens death and moves from threat to action: from the bloody sword of the Israelites killing off the Canaanites to the use of airliners as flying bombs in New York, stopping off on the way to release an atomic cargo over Hiroshima and Nagasaki. Everything is done in the name of God, blessed by him, but blessed most of all by those claiming to act in his name." Ibid., 176. And further he adds the following: "Fired by the same inborn death drive, the three monotheisms share a series of identical forms of aversion: hatred of reason and intelligence; hatred of freedom; hatred of all books in the name of one book alone; hatred of sexuality, women, and pleasure; hatred of the feminine; hatred of the body, of desires, of drives. Instead Judaism, Christianity, and Islam extol faith and belief, obedience and submission, taste for death and longing for the beyond, the asexual angel and chastity, virginity and monogamous love, wife and mother, soul and spirit. In other words life crucified and nothing exalted." Ibid., 67.

8 Ibid., 131.

9 Ibid., 12–13.

10 Ibid., 17.

11 Ibid., 19.

12 Ibid., 23.

13 Ibid., 20–21.

14 Ibid., 45.

15 Ibid., 48. Alan Tacca, writing in the *Kampala Monitor*, also advocates the abolishment of Christianity: "Most Western societies are not only nominally Christian" he argues. Even for churchgoers, "God is clearly a cultural construct. True believers are a dying breed, and Catholic and Protestant churches alike are struggling with a chronic shortage of priests and ministers." Rather the bemoaning

this trend, Tacca believes "the West should embrace it. Religion is doing little these days but provide fuel for conflicts: Muslims against Christians, Hindus against Buddhists, and everyone against the Jews. So let us dispose of the Christian God, the way Western colonial powers got rid of African deities long ago. Back then, colonizers actively undermined those gods until they were stripped of all dignity. Is it now time to declare their God also primitive? References to God should be removed from currencies and national anthems and sand-blasted off government buildings. Only after faith in the supernatural is gone can people take responsibility for generating virtue and beauty in the human realm." Alan Tacca, "When a Faith Outlives its Usefulness," *The Week*, April 14, 2006, 12.

16 Richard Dawkins, *The God Delusion* (New York: Houghton Mifflin, 2006), 5.
17 Ibid., 31. Italics in original.
18 Harris, *The End of Faith*, as quoted in Ibid., 88.
19 Ibid., 113–159.
20 Ibid., 227.
21 Ibid., 282–283.
22 Ibid., 327.
23 Ibid., 308.
24 Ibid., 347–374.
25 Daniel C. Dennett, *Breaking the Spell: Religion as a Natural Phenomenon* (New York: Viking, 2006).
26 Ibid., 9.
27 Ibid., 11–12.
28 Ibid., 17.
29 Ibid., 25.
30 Ibid., 30–31.
31 Ibid., 103.
32 Ibid., 160–161.
33 Ibid., 198–199.
34 Ibid., 199.
35 Ibid., 246.
36 Ibid., 277.
37 Ibid., 307.
38 Ibid., 324.
39 Ibid., 339.
40 Free Speech, *onegoodmove*, March 2007.
41 Jerry Coyne, "The Best Arguments for God's Existence Are Actually Terrible," *New Republic*, January 16, 2014.
42 Christopher Hitchens, *God Is not Great: How Religion Poisons Everything* (New York: Twelve Books, 2007).
43 Ibid., 44–45.
44 Ibid., 45–46.
45 Ibid., 49.
46 Ibid., 47.
47 Ibid., 111–127.
48 Ibid., 115.
49 Ibid., 122.
50 Ibid., 13.
51 Victor J. Stenger, *God: The Failed Hypothesis. How Science Shows that God Does not Exist* (Amherst, NY: Prometheus Books, 2007), 10–11. Stenger has written a more recent book titled *God and the Folly of Faith* (Amherst, NY: Prometheus Books, 2012), in which he again examines the intersection of religion and science. He states in the preface that science and religion are fundamentally incompatible because of their unequivocally opposed epistemologies. Science

based on careful observation is our only reliable source of knowledge about the world. Religion goes further in giving credence to additional sources of knowledge such as Holy Scripture, revelation, and spiritual experiences. Stenger wants to show how faith in these sources of knowledge is folly and science is the only reasonable alternative.

52 Ibid., 13, 18.
53 Ibid., 29.
54 Ibid., 43. Stenger claims that these steps are a modified form of the lack-of-evidence argument.
55 Ibid., 68.
56 Ibid., 50.
57 Ibid., 71.
58 Ibid., 84.
59 Ibid., 85.
60 Ibid., 106.
61 Ibid., 127.
62 Ibid., 128.
63 Ibid., 131.
64 Ibid., 161.
65 Ibid., 188.
66 Ibid., 195–196.
67 Ibid., 210.
68 Ibid., 216.
69 Ibid., 224.
70 Ibid., 250.
71 Ibid., 252.
72 Ibid., 255–258.
73 Stenger, *The New Atheism*, 13–14.
74 Ibid., 15.
75 Ibid., 14, 16–17.
76 Ibid., 41.
77 Alex Rosenberg, *The Atheist's Guide to Reality: Enjoying Life without Illusions* (New York: W.W. Norton, 2011), viii–xiii.
78 Ibid., 6–7.
79 Ibid., 8.
80 Ibid., 9.
81 Ibid., 14–20.
82 Ibid., 25–26.
83 Ibid., 46, 56, 92.
84 Ibid., 94–98.
85 Ibid., 103–113.
86 Ibid., 147–148.
87 Ibid., 147.
88 Ibid., 170–193.
89 Ibid., 194–195.
90 Ibid., 205.
91 Ibid., 219–220.
92 Ibid., 222–223.
93 Ibid., 235, 239.
94 Ibid., 243–246.
95 Ibid., 246–247.
96 Ibid., 260–274.
97 Ibid., 280–283.
98 Ibid., 292–299.
99 Stenger, *The New Atheism*, 46.

100 Ibid., 47, 55.
101 Ibid., 73.
102 Ibid., 107.
103 Ibid., 153–155.
104 Ibid., 221.
105 Ibid., 229.
106 Ibid., 233.
107 Ibid., 235.
108 Ibid., 244.

6 Secular Sources of Spirituality

In this chapter I want to present some secular ways of developing a sense of spirituality that will enable people to reconnect with nature and each other. This is not a how-to book, however, and I am not going to describe various exercises that can be done to get in touch with a spiritual dimension. Instead I describe some ideas that come from various sources as to what needs to be done in order to overcome the disenchantment with the world that has resulted from a scientific approach to reality and from an objective outlook that is part and parcel of capitalism, which, by and large, treats both nature and humans being as objects to be exploited for purposes of economic growth. There are various approaches that hold a great deal of promise regarding spirituality, including a reinvention of the sacred, the role of artistic expression in recovering spirituality, and other such ideas that can serve as a source of spirituality.

Reinventing the Sacred

In a book titled *Reinventing The Sacred: A New View of Science, Reason, and Religion*, Stuart A. Kauffman, founding director of the Institute for Biocomplexity and Informatics and a professor at the University of Calgary, claims to be offering a different worldview from the contemporary reductionist perspective, where all phenomena in the world can be explained by interactions of fundamental particles. Within this reductionist worldview, societies are to be explained by laws about people, which, in turn, are explained by laws about organs, then about cells, then biochemistry, chemistry, and finally physics and particle physics. Kauffman's worldview is based on a new view of the sacred that reaches further than science itself and involves a new understanding of not only the sacred but also science, art, ethics, politics, and spirituality. His field of research is complexity theory that involves a reintegration of science with the Greek view of the good life that is a life well lived.[1]

Emergence is a major part of this new worldview that holds that life, agency, value, and doing are real phenomena in the universe and cannot be reduced or derived from physics alone. Life as we know it, the evolution of the biosphere in which we live, the fullness of history, and our practical everyday worlds are real and not reducible to the laws of physics. The web of life is partially lawless and ceaselessly creative, yet it breaks no laws of physics. Our lives move forward into such a ceaseless creativity that we cannot fully understand, making reason alone an insufficient guide to the path our lives take. Science is not the only pathway to truth, according to Kaufman, as history and the situated richness of the humanities also provide important truths. Spirituality needs to have a place in our lives to help us reinvent the sacred based on a conception of God as the natural creativity in the universe.[2] Accomplishing this task involves the healing of injuries that are the result of the 350-year reign of reductionism as an explanation of the universe. According to Kaufman,

> [i]f we are members of a universe in which emergence and ceaseless activity abound, if we take that creativity as a sense of the God we can share, the resulting sense of the sacredness of all of life and the planet can help orient our lives beyond the consumerism and commodification the industrial world now lives, heal the split between reason and faith, heal the split between science and the humanities, heal the want of spirituality, heal the wound derived from the false reductionist belief that we live in a world of facts without values, and help us jointly build a global ethic. These are what are at stake in finding a new scientific worldview that enables us to reinvent the sacred.[3]

There is no scientific basis for values in the reductionistic worldview as one cannot deduce an ought from an is; there is a complete separation of facts and values. And the facts about our world come from physics, which is considered to be the basic science from which all other sciences can ultimately be understood. All higher-order processes in the universe can ultimately be explained as nothing but particles in motion. The universe operates without meaning and purpose, and its beginning and end can be explained by science without a need for religious explanations or superstitious beliefs that involve an active God who intervenes in history.[4]

Physicists themselves have questioned the adequacy of the reductionist approach to explain all phenomena in the world.[5] Some question whether biology can really be reduced to physics and whether organisms are just particles in motion.[6] The origin of life itself lies beyond reductionism. Just because life can be viewed as having emerged without the intervention of a Creator God does not lessen the wonder of it all: the evolution of life and the biosphere. If life is to be seen as sacred, we must reinvent the sacred as the creativity we see in nature itself.[7]

Rather than just brute facts, the agency that arises with the creation of life brings value, meaning, and action into the universe, according to Kauffman, and takes us beyond reductionism to a broader scientific worldview. As agents, we can alter the way the universe develops through the actions we take with respect to certain features of our world. We alter the climate of the earth by continuing to burn fossil fuels; we change the courses of rivers and tear mountains apart to get at the minerals inside. All this activity matters to some entities; it means something to them, and thus, value emerges based on the choices we make about our actions. What we ought to do is central to these decisions and involves moral considerations.[8]

People are not ready to give up on those things that are held to be sacred such as meaning, values, and purpose and to consider them to be mere illusions. But if the natural world has no room for sacred things because of the dominance of the traditional scientific worldview, then they must be located outside of nature in some supernatural realm where God infuses them into the universe. The conflict between science and religion is, in part, a disagreement over the existence of the sacred. Science has no place for the sacred while religion holds the sacred as central to its concerns.

But if something like meaning, for example, were to be discovered scientifically, the conflict might be resolved. Kauffman argues that we appear to be living in an emergent universe where life and agency arise without the need for some supernatural explanation. He makes what he calls an outrageous claim that the evolution of the biosphere is radically nonpredictable and ceaselessly creative. The universe is not completely governed by natural laws as traditional science would have us believe, and its evolution is partially beyond scientific laws and is therefore unpredictable.[9]

This new scientific worldview Kauffman advocates is, as he calls it, a stunningly creative biosphere that we help to co-create through our own actions. This new scientific worldview is very different, so he claims, from that envisioned by pure reductionism: "These, I hope, are long steps towards reinventing the sacred. If we contemplate the diversity and complexity of the biosphere, and the human mind, consciousness, economy, history, and culture—our emergent historicity—the ceaseless, partially lawless, every creative exploration of the adjacent possible on all these levels, how can we be less than awestruck?"[10] From this new sense of the sacred, there is hope to invent a new global ethic to orient our lives in an emerging global civilization. Reason alone cannot be a sufficient guide for our lives but is part of the mystery in which we live, where we cannot always know what will transpire but must act courageously in the face of uncertainty.[11]

The economic sphere provides a good example of the limits of reason. The way in which the economy evolves is not always foreseeable. Only a handful of people, for example, predicted the downfall of the economy in 2008 and made a bundle of money in the process by betting against the continued growth of the housing market. Traditional scientific predictability cannot be extended to the economic realm, yet we manage to make economic decisions in the face of inescapable ignorance, where reason alone is not sufficient to guide our actions. We only partially understand how to promote economic growth and have only partially succeeded in restoring the economy since the Great Recession. The evolution of the economy, like that of the biosphere and human culture and history, is part of the endless creativity in the universe that is partially unpredictable and not completely subject to the laws of nature.[12]

With respect to the mind, Kauffman does not believe the mind is merely a "computational machine;" an information processing system or an information computational network. The mind is not always algorithmic, which he defines as *an effective procedure to calculate a result,* as many neurobiologists and cognitive scientists believe. The human mind is much more than this and keeps breaking the boundaries of a computational model. It is essentially nonalgorithmic and is rather a *meaning and doing organic system.* As such, it is free to go where it will and is part of a creative universe. The mind makes the world meaningful and enables us to understand our place in the world. It is inventive and cannot be bound and circumscribed by a computational model.[13]

Regarding consciousness, Kauffman states that the mind–brain identity theory is the most acceptable philosophic view of consciousness and the basis of most neurobiological research on the subject. This theory does away with the mind–body dualism of Descartes by reducing everything to the brain and making consciousness, experiences and all other internal mental states disappear. Conscious experiences are an emergent property of neurons firing in the brain and thus have a physical basis. Kauffman takes issue with this theory and argues that consciousness is real; it is emergent in evolution and may arise naturally. Reductionism is limited in explaining agency, meaning and value, and consciousness. We are conscious beings and have internal mental states, even if it is a mystery how these states arise. While the true meaning of consciousness is not yet understood, there is reason to believe that it is fully natural.[14]

The new scientific worldview that Kauffman has been developing is thus an emergent universe of ceaseless creativity in which life, meaning, agency, ethics, and consciousness have emerged: "Our entire historical development as a species, our diverse cultures, and our embedded historicity, have been self-consistent, co-constructing, evolving, emergent, and unpredictable. Our histories, inventions, ideas, and actions are also parts of the creative universe . . . *None of this self-consistent co-construction seems to be what we mean as describable in its detailed becoming by natural law. Yet it is, in fact, truly happening all the time.*"[15]

Western culture is split between reason and the rest of our sensibilities, but we are at a juncture, according to Kauffman, where we have the communication tools to heal this split and invent a global ethic for a globally diverse and creative ongoing civilization and reinvent the sacred. Since the rise of modern science, is has been seen as the highest form of reason and viewed as the preeminent self-correcting path to knowledge. But what if rationality is only part of the process of how humans find their way in the world, and science itself suggests that reason alone is an insufficient guide to living our lives forward into the future. Perhaps it is time to reexamine and reintegrate the arts and humanities along with science, practical action, politics, ethics, and spirituality.[16] Kaufman goes on to say that

> [b]eing in the world in not merely cognitive, it is the full integration of all of our humanity, imagination, invention, thinking, feeling, intuition, sensation, our full emotional selves, and whatever we bring to bear. We could not make our way without all of these . . . Living involves knowing, judging, understanding, doing, caring, attending, empathy, and compassion, whether science, business, the law, the humanities, the arts, sports, or other ways of going about our lives. If we cannot marvel in our own created, lived, meaningful, unforeseen, human culture, we are missing part of the sacred that we have created and we can instead celebrate. Just because science replaced legal reasoning as the model of rationality hundreds of years ago, we need no longer to live with that view. Why limit ourselves, as magnificent as science is?[17]

A major threat to reinventing the sacred according to Kauffman is religious fundamentalism, including the Christian religion, Islamic, and an emerging Hindu fundamentalism. Fundamentalists cannot tolerate divergent views on many issues relating to human life, including its beginning and ending, as to admit that other views than their own may contain some truth would be compromising with the devil. If one claims to know the ultimate truth about the world and humans, as fundamentalists do, compromise and toleration are out of the question. They cannot modify their own views and remain true to their faith and will kill each other if necessary to defend their faith.[18]

Dealing with diverse fundamentalist cultures across the planet is a challenge we do not know how to meet says Kauffman. If we fail to create enough of a shareable worldview that goes beyond reductionism, is filled with value and meaning, and is open to the best of a shared wisdom across cultures, we face a darker world and starker clash of civilizations that involves striving for political and economic power. What is a high priority for the future of the human race is to create a nonthreatening spiritual space for believers and nonbelievers so that we can talk to each other, reason together about our different views of morality, and seek to convince each other through rational argument rather than killing each other?[19]

The keystone for moral reasoning in Western culture, which started with the Greeks and Romans and which lasted until the Enlightenment, was "natural law;" the view that there is order in the universe and that right living and action in accordance with natural laws were meant to create harmony in the universe. With the Enlightenment and the rise of modern science moral claims became problematic. Moral claims were not considered to be factual in the same way as so-called value-free scientific facts about the world that were given a privileged position. Facts and values became separated, and values and moral considerations became noncognitive and emotive in nature. Furthermore, one cannot deduce an "ought" for an "is";

in other words, the facts of science do not lead to moral principles. This has been called the naturalistic fallacy. But Kauffman disagrees with this view of values and thinks that

> [l]ife, agency, values, and therefore "oughts" are real in the universe. With values, human reasoning, as well as emotions, intuitions, experience, and our other sensibilities about values become legitimate, not mere emotive utterances, and not mere statements of fact, but instead reasoning about values. Reasoning about what we ought to do in concrete situations is a large part of how we orient ourselves in our real lives. Our moral reasoning in a genuine aspect of living our lives forward, and surely not reducible to the physics of Weinberg.[20]

There have been two major secular ethical traditions that emerged since the Enlightenment in Western cultures. One is the categorical imperative of Immanuel Kant, which was an effort to develop a consistent deontological logic and an ethics that could be universalized, and the other the utilitarian philosophy of Jeremy Bentham and John Stuart Mill, which advocated acting in a way that promoted the greatest good for the greatest number. Kauffman has serious problems with these traditions, which leads him to conclude that "there appears to be no set of self-consistent moral 'laws' or axioms that can self-consistently guide all moral choices by a kind of deductive moral logic." Moral reasoning thus enters the picture as the "needs, aims, and rights that we have come into conflict in specific moral settings."[21]

Neither morality nor the law is fixed for all times and places. Morality and law are ceaselessly changing and evolving and evoke creativity in dealing with new situations where there is little or no precedent to rely on for making decisions. To say that morality evolves, however, is not to fall into moral relativism where one cannot make moral judgments as to the "rightness" of particular actions over others. Rather, it invites respect for past moral wisdom, the view of others who may disagree over what course of action is moral, and flexibility to adapt to new facts as they emerge.[22]

We lack a global ethics, but Kauffman argues that we must develop one to prepare for the global civilization that is emerging. We must develop an ethical framework that will allow humanity to unite with a reinvented sense of the sacred and provide a foundation for the global civilization that is being created. Such an ethic is ours to create, but it must encompass far more than a sense of oneness with all of life and taking responsibility for a sustainable planet. With the rise of a global civilization, cultures with all their differences come into conflict, and it becomes difficult to find common ground, particularly with the rise of fundamentalist religious and political movements throughout the world. Kauffman thinks that the task of finding a common spiritual, moral, and ethical space that spans the globe could not be more urgent. We must come together to find reverence, meaning, awe, wonder, orientation, and responsibility in the world that we all share.[23]

Recognizing the dangers of using the word *God*, Kauffman thinks it would be wise to use this ancient symbol of reverence and give it a new and natural meaning. He would like to use the word *God* as the name for creativity in nature and thinks it would help bring us to the awe and reverence that creativity deserves. This conception of God refers to the way in which our universe unfolds and is our own humanity. The word *God* does not have to be used, he states, but it may be wise to use it to help orient our lives and create a safe and spiritual space in which we can all share. It could be used to allow the creativity in the universe to be a further source of meaning and membership for people of diverse cultures.[24] He goes on to say that

> [i]t is up to us to choose what we will build together across our traditions, across science and the rest of our cultures and histories. In reinventing the sacred, with God our chosen symbol for the creativity in the universe including our own capacity for our inventions of religion, I believe we can, at last, take responsibility for what we call sacred, and thus treat as sacred.[25]

Kauffman admits that his conception of God is not far from the God of Spinoza, where God is the unfolding of nature itself, or the intelligibility of nature, as Spinoza puts the matter. But Kauffman wants to go beyond the traditional scientific belief that the universe is governed by laws and broaden the sense of God from the creativity in nature to all of nature. All the unfolding of nature is then God as a fully natural god that does not reside in some supernatural realm. Kauffman wants to promote the idea of a natural god that is not far from an old idea of God *in* nature, an imminent god that is found in the unfolding of nature. This is his idea of a new science and a new worldview that includes a god with which we can live our lives forward into mystery. This new worldview "holds the promise of enriching us all as we discover, and choose, what we wish to hold sacred."[26]

Aesthetics and Philosophy

In the *Dialectic of Enlightenment* Theodore W. Adorno, of critical theory fame (see Chapter 13), gives aesthetic experience a privileged position regarding other forms of knowledge. The conceptual objectification of natural processes results in man's domination over external nature, as well as over his inner nature and social world. The idea of a nonconceptual approach to nature allows for freedom and social emancipation only if its members are able to encounter themselves and others in a noncoercive fashion where they relate to nature with a readiness for communicative surrender rather than seeking technical control. A society free from the repression of individual instincts and social power can value things not as objects for manipulative intervention but as counterparts to sensory experiences. Art represents an artificial form of such a civilizing approach to the world of nature as it is a unique type of experience through which the individual can acquire his or her substantiality without coming under the conceptual scheme of instrumental control.[27] According to Adorno,

> [i]f the work of art is today able to represent the only model of an experience in which, as in aesthetic perception, sensible impressions are no longer filtered through instrumental conceptual schemas, and if the emancipation of society is tied to the presupposition of a nondominating appropriation of the natural environment, then only the work of art is still able to represent in undiminished form the normative claim of social freedom. That is, so long as the compulsion toward the domination of nature is extended into the dominating order of social life, only artistic activity, since it represents an alternative to the prevailing practice of self-preservation, promises in the "idea of the redemption of historically repressed nature" the possible future of an emancipation from civilizing domination.[28]

Adorno makes the question of why art matters his central question. The analytical approach to aesthetics is dominated by the paradigm of scientific knowledge, where more and more such knowledge replaces mythological and metaphysical accounts of natural phenomena. Science is bound to the conditions of control-oriented action as all types of scientific knowledge, regardless of the methodological peculiarities, is aimed at control and domination. The whole of science, according to Adorno, is an instrument of technical or social control.[29] Aesthetics, however, should be concerned with finding ways to articulate and express our relations to ourselves and the world in ever-new ways that differ from objective scientific causal accounts.[30] The value of modernist art, for example, lies in its opposition to forms of artistic expression that support the status quo by "providing reassuring emotional experiences that reconcile people to unjust and inhumane situations to which they should not be reconciled."[31]

The problem with the aesthetic perspective, as Kant insisted some time ago, is that it is based on a noncognitive subjective relationship with the world and so inherently lacks objective determinacy: "Because the content of art cannot be wholly conveyed in the discursive terms which are the condition of something being conscious of itself, it is a reminder to disciplines which are essentially discursive that they may fail to articulate certain dimensions of experience." What philosophy has to explicate is that what art conveys to people is not reducible to what can be said about what it conveys.[32]

Adorno's focus on the beauty of nature stems from his awareness of the significance of art in modernity must reside in a noncognitive relationship of the subject to the world, and this difference must depend on changes in the relationship between subject and object that are not explained by natural causality.[33] Nature as an object of aesthetic experience seems to be able to say something to us without our being able to precisely way what that something is. Natural beauty offers a model, according to Adorno, of a relationship to things where we do not seek to objectify and appropriate them and allows them to "speak" to us by making us aware of things we may have repressed. Nature is more and more open to abuses characteristic of the modern period once it ceases to be sacred. This generates a different kind of apprehension of nature that he describes as follows:[34]

> The nature that is "given its voice" in modern art is not, then, nature as a "romantically" conceived unsullied state of past innocence, but rather what is repressed, both in human beings and in the environment, by forms which no longer allow certain things to speak.[35] The promise of the beauty of nature which art is to honor is not a realization of something concrete, but rather the sustaining of a relationship to things that can make sense of them in a way which is otherwise increasingly lacking in the secular world. Whereas cognitive relationships to things specify aspects of them that remain identical, thus enabling them to be better manipulated, aesthetic relationships rely precisely on things being able to become manifest in ways that do not depend on them being conceptually determinable. The idea of our not "being able to say what it is" means that the beauty of nature's ways is echoed in art's resistance to conceptual determination, and to commodification.[36]

In a world where more and more of nature is explained and controlled, Adorno thinks that art must be able to give a voice to what falls outside of those forms of explanation and control.[37] The nature explored by the modern physical sciences is often attached to a metaphysics, which denies a "temporal quality" to reality, which leads to a neglect of the qualitative aspects of nature. The idea of doing damage to nature is unlikely to gain much support in this worldview, leading to a counter that there is something to be damaged that is deeply connected to essential aspects of human existence that is based on the experience of natural beauty. The relationship is thus dialectical in that the objectification of nature in modern science produces a new subjective dimension that rather than seeing nature as a threat to human existence sees nature as being threatened.[38] As Adorno goes on to say,

> [t]he pre-modern relationship to natural beauty was, in one sense of the word, essentially an "objective" one, insofar as natural beauty was generally seen as part of the order of God's creation. As secularization gets underway, this idea of an objective order gives way to the sense that beauty in nature has to do with feelings of the subject. That change, as Hume and Kant suggest, leads to the problem of how subjective feeling has more than individual significance . . . The attempt to reconcile the subjective and the objective will eventually result in Hegel's argument

that appreciation of nature is in fact mediated by the beauty which is a product of spirit. People only appreciate natural landscapes when they become an object of artistic representation in their own right, rather than the scene for human action or the repository of religious symbols.[39]

The philosophical significance of art for Adorno lies in its offering a way of relating to the world that can easily be lost if the world is dominated by economic and technical imperatives. In the very act of labor humans learn to overcome the ever-present threat of nature by forcing its sensory manifold into a conceptual schema that provides them with a surveyable and controllable world. Men distance themselves from nature in their thinking in order to imaginatively present it to themselves but only in order to determine how it is to be dominated. Under the guiding perspective of social self-preservation, the natural environment is objectified, and with the goal of augmenting social power, it is gradually developed.[40]

Art can sustain and create meaningful relations of things in the face of growing disenchantment with the world of the kind that are present in everyday life. But these relations become increasingly neglected when the dominant aim of a society becomes control and exploitation of nature and the associated commodification of the objective world. Art creates a context of meaning that draws on the most basic experiences of being in the world such as when we are gripped by a natural scene of great beauty or falling in love. These experiences have become lost, neglected, repressed, or commodified in many areas of modern society and are in need of being articulated or expressed.[41] Adorno believes that

> [t]he failure to give definitive answers to aesthetic questions points, then, to kinds of experience and to aspects of the world without which art would not "speak." These can be illuminated by conceptual analysis but not replaced by it. Just as natural beauty speaks without us being able to translate it into discursivity, works of art speak by making sense of things, without us finally being able to specify their meaning in semantic terms. That is why art can also, for Adorno, be a repository of hope. Hope resides not in what we know and control, but in the sense that the world may yet offer something beyond what we know and control. Such hope can be generated by an experience in nature, or by a profound aesthetic experience.[42]

Art, which provides us with experiences that go beyond the solely cognitive, is so important in that a culture that increasingly functions only on the basis of a reality that can be "scientifically proved" distorts the human world. In such a culture, rational appraisal is reduced to various forms of quantification, according to Adorno, and the justified esteem that accrues to well-warranted science can be transferred to issues where it has no place. The fact/value distinction, for example, "is regularly invoked in order to consign anything which cannot be quantified to the realm of the merely subjective, so cutting off debate about essential social, cultural, and political matters, even though that distinction is more and more called into question by philosophical reflection."[43] As he says,

> [t]he idea that taste is "just subjective," and so outside the sphere of social legitimation, is contradicted almost everywhere by the fact that people get so agitated about issues of taste: just read the comments by readers in newspapers about new architectural plans, for example. Either we see such readers as just a locus of "will to power," seeking to assert themselves against the other by having their subjective preference approved, or we realize that they are part of a culture of judgment which, for all its problems, can result in something socially valuable. If this were not the case, why would people be so concerned to argue for their assessment, rather than simply bathing in solipsistic self-righteousness, or assuming that such matters are "merely subjective"?[44]

The lack of any real dialogue between those who are involved in the reductive naturalist end of philosophy and those involved in the humanities in a manifestation of the deeper connection between reductive directions in philosophy and dangerous social trends that attempt to reduce issues of cultural and social justice to issues of economic management and technological control. The irrational rejection of good science in the United States is a philosophical tension where "metaphysical faith in natural science as the only source of warrantable truth helps to create the space of arbitrary rejection of precisely the science which those who have such faith argue for so emphatically. While abstraction and objectification are essential to scientific progress, making them the basis of the understanding of all forms of relationship to the world adds to the social alienation that results from the dissonances between scientific and social and political developments in modernity." Thus, Adorno insists that philosophy must pay more attention to the truth of expressive forms of sense-making.[45]

Metaphysics, as it was understood in the Western philosophical tradition since the Greeks, has become modern natural science. The analysis and explanation of what there is that was traditionally sought by philosophy have been usurped by experimental science that has had unparalleled success in achieving an understanding of what there is in the world.[46] Natural science is better at telling us what kinds of things there are in the world than is analytical metaphysics and has enormous effects on what we do in the world that is not true of contemporary metaphysics.[47]

> [t]he real issue here is, then, once again, how one thinks about meaning. What is in question is the nature of philosophical responses to Max Weber's idea of the disenchantment of the world in modernity, hence the divergences over questions of meaning between, on the one hand,

narrow semantic and realist approaches which try to develop theories which mimic those in the sciences while doing no empirical research and, on the other, approaches, like Adorno's, that have a much wider sense of what it is for something to mean something . . . The Adornian question is how one responds to what is lost and gained, from disenchantment.[48]

Adorno is aware that the modern world is capable of radical destruction of meaning in ways that were not possible prior to modernity. The culture industry relentlessly promotes the saleable over the aesthetically significant, which leads to ecological devastation and a rapacious capitalism.[49] The commodity form has effects on the nature and content of artistic production and undermines individual discrimination by producing ideological norms of judgment and enjoyment that determine whether a cultural product becomes a successful commodity and thence part of the wider culture.[50] With regard to nature and ecology he says that

[t]he ecological crisis was not a theme for natural science until the crisis was already massively advanced. The realization of the threat posed to civilized life on earth is not necessarily most effectively communicated by scientific or philosophical theories, even though such theories must play a role in the change of awareness required . . . It is by taking account of "the really existing alienation between subject and object" in the form of an artistic response that "restores something like the ability to see nature." Art should involve the "dismantling of the conventional, the dismantling of everything which, so to speak, is interposed between the thing itself and consciousness."[51]

The core of Adorno's approach to meaning is the need to transcend given states of the world. The future philosophical significance of Adorno, according to Andres Bowie, will depend on the extent to which his work on the aesthetic dimension can inform the growing awareness in contemporary philosophy that it is too exclusively focused on semantic and cognitive considerations that may obscure our understandings of meanings that can both motivate and sustain lives but at the same time inhibit, distort, and destroy them.[52] The ever-expanding domain of explanatory science, the global commodity exchange, and modern technology obstructs the ability of the subject to see through these circumstances and determine the right course of action to take in relations to issues that arise in modern society.[53] He goes on to say that

[t]his is between the appeal to kinds of transcendence that are a source of the meanings that motivate human lives, on the one hand, and the idea that the very idea of transcendence is mere illusion that is invalidated by the fact of disenchantment of nature, on the other.[54]

Adorno thus gives aesthetics the leading role in the construction of a critical theory as art does two things that are important for critical theory: (1) it is the representation of a kind of reason that avoids the constrictions of instrumental rationality in taking up the mimetic capacity of aesthetic experience, and (2) it is the cognitive medium through which substantive insights that provide information about the social situation can be gained without succumbing to instrumental reason.[55] Critical theory is joined to the logic of art, as the cognitive capacity of the work of art is considered to be higher than that of theoretical reflection.[56]

Re-Enchantment of the World

Humanity is faced with numerous challenges such as global warming and terrorism and unless these are dealt with successfully human beings will be transformed into *inhuman* beings as billions of people experience shortages and famines. We must declare an "age of less," overcome excessive consumption, and focus on qualitative growth that does not rest on an "ever more" but upon an "ever better" and involves a better distribution of resources between and within nations. We must become more spiritual and more responsible even as we seem to be more brutish and irresponsible.[57] Politics must become capable of promoting an industrial economy of spirit by providing economic initiative with a framework of social rules and public investment that raises the level of individual and collective intelligence.[58] The "life of the spirit" has been subjected to the imperatives of a market economy and to the imperatives of technological developments linked to the fastest-possible return on investment for shareholders. But capitalism will not survive unless it can awaken a new spirit of capitalism to overcome the carelessness that leads to a destruction of society.[59] According to Bernard Stiegler, the director of the Institute of Research and Development at the Georges Pompidou Center in Paris and an associated professor at Goldsmith College at the University of London,

> [i]t is in such a context that the question of *care* can be posed in a new and political way, one not confined to the fields of medicine and ethics: *the question of care must return to the heart of political economy*, and with it, clearly, a new cultural, educational, scientific, and industrial politics capable of *taking care of the world*. This is why we propose an axiom of our reflections and our actions that—as the primary meaning of the verb "economize tells" us, and as each of us knows deep down— *to economize means first of all and before all else to take care.*[60]

Even those people who fight the consumerist economy are dependent on it even though we know it cannot last. An organization of innovation founded on disposability, carelessness, waste, and blindness is in contradiction with the future. Because we know this it is possible to conceive of a new industrial economy that is founded upon care that requires thought as well as radically new political, economic, and industrial propositions. This change does not involve the rejection of technical possibilities but, rather, aims to socialize these possibilities and put them in the service of society instead of in the service of a destructive system founded on disposability. The evolution of science and technology needs to be socialized in a manner that allows them to be directed toward taking care of the world and its future.[61]

Because of globalization, people all over the world are deprived of the possibility of deciding upon their style of living but, rather, are a slave of the system in sort of a Hegelian master/slave dialectic. We reproduce a way of life inherited from our family and relatives and reinforced by the culture in which we are raised. The process of individuation is destroyed as producers fade into the machine and become pure labor power and the consumer has become a mode of employment and becomes only a buying power. Capitalism has liquidated all forms of knowledge to produce entropy and distaste, where the cognitive industries place knowledge in the exclusive service of the economy and the culture industries have transformed arts and letters into entertainment.[62]

Despite recent trends toward individualism in American society, both producers and consumers have become disindividuated and have been subjected, according to Stiegler, to the loss of individuation. This is why a "re-enchantment" of the world has become necessary. What Stiegler calls hyperindustrialized capitalism has reached its limits, and we need a jump start that will countervail the "drop in the value of spirit." What is needed is a new *spirit of enterprise* that must not be a "rotten spirit" nor a "debilitated spirit" nor even a "servile spirit," but that involves a *refounding of the human enterprise in general*. This refounding must include an association of public power with private economic power to transform individuation with an eye to the long term. Public politics must be headed by a new form of public strength to open up a future for humankind.[63]

Public power is in charge of forging the long-term vision for a society that is seriously lacking when it comes to the economic actors in a capitalistic system. The stake of all public power is to counter *tendencies toward dissociation*, which can lead to incivility, to war, and even to barbarism. Industrial exploitation tends to reproduce dissociated milieus that are at the root of industrialization such as the division of labor and the opposition between producers and consumers.[64] The individual does not exist as a singularity but instead participates in a collective individuation, where individuals find themselves associated with others as a social being rather than as a singular atom bumping up against others in a competitive system.[65]

The evolution of neoliberalism constitutes "an abandonment of public responsibility for directing and incentivizing the social future to the prescriptions of the market alone, which is to say, in short, the renouncement of all political ambition in favor of an exclusively economic logic of development."[66] Thus, we live in an age of what Stiegler calls hyperindustrial capitalism, where knowledge has been adapted to the imperatives of production and consumption and in the process has become intrinsically debilitated. But if this kind of capitalism, according to Stiegler, does not invent a new model of development that overcomes dissociation that is inherent in a consumption society in favor of a society of association, it will eventually destroy itself as sociation.[67]

Contemporary society has seen the growth of information because of the development of digital technologies, but this growth has been at the determent of true knowledge; thus, ignorance has grown in the society at large rather than knowledge. Information is not transformed into knowledge but into an accumulation of hard data that are largely quantitative in nature. The crisis of knowledge this produces involves the fact that knowledge no longer speaks to being but instead has become a kind of merchandise that is freely distributed but is yet adulterated, having lost its power of individuation. This crisis combined with a new instrumentality of the intellect that is the result of the techno-scientific becoming of science consists more of an extension of ignorance rather than a development of societies of knowledge.[68]

The future of capitalism depends upon a growth of intelligence and knowledge, as well as an improvement of *the life of the spirit for the entire population of the world*. Contemporary capitalism produces nothing but a regression of mental, moral, intellectual, and aesthetic life, all of which are domains of the spirit. Faced with this kind of spiritual misery, which has been characterized as a disenchantment of the world, "man feels that he is irreducibly in need of spirit," but the danger of situating spirit exclusively on the side of religion and hoping for salvation of the soul in an afterlife is to be avoided. The life of spirit cannot be entirely reduced to a religious world; on the contrary, the life of spirit plays itself out first and foremost in daily work, in the relations between individuals, and in the instruments of communication including television, mobile phones, the Internet, and "all the cultural and cognitive information and communication technologies that are being deployed today."[69] Stiegler thinks that

> [i]t is clear that everyone's habitual behaviors will soon have to change profoundly, and that such a change will presuppose a formation and enhanced acuity of individual and collective intelligence and spirit. The question of a new spirit of capitalism is thus raised, and of a new industrial age, of an industrial *renaissance* that is capable of constituting a new social organization resting upon an implementation of cognitive and cultural technologies in the service of an elevation in the standard of social, that is, spiritual life. The standard of social life is not measured by the quantity of protein consumed—which, consumed in excess, leads without fail to physiological accidents, but also, as a hyperconsumptive behavior, to processes of depression and demotivation, and finally, to the congestion of industrial society. The elevation of the standard of living is in the first place that of the life of its spirit.[70]

Capitalism has lost its spirit and arouses nothing but mistrust, anxiety, and demotivation. It has become irrational. The reality of the information and knowledge society is "that of a society in which individuals from all walks of life spend more and more time in front of screens of their devices" such as television screens, computer screens, iPad screens, iPhone screens, and what-not. The technologies of reasoning, information, memory, and creation that are implemented by the cognitive and cultural industries will have to become technologies of a new spirit of capitalism.[71]

A Scientific Basis for Spirituality

In a book titled *Measuring the Immeasurable: The Scientific Case for Spirituality*, some of the most prominent authorities on what is called the new frontier, where science and spirit intersect present their ideas and scientific findings to bolster the case for a spiritual approach to reality. There is no editor or editors of this book, but in the introduction Tami Simon, who is not listed as one of the contributing authors, states that science and spirituality have never had an easy relationship and that their views on the nature of reality have often clashed. As the scientific understanding of the world has grown, this clash has become deeper. Science has in some sense discredited spirituality as a reality in our world and rendered it obsolete and unnecessary.[72] As stated by Simon,

> [w]e need scientific evidence of the results of spiritual practice so that experts in such fields as education, healthcare and medicine, psychology and psychiatry, can seriously consider the inclusion and integration of spiritual approaches in their work . . . Additionally, many people already on a spiritual path may draw strength and validation from having subjective experience confirmed by the objective tools of science. For some people, the language of science is the prevailing authority of our time and if there are scientific studies that confirm and validate spiritual experiences, this may provide important support and encouragement to some spiritual practitioners.[73]

The first author in this book, Peter Russell, whose work attempts to integrate Eastern and Western understandings of the mind, blames Descartes again for the dualism of mind and matter. Descartes split the cosmos into two realms: (1) the world of time, space, and matter; things that could be physically measured and (2) the realm of thought, consciousness, and spirit. Russell claims that Descartes wanted to avoid coming into conflict with the Catholic Church, which for centuries had been the principal arbiter of truth. Thus, his "natural philosophy" would focus on the world of matter and leave the world of spirit to the church.[74]

Thus, for some 350 years Western science has ignored the world of conscious experience because (1) the mind cannot be measured and weighed the way matter can, (2) science has sought to discover universal and objective truths about nature that are independent of an observer's state of mind and so have largely avoided subjective considerations, and (3) there was no need to explore the working of the mind as the universe could be explained without having to consider the troublesome subject of consciousness.[75] Russell goes on to state,

> So successful has this materialistic science been, it appears to have triumphed over religion. Astronomers have looked out into deep space, to the edges of the known universe; cosmologists have looked back into "deep time," to the beginning of creation; and physicists have looked down into the "deep structure" of matter, to the fundamental constituents of the cosmos. From quarks to quasars, they find no evidence of God. Nor do they find any need for God. The universe seems to work perfectly well without any divine assistance. In doing away with the notion of some almighty supernatural being, Western science would appear to have done away with religion, and hence with spirituality.[76]

Neuroscientific research seems to conclude that spiritual experience itself can be explained in terms of brain function. However, Russell claims that there is nothing surprising about these findings as it is a fundamental assumption of the neurosciences that brain activity and conscious experience is closely correlated. Thus, we should expect that changes in consciousness that involve a spiritual experience such as a feeling of deep serenity would show corresponding changes in the brain. This does not mean, however, that these spiritual experiences can simply be reduced to brain activity. Experience moves us and the "most significant aspect of the current scientific studies of meditation and spiritual experience is not that they can explain these experiences in terms of brain function, but that they are corroborating the claims of many spiritual teachings,"[77]

The scientific knowledge we have acquired over the centuries has led to a plethora of technologies that have given us the ability to control and manipulate many aspects of our world. The goal of this activity has been to free ourselves from suffering that is unnecessary and to increase our well-being in the world. While this material approach to reality has been successful in many ways, it has not achieved all that humankind has hoped for in this world as despite our abundant luxuries and freedoms. Russell sees little evidence that people are any happier than they were several decades ago and states that "our incessant chasing of worldly satisfactions has brought us to the brink of global catastrophe."[78]

Spiritual teachings also seek to liberate people from suffering and promote well-being, but they take an inward path and seek to understand how our minds become trapped in dysfunctional patterns. These teachings have developed various techniques and practices over the years, what Russell calls spiritual technologies, that can free us from inner causes of suffering and bring us deep relief. Thus, we must recover our respect for spirituality and acknowledge its critical value for the world today.[79]

Larry Dossey, a physician of internal medicine and former chief of staff of Medical City Dallas Hospital, presents evidence that he claims suggests that compassion and empathy are correlated with positive health outcomes and that as a consequence, "they should not be regarded as optional niceties in medical care, but as fundamental factors promoting recovery from any illness."[80] Compassion is good both for the person experiencing it and for the person to whom it is directed. It conveys a sense of connectedness with the person in need and refutes those who think that pain and illness should be endured with a stiff upper lip, that is, without complaint or whimper.[81]

Other authors argue that emotions are like a bridge linking both the material and immaterial realms. They are both physical and psychological in nature, linking the brain to the body in one vast communications network that coordinates the entire body–mind. Emotions determine which memories are conscious or not as they decide what becomes a recollection that rises to the surface or whether that memory becomes deeply buried in the unconscious where it can affect perceptions, decisions, behavior, and even health. Health and well-being involve not just the physical body but the mental, emotional, and spiritual self as well; human experiences that need to be taken into account in treating illness as a state of well-being can change depending on one's emotional state.[82]

Dan Siegel, a graduate of Harvard Medical School, director of the Mindsight Institute, and co-director of the UCLA Mindful Awareness Research Center, believes that research on some dimensions of mindful awareness practices shows that the body's functioning is greatly enhanced in that healing, immune response, stress reactivity, and a general sense of physical well-being are improved with mindfulness. By mindfulness he means "the awareness that emerges through paying attention on purpose, in the present moment, and nonjudgmentally to the unfolding of experience moment by moment." Mindful awareness is a human capacity not limited to one religious or contemplative practice but can be practiced by and made available to the full spectrum of our human family. Mindfulness enables us to not only refine our awareness of the present moment; it also helps the mind to know itself as mindful awareness involves awareness of awareness.[83]

Robert A. Emmons, a professor of psychology at the University of California, Davis, focuses on gratitude as a dimension of spirituality that many hold to be of extreme importance. Gratitude in a worldly sense is the feeling that one experiences in interpersonal exchanges when somebody acknowledges receiving a valuable benefit from another. Such feelings come from two stages of information processing: "(1) an affirmation of goodness or 'good things' in one's life, and (2) the recognition that the sources of this goodness lie at least partially outside of the self. In gratitude, we humbly acknowledge the countless ways in which we have been and are supported and sustained by the benevolence of others."[84] Emmons believes that there is a fundamental spiritual quality to gratitude that transcends religious traditions:

> in this attitude people recognize that they are connected to each other in a mysterious and miraculous way that is not fully determined by physical forces, but is part of a wider, or transcendental context. The spiritual core of gratefulness is essential if gratitude is to be not simply a tool

for narcissistic self-improvement. True gratefulness rejoices in the other. Is has as its ultimate goal reflecting back the goodness that one has received by creatively seeking opportunities for giving. The motivation for doing so resides in the grateful appreciation that one has lived by the grace of others. In this sense, the spirituality of gratitude is opposed to a self-serving belief that one deserves or is entitled to the blessings that he or she enjoys. Knowing the grace by which one lives is itself a profound spiritual realization.[85]

According to Emmons, gratitude brings benefits into the lives of those who are grateful. Research has shown that health benefits can accrue from grateful thinking. Rather than focusing on complaints, people who reflect on those aspects of their lives for which they are grateful can lead to higher levels of a pleasant effect.[86] People who are grateful are also more loving, forgiving, joyful, and enthusiastic. They are also rated by others to be more helpful, more outgoing, more optimistic, and more trustworthy.[87] Gratitude depends on receiving things that are not expected and are not earned or receiving more than we believe we deserve. This kind of awareness is both humbling and elevating.[88] Gratitude helps people feel closer and more connected to others. It takes us outside ourselves and helps us to see that we are part of a larger network of sustaining and mutually reciprocal relationships.[89] Grateful people draw upon the memories they have of being the recipients of benevolence themselves than a positive feeling about themselves and others.[90]

When we can be connected to our own purpose and the community around us, as well as our spiritual wisdom, say two other authors who focus on the role of nature in restoring health, we are able to live and act with authenticity in all our relations.[91] In an article titled "Nature and Spirit," Sara L. Warber and Kathrine N. Irvine claim that nature helps restore individuals to their authentic self, which helps them to think clearly, take in new information, and to function more effectively.[92] Research shows that people have a preference for natural settings, which can positively influence stress levels as well as one's emotional well-being.[93] Participants in outdoor programs report feelings of wholeness and being connected to a larger reality as well as being more in touch with what is really important to them.[94] Interaction with nature may no longer be a luxury but, rather, a vital and necessary part of being whole persons.[95] According to the authors,

[a]s one experiences nature through these multiple sensory modalities, the body may change its rhythm, modulating the cascades of neurotransmitters or immune system warriors in such a way that health is enhanced. Additionally, these interactions may touch us at a deeper level that some call the spirit, inviting us to realign our actions with what is truly important to us. Cultural wisdom, history, theory, and

research can provide insight into the potentially profound impact natural settings can have on these multiple levels of well-being.[96]

Changing our inner environment means learning how to change our thoughts, beliefs systems, and attitudes and this change is reflected back to us in the outer environment in which we live, states Sandra Ingerman, the author of several books on spirituality known for bridging ancient cross-cultural healing methods into our modern culture. In order to create the inner reality of a clean environment, she says, we must be able to see the beauty in all things we encounter and live in a state of appreciation and gratefulness.[97] It is who we become that changes the world, she claims; that we can change the environment as we change ourselves. All spiritual traditions teach us that things manifest themselves on a spiritual level before they affect the physical environment, thus making it important to understand that we can "create change on the planet by incorporating spiritual practices into our lives."[98]

In an article titled "Revealing the Wizard" Bruce Lipton, who is an internationally recognized authority on bridging science and spirit, argues that advances in cell biology and biophysics are discovering that the mind and spirit are creative forces that control the character of our lives.[99] Genetic determinism holds that life's programs are encoded in the genes, and thus, we do not have much control over the path our life takes. But Epigenetic science has found that we are not "victims" but, rather, "masters" over our genes. Life is controlled by something above the genes, and that something provides a gateway to understanding our proper role as participatory creators in the way in which our life unfolds.[100]

Consciousness is often referred to as that state of being awake and aware of things that are going on around a person. Self-consciousness refers to a state in which one is both a participant and an observer of life that unfolds.[101] The latter enables us to be co-creators of our life and not merely responders to stimuli from the environment.[102] The self-conscious mind expresses free-will while the subconscious expresses prelearned habits. Once a behavior pattern such as walking or driving a car is learned, the subconscious mind can carry out these rather complex functions without paying much, if any, attention to them. The role of the subconscious mind is to control every behavior that is not attended to by the conscious mind.[103]

Cognitive neuroscientists have discovered that the subconscious mind is responsible for 95 to 99 percent of our cognitive activity and therefore is controlling almost all of our decisions, actions, emotions, and behaviors.[104] The subconscious mind is therefore running the show and often undermines the desires of the conscious mind to progress and live a better life.[105] These subconscious programs are derived from observing our parents, siblings, teachers, religious leaders, and others in our local community, and many of these perceptions are limiting and self-sabotaging beliefs.[106] If we can keep our conscious mind from wandering into the past or future and keep it focused on the present, we can take control of our mind and use empowering thoughts that can lead to our desired aspirations.[107]

There are several what William Tiller, a fellow to the Academy for the Advancement of Science and professor emeritus of Stanford University's Department of Material Science, calls categories of phenomena and information, where we need to attain reliable understanding so as to enhance one's life journey. These include (1) things of the physical, (2) things of the psyche, (3) things of the emotion, (4) things of the mind, and (5) things of the spirit.[108] Descartes realized that in order to gain knowledge of our outer world a clear separation between mind and physical matter or between the soul and body was needed. Over time it became an *unstated assumption* of physics that consciousness was not a significant experimental variable. The acceptance of this assumption resulted in establishment science becoming almost totality reductionistic and materialistic.[109]

The important question for Charles Tart, a professor emeritus of psychology at the University of California, Davis, and a senior research fellow at the Institute of Noetic Sciences, is whether consciousness has properties of its own or is it simply an epiphenomenon of the physical brain and nervous system?[110] Because of the dominance of behavioristic/cognitive and psychoanalytical approaches humans are seen as nothing but a combination of robots and instinctively driven animals whose instincts for destructive behavior are held in check by civilization.[111] Empirical data show that consciousness is not reducible to a physical variable but must be investigated as a factor in its own right with real properties.[112] Thus, to automatically reject such transforming experiences as love, unity, and compassion as having no scientific basis is fallacious.[113]

More and more people are coming to believe that spiritual health is an integral part of their general and physical well-being and are asking health care providers to include a greater emphasis on the spiritual element in the treatment of illness. Thus, there is a necessity to rely on research, according to Andrew Newberg, an associate professor in the Department of Radiology and Psychiatry at the Hospital of the University of Pennsylvania and a staff physician in nuclear medicine, to fully understand the relationship among spirituality, the brain, and health.[114]

According to Newberg, the most important measures of spiritual phenomena are subjective in nature and usually described by people in terms of various cognitive, behavioral, and emotional parameters. There are many difficulties with this approach as people have many different kinds of spiritual experiences that are not comparable. It is very difficult to capture spiritual experiences let alone measure them in some fashion. How can one be sure that researchers are indeed measuring what they claim to be measuring? An additional difficulty is generalizing from one study to another when there are so many different approaches to spiritual phenomena. Given these problems it is important to supplement subjective measure with more objective measures such as blood pressure, heart rate, and hormone and immune functions. Newberg thinks it is important to link these kinds of physiological changes to health-related changes. For example, if it could be shown that meditation changes the immune system, it would be helpful to know if that translated into beneficial health outcomes such as reduced risk of getting the flu or maybe even cancer.[115]

Newberg goes on to discuss both positive and negative effects of religion on health and mentions the problem of discussing religion in a health care setting where some people fear "that it gives health care workers the opportunity to impose personal religious beliefs on others and that necessary medical interventions may be replaced by religious interventions . . . Moreover there is considerable debate over the way in which religion should be integrated with health care and who should be responsible, especially when health care providers are agnostic or atheist."[116] For these reasons it seems best to separate religion and spirituality and approach spirituality on a strictly secular basis.[117]

He mentions several secular practices, such as meditation, which is widely used as a therapeutic technique to deal with physical ailments, and claims that many of what he calls preliminary studies suggest that meditation may have a number of health benefits. However, given that there are many types of meditation it is not clear which forms may be beneficial and what specific aspect of meditation are providing the benefits. Yoga is also widely used for exercise and therapeutic benefits, but Newberg claims it is based on a set of theories that are not yet scientifically proven. In conclusion Newberg states that the relationship between spirituality and health is complicated but that the existing paradigm of medicine could be drastically changed with a new, more highly integrated way of healing.[118]

Finally, meditation as a spiritual practice is the focus of an article by Joan Hageman, the chair of research with PSYmore Research Institute in Tampa, Florida. Meditation has been defined as an intentional self-regulation of one's attention to be used for self-inquiry or self-reflection. It may involve self-realization or the discovery of some kind of ultimate truth.[119] According to Deane H. Shapiro, whom she cites in the article, there are three primary categories of attentional strategies: (1) mindfulness, (2) concentrative, and (3) integrated. Another way of classifying meditative practice is into the two basic categories of passive and active.[120] And according to John L. Craven, whom she also references, meditation can be experienced as (1) an altered state of awareness, (2) concentration, (3) maintenance, (4) relaxation, and (5) suspension of logical thought processes.[121] Meditation may be practiced in silence when sitting or walking or other exercises, or it may involve certain breathing techniques, prescribed behaviors, bodily postures, and/or other specific exercises that are focused on promoting awareness, harmony, balance, and/or enlightenment.[122] Hageman goes on to say that

> [i]n this author's opinion, higher states of consciousness that may be achieved through a meditative practice offer the potential for the

individual to open the self to a connection with the divine no matter how the individual might his or her own sense of the divine and reality. Meditation is not a "cure-all," but it does offer another way to enhance one's well-being physically, mentally, and spiritually.[123]

The human experience of consciousness is the quality of mind. It includes self-awareness, your relationships to your environment, the people in your life, and your worldview or model of reality. Simply put, your consciousness determines how you experience the world. Your consciousness, or your perception of reality, is created by the interactions of your subjective and objective lives. Your subjective life is what exists in your inner experience; your objective life is what's "out there" in the world. The convergence of your self-identity and your perceptions of the world gives rise to your worldview—and thus how you relate to, mediate, and ascribe meaning to both these inner and outer worlds.[124]

This attempt to provide a scientific basis for spirituality by linking spiritual practices to positive health outcomes is a noble and important effort that might make the whole concept of spirituality acceptable for many people. In this scientific and technological world, the language of science is an authoritative language, and if some illusive concept like spirituality can be subjected to scientific research, this should help the whole idea gain some measure of credibility. However, these studies that show some kind of positive relation between spiritual practices and health outcomes have problems, not the least of which is that spirituality is a philosophical concept and to operationalize it in the manner done in these studies does not do justice to the richness of the concept and its applicability to human beings. The scientific approach to spirituality has little to say about establishing connections between humans and humans with nature, which is what seems to be lacking in today's world.

The Sociological Imagination

In the ordinary course of their lives, says C. Wright Mills, a former professor of sociology at Columbia University, people do not usually think of historical change or institutional contradictions when dealing with the troubles they have to endure. They remain unaware of the connection between the path world history is taking and the pattern of their own existence. They ordinarily are not able to make a connection between human and society, biography and history, and self and world. After some two centuries of development, capitalism has become only one way of making society into an industrial apparatus as alternative ways of organizing society have grown. Even formal democracy, at least at the time this book was written, is restricted to a relativity small portion of humankind as alternative political systems have appeared. Ancient ways of living have disappeared in the underdeveloped world, and vague expectations have become urgent demands. These kinds of historical changes outpace the ability of people to keep their orientation in line with cherished values. It is no wonder that average people feel that they cannot cope with this kind of a changing world and thus turn inward to a private self in isolation from the world.[125]

What people need is a quality of mind that will help them understand what is going on in the world and what is happening to themselves in light of historical changes. This quality of mind, what Mills calls the sociological imagination, enables people to understand the larger historical context in terms of its meaning for themselves and enables them to take into account how individuals who are wrapped up in their daily experience often develop a false consciousness related to their social positions. Within the framework of modern society, their individual psychologies are formulated; by such means, Mills says, their uneasiness is focused upon explicit troubles, and their indifference is transformed into involvement with public issues.[126]

There are several benefits from this kind of imagination, the first of which is that by locating themselves within a particular historical period, people can understand their own experience, gauge their own fate, know their own chances in life, and become aware of all the other people who share in their circumstances. By the very fact of living every individual contributes, however minutely, to the shaping of society in which they live even as they in turn are shaped by that society. The second benefit is that the sociological imagination enables people to grasp history and biography and how the two relate to each other within society. Recognition of this task and this promise is them mark of the classic social analyst. A social study that does not return to the problems of biology and history and their interactions within a society has not completed its intellectual journey. Those analysts who have been imaginatively aware of the promise of their work have consistently asked the following questions:[127]

1. What is the structure of this particular society as a whole?
2. Where does this society stand in human history?
3. What varieties of men and women now prevail in this society and in this period?[128]

These are the questions that Mills claims are raised by any mind that possesses sociological imagination. Such a mind has the capacity to shift from one perspective to another and the capacity to range from the most impersonal and remote transformations to the most intimate features of the human self and to see their relations. This is how people can grasp what is going on in the world and understand how they fit into the larger picture of historical change. Mills claims that the sociological imagination is the most fruitful form of self-consciousness and enables people to acquire a new way of thinking and by their reflection and sensibility realize the cultural meaning of the social sciences.[129]

According to Mills, the difference between "the personal troubles of milieu" and "the public works of social structure" is the most fruitful distinction that the sociological imagination involves. *Trouble* is a private matter and occurs when values that are cherished by the individual are felt to be threatened. *Issues*, on the other hand, have to do with matters that transcend local concerns and are public matters that occur when a value cherished by the public is felt to be threatened. An issue often involves a crisis in institutional arrangements and sometimes relates to what Marxists call "contradictions." As an example of such issues Mills treats unemployment, war, marriage, and the metropolis. These are structural issues and to solve them requires consideration of political and economic issues that affect innumerable milieu. To be able to trace linkages among a great variety of milieu and to be aware of the idea of social structure and to use it with sensibility is to possess the sociological imagination.[130]

When people do not feel any threat to their cherished values, they experience *well-being*, but when they do feel them to be threatened, they experienced a crisis either as a personal trouble or as a public issue. When all of their values seem to be threatened they most likely will feel panic. However, people can be unaware of a threat and experience *indifference*, or they may be aware of a threat but unaware that any cherished values are at stake in which case they experience *uneasiness* that, if it is total enough, can result in a deadly unspecified malaise. Mills believes that his time was characterized by uneasiness and indifference and that instead of explicit issues, there was a vague sense of uneasiness and a general feeling that all was not right. The values that were threatened nor whatever threatens them were not clear and much less formulated as problems of social science. Yet it was the uneasiness itself that was the trouble and the indifference that was the issue. The social scientist's foremost political and intellectual task, says Mills, is to make clear the elements of contemporary uneasiness and indifference. In this regard, Mills thinks that the chief danger in his time lie in the unruly forces of contemporary society itself, with its alienating methods of production, its enveloping techniques of political domination, its international anarchy—in a word, its pervasive transformations of the very "nature" of man and the conditions and aims of his life.[131]

The sociological imagination, he believes, is becoming the major common denominator of cultural life and its signal feature. This quality of mind goes far beyond the social sciences, but its acquisition by individuals and by the cultural community at large is often slow and fumbling. The sociological imagination is not merely a fashion but also a quality of mind "that seems most dramatically to promise an understanding of the intimate realities of ourselves in connection with larger social realities." It is not merely one quality of mind among others, but according to Mills "it is the quality whose wider and more adroit use offers the promise that all such sensibilities—and in fact, human reason itself—will come to play a greater role in human affairs."[132]

Esteem for science has long been assumed, but currently the technological ethos and the kind of engineering imagination associated with science rather than being experienced as hopeful and progressive are more likely to be seen as frightening and ambiguous. The human meaning and social role of science, its military and commercial use, and its political significance are undergoing reappraisal. Much that has recently passed for "science" is felt to be dubious metaphysics that no longer tries to picture reality as a whole or present a true outline of human destiny. Philosophers who deal with science often transform it into "scientism," making its experience to be identical with all of human experience and claiming that life's problems can only be solved by use of the scientific method.[133]

Mills states that because social science has not been adequate to the task, critics and novelists, dramatists and poets have been the major and often the only way that private troubles and public issues can be formulated. Art, however, cannot accomplish this task because it does not provide the intellectual clarity that can help people overcome their uneasiness and indifference. Thus, it is important for the social sciences to aid in the development of sociological imagination. The problems that are examined in classical social analysis are of direct relevance to urgent public issues and insistent human troubles, but there are many obstacles to be overcome not the least of which is the reluctance of many practitioners of social science to take up the challenge. What is known as sociology has become in recent years the center of reflection about social science. It has become the center for interest in methods, as well as general theory. Yet sociology has tended to move in one or more of three general directions, each of which is subject to distortion or to being run into the ground:[134]

1. Toward a theory of history where the materials of human history are forced into a trans-historical strait-jacket out of which issues prophetic views of the future.
2. Toward a systematic theory of "the nature of man and society" where history is altogether abandoned and the nature of man and society becomes an elaborate and arid formalism.
3. Toward empirical studies of contemporary social facts and problems where studies of contemporary fact can easily become a series of rather unrelated and insignificant facts of milieu.[135]

The promise of sociology may be understood in terms of these tendencies. There has been an amalgamation in sociology that embodies elements and aims of various Western societies, but this presents a danger that amidst such abundance sociologists will be in such a hurry to do research that they will lose this legacy. This tradition contains the best statements that can help the social sciences attain their full promise. Any social scientist that takes them into account will be richly rewarded, and mastery of them can be turned into new orientations for work in the social sciences.[136]

Social scientists cannot avoid making choices about values and having them appear in their work as a whole. Threats to values cannot be clearly formulated without acknowledging these values. This brings up important question like whether they are aware of the uses and values of their work, whether these are subject to their control, and whether they even care about controlling them. How they deal with these questions determines the answer to what Mills calls the final question, which is "whether in their work as social scientists they are (a) morally autonomous, (b) subject to the morality of other men, or (c) morally adrift." Mills believes social scientists must confront these fateful questions.[137]

The social scientist is not suddenly confronted with the need to choose values as he or she is already working on the basis of certain values. What is called moral judgment is a desire to generalize and make available for others the values that he or she has come to choose. Three overriding political ideals are inherent in the traditions of social science and involved in its intellectual promise. These are (1) the value of truth, (2) the value of the role of reason in human affairs, and (3) human freedom. Freedom and reason are critical to the civilization of the Western world, but in any given application they can lead to much disagreement. Social scientists have as one of their intellectual tasks the clarification of the ideals of freedom and reason.[138]

There are three political roles involved in this task. The first is that much of social science, and, in particular, sociology, contains the theme of the *philosopher-king*. The enthronement of reason means the enthronement of the "man of reason." This idea goes against the grain of democracy as it involves an aristocracy if it is based on talent rather than birth or wealth. The quality of politics depends very much on those who are engaged in it, and Mills says that if the philosopher were indeed king, he would be tempted to leave his kingdom, but on the other hand, when kings are without any "philosophy" they are unable to rule responsibly.[139]

The second role is to become an *advisor* to the king. This role need not become bureaucratized where social science becomes a functionally rational machine and the social scientists loses his moral autonomy and his substantive rationality and is merely used to refine the techniques of administrative control. But Mills thinks it is difficult to fulfill this role in such a way to retain moral and intellectual integrity. It is easy for consultants to imagine themselves philosophers and their clients enlightened rulers. Some consultants remain loyal to enlightened despots. Nonetheless, it is possible to perform this role well, but the third role is much less burdensome.[140]

This third role is where social scientists remain independent to do their own work and select their own problems, but their work is directed *at* kings as well as *to* "publics." In this role the social scientist can be imagined as a member of a self-controlled association, which we call the social sciences. This role involves acting upon the value of reason in assuming that man is free and that by his rational endeavors, he can influence the course of history. Some men, however, are freer than others and have access to decision makers and sources of power that make history. How large a role explicit decisions play in the making of history depends on the means of power that are available at any given time in any given society.[141]

There are some events in history that are beyond the control of human beings which Mills calls fate or "inevitability." These events have three characteristics: (1) they must be compact enough to be identifiable, (2) they must be powerful enough to have consequences, and (3) no one can be in a position to foresee these consequences and so to be held accountable for them. Fate, however, is not a universal fact and is not inherent in the nature or the nature of man. It is rather a feature of a historically specific kind of social structure. In Mills's time, there was a centralization of international, as well as national means of, history making. This centralization signals that men can now make history and are not necessarily in the grip of fate. But the ideologies that help men make history have declined and collapsed in Western societies. The intellectual and political communities have defaulted, and neither raise demands on the powerful for alternative policies nor set forth such alternatives before publics.[142]

Social scientists have the task of determining the limits of freedom and the limits of reason in history. By assuming the third role they do not see themselves as some autonomous being that is standing "outside society." Indeed, no one can adopt this position, and the important question is where one stands within society. The social scientist is not just an "ordinary man" who feels that he stands outside the major history-making decisions of his period. His task is to intellectually transcend the milieu in which he happens to live. By the very nature of his work he is aware of the social structure of society and the historical mechanics of its movement. He may not have access to the major power centers of society, but in a sense he can speak the truth to power by making those in power aware of the consequences of their decisions and the responsibility they have for those consequences.[143]

The aim of social scientists is to help individuals become self-educating and self-cultivating and in the process become free and rational individuals. They ought to combat all those forces that are destroying genuine publics and are creating a mass society. A democratic society is one in which individuals are transcendent and in which genuine publics rather than masses prevail. People in a mass society are not able to turn personal troubles into public issues; it is the political task of the social scientists to translate these troubles into public issues, and these public issues into their human meaning. Those that are vitally affected by any decision made in society should have an effective voice in that decision. The power to make decisions in society must be publicly legitimated and the makers of decisions must be held publicly accountable. This cannot be done unless free and rational individuals are dominant in society.[144]

Mills holds that the social structure of the United States in his time was not altogether democratic. He believed it was generally democratic mainly in form and in the rhetoric of expectation. But in substance and practice it was often nondemocratic and in many institutional areas it was clearly nondemocratic. He mentions corporations and the military machine as examples of centers of power that were not accountable to those whom their activities affect very seriously. How well the political role of the social scientist in enacted and how effectively were relevant to making these power centers accountable and the extent to which democracy prevails. The social sciences are a prime carrier of the role of reason in public affairs.[145]

Mills does not believe, however, that given the political structure currently in place, social scientists will become effective carriers of reason. Two characteristics must be present in parties, movements, and publics for this to happen: (1) within them ideas and alternatives of social life must be truly debated, and (2) they have a chance really to influence decisions of structural consequences. If such organizations existed we could be hopeful about the role of reason in public affairs. In the absence of these characteristics people lived in a society that was democratic mainly in its legal forms and its formal requirements. The absence of democratic parties and movements and publics does not mean, however that social scientists are off the hook, so to speak. They must continue to be one of the chief carriers of reason and ought to try make the educational institutions of which they are a part a framework in which the public might be liberated and their discussions encouraged and sustained.[146] Social scientists must encourage controversy and debate that is wide open and informed. They must

> help cultivate and sustain publics and individuals that are able to develop, to live with, and to act upon adequate definitions of personal and social realities. The role of reason requires only that the social scientist continue on with the work of social science and avoid contributing to the bureaucratization of reason and discourse. To know the intellectual and political role of the social sciences within the societies being studied, the social scientist must come to grips with his own view of the nature of historical and the place of free and reasonable men with society. He then finds out what he himself thinks of the values of freedom and reason which a critical part of the tradition and promise of social science.[147]

Mills does not think that social science will "save the world," but he sees nothing wrong with trying. By the phrase "save the world" he means the avoidance of war and the arrangement of human affairs to be consistent with the ideals of human freedom and reason. An appeal to the powerful people in society he holds to be utopian and relations with them are likely to be ones that they find useful for their purposes. But it is not utopian for even one social scientist to appeal to his or her colleagues to undertake a reconsideration of their collective role as social scientists.

Any social scientist who is aware of what he or she is about must confront the difference between what people are interested in and what is to people's interest.[148] The simple democratic view that we should focus only on *what men are interested in*, which to Mills means accepting the values that have been inculcated in people either accidently or deliberately by vested interests. Focusing on *what is to men's interest*, however, may violate democratic values, and social scientists may become manipulators and coercers rather than persuaders who are trying to get men to reason together. In conclusion Mills suggests that social scientists much address themselves to issues and troubles and formulae them as problems of social science. This is the only chance, he believes, "to make reason democratically relevant to human affairs in a free society, and to realize the classic values that underlie the *promise* of our studies."[149]

Native American Philosophy

There is much to learn from Native American rituals and practices and the philosophy behind them that has to do with things of the spirit. Native Americans had a connection with nature and each other that those of us born into an individualistic culture find difficult to understand. Theirs was a spiritual connection with the environment in which they were embedded that extended in some ways to the entire universe. Remnants of their culture managed to survive despite the best efforts of the white man to destroy it and make the Native Americans into good Christian Americans. In the name of Manifest Destiny treaties with them were broken when the white man wanted the land on which they resided, and they were moved farther and farther west and finally settled into reservations on land the white man didn't want. The story of their removal from places where they had lived for thousands of years is indeed a story about a trail of tears.

Vine Deloria, Jr., a practicing lawyer and professor at the university in Boulder, Colorado, points out in a book titled *God Is Red* that the differences between political conservatives and liberals are not fundamental. While conservatives may emphasize individual responsibility and self-help doctrines and the liberals may seem to have more sympathy for humanity, they both share an idea of history that justifies their actions and validates their ideas about the place of the United Sates in the grand scheme of things. When Native American (NA) ideology is compared with that of the Western Europeans (WE) who immigrated to this country, the difference is of great philosophical importance.[150]

Native Americans believe that land has the highest possible meaning and that they belong to the land in contrast to Western Europeans, who think of time as most important and believe that the land belongs to them. Thus, the former is concerned with the philosophical problem of space and the other with time. The essence of WE identity is the assumption that time proceeds in a linear fashion and that at some point in this progression of time they became the guardians of the world. This ideology, according to Deloria, sparked the Crusades, the Age of Exploration, the Age of Imperialism, the crusade against the spread of communism with a policy of containment, the war in Vietnam, and, of course, the idea of Manifest Destiny to settle the western part of the United States.[151]

There is also a difference in regards to religion as WE consider revelation as the communication of a divine plan that is mistaken as a truth applicable to all times and places so that it must be impressed upon people who have no connection with the cultural complex in which this revelation manifested itself. Religious experience is thus taken from its original cultural context and made into an abstract principle applicable to all peoples of the world. NA, on the other hand, take their religious traditions from the world around them and their relationships with other forms of life in the world. The places where revelations were experienced were set aside as special places where, through rituals and ceremonies, people could reconnect with the spirits. Revelation "was seen as a continuous process of adjustment to the natural surroundings and not as a specific message valid for all times and places."[152] While religions that are spatially determined can create a sense of sacred time that is tied to a specific location, it is difficult for a religion that is bound to history to incorporate sacred places into its doctrine. Thus, space can generate a sense of time, but time itself has little relationship to space.[153]

Spatial thinking requires, according to Deloria, that ethical systems relate directly to the physical world and real human situations. Ethics is not considered to be a series of abstract principles that are valid for all times and circumstances but instead involves real people in real concrete situations. If time is the primary consideration, we never can come to grips with the reality of our existence in places and are directed to abstract interpretations of reality rather than to the experiences themselves. It is direct, concrete experience that is of ultimate importance in NA thinking, again reflecting its focus on space rather than time.[154]

Ecology involving the politics of the new left in American society and the movement to local self-determination along with increased citizen participation are efforts to recapture a sense of place in American practice and manifest a rejection of the traditional American sense of progress. But Deloria believes that it is doubtful that American society can move very far or very significantly without a major revolution in theological concepts that lead to a new religious conception of the world. Before any final solution to the problem of American history can occur, a reconciliation of some kind must occur between what he calls the spiritual owner of the land, who, of course, are the NA, and the political owner of the land, who, of course, are the American whites.[155]

For Christians, the creation story is the beginning event of a linear time sequence in which God works out his divine plan the conclusion of which is an act that destroys the world and brings history to an end. For NA the beginning and end of time are of no concern as time is cyclical and there is no sense of a process of history that has a final ending. In the Christian religion man and the rest of creation are doomed soon after the creation event because of the fall of Adam when evil enters the world and this sinful world continues until the end of the world takes place. For NA their fall and the whole creation are considered to be good and man, and the rest of creation is cooperative and respectful of the task to take care of the world and do no harm, a task given to them by the Great Spirit.[156]

The idea that man receives domination over the rest of the world also comes from the creation story and has led to the economic exploitation of the earth, according to Deloria. The creation thus becomes a mere object in Western thinking to be exploited for human purposes, which is a view that is directly opposite to that of NA religions. All in all, the creation story of Christianity has serious shortcomings for NA as it is considered by Christians not only as a historical event that for literalists actually took place but also as an event that determined all other facts of our existence as it sort of set the stage, so to speak, for the progression of history toward its final end when Christ would return to establish his Kingdom.[157] As Deloria says,

> [i]t is bad enough to consider Genesis as a historical account in view of what we know today of the nature of our world. But when we consider that the Genesis account places human and nonhuman life systems in a polarity with us, tinged with evil and without hope of redemption except at the last judgment, the whole idea appears intolerable.[158]

In contrast to the domination thesis of Christianity, the task of NA religion is to determine the proper relations of NA people with other living things and to develop a discipline within the tribal community that will enable them to live harmoniously with other creatures. The recognition that humans hold a special place in creation which is characteristic of Christianity is tempered with the thought in NA religion that humans are dependent on everything in creation for their existence. Each form of life has its own purpose in the grand scheme of things, and "there is no form of life that does not have a unique quality to its existence."[159] This view of creation did not produce a fear of nature nor was there a sense of wilderness that needed to be conquered and developed. Deloria quotes Chief Standing Bear who makes this point:

> We did not think of the great open plains, the beautiful rolling hills, and the winding streams with tangled growth as "wild." Only to the white man as nature a "wilderness" and only to him was the land "infested" with "wild" animals and "savage" people. To us it was tame. Earth was bountiful and we were surrounded with the blessings of the Great Mystery. Not until the hairy man from the east came and with brutal frenzy heaped injustices upon us and the families that we lived was it "wild" for us. When the very animals of the forest began fleeing from this approach, then it was for us the "Wild West" began.[160]

Deloria believes that the alienation of humans from nature is caused in part by the action of humans against nature rather than the result of a corrupted relationship that resulted from their inability to relate to its creator. But he is also doubtful that Christians can change their understanding of creation, as their religion is firmly grounded in an escape from a fallen nature, and it is highly unlikely to suppose "that they can find reconciliation with nature while maintaining the remainder of their theological understanding of salvation." In sum, the religions of the NA certainly appear to be more at home in the modern world than do the Western religions with their traditional religious concepts of the creation.[161]

Indian tribes, says Deloria, had little use for a detailed recording of past events or keeping a chronological record of past events as history had virtually no place in the religious life of the tribes. In contrast, Christianity has always had a major emphasis on the idea of history as it believed that the experiences of humans could be recorded in a linear fashion that would show the whole purpose of creation revealing how the end of the world would take place and the existence of a future world where the faithful would be welcome. Thus, again the notion of time is all important to Christians whereas it has a casual, if any, importance to tribal peoples.[162] As Deloria says,

> [t]he Christian religion looks toward a spectacular end of the world as a time of judgment and thus an end of history. It is thus theologically an open-ended proposition because it can at anytime promote the idea that the world is ending; when such an event fails to occur, the contentions can easily be retracted by resorting to philosophical warnings about the nature of time. Time thus becomes a dualistic concept for Christians. It is both divine and human; prophecies given with respect to divine time and promptly cancelled by reference to human time and its distinction from divine time.[163]

World history as conceived by Christianity is the story of how the Western nations conquered the rest of the word and the subsequent development of a sophisticated technology. There is little or no appreciation of the cultures and religions of other nations, and they do not have status in the Christian interpretation of world history. Western man, however, must quickly come to grips with the breadth of human experience as new discoveries are made about the origin of human beings in Africa that challenge the Old Testament stories. He must downgrade the ancient history of the Near East, which will cut more subject matter from the Christian religion. This involves a surrender of the historical Adam and his successors to adapt to what science is discovering about the origins of the human species and its subsequent dispersal throughout the world.[164]

The difference between Christianity and its interpretation of history and the spatially located Indian tribal religions is well illustrated when the sacred places of NA are taken into account—the sacred mountains, the sacred hills, sacred rivers, and other geographical features that are sacred to Indian tribes. For example, the Navajo tribe has four sacred mountains that are believed to have risen from the underworld. There is no doubt in their minds that there are particular mountains, like Mount Taylor in New Mexico, where the creation story took place. They cannot say *when* it happened, but they are fairly certain *where* the emergence of the world took place.[165]

Of great importance is the relationship to the natural world between the two groups. In Christianity the physical world is not often seen as a positive place but is a vale of tears filled with human suffering and tragedies. The human body and its fleshly temptations, along with the world in which humans live, are often seen as an evil to be overcome by accepting God's grace and being saved for the sins of the flesh and worldly temptations. Animals are placed below humans in the hierarchy of existence, and religious ceremonies often do not acknowledge the existence of the material world. NA, on the other hand, regard the physical world as integral to human ambitions and activities and tribulations of everyday life.[166]

Christians erect gigantic cathedrals and churches to separate themselves from the sinful secular and natural world and as a haven from the trials and tribulations of everyday life. The Indian religions hold their ceremonies and rituals by and large in a natural setting and do not think of establishing a separate building for religion's activities.[167] Christians seek salvation as an escape from this planet to a place where they can enjoy eternal life filled with the delights they were denied during their lifetime, while NA use the forces of nature for their benefit and are not fearful of natural processes. They have no reason to reduce religion to systematic thought and elaboration of religion's concepts as such an activity would separate them from their experience of the natural world.[168]

Tribal peoples, at least according to Deloria, have no difficulty with death, and view it as a natural progression through the stages of life, and entertain no promises of delights and rewards. They live within the normal cycles of life and death that constitute earthly life. Christians, on the other hand, should have no trouble with death either since this earthly life is so difficult for them, temptations to sin are ever present, and the promise of eternal life as a reward for being faithful should make them wish for the final passage to a better life. Yet, as Deloria points out, Christians fear death most likely because death is associated with a judgment day when the kind of life they have lived will be evaluated from on high and the wheat will be separated from the chaff, with the latter burning in the fires of eternal hell. The problem is that no one can be certain that they have lived a good enough life to be sent to heaven.[169]

Christianity thus focuses on the afterlife and Christian's behavior in this world had sort of a testing aspect to it as what mattered was the next life that awaited them if they had been good and passed the test at their death. Thus, personal responsibility was focused on a set of behaviors that would as much as possible guarantee them eternal life, and it was not an ethic that focused on dealing justly with their fellow contemporaries. Salvation became something of a confusing thing as it became mixed up with the idea of predestination, where the elect were selected for eternal life without having to do anything. Thus, justification by faith alone was discredited and offered no guidelines for living the good life. People were then motivated to find some way of convincing themselves they were in the elected group, and the accumulation of wealth became this kind of marker to provide some degree of certainty about where they would go after death.[170]

For tribal people, according to Deloria, the afterlife was not of great concern, and while there may have been vague references to the lands of the spirits in some tribes, no highly articulated or developed theories of the afterlife were necessary. Death for them fulfilled their destiny as the deterioration of their bodies contributed to the ongoing life cycle of creation. Death is an event that every person is faced with at some point and is not an arbitrary capricious divine wrath. The tribal community regroups after the death of one of its members and continues to exist and while the members left behind may be lonely they are not alone and are cared for by the tribe.[171] There is a strong sense of relationship in NA life that extends to all aspects of the world so that one need never feel alone as enunciated by Joseph Epes Brown, who was a professor of religious studies at the University of Montana:

> This sense of relationship pertains not only to members of a nuclear family, band, of clan. It also extends outward to include all beings of the specific environment, the elements, and the winds, whether these beings, forms, or powers are what we would call animate or inanimate. In Native American thought no such hard dichotomies exist. All such forms under creation are understood to be mysteriously interrelated. Everything is relative to every other being or thing; thus nothing exists in isolation.[172]

In Christianity there is the belief that when one accepts Jesus Christ as one's personal savior there is a radical change in his or her constitution and behavior. This is the personal testimony of those who have been through a conversion experience and consider themselves to have been born again. Evangelists "orchestrate their crusades with hymns, angry sermons, threats of judgment, soothing words of comfort, efforts at healing, and psychological tricks" to get their audience to make a decision for Christ and proceed to kneel at the altar in what for some is a highly emotional experience. One must accept a personal relationship with Christ in order to be saved.[173]

For NA, however, religion does not involve such a personal relationship with the deity but is rather a covenant between a particular god and a particular community. There is no salvation apart from the continuance of the tribe itself. Religious doctrine is not needed, and one cannot "join" a tribal religion by agreeing to its doctrines. Religion is a tribal phenomenon that supports the individual in a community context and does not attempt to abstract an individual from his or her community context in contrast to Christianity, which is concerned with salvation of the individual soul. This soul is abstracted from any kind of social context as each individual is held responsible for the state of his or her soul and cannot blame social or economic conditions.[174]

A tribal religion is integrated with other functions of the community, so there is no issue of church and state as exists with Christianity and other religions in the United States as both church and state in NA experience are two complementary aspects of community life.[175] Government does not need to expand into the social welfare field as religion's duties cover those aspects of community concern. The coercive power of the government is blunted by the religious understandings of life within the tribal community. Religious wars are avoided as other peoples are regarded as having special powers and medicines that have been given to them, which precludes the development of an exclusive franchise that has been issued to any one group of people.[176]

For the NA sacred places must be preserved as they are the foundation of all other beliefs and practices of NA religion, reminding tribal members that they are not larger than nature and have responsibilities to the natural world that transcend personal desires and wishes. This lesion must be learned anew by each generation as the technology of industrial society always leads in the other direction. If we foul our planetary nest we shall have a most bitter lesson to learn. Deloria is not very optimistic, however, about the time available "for the non-Indian population to understand the meaning of sacred lands and incorporate the idea into their lives and practices." The best that can be hoped for, he says, is that some protection can be given to these sacred places before the world is destroyed.[177]

Unless these sacred places are discovered and protected, a nation can never come to grips with the land itself, and without this basic relationship, says Deloria, national psychic stability is impossible. While ecologists predict a severe environmental crisis in the near future unless we come to grips with issues such as climate change, the Christian religion continues to project the end of our present existence and the creation of another world where the chosen people will live happily ever after. The destruction of the world can be prevented by changing what Deloria calls a "naïve conception of this world as a testing ground of abstract morality to a more mature view of the universe as a comprehensive matrix of life forms." This shift involves primarily a change in religious beliefs rather than being economic or political in nature.[178]

The problem contemporary societies face is to grasp the essential meaning of their existence within the world as it is directly experienced, what I would call a naturalistic approach to understanding one's place in this world. Yet Deloria believes this task is virtually impossible for people from a European background of deeply imbued with Christian beliefs.[179] The meaning of life for Christians is tied to salvation from the temptations they are confronted with in this sinful world and to preparing themselves for the afterlife, which is where they can then live a truly fulfilled life with God the father almighty. This world is more or less just a place where their faith is tested, and if they remain steadfast, they will be one of the chosen to enter into eternal life. Such is the nature of belief for those who adhere to Christian doctrine.

The land calls out to humans for redemption, but this redemption involves a restoration of sanity rather than what Deloria calls a supernatural reclamation project at the end of history. Religion cannot be limited to sermons and scriptures as it is a force in and of itself that "calls for the integration of lands and peoples in harmonious harmony. The lands wait for those who can discern their rhythms." On each continent, rivers, mountains, and lakes "all call for relief from the constant burden of exploitation."[180] In the concluding paragraph Deloria makes a very moving statement about the land that refers back to the title of the book:

> Who will find peace with the lands? The future of humankind lies waiting for those who will come to understand their lives and take up responsibilities to all living things. Who will listen to the trees, the animals and birds, the voices of the places of the land? As the long-forgotten people of the respective continents rise and begin to reclaim their ancient heritage, they will discover the meaning of the lands of their ancestors. That is when the invaders of the North American continent will finally discover that for this land, God is red.[181]

By way of summary, Kaufman sees the reinvention of the sacred and its focus on meaning, values, and purpose, as an alternative to scientific reductionism, which despiritualizes our world. Adorno wants aesthetic experience to play a leading role in critical theory and holds that art matters to introduce a spiritual dimension in a world dominated by economic and technological imperatives. Stiegler argues that hyperindustrialized capitalism had reached its limits, and we must engage in a re-enchantment of the world involving a life of the spirit in order to take care of it adequately. The scientific case for spiritually rests on the assumption that science has rendered spirituality obsolete and unnecessary in our world so an attempt to provide a scientific basis for spirituality by linking spiritual practices to positive health outcomes is a noble and important effort that might make the whole concept of spirituality acceptable for many people. Mills argues that we need a quality of mind, what he calls the sociological imagination, that allows us to cope with change, to find personal meaning in history, and to make reason relevant to human affairs in a free society. Finally, Native American philosophy focuses on space, which is exemplified in the notion of sacred places, in contrast to the Western Europeans who settled the country and emphasized time as a linear progression, which was operative in the notion of Manifest Destiny. The following quote from Joseph Epps Brown on the value of a spiritual approach to life to provide a balance with materialism seems an appropriate way to end this chapter:

> We are so blinded by the perspectives of our own society that we cannot realize that complex material achievements of the type we possess, or rather by which we are often possessed, are usually had at the expense of human and spiritual values. A minimum of material possessions does not necessarily mean a corresponding poverty in mental and spiritual achievements. The nomadic type of culture offers valuable lessons to the contemporary industrial person who is in danger of being crushed by the sheer weight of civilization, and who therefore often sacrifices the deepest and most meaningful values of life by identifying with an endless series of distracting and often destructive gadgets.[182]

Notes

1 Stuart A. Kauffman, *Reinventing the Sacred: A New View of Science, Reason, and Religion* (New York: Basic Books, 2008), ix.
2 Ibid., x–xiii.
3 Ibid., 9.
4 Ibid., 11–14.
5 See Philip W. Anderson, "More Is Different," *Science*, Vol. 177 (1972), 393; Robert Laughlin, *A Different Universe: The Universe from the Bottom Down* (New York: Basic Books, 2005); and Leonard Susskind, *The Cosmic Landscape: String Theory and the Illusion of Intelligent Design* (New York: Little-Brown, 2006).
6 Kauffman, *Reinventing the Sacred*, 31–43.
7 Ibid., 71.
8 Ibid., 72–74, 87.
9 Ibid., 129–131.
10 Ibid., 141.
11 Ibid., 149.
12 Ibid., 151, 175.
13 Ibid., 177–196.
14 Ibid., 199–200, 229, 230.
15 Ibid., 231.
16 Ibid., 246–250.
17 Ibid., 252–253.
18 Ibid., 257.
19 Ibid., 257, 260.
20 Ibid., 264.
21 Ibid., 266. See 264–266 for Kauffman's critique of the categorical imperative and utilitarianism.
22 Ibid., 271.
23 Ibid., 273–280.
24 Ibid., 284–285.
25 Ibid., 287.
26 Ibid., 287–288.
27 Andres Bowie, "Introduction: Contemporary Alternatives," in Andrew Bowie, ed., *Adorno and the Ends of Philosophy* (Cambridge, UK: Polity Press, 2013), 65–66.

28 Axel Honneth, *The Critique of Power: Reflective Stages in a Critical Social The-ory* (Cambridge, MA: The MIT Press, 1991), 66.
29 Bowie, *Adorno and the Ends of Philosophy*, 60.
30 Ibid., 136–137.
31 Ibid., 138.
32 Ibid., 141.
33 Ibid., 142.
34 Ibid., 146–148.
35 Ibid., 151.
36 Ibid., 154.
37 Ibid., 156.
38 Ibid., 144–145.
39 Ibid., 142.
40 Ibid., 42.
41 Ibid., 167.
42 Ibid., 157–158.
43 Ibid., 170.
44 Ibid., 171.
45 Ibid., 173–174.
46 Ibid., 175.
47 Ibid., 176.
48 Ibid., 177.
49 Ibid., 184.
50 Ibid., 140.
51 Ibid., 162.
52 Ibid., 188.
53 Ibid., 192, n7.
54 Ibid., 188.
55 Ibid., 67.
56 Ibid., 68–69.
57 Bernard Stiegler, *The Re-Enchantment of the World: The Value of Spirit against Industrial Populism* (London: Bloomsbury, 2014), 3–4.
58 Ibid., 7.
59 Ibid., 11.
60 Ibid., 18.
61 Ibid., 23–24.
62 Ibid., 31–33.
63 Ibid., 44–52.
64 Ibid., 53–55.
65 Ibid., 60.
66 Ibid., 63.
67 Ibid., 72–74.
68 Ibid., 83–89.
69 Ibid., 95–96.
70 Ibid., 98–99.
71 Ibid., 100.
72 Tami Simon, "Introduction," in Daniel Goleman, ed., *Measuring the Immeasur-able: The Scientific Case for Spirituality* (Boulder, CO: Sounds True, 2008), ix.
73 Ibid., x.
74 Peter Russell, "Exploring Deep Mind," in Daniel Goleman, ed., *Measuring the Immeasurable: The Scientific Case for Spirituality* (Boulder, CO: Sounds True, 2008), 1–2.
75 Ibid., 2.
76 Ibid.

77 Ibid., 7–8.
78 Ibid., 12.
79 Ibid., 12–13.
80 Larry Dossey, "Compassion and Healing," in Daniel Goleman, ed., *Measuring the Immeasurable: The Scientific Case for Spirituality* (Boulder, CO: Sounds True, 2008), 50.
81 Ibid., 56.
82 Candace Pert with Nancy Marriott, "The Science of Emotions and Consciousness," in Daniel Goleman, ed., *Measuring the Immeasurable: The Scientific Case for Spirituality* (Boulder, CO: Sounds True, 2008), 15–33.
83 Dan Siegel, "Reflections on the Mindful Brain," in Daniel Goleman, ed., *Measuring the Immeasurable: The Scientific Case for Spirituality* (Boulder, CO: Sounds True, 2008), 64–69.
84 Robert A. Emmons, "Gratitude: The Science and Spirit of Thankfulness," in Daniel Goleman, ed., *Measuring the Immeasurable: The Scientific Case for Spirituality* (Boulder, CO: Sounds True, 2008), 122.
85 Ibid., 122–124.
86 Ibid., 124–125.
87 Ibid., 126.
88 Ibid., 128.
89 Ibid., 129–130.
90 Ibid., 133.
91 Sara L. Warber and Katherine N. Irvine, "Nature and Spirit," in Daniel Goleman, ed., *Measuring the Immeasurable: The Scientific Case for Spirituality* (Boulder, CO: Sounds True, 2008), 140.
92 Ibid., 147.
93 Ibid., 148–149.
94 Ibid., 151.
95 Ibid., 155.
96 Ibid., 138.
97 Sandra Ingerman, "Medicine for the Earth," in Daniel Goleman, ed., *Measuring the Immeasurable: The Scientific Case for Spirituality* (Boulder, CO: Sounds True, 2008), 158–159.
98 Ibid., 161.
99 Bruce Lipton, "Revealing the Wizard behind the Curtain," in Daniel Goleman, ed., *Measuring the Immeasurable: The Scientific Case for Spirituality* (Boulder, CO: Sounds True, 2008), 185.
100 Ibid., 186.
101 Ibid., 189.
102 Ibid., 190.
103 Ibid., 191.
104 Ibid., 192.
105 Ibid., 194.
106 Ibid., 192.
107 Ibid., 197.
108 William Tiller, "Toward a Reliable Bridge of Understanding between Traditional Science and Spiritual Science," in Daniel Goleman, ed., *Measuring the Immeasurable: The Scientific Case for Spirituality* (Boulder, CO: Sounds True, 2008), 288.
109 Ibid., 290.
110 Charles Tart, "Consciousness: A Psychological, Transpersonal, and Parapsychological Approach," in Daniel Goleman, ed., *Measuring the Immeasurable: The Scientific Case for Spirituality* (Boulder, CO: Sounds True, 2008), 313.
111 Ibid., 314–315.

112 Ibid., 325.
113 Ibid., 326.
114 Andrew Newberg, "Spirituality, the Brain, and Health," in Daniel Goleman, ed., *Measuring the Immeasurable: The Scientific Case for Spirituality* (Boulder, CO: Sounds True, 2008), 349.
115 Ibid., 351–354.
116 Ibid., 357.
117 This is my opinion, not Dr. Newberg's.
118 Ibid., 367–371.
119 Joan H. Hageman, "Not All Meditation Is the Same: A Brief Overview of Perspectives, Techniques, and Outcomes," in Daniel Goleman, ed., *Measuring the Immeasurable: The Scientific Case for Spirituality* (Boulder, CO: Sounds True, 2008), 374.
120 Ibid., 375.
121 Ibid., 376.
122 Ibid.
123 Ibid., 384.
124 Marilyn Mandala Schlita, Cassandra Vieten, and Time Amorok, "Living Deeply: The Art and Science of Transformation in Everyday Life," in Daniel Goleman, ed., *Measuring the Immeasurable: The Scientific Case for Spirituality* (Boulder, CO: Sounds True, 2008), 448.
125 C. Wright Mills, *The Sociological Imagination* (London: Oxford University Press, 1959), 3–5.
126 Ibid., 5.
127 Ibid., 5–6.
128 Ibid., 6–7.
129 Ibid., 7–8.
130 Ibid., 8–11.
131 Ibid., 11–13.
132 Ibid., 13–15.
133 Ibid., 16.
134 Ibid., 18–22.
135 Ibid., 22–23.
136 Ibid., 24.
137 Ibid., 177–178.
138 Ibid., 178–179.
139 Ibid., 179–180.
140 Ibid., 180–181.
141 Ibid., 181.
142 Ibid., 182–184.
143 Ibid., 184–185.
144 Ibid., 186–188.
145 Ibid., 188–190.
146 Ibid., 190–191.
147 Ibid., 192.
148 Ibid., 193–194.
149 Ibid., 194. Italics mine.
150 Vine Deloria, Jr., *God Is Red: A Native View of Religion* (Golden, CO: Fulcrum Publishing, 1994), 62.
151 Ibid., 64.
152 Ibid., 66–67.
153 Ibid., 71.
154 Ibid., 73.
155 Ibid., 74–76.

156 Ibid., 78–82.
157 Ibid., 82, 87.
158 Ibid., 87.
159 Ibid., 88.
160 Luther Standing Bear, *Land of the Spotted Eagle* (Boston: Houghton Mifflin, 1993), as quoted in Ibid., 91.
161 Ibid., 91, 95.
162 Ibid., 98, 103.
163 Ibid., 106.
164 Ibid., 108–109.
165 Ibid., 122.
166 Ibid., 153–154.
167 "For the Indians, however, the world of nature itself was their temple, and within this sanctuary they showed great respect to every form, function, and power. That the Indians held as sacred all the natural forms surrounding them is not unique, for other traditions respect created forms as manifestations of God's works. But what is almost unique in the Indian's attitude is that their reverence for nature and for life is *central* to their religion: each form in the world around them bears such a host of precise values and meanings that taken all together they constitute what one could call their doctrine." Joseph Epes Brown, *The Spiritual Legacy of the American Indian* (Bloomington, IN: World Wisdom, Inc. 2007), 27.
168 Deloria, *God Is Red*, 154–155.
169 Ibid., 163, 167–168.
170 Ibid., 168–169.
171 Ibid., 179, 183.
172 Brown, *Spiritual Legacy*, 39.
173 Deloria, *God Is Red*, 185, 194.
174 Ibid., 194–197.
175 "It has now become abundantly clear that it is a fundamental and universal characteristic of Native American cultures . . . that 'religion' is not a separate category of activity or experience that is divorced from culture or society." See Brown, *Spiritual Legacy*, xiii. This author claims that there is no equivalent for *religion* in any American Indian language.
176 Deloria, *God Is Red*, 211.
177 Ibid., 281–282.
178 Ibid., 284, 287.
179 Ibid., 284.
180 Ibid., 292.
181 Ibid., 292.
182 Brown, *Spiritual Legacy*, 23.

7   Spirituality in the Workplace

The final source of spirituality to be considered is the workplace itself where there has been something of a movement to find a spiritual dimension in the work people do for a living. The great majority of people spend most of their waking hours working, making the work people do and the environment in which it is done of great importance. The concept we have of ourselves as human beings is largely shaped by our work activity and what we do there affects our lives outside of the work environment. We seek satisfaction through our work, have an intrinsic drive to grow, and, for the most part, desire opportunities to learn new things and advance ourselves. We want to find meaning in our work since it takes up such a great portion of our time, and this meaningfulness carries over into our personal lives and makes us feel better about ourselves and our interactions with other people.[1]

Yet for many people work is a necessary evil because of the need for a paycheck to support oneself and one's family. They have come to accept the lack of fulfillment at work as normal and do not expect much out of their work beyond the necessary monetary reward and an occasional step up the ladder. They are disconnected from their work and do not find much if any meaning in it or satisfaction for themselves. They more or less perform their work mechanically, particularly if it is somewhat repetitive in nature, and look forward to the weekend when they can do something more enjoyable. One could say that in these situations the connection between spirituality and work is missing or most certainly has diminished.[2]

This connection between work and spirituality is a relatively new concern of scholars in business and management and like any new concept has many different definitions and is used in many different contexts. For example, J. G. Allegretti, writing in an article titled "Work and the Spiritual Life," defines spirituality as a kind of shorthand expression that refers to the deepest urgings and impulses of the human self that have to do with giving meaning and depth to everyday life. The concept encompasses the need for creativity on the part of human beings, the desire for self-expression, and a hunger for love and service. A spirituality of work refers to making work a part of one's spiritual life, finding opportunities for self-expression through one's work, bringing moral values into the workplace, and developing a sense that all of life is sacred, including the time one spends working.[3]

W. A. Guillory, in his article "Spirituality and the Workplace," thinks of spirituality as referring to one's inner consciousness, the source of inspiration, creativity, and wisdom. Spirituality thus comes from within and goes beyond one's programmed beliefs and values. Spirituality related to the workplace is the life force that permeates and creates a living organization in the pursuit of business objectives. He believes that in order to be creative and innovative in today's workplace, people must reunite with their spirituality and make it a legitimate part of the working environment. It must not be isolated to a particular religious expression but must be integrated into the workplace as well to be a meaningful part of one's life experience.[4]

Robert A. Giacalone and Carole L. Jurkiewicz, professor of human resource management at the Fox School of Business at Temple University and Woman's Hospital Distinguished Professor of Healthcare Management at the E. J. Ourso College of Business at Louisiana State University, respectively, point out that many definitions of spirituality include some notion of transcendence, ultimacy, or divinity but from these common elements the definitions vary greatly. Spirituality is sometimes treated as a behavior or personal expression; others see it as being objective in nature while still others describe spirituality as a "subjective" experience. Others see spirituality as a search for meaning while some see it as an animating force that inspires one toward purposes that are beyond one' own personal concerns.[5] Barry Z. Posner, a professor of leadership in the Leavey School of Business at Santa Clara University, sees spirituality as involving the following questions:

- What do I *stand* for?
- What do I *believe* in?
- What am I *discontent* about?
- What makes me *weep* and *wail*?
- What makes me *jump for joy*?
- What *keeps me awake* at night?
- What has *grabbed hold* and won't let go?
- Just what is it that I really *care about*?[6]

The lack of consensus in defining spirituality itself is a conceptual impediment to the achievement of an understanding of workplace spirituality. This lack of clarity is compounded when it is applied to the workplace. Some scholars try to get around this difficulty by breaking the term down into some component parts, such as (1) a recognition that employees have an inner life, (2) an assumption that employees desire to find work meaningful, and (3) a commitment on the part of the organization to serve as a context or community for spiritual growth. But should these components be accepted as the only viable ones of should others be included? Does workplace spirituality constitute either distinctly individual components, or does it include organizational components as well making it something of an amalgamation of both? These distinctions are important if workplace spirituality is to be distinguished from the study of spirituality in other contexts[7]

Most scholars of in this area make a distinction between workplace spirituality and religion. For Guillory spirituality is a way of being that predetermines how one responds to life's experiences whereas religion deals with the incorporation and implementation of organized belief systems. Religion is a vehicle that spirituality takes in practice while spirituality is the source behind that form of expression.[8] Others argue that viewing workplace spirituality through the lens of a particular religious tradition is divisive as it excludes those who do no share that tradition. Still others are concerned that since religious doctrine is based on faith, it cannot be studied scientifically. Since the disciplines of management and administration are based on a scientific model and religion is not subject to being tested by scientific method it cannot contribute to a scientific body of knowledge. Principles that are derived from religion cannot and should not usurp principles of management and administration, which are the backbone of current scholarship and practice.[9]

Giacalone and Jurkiewicz believe that a scientific approach to workplace spirituality is feasible and mention several decades of research that has employed the scientific method to study spirituality in itself. They also mention what they call key weaknesses that serve to hamper the development of a scientific approach to workplace spirituality. These include (1) the lack of a an adequate conceptual definition mentioned earlier, (2) inadequate measurement tools, (3) limited theoretical development, and (4) legal concerns that involve biases against spirituality.[10]

Regarding the first weakness, a working definition of workplace spirituality must have a substantive dimension that evokes manifestations of beliefs, emotions, practices, and relationships and a functional dimension that deals with the practical purpose that spirituality serves for an individual in an organizational context such as the connection between spirituality and productivity, turnover, health, and other such variables. With this in mind, Giacalone and Jurkiewicz offer the following definition of workplace spirituality: "*aspects of the workplace, either in the individual, group, or the organization, that promote individual feelings of satisfaction through transcendence.*"[11]

With respect to the second weakness, the authors examine the question of the utility of workplace spirituality by positioning it within a system context. Thus, its utility can be demonstrated by linking it to tangible aspects of the work environment that can be most easily measured such as performance on the job, turnover, and productivity. Others, however, argue that workplace spirituality must be seen in a broader and holistic context as a system of interwoven cultural and personal values that impact all levels of personal and organizational life. To get an understanding of the full utility of workplace spirituality one must look at the interplay of individual and organizational values, as it is most likely that a divergence between organizational and personal values has led to an interest in workplace spirituality.[12]

There is a good deal of research to suggest that interest in workplace spirituality appears to mirror changes in values across the globe that involve a greater propensity to favor what are called postmaterialistic values such as concern for quality of life, self-expression, community, and the like over materialistic values such as prosperity, security, and control. The implications of this shift are far-reaching and represent a cultural shift in which quality-of-life issues are more of a motivating force than are material possessions. Value changes that focus on spirituality are being embedded in societies around the world and organizations need to take this into account. To adequately take these changes into account, theory development and research related to workplace spirituality must be grounded and placed within an interdisciplinary or multidisciplinary context.[13]

Finally, concern about legal issues can arise when the terms *workplace* and *spirituality* are linked. There is a potential antagonism that can result from the intersection of work and spiritual domains. There can be a conflict between a rationalistic and positivistic approach to the world and one based on transcendent intangibles. In other instances, allowing nonreligious views of spirituality into the workplace might clash with deeply held personal religious beliefs. In either case, legal issues could arise that involve stockholders and workers themselves.[14]

However, the authors believe and integrative approach to the workplace and spirituality can overcome these conflicts. First of all, there is a long history of organizational research into intangibles such as leadership and power, which makes rejecting spirituality because it is intangible as not being consistent with ongoing research. And second, the integrative stance does not assume that religious faith is a substitute for the scientific approach when studying the organization. If organizational research has been based to date on the development of scientific principles, a different yardstick cannot be used for spiritual variables. The authors conclude that "[c]arefully designed research focusing on these and other variables can move us toward a new paradigm of study that is based on the same scientific principles that have historically characterized the organizational sciences . . . The scientific study of workplace spirituality may being forth a new development in the organizational sciences, one hopefully unfettered by legal and religious phobias."[15]

Other Views of Workplace Spirituality

Jeffrey Pfeffer, a well-respected management scholar who is the Thomas D. Dee II Professor of Organizational Behavior at the Graduate School of Business at Stanford University, sees the word *spirit* as referring to a vital force that animates human beings and is part of their being rather than being something external to themselves. He sees four elements that define this force as far as it is manifest in workplaces. These include (1) people often want a kind of work that provides them with the opportunity to develop and master new skills and competencies and that allows them to learn new things about themselves and in the process becoming more competent and knowledgeable all of which helps them to realize their full potential as human beings; (2) people want work that has some social value and meaning, a dimension that is consistent with organizations that stand for something beyond profit and have an overarching purpose or mission that gives people a sense that their work has meaning and purpose beyond simply working for a living; (3) people want to be interconnected with others and feel that they are part of a community; and (4) people want to live and work in an integrated fashion and perform work that is consistent with their basic beliefs and their concept of themselves.[16]

Keeping these four elements in mind, Pfeffer then discusses a number of management practices in relation to whether they work or not in enabling these elements of the workplace. The first practice he examines is the traditional emphasis on running companies solely for the benefit of shareholders. There are several problems with this narrow focus that ignores other missions and values that are of importance. First of all, maximizing profit or shareholder value does not stir people's imaginations or emotions and does not inspire people who want to make a difference in the world and engage in meaningful activities. Second, what is really scarce is not capital but talent and people with knowledge so focusing solely on returns to capital and ignoring people makes no economic sense.[17]

Third, better decisions can result by operating companies for the benefit of both shareholders and employees as the commitment of both is needed for a successful business. Fourth, why capital should receive a higher priority than other stakeholders in not clear from either a logical or legal standpoint. Capital is the result of past labor, so why should *past* labor receive a higher priority than *current* labor. Thirty states have relaxed the legal obligation to maximize shareholder returns by allowing other constituencies to be considered in corporate decision making. And finally, stock price and profits are outcomes of managerial decisions which need to also focus on the process by which those outcomes were produced. Not focusing on the process that produces results, that is, employees and customers, and focusing exclusively on the goal can lead to poor performance.[18]

The second management practice Pfeffer discusses is the traditional way of managing employees by controlling and directing them to achieve corporate objectives. This involves telling employees what to do and making and keeping them submissive. This way of managing does not do much to develop employees belief in their worth, competence, or value to the company. The alternative is to encourage autonomy and decision-making responsibility in the organization and in this manner build the spirit of employees by letting them actually make important decisions about the direction of the organization and the allocation of resources within the organization. This enables employees to flourish and grow allowing them to realize more of their untapped potential and increasing their commitment to the organization and engagement within the organization itself.[19]

Relying on self-management teams is a third management practice that Pfeffer discusses. Workers in self-managed teams have greater autonomy and discretion in the direction of their work and this translates into better performance on the job as well as greater job satisfaction. Teams give people a greater sense of connection to their colleagues because they work together to achieve common objectives. The substitution of peer support for the traditional hierarchical control gives employees a better self-image and feeling of worth to the organization. They have a sense of control over their work environment, which helps to enhance their spirit in the workplace.[20]

Another management practice that has implications for workplace spirituality is the design and compensation of reward systems. The typical system is based on individual performance which leads to inequalities in the workplace. This inequality has been shown to result in lower productivity, lower job satisfaction, and higher turnover, particularly for those at the lower end of the pay scale. The alternative is a collective pay system that is not based on how well an individual does in relation to another but on how well the entire system performs. A collective reward structure de-emphasizes internal competition that retards sharing knowledge and helping colleagues and develops a greater sense of community, "increasing the strength of social bonds between employees and their connection to the organization."[21]

In many companies emphasis is placed on controlling people, telling them what to do, and monitoring them to make sure they do what they are told. This is a typical way of understanding the role of management. What message is conveyed to employees by this type of control system is that they cannot be trusted to use their knowledge and talents in the interests of the organization. They need to be controlled and monitored. This becomes a self-fulfilling prophecy, and people who are not trusted sometimes come to act in an untrustworthy manner. An organization that is serious about nurturing people's spirit in the workplace will let employees know what is expected of them and then trust them to figure out how best to contribute in their own way to the success of the organization. They are allowed to be themselves without constant control and monitoring as they interact with their colleagues and contribute to the success of the whole.[22]

Companies that are serious about workplace spirituality, according to Pfeffer, will recognize that employees have a life outside of work and provide a way for their employees to fulfill their family and other social obligations. Some organizations require a commitment that leaves no time for any kind of social life and compel employees to choose between having a successful career and being loyal to the company and having a life outside of work that may involve commitments to friends and family. This creates a severe conflict over which roles the employee chooses to fulfill and impoverishes their lives and spirit in and out of the workplace. Companies that allow an employee to have both a job and a life without creating such a conflict nurture the spiritual dimension of its employees, which may lead to greater loyalty and productivity.[23]

Finally, to create a workplace where spirituality is nurtured, fear and abuse must be driven out of the workplace. Some managers believe that fear motivates people, but Pfeffer believes that a management style based on fear does not work because it discourages employees from telling the truth about things going on in the workplace, it drives people to look out only for themselves and their self-preservation, it drives good people out of the organization, and finally it demoralizes employees, causing them to withdraw reducing the amount of effort they will expend on behalf of the organization. Fear and intimidation do not foster the spiritual dimension, according to Pfeffer, and makes people feel bad about themselves. Companies that foster the spiritual dimension of the workplace treat employees with dignity and respect and make them feel good about themselves and the workplace environment.[24]

Organizations have become more important in industrial societies over the years and the majority of people in these societies spend a great deal time in these organizations earning their livelihood. These organizations have an ever more impact on the communities where they are located. Fundamental human rights and moral precepts do not disappear when one becomes an employee in these organizations and societies have a moral obligation, according to Pfeffer, to ensure that these places of employment build up rather than break down the human spirit. The ends do not justify the means, and the employees right to be treated with dignity at work, to be able to grow and learn on the job, to be connected with others, and to be a whole integrated person at work, cannot be sacrificed for economic expediency. The spiritual dimension of the workplace must be considered in economic decisions.[25]

Blake Ashforth, the Rusty Lyon Professor of Business in the W. P. Carey School of Business at Arizona State University, and Michael Pratt, professor of organizational studies at the Carroll School of Management at Boston College, hold that workplace spirituality has three major dimensions: (1) a connection to something greater than oneself, or what they call the *transcendence* of self; (2) *holism and harmony*, where the various aspects of oneself are integrated into a roughly coherent and consistent self; and (3) growth understood as self-development or self-actualization, a realization of one's aspirations and potential. While *spirituality* is often conceptualized as a noun, it can also be understood as a verb referring to a process where the journey itself is part of the meaning of the term. Spirituality as a process is highly subjective and fluid and often idiosyncratic.[26]

They argue that strivings for spirituality in the workplace are *in*consistent with the institutionalized settings in which they are sought in at least two ways. The first concerns the locus of spirituality, which, for Ashforth and Pratt, resides in the individual. Thus, seeking spiritual fulfillment may be at odds with the mandate of the organization that is a collective that requires its members so share a common culture and perspective and be committed to the goals of the organization. An unbridled individuality that takes the form of a spiritual journey may thus be a threat to the coherence of the organization.[27]

The second problem concerns the focus of spirituality, which, as a process, is considered to be an end in itself. However, business organizations focus on outcomes and such a process is considered to be a means to an end not an end in itself. Furthermore, organizations define the individual as a member of the organization fulfilling a particular role rather than as a unique person. They tend to view individuals in an atomistic sense rather than having a holistic vision of the individual. Finally, spiritual concerns tend to be squeezed out by the urgent press of pragmatic and concrete concerns that the organization has to address in order to survive and prosper.[28]

Because of these two problems, Ashforth and Pratt conclude that work organizations are not readily compatible with spiritual strivings. However, these organizations can approximate spirituality through the use of an array of approaches that differ in the degree of control exercised by the organization. At one end of the spectrum is an enabling approach that allows individuals, if they wish, to pursue their own spiritual journeys. At the other end of the spectrum are directing organizations that exercise a great deal of control by imposing a preferred cosmology on all its members. In between are partnering organizations in which spiritually is mutually authored by both the individual members and the institution. The authors discuss the advantages and disadvantages of each approach, but they cannot say which is the best approach. Individuals are going to resonate with different approaches.[29]

What they can say, however, is that directing organizations and perhaps some forms of partnering organizations seem to incur the most costs for individuals and organizations. Given the inherent incompatibility between spiritual and organizational concerns, success in approximating spirituality for some members of the organization may mean failure in achieving certain organizational interests. Furthermore, they predict that most individuals will prefer enabling and some forms of partnering over directing organizations because of their emphasis on individualism. Finally, the authors predict that there will likely be increases in all three forms of spiritual approximation as spiritual socialization in organizations evolves.[30]

Gordon E. Dehler, an associate professor at the College of Charleston, and M. Ann Welsh, professor of management at the University of Missouri, writing in "The Experience of Work: Spirituality and the New Workplace," state that an important lesson for organizations to learn is that people bring their *whole* selves to the workplace, thus "organizations *must* address the physical, mental, emotional, *and spiritual* needs of their workers."[31] The nature of work in the new economy has changed from the traditional relationship based on mutual loyalty between the organization and the worker to one where employees are essentially "free agents" and make careers for themselves based on their skills and expertise rather than on organizational membership. Work becomes more of an end in itself, and *doing the work* serves as a source of enjoyment, satisfaction, and fulfillment, making spirituality all the more important.[32]

When spirit is described as a search for meaning, Dehler and Welsh state that writers are actually defining spirit in terms of emotion, the internalized and personal feelings of meaning, purpose, knowing, and being. This kind of emotion energizes action, and thus, spirit is a form of energy. Spirit represents an inner source of energy, and spirituality is the outward expression of that force. The most serious danger to spirituality is when managers embrace this emotional side of work and turn it into an instrumentality; that is, they embrace workers' spirituality because it contributes to the bottom line. This practice does not treat workers as complete human beings who see the workplace as a site for expression of their inner selves and a place for fulfilling experiences that contribute to their personal growth. The purposes and values of the organization must be congruent with the purposes and values of the individuals who make up its workforce for workers to do *in*spirited work.[33]

Dehler and Welsh conclude that spirituality not only has a place in the contemporary workplace; it is also integral to what the workplace represents. However, spirit and spirituality do not involve the application of certain prescriptions and techniques. Workers bring their whole selves to the workplace, and their jobs need to be designed to be challenging to their whole selves in order to energize them to do their tasks appropriately. If spirituality is invoked by management because it is the right thing to do in creating a thriving workplace where individual and organizational values and outcomes are integrated, then the future of that organization is more promising than if spirituality is only invoked because it enhances the bottom line.[34]

Raymond F. Paloutzian, Robert A. Emmons, and Susan G. Keortge, in a paper titled "Spiritual Well-Being, Spiritual Intelligence, and Healthy Workplace Policy," hold that when workers are motivated to pursue transcendent goals they are likely to continue to work at even mundane tasks for long periods. They are also likely to engage in interpersonal behaviors that foster trust and commitment to the employer and the goals of the organization. People have a built-in tendency toward spirituality and have a need to contribute to something bigger than themselves. This gives a sense of fulfillment to workers, a sense of well-being that can be attained in no other manner.[35]

Spirituality, according to the authors, refers to a tendency to strive for those values and purposes that the individual finds ultimately meaningful. *Spiritual well-being*, in a nonreligious sense, refers to a sense of purpose and direction, while *spiritual intelligence* refers to the degree to which a person has the mental and emotional properties that enable a person of see an overall and guiding purpose, to see whatever tasks they are performing as linked to a larger purpose, and to sustain behavior in order to serve these purposes. Spiritual well-being can be seen as a social indicator, a way of measuring the level at which individuals are functioning in society. It also contributes to a sense of self-esteem, that they feel better about themselves when they are connected to a larger purpose that lies outside themselves rather than focusing on their own narrow and self-interested concerns.[36]

Spiritual intelligence allows workers to be sensitive to transcendent realities and gives them the ability to use spiritual information to solve real-life problems and thus has relevance for understanding manifestations of spirituality in the context of the workplace. Virtues such as humility, compassion, and wisdom contribute to the health and effective functioning of the organization. More than any other virtue attached to spiritual intelligence, gratitude appears to have important implications for individual and collective functioning in organizations. Gratitude is the positive recognition of benefits received, but it is also a felt sense of wonder, thankfulness, and an appreciation for life that can be expressed toward others. These are all crucial elements of well-being.[37]

A healthy workplace policy will support these elements of spiritual intelligence. On one hand, a seamlessness should be promoted between home life and work life as they can be seen as two pieces of one puzzle to find meaning and purpose. On the other hand, a distinction between the two must also be maintained, and an appropriate balance between home and work must be promoted by management. Managers must trust their employees and promote commitment to the goals of the organization rather than compliance with management directives. Teamwork and communication must be promoted to make employees feel that they are working toward a common goal. Communication between management and employees must be unambiguous and affirming as well as nonjudgmental. There should be no hidden messages or agendas. Finally, the organization must help employees in time of need, when there is a personal crisis or tragedy that makes them vulnerable. All of these actions will contribute to the well-being of workers and motivate them to respect management and contribute to the well-being of the organization.[38]

K. Praveen Parboteeah, associate professor of management at the University of Wisconsin at Whitewater, and John B. Cullen, professor of strategy at the Amsterdam Business School, in an article titled "Ethical Climates and Spirituality," examine how the ethical climate of an organization can contribute to spirituality in the workplace. The ethical climate refers to the prescriptive dimension that reflects the prevailing organizational practices that have moral consequences. An ethical climate helps employees identify ethical issues within the organization and serves as a perceptual lens through which employees diagnose and assess ethical situations. An ethical climate helps workers resolve and find answers when faced with a moral dilemma that has no immediate and obvious solution. Such a climate also helps corporations to follow a morality that demands more out of them than simply adhering to the minimal standards of acceptability involved in following conventional business practices.[39]

Spirituality is defined by the authors as a feeling of being connected with oneself and others; it involves a sense of connectedness and wholeness in the workplace. Spirituality can benefit employees by helping them deal with the realities of the workplace and find meaning in their work as they connect with other people. Spirituality can benefit the organization as well by enhancing organizational performance. Given this sense of spirituality, the authors rely on a study that identified three distinct factors that reflect spirituality. These include conditions for community, meaning at work, and the inner life of workers.[40]

The first factor involves the extent to which employees feel that they are allowed to be part of a community rather than just a lone individual working at a particular task. As part of a community workers can grow personally, feel they are valued as individuals, and find a sense of belonging. If such conditions are present, workers can bring their whole self to work and develop meaningful interpersonal relations. Regarding finding meaning at work, if the right conditions are present workers can go beyond regarding work as merely interesting and satisfying and achieve personal fulfillment and spiritual growth in the workplace itself. Finally, the inner life refers to a sense of hopefulness and an awareness of personal values. Recognition of this inner life means seeing workers as having both a mind and a spirit and that both are equally important.[41]

To establish a link between and ethics in organizations and these three manifestations of spirituality, the authors rely on a typology of ethical climates from a previous study. The first climate, labeled the *egoistic* climate, is one where organizational norms support the satisfaction of self-interest. Within this climate the individual's self-interest is the primary source of moral reasoning when they have to make a moral decision. The needs and interest of others are ignored; thus, within this kind of ethical climate a sense of community is less likely to develop. Within this climate it is also difficult to develop a sense of meaningful work as selfish interests alienate the worker from a transcendent dimension of the workplace. And such a climate does not promote the development of an inner life as workers are seen as coldly self-serving in their behavior.[42]

The second kind of ethical climate is called the *benevolent* climate, where company norms support maximization of joint interests even if it means that individual needs will be ignored. Within this climate people are encouraged to make utilitarian decisions that provide the greatest good for the greatest number of people. Individuals are encouraged to have a sincere interest for the well-being of everyone. Obviously this climate fosters the development of a sense of community through encouraging a deep connection and relationship between people. Caring for others and helping them also facilitate finding meaning in the workplace. And finally, the benevolent climate fosters the development of the inner life aspect of spirituality as it provides a counter to the egoistic and selfish nature of human beings in Western societies.[43]

The third ethical climate, the *principled* climate, is one in which company norms support following abstract ethical principles that are independent of situational outcomes. Within this climate there is an expectation that workers will rely on their own personal morality in making ethical decisions. It is assumed that workers will reach a higher level of ethical maturity by relying on their own values and standards in reaching conclusions about ethical behavior. In a principled climate, morality comes from analyzing the act rather than the consequences, which is consistent with Kantian universal moral judgment rather than with utilitarianism. Within this climate it is argued that workers can gain a sense of trust and respect for others which fosters a sense of community. Such a climate can also contribute to a sense of meaning through a deeper understanding of a job and organizational issues. And workers in this kind of climate are more likely to reach higher levels of moral development that involves the inner self.[44]

In sum, the authors suggest that the benevolent and principled ethical climates are more strongly linked to workplace spirituality. The egoistic climate with its emphasis on self-interest at the expense of other individuals seems to be the least desirable climate for the development of workplace spirituality. To encourage all aspects of workplace spirituality managers need to promote the benevolent and principled ethical climates and convey that the organization is concerned with more than just maximizing profits. They need to create a climate where workers feel they belong and connect with their coworkers, where workers feel their work contributes to society and has a higher meaning beyond the immediate workplace, and where they can develop their inner life and find deeper reasons for their existence than mere survival.[45]

Michael G. Bowen, Gerald R. Ferris, and Robert W. Kolodinsky examine the effect organizational politics has on workplace spirituality and how certain leadership attributes may be most effective in promoting spirituality in the workplace. They argue that the self-serving aspects of organizational politics often produce detrimental effects and can adversely affect workers and work environments. However, political skill, which they see as a separate construct from organizational politics, is a set of political competencies that can promote spirituality in the workplace and neutralize the dysfunctional consequences that often result from organizational politics. According to the authors there are two emerging areas of leadership that are most relevant to the development of spirit-based organizations while at the same time are helpful in reducing the negative effects of organizational politics. Leaders who are both politically skilled and servant oriented inspire trust and confidence in allowing workers to achieve a sense of balance, meaning, and personal fulfillment in the workplace.[46]

Political skill has been defined as the ability to understand the needs and aspirations of other people and to use this knowledge to influence others to act in ways that enhance personal and organizational objectives. They combine social astuteness with the ability to adjust their behavior to changing situations in a manner that inspires support and trust from employees. They are more likely to see the benefits of promoting workplace spirituality and its relation to effective organizational functioning than leaders who are rigid and unaccepting of diverse views of spirituality. They make it easier for workers to embrace the notion of a spiritually rich workplace.[47]

Servant leadership is grounded in the idea that the best leadership is provided by those who seek to serve others. The clear articulation of a vision that inspires workers is often associated with servant leadership. Thus, a key challenge for such leadership is to articulate a vision that is sufficiently clear and focused and yet flexible enough to reconcile the organization's need for effectiveness with the employee's needs for personal growth, purpose, and meaning in their work. Servant leaders are able to articulate goals for the organization, inspire trust in followers, know how to listen to people, give positive feedback, and emphasize personal development of employees. Servant leadership is most likely to embrace workplace spirituality, which emphasizes listening to workers and understanding their needs, values, desires, and issues.[48]

The authors believe that leaders can be both politically skilled and servant-oriented at the same time. Both types of leaders inspire trust in workers and are able to make the kinds of connections that are important for developing a sense of community that is characteristic of a spiritual workplace. Both leadership types can be socially and emotionally connected with workers with the ability to listen and discern workers' needs and concerns and enable workers to feel connected and understood as valued members of the organization. Leaders who exemplify both political skills and are servant oriented are best positioned to develop a spiritually rich workplace and reduce organizational politics, creating a workplace where more positive outcomes such as increased job satisfaction and commitment to the organization are likely.[49]

Bennett J. Tepper, a professor at Georgia State University, introduces a new construct called *organizational citizenship behavior* (OCB) into the discussion of workplace spirituality. This construct refers to discretionary actions on the part of workers that are not necessarily formally rewarded but that, in the aggregate, promote organizational effectiveness. For example, some research has shown that workers who are more satisfied with their jobs exemplified OCB behaviors such as helping colleagues and speaking favorably of the organization with greater frequency. Since its introduction there has been a good deal of empirical research into OCB that has found that employees perform OCB behaviors to reciprocate to their organization for fair treatment and to manage favorable impressions.[50]

Tepper proposes a third antecedent to OCB that is linked to workplace spirituality, that is, that employees perform OCB more frequently if they find sacred meaning and purpose to their existence. According to Tepper, spirituality influences OCB through three mediating psychological states: gratefulness, sensitivity to the needs of others, and tolerance for inequity. He argues that spiritual individuals are more likely to experience gratefulness in doing ordinary activities. One way individuals can express this gratefulness is by doing things that benefit other people; hence, spirituality can produce gratefulness in individuals, which, in turn, produces OCB behaviors that benefit other workers and the employer. Thus, gratefulness mediates the relationship between spirituality and OCB; employees who are more spiritual will also be more grateful, which motivates them to perform OCB with greater frequency.[51]

According to the author individuals look to others for validation of their spiritual strivings and, in turn, serve to validate other people's spiritual strivings. In order to validate their own spirituality, individuals must be sensitive to what other people think, but in order to validate other people's spirituality, they must be sensitive to what other people need. This sensitivity to other people's needs should translate into OCB, which can take the form of helping others when they need assistance, being courteous by informing people of decisions or policies that will affect them, and encouraging other people to do their best in the workplace. Sensitivity to the needs of other thus mediates the relationship between spirituality and OCB; employees who are spirituality inclined will be more sensitive to the needs of others which will motivate them to perform OCB with greater frequency.[52]

Finally, spiritual individuals should be able to accept experiences that fall short of expectations, to persist in the face of failure, and to forgive organizations and coworkers for minor mistakes and indiscretions. This capacity to accept less than ideal outcomes should produce greater OCB on the part of those workers. Even in the face of unfair allocations of decision-making processes individuals with a high tolerance for inequity should be more forgiving and willing to continue their commitment to the organization. This tolerance will thus mediate the relationship between spirituality and OCB; employees who have a greater degree of spirituality will have a higher tolerance for inequities in the workplace and be motivated to perform OCB with greater frequency.[53]

These mediating relationships will be stronger when there is a greater convergence between the spirituality of the employee and the target's values whether it is the employer or some other specific individual in the workplace. For those individuals that demonstrate spirituality, the search for meaningfulness that is involved in spiritual behavior influences their willingness to perform desired work behavior (OCB) regardless of their relationship with the organization and their desire to manage favorable impressions. In conclusion, Tepper argues that from both practical and scholarly perspectives, the OCB literature represents one of the most promising and useful areas of management research. The organization depends on employee's willingness to perform OCB behaviors; thus, understanding the factors that contribute to the performance of OCB, such as spirituality, has important implications for organizational effectiveness.[54]

Andrew J Hoffman, Holcim Professor of Sustainable Enterprise at the University of Michigan, focuses on the management function and notes that an increasing number of managers who find that the values of the organization they work for clash with their personal values choose to remain in the organization acting as change agents or organizational entrepreneurs to alter the firm's cultural values rather than leave the organization for a new position elsewhere. In doing so they are striving to develop their complete self in the workplace by bringing their personal values, which Hoffman thinks are synonymous with spiritual beliefs, into the workplace. These personal values represent a higher purpose and a higher sense of service in making a contribution to society as a whole rather than just a narrow focus on the profits of the organization; hence, they are spiritual in nature.[55]

Managerial action is strongly influenced by the organizational culture of the organizations to which they belong and by the social institutions in which they reside. These cultures shape individual consciousness and guide the perceptions and behavior of their members and give collective value and meaning to particular events and activities. Since managers are members of multiple social groups, they often find that the cultural demands of these groups are in conflict. Organizational life becomes an attempt to mediate between these demands. They seek to make a success in their job and thus are committed to their professional workplace values, but they are also committed to their personal social values that may clash with these values of the workplace. In the face of such conflict there is a tendency to change those cultural elements that are easiest to change.[56]

With regard to environmental values, changes to the organization to incorporate environmental values came about primarily because of external pressures brought by environmental groups. But beginning in the 1990s, according to Hoffman, drivers for environmental responsibility came from within the organization itself as younger managers began to pressure top management to positively respond to environmental issues. While environmental groups continued to influence the belief systems of these managers, education and religion also came to create a powerful link between personal and environmental values. Educational institutions, claims Hoffman, indoctrinate their students in the appropriate way to think and act within society and have educated youth about the environment that is far different from that of previous generations. Religious values regarding the environment are also changing as the religious leaders of many different faiths have adopted environmental protection as a religious and moral issue. These religious values in combination with changes in educational values have become a potent force in influencing the thinking and values of individual managers.[57]

To mediate the conflict between professional and personal values managers try to fit within both cultural domains. On one hand, they may simply try to model new beliefs about appropriate behavior in the workplace without attempting to change the organization itself. On the other hand, they may act as change agents attempting to alter the culture of the workplace to be more consistent with their personal values. The spiritually motivated manager then becomes an organizational entrepreneur. They may draw a great deal of personal satisfaction by introducing environmental values into the workplace as a way of meeting their spiritual objectives.[58]

There are two tactics they can use in this regard. The first is to reframe environmental issues into the terms, language, and rhetoric of the workplace by showing how taking environmental issues into account can improve operating efficiency, reduce the costs of risk management, reduce costs of capital, increase market demand, improve strategic direction, or improve human resource management. However, when spiritual values do not fit with accepted notion of acceptable business practices, the manager may seek to change the measures of success within the organization and articulate different values about what is important and unimportant and what is right and wrong within the organization.[59]

The second tactic is the maintenance of multiple affiliations both inside and outside the organization. Managers may remain firmly connected to those environmental, educational, and religious groups which have influence their beliefs and behavior as these groups can continue to provide support and information vital to the role of a change agent. Inside the workplace the spiritually motivated manager can establish networks with key constituents who are necessary to make change happen within the organization. They must understand the politics of change within the organization and draw resources from within to support their objectives.[60]

Organizations themselves must help their employees revolve these tensions between professional and personal values. Unresolved tensions inhibit commitment to organizational goals and thus adversely affect organizational performance. Resolving these tensions can improve productivity by channeling behavior toward activities that benefit both the individual and the organization. They must develop new proficiencies to understand the motivation of a manager who chooses to act as a change agent and be an organizational entrepreneur. Organizations and employees can work together to create a highly committed workforce by actively seeking to align professional and personal values.[61]

Religion and Workplace Spirituality

The issue of religion and spirituality and how this relationship affects the workplace is an important issue that is addressed by several authors. Since religion is an important source of spirituality for many people it is important to address the question of what place, if any, religion has in the workplace. While many social scientists believe that with the rise of science during the Enlightenment modern scientific truth has superseded all previous belief systems and secularization has taken hold in modern societies, many surveys suggest that religion is alive and well in contemporary American society. Thus, the secularization model has been revised to take this into account.

Nonetheless, while religion has not been eliminated in American life it has been transformed as mainstream institutional religion has lost much of its influence over people. This transformation has been described as a privatization of religion where human experience has been divided into public and private spheres. The rational character of the public sphere makes it less likely that religious beliefs will be relevant in such a setting and is more viable in ordering personal affairs.[62]

In light of this transformation, the term *spirituality* has been used more frequently to describe such experiences as meaningfulness, purpose, transcendence, connection with others, well-being, and the like, components that were once understood to be part of one's religious experience. This allows for the possibility of a spirituality that is not connected with religion and the emergence of a conceptual distinction between religion and spirituality. Yet there are many commonalities between religion and spirituality that must not be overlooked. Both consider life to be sacred, which involves a transcendent dimension that goes beyond mere pleasure or comfort. Both religion and spirituality involve questions of meaning and purpose and consider any culture that is based on science and rationality to be impoverished because of science's limited capacity to fulfill the human search for meaning.[63]

Some authors find a distinction between a dwelling spirituality and a seeking spirituality to be useful in a further analysis of spirituality in the workplace. A dwelling spirituality emphasizes security and promotes a sense of community interrelatedness with others and a spiritual home where one can feel secure. This sense of certainty and stability reduces the chaos and confusion of life. A seeking spirituality, on the other hand, offers individuals a greater sense of freedom from the constraints of community expectations and a willingness to explore one's inner life in a search for personal fulfillment. Spiritual seekers are more likely to stress personal growth and inner development than are dwellers and see truth as more subjectively determined and therefore less certain and absolute.[64]

With regard to the workplace, spiritual dwellers focus more on the theological and spiritual basis of work and may, in some cases, see work as a form of worship: that they should see their work as a service to God and others. The idea that work is a calling to serve and love God is common to dwellers and motivates them to use their skills and talents more fully. They are primed to pursue excellence in their jobs and respond positively to any corporate campaigns to promote this virtue in the workplace. Their faith can provide a supportive network of like-minded people that can help them cope with job-related pressures. Dwellers often find stability and security in their work and coworkers become something like a family and the workplace becomes a quasi-spiritual home for them.[65]

Spiritual seekers, on the other hand, prize freedom and individuality and enjoy work that gives them at least a sense of freedom and allows them to express this individuality and provides them with a sense of personal fulfillment. Work needs to provide them with the opportunity to give a legitimate account of themselves. The sense of accomplishment work can provide is more important to them than salary, fringe benefits, time off, and other such extrinsic factors. Some companies report that by enhancing spirituality in the workplace people can reach a relaxed centeredness, a heightened awareness of their surroundings, get along better with their coworkers, and make better business decisions. In short, seekers have more of a process orientation and focus more on the personal benefits they can receive through work and how it affects their inner selves.[66]

Any workplace is likely to have both dwellers and seekers, and thus, organizations that want to respond to the spiritual needs of their employees must be flexible and inclusive of both orientations. They need to respect dwellers' need for moral order and the social support the workplace can provide, while at the same time respond to seekers' needs for freedom and individuality and guard against being too legalistic by having too many formal rules and procedures that constrain workers' behavior. Organizations can encourage both groups to see their work as more of a vocation by informing workers about the way in which their products or services benefit society and point out how important the jobs the workers have contribute to that product or service. In any event, companies need to better understand the needs of both dwellers and seekers, how these two orientations differ, and what impacts they have on the workplace.[67]

Richard D. White Jr., the Marjory Ourso Excellence in Teaching Professor at Louisiana State University, focuses on the conflicts that can arise when organizations attempt to respond to the spiritual needs of employees. While there may be many benefits to promoting spirituality in the workplace, there are also limitations to encouraging spirituality that employers need to consider. Employees can tap into spirituality employing secular means and methods or turn toward religious sources for their spiritual nourishment. The line between these two approaches if often blurred and fuzzy. Secular methods include things like yoga exercises or meditation of some sort that would seem to be easier for employers to accommodate. Bringing religion into the workplace, however, can involve accommodating different kinds of clothing that may offend some workers, respecting holidays and holy days by giving employees time off for religious observances, and other such measures. When employees transform their spirituality into specific behaviors, conflicts can arise between the right of employees to practice their religion and the employer's right to efficiently conduct a business.[68]

According to White, the development of workplace religious policy falls into three distinct periods with each period having a different emphasis. In the first period, which ran from the formation of the nation to the 1950s, the emphasis was on the rights of the employer and an employee could be fired because of his or her religious beliefs with no regard for due process. The courts made a distinction between religious thought and religious behavior. The freedom to act on one's beliefs could be restricted while the freedom to believe, of course, could not be affected by any policy as people are free to believe whatever they want. They just couldn't act on their beliefs without exposing themselves to being fired or whatever else the employer deemed necessary.[69]

The second period, which ran from the 1950s through the 1960s, saw a shift in emphasis toward the rights of the employee. Various decisions of the Supreme Court forced states to recognize the unique requirements that various religious traditions imposed on its adherents. The burden of proof in disputes was shifted from the employee to the employer altering the balance of power in these disputes. The third period began in the late sixties and continues to the present and involves more of a balance between the rights of the employer, the employee, and the public interest. There were three concerns to take into account: (1) the constitutional rights of the employee; (2) the organization's responsibility to function in an efficient, effective, and economical manner; and (3) the impact on the public interest. The courts have to decide which of these concerns takes precedence in any particular case that comes before them.[70]

The Civil Rights Act of 1964 was modified in 1972 to require employers to "reasonably accommodate" employee's religious beliefs meaning any action that does not impose "undue hardship" on the employer. However, there has been continuing confusion about the meaning of these terms and whether the Civil Rights Act actually gives an advantage to either the employee or employer. The act itself provides little guidance for determining what level of accommodation is required of the employer and what creates an undue hardship. Court decisions involving these issues have muddled the boundaries of religious freedom and have been of little help in defining what constitutes an undue hardship on the employer. Executive orders of the president have fared no better in this regard.[71]

This confusion affects public employers in particular but also has implications for private employers. White offers several suggestions to cope with this situation. Where religious convictions can be easily accommodated with little financial impact or loss in efficiency or infringement on the rights of other employees, it seems obvious that religious expression can be accommodated. The more difficult cases require a balance between the rights of the employee and employer and can be evaluated with regard to any impact on the efficiency and effectiveness of the organization. The employer must walk a fine line to avoid litigation that could adversely affect the organization.[72]

Religious expression should be handled the same as any other kind of expression, and supervisors must be careful not to treat employees differently because of their religion. Training of leaders is essential and they must base their decisions regarding religious expression mainly on the requirements of the job rather than on prejudices or other irrelevant factors. Policies with respect to religion in the workplace must be clear to provide guidance for supervisors and those they are supervising. Employees have a responsibility to not abuse whatever accommodations are made for his or her religious beliefs. In the final analysis, the employer's commitment to promoting spiritual health, including religious expression, can serve as a reminder that the employees of that organization are valued and are an important part of the organization.[73]

Other Aspects of Workplace Spirituality

Several authors treat the relationship of spirituality to certain outcomes in the workplace. Adrian Furnham, professor of psychology at University College in London, for example, examines spirituality in relation to money and happiness. While many people report that more money would improve the quality of their lives, research, for the most part, shows only a modest correlation between income and happiness. The research results show that after a certain point, there is no relationship between personal wealth and happiness. Personality traits such as stability, extraversion, agreeableness, and high self-esteem were found to be the strongest predictors of happiness. People who are into spirituality should not be surprised at these findings as the term implies that nonmaterial things such as personal fulfillment, meaningful work, and purpose in life are more likely to bring happiness and contentment rather than the accumulation of more and more wealth.[74]

Furnham then goes on to describe various ethical approaches one can adopt that relate to how one understands the role of work in one's life and that prescribe appropriate conduct in the workplace. Some of these approaches are definitely spiritualistic in nature while others are more materialistic. It is not clear how this analysis of ethical approaches links up with the first part of the paper that deals with happiness and well-being in the workplace other than perhaps some of these approaches can implicitly be seen as encouraging better outcomes in the workplace and in one's life in general.[75] In any event, it seems that what Furnham really has here is two different papers that address different aspects of happiness and well-being.

The author first describes the *Protestant work ethic*, which emphasizes the concept of the calling where individuals are called to fulfill their duty to God by working in this world; the doctrine of predestination, which motivated people to prove they were one of the elect by accumulating wealth; and a worldly asceticism, which stressed saving and investment rather than consumption. The *wealth ethic* stresses the need to have sufficient wealth so one is not dependent on others and work is a means to this end of wealth accumulation. Some scholars argue that the work ethic was incorrectly perceived and is, in fact, the wealth ethic, where wealth should be acquired honestly because of its obvious and manifest benefits. The *welfare ethic*, on the other hand, argues that people should enjoy the good life by living off payments received from the welfare system.[76]

The *leisure ethic* holds that work cannot be made meaningful and fulfilling and is only a means to earn money to pursue leisure activities in which personal fulfillment and pleasure can be found. The *sports ethic* is where human fulfillment is found in sports, either in competitive sports such as tennis and handball or in individual activities such as hiking and snowshoeing. In the *narcissistic ethic* the culture of competitive individualism has changed into a narcissistic preoccupation with the self as the source of happiness. This ethic involves the care and training of the mind and body to project a certain self-image, where the symbols of success are more important than actual achievements.[77]

The *romantic ethic* is believed to be responsible for modern consumerism as it has created and justified consumer hedonism. The romantics believed people could be morally improved through consuming cultural products that yielded pleasure. Finally the *being ethic* stresses shared experienced and the affirmation of living. The materialistic way of life has failed to provide happiness, it is said, and economic progress is not conducive to well-being. The ethic of being involves an inner security that is not based on wealth or success in materialistic terms, a sense of identity and confidence based on what one is than what one has, a need for relatedness and for solidarity with the world around one without a need to control it and possess it for one's own interests.[78]

R. Elliott Ingersoll, professor of counseling and counseling psychology at Cleveland State University, maintains that spiritual wellness and spiritual well-being have been a concern of researchers in sociology and psychology for more than thirty years, and the constructs they have developed are directly applicable to the workplace. Ingersoll chooses to focus on spiritual wellness, which he claims has its origin in the medical wellness movement, where wellness is defined "as the optimum integration of the various dimensions of human functioning," which includes spirituality. The author discusses various dimensions of spiritual wellness in the article that were developed by using a panel of experts from eleven different spiritual traditions. These dimensions include (1) a conception of the absolute or divine, (2) meaning, (3) connectedness, (4) mystery, (5) present-centeredness, (6) spiritual freedom, (7) forgiveness, (8) hope, (9) knowledge and learning, and (10) ritual.[79]

Many people maintain that whatever they believe the concept of *divinity* helps them develop ethically and helps guide their actions as they live and work in the world. In many traditions, honesty in business dealings and promoting practices that have a positive impact on society are stressed. The challenge for managers is to create a workplace where a spiritual worldview can be expressed. They may find that in many instances, this practice also fosters a healthy workplace with less friction among employees and greater productivity. In general, however, organizations that would most benefit from such a workplace are less likely to foster such an acknowledgment where spirituality is encouraged.[80]

Meaning, according to Ingersoll, involves a sense that life is worth living and that work can serve purposes beyond physical existence. Ingersoll suggests that managers may well wish to explore the meaning their own work provides and do the same with their employees. Honesty is an important ingredient for this kind of dialogue, and if it is not present, little of value will result from such discussions. But it can be important for employees to know the key values of those running the company as it may help them assess if they can find meaningful work in the organization or whether they may be better off seeking employment in another company.[81]

The dimension of *connectedness* can refer to one's sense of being connected with the divine, with other people, with nature, or perhaps with all three. Most people live some distance from their work and have to spend time commuting and thus have less time to spend with family and neighbors or get involved in their communities. This increases the value of their connectedness in the workplace and makes an organization that can foster this connectedness all the more important. Competition certainly affects connectedness and if not directed properly can become destructive, but a healthy competition can contribute to the success of the organization and its employees. Connectedness can promote an awareness of the needs of others and enable one to empathize with others, an ability that Ingersoll thinks is important to people in management positions.[82]

The dimension of *mystery* is something of a mystery itself, but Ingersoll takes it to refer to a capacity for awe and wonder and how one deals with ambiguity and uncertainty. Uncertainty and risk often go together and if managers are quick to blame workers when things go wrong this may cause the workers to minimize risk in the future and resist change which may decrease performance. The ability to tolerate uncertainty should be promoted as it frees energy to focus on the task at hand with all its attendant risks and challenges.[83]

Present-centeredness refers to the ability to focus and respond to every moment as it unfolds, which is a valuable skill for any job but particularly those that involve machinery and repetitive actions where death and injury is a possibility. This dimension also involves the ability to stay attentive which is a valuable characteristic in employees. Meditation is one of the oldest practices that can be used to increase the ability to be attentive, and since it is by and large a secular practice it can be easily implemented in the workplace without getting involved in religious entanglements that can be detrimental to the organization.[84]

Spiritual freedom refers to the lack of coercion either from within, where one may punish oneself for certain behaviors and from without where one may be punished by an authority for certain things one is doing. Always having to be vigilant regarding the source of the coercion takes a good deal of energy and does not make a person feel safe. And it reduces the ability of a person to see all the options that are available as one can feel trapped and unable to see a way out of the situation. Lack of freedom does not contribute to spiritual well-being or to a sense of well-being in the workplace.[85]

Forgiveness had positive correlations with health and wellness and involved working through the negative emotions connected with getting

214 Sources of Spirituality

hurt by another rather than just trying to bury the hurt and forget about it to get on with things. This can result in having one's life ruled by memory of the incident for a very long time. Expressing anger toward a coworker who precipitated the incident can often result in regret over a ruined relationship. Working through that anger and making an effort to forgive and understand the situation of the coworker can be a form of self-care and allow redirection of one's energy in a more positive manner.[86]

Hope is essential to navigating life and dealing with all the adversities that life involves. It is certainly essential to the workplace as one's work can be a source of hope or a place to lose it because of some negative incident. Hope has been described as "positive expectation" and as what some have called "hopeful thought" that involves goals, agency, and pathways. People require pathways in order to pursue their goals and the agency to pursue those pathways. Managers can assess whether the workplace provides such pathways where employees can achieve their goals and thus find hope in the workplace or whether the workplace is a place where such hopes are squashed.[87]

Hope, says Ingersoll, is often tied up with the ability to gain new *knowledge* and *learn* new things in and away from the workplace. People who are interested in their life and life in general are less likely to be bored and more likely to engage in new things with interest and curiosity even if the work they do is repetitive and offers no opportunities for lifelong learning. When people become hopeless they may be more likely to spend whatever downtime they have from work in front of the television set rather than engaging in learning activities that may be available to them. Even if these activities are not work related, they will have positive benefits for employees that carry over to the workplace.[88]

Finally, *ritual* refers to practices that people engage in that are related to their spiritual being or worldview. Ritual can be narrowly defined to refer only to religious practices or more broadly to include secular activities. Ingersoll thinks of ritual as a regular activity that focuses one's mind on the transcendent which can be a totally secular undertaking. Related to the workplace, ritual could take the form of sessions during the day devoted to meditation or yoga and other such practices. Going to work itself can be something of a ritual is it connects people with something larger than themselves and provides meaning to their lives, but it is not good for people to become identified almost exclusively with their work and have nothing else in their life that provides meaning and purpose.[89]

In conclusion, Ingersoll thinks that the construct of spiritual wellness provides a meaningful way to talk about spirituality in the workplace without being bound by the language and practices of a particular religious tradition. Every one of the ten dimensions he mentions can focus on individually as a source of research, as well as the umbrella construct of spiritual wellness itself. However, an application of spiritual wellness to the workplace need not wait for such research as anecdotal and clinical evidence suggests the usefulness of this construct to enhance the functioning of humans both inside and outside of the workplace. The potential benefits of this construct need to be explored by management in the interests of both employees and the organization.[90]

In an article titled "The Multiple Roles of Spirituality in Occupational Stress and Well-Being," Kelly L. Zellars, Pamela L. Perrewe, and Jeremy R. Brees, focus on spirituality and its relation, as the title suggests, to the occupational stress process. Occupational stress refers to the physiological and psychological reactions of employees to conditions in the workplace that produce stress. It is a feeling that the demands of the job someone is doing exceed his or her capacity to cope with these demands. The literature on occupational stress shows that stressful demands of a job can have debilitating consequences for employees and is associated with numerous health problems while it costs employees billions of dollars in disability claims, absenteeism, and lost productivity.[91]

The authors define spirituality as the search for and experience of the sacred, which includes a desire to find one's place in the world and a search for meaning in one's existence. The authors consider this definition to be broader than any particular organized religion as not all those who embrace spirituality believe in a higher being. However, spirituality does emerge through the awareness of a transcendent dimension to life as spirituality involves a respect and concern for the well-being of others and a reverence for the universe and its creation. It involves a sense of interconnectedness with other living things, including animals, and a realization of the potential they have to contribute to life in general.[92]

The authors consider two categories of what they call antecedents to job stress. These are personality characteristics and job or organizational conditions. With regard to the former, the most frequently examined characteristic in the literature is negative affectivity. Workers with this characteristic focus on the negative aspects of all situations including their jobs and thus report greater levels of stress on the job. People with positive affectivity, on the other hand, behave in a manner that elicits positive emotions that help them cope with job stress and enables them to perform better and be less likely to experience all the negative effects the job can produce. Organizational factors that can contribute to job stress include insecurity about the job itself, interpersonal conflicts, technological changes, abusive supervisors, ambiguous requests from management, and work-family conflicts. The greater number of these stressors that are present in the work situation the more likely employees are likely to feel stress.[93]

Not all potential stressors in the job situation actually produce stress in individuals as they differ in their assessment of the relevance of a potential stressor and hence in what they believe is stressful. One reason for this difference may be people's sense of spirituality as spirituality can moderate the relationship between the personality characteristics of the worker and the job stressors that are present. They may be guided by a sense of purpose and believe there is a transcendent reason for or meaning in the events that occur in the workplace. Spirituality may also minimize the perceived threats for those employees who are high in negative affectivity. Spirituality can give these individuals a sense of coherence and control that they may not have otherwise.[94]

When workers feel or experience stress they often attempt to discover the cause of the stress and spirituality moderates the relationship between the perceived stressors and the attribution of causes. Spirituality differs from luck as the latter is arbitrary and random while spirituality conveys a sense of order and purpose. An attribution based on a sense of spirituality can positively affect the acceptance of a stressful situation and help reduce the stress to acceptable levels. It helps the individual adopt a broader view of the current situation and accept a stressful situation as simply one of life's experiences. Stress is perceived as part of a greater scenario of events and helps workers regain some sense of control over their environment making it more predictable and less random.[95]

The authors conclude that spirituality can be effective in helping workers cope with stressful situations. They again mention that they separate specific religious practices from the construct of spirituality and focus on the personal search for meaning and sacredness that is relevant to the workplace. They also claim that much of research on workplace spirituality has been anecdotal and conceptual in nature and that it is time for more systematic and empirical examination of the relation between spirituality and stress in the workplace. While spiritual activities in the workplace may promote physiological and psychological well-being in the workplace, more empirical research is needed before such propositions can be used to guide managerial behavior.[96]

Hope in the workplace is another dimension that is discussed in the literature on workplace spirituality. Since the Great Recession many people in American society have still not found a job and have given up hope of ever finding employment. Many of the jobs that people have are low paying with little security as the economy has shifted from a manufacturing- to a service-based economy. The unfortunate reality about work in the modern economy is that many workers see a lack of opportunity in the work they do and the workplace as a place of mundane misery. People have lost hope in a better future for themselves and their children, and the American dream of continued growth and prosperity for all has faded. These factors lead some authors to develop a theory of hope and its relationship to the workplace with the hope of reestablishing it to bring greater happiness to the workplace.[97]

For some authors, the definition of hope includes both pathways and agency thought, where pathways thinking involves the *perception* that effective routes to personal goals can be achieved that does not necessarily mean concrete plans have been developed and where agency thought provides the motivation for people to pursue their goals by tapping into perceptions that people can actually *begin* and *sustain* goal-directed movements. Pathways and agency, it is argued, are the two primary components of hopeful thinking, and if either is missing the likelihood of attaining one's goals is impaired or blocked.[98]

Research on hope and the workplace shows that high-hope employees are better able to find alternate routes to goal attainment when normal routes are blocked by things like corporate restructuring and downsizing. There is also evidence that taking the time and effort to build hope within employees can enhance the mission of the organization. Placing managers into work groups that are cohesive where tasks and goals are shared can lead to an increased sense of social support and career optimism. Research also shows that if people are happy at work, they are also more likely to be happy with their lives outside of work. The reverse is also true as life is a whole, and if it is difficult to be happy with life in general, one's work is also likely to be not meaningful and enjoyable.[99]

Hope is related to job stress; as such stress can result from impeded pursuit of goals in the workplace. People who are high in hope are less likely to view obstacles of this nature as stressful and are better able to cope with obstacles than low-hope people. Hopeful workers are likely to be more productive and happier making the creation of hopeful work environments of great importance. The authors believe that the creation of this kind of climate will become more important as the economy shifts to a more service and information orientation. A key aspect of a hopeful work environment is social support as supportive and open relationships with coworkers can foster productivity and creativity. Workers who have little control over their work can experience stress and burnout. Companies who give workers greater control over their work can not only foster hope in this manner but also trust between employees and the corporation. Finally, the authors think it is important to note that it is not stress as such that is harmful but how one interprets it that is crucial to coping with adverse situations in the workplace. One can see these situations as providing new challenges and opportunities or as a threat to one's self and existence.[100]

Within hope theory, people are thought to feel good about themselves, that is, have high self-esteem, when they perceive themselves as being successful in attaining their goals, and conversely, having low self-esteem when they think they are blocked or unsuccessful in reaching goals that are important to them. Hope is believed to be the source of self-esteem, and high-hope people believe that the career they have chosen is the right pathway for reaching their goals and that they have the necessary agency to succeed both of which leads to higher self-esteem. People with high self-esteem are likely to be more satisfied with their jobs and less likely to be absent from work and stay with their employer longer. Companies that foster hope in the workplace are thus more likely to see enhanced performance and productivity leading to greater profitability.[101]

In the spring of 2000, a survey was completed that appeared in *Success* magazine that used a Hope Scale to identify the top ten companies as far as hopefulness was concerned and found several commonalties across these companies. The first commonality was that all ten companies were profitable and reported financial success along with projected growth. Thus, the most hopeful companies appeared to be prospering. Second, these companies anchored hope to concrete goals and shared ownership of these goals between management and employees, which seemed to increase creativity and pride in their companies. These companies also had CEOs that were not dictatorial and worked hard to create trust, respect, and affection among their employees. Almost all of the ten top companies also mentioned innovation as a key factor in hiring and keeping good employees, and all said they worked at creating and maintaining an environment that encouraged independent thought and discourse and gave their employees the opportunity to communicate across various levels of the company.[102]

The authors maintain that these ten companies collectively illustrate the power of hope in the workplace and demonstrate that encouraging hopefulness throughout the company can be a key to financial success. These hopeful cultures make people want to work for these companies and be productive employees. Hard work is rewarded in these companies, and employees are given responsibility for finding solutions to problems and implementing changes. High-hope employees motivate themselves, and management helps these employees set clear and realistic goals for themselves and enables them to achieve success by getting out of the way and not putting roadblocks and impediments in their way. The organization benefits from this success of their employees.[103]

Thus, there is a vast literature on the topic of workplace spirituality. In general, it seems to involve a sense of purpose to one's work that goes beyond merely earning a living, that there needs to be a transcendent dimension to work for it to be meaningful, and that employees need to feel they are making an important contribution to society. Workplace spirituality also involves the opportunity for growth of the self, the development of an inner life that is connected with others, a sense that one is part of a community rather than an isolated individual. Trust is also important and involves confidence in one's coworkers, as well as management, that one can rely on those around oneself for help and support and that management has an interest in the well-being of workers. Workplace spirituality also involves integrity in the sense that there is some degree of correspondence between one's personal values and the values of the organization.

The most important question, however, is the relation of workplace spirituality to the goals of the organization. Management has to be ultimately concerned about the bottom line and is highly unlikely to promote concerns that do not contribute to the profitability of the organization. Thus, it is most likely to support programs promoting workplace spirituality that enhance productivity and thus contribute to the profitability of the organization itself. Yet workers who perceive that this is the case are most likely to be turned off by attempts to promote workplace spirituality if they perceive that this is just another attempt by management to get them to work harder and longer. This basic distrust between workers and management is a fact of life in corporate organizations and is a rift that is unlikely to disappear unless and until there is a complete reorientation of bottom-line thinking.

Notes

1 Robert A. Giacalone and Carole L. Jurkiewicz, "Preface," in Robert A. Gia-calone and Carole L. Jurkiewicz, eds., *Handbook of Workplace Spirituality and Organizational Performance*, 2nd ed. (New York: M.E. Sharpe, 2010), xv.
2 Ibid.
3 J.G. Allegretti, *Loving Your Job, Finding Your Passion: Work and the Spiritual Life* (New York: Paulist Press, 2000).
4 W.A. Guillory, *Spirituality in the Workplace* (Salt Lake City, UT: Innovations International, 2000).
5 Robert A Giacalone and Carole L. Jurkiewicz, "The Science of Workplace Spirituality" in Robert A. Giacalone and Carole L. Jurkiewicz, eds., *Handbook of Workplace Spirituality and Organizational Performance*, 2nd ed. (New York: M.E. Sharpe, 2010), 5–6.
6 Barry Z. Posner, "Forward to the First Edition," in Robert A. Giacalone and Carole L. Jurkiewicz, eds., *Handbook of Workplace Spirituality and Organiza-tional Performance*, 2nd ed. (New York: M.E. Sharpe, 2010), xii.
7 Giacolone and Jurkiewicz, "The Science of Workplace Spirituality," 6.
8 Guillory, *Spirituality in the Workplace.*
9 Giacolone and Jurkiewicz, "The Science of Workplace Spirituality," 4–5.
10 Ibid., 4–5.
11 Ibid., 12–13.
12 Ibid., 13–14.
13 Ibid., 14–16.
14 Ibid., 18.
15 Ibid., 18–20.
16 Jeffrey Pfeffer, "Business and the Spirit: Management Practices that Sustain Values," in Robert A. Giacalone and Carole L. Jurkiewicz, eds., *Handbook of Workplace Spirituality and Organizational Performance*, 2nd ed. (New York: M.E. Sharpe, 2010), 29–30.
17 Ibid., 31.
18 Ibid., 31–32.
19 Ibid., 33.
20 Ibid., 34.
21 Ibid., 34–35.
22 Ibid., 35–37.
23 Ibid., 37–38.
24 Ibid., 38–39.
25 Ibid., 39–40.
26 Blake E. Ashforth and Michael G. Pratt, "Institutionalized Spirituality: An Oxy-moron?" in Robert A. Giacalone and Carole L. Jurkiewicz, eds., *Handbook of Workplace Spirituality and Organizational Performance*, 2nd ed. (New York: M.E. Sharpe, 2010), 44–45.
27 Ibid., 45–46.
28 Ibid., 46.
29 Ibid., 47–53.
30 Ibid., 54–55.

31 Gordon E. Dehler and M. Ann Welsh, "The Experience of Work: Spirituality and the New Workplace," in Robert A. Giacalone and Carole L. Jurkiewicz, eds., *Handbook of Workplace Spirituality and Organizational Performance*, 2nd ed. (New York: M.E. Sharpe, 2010), 60.
32 Ibid., 65.
33 Ibid., 65–67.
34 Ibid., 69.
35 Raymond F. Paloutzian, Robert A. Emmons, and Susan G. Keortge, "Spiritual Well-Being, Spiritual Intelligence, and Healthy Workplace Policy," in Robert A. Giacalone and Carole L. Jurkiewicz, eds., *Handbook of Workplace Spirituality and Organizational Performance*, 2nd ed. (New York: M.E. Sharpe, 2010), 73–74.
36 Ibid., 74–77.
37 Ibid.77–79.
38 Ibid., 81–85.
39 K. Praveen Parboteeah and John B. Cullen, "Ethical Climates and Spirituality: An Exploratory Examination of Theoretical Links," in Robert A. Giacalone and Carole L. Jurkiewicz, eds., *Handbook of Workplace Spirituality and Organizational Performance*, 2nd ed. (New York: M.E. Sharpe, 2010), 100.
40 Ibid.
41 Ibid., 100–101.
42 Ibid., 101–102.
43 Ibid., 103–104.
44 Ibid., 104–105.
45 Ibid., 109–110.
46 Michael G. Bowen, Gerald R. Ferris, and Robert W. Kolodinsky, "Political Skill, Servant Leadership, and Workplace Spirituality in the Creation of Effective Work Environments," in Robert A. Giacalone and Carole L. Jurkiewicz, eds., *Handbook of Workplace Spirituality and Organizational Performance*, 2nd ed. (New York: M.E. Sharpe, 2010), 127.
47 Ibid., 133–135.
48 Ibid., 131–133.
49 Ibid., 135–136.
50 Bennett J Tepper, "Organizational Citizenship Behavior and the Spiritual Employee," in Robert A. Giacalone and Carole L. Jurkiewicz, eds., *Handbook of Workplace Spirituality and Organizational Performance*, 2nd ed. (New York: M.E. Sharpe, 2010), 143.
51 Ibid., 146–147.
52 Ibid., 148.
53 Ibid.
54 Ibid., 149–150.
55 Andres J. Hoffman, "Reconciling Professional and Personal Value Systems: The Spiritually Motivated Manager as Organizational Entrepreneur," in Robert A. Giacalone and Carole L. Jurkiewicz, eds., *Handbook of Workplace Spirituality and Organizational Performance*, 2nd ed. (New York: M.E. Sharpe, 2010), 155–156.
56 Ibid., 158.
57 Ibid., 158–161.
58 Ibid., 162.
59 Ibid., 162–164.
60 Ibid., 164–165.
61 Ibid., 167.
62 Peter C. Hill and Gary S. Smith, "Coming to Terms with Spirituality and Religion in the Workplace," in Robert A. Giacalone and Carole L. Jurkiewicz eds.,

Handbook of Workplace Spirituality and Organizational Performance, 2nd ed. (New York: M.E. Sharpe, 2010), 171–172.

63 Ibid., 173–176.

64 Ibid., 176–178.

65 Ibid., 180.

66 Ibid., 181.

67 Ibid., 181–182.

68 Richard D. White, "Drawing the Line: Religion and Spirituality in the Workplace," in Robert A. Giacalone and Carole L Jurkiewicz, eds., *Handbook of Workplace Spirituality and Organizational Performance*, 2nd ed. (New York: M.E. Sharpe, 2010), 185.

69 Ibid., 187–188.

70 Ibid.

71 Ibid., 191–193.

72 Ibid., 194–195.

73 Ibid.

74 Adrian Furnham, "Ethics at Work: Money, Spirituality, and Happiness," in Robert A. Giacalone and Carole L. Jurkiewicz, eds., *Handbook of Workplace Spirituality and Organizational Performance*, 2nd ed. (New York: M.E. Sharpe, 2010), 199–204.

75 See Ibid., 213 for a table that show the relationship of these different ethical approaches to seven different dimensions of life including work, success, development, money, happiness, spirituality, and competitiveness.

76 Ibid., 204–207.

77 Ibid., 207–210.

78 Ibid., 210–213.

79 R. Elliott Ingersoll, "Spiritual Wellness in the Workplace," in Robert A. Giacalone and Carole L. Jurkiewicz, eds. *Handbook of Workplace Spirituality and Organizational Performance*, 2nd ed. (New York: M.E. Sharpe, 2010), 216–218. At the beginning of the article the author cites four sayings in regard to work that are very insightful: (1) Diane Fassel: Everywhere I go it seems that people are killing themselves with work, (2) Bhagavad Gita: They all attain perfection when they find joy in their work, (3) Thomas Aquinas: There can be no joy in living without joy in work, and (4) Timothy Leary: You can't do good unless you feel good.

80 Ibid., 217–218.

81 Ibid., 219.

82 Ibid., 220.

83 Ibid.

84 Ibid., 220–221.

85 Ibid., 221.

86 Ibid., 220–221.

87 Ibid., 222–223.

88 Ibid., 223.

89 Ibid., 223–224.

90 Ibid., 224.

91 Kelly L. Zellars, Pamela L. Perrewe, and Jeremy R. Brees, "The Multiple Roles of Spirituality in Occupational Stress and Well-Being," in Robert A. Giacalone and Carole L. Jurkiewicz, eds., *Handbook of Workplace Spirituality and Organizational Performance*, 2nd ed. (New York: M.E. Sharpe, 2010), 227.

92 Ibid., 228.

93 Ibid., 229–230.

94 Ibid., 230–231.

95 Ibid., 231–233.

96 Ibid., 235–236.
97 Virgil H. Adams III, C.R. Snyder, Kevin L. Rand, Elisa Ann O'Donnell, David R. Sigmon, and Kim M. Pulvers, "Hope in the Workplace," in Robert A. Giacalone and Carole L. Jurkiewicz, eds., *Handbook of Workplace Spirituality and Organizational Performance*, 2nd ed. (New York: M.E. Sharpe, 2010), 241–242.
98 Ibid., 242–243.
99 Ibid., 243–244.
100 Ibid., 244–245.
101 Ibid., 245–246.
102 Ibid., 247–248.
103 Ibid., 248–249.

Part III
Critiques of Capitalism

8   Marxist Theory

There was some renewed interest in Marxist theory during the 2008 economic crisis affecting Western societies. New classes were taught in Marxist thinking, and some books were written both for and against the idea of communism and the applicability of Marxist thought to the economic problems facing the United States and other capitalistic countries.[1] A *Harvard Business Review* blog post written by Umair Haque titled "Was Marx Right?" reviews several aspects of Marx's thought including exploitation and alienation of workers, crisis of overproduction, stagnation, false consciousness, and commodity fetishism for their relevance to today's economy. He concludes that these critiques of Marx seem more relevant to today's world than we might have guessed. While calling Marx's prescriptions for capitalism poor, Haque suggests it may nonetheless be worthwhile to explore the critiques and prophecies of Marx even if we don't agree with them.[2]

An article about Marx in *Bloomberg Businessweek* mentions several aspects of Marx's thinking that it calls "shockingly perceptive."[3] One of these aspects is Marx's observation that capitalism is inherently unstable, an observation that went against the prevailing wisdom at the time he lived. Another aspect is Marx's idea of the "reserve army of the unemployed," whose existence would keep downward pressure on wages for the employed because the unemployed would work for any wage they could get in order to survive. Marx also thought that capitalism tended toward overproduction because workers would never be paid enough to buy all the stuff that is produced by capitalism. Finally, unfettered capitalism results in wild excesses that eventually may destroy the system unless it is regulated to keep these excesses in check.

All of these aspects have applicability to the United States and other European countries. Instability was the order of the day during the worldwide financial crisis of 2008 as stock markets had wild swings up and down and several countries teetered on the edge of bankruptcy. The United States experienced great political and economic instability, and the future was kind of up for grabs for a time. The unemployment rate remained unreasonably high for some time and not enough jobs were being created by the private sector to keep everyone working. The middle class has seen its income decline for the past several decades while the very rich keep getting richer.[4] Such growing inequality means that working people do not have enough income to buy what the system produces.[5] Finally, deregulation of the financial sector allowed wild speculation in new financial instruments that were based on false assumptions and led to a financial crisis that brought the system to its knees.

The article points out, however, that we also should not forget what Marx got wrong. The workers' revolution that was supposed to overthrow capitalism and usher in communism hasn't happened and isn't likely to happen under current conditions. The kind of communism that emerged in the former Soviet Union and China collapsed under its own weight, and some kind of capitalism, guided and fenced in by the political system, has led to rates of economic growth, particularly in China, that were the envy of the Western world for several years. Communism didn't work to provide for the needs of people in these counties, and capitalism in some form or other has replaced old forms of socialism based on Marxist thinking. This development alone should give pause to people who hope to find something in Marxist thought that could help us deal with the current crisis and provide a spiritual dimension that is sorely needed.

Dialectal Materialism

There are several aspects about Marxist thinking that deserve to be looked at that makes it applicability to current problems questionable. Marx took the idea of the dialectic from Hegel and made it applicable to the material world. Hegel was an idealist and stood firmly within the tradition of German idealism. Marx, however, asserted that the Hegelian dialectic was standing on its head, so to speak, and needed to be put on its feet by being transformed from idealist to materialist. Thus, he developed the notion of dialectical materialism that he used to explain the eventual rise of communism. The contradictions of capitalism would lead it to collapse, and out of the ashes communism would emerge.[6] The transition from feudalism to capitalism and then communism was a historical inevitability.

Both Hegel and Marx were scientific philosophers and not social critics. Neither were they normative and concepts like rights and justice, which are normative concepts, were not part of their thinking. The contradictions in any system were objective in nature and they were engaged in an analysis of what is going to happen, not what should happen. They were about prediction, not prescription. When concepts like freedom are actualized in history as in the free-enterprise system, this actualization falls short of the full meaning of the concept, and eventually enough of a contradiction develops that the system has to be reformed or overthrown. The dialectic is like an algorithm that grinds it way through history and brings about social change.[7]

For example, the United States was founded on the concepts of freedom and equality, where all men were said to be created equal and have the right to life, liberty, and the pursuit of happiness. The contradiction between what this country said it stood for in its Declaration of Independence and the fact that for the country to be established as one nation, the founders had to compromise and allow slavery to exist in the southern part of the country and then be extended as the nation pushed west, was a contradiction that eventually resulted in the Civil War. When this war did not give blacks their full rights as citizens of the United States, the civil rights movement of the 1960s arose, which abolished institutional segregation throughout the country.

Thus, Marx claims to be scientific in his analysis of history through the use of the Hegelian dialectic, what he calls dialectical materialism. His analysis has no normative dimension as Marx believes that he is describing how the contradictions of capitalism will inevitably lead to communism without human interference. He is describing what he sees as historical necessities and describes a logic in history that will lead to communism where the alienation of workers that takes place in capitalism will be overcome. They "would no longer be confronted by an alienated world of objects appropriated as private property . . . Man would realize his human nature as a free conscious producer, engaging in a variety of creative activities no longer actuated by the drive to accumulate property."[8]

While Marx talks constantly about the exploitation of the worker in a capitalistic system and sees surplus value as an appropriation of unpaid labor by capital, one searches in vain for an argument that capitalism is unjust or inequitable and that it violates the rights of workers. Marx's descriptions of capitalism may strike most people as unjust, but according to Allen W, Wood, whatever else capitalism may have meant for Marx, it does not seem to be unjust.[9] As Engels says, "social justice or injustice is decided by the science which deals with the material facts of production and exchange, the science of political economy."[10] For Marx, "the justice or injustice of an action or institution does not consist in its exemplification of a juridical form or its conformity to a universal principle . . . but by the concrete requirements of a historically conditioned mode of production."[11] Thus, capitalism is but a necessary stage of productive activity that will eventually usher in a communist society, and a concept of justice is not necessary as the logic of dialectical materialism will have its way in history. As Louis Althusser, a French Marxist philosopher who taught for many years at École normale supérieure in Paris states,

> If we take seriously what Marx tells us about the real dialectic of history, it is not "men" who make history, although its dialectic is realized in them and in their practice, but the masses in the relations of the class struggle.[12]

One can argue, however, that there are no inexorable laws of history that operate independently of human behavior, human choices, and human intentions, all of which can be judged from a normative perspective. The dialectic needs a normative dimension in order to work, as contradictions will not be resolved unless enough people see the contradiction and act to resolve it in some fashion. The Civil War would never have happened without the abolitionists and others in the country who wanted to end slavery, not because of some inexorable law of history but because it was morally wrong. And when Reconstruction failed and blacks were still not allowed to participate as full citizens because of segregation throughout the south, it took the moral fervor of both blacks and whites who laid their lives on the line to open up the south in the 1960s and to assure passage of civil rights laws to finally remove some of the most egregious barriers that prevented blacks from being full citizens of this country with all the rights and privileges that go along with such citizenship. The contradiction between freedom and slavery would never have been resolved, or even attempted to be resolved, unless enough people became outraged by the way blacks were being treated in this country.[13]

The lack of a normative dimension was a serious omission in Marxian theory as it created an amoral climate in which ruthless leaders could emerge in communist societies and kill tens of millions of their own people in the interests of promoting communism. Stalin allowed millions of people in Ukraine and Belarus to starve or be beaten to death through the forced collectivizing of agriculture. Starting in the 1930s, Stalin conducted his first utopian agricultural experiment in Ukraine, where the land was collectivized and the kulaks, who were called the "wealthy" peasants, were the victims of beatings and starvation. This experiment amounted to a war with Ukrainian peasant culture itself, which resulted in a mass famine in 1933 where millions of Ukrainians needlessly perished.[14]

In China, the chairman of the Chinese Communist Party Mao Zedong allowed as many as 45 million people to be killed by collectivizing agriculture and forcing people to work on projects such as the backyard furnaces that were supposed to increase steel production. Between 1958 and 1962 Mao implemented his Great Leap Forward, which he hoped would catapult China past it competitors. China's greatest asset, a peasant labor force that was estimated in the hundreds of millions, was mobilized to "transform both agriculture and industry at the same time . . . In the pursuit of a utopian paradise, everything was collectivized, as villagers were herded together in giant communes which heralded the advent of communism. People in the countryside were robbed of their work, their homes, their land, their belongings, and their livelihood."[15]

Some 6 to 8 percent of the victims of Mao's program were tortured to death or summarily killed. Many other victims simply starved to death by being deprived of food. Others vanished because they were too old, weak, or sick to earn their keep. People were killed because they were rich, because they could not keep up with the workload, because they spoke out against the way they were being treated, or simply because they were not liked by the people in power. Because the local cadres were pressured to keep their attention focused on figures rather than people, making sure the targets they were handed by the top planners were fulfilled, countless others died because of neglect. This vision of a utopia led to one of the most gruesome mass killings of human history and inflicted serious damage on agriculture, trade, industry, and transportation throughout China that took years to overcome.[16]

These acts were the acts of ruthless leaders who would stop at nothing to get their way and had no concern about the effects of their practices on their own people as they were a part of history in advancing the communist idea and creating a communist society. Marxist theory with its focus on a scientific mechanism had no normative guidelines or principles that could be used by people with a moral sensibility to try to stop these senseless killings. It is a theory that has no sense of justice, no sense of rights, and no sense of morality. It is completely devoid of moral content and as such is not a humanistic theory at all but is an amoral and heartless analysis of history in which human beings are reduced to mere cogs in a dialectical machine that operates in history like an algorithm that grinds along irrespective of humans and their needs and concerns.

The Mode of Production

The basic unit of analysis for Marx was the way in which a society organized itself to provide for its material needs. A society can only be understood by analyzing its basic mode of production, its economic system that structures how goods and services are produced in that society. Humans have no soul, according to Marx; there is no spiritual or nonmaterial essence to human identity. What humans are, the contents of their consciousness and by extension their identity, is shaped by the demands of the physical and social system in which they exist. The social and economic context in which they live out their lives constructs the consciousness and identity of human beings.[17]

History is a succession of economic systems or modes of production, if you will, where new societies evolve out of the antagonisms between different classes of people that are inherent in the previous society. Historical change derives from differences in the way humans ensure their continued physical existence. History can thus be divided into stages, where each stage corresponds to a particular economic mode of production that is differentiated by the unique way the physical needs of its inhabitants are met and the nature of the social relationships which are associated with that economic organization. This gives rise to an institutional and ideological superstructure that consists of a particular set of political, religious, legal, and other structures, as well as their concomitant ideologies. This superstructure includes a particular conception of the state and its role in the economy, of what is lawful and unlawful in the society, and a set of religious beliefs that provide further support for the economic organization of society.[18] As Karl Marx himself says,

> [i]n the social production of their life, men enter into definite relations that are indispensable and independent of their will, relations of production which correspond to a definite stage of development of their material productive forces. The sum total of these relations of production constitutes the economic structure of society, the real foundation, on which rises a legal and political superstructure and to which correspond definite forms of consciousness. The mode of production of material life conditions the social, political, and intellectual life process in general. It is not the consciousness of men that determines their being, but on the contrary, their social being that determines their consciousness.[19]

Each stage of history sows the seeds of its own undoing and produces its own contradictions that progressively through the dialectical process lead to communism. The different elements that compose the economic mode of production, including the social, technological, and material, reach a point where they contradict each other and come into conflict. Capitalism was the antithesis of feudalism, out of which it emerged because of new technologies that gave rise to the factory system and the increasingly oppressive relations between landowners and peasants. History has a purpose or teleology as it is inevitably heading toward communism and abolition of private property and the communal ownership of the means of production. Class divisions on the basis of wealth would be abolished, and a classless society would emerge.

Under capitalism, society became divided into two major classes, the bourgeoisie which was the emergent middle class that became wealthy because they owned the factories that were created during the industrial revolution, and the proletariat or working class, whose labor was exploited by the capitalists who extracted their profits out of the surplus value created by the proletariat by paying them less that what they deserved. Out of this economic arrangement arose a particular set of political, legal, religious, philosophical, and other institutions and ideologies that legitimized the system. The views of the bourgeoisie came to be assimilated by the proletariat as the natural and inevitable way of seeing things and because the particular interests of the bourgeoisie came to be identified with the interests of all their ideology prevailed and served to help them maintain their economic and political power.

Eventually, however, the dependency of the bourgeoisie on the proletariat would bring about capitalism's demise. The mass of the laboring class would become conscious of its indispensability to those who owned the means of production and they would erupt into revolution and seize ownership of the means of production. Private property would thus be abolished when the working class seized the capital of the capitalists, and a communist society would emerge that Marx saw as the inevitable consummation of the march of history. The stranglehold that the capitalists had on society would be overthrown, and a worker's paradise would emerge out of the wreckage.

Value

Under capitalism we are surrounded by a proliferation of commodities that have been created expressly for the sake of being exchanged for money. A commodity is an object outside of us that by its properties satisfies human wants of one sort or another. For Marx the questions are, "What makes these commodities valuable?" and "How is value determined in a capitalistic society?" Marx analyzes the value that these commodities are deemed to have in order to discover the exact composition of this value and the role it plays in a capitalist system. Thus, Marx comes up with various kinds of value that commodities have at various stages of production and exchange.

Use-Value: This term refers to the utility of a thing and is tied to the physical properties of the commodity and does not exist apart from the commodity. This property of a commodity is independent of the amount of labor that is expended to create its useful qualities. Thus, use-value is essentially qualitative in that commodities have a quality that is perceived to be useful to those who find that quality fills a certain need or desire that they have. Thus, a car, for example, is useful for people who need transportation from one place to another. The car may also be useful to express a certain characteristic of the user who likes a certain flashy color or design or likes the feeling of power that the car gives him or her if it has a high horsepower. The car or any other commodity may have different uses for different people.[20]

Exchange-Value: This value presents itself as a quantitative relation, "as the proportion in which values in use of one sort are exchanged for those of another sort, a relation constantly changing with time and place." It is a total abstraction from use-value and appears to be something accidental and purely relative. This value is established socially and is the product of the way in which people have organized themselves to produce commodities in a given society. While a car may have a certain use-value to the owner, if he or she wants to sell it or trade it in for a new model, exchange-value comes into play that has no relation to use-value as exchange-value is socially determined by all the people who are active in the market at any given time. Thus, it also could be called market-value as it is the value any given commodity has when it is bought and sold on the market.[21]

Labor-Value: The ultimate standard of value for Marx and common to all other measures of value is the labor that goes into producing particular commodities, the energy and effort that are expended in making them. Commodities only have value because of the labor that is embodied or materialized in them. Marx defines this value as "[t]he labour-time socially necessary is that required to produce an article under the normal conditions of production, and with the average degree of skill and intensity prevalent at the time." Thus, the "value of any article is the amount of labour socially necessary, or the labour-time socially necessary for its production and the total labour-power of society is embodied in the sum total of the value of all commodities produced by that society."[22] To quote from Marx again:

> In general, the grater the productiveness of labour, the less is the labour-time required for the production of an article, the less is the amount of labour crystallized in that article, and the less is its value, and *vice versa*, the less the productiveness or labour, the greater is the labour-time required for the production of an article, the greater is its value. The value of a commodity, therefore, varies directly as the quantity, and inversely as the productiveness, or the labour incorporated in it.[23]

Surplus-Value: Under capitalism the worker sells his labor power to the capitalist in exchange for a wage which supposedly reflects the value of this commodity. However, this labor power is capable of producing a certain amount of value over and above its own value as a commodity. This is surplus value that the capitalist appropriates for him- or herself and is driven to maximizing this value by an ever intensifying exploitation of this labor-power.[24] Surplus value has two forms: *absolute surplus-value* is produced by prolongation of the working day, and *relative surplus-value* arises "from the curtailment of the necessary labour-time and from the corresponding alteration in the respective lengths of the two components of the working day."[25] This latter value arises out of improvements in technology that can reduce the necessary labor time invested in the production of commodities for sale on the market.

By way of summary, then, people buy commodities on the market because they have a certain utility to them, these commodities are fulfilling some need or desire on the part of the person buying them. However, the value that has to be given up to purchase these commodities is determined by the market, where the exchange-value reflected in the price of the commodity is a social product that reflects the value of all the people participating in the market. This may or may not correspond to the use-value of any given participant. The most fundamental value for Marx, however, is the labor that went into the production of any given commodity. This labor-power is considered to be a commodity by Marx that receives a wage for its efforts, but the value produced by this labor-power can be greater than this wage creating a surplus-value that is appropriated by capitalists who are driven to maximize this value by exploiting the worker.

Alienation

This exploitation leads to alienation where the worker sinks to the level of a commodity, and indeed, according to Marx, the most wretched of commodities. The "wretchedness of the worker is in inverse proportion to the power and magnitude of his production."[26] The object that labor produces, that is, labor's product, confronts him or her as *something alien*, as a *power* that is *independent* of the producer. The more objects the worker produces, the more he or she falls under the dominion of capital, who tears the product away from him or her, and this estranged labor makes the worker feel outside his or her work and his or her work feels outside himself. The separation of things in the world that come from labor is the separation of the worker from his human nature. This constitutes a loss of reality, the theft of the objects most necessary not only for life but for his work, and the production of an alien objective world that confronts the worker as something alien and hostile.[27] This alienation can take several forms.

Alienation from the products of labor: "The relation of the worker to the *product of labour* as an alien object exercising power over him. This relation is at the same time the relation to the sensuous external world, to the objects of nature as an alien world antagonistically opposed to him." Nature provides labor with the *means of life* in that labor cannot *live* without objects on which to operate and provides the means for the physical subsistence of the *worker* him- or herself.[28]

Alienation from the laboring activity itself: "The relation of labour to the *act of production* within the *labour* process. This relation is the relation of the worker to his *own* activity as an alien activity not belonging to him; it is activity as suffering, strength as weakness, begetting as emasculating, the worker's own physical and mental energy, his personal life for what is life other than activity—as an activity which is turned against him, neither depends on nor belongs to him. Here we have *self—estrangement*, as we had previously the estrangement of the *thing*."[29]

Alienation from man's species being: Estranged labor turns "both nature and his spiritual species property, into a being *alien* to him, into a *means* to his own *individual existence*. It estranges man's own body from him, as it does external nature and his spiritual essence, his *human* being . . . Every self-estrangement of man from himself and from nature appears in the relation in which he places himself and nature to men other than and differentiated from himself."[30]

Alienation from each other: "An immediate consequence of the fact that man is estranged from the product of his labour, from his life-activity, from his species being is the *estrangement of man* from *man*. . . In fact, the proposition that man's species nature is estranged from him means that one man is estranged from the other, as each of them is from man's essential nature. . . Hence within the relationship of estranged labour each man views the other in accordance with the standard and position in which he finds himself as a worker."[31]

Thus, the loss of reality, of one's objectified activity, of one species being, results in estranged or alienated labor:

> If the product of labour does not belong to the worker, if it confronts him as an alien power, this can only be because it belongs to *some other man than the worker* . . . If his own activity is to him an unfree

activity, then he is treating it as activity performed in the service, under the dominion, the coercion and the yoke of another man . . . Just as he begets his own production as the loss of his reality, as his punishment; just as he begets his own product as a loss, as a product not belonging to him; so he begets the dominion of the one who does not produce over production and over the product.[32]

Alienation happens because of private property since people have to work for someone that owns the property the worker needs to produce something. The appropriation of surplus value enriches the controlling person, and the harder a worker works, the more he or she enriches the owner of the property, who has an incentive to get as much surplus-value as possible out of the worker. The different forms of alienation eventually produce a class that will lead or promote a revolution that will emancipate society from private property. This emancipation of the workers leads to universal human emancipation "because the whole of human servitude is involved in the relation of the worker to production, and every relation of servitude is but a modification and consequence of this relation."[33] According to Robert C. Tucker, this emancipation means that

> "[l]abor" will have been abolished, not in the sense that individuals will sink into indolent activity, but that their productive activities will take on the character of free creative self-expression not performed for wages or acquisitive purposes.[34]

Marx has much more to say on various topics that help in understanding how the capitalist system exploits the worker. With respect to *capital*, for example, he states that

> [c]apital can only increase by exchanging itself for labour power, by calling wage labour to life. The labour power of the wage-worker can only be exchanged for capital by increasing capital, by strengthening the power whose slave it is . . . If capital grows, the mass of wage labour grows; in a word, the domination of capital extends over a greater number of individuals. To say that the worker has an interest in the rapid growth of capital is only to say that the more rapidly the worker increases the wealth of others, the richer will be the crumbs that fall to him, the greater is the number of workers that can be employed and called into existence, the more can the mass of slaves dependent on capital be increased.[35]

As Marx states,

> [t]he faster capital intended for production, productive capital, increases, the more, therefore, industry prospers, the more the bourgeoisie enriches

itself and the better business is, the more workers does the capitalist need, the more dearly does the worker sell himself.[36]

With regard to the *class struggle* Marx says that "[l]ong before me bourgeois historians had described the historical development of this class struggle and bourgeois economists the economic activity of the classes. What I did that was new was to prove: 1) that the *existence of classes* is only bound up with *particular historical phases in the development of production*, 2) that the class struggle necessarily leads to the *dictatorship of the proletariat*, 3) that this dictatorship only constitutes the transition to the *abolition of all classes* and to *a classless society*."[37] Not only are class privileges to be abolished, but class distinctions themselves and equality would also be extended to the social conditions of individuals. The notion of a class struggle is fundamental to Marxist thought.

Critique of Marx

In a book titled *Marxism and Socialist Theory*, the authors Michael Albert and Robin Hahnel attempt to address certain methodological problems that they believe plague most Marxist thinkers, namely, the questions of whether Marxism is indeed a science, whether the dialectical process a useful and sufficient way to analyze history, and whether Marxism rests on a sound foundation rather than being too narrow and leaving out some important elements.[38] Their first volume, which is of concern in this chapter, deals with theory and focuses on broad, abstract issues of methodology and philosophy in response to these questions about Marxism. The second volume focuses on the United States, the Soviet Union, China, and Cuba and deals with the internal arrangements of the institutions in these societies and the different theories people use to understand how these societies function.[39]

According to the authors, there are four major theories that can be considered on the left side of the spectrum including orthodox Marxism, radical feminism, nationalism, and anarchism. One way to approach this menu is to assume one of these theories is basic and the others are derivative and thus less important, what the authors call a monist orientation. Another way is to see these four theories as separate pieces of a whole that are complementary and must be used in turn to explain the problem that is under consideration. A third way is to agree that these theories are complementary but that they must interpenetrate each other to form an encompassing orientation that embodies all four theories where the whole is more than the sum of the parts. The authors take this last approach, call it a *totalist* approach, and argue that the division of analysis into separate "disciplines" impedes a clear understanding not only of the "whole" phenomenon but also of its component parts.[40]

The world is an interconnected whole, they argue, and as finite human beings we have to break the whole down into smaller parts so that we can conceptualize and analyze something that is doable. But then we hope to be able to reconstruct the whole again with this knowledge in hand and usually do so from a single perspective or worldview, what the authors call monism. This kind of approach, however, is no longer sufficient, and it is essential that theory development embodies complimentary viewpoints that can eventually be merged into a single philosophy. The idea of "complementarity" came from the work of Niels Bohr in theoretical physics, who argued that perhaps the world was more complex than we had thought, and no single viewpoint was sufficient to explain this complex reality. Thus, to understand the world we needed to understand it from different and complementary viewpoints as it has aspects that are irreducible to one another and requires diverse approaches for a full understanding.[41]

We also need to approach reality relationally rather than seeing it as a sequence of isolated and separate events that impinge on one another from without. Instead, we need to view each event in the context of its relation to other events, seeing that the character and meaning of any event depend on their interrelations with other events. Mechanical thinking, which has revealed much about the world, involved analyzing events separately and viewing situations in terms of cause and effect. Dialectical thinking, on the other hand, involves an approach that sees events as part of a relational network and a time-spanning historical process. The authors see both of these methods as complementary, and their dual use is beneficial if one wants to understand the history and dynamics of social change. With regard to Marxist theory, both of these approaches should guide its development in the future.[42]

Orthodox Marxism, understood as the materialistic theory of history and the labor theory of value, has reached the limits of its applicability, according to Albert and Hahnel, and is in a crisis situation. The predictions of this kind of Marxism have not happened as the working class is not in control of its situation and the state is not withering. There is a need for a new theoretical approach based on a fuller theory of human nature where the human agent is endowed with sociality, consciousness, self-consciousness, and something the authors call "praxis." The locus of Marxism must be moved from a focus on economic activity to activity, in general, and away from a single sphere of analysis and a single kind of human praxis to a different approach.[43]

This approach involves something along the lines of what the authors call a *totalist* orientation and aims not for synthesis but complementarity in conceptual development. As the authors state, "[t]o overestimate the monist importance of the economy as a sole determining sphere of activity alone or fail to perceive that the economy itself is fundamentally affected by other spheres is debilitating."[44] Yet in orthodox Marxism the mode of production, that is, the manner in which a society organizes itself to provide for its material needs, is considered the "base" and includes both the forces and social relations of production. The "superstructure," which includes political, familial, cultural, legal, religion and other institutional and ideological relations, is derivative and reflective of this base mode of production. Thus, economic relations are most basic in orthodox Marxism, and contradictions in the economic sphere are most critical when it comes to social change and economic classes are the most important collective agent when it comes to revolution.[45]

The authors, however, want to go beyond this economic interpretation of history and argue that kinship, community, and politics are also central to social change. It is not only economic classes that are important, but also kin, race, national, religious, ethnic, and political divisions that can create groups that can play critical revolutionary roles. In particular, they identify a new class that they call "coordinators," who often control the work of others and have more status because of specialized knowledge and whose work is more conceptual than executionary. This new class includes managers, engineers, social planners, philosophers, and various kinds of "intellectuals." This class, so say Albert and Hahnel, is located between capital and labor under both capitalism and socialism and often attains a dominant economic position.[46]

In the totalist perspective, the authors argue that the four principle spheres of human activity, the political, economic, community, and kinship spheres, are intricately interrelated and are linked together in a single social formation. These four spheres have the same elementary components and roots, which are individual people with their human needs that we all share due to our species nature and institutions with their social role structures. We have economic needs related to survival and sustenance, kinship needs associated with reproduction and sexual/emotional requirements, community needs involving social identities, and political needs involving establishment of regularity and clarity of norms of acceptable activity. Any one of these needs is always entwined with the presence of the others so the four different types of activity are always carried out in the context of one another.[47]

There are several implications of this totalist approach for further theoretical work regarding socialism, according to the authors. The idea of categorizing societies solely along economic lines or any other single axis will be seriously undermined. Every society has these four spheres of human activity that must be described. Furthermore, while these spheres affect each other's historical development, they need not always change simultaneously. Major alterations in one sphere may cause only minor alterations in the other spheres. This renders a simple stage theory of history obsolete, and the laws of motion for any particular sphere cannot be mistaken for the laws of motion for the entire society.[48]

In orthodox Marxist theory the state is part of the "superstructure" and is derived from the requirements of the "economic base." The state is but the reflection of the economy in political institutions and is not in itself a realm of political power or a cause of special oppressions that may supersede the oppression of economic classes. To understand the state one must understand the economic pressures it is subjected to and the economic requirement it must fulfill; there is no need to consider something like political power that is not derived from economic power or political oppression that does not come from the dynamics of the oppression of economic classes. Class struggles within the state itself are ignored, and the existence of a state role in community, kinship, and the reproduction of authority is largely ignored.[49]

In keeping with their totalist approach, the authors state that a new approach to the capitalistic state must address both the interface between political decision making and institution of the other spheres and the inner structure of political institutional themselves.

Political analyses must deal with social relations within the state and how these relations define the different social actors within society. Undermining the traditional Marxist notion that abolishing private property can automatically lead to a superior society, a totalist analysis shows that an authoritarian approach to social change will only tend to reinforce characteristics of the old regime and may well lead to a different society from the egalitarian one that socialists hope to create. It may instead lead to a centralized, bureaucratic one-party state, such as existed in the former Soviet Union, where the worker is exploited as much as under capitalism.[50] As the authors state,

> [i]n fact, for all his/her alleged leading role, the Soviet worker has just as little to say in the high or low level decisions of his/her enterprise as the worker in a capitalist plant. He/she has no voice in deciding whether operations will be expanded or cut back, what will be produced, what kind of equipment will be used and what technical advances (if any) will be enacted, whether there will be piece-rates or hourly wages, how performance will be measured and production norms calculated, how worker's wages will evolve relative to increases in productivity, how the authority structure of the plant from director to foremen will operate.[51]

A centrally planned economy where a small group of bureaucrats decide what is good for society and its members is antithetical to any notion of collective self-management. When power is concentrated in this fashion a new stratum of bureaucrats emerge that, in all respects, resembles the capitalist class of owners and managers. While this group claims to rule in the name of the working class, it actually makes itself into a privileged class that lives at the expense of society as a whole. If the state insists upon central control of the means of production, the position of the workers is identical to what it would be under capitalism. State management of the economy alienates workers from the means of production every bit as does its rival.[52]

After debunking central planning the authors then engage in a discussion about whether market socialism is a realistic alternative, that is, whether social ownership of the means of production can be linked up with a market economy. While markets coordinate the activities of different economic units through an exchange process, they also disguise the fact that people in these different economic units are actually engaged in a social activity with one another. Since the activities of these economic units are not consciously coordinated by anyone we fail to understand that workers in these different units are involved in a shared activity. Instead it appears that they are engaged in isolated productive activity and have relations only with the material things they need as inputs to produce the outputs they create.[53] According to the authors,

> [r]elations between people and other people either disappear from sight or are confined to recognition of relations between people within the same economic unit. By focusing on this surface appearance we lose sight of the fact that in social economic activity people must have relations with other people and that it is precisely these human relations that are disguised as relationships between commodities in exchange. This information disguising character of markets which causes people to attribute to things the creative power that actually resides only in themselves is called "commodity fetishism."[54]

Albert and Hahnel think that the only information the market provides relative to the relations between different economic units such as autoworkers, steelworkers, and coal miners, for example, is a price that goes along with the actual physical commodities that are exchanged. This information, so say the authors, is totally insufficient to allow the autoworkers to evaluate and understand the social relations they have with the steelworkers and miners. The price does not reveal everything that went into a commodity's production as it does not tell us anything about the concrete pleasures and character development that were produced in the workers and hides information about things like morale and empathy. Markets make it almost impossible to think relationally about the individual worker's involvements with other productive units and preclude the development of anything like solidarity based on each unit's concern with the well-being of others.[55]

Concern with the human situation of other workers in different economic units would undermine the functioning of the market and a concern about efficiency as the essence of every market exchange is that each party to the exchange tries to take maximum advantage of the other. Markets establish an institutional setting, where the outcome is a war of each against all the others, something of a Hobbesian view of society.[56] They create incentives for individuals to pursue their own well-being at the expense of society's well-being and do not foster a consciousness that extends beyond this self-interested behavior. Under market socialism, decisions within firms become technical in nature as quantitative data are used to calculate the "bottom-line," and appeals to greater work enjoyment and sociality will lose out to appeals to higher income per employee. This process will enhance the powers of the managerial class, who will increasingly monopolize decision making within the firm and substitute their own bottom-line orientation for the goals of the workers in a self-managed firm.[57] Thus, the authors conclude,

> far from being an appropriate institution for socialism—one that embodies cooperation, diversity, and solidarity as core characteristics—markets are instead an inter unit form embodying individualism, greed, and competition, and suited not to the enhancement of the power of the direct producers over their own workplace activity and its product, but to the development of economic hegemony by a new class of managers and other intellectual workers or coordinators.[58]

Markets also promote the expression of individual needs, according to the authors, and dampen the expression of social needs, which leads to an overproduction of private goods with negative externalities and a scarcity of public goods with positive externalities. Over time people will adjust their consciousness to this scarcity of public goods, tend more and more to overlook public bads, and increase their needs for private goods ensuring an oversupply to these goods. Markets provide an institutional boundary that prevents people from exercising their social qualities and developing what social potential they have and steers them toward "materialistic individualism in a snowballing way that leads to a cumulative divergence from maximum fulfillment."[59]

Thus, if markets are used instead of central planning to coordinate the activities of different productive enterprises, an ever-increasing individualism will result along with desires for private as opposed to public goods. Even if social ownership of the means of production exists, the society will steadily progress toward individualistic materialistic values and workers will want ever increasing levels of personal income for purposes of consumption and humanization of the workplace will be of lesser importance. The pressure of market competition that forces capitalists to accumulate more and more assets and grow their enterprises, lest they be outcompeted, is not mitigated by social ownership of the means of production. Even in worker self-managed firms the trend is to hire a managerial staff to assure efficient outcomes. The result is that this managerial class is granted more and more authority over the workplace even as workers become more and more alienated.[60]

Having concluded that both central planning and markets are not consistent with building a socialist society and propel postcapitalist society toward different economic outcomes from those of socialism, the authors propose a different economic arrangement that is not dominated by the emergence of a new managerial class that stands between workers and capitalists. This new approach, which they call "decentralized socialist planning," does not create a new class division but, instead, leads to dissolution of classes and the "emergence of collective self-management on the part of all economic actors." They try to envision institutions that will advance human potentials for diversity, self-management, and interpersonal solidarity.[61]

The authors start this discussion with a chapter on the history of kinship where kinship activity refers to the process by which children become adults and acquire adult demeanor, personality, and capabilities. We must extend our understanding of kinship networks throughout society, they argue, as the kinship network is socially embedded and exists only in the context of economic, political, and community relations. Thus, kinship networks such as the family do not exist in isolation from the rest of society and cannot be fully understood in the abstract. The problem with orthodox Marxism is that is does not recognize "the existence of a kinship sphere that has implications of its own for human development and organization" and "seeks to relegate this sphere to a secondary and derivative position." It forgets that workers come from particular kinds of families that shape the way they see the world and where they developed their understanding of social relations.[62]

The labor market is segmented in both capitalism and socialism. There are jobs that are considered to be "women's" work and women are channeled into these jobs where they compete with one another. Doing such women's work can reproduce sexism rather than eliminate it, and women's entry into the workforce does not necessarily guarantee them liberation from oppression. Studies show that under socialism women are still subordinate in the workplace and work in jobs that are considered to be inferior and that have less pay and status. They are also primarily responsible for the home and rearing children and are subject to physical and mental abuse from men. This kind of sexism is not the result of the economic system in which men and women work to provide for their economic needs, it starts in the family, where male–female relations are developed in a patriarchal situation, where the father is usually the authority figure to be obeyed and feared. Here is where male and female roles that carry over into adult life and into the workplace are learned. Authoritarian patterns present in the family produce a respect for authority and power and a willingness to obey orders from superiors as well as a disdain for subordinates and an insistence on their obedience.[63]

Sexism produces a male and a female "mode" that governs how men and women perceive each other and how they relate to the world. Differences in work and pay and *in expected behavior and workday attitudes* tend to reproduce male and female attributes and define the male and female modes that pervade our society as a whole. What it is to be a man is perceived to be different from what it is to be a woman, and both are alienated from what it is to be human. Such a socialization process molds children to fit preconceived social roles rather than freeing them to develop as they will and become human beings that can choose whatever roles they deem appropriate for themselves under the conditions in which they find themselves.[64]

Orthodox socialist approaches to this problem are concerned only with "material economic relations," treating kinship relations as secondary that will follow socialist transformations in the economy. The reality is that the same old family will produce the same old kinship relations even under a socialist economy. What is needed is a totalist framework that does not subordinate kinship dynamics to other spheres or ignore the impact of economic, political, and community forces on the kinship sphere. Such an approach will help with understanding how male supremacy can be eliminated and how sexism can be overcome in society as a whole. Organizations must adopt norms and techniques that *counter sexist modes of conduct* and aim for both solidarity and particularity, collectively and autonomy, that is, complementarity within a framework of totality.[65]

Community is the last of the four critical spheres of human activity to be addressed as both Marxism and feminism consistently underestimate the importance of issues that arise in the community. This sphere is frequently more diffuse that the other spheres as it if often not centered around one key institution. The authors briefly discuss the role that art plays in cultural development and then spend much more time discussing racism, arguing that a reductionist approach to this phenomenon is far-fetched. Attempts to overcome racism need to understand the community roots of white supremacy and Black Nationalism and not assume these are merely ideological reflections of economic factors. Likewise orthodox Marxists are insensitive to the importance of regional diversity as well as to the role that religion plays in the development of culture.[66]

Culture is rooted in the sphere of community activity and is a *human product* aimed toward the fulfillment of basic human needs. Cultural attributes are a product of social interaction within a community and have deeper roots than the rationalization of economic circumstances. The development of community involves the emergence of a common identity and language, as well as a shared heritage. How we see ourselves, how moral issues are dealt with, and solutions to life's problems are all community matters. Communities may be culturally enriching and supportive of human development, or they may be destructive of human potentials. Most likely they are some of both. In any event, while community activity is not an isolatable sphere, it warrants designation as a core element in the development of social life:[67] "The sphere of community activity and the network of community institutions are often as central to the character of social life and social possibilities within a country as are the spheres of kinship, economics, and politics."[68]

In conclusion Albert and Hahnel state that the central thesis of their book is "that a rejuvenated social theory sufficient to contemporary socialist needs would have to transcend economism in all its guises and weave a number of complimentary analyses into a totalist framework."[69] The orthodox Marxist paradigm, they argue, is not sufficient to the needs of socialists and is better suited to the needs of coordinators, bureaucrats, and members of the dominant community than the oppressed groups Marxism is supposed to serve. The vision they presented of what socialism might be like involved a transformation of all four spheres of social activity, the economic, political, kinship, and community, into what they called a totalist approach that they say must be unswerving if socialism is to be realized in practice.[70]

This book presents a powerful critique of traditional Marxism that pretty much demolishes the whole Marxist assumption about the base of social and historical development being the way the economy is organized to provide for the material needs of its people with political, religious, and cultural institutions being derivate and stemming from this base organization, what in Marxism is called the superstructure. They argue for a much broader and interrelated understanding of the way these institutions develop with no one of what they call the four spheres of social activity forming a so-called base from which the other are derivative. The totalist approach they advocate sees all of them as interrelated and affecting each other in the course of historical development.

But the authors also provide a strong critique of central planning and markets as ways of making essential economic decisions about what to produce and how much to produce. Social ownership of the means of production will not work if it is connected to either one of these institutions, they argue, and critique both the central planning mechanism that existed in the former Soviet Union as well as the self-managed system that existed in the former country of Yugoslavia. Neither accomplished the goal of socialism as central planning became bureaucratic and alienated the workers just as much as they were alienated under capitalism, and markets led to the emergence of a managerial class that came to control worker owned productive facilities and again left the workers in a subordinate and alienated position.

There are other problems with Marxist thought. He did not foresee the development of labor unions that did not seek an overthrow of the capitalist system but, rather, sought to better the lot of the workers within capitalism by focusing their efforts on getting increased wages for their members as well as better working conditions. For many years, unions and corporations worked hand in glove to reduce conflict between labor and management and engaged in collective bargaining that, in many cases, resulted in higher wages that were passed on to the consumer in the form of higher prices. The demise of unions in the past several decades is one of the reasons wages have stagnated for workers and inequality has increased.

Marx also did not foresee that the state would intervene in the workings of the market and make child labor illegal, for example, and pass legislation regulating wages and hours worked, promote health and safety concerns, address discrimination in the workplace, and deal with many other problems as described in the first chapter. All of these measures have helped to keep capitalism functioning in the interests of the entire society rather than just capitalists. Marx had nothing good to say about state-sponsored economic remedies and was intensely suspicious of any such measures taken by the German government in his time.[71]

The labor theory of value also proved difficult to determine and transfer into actual prices and was rejected by marginal utility theorists whose ideas form the basis of contemporary mainstream economics. They asserted "that the value of a good or service was determined by consumers' subjective appraisal of the usefulness of purchasing and additional one of these goods or services as against the purchase of any other good or service." They combined use-value and exchange-value that Marx had considered as separate and identified value with market price. The interaction of supply and demand determined the value of goods and services, not labor time, as Marx had asserted.[72]

Another questionable assumption of Marxism, as well as of Hegelianism, is that there is an end to history and that history is inevitably moving toward some ideal or perfect state of affairs where the full realization of history's purpose will be realized. For Hegel it was absolute spirit whereas for Marx it was communism. This has been true of other writers as well that there is a teleology or purpose to history that culminates in some perfect realm where no more change is necessary resulting in an end to history. But an equally valid assumption is that history never ends and change continues indefinitely and that the story of history is one dam thing after another. These are equally valid assumptions, and there are not necessarily any laws of history that are leading it anywhere.

As for the breakup of the Soviet Union, Gorbachev designed and sold his programs of *perestroika* and *glasnost* as reforms of the communist system and not as a replacement. He could not have done otherwise, given his beliefs in the system and the political realities of his time. But by opening the closed pages of the Soviet past, he chiseled away at whatever legitimacy the system yet retained and added to the certainty of failure.[73] The problem was that Marx and Lenin could not be combined with Hayek and Friedman, and there could be no "Communism with a human face." Once the system began to be humanized it could no longer stand, and real reform would end up in regime change.[74] Ken Adelman writing in *Reagan at Reykjavik* does not believe this was a historical inevitability, however, and Marx's methodology may not apply:

> To assert the inevitability of the Soviet breakup . . . presumes that economic factors people history to its inevitable outcome. While it may seem fitting to apply Karl Marx's methodology to Soviet history, his may not be the best tools of analysis. For this approach takes real people out of history. It substitutes grand trends and great waves for real, live decision makers, who grapple as best they can to the predicaments they confront. That approach assumes an inevitability to history's unfolding that sure doesn't feel that way to those in it at the time.[75]

However, with all these problems, Marxism may still have some relevance. The problems that were mentioned in the first chapter as constituting the material crisis of capitalism can be seen as contradictions in the Marxian sense, and the question raised there is, "How long the country can continue to go into debt to correct these contradictions?" What can it do about current inequalities, for example, and resolve this issue to the satisfaction of the society at large? Wages for workers have been stagnant for several decades while the rich have gotten richer and exercise more and more influence in the political system. How long will this situation be tolerated, and will it result in major changes to the capitalistic system? These are critical questions that have some basis in Marxist thought. As seen by David Harvey, Distinguished Professor of Anthropology at the Graduate Center of the City University of New York, technological developments offer the possibility of realizing the freedom for workers Marx envisioned:

> But if, said Marx, the true realm of freedom begins when and where necessity is left behind, then a political economic system that is based on the active cultivation of scarcity, impoverishment, labour surpluses and unfulfilled needs cannot possibly allow us entry into the realm of freedom, where individual human flourishing for all and sundry becomes a real possibility. The paradox is that automation and artificial intelligence now provide us with abundant means to achieve the Marxian dream of freedom beyond the realm of necessity at the same time as the laws of capital's political economy put this freedom further and further out of reach.[76]

In keeping with the main theme of this book one of the main problems of Marxism is its materialistic and scientific orientation that leaves out any consideration of spirituality. Its notion of dialectical materialism is based solely on the way in which societies organize themselves to provide for the material needs of its citizens. While Albert and Hahnel want to broaden this approach by including the political, kinship, and community along with the economic dimension and see these spheres as interacting rather than derivative they still do not discuss a spiritual dimension that runs through all these spheres. It is a spiritual dimension that is needed to overcome the problem we currently face and establish a connection with each other where the good of the whole supersedes the interests of any particular group or class, a realization that we are all in this together and need each other to succeed as a society.

Notes

1 See Louis Althusser and Etienne Balibar, *Reading Capital* (London: Verso, 2009); Vincent Barrett, *Marx* (New York: Routledge, 2009); David A. Harvey, *A Companion to Marx's Capital* (London: Verso, 2010); Amy Wendling, *Karl Marx on Technology and Alienation* (New York: Palgrave Macmillan, 2009); Terry Eagleton, *Why Marx Was Right* (New Haven: Yale University Press, 2011); David Harvey, *The Enigma of Capital and the Crisis of Capitalism*, 2nd ed. (New York: Oxford University Press, 2011).
2 Umair Haque, "Was Marx Right?" *Harvard Business Review* Blog Post, http://hbr.org/2011/09/was_marx_right.html, Wednesday, September 7, 2011. Haque

has also written a book titled *The New Capitalist Manifesto: Building a Disruptively Better Business* published by the Harvard Business Press in 2011.

3 Peter Coy, "Opening Remarks: Marx to Market," *Bloomberg Businessweek*, September 10–25, 2011, 10–11.

4 In October 2011, the Congressional Budget Office released a report that showed that average inflation-adjusted after-tax income for the richest 1 percent of the population had grown 275 percent during the last three decades. The poorest fifth of the population showed an income increase of only 18 percent while the three-fifths of the population in the middle of the income scale showed a growth of just under 40 percent. "America's Rich Have Dominated Income Increases, Study Says," *The Denver Post*, October 26, 2011, p. 5A. See also "The Great American Divide," *Time*, October 10, 2011, 26–32. Meanwhile, a Census Bureau report showed that 15.1 percent of the population—46.2 million Americans—were living in poverty. See "Poverty: Decades of Progress, Slipping away," *The Week*, September 30, 2011, 21; Rana Foroohar, "The Truth about the Poverty Crisis," *Time*, September 26, 2011, 24.

5 See Nicholas D. Kristof, "America's Primal Scream," *New York Times*, October 16, 2011, SR11; Chrystia Freeland, "Capitalism Is Killing the Middle-Class," *The Week*, September 30, 2011, 14; Aldo Svaldi, "The Vanishing Middle Class, *The Denver Post*, October 23, 2011, 1A.

6 Robert C. Tucker, "Introduction," in Robert C. Tucker, ed., *The Marx-Engels Reader*, 2nd ed. (New York: W.W. Norton, 1978), xix–xxxviii.

7 See Ernesto Laclau, *Politics and Ideology in Marxist Theory* (New York: Verso, 2011).

8 Tucker, "Introduction," xxv.

9 Allen W. Wood, "The Marxian Critique of Justice," in Marshall Cohen, Thomas Nagel, and Thomas Scanlon, eds., *Marx, Justice, and History* (Princeton, NJ: Princeton University Press, 1980), 3.

10 Ibid., 15.

11 Ibid., 16.

12 Louis Althusser, *Politics and History*, Ben Brewster, trans (New York: Verso, 2007), 168.

13 See Bruce Watson, *Freedom Summer* (New York: Viking, 2010).

14 Timothy Snyder, *Bloodlands: Europe between Hitler and Stalin* (New York: Basic Books, 2010). See also Norman M. Naimark, *Stalin's Genocides* (Princeton, NJ: Princeton University Press, 2010).

15 Frank Dikotter, *Mao's Great Famine: The History of China's Most Devastating Catastrophe, 1958–1962* (New York: Walker & Co., 2010), ix.

16 Ibid., xi.

17 Karl Marx, "The German Ideology: Part I," in Robert C. Tucker, ed., *The Mark-Engles Reader*, 2nd ed. (New York: W.W. Norton, 1978), 150.

18 Ibid., 151–154.

19 Karl Marx, "Marx on the History of His Opinions," in Robert C. Tucker, ed., *The Mark-Engles Reader*, 2nd ed. (New York: W.W. Norton, 1978), 4.

20 Karl Marx, "Capital, Volume One," in Robert C. Tucker, ed., *The Mark-Engles Reader*, 2nd ed. (New York: W.W. Norton, 1978), 303.

21 Ibid., 304–305.

22 Ibid., 306.

23 Ibid., 307.

24 Tucker, "Introduction," xxx.

25 Marx, "Capital," 379.

26 Karl Marx, "Economic and Philosophic Manuscripts of 1844," in Robert C. Tucker, ed., *The Mark-Engles Reader*, 2nd ed. (New York: W.W. Norton, 1978), 70.

27 Ibid., 71–74.
28 Ibid., 74.
29 Ibid., 74–75.
30 Ibid., 77–78.
31 Ibid., 77.
32 Ibid., 78.
33 Ibid., 80.
34 "Introduction," xii.
35 Karl Marx, "Wage Labour and Capital," in Robert C. Tucker, ed., *The Mark-Engles Reader*, 2nd ed. (New York: W.W. Norton, 1978), 210–211.
36 Ibid., 210.
37 Karl Marx, "Class Struggle and Mode of Production," in Robert C. Tucker, ed., *The Mark-Engles Reader*, 2nd ed. (New York: W.W. Norton, 1978), 220.
38 Michael Albert and Robin Hahnel, *Marxism and Socialist Theory* (New York: South End Press, 1981).
39 See Michael Albert and Robin Hahnel, *Socialism Today and Tomorrow* (New York: South End Press, 1999).
40 Albert and Hahnel, *Marxism and Socialist Theory*, 5–6.
41 Ibid., 14–26.
42 Ibid., 28–29.
43 Ibid., 39. "Orthodox Marxist economics is *not* an economic theory of praxis, the labor theory of value fails to be a social relations theory of value, and the orthodox Marxist theory as a whole is permeated by 'economism' in two senses: 1) it exaggerates the lone centrality of economic relations in determining the rest of social life, and 2) it minimizes the effects of non-economic realms back upon the very definition and character of the economy itself." Ibid., 129.
44 Ibid., 45.
45 Ibid., 52.
46 Ibid., 84. This new class the authors mention is very similar to what has been called managerialism by another author who argued that traditional notions of capitalism were disappearing and socialism remained an abstract Marxian ideal. What was emerging in industrial societies all over the world was a managerial class that was achieving social dominance and becoming the ruling class in society. The legitimacy of this class was not dependent on ownership of private property but on their ability to manage the technical nature of the processes of modern production. See James Burnham, *The Managerial Revolution* (New York: John Day Co., 1941).
47 Ibid., 86–87.
48 Ibid., 89.
49 Ibid., 104–109.
50 Ibid., 113–114.
51 Ibid., 165.
52 Ibid., 174. Richard D. Wolff, Professor of Economics Emeritus at the University of Massachusetts at Amherst, agrees with this assessment. He says, "I would argue that in the Soviet Union, for example, because they never changed the internal structure of the enterprise, workers were as alienated from their outputs in the Soviet Union as they had been in Russian private capitalism before. Soviet workers were as adversarially linked to the managers of their enterprises that were state officials as they had been before to private officials." See Richard Wolff, *Occupy the Economy: Challenging Capitalism* (New York: City Lights Books, 2012).
53 Ibid., 176.
54 Ibid., 177.
55 Ibid., 177–178.

56 See Thomas Hobbes, *Leviathan*, Richard E. Flathman and David Johnston, eds. (New York: W.W. Norton, 1997).
57 Albert and Hahnel, *Marxism and Socialist Theory*, 179–181.
58 Ibid., 181.
59 Ibid., 185–186.
60 Ibid., 186–189. "In sum, it seems to us that the data we have seen corroborates rather than contradicts the accounts of visitors to Yugoslavia, namely that there is a level of individualism, materialism, and apathy toward the work process among Yugoslavians very similar to that among citizens in capitalist societies." Ibid., 190.
61 Ibid., 190–195.
62 Ibid., 198–209.
63 Ibid., 213–220.
64 Ibid., 221–224.
65 Ibid., 226–228.
66 Ibid., 231–252.
67 Ibid., 231–263.
68 Ibid., 263.
69 Ibid., 269.
70 Ibid., 269–274.
71 Jonathan Sperber, *Karl Marx: A Nineteenth-Century Life* (New York: Liveright Publishing Corporation, 2013), 459–460.
72 Ibid., 460.
73 Ken Adelman, *Reagan At Reykjavik: Forty-Eight Hours That Ended the Cold War* (New York: Broadside Books, 2104), 317.
74 Ibid., 317–318.
75 Ibid.
76 David Harvey, *Seventeen Contradictions and the End of Capitalism* (New York: Oxford University Press, 2014), 208.

9   Critical Theory

Critical theory began in 1937 with the publication of Max Horkheimer's article titled "Traditional and Critical Theory"[1] which was also the inaugural address for the founding of the Institute for Social Research at Frankfurt, Germany, where this school of thought took shape. Also known as the Frankfurt School it was subsequently represented in the writings of Theodor Adorno, who, along with Horkheimer, became a leading spokesperson for the movement. Since then it has been the paradigm of theory for many scholars in which the intention of a philosophically guided diagnosis of current events is combined with an empirically grounded social analysis.[2]

The most prominent members of this school of thought included Theodor W. Adorno, Herbert Marcuse, Jürgen Habermas, and Max Horkheimer. In addition to Adorno, Marcuse, and Horkheimer, other first-generation theorists included Walter Benjamin, Leo Lowenthal, Erich Fromm, Franz Newman, Friedrich Pollock, Otto Krichheimer, Henryk Grossman, and Arkadij Gurland. The most important second-generation theorists included Klaus Elder, Claus Offe, Albrecht Wellmer, and Axel Honneth, as well as Habermas. During the Second World War most members of the institute left Germany for Columbia University in New York City; however, Horkheimer moved to Pacific Palisades near Los Angeles and was eventually joined by Adorno. The institute was reconstituted in 1953 back in Frankfurt.[3]

Critical theory was conceived from the outset as a continuation of Marx's intentions under altered historical circumstances. The National Socialists' seizure of power in Germany and Stalin's seizure of power in the Soviet Union raised doubts about whether the proletariat still bore the potential for transforming postliberal capitalism as the Marxist theory of revolution assumes. A major portion of activity at the Institute was devoted in the 1930s to an attempt to provide an empirical answer to the problem expressed in this tension. It was believed this task could only be fulfilled within an interdisciplinary context that the Institute for Social Research provided.[4]

What Is Critical Theory?

Critical theory has been called a radical social theory that is critical of both capitalism and Soviet socialism. Critical theorists responded to the historical events of their day, which initially included the changing composition and direction of the European labor movement, the evolution of Soviet communism, and the development of Western capitalism. Many of them did not believe that traditional Marxist theory could adequately explain the unexpected development of capitalism in the twentieth century. They were influenced by the failure of the working class to generate a revolution in Western Europe, as this is where Marx had predicted that a communist revolution would take place, and by the rise of Nazism in such an economically and technologically advanced nation such as Germany. Their writings pointed to the possibility of alternative theories of social development that were independent of the Communist Party and divorced from the organized working class.[5]

Some of the core issues that critical theory has been concerned with include a critique of modernity and capitalist societies and emancipation from the pathologies of modern society. They drew answers from other schools of thought to fill in some of the blanks of traditional Marxism using the insights of sociology, psychoanalysis, existential philosophy, and other disciplines, making critical theory something of an interdisciplinary effort. Eventually the focus of critical theory was expanded to include the decline of patriarchy in the nuclear family, the psychosocial dynamics that underlie authoritarian, anti-Semitic and fascist movements and the potential for totalitarian mind control in the mass production and consumption of "culture."[6]

According to Horkheimer in his seminal article, theory is the sum total of propositions about a subject, the validity of which depends on the propositions being consonant with the actual facts that are examined. If theory and experience are in contradiction with each other, one of the two must be reexamined. Something is either wrong with the theory, or the experience has not been observed correctly. This traditional conception of theory has shown a tendency toward a purely mathematical system of symbols, and in the natural sciences, theory formulation has largely become a matter of mathematical construction. The social sciences, including sociology, have attempted to follow the lead of the natural sciences, and "establishing a relationship between the simple perception or verification of a fact and the conceptual structure of our knowing is called its theoretical explanation."[7]

Understanding nature and economic and social mechanisms both demand amassing of a body of knowledge supplied in an ordered set of hypotheses. Such work, says Horkheimer, undoubtedly contributes to the continuous transformation and development of the material foundations of society. But this conception of theory has been made into an absolute and treated as if it were grounded in the nature of knowledge as such and became a reified, ideological category.[8] Horkheimer claims that traditional scientific theories are ideological in two senses: (1) they falsely assume that "facts" exist independently of theoretical concepts and that the formation of these concepts is detached from historical circumstances and that the independence of "objective" reality reflects the abstract individualism and alienation of capitalist society of which modern science is a product, and (2) they reduce society to a system of ahistorical, lawlike regularities that are resistant to change and lend themselves to forms of social engineering that enhance the power of those at the top such as managers and bureaucrats who seek better and more efficient methods of controlling those at the bottom such as the average worker.[9]

Critical theory seeks to emancipate people from this ideological strait-jacket by combining the explanatory methods of traditional theory with an empathetic understanding of the subjective attitudes and experiences of actual historical agents.[10] Knowledge and the application of knowledge to experience do not come from purely logical or methodological sources but can rather be understood only in the context of real social processes. Science has a social function that is not made manifest in the traditional approach to theory, "which speaks not of what theory means in human life, but only of what it means in the isolated sphere in which for historical reasons it comes into existence."[11]

There is, however, a human activity whose object is society itself and is focused on the way in which the social structure is organized. Critical theory examines these structures and is wholly distrustful of the rules of conduct that are provided for each member of society as it is presently con-stituted. Critical thinking seeks to abolish the opposition between an indi-vidual's purposefulness, spontaneity, and rationality and the work–process relationships on which current society is structured. The proletariat may indeed experience meaninglessness in the form of continuing and increasing wretchedness and injustice, but this awareness is prevented from becoming a force in society by the differentiation of the social structure that is imposed from above and by the opposition between personal class interests.[12]

Critical theory derives from a historical analysis of the goals of human activity, focusing on what Horkheimer calls the idea of a reasonable orga-nization of society that meets the needs of the whole community. If critical theory involved simply dealing with the feelings and ideas of any one class at any given moment, it would be merely describing the psychological contents of certain social groups and would be akin to social psychology. But if the theoretician and his object of interest are instead seen as forming a dynamic unity with the oppressed class so that the presentation of social contradic-tions is not merely an expression of the concrete historical situation but also a force within it to stimulate change, then the real function of theory emerges.[13]

In traditional theory the object with which science deals is not affected by theory as subject and object are kept apart. The objective phenomenon is independent to the theory and the observer can effect no change in the object. A critical attitude, however, is part of the development of society, and every part of the theory involves a critique of the existing order and a struggle against it, which is determined by the theory itself. Knowledge and action are not distinct concepts, and the theoretician does not isolate him- or herself from the social struggles in which he or she exists.[14] The understanding of a social experience is shaped by ideas that are in the researchers themselves. As Horkheimer says,

> [t]he facts which our senses present to us are socially performed in two ways: through the historical character of the object perceived and through the historical character of the perceiving organ. Both are not simply natural; they are shaped by human activity, and yet the individual perceives himself as receptive and passive in the act of perception.[15]

The perceived fact is codetermined by human ideas and concepts even before it is consciously elaborated in theory by the knowing individual. The so-called purity of an objective event is connected with technological conditions as well as the material process of production. It is easy to confuse the question of the mediation of the factual through the activity of society as a whole and the question of the influence of the measuring instrument, that is, the influence of a particular action upon the object being observed, a problem that particularly plagues physics. As a researcher records reality he or she separates it for purposes of analysis, rejoins pieces of it to form larger areas for research, and concentrates on some aspects while failing to notice others.[16]

In traditional theory, objective facts and the conceptual system by which the facts are grasped are external to theoretical thinking itself. This alienation finds philosophical expression in the separation of fact and value, knowledge and action, and other such polarities. Critical thinking is motivated to transcend these tensions and abolish the opposition between the individual's purposefulness, spontaneity, and rationality. Critical thought holds a concept of humans that are in conflict with themselves until this opposition is removed: "Critical thinking is the function neither of the isolated individual nor of a sum-total of individuals. Its subject is rather a definite individual in his real relation to other individuals and groups, in his conflict with a particular class, and, finally, in the resultant web of relationships with the social totality and with nature."[17]

Critical theory develops a viewpoint that is derived from historical analysis, where the goals of human activity are immanent in the work that humans perform, especially the idea of a reasonable organization of society that will meet the needs of the whole community. Bourgeois society, however, is not governed by any plan that is consciously directed to a specific goal; it proceeds as a whole more or less accidentally through history. The work of individuals and its results are alienated from them, and the whole process seems to be an unchangeable force of nature that is beyond anyone's control. Individuals must accept the basic conditions of their existence and find satisfaction and praise in accomplishing the tasks connected with their place in society and courageously doing their duty. The world is not their own but rather is the world of capital.[18]

The situation of the proletariat, however, is no guarantee of correct knowledge. They may indeed experience meaninglessness in the increasing wretchedness and injustice in their lives, but this awareness is prevented from becoming a social force by the differentiation of social structure imposed from above and by the opposition between personal class interests. A systematic analysis of proletarian consciousness and self-awareness does not provide a true picture of proletarian existence and interests.[19] The whole of society must be critically analyzed, showing how an exchange economy must necessarily lead to an increase of social tensions. In a rather pessimistic view Horkheimer makes the following observation:

> To put it in broad terms, the theory says that the basic form of the historically given commodity economy on which modern history rests contains in itself the internal and external tensions of the modern era; it generates these tensions over and over again in an increasingly heightened form; and after a period of progress, development of human powers, and emancipation for the individual, after an enormous extension of human control over nature, it finally hinders further development and drives humanity into a new barbarism.[20]

The doctrinal substance of critical theory does not shift as long as the age itself does not radically change. The decisive substantive elements of the theory cannot change until there has been a historical transformation of society. While history does not stand still, historical development only leads to a reassignment of degrees of relative importance given to individual elements of the theory. Horkheimer illustrates this proposition with the change in focus from the legal owners of the means of production when factories were small to the management of large-scale enterprises that control the means of production in today's world, the so-called separation of ownership and control. Society is no longer dominated by independent owners but by cliques of industrial and political leaders. Critical theory does not fall victim to the illusion that profit and property no longer play a key role, an illusion that Horkheimer claims is carefully fostered in the social sciences. Profit comes from the same social sources and must be increased by the same means as before.[21]

Since critical theory is a unified whole that is related to the contemporary situation, the theory as a whole is caught up in evolution. Yet this does not change the theory's foundations and its concern for the abolition of social injustice. The future of humanity depends on the existence of a critical attitude toward our declining culture. The nature of critical theory involves a changing of history and the establishment of justice between and among individuals and the institutions in which they function. The opposition between the individual and society grows ever greater as science grows ever more abstract. Conformism in thought, the idea that one should adhere to conventional wisdom "and the insistence that thinking is a fixed vocation, a self-enclosed realm within society as a whole, betrays the very essence of thought."[22]

In Horkheimer's thinking all social practice is reduced to the productivity of the human species. Social labor has emancipated humans from the power of nature and produced a civilization that has come to dominate nature and continually expand in relation to nature.[23] But at the same time humans are alienated from their work and its results, and the whole process in which they exist, where labor power and human life are largely wasted, itself seems to be an unchangeable force of nature beyond human control. This contradiction between productive forces and productive relations governs Horkheimer's attempt to provide a foundation for a critical theory of society.[24]

The materialistic interpretation of history, according to Horkheimer, is indebted to the concept of history contained in Hegel's work as it contains the notion of a context of history that goes beyond the intentions of individual agents. But it is also opposed to it in that it traces the development of human history back to the domination of nature rather than the unfolding of absolute Spirit. This Spirit is dethroned as an autonomous power shaping history and in its place as the motor of history is the domination of nature and self-preservation solely through the processes of social labor, which is the only dimension in which sociocultural progress takes place.[25]

Other Concerns of Critical Theory

The social rationalization of society has resulted in a division of labor into efficient units of production that transforms society into an organism that is held together by functional interdependencies that are arranged hierarchically and controlled from the top that extracts a huge amount of remuneration for its services. Exchange relationships governed by the price system reduce all human and material values to quantifiable commodities. As this capitalist system extends its hegemony throughout the world, it achieves higher levels of integration and adaptation thanks in large part to the intervention of the state on capitalism's behalf. And the "culture industry," in turn, provides consumer goods that give individuals a false sense of happiness.[26]

Critical theory must penetrate this false consciousness of harmony and happiness that pervades the consumer culture. Society in reality appears to be something alien and overwhelming, a kind of fate that stifles people's desire for self-determination: "The repetitiveness, sameness, and ubiquity of modern culture make for automated reactions to issues and weaken the forces of individual resistance. The reduction of culture to popular consumer commodity reinforces authoritarian and conformist patterns of behavior. Resignation, avoidance of conflict, anti-intellectualism, and stereotyping, which are all part of modern mass culture, lend themselves to political propaganda, whether in a fascist or democratic society, which transforms autonomous individuals into a mass requiring organization by a leader."[27]

Critical theory is largely focused on the evaluation of the freedom, justice, and happiness of societies rather than on a description and explanation of social phenomena and, in this sense, is more of a moral philosophy than a predictive science. It is critical of both existential philosophy and logical positivism as having abandoned critical thought. The former was uncritical with regard to speculative reference to empirically verifiable "essences" while logical positivism was uncritical in its assumption that true knowledge corresponds to conceptually unmediated "facts." It is also critical of idealism as this way of thinking tends to hold that individuals can achieve their goals in abstraction from social change and that freedom and happiness are reduced to "states of mind" divorced from material conditions and thus never fully realized. Idealism also ends up justifying the validity of practices and institutions that sustain historically contingent forms of class domination. The contradiction between idealism and materialism in which philosophy finds itself "is but a reflection of a society 'in crisis' torn between its transcendent ideals and its historical imperfections."[28]

Critical theorists maintain that philosophy (theory) and social reform (practice) are inseparable. Philosophical reflection must guide construction of a free, just, and happy society where we are emancipated from ideology and dogma. Reason understood as a collective enterprise of mutual critique creates a society of free individuals who are free from want and from the domination that comes from social injustice and inequity.[29] However, critical theory must be critical of its own philosophical assumptions by using the method of historical materialism conceived as a dialectical movement within existing social reality. This dialectical method is self-correcting and enables a change of previous interpretations that are seen to be false. Critical theory thus rejected what it saw as the dogmatic historicism and materialism of orthodox Marxist thought. Critical theorists came to believe that the material tensions and class struggles of which Marx spoke no longer had the same revolutionary potential in contemporary Western societies. This meant that Marx's dialectical interpretations and predictions were either incomplete or incorrect. Thus, there was a need for new theories of the economic, political, cultural, and psychological domination structures of advanced industrial societies.

Marcuse, for example, argues that the critical theory of society as understood by its founders is linked with materialism and is an economic rather than a philosophical system of thought. The two basic elements that link materialism to social theory are a concern with human happiness and the conviction that such happiness can only be attained through a transformation of the material conditions of society. One must look at an analysis of economic and political conditions to discern the actual course this transformation is taking and what measures must be taken to attain a rational organization of society. Reason is necessary to create a sense of universality and community that goes beyond mere self-sufficiency and develop a common life in a common world where rational subjects participate with other rational subjects.[30]

This demand for reason "means the creation of a social organization in which individuals can collectively regulate their lives in accordance with their needs." In such a society the labor process itself should not determine the existence of those who labor; rather, their needs should determine the labor process. The labor process should be regulated in the interests of the freedom and happiness of the masses, and without this element even an increase of production and the abolition of private property do not overcome the old injustices in the means of production. The transformation of social existence must be guided by this ultimate goal at its inception in order for humankind to be liberated and for freedom and happiness to be realized in everyday existence.[31]

Critical theory maintains that man can be more than simply a manipulable subject in the production process of class society. It opposes every form of production that dominates individuals instead of individuals dominating the production process. This idealism underlies the materialism of critical theory. When concepts like freedom and happiness are transformed from abstract concepts into reality the association of free men with competitive, commodity-producing society will also be transformed. This will also take the disengagement of science from the established patterns of domination and free it from serving the development of capitalistic productive forces to open up new potentialities for a richer existence. Transformation of the economic structure of society must also reshape the organization of the entire society so that when economic antagonisms between groups and individuals are abolished the political sphere can become independent and determine the development of society.[32]

Adorno believes that philosophical speculation should not hide behind the facts of its own history, where many areas of study involving science were withdrawn from its influence and subjected to the scientific method. Modern scientific intelligence, Adorno claims, came to regard philosophy as an archaic relic that was carried over from early Greek speculation where explanation of natural phenomena and metaphysical insight into the nature of things were inextricably interwoven. As science advanced, philosophy was more or less forced to become a "tiny, tolerated enclave, opposed thereby to what it set out to be—a universal system of truth." However, philosophy cannot reunite with its past glories and restore its preeminence, nor can it become a specialized discipline that follows along the lines suggested by scientific method.[33]

A philosophical method that frees itself from all these encumberments will find itself opposed to current thinking. Adorno thinks "that philosophical speculation that satisfies the aims of genuine metaphysical inquiry . . . draws its strength from its resistance to modern methodology and serves to counter the present-day acceptance of the material world around us." A philosophy that abandons its claim to omniscience and gives up the idea of crystallizing all truth within itself and renounces claims to a mastery of the absolute can still be guided by a sense of responsibility for everything and need not sacrifice the concept of truth itself. From the pre-Socratic onward, philosophers have always played a critical role; however, the critical idea has also been disrupted by modernity along with many other philosophical traditions. Such criticism has been a unifying factor in the history of philosophy and has been an important counter to passive acceptance of received theory.[34]

Our current world has become more and more reified and the veil under which we hide the face of nature has become thicker, which has led to an acceptance of the ideas connected with that veil as the only true experience of this world and of natural phenomena. This reified consciousness is entirely naïve, according to Adorno, and appeals to the authority of science, the rules by which it functions and the absolute validity of its methods, which together do not "allow the minds of men to dwell on matters that do not bear the stamp of its approval." Science, which is supposed to liberate ideas from the tutelage of dogma and be the means of autonomy to free man from any means of unseeing authority, has itself degenerated into an instrument of heteronomy. The task of philosophy is to break up the seemingly obvious and the apparently incomprehensible and to diagnose the malady that is driving the world to disaster. It must liberate itself from the "scientific compulsion to think solely along paths in line with the dictates of approved scientifically tested principle."[35]

Habermas's essay "Knowledge and Human Interests" shares many similarities with Horkheimer in that both develop a critique of positivism and both present a vision of critical social science, yet their conclusions are quite different. According to Habermas, knowledge that frees itself from mere human interests and is based on ideas, that has taken a theoretical attitude, is the only knowledge that can truly orient action. While Horkheimer had distinguished between a traditional theory and theory in the sense of critique; Habermas wants to start with Husserl's notion about the crisis of the sciences, by which he did not mean a crisis in the sciences but with their crisis as science. That which produces a scientific culture is the formation of a thoughtful and enlightened mode of life, not the information content of theories. Yet modern science has dissociated values from facts and has made a distinction between descriptive and prescriptive statements, and the conception of theory as a process of cultivation of the person has been abandoned.[36]

Husserl criticizes the objectivism of the sciences, where the world appears as a universe of facts whose lawlike connection can be grasped descriptively. This objectivist illusion conceals the constitution of those facts and thereby prevents, according to Husserl, the interlocking of knowledge with interests from the lifeworld. Seeing itself as free from such interests, science can unjustly claim to be dealing with pure theory. Husserl thinks only phenomenology can break with this naïve attitude in favor of a rigorously contemplative one that frees knowledge from interest. However, phenomenology is a transcendental philosophy that conserves something like the theoretical attitude but only in an abstract manner. Thus, Habermas thinks that Husserl, while criticizing the objective self-understanding of the sciences, succumbs to another objectivism attached to the traditional concept of theory.[37]

Science claims that the facts is discovers and the relation between them can be apprehended descriptively, but Habermas argues that such basic statements are not simple representations of facts in themselves but express the success or failure of our operations. Facts that are relevant to the empirical sciences are constituted through an a priori organization of our experience subject to a constitutive interest in technical control over objectified processes. What Habermas calls the historical-hermeneutic sciences gain their knowledge using a different methodological framework. Access to relevant facts is gained through an understanding of meaning rather than objective observation. This involves an interpretation of texts where the rules of hermeneutics determine the possible meaning of the validity of statements in the cultural sciences.[38]

Critical theory incorporates a reflective method that combines both objectifying and interpretative procedures in determining when theoretical statements grasp invariant regularities of social action or when they express ideologically frozen relations of dependence. Only in such reflection does knowledge have emancipatory consequences in achieving freedom from domination and thus knowledge is shown to be necessarily dependent on interests. Self-preservation, along with knowledge and freedom, and united in such emancipatory reflection on the validity of statements can be determined in rational discussion that is free from ideological constraint. Habermas concludes that "the truth of statements is based on anticipating the realization of the good life."[39]

The Dialectic of Enlightenment

In *Dialectic of Enlightenment*, Adorno and Horkheimer take something of a pessimistic turn in their thinking. Having witnessed the rise of fascist forces in Germany and Europe, the failure of the working class to revolt in Germany, the creation of a welfare state, and the rise of the culture industry to support capitalism, they became much more theoretically pessimistic about the possibilities for revolutionary progressive change and came to see that the contradictions within the social totality were becoming more difficult, if not impossible, to exploit for critique and thus social change. In this writing they attempt to account for the reasons all of these tragic developments had taken place.

In the introductory essay to this book the authors state that the program of the Enlightenment resulted in the disenchantment of the world, the dissolution of myths and the substitution of knowledge for fancy. They consider Bacon's view of the Enlightenment to be appropriate to the scientific attitude that continued after his death. The human mind, which overcomes superstition and myth, is to hold sway over a disenchanted nature where any notion of sacredness is not relevant. Knowledge is power and knows no obstacles and technology is the essence of this knowledge. What we want to learn from nature is how to use it for our interests and wholly dominate it and other people. The authors claim that this is the only aim of the Enlightenment. This scientific worldview eliminated any claim to meaning, and matter would be mastered without any reference to ruling or inherent powers in nature such as were present in the mythological worldview. Whatever does not conform to the rule of computation and utility is suspect. Enlightenment becomes totalitarian as scientific rationality becomes the dominant worldview.[40]

Science largely replaced the mythological worldview that enabled people in the pre-scientific era to make sense of their world and cope with their tenuous existence in it. Myth is a collection of such stories that deal with the human condition, the origins of life as well as death and the afterlife, supernatural beings such as nymphs and mermaids, and the gods that govern the universe. These myths are thus an expression of the beliefs and values about these subjects that are held by a particular culture in an effort to explain complex natural phenomena that are difficult to understand and are frightening to people. Many of these myths are still prevalent in the modern world, particularly in the area of religion, as people are under no obligation to abandon mythology for science.

Nature can be terrifying in many different ways as it sometimes confronts people with situations they cannot fathom and which threaten to destroy them and the environment in which they exist. There are hurricanes that have enormous potential for destruction, tornadoes that do not give people much warning in some circumstances, earthquakes that can destroy the very foundations of people's existence, floods that engulf whole communities, volcanic eruptions that block out the sun, and other forces in nature that pose major threats. And before modern medicine there were diseases that could wipe out whole civilizations without warning. There were many such things that were beyond the control of humans in the pre-scientific age and produced anxieties beyond imagination. Even today many of these same threats exist and with all our scientific knowledge pose significant threats to human existence.

Science attempts to demythologize nature, allowing for greater control over nature and giving humans the ability to manipulate it in such a way as to reduce the anxiety nature can cause and make it seem less terrifying. Science gives us the means to predict where hurricanes and tornadoes might strike so we can prepare for them and get out of the way if possible. Modern medicine develops ways to combat diseases that can threaten vast numbers of people and gives us vaccines to keep them in check. Thus the scientific worldview becomes dominant in modern societies because it works so well and has vastly improved the human condition. But it can become something of a myth itself.

Horkheimer and Adorno state that the old mythological worldview turned into enlightenment and nature turned in mere objectivity. But enlightenment becomes something of a myth itself and with every development becomes more engulfed in mythology. "The principle of immanence, the explanation of every event as repetition, that the Enlightenment upholds against mythic imagination is the principle of myth itself." Power over nature is increased, but alienation from nature is the result. Nature is known so that it can be manipulated, and its potentiality is turned to the ends of humans. The possibility of world domination is realized only in terms of a more skilled science. Such domination tends toward a division of labor that serves the dominated whole for the end of self-preservation.[41]

Nature is comprehended mathematically, and this mathematized world is conceived as the truth about nature and in this way enlightenment intended to secure itself against the return of the mythic. Thinking becomes objectified and turns into an automatic process that impersonates a machine such that ultimately the machine can replace thinking. Mathematical procedure becomes the ritual of thinking. Thought is turned into a thing or an instrument, and the more the machinery of thought subjects existence to itself, the more blind its resignation in reproducing existence. Enlightenment thus returns to mythology as the mathematization of nature as being the final truth about nature is itself a myth.[42]

Domination is not only paid for by the alienation of people from the objects dominated, but spirit itself is objectified bewitching the relations between people. Even the individual is reduced to conventional responses and modes of operation that are expected. This objectification of spirit leaves the individual subject to the countless agencies of mass production, which, along with its culture, impresses conventional modes of behavior on the individual, who comes to see this behavior as the only respectable, natural, and rational way to behave. Humans come to be defined as things and the technical process into which the subject has objectified itself is free from the ambiguity of mythical thought and meaning "because reason itself has become the mere instrument of the all-inclusive economic apparatus."[43]

The authors believe that the more complicated and precise this apparatus becomes, the more impoverished are the experiences that it can offer. The working conditions in society compel conformity, and the impotence of the worker is but the logical consequence of industrial society. The reduction to mere objects of the administered life that informs every aspect of modern existence, including language, and perception represents an objective necessity against which they believe nothing can be done. Misery as the antithesis of power and powerlessness grows immeasurably together with the capacity to remove misery permanently. While life is made easier though the production of material things the process of capitalist production produces more alienation on the part of the people who are trapped in the system.

The social rationalization of society has resulted in a division of labor into efficient units of production that transforms society into an organism that is held together by functional interdependencies. These are arranged hierarchically and controlled from the top, which, in turn, extracts a huge amount of remuneration for its services. Exchange relationships governed by the price system reduce all human and material values to quantifiable commodities. As this capitalist system extends its hegemony throughout the world it achieves higher levels of integration and adaptation thanks in large part to the intervention of the state on capitalism's behalf. And the "culture industry" in turn provides consumer goods that give individuals a false sense of happiness.[44]

Critical theory, according to Horkheimer and Adorno, must penetrate this false consciousness of harmony and happiness that pervades the consumer culture. Society in reality appears to be something alien and overwhelming, a kind of fate that stifles people's desire for self-determination: "The repetitiveness, sameness, and ubiquity of modern culture make for automated reactions to issues and weaken the forces of individual resistance. The reduction of culture to popular consumer commodity reinforces authoritarian and conformist patterns of behavior. Resignation, avoidance of conflict, anti-intellectualism, and stereotyping, which are all part of modern mass culture, lend themselves to political propaganda, whether in a fascist or democratic society, which transforms autonomous individuals into a mass that can be manipulated and dominated by the leaders of society."[45]

People distance themselves from nature through thought in order to determine how it is to be dominated. Thought becomes illusory whenever it denies this divisive function, which involves distancing and objectification. Bacon's utopian vision that we should "command nature by action" has been realized, and the nature of the thralldom that he ascribed to unsubjected nature is domination itself. Knowledge, which Bacon believed to be important for the sovereignty of individuals, has itself fallen under domination and is used in the interests of capitalist society. Enlightenment, instead of freeing individuals from mythological thinking and promoting a more rational and just society, has been made to serve the present-age ideology and results in wholesale deception of the masses.[46]

As philosophy emancipated itself from religious dogma reason became increasingly linked to the calculation of the most efficient means for attaining any end whatsoever. Reason became limited instrumental calculation and its moral content disappeared as people who were rational used formal procedures to calculate the most efficient means possible. Reason thus became subjective in that it served the subject's interest in self-preservation, be it that of the single individual or of the community on whose maintenance the individual depends. Freedom and justice are no longer valued for their own sake but are "means" that can be discarded whenever it is prudent. As Horkheimer and Adorno argue in "The Concept of Enlightenment" this reduction of reason to means-end calculation has far-reaching consequences for the organization of society. The dissemination of means–end rationality has promoted the one-sided growth of modern science and technology in ways that are thoroughly undemocratic.[47]

The techniques of rational management and efficient administration require forms of hierarchy and segmentation that increase domination. Governed by the market the economy produces unintended side effects such as recessions, uneven development, uncontrolled growth and waste, and pollution, which confront society with a new form of unfreedom that may be more insidious than that imposed by either religion or personal tyranny. Modern capitalism embodies a form of totalitarianism that is not that much different from that prevalent in bureaucratic socialist societies. For critical theorists East and West converge in the reduction of nature and humanity to an objectified system of mathematical quantification and exchange relationships that are predictable and controllable.[48]

Horkheimer and Adorno assert that the steering of the entire economic process has been turned over to the centralized administrative apparatus of domination. The interests of major corporations and the planning capacity of state organs have joined in a kind of "technical rationality to which all domains of social action are uniformly subordinated."[49] Adorno regards the development of a centrally administered thoroughly organized society as the definitive event in the formation of highly developed societies.[50] In such a society the techniques of modern film, radio, and television become fused with the entertainment industry to form a cultural-industrial complex, whose manipulative products make it possible to control individual consciousness and affect the members of society in such a manner that they willingly undertake administratively sanctioned tasks.[51]

The culture industry produces conformity-creating messages that influence individual members of society by penetrating to the deepest level of consciousness and guiding them along paths suggested by the mass media and creates a passive non-reflective consumer.[52] Under the influence of what Adorno calls the pseudo-worlds of the media, "subjects become willing recipients of conformity-inducing messages."[53] The members of this kind of society no longer have the strength to master their individual instincts. The loss of parental authority allows the child to be directly socialized through administrative power. When the growing child could form a moral conscience by internalizing the norms and sanctions authoritatively represented by the father, he or she had some independence that secured them from behavioral requirements stipulated from the outside.[54]

As the father's authority has been shaken the culture industry has been able to act as a surrogate in regulating instincts and has created the "outward directed character" that is dominated by a centrally administered system.[55] This domination produces an individual with a conscience that has internalized the capacities for controlling the environment. The growing individual is thus confronted with an objective world of natural objects which in the process of socialization he or she learns to dominate.[56] The oppressed individual becomes a victim of the techniques of domination in a totally administered society where the ruling bureaucracies are able to regulate the entire process of social production through the means of technical rationality.[57]

Means and Ends

In an article titled "Means and Ends," Horkheimer thinks of subjective reason as being concerned with means and ends, with the adequacy of procedures for purposes that are more or less taken for granted. Subjective reason does not consider the question whether purposes as such are reasonable and assumes that they serve the subject's interest in self-preservation. The idea that a purpose can be reasonable for its own sake without reference to some kind of subjective gain or advantage is alien to subjective reason. When it is used to refer to an idea or a thing rather than an act, it refers to the relation of that object or concept to a purpose and not to the object or concept itself.[58]

Objective reason, on the other hand, considers reason to be a force not only in the individual mind but also in the objective world in relations among human beings, in social classes and social institutions, and in nature. Objective reason aims at developing a comprehensive system of hierarchy of all beings and the degree of reasonableness of an individual's life is determined with respect to its harmony with this totality. The objective structure is the focus, not just individuals and their purposes, and the end result of this kind of thinking is to reconcile the objective order of the "reasonable" as conceived by philosophy within human existence. There is a fundamental difference between objective theory, where reason is a principle inherent in reality, and the view that reason is a subjective faculty of the human mind.[59]

Both the subjective and objective views of reason have been present in history from the outset but subjective reason eventually emerged into a dominant position which Horkheimer thinks produces a crisis in that at some point thinking becomes incapable of considering objectivity or begins to negate it as a delusion. Reason became subjectivized, and no particular reality could be seen to be reasonable in itself as all the basic concepts were emptied of content. Thinking cannot determine the desirability of any goal in itself and the criteria for our actions and beliefs came to depend on factors other than reason. It became meaningless to talk about truth in relation to practical, moral, or esthetic decisions. Ethical values came to be seen as subjective, and reason cannot be used to pass judgment on actions and ways of life as such judgments are subjected to conflicting interests to resolve.[60]

This relegation of reason to a subordinate position contrasts with the so-called pioneers of bourgeois civilization who believed that reason played a leading, if not predominant, role in human behavior. Reason was seen as a spiritual power that was supposed to regulate our preferences and relations with each other and with nature. When reason was first conceived, it was intended to do more than just regulate the relation between means and ends; it was supposed to be the instrument for understanding and determining the ends themselves. Objective reason refers to a structure inherent in real-ity itself that calls for actions that are independent of personal wishes and interests. Objective reason looks to replace traditional religion with philo-sophical thought and insight, and since it holds to the concept of objective truth it must take a positive or negative stance regarding the content of established religion.[61]

The controversy between religion and philosophy eventually ended in a stalemate, and both came to be regarded as separate branches of a common culture. But the fundamental unity of all beliefs rooted in a common Chris-tian ontology was shattered, and the neutralization of religion reduced it to the status of one cultural good among others. This paved the way for the elimination of religion as the medium of spiritual objectivity and the idea of the absoluteness of religious revelation. Philosophy was also affected as when the philosophers of the Enlightenment attacked religion in the name of reason what they really killed was not the church but metaphysics and the objective concept of reason itself. The use of reason to perceive the true nature of reality and for determining guiding principles of our lives came to be seen as obsolete. Reason was no longer useful for ethical, moral, and religious insight.[62]

An attitude of neutrality toward all spiritual content was furthered as the search for universal objective truth was replaced by a formalized and inher-ently relativist reason. Given this vacuum, the idea of self-interest gained the upper hand during the industrial age and suppressed other motives con-sidered fundamental to the functioning of society. But this theory of self-interest involved a contradiction with the idea of the nation, and philosophy was subject to falling prey to an irrational nationalism tainted with romanti-cism. The political constitution was originally thought of as an expression of concrete principles that were rooted in objective reason. Ideas of justice, happiness, equality, democracy, property, were all believed to stem from reason, but when reason was reduced to the subjectivist principle of self-interest the particular preempted the place of the universal.[63]

Reason thus became an instrument completely harnessed to the social process, according to Horkheimer, and its role in the domination of men and nature became the sole criterion in judging its pragmatic value. Think-ing itself was reduced to the level of industrial processes as concepts became rationalized, labor-saving devices. Ideas were considered to be things and language was just another tool in the gigantic apparatus of production in modern society. The meaning of words was supplanted by their function or effect in the world of things and events. Words that are not used for practi-cal purposes were suspected of being sales talk of some kind as truth that was no end in itself. Science, conceived as the classification of facts and the calculation of probabilities, became the sole authority. Statements that justice and freedom were better than their opposites were not scientifically verifiable and were therefore considered useless.[64]

Subjective reason, claims Horkheimer, can conform to anything and can be used by both adversaries and defenders of traditional human values and can support the ideology for profit and reaction as well as the ideology for progress and revolution. Without a rational foundation, the democratic principle depends on the so-called interests of the people and the principle of the majority, which is inseparable from the principle of democracy, is not only a substitute for but is also considered to be an improvement upon objective reason. Men are considered to be the best judges of their own interests, and the interests of the majority, so it is thought, are considered as valuable to a community as the intuitions of a so-called superior reason. But Horkheimer questions whether men can know their own interests. How is this knowledge gained, and what assurances do we have that this knowledge is correct?[65]

The framers of the Constitution were far from substituting majority rule for those of reason. There was no principle for these people that did not derive its authority from a metaphysical or religious source, including the majority principle itself, which was only one among many ideas of similar dignity. For example, the majority principle was not considered to be a guarantee of justice and the rights of a minority were considered to be an intuitive truth coming directly or indirectly from a philosophical tradition that was still alive at the time.[66]

Subjective reason has no such inheritance and considers truth as habit and strips it of its spiritual authority. In today's world, according to Horkheimer, the majority principle has become the sovereign force to which thought must adhere and is the arbiter of cultural life. Public opinion has become a mere tool for obscure forces that manipulate it in their interests and make it appear as a substitute for reason. Since ends are no longer determined by reason it is impossible to judge one political or economic system as better than another. Even if a group of enlightened people were to fight the greatest evil imaginable, subjective reason would make it almost impossible to judge it as evil and make the fight morally imperative. The motives of the group would be questioned and the personal interests of the groups would be examined.[67]

Tradition cannot be invoked as the measure of any ethical or religious truth as it suffers from a lack of authenticity. Civilized society has been living on the residue of these truths, but they gradually over time lose their power of conviction. Subjective reason has destroyed the theoretical basis of these truths and empties them of any objective content. In the modern world, those who cherish the old ethical and religious doctrines are deprived of an adequate philosophy to support these doctrines. They are regarded as either "expressions of mere subjective desires or as an established pattern deriving authority from the number of people who believe in it and the length of time of its existence."[68]

Instrumental Reason

From this critique of reason as it emerged during the Enlightenment, critical theory went on to develop the notion of instrumental reason. The primary roles that people play in Western culture have been reduced to production and consumption. These roles also involve the use of what has been called instrumental reason, which is a way of thinking that provides direction for the path that science and technology take in our society. Such an understanding of instrumental reason has to do with dominance over nature and other human beings that is the essence of management in a capitalistic society. Such reasoning is used for the purpose of increasing the profits of the organization and the economic wealth of society. It is concerned with economic exploitation of nature and humans to attain certain materialistic ends that are believed to create a good society based on an ever-increasing supply of goods and services.

There are many different ways to think about the reasoning process humans employ, but critical theorists believe that instrumentality has become the dominant form of reason in the modern world. Instrumental reason, at least as defined in critical theory, is reason used for the particular end of dominating and exploiting nature and people in the interests of capitalist production and consumption. People are seen as human resources that are necessary elements in the production process and are to be managed so as to contribute to the goal of profit making for capitalistic enterprises. Likewise, nature is seen as merely something that contains resources that are necessary to production so that things can be made for sale on the market. Instrumental reason is not concerned with any other meanings in life except those that are associated with production and consumption of commodities produced for sale on the market. It does not allow for self-reflection on deeper meanings of life that may come from philosophy or religion but reduces things to matter, history to fact, and everything to a number. Commodity exchange is merely the historically developed form of instrumental rationality.[69]

Social relations are reduced to administration, and the role of a manager is to manipulate people to work toward the goals of the corporate organization. Organizations are thus totally administered and the freedom of individuals to pursue their own goals and interests is curtailed in the interests of the organization's objectives. Nature is raped for resources and used as a dumping ground for waste material. No thought is given to the ecological health of the environment or the long-term implications of this continued exploitation. The potentiality of humans and nature is thus utilized to pursue the goals of capitalism. All that matters is more and more production and consumption, and the entire society is subject to the logic of the capitalistic system. Thought itself is thus turned into a thing, an instrument that is directed to the ends of capitalistic society; it is restricted to organization and administration. Reason becomes a mere instrument of an all-inclusive economic apparatus.[70]

Manipulative intervention into natural processes replaces a passive defense against natural dangers with active control of nature. Under the imperative of self-preservation, humans place the natural environment under their conceptual and practical control. It is made into an objectified reality suited to the goals of manipulative intervention and becomes more and more a product of human activity. We reshape nature to suit capitalistic interests, even to the extent of creating our own climate. This manipulation of nature results in the neutralization of its sensible qualities and its variety as nature becomes subject to standardization and uniformity by being developed to suit human interests. The cost is the exclusion of living nature as it is gradually despiritualized and cognitively deprived of its sensory richness and loses any sense of the sacred. Industrialization turns the natural environment into a lifeless and barren wasteland.[71]

Labor requires a single-minded vigilance and directed energy to accomplish the goals of the organization. Only those instinctual impulses that can be channeled into instrumental performance are allowed. All the diverting, distracting, or superfluous instincts of workers must be sublimated or suppressed. In the corporation, labor is directed by a privileged class called management that dominates the other employees and extracts a disproportionate remuneration for its services. Control is exercised through socially allocated work assignments as workers are made into objects subject to goal-oriented manipulations. This is analogous to the objectification of nature, making it subject to repeatable operations of exploitation. Money commands the obedience of the dominated subjects as submitting to corporate goals is the only way most employees can attain the resources they need to sustain themselves and their families.[72]

This domination of a privileged class is a social extension of the human domination of nature, and the despiritualization of nature that results is analogous to the cultural impoverishment of employees, many of whom do boring and meaningless tasks in the corporation. The employee is a passive and intentionless victim of the same techniques of domination that are aimed at nature. Thus, instrumental reason is used to both control and dominate the employees of the organization and to control and dominate nature, all in the interests of increasing production and consumption and growth in a capitalistic society. This use of reason has undermined moral considerations and has helped create a moral vacuum that is only too evident in the business community. It has led to an acceptance of the economic model of the firm as the ultimate justification for business activities. It also involves a certain view of government, as well as culture and nature, and determines the way business relates to these aspects of society.[73]

This privileged class is exempted from all manual labor while the socially oppressed class is encumbered with all manual labor. This socially oppressed class must continue in itself the blind irregularities of nature and extend them to humanity as a whole. Thus, the social domination of the working class by the privileged class is a kind of intra-social extension of the human domination of nature. If the oppressed class is seen as an unresisting object of technical control in the same way nature is dominated, one can speak of the cultural impoverishment of laborers as a direct product of social domination in the same way the despiritualization of nature is the direct product of the social domination of nature.[74] According to Axel Honneth,

> [i]n both processes a collectivity represented as a subject—that of the human species in the first, that of the privileged class in the second—dissociates itself from its own natural and social environment by making it into an object of control-oriented action. Just as the instrumentally acting subject subsumes natural processes under the abstract perspective of control in order to be able to make it subject to his goal-oriented manipulations, so too the socially privileged subject arranges all other members of society according to the perspective of control in order to let them become organs for the execution of socially allocated work assignments . . . Social organization in which the successful procedure of control and manipulation of the oppressed member of society are embedded correspond, on the side of social domination, to the technical instruments in which rules are gradually embodied in repeatable operations upon nature.[75]

Thus, the natural environment is objectified and gradually deprived of its sensory richness as it comes under control and domination by humans. But this objectification of nature also involves the self-objectification of humanity. For the sake of labor, "individuals must forcibly constrict their capacity for sensory experience as well as their organic instinctual potential in order to realize the discipline of instrumental functions." As humans increase their control over external nature they gradually forfeit their inner nature since they must treat it in the same way as external nature.[76]

The development of productive forces that dominates nature dilutes it to a mere projection of social control, but this increase in the power of humans alienates them from that over which they exercise their power. Humans know each other and nature only insofar as they can be manipulated. The subject that is produced by instrumental intervention cannot respond openly and flexibly to the sense impressions it receives from nature, and its sensory possibilities are limited to those that fit in with the conceptual schematism of control. All sense experiences that threaten the direct pursuit of control are excluded.[77] Honneth says,

> Beyond making sense perception rigidly one-sided, social labor also demands the permanent channeling of amorphous natural impulses . . . The motivational basis for the domination of nature arises with the repression and rejection of all instinctual impulses the impede labor. Since labor requires single-minded vigilance and directed energy, the subject is allowed to take up in his ego only those instinctual impulses that can be channeled into his instrumental performance. All diverting, distracting, or superfluous instincts, by contrast, must be either sublimated

of suppressed . . . The process of the domination of nature repeats itself in the control of instincts, as the individual conquest of inner nature.[78]

Instrumental rationality provides the key for a critical theory of society. Instrumental reason deprives the acting subject of purposive-rational thinking and serves the technical domination of external nature as well as the prudential disciplining of one's inner nature.[79] "Commodity exchange is merely the historically developed form of instrumental rationality."[80] Humans employ their knowledge of the natural environment to make the regularities of nature into a means to acquire their own livelihood. As they learn to master and control nature they abstract form the majesty of nature and make it into "an objectified reality in accordance with repeatable experiences suited to the goals of manipulative intervention."[81]

Ethics

Critical theorists continually remind readers that rationalism promises freedom, justice, and happiness but ends up giving legitimacy to the domination of contemporary society. Some of them address the source of this contradiction and suggest possibilities for a more enlightened morality. Horkheimer starts with bourgeois morality whose ideals reflect social relations that are particular to a capitalist society. This morality is largely dependent on Kant's formulation of morality, where morality consists of acting in a manner that is consistent with the actions of all like-minded rational persons: the universalization principle. It requires that we refrain from violating the rights of others and treat them as possessing dignity and worth; treating people as ends and not means.[82]

The main problem Horkheimer finds with Kant's ethical formulation is that it opposes reason (duty) to happiness, universal interest to particular interest, freedom to instinctual motivation, and the individual to society. He shows how the tensions in this idealistic philosophy mirror the tensions within a capitalistic society regulated by contractual agreements. Horkheimer's materialistic analysis holds that in a capitalistic society, individuals are caught between the competing demands of self-interest and morality and identify their own particular interests with the good of society (Adam Smith's invisible hand). At the same time they experience their freedom and individuality as things that are internal or private as opposed to the unfreedom and uniformity of their physical or everyday existence.[83]

From the materialistic perspective of Horkheimer, bourgeois morality points beyond itself and the capitalistic society it reflects. Historical materialism emphasizes the connection between private morality and public life and holds that Kant's universal goals of freedom and happiness for the isolated individual can only be realized in a just society. True freedom presupposes the satisfaction of human needs under democratic conditions in society guaranteeing an equality of power. Under these conditions, the opposition between the is and the ought, particular and universal interest, and freedom and happiness will no longer be necessary.[84]

Marcuse's concern is with the contradiction between happiness and reason that exists in modern moral philosophy. He argues that reason and happiness are opposed to one another under capitalism and that moral duty confronts pleasure as something subjective, particularistic, and instinctual. Rational behavior requires the suppression of desire that encourages an untrammeled pursuit of material goods and wasteful consumption that perpetuates unfreedom and unhappiness for the masses. "True" pleasures are those that allow for the development of human faculties both intellectual and sensual. The precondition for this development is the creation of a just society.[85]

The determination of which pleasures are "true" depends on the establishment of an emancipated democratic society where all people can rationally agree on common interests. The current regime of social production based on profit and consumption does not promote true freedom, justice, and happiness. However, science and technology need not result in increased domination. Once having achieved the mechanization of all socially necessary but repressive labor, science and technology could be emancipated by transforming it into a means for pacifying and freeing nature. This would mean a qualitative change in science and technology from an instrument of objectification and domination into a medium of receptivity.[86]

Habermas, however, believes this kind of transformation is all but inconceivable. He believes that this kind of emancipation can only occur when the existence of a different kind of rationality is acknowledged. Emancipation must begin with the democratization of society where self-determination is nurtured in free and open discussion among social and political equals. There must be a fundamental interest in achieving an integrated identity through free and undistorted communication.[87] Rational justification of prescriptive statements must be seen as a dialogical process of reaching agreement on contested statements. What establishes the validity of a prescriptive statement or norm is not its correspondence with facts or derivation from more basic principles but what people would agree is in their common interest under egalitarian conditions that permit free and open discussion. Questions about rights and duties cannot be answered in the abstract apart from historical needs and interests. But Western societies suppress discussion of common interests. Parties of unequal bargaining strength reach compromises that express a weighing of particular interests without determining whether such interests are rational or "generalizable."[88]

Culture and Technology

While positivistic trends in sociology tend to dismiss the notion of society as mere philosophical survival, Adorno claims that such realism is itself unrealistic, "[f]or while the notion of society may not be deduced from any individual facts, nor on the other hand be apprehended as an individual itself, there is nonetheless no social fact which is not determined by society as a whole. Society appears as a whole behind every concrete social situation." Society must be defined through theory that recognizes society as a product of human activity where living subjects are able to see themselves as part of society that constrains their individual behavior.[89]

The market system in modern industrial societies fashions humanity into a vast network of consumers and producers but is itself an objective abstraction that involves a universal development of an exchange system that operates independently of the qualitative attitudes of producers and consumers. The market system represents the domination of the general over the particular, according to Adorno, and of society over its membership and reduces humanity to agents and bearers of exchange value. The total system requires everyone to respect the law of exchange if they do not wish to be destroyed irrespective of whether they are motivated by profit. The institution of exchange creates and reproduces an antagonism that could at any time bring society to an ultimate catastrophe.[90]

The difference between classes in society grows with the increasing concentration of capital and results in a separation of social power from social helplessness. From personal experience almost everyone knows that social existence is not the result of personal initiative as most people have to take a job in order to make a living irrespective of their own human talents and possibilities. A rational and genuinely free society cannot do without administration and a division of labor, but all over the world, according to Adorno, administrations have tended toward a greater self-sufficiency and independence from their administered subjects, reducing these subjects to abstractly normed behavior. These subjects, both deliberately and automatically, are hindered from coming to a consciousness of themselves as subjects. They owe their life to what is being done to them and are trapped in the system. People must act to free themselves from what Adorno sees as the "present petrified conditions of existence," but this existence has left its mark on people and deprived them of so much of their life and individuation that they scarcely seem capable of the spontaneity that is necessary to change that existence.[91]

Adorno is also concerned with the effect of television on society and focuses on the nature of present-day television and its imagery rather than on any particular show or program. He refers to the current culture industry and states that the commercial production of cultural goods has become streamlined, thereby increasing the impact that popular culture has on the individual. This popular culture is not confined to one particular form of expression but has seized all media of artistic expression and therefore cannot be avoided. The repetitiveness, selfsameness, and ubiquity of modern mass culture has made it into a medium of psychological control and weakens the forces of individual resistance. The strength of modern mass culture has been further increased by changes in the sociological structure of the audience that have become cultural "consumers."[92]

Television, in particular, has a multilayered structure that consists of various layers of meaning superimposed on each other that contribute to the effect of television on the viewer. Meaning has been taken over by the culture industry and what it conveys has become organized in order to enthrall viewers on various psychological levels simultaneously. In fact, says Adorno, the hidden message may be more important that the overt message, as the hidden message will escape the controls of consciousness and since it is not warded off by sales resistance will more likely sink into the mind of the viewer. The concept of a multilayered personality has been used by the culture industry to snare the consumer as completely as possible in order to produce the intended effects through both surface and latent messages.[93]

Television lends itself to stereotyping, what Adorno calls inducing people to engage in mechanical simplifications that distort the world in ways that seem to fit into preestablished pigeonholes. Many shows enforce what he calls the psychologically extremely dangerous division of the world into black (the out-group) and white (the in-group) and in doing so simplifies and distorts any real social issues. One of the most typical stereotypes is that of the artist who is usually portrayed as maladjusted, introverted, and is often identified as being homosexual while the "man of action" is most often portrayed as a real strong man. To overcome the effects of television Adorno states that we must knowingly face psychological mechanisms operating at various levels in order to avoid becoming blind and passive victims of television.[94]

In an article titled "Freudian Theory and the Pattern of Fascist Propaganda," Adorno argues that mass culture and authoritarianism go together. The problem of mass psychology, according to Freud, is that it leads to the decline and subsequent weakness of the individual. Freud is interested in finding which psychological forces result in the transformation of individuals into mass society. Fascist demagogues have to combine individuals into a mass unity by artificially creating a bond between individuals, and Freud believes that this bond that integrates individuals is libidinal in nature. The coherence of masses can be explained by referring to the pleasure principle, the actual or vicarious gratifications individuals experience by surrendering to mass psychology. As part of a mass movement individuals can throw off the repressions of their unconscious instincts and display primitive attitudes that are contrary to their normal rational behavior. The creation of mass or herd instincts creates a potential shortcut from violent emotions to violent actions.[95]

Fascism as a rebellion against civilization is a reproduction of the archaic in and by civilization itself and gets its energy from psychological agencies that are pressed into the service of the unconscious. One such agency that helps hold the masses together is an unconscious "love relationship" that can be expressed only in a sublimated and indirect way. Another is the psychological image that surrounds a leader who taps into the unconscious need for a powerful and threatening father and an extreme passion for authority. A bond between leaders and followers is formed based on the need for identification, which is an early expression of an emotional tie with another person. Idealization is another unconscious element and is used by a fascist leader to promote the idealization of himself in his followers. This pattern of identification through idealization is collective, where followers make the leader their ideal and thus come to love themselves and get rid of the frustration and discontent that mar the picture of their empirical selves.[96]

The leader must, however, appear as both an idealization, a superman if you will, and as an average person in order to identify with the masses. The superman must resemble the follower and appear as his "enlargement" at the same time. He must be both omnipotent and just one of the folks, a plain, red-blooded American untainted by material wealth. The leader gratifies the followers wish to submit to authority and to be the authority himself.[97] He has the ability to guess the psychological wants and needs of the followers who are susceptible to his propaganda and has the capacity to express without any inhibitions things that are latent in the followers. The spell that leaders have over their followers largely depends on their oral ability as language itself can function in a sort of magical manner in reducing individuals to members of crowds.[98]

Fascist propaganda must continually suggest to the followers that simply belonging to the in-group is better, higher, and purer than those people who are excluded to the out-group. Any kind of critique or self-awareness of these psychological mechanisms is resented as a narcissistic loss and elicits rage against anyone or anything that questions their stubbornly maintained values. Concentrating hostility on the out-group does away with intolerance within the in-group.[99] Fascists play down differences with the in-group and level out distinctive qualities among members of the group except the hierarchical one involving the leaders. No member of the in-group should indulge in individual pleasures as repressive egalitarianism is part and parcel of the fascist mentality. Coherence of the in-group is a reaction against their jealousy of each other, which is pressed into the service as in-group coherence.[100]

The objective aims of fascism are largely irrational and contradict the material interests of a great number of their adherents. Since fascism cannot win over the masses through rational arguments its propaganda must be oriented psychologically to mobilize the unconscious, irrational, and regressive processes in the individuals that are the target of their propaganda. Such tactics assume people have been robbed of autonomy and spontaneity by standardized mass culture and can be manipulated in the interests of fascism. The psychology of the masses has been taken over by fascist leaders and transformed into a means for their domination. The individual has lost his substance and has become part of a hoard driven by a "group psychology" that can be merciless and unapproachable.[101]

Marcuse claims that in the analysis of an economy, whether capitalistic or otherwise, the negative effects such as overproduction, unemployment, insecurity, waste, and repression, are overlooked as long as they are considered to be inevitable byproducts of the economic system and growth and progress continues. This focus on positive thinking is enforced by the anonymous power and efficiency of the technological society. This absorption of the negative by the positive is validated by daily experience, and this kind of thinking permeates the general consciousness of society and even affects the consciousness of the critic who may see the negative effects of the economy but is also swept up in the general commitment to growth and progress.[102]

Critical thought, however, strives to define the irrational character of the established rationality, the kind of thinking that supports the status quo in society, and to define the tendencies that cause this rationality to generate its own transformation. The transition to a new technology would, according to Marcuse, involve a transition to a higher stage of civilization and would be catastrophic for the established technology. It would also involve a new idea of Reason both on the theoretical and practical levels. Marcuse thinks that Whitehead best captures this new idea of Reason in the statement "The function of Reason is to promote the art of life," which entails the threefold urge to live, to live well, and to live better.[103]

In advanced industrial societies, however, scientific abstractions came to dominate and prove their worth in the actual conquest and transformation of nature. Philosophical abstractions did not and could not transform nature in this manner, and the truth of metaphysical propositions came to be rooted in their historical content, that is, by the degree to which they define historical possibilities. According to Marcuse, scientific rationality translated into political power is the decisive factor in the actual development of these historical possibilities. In constituting themselves as a political enterprise, science and technology could enter a new stage where the construction, development, and utilization of material and intellectual resources could be freed from particular interests which have impeded the satisfaction of human needs and the evolution of human faculties and could open up "a universe of qualitatively different relations between man and man, and man and nature."[104]

Industrial civilization has largely treated nature as it has treated man himself, as an instrument of destructive productivity. The standard of living attained in the most advanced industrial societies is not, according to Marcuse, a suitable model of development if the goal is the pacification of existence. To attain this existence man must be liberated from the affluent society. This does not mean, however, a return to poverty and simplicity. The elimination of profitable waste would, on the contrary, increase the social wealth available for distribution. The energy that would be liberated from those performances that are necessary to sustain destructive prosperity could result in a decrease in the degree of servitude to that prosperity and free individuals to live a rational and pacified existence. They could be free from the repressive needs created by advertising and all the indoctrinating media of information and entertainment and attain an autonomy where the repressed dimensions of experience could come to life again. No less than the material base of domination is at stake.[105]

According to Habermas, society has become progressively rationalized and this rationalization is linked to the institutionalization of science and technology. By rationalization Habermas means the extension of criteria of rational decision making into all areas of society, and the industrialization of social labor subjecting it to the criteria of instrumental action which also penetrates other areas of society. Marcuse has written that purposive-rational action is the exercise of control and the rationalization of the conditions of life was synonymous with the institutionalization of a form of domination of nature and society where its political character becomes unrecognizable. This form of domination is rational in that it helps to maintain a system whose legitimacy stems from continued growth of the forces of production along with scientific and technological progress.[106]

Emancipation from this domination cannot happen without a revolutionary transformation of science and technology themselves. Marcuse envisions both different modes of theory formation and a different scientific methodology, in general. Nature would no longer be subjected to instrumental action but "technical control would be replaced by the objectives of preserving, fostering, and releasing the potentialities of nature." Marcuse has in mind an alternative attitude toward nature where nature can be encountered as an opposing partner in possible interactions rather than nature being the object of possible technical control, a fraternal rather than an exploited nature. Habermas, however, believes that the achievements of technology cannot be dispensed with and that an awakened nature could not be substituted for these achievements. Modern science is inherently oriented to possible technical control, and for scientific-technical progress in general there is no more "humane" substitute.[107]

In refuting Marcuse's ideas Habermas attempts to reformulate the concept of rationalization in another frame of reference. In this attempt he takes as his starting point what he claims is a fundamental distinction between work and interaction. Work or what could also be called purposive-rational action can refer to either instrumental action or rational choice or their conjunction. Instrumental action is governed by technical rules based on empirical knowledge while rational choice is governed by strategies based on analytical knowledge. Interaction, on the other hand, refers to communicative action or symbolic interaction and is governed by binding consensual norms that define reciprocal expectations about behavior. These norms are internalized with personality structures and deviant behavior which violates these norms and provokes sanctions.[108]

With these distinctions in mind, social systems can be distinguished as to whether purposive-rational action or interaction predominates. At the analytic level Habermas goes on to distinguish between the institutional framework of a society or what he calls the lifeworld and the subsystems of purposive-rational action that are embedded in that world. Actions that are determined by the institutional framework are both guided and enforced by norms. Actions that are determined by subsystems of purposive-rational action conform to patterns of instrumental or strategic action.[109]

Traditional societies that had a precapitalist mode of production tolerated technical innovation and organizational change only within definite limits. A traditional society is grounded and legitimized by mythical, religious, or metaphysical interpretations of reality. The stock of accumulated technical exploitable knowledge in a traditional society never reached the point where their "rationality" would have constituted a threat to the authority of the cultural traditions that legitimize political power. These societies continued to exist as long as these limits were respected. The appearance of the capitalistic mode of production, however, equipped the economic system with a self-propelling mechanism that ensures long-term economic growth and innovation as such that has been institutionalized. Capitalism guaranteed the permanent expansion of purposive-rational action and overturned the traditional institutional framework to the forces of production which had to be freed from institutional constraints to realize its potential.[110]

Capitalism provides a legitimation of political domination which is not called down from the heights of cultural tradition but is summoned up from the base of social labor. The notion of property changes from a political relation to a production relation because it is legitimated through the rationality of the market. The political system becomes justified through the legitimate relations of production, and its function becomes one of providing a legal framework to protect private property and the workings of the market. The institutional framework of society is immediately economic and only moderately political.[111] According to Habermas,

> [t]he superiority of the capitalist mode of production to its predecessors has these two roots: the establishment of an economic mechanism that renders permanent the expansion of subsystems of purposive-rational action, and the creation of an economic legitimation by means of which the political system can be adapted to new requisites of rationality brought about my these developing subsystems . . . Within it we can distinguish between two tendencies: rationalization "from below" and rationalization "from above."[112]

Mythological interpretations and religious worldviews lose their cogency in capitalism as modern science develops a methodological frame of reference that reflects the transcendental viewpoint of possible technical control. Modern science is taken into the service of capital and produces knowledge that is technically exploitable to further the growth of capitalism. Since the last quarter of the nineteenth century, according to Habermas, there has been an increase in state intervention into the market in order to secure the system's stability and a growing interdependency of research and technology turning the sciences into the leading productive force. Regulation of the economic processes by the state arose as a defense mechanism against the dysfunctional tendencies that capitalism produces when left to itself.[113]

Politics then was no longer only a phenomenon of the superstructure that Marx described, as society no longer perpetuates itself through self-regulation as a domain that precedes and forms the basis of the state. "A point of view that methodically isolates the economic laws of motion of society can claim to grasp the overall structure of social life in its essential categories only so long as politics depends on the economic base. It becomes inapplicable when the 'base' has to be comprehended as in itself a function of governmental activity and political conflicts." A critical theory of society can then no longer be based exclusively on political economy as when the ideology of a just exchange process disintegrates the power structure can no longer be criticized only at the level of the relations of production. Political power thus requires a new legitimization as it can no longer be derived from the unpolitical order constituted by the relations of production. The political system is obliged to maintain stabilizing conditions to secure employment and a stable income guaranteeing social security and the chance for individual upward mobility.[114]

Politics takes on a negative character as it is directed toward the stability and growth of the economic system and the elimination of the dysfunctions and avoidance of risks that threaten the system. It becomes oriented toward the solution of technical problems rather than the realization of practical goals directed toward attaining the good life that requires a democratic decision-making process. The solution of technical problems does not require public discussion; therefore, the new politics of state intervention depolitcizes the mass of the population. However, the institutional framework of society is still distinct from the system of purposive rational action, and its organization continues to be a problem of practice linked to communication and not one of technology.[115]

However, technology and science have become a leading productive force, according to Habermas, rendering Marx's labor theory of value inoperative. Scientific-technical progress has become an independent source of surplus-value and labor-power plays an ever smaller role in producing surplus value for capitalists. The autonomous progress of science and technology appears as an independent variable on which economic growth depends. The self-understanding of modern society has been detached from communicative action and the concepts of symbolic interaction and have been replaced with a scientific model where the "social life-world is replaced by the self-reification of men under categories of purposive-rational action and adaptive behavior. This technocratic intention could lead to a creeping erosion of the institutional framework where it could be absorbed by the subsystems of purposive-rational action, a reversal of the usual situation."[116]

State regulated capitalism suspends class conflict and secures the loyalty of the wage-earning masses through rewards and keeps them in a state of latency, making this aspect of Marxian theory no longer relevant in producing a revolution of the proletariat. Class antagonisms have not been abolished, but they have become latent. Furthermore, technocratic consciousness is "less ideological" than all previous ideologies, but it does involve the repression of "ethics" as such as a category of life. According to Habermas, the ideological nucleus of this consciousness "is the elimination of the distinction between the practical and the technical. The institutional framework is disempowered as purposive-rational action takes on a life of its own. Practical interest disappears behind the interest society has in the expansion of the power of technical control." Eventually this way of thinking that Habermas calls technocratic consciousness begins to functions as a substitute ideology for the diminished bourgeois ideologies.[117]

We now know how to bring the relevant conditions of life under control, for example, and adapt the environment to our needs rather than adapting ourselves to an external nature. Marx recognizes this development in stating that the "bourgeoisie during its rule of scarcely one hundred years, has created more massive and more colossal productive forces than have all the preceding generations together. Subjection of nature's forces to man, machinery, application of chemistry to industry and agriculture, steam navigation, railways, electric telegraphs, clearing of whole continents, canalization of rivers, whole populations conjured out of the ground." The intention of the technocrats in both capitalism and socialism was to use psychological manipulation to bring society as well as nature under control by reconstructing it according to the pattern of self-regulated systems of purposive-rational action and adaptive behavior.[118]

Eventually Habermas believes that the structural elimination of practical problems from a depoliticized public realm must become unbearable, but this will only give rise to a political force if this kind of sensibility comes into contact with a problem the system cannot solve. He sees one such problem in that the "amount of social wealth produced by industrially advanced capitalism and the technical and organizational conditions under which this wealth is produced make it ever more difficult to link status assignment to the mechanism for the evaluation of individual achievement." Student protest could destroy this crumbling achievement ideology and bring down an already-fragile legitimating basis of advanced capitalism which Habermas states rests only on depoliticization.[119]

Critiques of Critical Theory

The three trends of poststructuralism, postmodernism, and feminism deal with current forms of domination based on race, gender, class, and technical expertise and challenge critical theory's faith in the emancipatory potential of reason. Writers in these areas are skeptical about the notion of universal reason and hold that the basic rules, norms, and structures that govern linguistic and cultural practices undergo constant mutation. They emphasize the contextuality and relativity of all structures including those which govern the determination of "rational behavior." They oppose the overextension of bureaucratic domination, the totalitarian subordination of dissident subcultures to the dominant culture, and the marginalization of ethics and aesthetics with respect to the scientific and technological.[120]

Michel Foucault, for example, a French philosopher who at the time of his death held a chair at the College de France, shares with critical theory a concern with the manner in which humans are constituted as autonomous subjects who are subject to control by other persons and themselves. He does not take to any global theory of social rationalization but, instead, undertakes an empirical analysis of power struggles and power relations. These power relations cannot be reduced to economic exploitation and domination. The ethical and political goal of today's struggles, Foucault claims, cannot be liberation from power per se but from the peculiar power relationship associated with certain practices of the state, and since power relations are as diffuse as they are concentrated, liberation must take on the form of local struggles and strategies.[121]

According to Jean-Francois Lyotard, another French philosopher but also a sociologist and literary theorist, the social bond "consists of an interweaving of heterogeneous 'language games' whose structure conforms neither to the technical transfer of information nor to the unconstrained achievement of mutual understanding between disinterested interlocutors."[122] A critical theory that is guided by the criterion of unconstrained consensus will be useless to provide legitimation for society's norms and values. Habermas's theory, he claims, rests on two false assumptions: (1) "that it is possible for all speakers to come to an agreement on which rules of metaprescriptions are universally valid for language games, when it is clear that language games are heteronomous, subject to heterogeneous sets of pragmatic rules," and (2) that "the goal of dialogue is consensus."[123]

Habermas replies to these criticisms by underscoring the subversive nature of modern culture which seems to continually undermine its own normative standards. However, he states that the postmodernists revel in anarchy and welcome the disruption of science, technology, and a unifying reason. Poststructuralism dissolves universal reason into a plurality of language games and power relations that makes political resistance meaningless. Neoconservatives desire a return to traditional moral authority and the capitalistic work ethic and also show a postmodern disdain for reason either in its scientific form or in its moral-aesthetic form. Habermas does not think that the subversive nature of modern culture is so radical that it undermines the very standards of rationality that lend it cohesion.[124]

He argues that a common thread of communicative rationality runs through all the specialized disciplines and that this kind of rationality is responsible for ensuring the transmission of tradition, integration of society, and the socialization of free and responsible agents. He thinks it is wrong to dismiss the unifying tensions of the Enlightenment because these intentions make it possible for the average person to revitalize their capacity to relate critically to existing traditions. By communicating specialized knowledge in a manner that is accessible to popular experience, the average person can learn to critically and examine his own cognitive, moral, and expressive sensibilities. The completion of the modern project demands the enlightenment of the average citizen so they can hold those who possess technical expertise accountable for the use of their power.[125]

Regarding the feminist critique of critical theory, Nancy Fraser, the Henry A. and Louise Loeb Professor of Philosophy and Politics at the Graduate Faculty of the New School in New York, deals with the distinction that Habermas makes between a communicatively structured "lifeworld" that is oriented toward "symbolic reproduction" that includes transmission of culture and social integration and an instrumentally structured economic-bureaucratic "system" oriented toward "material reproduction." Habermas assigns the family and its childrearing capability to the lifeworld and the economy and state to the system. Fraser claims that this interpretation ignores the extent to which the family contributes to material reproduction and undercuts the feminist critique of homemaking as unremunerated labor that does not count in gross national product. The emancipation of homemakers would require a restructuring of the family along the lines of an economic wage relationship, but this restructuring would disrupt the socialization process.[126]

Fraser also claims that Habermas neglects the way gender roles have been institutionalized in our society. The institutionalized role of the worker in our society is primarily masculine and men are raised to be independent and self-sufficient while women are marginalized in the so-called helping professions where they can utilize their nurturing and caring skills. Women are not taught to think of themselves as fully independent and self-sufficient "breadwinners," and consequently, if it is necessary for them to go on welfare, they experience such state paternalism as but another extension of the patriarchal domination they have suffered under for their entire lives as welfare undermines their freedom and dignity.[127]

Finally, Seyla Benhabib, professor of government at Harvard University and Senior Research Associate at the Center for European Studies, argues that Habermas tends to distinguish between moral-practical discourses, whose purpose is to discover universalizable rights and duties, and aesthetic-expressive discourses that are aimed at discovering common needs shared by particular communities. This separation, Benhabib claims, displays a gender bias in that female moral development stresses the competencies of caring, solidarity, love, sympathy, and bonding that has traditionally been associated with the family, while males develop along a path that focuses on separation, independence, and competition. Males are thus more likely to develop aptitudes that favor abstract procedures of conflict resolution that better prepares them for management roles in societal institutions.[128]

Summary

Critical theory is critical of the Enlightenment with its emphasis on rational thought and action which is supposed to lead to freedom, justice, and happiness by freeing humankind from the mythologies of the past and encouraging people to think for themselves. But rationalism came to serve the interests of the capitalist system of domination and gave legitimacy to the exploitation of both workers and nature by capitalistic interests in ever increasing production and consumption. The world of workers is not their own but is a world of capital. All human and material values have been reduced to quantifiable commodities that can be bought and sold on the market. Domination is a theme that runs through all the critical theorists and along with instrumental reason allows capitalists to run the show in the in the interests of making more and more profit. As summed up by Johanna Oksala, a senior research fellow at the University of Helsinki,

> Adorno and Horkheimer see fascism in their native Germany as well as the consumer capitalism and 'candy-floss entertainment' of California as different manifestations or the Enlightenment project. When reason is elevated as the sole, highest principle organizing politics, we end up with new and devastating forms of domination: political systems that are maximally effective and functional, but empty of meaning and capable of the most horrendous atrocities . . . The advancement of reason made it possible to explain and control both nature and society, but at the same time this control became a new form of domination. Enlightenment reason was essentially *instrumental* reason: it was a tool of domination empty of any substantive goals or meanings.[129]

Adorno, for example, views the social situation of his time as one of totalized domination and sees the unity of a single process of domination in systems of political power ranging from the Stalinist Soviet Union through fascist Germany to what he calls state capitalism in the United States. For Adorno these are barely distinguishable forms of one historical process, the result of which is a system of total domination. Relations of domination form a structural paradigm from which the hidden logic of the whole process of civilization can be understood. He was indifferent if not skeptical toward the multidisciplinary investigation of the crisis of capitalism and ambivalent toward an empirically controlled and interdisciplinary theory of society. His conception of critical theory was a philosophy of history in which the historical genesis of total domination could be clarified. Relations of domination were viewed as a structural paradigm from which one can read the hidden logic of the whole process of civilization.[130]

Emancipation from this domination comes from having science and technology serve different ends than an increase in production and consumption. People do not need to live in poverty, but they also could consume much less and be perfectly happy. The labor process should not determine the existence of those who labor, but their needs should determine the labor process. There is a hint of Marxism here in that the needs of those who labor to produce profits for capitalists should take priority. They should not be made slaves to capital and dominated by capitalistic interests. Critical theory has tried to carry on some of the tenants of Marxism that are still viable even though Marx's predications about the fall of capitalism did not prove true and there has been no revolution of the proletariat.

The problem with critical theory is in the title of the movement. It has been primarily a critique of contemporary capitalism and has no real program that would produce change and emancipate workers and consumers from domination. While the movement has developed some important ideas about modern capitalism it offers no realistic alternative. It advocates no overthrow of the dominant classes in capitalistic society and offers no vision of an alternative future to replace continual growth in production and consumption that would capture the imagination of people and motivate them to change their behavior. Critical theorists do not seem to be in favor of socialism as that did no work out too well in the former Soviet Union, so it seems that capital will remain in private hands and the market system will continue to allocate resources. There is no concern with a spiritual dimension in these institutions to connect people with each other and to connect people with nature. Critical theory helps in understanding the nature of the despiritualization of humans and nature that has taken place under capitalism, but it remains by and large what its title implies, a critique of contemporary society. It fails to offer substantial perspectives for positive social and political change nor does it provide meaningful alternatives for the practice of philosophy

As regards the future of critical theory, Axel Honneth, a professor of Philosophy at the Johann Wolfgang Goethe University in Frankfurt, Germany, attempts to establish a recognition-based framework for critical theory that targets injustices it understands as culturally rooted in social patterns of interpretation, representation, and communication. Rather than focusing on a more just distribution of resources and wealth, the recognition paradigm involves the creation of a difference-friendly world where claims for the different perspectives of ethnic, racial, and sexual minorities as well as of gender differences are given due consideration. Discussions about social justice, which were once centered on distribution, are now becoming increasingly divided between claims for redistribution and claims for recognition with the latter beginning to dominate the discussion.[131]

Honneth considers recognition to be the fundamental overarching moral category in discussions of social justice and treats distribution as a derivative category subsumed under recognition. What critical theory is faced with is a "multitude of politically organized efforts by cultural groups to find social recognition for their own value convictions and lifestyles." This struggle wants to change a nation's majority culture of the white, male, heterosexual citizen by overcoming stereotypes in such a way that social recognition can be won for one's own traditions and way of life."[132] The goal is for all members of society to be "equally included in the network of recognition relations by which society as a whole is integrated."[133]

Nancy Fraser disagrees with this approach and thinks that recognition alone cannot bear the entire burden of critical theorizing. It is not sufficient by itself, in her view, "to capture the normative deficits of contemporary society, the societal processes that generate them, and the political challenges facing those seeking emancipatory change" To think that recognition could do all this is to overextend the concept, in her view, and distort it beyond recognition depriving it of its critical force. Such as approach, she argues, cannot provide a suitable empirical reference point, nor does it constitute a viable account of culture and a defensible theory of justice. What is needed, she states, is to "*situate recognition as one dimension of a perspectival-dualist framework that also encompasses distribution.*"[134] There is thus some disagreement, at least between these two scholars, as to the direction critical theory should take in the future.

Notes

1 Max Horkheimer, "Traditional and Critical Theory," in David Ingram and Julia Simon-Ingram, eds., *Critical Theory: The Essential Readings* (St. Paul, MN: Paragon House, 1991), 239–254.

2 Axel Honneth, *The Critique of Power: Reflective Stages in a Critical Social Theory* (Cambridge, MA: The MIT Press, 1991), 3.

3 See David Ingram and Julia Simon-Ingram, eds., "Introduction," in David Ingram and Julia Simon-Ingram, eds., *Critical Theory: The Essential Readings* (St. Paul, MN: Paragon House, 1991), note 2, xxxviii–xxxix.

4 Honneth, *The Critique of Power*, 18.

5 Ingram and Ingram, "Introduction," xix.

6 Ibid.

7 Horkheimer, "Traditional and Critical Theory," 239–240.

8 Ibid., 241.

9 Ingram and Ingram, "Introduction," xxvii.

10 Ibid., xxvii–xxix. Horkheimer believes that capitalist society operates according to certain economic laws that contain internal contradictions that are reflected in the alienation and discontent of workers. This creates a "false" consciousness that requires a deeper philosophical reflection on the cultural ideals that legitimate existing patterns of domination in capitalist society. Once people are enlightened about their real interests and the prospects that exist for realizing them they will be freed from the compulsion of habits that are based on false consciousness.

11 Horkheimer, "Traditional and Critical Theory," 241–242.

12 Ibid., 244–247.

13 Ibid., 246–247.

14 Ibid., 249–250.

15 Ibid., 242.

16 Ibid., 243.

17 Ibid., 245–246.

18 Ibid., 243–244.

19 Ibid., 246–247.

20 Ibid., 249.

21 Ibid., 251–252.

22 Ibid., 253.

23 Honneth, *The Critique of Power*, 6.

24 Ibid., 8–9.
25 Ibid., 19.
26 Ingram and Ingram, "Introduction," xxiii.
27 Ibid., xxiii–xxiv.
28 Ibid., xxi.
29 Ibid., xx–xxi.
30 Herbert Marcuse, "Philosophy and Critical Theory," in David Ingram and Julia Simon-Ingram, eds., *Critical Theory: The Essential Readings* (St. Paul, MN: Paragon House, 1991), 5–8.
31 Ibid., 9–10.
32 Ibid., 16–18.
33 Theodor W. Adorno, "Why Philosophy?" in David Ingram and Julia Simon-Ingram, eds., *Critical Theory: The Essential Readings* (St. Paul, MN: Paragon House, 1991), 21. Adorno claims that even Newtonian physics had once been known as philosophy.
34 Ibid., 21–22.
35 Ibid., 22–27.
36 Jürgen Habermas, "Knowledge and Human Interests: A General Perspective," in David Ingram and Julia Simon-Ingram, eds., *Critical Theory: The Essential Readings* (St. Paul, MN: Paragon House, 1991), 255–256.
37 Ibid., 256–259.
38 Ibid., 260–261.
39 Ibid., 264.
40 Theodor W. Adorno and Max Horkheimer, "The Concept of Enlightenment," in David Ingram and Julia Simon-Ingram, eds., *Critical Theory: The Essential Readings* (St. Paul, MN: Paragon House, 1991), 49–50.
41 Ibid., 51–53.
42 Ibid., 53–54.
43 Ibid., 54.
44 Ingram and Ingram, "Introduction," xxiii.
45 Ibid., xxiii–xxiv.
46 Adorno and Horkheimer, "The Concept of Enlightenment," 56.
47 Ingram and Ingram, "Introduction," xxii.
48 Ibid., xxii–xxiii.
49 Honneth, *The Critique of Power*, 72.
50 Ibid., 74.
51 Ibid., 77.
52 Ibid., 78.
53 Ibid., 79.
54 Ibid., 84–86.
55 Ibid.
56 Ibid., 89.
57 Ibid., 93–95.
58 Max Horkheimer, "Means and Ends," in David Ingram and Julia Simon-Ingram, eds., *Critical Theory: The Essential Readings* (St. Paul, MN: Paragon House, 1991), 35–36.
59 Ibid.
60 Ibid., 36–38.
61 Ibid., 38–39.
62 Ibid., 39–40.
63 Ibid., 40–41.
64 Ibid., 41–42.
65 Ibid., 42–43.

66 Ibid., 44.
67 Ibid., 44–45.
68 Ibid., 46.
69 Alex Honneth, "The Turn to the Philosophy of History in the Dialectic of Enlightenment: A Critique of the Domination of Nature," in Honneth, *The Critique of Power*, 32–56. See also Adorno and Horkheimer, "The Concept of Enlightenment," 49–56; and Theodor Adorno and Max Horkheimer, "The Culture Industry: Enlightenment as Mass Deception," in Theodor Adorno and Max Horkheimer, eds., *Dialectic of Enlightenment*, trans. John Cumming (New York: Continuum, 1990), 120–167.
70 Ibid.
71 Ibid.
72 Ibid.
73 Ibid.
74 Ibid., 50–52.
75 Ibid., 53.
76 Ibid., 48.
77 Ibid., 42–45.
78 Ibid., 46–47.
79 Ibid., 35.
80 Ibid., 38.
81 Ibid., 39.
82 Max Horkheimer, "Materialism and Morality," in David Ingram and Julia Simon-Ingram, eds., *Critical Theory: The Essential Readings* (St. Paul, MN: Paragon House, 1991), 176–202.
83 Ibid.
84 Ibid.
85 Herbert Marcuse, "On Hedonism," in David Ingram and Julia Simon-Ingram, eds., *Critical Theory: The Essential Readings* (St. Paul, MN: Paragon House, 1991), 151–175.
86 Ibid.
87 Jürgen Habermas, "Selections from Legitimation Crisis," in David Ingram and Julia Simon-Ingram, eds., *Critical Theory: The Essential Readings* (St. Paul, MN: Paragon House, 1991), 203–216.
88 Ibid.
89 Theodor W. Adorno, "Society," in David Ingram and Julia Simon-Ingram, eds., *Critical Theory: The Essential Readings* (St. Paul, MN: Paragon House, 1991), 61–62.
90 Ibid., 63–65.
91 Ibid., 65–68.
92 Theodor W. Adorno, "How to Look at Television," in David Ingram and Julia Simon-Ingram, eds., *Critical Theory: The Essential Readings* (St. Paul, MN: Paragon House, 1991), 69–71.
93 Ibid., 73–77.
94 Ibid., 79–82.
95 Theodor W. Adorno, "Freudian Theory and the Pattern of Fascist Propaganda," in David Ingram and Julia Simon-Ingram, eds., *Critical Theory: The Essential Readings* (St. Paul, MN: Paragon House, 1991), 84–87.
96 Ibid., 87–90.
97 Ibid., 90–93.
98 Ibid., 95.
99 Ibid., 90–93.
100 Ibid., 94.

101 Ibid., 97–98.
102 Herbert Marcuse, "The Catastrophe of Liberation," in David Ingram and Julia Simon-Ingram, eds., *Critical Theory: The Essential Readings* (St. Paul, MN: Paragon House, 1991), 103.
103 Ibid., 104–105.
104 Ibid., 105–109.
105 Ibid., 112–115.
106 Jürgen Habermas, "Technology and Science as 'Ideology'," in David Ingram and Julia Simon-Ingram, eds., *Critical Theory: The Essential Readings* (St. Paul, MN: Paragon House, 1991), 117–120.
107 Ibid., 120–122.
108 Ibid., 123–124.
109 Ibid., 125.
110 Ibid., 126–127.
111 Ibid., 127–128.
112 Ibid., 128.
113 Ibid., 128–130.
114 Ibid., 130–131.
115 Ibid., 131–132.
116 Ibid., 132–133.
117 Ibid., 134–138.
118 Ibid., 139–140.
119 Ibid., 144.
120 Ingram and Ingram, "Introduction," xxxii–xxxiii.
121 Michel Foucault, "The Subject and Power," in David Ingram and Julia Simon-Ingram, eds., *Critical Theory: The Essential Readings* (St. Paul, MN: Paragon House, 1991), 304–319.
122 Ingram and Ingram, "Introduction," xxxiv.
123 Jean-Francis Lyotard, "From the Postmodern Condition: A Report on Knowledge," in David Ingram and Julia Simon-Ingram, eds., *Critical Theory: The Essential Readings* (St. Paul, MN: Paragon House, 1991), 320–341.
124 Jürgen Habermas, "Modernity: An Unfinished Project," in David Ingram and Julia Simon-Ingram, eds., *Critical Theory: The Essential Readings* (St. Paul, MN: Paragon House, 1991), 342–355.
125 Ibid.
126 Nancy Fraser, "What's Critical about Critical Theory?" in David Ingram and Julia Simon-Ingram, eds., *Critical Theory: The Essential Readings* (St. Paul, MN: Paragon House, 1991), 357–387.
127 Ibid.
128 Seyla Benhabib, "The Utopian Dimension in Communicative Ethics ?" in David Ingram and Julia Simon-Ingram, eds., *Critical Theory: The Essential Readings* (St. Paul, MN: Paragon House, 1991), 388–399.
129 Johanna Oksala, *Political Philosophy: All that Matters* (New York: McGraw-Hill, 2013), 76.
130 Honneth, *The Critique of Power*, 35–37.
131 Nancy Fraser and Axel Honneth, *Redistribution or Recognition: A Political-Philosophical Exchange* (New York: Verso, 2003), 7–9.
132 Ibid., 117–118.
133 Ibid., 260.
134 Ibid., 233.

Part IV
Spirituality and Society

10 The Scientific Worldview

We view the world in a certain manner that enables us to live in the world and work out some kind of meaningful existence. The way we think about the world reflects the dominant worldview of our time which in our country and Western countries in general is largely scientific and technological in nature. This scientific and technological culture we live in involves a certain way of viewing the world that shapes our language and concepts and the way we relate to the world. This way of thinking influences everything we do and is reflected in every aspect of our lives, including ethics, economics, politics, and the way we relate to nature. In this kind of world, the knowledge attained by science and the tools and techniques of technology are used to manipulate and shape the natural world in our interests. This manipulation is based on a certain understanding of the way in which the world works and functions.

This scientific worldview is based on the assumption that the world is made up of individual elements that relate to each other through laws that can be discovered in scientific inquiry.[1] The behavior of the world is not random but operates according to laws that function in nature to produce regularities that can be counted on to continue. These laws allow us to send shuttles into space to dock with the international space station and land people on the moon. They enabled us to develop the atomic bomb and nuclear power plants. They exist in all parts of our material world and form the basis of our ability to understand how the world works and allow us to manipulate it to accomplish our own goals and objectives.

Science deals with the natural world and involves a search for natural causes and explanations of things that happen in the world. It does not deal with supernatural explanations or beliefs but concerns itself solely with the natural world and assumes that everything can be explained on the basis of natural causes without an appeal to the supernatural. Science is materialistic in assuming that there is a real external world out there that can be accessed through scientific methods. Science is a way of knowing this reality; it involves a method that systematically investigates and organizes aspects of this reality that we can access through our senses. Knowledge that comes to us in other ways is not scientific knowledge.

The mythological worldview that science largely, but not completely replaced, consisted of a collection of stories that expressed the beliefs of a particular culture relative to the world in which they lived. For thousands of years people associated objects in the sky, the earth, and aspects of their physical world with supernatural beings. Myths often tell the story of ancestors, heroes, and gods or goddesses with special powers over the world and human existence. These stories sometimes contain mythical characters such as mermaids, unicorns, dragons, or angels that play certain roles in the stories. Myths were used to explain certain things that happened in the world and provided an understanding of complex natural phenomena that helped people cope with their existence.

Nature can be terrifying to humans. Imagine how primeval forests appeared to early peoples who populated the earth. These forests contained many unknowns such as animals and other things that posed a threat to human existence, much the same as jungles appear to us in today's world. There were hurricanes, tornados, earthquakes, floods, volcanic eruptions, and other forces in nature that posed major threats just as they do today. And there were diseases that could strike at any time and wipe out thousands of people as they can today. Nature can be quite terrifying and arbitrary and beyond the control of humans.

Mythology helped people cope with this tenuous existence and provided a means of understanding what was happening in their world. The idea of God, for example, puts nature under the control of a supernatural being. One can appeal to this being through prayer or other means to look favorably upon the petitioner. This helps reduce some of the anxiety involved in living in such an uncertain world. Science, on the other hand, demythologizes nature and provides another way of understanding the world that allows for greater control and manipulation of nature to reduce the anxiety and make it less terrifying. Science gives us the means to predict where hurricanes might strike so we can prepare for them. It allows us to develop medicines to combat diseases that threaten to wipe out vast numbers of people. It enables us to understand how tornados form and predict where they might develop.

This scientific worldview did not develop and win adherents overnight but had to struggle against the worldview of other authorities in society. For example, based on Aristotelian philosophy it was believed that the sun and other planets revolved around the earth and that human beings and the earth they lived on were the center of the universe. This belief was perpetuated by the church which placed its considerable authority behind such a view of the universe. Leading intellectual figures of the time supported the assumption that the earth was the motionless center of a system around which the sun and planets revolved. As observations began to be made about the movements of the planets and the sun, elaborate and complicated theories had to be invented to explain the observed irregularities of their rotation based on an earth-centered assumption.[2]

None of these explanations proved to be satisfactory, however, and they made less and less sense as time went on and became unworkable.[3] Finally, the only thing that did make sense was to abandon the old worldview about an earth-centered solar system and accept the view that the earth and other planets revolved around the sun instead. In attempting to develop an astronomical theory that would more accurately reflect the actual position of celestial bodies, Copernicus had to challenge the traditional view of the universe. In the Copernican system, the earth was not the center of the universe or even of our own solar system. Such a view constituted no less than a scientific revolution or paradigm shift and eventually became the accepted way of viewing the universe.[4]

Such changes in thinking do not come easily, however, and the early scientists who developed these new theories did so at considerable personal cost to themselves because of opposition from church authorities.[5] It took courage to publish these new ideas, especially when they challenged both Aristotelian physics and Holy Scripture. Church authorities officially banned the Copernican worldview in 1616 when his book, *On the Revolution*, was put on the Index of Forbidden Books by the Congregation of the Index.[6] When Galileo came along and made observations through a telescope that convinced him that the Copernican model of the universe had to be the true picture, the church commanded Galileo to abandon such a worldview and support the traditional assumptions about the earth and its place in the universe. While Galileo tried to comply with conditions laid down by the pope, he simply could not make a convincing case for the traditional worldview and was eventually brought before the Inquisition and sentenced to house arrest.[7]

But the damage had been done. It was widely perceived that science had demonstrated new truths about the universe through observation that could not be erased by religious dogma based on outdated philosophies. The church eventually had to reconcile itself to the results of scientific observation, which rapidly became the new authority in such matters. From these beginnings, science went on to become the established authority in matters pertaining to the physical universe and eventually was extended into other fields, such as medicine, biology, geology, and on into the social sciences, such as economics, political science, and sociology. Science thus became the basis for a new worldview of everything, not just the physical universe. The implications of the Copernican Revolution, as it has been called, thus affected far more than astronomy, according to Thomas S. Kuhn, ultimately affecting not only science but also philosophy, religion, and social theory:[8]

> Initiated as a narrowly technical, highly mathematical revision of classical astronomy, the Copernican theory became one focus for the tremendous controversies in religion, in philosophy, and in social theory,

which, during the two centuries following the discovery of America, set the tenor of the modern mind. Men who believed that their terrestrial home was only a planet circulating blindly about one of an infinity of stars evaluated their place in the cosmic scheme quite differently than had their predecessors who saw the earth as the unique and focal center of God's creation. The Copernican Revolution was therefore also part of a transition of man's sense of values.[9]

This scientific revolution involved a change in ways of securing our beliefs about the natural world. The philosophical basis for this revolution stressed the role that experimental method played in the development of scientific theories and held that the universe was a mechanical system that could be described by mathematical laws discovered through scientific observation. According to Steven Shapin, a professor of sociology at the University of California, San Diego, there were four interrelated aspects of this revolution: (1) the mechanization of nature; (2) the depersonalization of natural knowledge; (3) the attempted mechanization of knowledge, that is, following explicitly formulated rules of method in producing knowledge to eliminate the effects of human interests and passions; and (4) "the aspiration to use the resulting reformed natural knowledge to achieve moral, social, and political ends, the condition of which was agreement that the knowledge in question truly was benign, powerful, and above all *disinterested*."[10]

Reasoning was made subject to the findings of reliable observation conducted according to the rigors of accepted scientific methodology and mathematically disciplined thinking. What counted was reliably constituted observation of nature, not tradition or religious authority. Adherents of the scientific revolution were encouraged to believe what they saw with their own eyes rather than adhering to accepted tradition. This empirical content rested not just on direct observation of what went on in the world naturally, however, but also on artificially and purposefully contrived experiments that produced phenomena that might not be observed easily or at all in the normal course of nature.[11]

Principles related to the physical world rest on empirical claims that support hypotheses about the way the world is constituted. Scientific method is an inductive and empirically grounded procedure; it proceeds from accumulated knowledge of particulars (observational and experimental facts) to causal knowledge and general truths about nature.[12] The foundation of scientific knowledge are facts discovered in the course of scientific investigation, and these facts are established by reliable observation or experiment guided by hypotheses. These facts had to be guaranteed as authentic and protected from contamination by other less certain items of knowledge, hence the importance of adhering to a rigorous methodology. "A factually grounded approach to knowledge held out the prospect of a well-founded certainty and a well-conceived approach to knowledge of nature's underlying causal structure."[13]

Science, according to Timothy Ferris, an emeritus professor at the University of California, is inherently antiauthoritarian. Scientific propositions must be subject to experimental method and tested according to the rules of scientific procedure. If a proposition repeatedly fails such testing, it is dropped from further consideration regardless of who supports it and how much it may have made sense. Science is self-correcting as the results of such tests are subject to being replicated by other scientists, and if a new discovery cannot be replicated, the results are not considered to be valid.[14] In this manner cold fusion, which was supposedly discovered by two scientists at the University of Utah, was found to be a hoax as it could not be replicated by other scientists.

Science also utilized mathematics because nature was believed to be mathematical in structure. Scientific investigation of physical phenomena tried to make sense of physical evidence gathered from observation and experiments by establishing formal mathematical patterns that were believed to underlay and give rise to the natural world. Nature was believed to follow laws that were mathematical in form and that could be expressed in the language of mathematics. Newton, in fact, was concerned with the certainty of mathematical demonstration insofar as it could be legitimately attained in physical inquiry. Physical theories that could be mathematically expressed that were also supported by legitimate empirical observation or experiment could be spoken of with absolute confidence.[15] Thus, science was able to establish itself as the new authority with respect to the physical world, an authority that was eventually extended into the social realm and into human behavior itself.

Religion has not accepted this new worldview without difficulty. Galileo, for example, was not formally let off the hook by the Catholic Church until just a few short years ago in an official statement. Fundamentalist religions have still not accepted theories of evolution and battles between creationists and evolutionists continue in today's world. But when push comes to shove, science usually wins out with regard to our understanding of the world and developing solutions to problems simply because it makes better sense to most people and works better in solving problems. Scientific thinking dominates or world and shapes our perceptions of what the world is like and enables us to manipulate it in our interests through the development of new technologies.

Nature as a whole came to be viewed as a machine that was considered to be wholly intelligible. There was nothing mysterious or magical about a machine. It operated according to universal laws, and there was nothing capricious about the uniformities that were observed in nature. The machine metaphor was a "model of the form and scope that human knowledge of nature might properly have and of how human accounts of nature might properly be framed."[16] Matter was considered to be passive and inert, and while there were complexities in nature, these were not the result of purpose and design. This mechanical account of nature was in opposition to a tradition that saw purpose or intention in nature.

This classical vision of a machine-like world governed entirely by universal mathematical laws has no room for spontaneity or freedom. The world of nature is seen as an automatic machine with no soul, no spontaneous life, and no purposes of its own.[17] This desacralized, soulless vision of nature became the foundation for modern science and established itself as the reigning paradigm in the scientific revolution of the seventeenth century.[18] Nature came to be regarded as dead matter subject only to mechanical forces and governed by mathematical laws. The whole course of nature was thought to be determined as everything was believed to carry on inexorably and mechanically and was in principle completely predictable. The whole of nature was thought to be essentially knowable to the mathematical reason of scientists.[19]

Science thus views the world as a closed system that operates according to mechanical laws that can be expressed in mathematical terms. This worldview produces a quantitatively characterized universe that constitutes the way we perceive the world and the kind of sensibilities we develop as human beings. Knowledge becomes the building up of a storehouse of so-called objective facts gleaned from scientific studies. The way to know the world is through such studies that are based on a spectator theory of knowledge, where the researcher is only an observer of what's there in nature. The scientific approach to reality is one of breaking the whole of life down into its component parts in the interests of understanding how the world works so as to be able to manipulate those parts and shape the world to our advantage.

Characteristics of the Scientific Worldview

The way science operates is to reduce everything to its most fundamental elements on the assumption that everything that exists in the natural world can be explained through the interactions of a small number of simple elements whose behavior is governed by physical laws pertaining to those elements. This method is most often referred to as *reductionism*, which has been defined as "the endeavor of understanding any object of inquiry, such as physical objects, situations, phenomena, explanations, theories, concepts, language, and so forth, by specifying the elements that constitute it . . . The whole does not impart meaning to the parts, but rather, the parts are the meaning of the whole. The study of anything must be the study of its parts."[20]

While reductionism can be traced back before the rise of modern science, it was with the development of classical physics which incorporated the method of understanding an object of inquiry by analyzing its constituent elements that reductionism emerged into its full significance. Classical physics views the universe as composed of discrete particles that operate mechanistically and deterministically following universal laws of motion and gravity.[21] Thus, in particle physics, for example, the search is on for the fundamental building blocks of the universe, and physicists have gone way beyond protons, neutrons, and electrons that some of us were brought up to believe made up the atom. The so-called standard model of particle physics is an extremely complicated description of the fundamental elements and forces that make up physical matter.

In medical science, the human body is broken up into various systems such as the skeletal system, the muscular system, the nervous system, the circulatory system, the digestive system, the respiratory system, and so on, and each system is composed of various parts such as different kinds of bones, muscles, nerves, the heart and blood vessels, the digestive organs, and respiratory organs such as lungs. Doctors specialize in these different areas of the body, and if an internist cannot diagnose or heal our ailment, he or she will refer us to one of these specialists. The body is considered to be a mechanical and chemical system that can be examined and manipulated to make it function better.

In neuroscience human behavior is studied by looking at what parts of the brain are stimulated by certain human activities. The assumption behind this research is that everything can be reduced to neurons firing in certain parts of the brain. As stated by Nobel laureate Francis Crick, "You, your joys and your sorrows, your memories and your ambitions, your sense of personal identity and free will, are in fact nothing more than the behavior of a vast assembly of nerve cells and their associated molecules."[22] Since there are more than 100 billion neurons in the human body and each neuron is connected to hundreds of thousands of other neurons and each can fire signals hundreds of times a second across about 100 trillion synapses, understanding the human brain in this fashion is a daunting task.

In the social sciences human behavior is studied in a reductionist manner in that individual components of human and social behavior are identified and related to each other through some kind of statistical process to see if there are significant relationships. Variables that relate to the phenomenon under investigation are specified and data collected on these variables that are then analyzed with statistical methods to determine if there are relationships between these variables that can describe the behavior under examination and that can then be used to predict future behavior. Thus, the whole is broken down into various parts, and these parts are then examined for relationships with each other that can be expressed in statistical terms related to the behavioral process under investigation.

Each scientific area has its own methods to investigate problems in a rigorous manner. Thus, our knowledge of the world is broken up into different fields of study that have separate scholars, journals, and conferences, as well as standards. Science has become specialized to the extent that people in one field of study cannot really talk and understand what is going on in other fields. In the natural sciences there are different kinds of physical scientists, some looking for smaller and smaller particles in a search for the basic building blocks of the universe while other deal with larger natural structures such as the universe itself. In the social sciences there are economics, sociology, and political science, all looking at various aspects of human behavior in different contexts

Such a process has greatly increased our knowledge of particular areas of interest but it has also lead to a fragmentation of knowledge and a loss of the whole picture. It seems impossible to fit all this knowledge together in some unified theory of everything and so the world remains fragmented in our thinking. Some attempts have been made to link fields together as in areas of study that have a hyphen in their name such as socio-economics and astro-physics, but such hyphenated efforts do not really do the job of uniting knowledge into some kind of meaningful whole. It seems that over time science is becoming more and more specialized, with each specialization building its own knowledge base ever larger, a base that has to be learned by anyone entering the field.

The ultimate task of reductionism, however is to unite these different fields of knowledge by showing that they stem from a common ground. Paul Oppenheim and Hilary Putnam, for example, look toward a unity of the sciences through a reductive process and state that "the assumption that unitary science can be attained through cumulative micro-reduction recommends itself as a working hypothesis."[23] What they mean by this is that there is at least a possibility that all science may one day be reduced to the elementary particles of micro-physics. The different reductive levels that they employ start with social groups and proceed downward through multicellular living things, cells, molecules, atoms, and finally elementary particles.[24] They cite numerous examples where success in this reductionistic process has already been attained and mention other possibilities to show where this process may be applied:

> It is not absurd to suppose that psychological laws may eventually be explained in terms of the behavior of individual neurons in the brain; that the behavior of individual cells—including neurons—may eventually be explained in terms of their biochemical composition; and that the behavior of molecules—including the macro-molecules that make up living cells—may eventually be explained in terms of atomic physics.[25]

Thus, everything is reduced to the fundamental particles of atomic physics. This is the ultimate goal of reductionism; that we can understand everything about the universe and human beings by understanding how the so-called fundamental building blocks of nature relate to each other. Human beings become nothing more than a bunch of subatomic particles that behave in certain ways that science can discover. Questions can be raised, however, as to whether this is a satisfactory way of dealing with human behavior and whether such reductionism can even adequately explain the natural world. There have been complications at the subatomic level with the development of quantum mechanics mentioned in the next section that makes even our understanding of particle behavior problematic.

Classical science is thus *atomistic* in looking for individual components that make up nature and then trying to understand how these components relate to each other through some mechanistic process. This view of nature also pervades the social sciences where individual components of human behavior are identified and then related to each other through some statistical process to see if there are significant relationships. The reductionistic process thus forces us to think in terms of individual atoms and look for mechanisms through which these atoms relate to each other. In a philosophical sense this is called atomic individualism and it results in a view of society as a collection of independent self-sufficient individuals. Each person is like an atom that exists independently regardless of the social context. A society is simply the sum of these individualistic atomistic humans which provide the substance of society.

The term *atomism* comes from the Greek word *atoma*, which means things that cannot be cut or divided. Supposedly this philosophy originated with Democritus in 460 BCE and can be summarized in four propositions: (1) all bodies are composed of atoms and spaces between the atoms; (2) atoms are eternal, indivisible, infinite in number, and homogeneous in nature; all differences in bodies are due to a difference in the size, shape, or location of the atoms; (3) there is no purpose or design in nature, and in this sense all is ruled by chance; and (4) all activity is reduced to local motion.[26] With the rise of modern science, this philosophical conception of reality was applied to physics and became the basis of most of the sciences. Matter is not continuous but is considered to be atomically constituted.

Furthermore, these atoms were believed to be fixed and unchanging, and while they may change their position in space, they are unchangeable as far as their own being is concerned. An atom may change its direction and velocity of motion so that its relationship to other things is changed, but all this is external to its internal being which does not change. Changes that occur are between substances and these changes do not affect the atom's inner nature. The atom has no potentialities to become something else; it has no development or history of change. It is what it is and is the same yesterday, today, and forever. These immutable entities are the objects of any true knowledge of nature because they have the characteristic of a fixed certitude that is unchanging.[27]

Science thus deals with *discretes*; it breaks up space and time into discrete elements so that space can be measured and time broken into identifiable units. We experience space as continuous, yet when we measure it for whatever purpose we break it into parts that can be dealt with individually. Land, for example, is a continuous thing, but when we break it into lots we are able to allocate it for individual usage. This creates problems at a conceptual level, however, as with Zeno's paradox.[28] Time is broken up into hours and minutes and seconds so that we can organize our day and accomplish certain goals within time; patterns of human activity became regulated according to a mechanical conception of time rather that the rhythms of human life or natural seasons. But this creates the problem as to what holds all these minutes and seconds together and makes a continuous day or year or lifetime.

One of the most important characteristics of the scientific approach is its use of *quantitative* procedures to support its findings and identify what is considered to be true knowledge. Mathematics is considered to be the language of nature and the only knowledge worth considering from a scientific perspective is that which can be quantified and mathematized in some manner to arrive at a scientific conclusion. What lies outside the domain of science and cannot be quantified or mathematized is considered to be merely opinion, speculation, belief, feeling, or superstition. Quantification crowds out so-called subjective impressions since the reality science deals with is objectified and mathematized. Experience or common sense become disconnected from knowledge and become purely subjective in nature. There is no place for the sacred, for religious experience, or for the spiritual realm in a purely mathematical worldview. According to Christopher Dawson, writing in *Progress and Religion,*

> [f]rom the 17th century onwards, the modern scientific movement has been based on the mechanistic view of nature which regards the world as a closed material order moved by purely mechanical and mathematical laws. All the aspects of reality which could not be reduced to mathematical terms . . . were treated as mere subjective impressions of the mind.[29]

Quantification involves measurement as quantitative attributes are those it is possible to measure in some fashion. Physical quantities that can be measured include distance, mass, and time, while many attributes in the social sciences such as beliefs and values can also be studied as quantifiable properties. The assumption is that these properties have a quantitative structure where some kind of measurement can be made that will capture the reality of the property. Measurement is critical to quantitative research as it provides a connection between empirical observation of discrete entities and a mathematical expression of quantitative relationships between them.

A final characteristic of the scientific worldview is *determinism*, the idea that every event in the world, which includes human events and actions as well as events in the physical world, is causally determined by an unbroken chain of prior occurrences. If all of reality can be reduced to fundamental atoms the behavior of which is governed by mathematical laws, and if we have complete knowledge of physical matter and all of the laws governing that matter, then we should be able to compute every physical event that will ever occur in the world. All these events are predetermined by the nature of physical matter at a given point in time and the laws that govern the behavior of that matter. As John Dewey, the American Pragmatist states,

> The fundamental principle of the mechanical philosophy of nature is that it is possible to determine exactly (in principle if not in actual practice) both the position and velocity of any body. Knowing this for each particle which enters into any change, as a motion, it is possible to calculate mathematically, that is exactly, just what will happen. The laws or physical equations that express the relations of the particles and bodies under different conditions are then assumed to be a "governing" framework on nature to which all particular phenomena conform . . . The philosophy in question assumed that these positions and velocities are there in nature independent of our knowing, or our experiments and observations, and that we have scientific knowledge in the degree in which we ascertain them exactly. The future and the past belong to the same completely determinate and fixed scheme. Observations, when correctly conducted, merely register this fixed state of changes according to laws of objects whose essential properties are fixed.[30]

This idea of determinism finds in way into many areas of our existence. In biology it leads to the belief that all human behavior is fixed by our genetic endowment. In neuroscience it leads to the notion that human behavior is determined by neurons firing in certain parts of the brain, which, in turn, is determined by certain chemicals or lack thereof in the body. Environmental determinism holds that the physical environment determines the kind of culture people develop and the values that they believe in most strongly. Technological determinism is the belief that the technology we employ has certain outcomes that cannot be changed by any actions humans may take to alter those outcomes.

Determinism is related to prediction as strict determinism leads to prefect predictability. If we know all we need to know about the initial conditions regarding the nature of physical matter and the laws that govern the behavior of that matter, then obviously we can predict with perfect accuracy what will happen in the future. Lack of perfect predictability, however, does not mean lack of determinism. It may be that we simply do not have all the information we need to make such a prediction, we do not know everything we need to know about the initial conditions or about the laws of nature, which implies that sometime in the future when more research has been done, we may have such information and be able to make such predictions.

This idea of determinism obviously conflicts with notions about free will and human freedom. While we may like to think that humans have free will to make decisions about their future, if determinism is true then we may not have this kind of freedom, in particular, the freedom to have done otherwise given certain past states of affairs or initial conditions. This debate about determinism and human freedom has gone on for some time in philosophy, and there have been some creative attempts to resolve this problem.[31] The traditional way of dealing with this problem, however, continues the dualism of Cartesian philosophy, which made a separation between mind and matter. The mind was placed outside of nature, and thus, the uncertain and indeterminate were considered to be only subjective impressions of the mind and had no objective reality. According to John Dewey, this contrast between the doubtful and the determinate became one of the chief marks by which the subjective and objective were placed in opposition to each other.[32]

Our ability to put land rovers on Mars and send satellites into space based on our knowledge of the laws of motion governing the behavior of bodies in our solar system provides strong evidence to support a deterministic view of the universe. As long as we get things right we have confidence that the universe will act as it always has and our satellites will go where they are supposed to and do what has been planned. However, there have been relatively new developments in science itself that have raised questions about the idea of strict determinism as well as other aspects of the classical scientific worldview and have made the case for a probabilistic view of the universe particularly at the subatomic level.

New Developments in Science

There have been new developments in science, many taking place in recent years that have modified or perhaps even radically challenged the classical view of science and the characteristics of its worldview. The first such development came from *quantum theory*, which held that the energy in all heat, light, and radio waves existed in the form of tiny, discrete amounts called quanta. In classical physics, all changes in energy levels, and light were conceptualized as continuous. Quantum theory introduced discreteness into this picture, and for a while the orbits of electrons were believed to be another example of an unexplainable discontinuity in nature until an alternative view was discovered where atoms acted like waves, not particles, and this conception could then explain the orbits of electrons better than classical physics.[33]

There were now two radically different concepts of the atom that could not immediately be reconciled. Was the electron a wave or a particle?[34] This led to Werner Heisenberg's principle of uncertainty, which, along with Bohr's principle of complementarity, established the internal consistency of quantum theory.[35] Heisenberg theorized that the mere fact of observing an object inevitably changes its location, and it is therefore impossible to know where it really is; furthermore, the more you know about the particles position, the less you are able to know about its speed and direction, and the more you know about a particle's speed and direction, the less you can know about where it is located at any given time. Thus, it is fundamentally impossible to know both a subatomic particle's exact speed of movement and its exact position at the same time.[36]

This insight challenged the classical view of nature as an independent reality apart from any observation that could be known objectively through the methods of science. What we see, according to Heisenberg, depended on the conceptual net we used to capture nature and the context surrounding the observation. The observation itself affects what is observed, and thus, subjectivity enters into the experiments we conduct. As Heisenberg himself puts it, "[t]his again emphasizes a subjective element in the description of atomic events, since the measuring device has been constructed by the observer, and we have to remember that what we observe is not nature itself but nature exposed to our method of questioning."[37] Science is no longer the objective dispassionate method that classical physics assumes. The objective and the subjective interact with each other in examining the world we live in, and the subjective includes feelings, prejudices, biases, and all the other things that are not necessarily subject to the methods of science.

Thus, Heisenberg saw that the electron was a particle whose position and velocity could only be expressed as a probability. The classical view of Newtonian determinism, which claimed that all events could be described with infinite precision, was now replaced by probabilities and science moved from a world of fixed rules and laws to a world of chance and uncertainty. Heisenberg challenged the premise of the classical view by asserting that we cannot know the present in all its details as a matter of principle. And if we cannot know the initial conditions in all their detail the future becomes unpredictable.[38] As Heisenberg says,

> [f]or many people, the breakdown of perfect predictability is the troubling feature of quantum mechanics. (Einstein is among them; that's the origin of his complaint that "God does not play dice with the universe.") If the Copenhagen interpretation is right, there could be no such thing as Laplace's Demon in a quantum world; at least, not if the world contained observers. The act of observing introduces a truly random element into the evolution of the world. Not *completely* random—a wave function may give a very high probability of observing one thing, and a very low probability of observing something else. But *irreducibly* random, in the sense that there is no piece of missing information that would allow us to predict outcomes with certainty, if only we could get our hands on it. Part of the glory of classical mechanics had been it clockwork reliability—even if Laplace's Demon didn't really exist, we know he could exist in principle. Quantum mechanics destroys that hope. It took a long while for people to get used to the idea that probability enters the laws of physics in some fundamental way, and many are still discomforted by the concept.[39]

This view of how the world of subatomic particles acted was resisted by those who trusted in the certainties of a Newtonian universe and even had religious implications in that it challenged God's omniscience. If God cannot know where the electron is, then he cannot know what will happen in the future and free will is introduced into our world.[40] Matter is thus changing all the time because of its interaction with the act of observing, and a subjective element is introduced into the very heart of the notion of an objective nature that is independent of our existence. For many, according to John Dewey, this seemed to make the universe unintelligible and arbitrary:

> The idea of a universal reign of law, based on properties immutably inhering in things and of such a nature as to be capable of exact mathematical statement was a sublime idea. It displaced once for all the notion of a world in which the unaccountable and the mysterious have the first and last word, a world in which they constantly insert themselves. It established the idea of regularity and uniformity in place of the casual and sporadic. It gave men inspiration and guidance in seeking for uniformities and constancies where only irregular diversity was experienced. The ideal extended itself from the inanimate world to the animate and then to social affairs. It became, it may be fairly said, the great article of faith in the creed of scientific men. From this point of view, the principle of indeterminacy seems like an intellectual catastrophe. In compelling surrender of the doctrine of exact and immutable laws describing the fixed antecedent properties of things, it seems to involve abandonment of the idea that the world if fundamentally intelligible. A universe in which fixed laws do not make possible exact predictions seems from the older standpoint to be a world in which disorder reigns.[41]

The view of the passive scientific observer is thus challenged by a view of science as participatory. The scientific observer is involved in what is being observed as quantum theory discovered. What is being looked for and the way it is looked at affect what is found by the scientist. The expectations of the experimenter affect what is observed and the eventual outcome of the experiment. There is more of participatory sense on the part of some scientists, that our knowledge of nature is not entirely objective and that there is no such thing as unobtrusive measures or experiments that do not affect that which is being observed.[42] In spite of the objections to this view of nature, quantum theory has gone on to become the basis for many scientific and technological advances of recent origin.

New understandings in the *complexity sciences* that draw attention to the interactive effects and emergent properties of living systems also challenge the mechanistic paradigm of classical science. This approach is nonlinear in nature and provides a way of going beyond the limits of reductionism. The basic building blocks of nature cannot exist or be understood, so it is argued, apart from the cognitive context that frames their relationships.[43] Such scientists claim that we are living through a period of change in the natural sciences that involves a paradigm shift from the idea of nature as inanimate and mechanical to a new understanding of nature as organic and alive.[44] The world cannot be fully explained by just looking at its parts but is holistic and difficult to comprehend by classical scientific analysis.[45]

In the area of cosmology, the idea of the cosmos as a machine has given way in some instances to the image of the cosmos as a living organism. The big bang theory holds that the universe began as small as the point of a pencil and has been expanding ever since this small beginning. The discovery that the universe was expanding at all points, that everything was moving away from everything else, was a major change in thinking from the idea of a steady state universe. As the universe expands, a succession of new structures and forms appear that are nothing like a machine but more like the way an embryo develops or a tree that grows from a small seed. Thus, cosmology has adopted an image of a developing organism as opposed to a machine that operates according to universal laws of motion.[46]

The doctrine that everything is determinate and in principle predictable that began to be questioned by quantum theory has also been challenged by the development of *chaos theory* and chaotic dynamics has made the old idea of determinism untenable not just in the quantum realm, but in the predicting of weather, the development of spreading waves, and in most other natural systems.[47] The idea that very small changes in a system can have large and unexpected consequences is a fundamental tenant of chaos theory. Chaos and indeterminism have introduced a greater sense of freedom and spontaneity into nature than anything that prevailed for more than three centuries when science was under the spell of classical determinism.[48]

The concept of matter itself underwent some changes with the development of relativity theory and quantum mechanics that is sometimes described as dematerialization. In Einstein's theory of relativity, mass can be transformed into energy and vice versa, but both mass and energy retain separate identities. This implies that the world has two constituents, both mass and energy. According to quantum theory the position of a particle and its motion cannot be determined at the same time, and electrons seem to travel as waves but to interact as particles. This uncertainty leads to the conception of a virtual particle that is nonetheless considered to be real because its effects are measurable.[49]

The classical conception of matter where subatomic particles have a certain location at a certain time and a specific momentum at every moment of time collapses with the discovery of indeterminacy, where the particles do not have a precise location and momentum. Also the observer is believed to play a role in *"making the physical world become what we perceive it to be at the macrophysical level* as a collection of clearly defined and locatable objects." These new understandings of matter that view it as a kind of hybrid of matter and energy are incompatible with the view of materialism that dominated the physics of the modern period. While "primary matter' still serves as the basic stuff out of which everything else is composed, contemporary physics suggests that information can take over the roles that matter used to play and that matter and meaning are entangled. The deeper pursuit of the explanation of matter the more that nonmateriality reveals itself to be in or behind the solid objects we experience in nature.[50]

On closer inspection, solid matter is seen to be composed as almost all empty space and the particles of which matter is composed are ghostly patterns of quantum energy or possible vibrating loops of strings in a ten-dimensional view of space-time. The theory of relativity undermined the notion of absolute time and quantum mechanics demolished the concept that subatomic particles could be assigned well-defined values at all times. So a shift occurred in theoretical physics, where the universe was treated as if it is simply mathematics. Mathematics is considered by many physicists as the ground of being and agree with Galileo, who many centuries ago stated that "the great book of nature can only be known by those who know the language in which it was written and this language is mathematics."[51] According to Paul Davies, a professor at Arizona State University,

> Plato located numbers and geometrical structures in an abstract realm of ideal forms . . . Many mathematicians are Platonists, believing that mathematical objects have real existence, even though they are not situated in the physical universe. Theoretical physicists are steeped in the Platonic tradition, so they also find it natural to locate the mathematical laws of physics in a Platonic realm. The fusion and Platonism and monotheism created the powerful orthodox scientific concept of the laws of physics as ideal, perfect, infinitely precise, immutable, eternal, state-immune, unchanging mathematical form and relationships that transcend the physical universe and reside in an abstract Platonic heaven beyond space and time.[52]

An alternative view of reality, where information is regarded as the primary entity from which physical reality is constructed, is gaining in popularity among scientists and mathematicians who work on the foundations of computing and physicists who work on the theory of quantum computing. Placing information at the base of the explanatory scheme is a radical shift in worldview rather than merely a technical change in perspective.[53] If information is physical and ontologically real as well as fundamental to reality, then there are no physical laws that transcend nature, but rather, they are inherent in and emergent with the universe.[54] The mechanistic worldview of the universe as a machine is supplemented by the computational paradigm, where the universe if seen as a machine that processes information. The universe computes, and this is a mathematical fact not just a metaphor, and it is a quantum computer, where fresh and random bits are constantly injected into the universe. This gives rise to all sorts of complex order and structure.[55] According to Seth Lloyd, writing in "The Computational Universe,"

> [b]y contrast, the computational theory of the universe has a simple and direct explanation for how and why the universe became complex. The

history of the universe in terms of information processing revolutions, each arising naturally from the previous one, already hints at why a computing universe necessarily gives rise to complexity. In fact, we can prove mathematically that a universe that computes mush, with high probability, give rise to a stream of ever-more-complex structures.[56]

The concept of information is a central unifying concept in the sciences playing crucial roles in physics, biology, cognitive neuroscience, and the social sciences However, describing both physical and mental relationships in computational terms is problematic if any physical event in these sciences is considered to be a computation and the mind becomes a special-purpose computer. In this view, the mind–body problem disappears, and in such a uniformly informational universe, there is no meaning, value, purpose, or agency. Networks of informational causality are as blindly mechanical as in classical physics.[57]

Thus, the concept of matter has thus been enlarged to include not only the stuff-character of matter but also the energy of matter and the informational structures of matter. Relativity theory introduced energy into the equation while matter lost some of its primary qualities such as location, duration, and indivisibility in quantum theory. Finally, the new sciences of cybernetics showed that the informational properties of matter seemed to exert a causal influence, and should be seen as irreducible aspects of the material world. "In short, the new picture is that matter is not just the kind of physical brick-like stuff that Newtonian physicists used to think of, and that mass, energy, and information constitute three irreducible though inseparable aspects of the material world."[58]

These and other developments in the scientific community are leading to a shift in worldview to some kind of a post-mechanistic state, where the universe and the earth is an organism that is growing and changing, and even the laws that govern the behavior of more fundamental elements that make up the universe may be changing and evolving. However, these developments have not filtered down to other sciences, let alone the average person in society. The classical scientific worldview with its characteristics of reductionism, atomic individualism, discreteness, its quantitative approach, and its deterministic outlook has pervaded everything in our society and created a certain kind of consciousness that makes us look at everything through these kinds of glasses.[59]

Most of us still live in a world of scientific objectivity, where things happen in front of an observing and detached scientist. The idea that scientists are somehow disembodied and not bodily or emotionally involved in what they are doing is still the dominant scientific paradigm.[60] The idea that nature may be a living organism has been largely relegated to the realm of subjective experience and private life while mechanistic attitudes have been given scientific authority.[61] Thus, the traditional or classical scientific worldview is alive and well in our society and constitutes the way most people think about most aspects of life and the nature of existence. Humans and nature can be treated as objects subject to manipulation in the interests of capitalism to promote economic growth and make profits for the corporation. Any kind of a spiritual dimension is excluded from scientific investigation and is considered to be merely subjective impressions in the mind having no objective reality.

Notes

1 Louis Althusser discussed the development of the concept of law to apply to nature. "The long history of the concept of law is well-known. Its modern meaning (the sense of *scientific law*) only emerged in the works of physicists and philosophers of the sixteenth and seventeenth centuries. And even then it still carried with it the traits of the past. Before taking the new sense of a constant relation between phenomenal variables, i.e., before relating to the practice of the modern experimental sciences, law belonged to the world of religion, morality, and politics. It was, in its meaning, steeped in exigencies arising from human relations . . . The law was a commandment. It thus needed a will to order and a will to obey. A legislator and subjects. The law possessed thereby the structure of conscious human action: it had an end, it designated a target, at the same time as it required its attainment . . . Every case exhibited the same form of commandment and end. Divine law dominated all laws. God had given his orders to nature as a whole and to man . . . It was a long time before the idea that nature might have laws which were not orders could rid itself of this heritage . . . In the seventeenth century, this long effort succeeded in disengaging a special domain for this new meaning of law; the domain of *nature*, of *physics*. Louis Althusser, *Politics and History*, Ben Brewster, trans (New York: Verso, 2007), 31–32.

2 David Filkin, *Stephen Hawking's Universe: The Cosmos Explained* (New York: Basic Books, 1997), 26–27. "Ptolemy's model of the universe was founded on Aristotle's dictates, coupled with what the Alexandrian knew about the actual behavior of the heavenly bodies based on years of careful observation. A troubling conundrum that he had to explain was 'retrograde motion'—the concept that the wandering stars during their annual rotation around the earth, appeared to stop and then actually go in reverse before stopping again and then resuming their proper course. Ptolemy cleverly solved this mystery. In his conception, the planets revolved around the earth by being attached to one of two spheres. Each planet had two spheres. The main sphere, the one that had the earth at its center, was called the 'deferent.' The second, smaller sphere, to which the planet was attached, was called the 'epicycle.' The epicycle revolved around a point on the deferent. So the construct was a sphere whose center was on the edge of a much larger sphere: Picture (in two dimensions) a tambourine and one of the round cymbals attached to it; the perimeter of the tambourine is the deferent, and the small cymbal is the epicycle." There were other complications as well that had to be addressed. Since it was observed that the earth was not quite the center of the universe, Ptolemy created a point near the earth called the "eccentric" that was the center of all the planetary deferents. The planets did not move at a consistent and uniform speed either, necessitating the creation of another point called the "equant" (equalizing point) on the other side of the eccentric that was the point around which the planets revolved at a consistent and uniform speed. The complexity and cumbersomeness of this model should be apparent. See Jack Repcheck, *Copernicus' Secret: How the Scientific Revolution Began* (New York: Simon & Schuster, 2007), 14–15.

3 In a memorandum that Copernicus drafted sometime before 1514, he states, "Yet the planetary theories of Ptolemy and most other astronomers, although consistent with the numerical data, seemed likewise to present no small difficulty. For these theories were not adequate unless certain equants were also conceived; it then appeared that a planet moved with uniform velocity neither on its deferent (main orbit) nor about the center of its epicycle (second orbit). Hence a system of this sort seemed neither sufficiently absolute nor sufficiently pleasing to the mind. Having become aware of these defects, I often considered whether there could perhaps be found a more reasonable arrangement of circles, from which every apparent inequality would be derived and in which everything would move uniformly about its proper center, as the rule of absolute motion requires." Repcheck, *Copernicus' Secret*, 54. "The great success of Ptolemy's model represented both the best and worst of ancient Greek science. On the positive side, the model gained acceptance because if made predictions that agreed reasonably well with reality, and insistence on such agreement remains at the heart of modern science today. On the negative side, the model was so convoluted that it's unlikely that anyone, including Ptolemy himself, thought it represented the true nature of the cosmos. Indeed, the model was not even fully self-consistent, as different mathematical tricks needed to be used to calculate the positions of the different planets. Today, these negatives would weigh so heavily against any scientific idea that people would go immediately back to the drawing board in search of something that worked better. But in Ptolemy's time, these negatives were apparently acceptable, and it was another 1,500 years before they were revisited." Jeffrey Bennett, *Beyond UFOs: The Search for Extraterrestrial Life and Its Astonishing Implications for Our Future* (Princeton, NJ: Princeton University Press, 2008), 31.

4 See Thomas S. Kuhn, *The Structure of Scientific Revolutions*, 3rd ed. (Chicago: The University of Chicago Press, 1996) for his view of how scientific revolutions and paradigm shifts take place.

5 Copernicus's magnum opus, *On the Revolutions*, was published as he was dying. There is reason to believe that a copy of the publication arrived at his house the last day of his life so that he saw it before he died. See Repcheck, *Copernicus' Secret*, 167, 171.

6 Ibid., 194.

7 Filkin, *Stephen Hawking's Universe*, 38–47.

8 See Thomas S. Kuhn, *The Copernican Revolution: Planetary Astronomy in the Development of Western Thought*, revised ed. (New York: MJF Books, 1985).

9 Ibid., 2.

10 Steven Shapin, *The Scientific Revolution* (Chicago: The University of Chicago Press, 1996), 13.

11 Ibid., 85.

12 Ibid., 92.

13 Ibid., 105.

14 Timothy Ferris, *The Science of Liberty: Democracy, Reason, and the Laws of Nature* (New York: Harper Collins, 2010), 4.

15 Shapin, *The Scientific Revolution*, 116.

16 Ibid., 36.

17 "[A] universe whose essential characteristic is fixed order and connection has no place for unique and individual existences, no place for novelty and genuine change and growth." John Dewey, *The Quest for Certainty* (New York: Capricorn Books, 1960), 209.

18 "The rise of new science in the seventeenth century laid hold upon the general culture in the next century. Its popular effect was not great, but its influence upon the intellectual elite, even upon those who were not themselves engaged in

scientific inquiry, was prodigious. The enlightenment . . . testified to the wide-spread belief that at last light had dawned, that dissipation of the darkness of ignorance, superstition, and bigotry was at hand, and the triumph of reason was assured—for reason was the counterpart in man of the laws of nature science was disclosing." John Dewey, "Time and Individuality," in *The Later Works, 1925–1953*, Vol. 14, Jo Ann Boydston, ed. (Carbondale and Edwardsville, IL: Southern Illinois University Press, 1988), 100.

19 Matthew Fox and Rupert Sheldrake, *Natural Grace: Dialogues on Creation, Darkness, and the Soul in Spirituality and Science* (New York: Doubleday, 1997), 15–19.

20 Sandra Rosenthal, "Reductionsim," in Robert Kolb, ed., *The Encyclopedia of Business Ethics and Society* (Thousand Oaks, CA: Sage, 2008), 1784–1785.

21 Ibid.

22 Charles Barber, "The Brain: A Mindless Obsession," *The Wilson Quarterly*, 32 Winter 2008, 42. Some research questions whether there is such a thing as free will that drives our behavior or whether we are actually mechanistic creatures and what we claim to be self-aware consciousness is actually an illusion. Studies have shown that our unconscious brains are active in influencing our decisions milliseconds before a subject made what he or she thought was a "spontane-ous" decision. See "Health & Science: Is Free Will a Myth?" *The Week*, May 2, 2008, 19.

23 Paul Oppenheim and Hilary Putnam, "Unity of Science as a Working Hypoth-esis," in Janet A. Kourany, ed., *Scientific Knowledge*, 2nd ed. (Belmont, CA: Wadsworth Publishing Co., 1998), 270.

24 Ibid., 271.

25 Ibid., 269.

26 "Atomism," *Catholic Encyclopedia*, ed. Kevin Knight, http://www.newadvent.org/cathen/02053a.htm, accessed August 23, 2008.

27 Dewey, "Time and Individuality," 103. See also Dewey, *The Quest for Certainty*, 188–120.

28 Zeno's paradox involves getting from one place to another. For example, to get from where you are to the nearest door, you first have to cover half the distance. Then you have to cover half the remaining distance and so on ad infi-nitum, meaning you never can reach the door as you will always have an ever decreasing infinitesimal distance that remains to be covered. Yet in experience we do reach the door, so this phenomenon is simply the result of breaking space into discrete elements that can't be put back together into some continuous whole.

29 Christopher Dawson, *Progress and Religion: An Historical Inquiry* (London: Sheed & Ward, 1929), 219.

30 Dewey, *The Quest for Certainty*, 201–202.

31 Carl Hofer, "Causal Determinism," in *Stanford Encyclopedia of Philosophy*, http://plato.stanford.edu/entries/determinsim-causal/, accessed July 9, 2008.

32 Dewey, *The Quest for Certainty*, 231–232.

33 Charles Flowers, *A Science Odyssey: 100 Years of Discovery* (New York: Wil-liam Morrow and Company, 1998), 27–29.

34 See Charis Anastopoulos, *Particle or Wave: The Evolution of the Concept of Matter in Modern Physics* (Princeton, NJ: Princeton University Press, 2008).

35 See Henry J. Folse, *The Philosophy of Niels Bohr: The Framework of Com-plementarity* (Amsterdam: North-Holland, 1985), for a philosophical treat-ment of Bohr's attempt to reconcile wave–particle duality with his theory of complementarity.

36 Flowers, *A Sciency Odyssey*, 29–30.

37 Werner Heisenberg, *Physics and Philosophy: The Revolution in Modern Science* (New York: Harper Perennial, 1958), 32.
38 Anastopoulos, *Particle or Wave*, 186.
39 Sean Carroll, *From Eternity to Here: The Quest for the Ultimate Theory of Time* (New York: Dutton, 2010), 241.
40 Flowers, *A Science Odyssey*, 31–33.
41 Dewey, *The Quest for Certainty*, 208.
42 Ibid., 24.
43 Frank Capra, *The Web of Life: A New Scientific Understanding of Living Systems* (New York: Anchor Doubleday, 1996), 31.
44 Fox and Sheldrake, *Natural Grace*, 15–19.
45 Roger Lewin, *Complexity: Life at the Edge of Chaos* (Chicago: The University of Chicago Press, 1999), x.
46 Ibid., 21.
47 Edward Lorenz, who developed chaos theory, died in 2008. His paper titled "Predictability: Does the Flap of a Butterfly's Wings in Brazil Set Off a Tornado in Texas?" published in 1972 became one of the most referenced scientific papers in modern history. When he received the Kyoto Prize for earth and planetary sciences in 1991, the committee said he had "brought about one of the most dramatic changes in mankind's view of nature since Sir Isaac Newton." See "Obituaries: The Meteorologist who Formulated Chaos Theory," *The Week*, May 2, 2008, 35.
48 Lewin, *Complexity*, 23–24. Some scholars claim that James Clerk Maxwell, a scientist from the nineteenth century who helped to revolutionize physics with his work on electro magnetics, presented a premonition of chaos theory in essay he wrote in 1873, some hundred years before mathematicians began to develop the subject. See Nancy Forbes and Basil Mahon, *Faraday, Maxwell, and the Electromagnetic Field* (Amherst, NY: Prometheus Books, 2014), 235.
49 Ernan McMullin, "From Matter to Materialism . . . and (almost) Back," in Paul Davies and Niels Henrik Gregersen, eds., *Information and the Nature of Reality: From Physics to Metaphysics* (New York: Cambridge University Press, 2010), 23–27.
50 Philip Clayton, "Unsolved Dilemmas: The Concept of Matter in the History of Philosophy and in Contemporary Physics." in Paul Davies and Niels Henrik Gregersen, eds., *Information and the Nature of Reality: From Physics to Metaphysics* (New York: Cambridge University Press, 2010), 55–59.
51 Paul Davies, "Universe from Bit," in Paul Davies and Niels Henrik Gregersen, eds., *Information and the Nature of Reality: From Physics to Metaphysics* (New York: Cambridge University Press, 2010), 65–67.
52 Ibid., 72–73.
53 Ibid., 75.
54 Ibid., 83.
55 Seth Lloyd, "The Computational Universe," in Paul Davies and Niels Henrik Gregersen, eds., *Information and the Nature of Reality: From Physics to Metaphysics* (New York: Cambridge University Press, 2010), 102–103.
56 Ibid., 98.
57 Terrence W. Deacon, "What Is Missing for Theories of Information?" in Paul Davies and Niels Henrik Gregersen, eds., *Information and the Nature of Reality: From Physics to Metaphysics* (New York: Cambridge University Press, 2010), 150, 156.
58 Niels Henrik Gregersen, "God, Matter, and Information: Towards a Stoicizing Logos Christianity," in Paul Davies and Niels Henrik Gregersen, eds., *Information and the Nature of Reality: From Physics to Metaphysics* (New York: Cambridge University Press, 2010), 322.

59 For example, Capra argues that conventional social science is based on an outdated mechanistic paradigm of natural science that calls for objective analysis
   of discrete building blocks to aid in the erection of conceptual frameworks that
   allow for prediction and control of natural and social phenomena. See Capra,
   The Web of Life, 30.
60 Fox and Sheldrake, *Natural Grace*, 20.
61 Ibid., 26.

11 The Mind–Body Problem

The mind–body problem has been in existence for thousands of years going back to the ancient Greek philosophers such as Plato and Aristotle. The problem is rather simple to state but has been extremely difficult to resolve. The mind and the body seem to be very different kinds of entities. The mind has a consciousness that involves feelings, thoughts, imagination, and other such phenomena that many think cannot be reduced to material elements. The body, on the other hand, is a material substance that can be worked on and fixed in certain circumstances and follows the laws of physiology. The question is how these two different entities interact so that the mind is able to have effects on the body as when a person wills the body to perform some act and, in turn, how the body can affect the mind as in the experience of pain.

This problem became particularly acute with the rise of modern science and its mechanistic and materialistic worldview. Before the rise of modern science, Christian thinkers presupposed the world to be composed of two parts, the material and the spiritual, existing alongside one another as independent yet interacting realms. With the emergence of classical materialism in the eighteenth and nineteenth centuries, however, the world of material particles was claimed to be the sole reality, and all genuine knowledge about nature and humanity "must be reduced to the causal powers inherent in the interplay between basic physical constituents."[1] Thus, matter replaced God as the ultimate reality, and the realm of the mental was excluded as a genuinely existing thing.

Philosophy had to come to terms with this scientific worldview and incorporate modern science in its understanding of the world. It was Rene Descartes, a French philosopher who lived in the first half of the seventeenth century, who embodied this worldview in his philosophy. The body, for Descartes, was a mechanical entity that could be worked on and understood in a scientific sense. But Descartes did not want to reduce the mind to this state, so he located the mind outside of nature. This action created a mind–body dualism, where the mind became something separate from the body located in some nonmaterial realm. As Steven Shapin states, the mind was not a mechanical entity and could not be accounted for in this manner:

> For human beings, however, the scope of mechanical accounts was crucially limited. Explanations of the human *body* were, for Descartes, not the same thing as explanations of human *beings*, for there was something about human beings that could not be comprehended by an account of the body's matter and motion. We do not *feel* ourselves to be machines, and Descartes agreed that we are not. We feel ourselves to exercise will, to have purposes, to move our bodies in response to our purposes, to be conscious, to make moral evaluations, to deliberate and to reason (that is to *think*), and to express the results of our thought in language—none of which Descartes reckoned that machines, or animals can do.[2]

For Descartes, the I, with its characteristics, was a self-contained entity, a thing that thinks outside of nature and beyond the realm of scientific study. The material world is other than the I and can be observed and studied by science. Human beings thus have a dual nature. Their bodies are like machines and can be accounted for by matter in motion. But they also have a mind, which cannot be accounted for in this manner. The world itself thus is made up of two different realms, that of matter and that of mind, and it is only in human beings that these two realms meet. Exactly how mind and matter meet in the human being remained something of a mystery. The body is extended in space, but the mind is not so extended. However, if the mind is not extended into space, then where is it located? And how do the two realms make contact with each other?[3] Put another way, the immaterial mind is not located anywhere in space, and because of this property how can it touch and affect the body at any particular place.

This mind–body dualism and the dichotomies that came with it such as the split between the spiritual and material world and the subject–object dichotomy have plagued philosophy ever since as they have been struggling with these issues for centuries. Those scientists who wanted to reject dualism and study the mind as an object had to treat it as part of scientifically defined nature and so the mind in modern times has been reduced to the brain, which can be scientifically studied as some kind of a mechanical entity. Things like love, ethics, freedom, and so on have become nothing more than neurons firing in certain parts of the brain that can be observed with modern technology.[4]

Nature as a whole came to be viewed as a machine that was considered to be wholly intelligible. There was nothing mysterious or magical about a machine. It operated according to universal laws and there was nothing capricious about the uniformities that were observed in nature. The machine metaphor was a "model of the form and scope that human knowledge of nature might properly have and of how human accounts of nature might properly be framed."[5] Matter was considered to be passive and inert, and while there were complexities in nature, these were not the result of purpose and design. This mechanical account of nature was in opposition to a tradition that saw purpose or intention in nature.

This classical vision of a machinelike world governed entirely by universal mathematical laws has no room for spontaneity or freedom. The world of nature is seen as an automatic machine with no soul, no spontaneous life, and no purposes of its own.[6] This desacralized, soulless vision of nature became the foundation for modern science and established itself as the reigning paradigm in the Scientific Revolution of the seventeenth century.[7] Nature came to be regarded as dead matter subject only to mechanical forces and governed by mathematical laws. The whole course of nature was thought to be determined as everything was believed to carry on inexorably and mechanically and was in principle completely predictable. The whole of nature was thought to be essentially knowable to the mathematical reason of scientists.[8]

Science thus views the world as a closed system that operates according to mechanical laws that can be expressed in mathematical terms. This worldview produces a quantitatively characterized universe where knowledge becomes the building up of a storehouse of so-called objective facts gleaned from scientific studies. The universe, including humans, is thus entirely materialistic and there is no room for anything like the soul or spirituality or some kind of nonmaterialistic consciousness. The subjective element is not reliable as a source of knowledge as it is based on opinion rather the hard facts of science. It is interesting to see how this separation of mind and body was dealt with by philosophers and scientists over the years as it constitutes one of the most vexing problems facing these scholars.

The existence of the mind does seem to depend on the brain as we have no solid evidence that something like a disembodied mind exists. Yet the mind is often believed to be the one object of study for which the third person experimental approach is inappropriate. The mind is considered to be more than a behavioral–material–functional entity which can be studied by the hard psychological sciences. The problem for philosophy is whether it can go beyond third-person observational and experimental science to say anything meaningful about the mind and it properties.[9] How can we even talk about a nonmaterial something that is somehow connected to the material body and provides it with some kind of motivating or spiritual force? Does spirituality have any meaning in this context? This question may not be of much interest to business school students and faculty, but it is of critical importance to anyone that considers spirituality to have some kind of reality in the contemporary world and a force that is necessary for human flourishing and survival. As stated by Deepak Chopra, the author of more than sixty books and a leading figure in the field of emerging spirituality,

[f]or centuries the mystery of how the mind relates to the body has been a philosophical question, not a practical one. So far as ordinary life goes, brain vs mind isn't a pressing debate. We say, "I've made up my

mind," not "I've made up my brain." The average person goes through life never questioning that it takes a mind to be human. But this seemingly ivory-tower issue has incredibly practical implications. You cannot be indifferent to the question of mind versus brain if the mind serves as a portal to a deeper reality; if reaching that reality can transform your life, mind versus brain turns into the most urgent question of all.[10]

Vitalism

One of the first attempts to deal with this problem was called Vitalism, a movement that arose as a strictly materialistic view of reality began to gain credence. Vitalism was a school of thought based on the idea of a life force or life principle that was somehow inherent in or associated with the motions that were part of human physiology such as pulses of the heart and circulation of the blood. This life force came from some realm outside the powers of humans and as a universal vitality was an invisible substance added to the matter of the body as electricity is to the various things with which it may be connected. This theory was said to bring some scientific evidence to the notion of the soul that came from theology and challenged the emerging notion of a purely materialistic basis for life itself.[11]

Vitalism became a controversial issue in Britain that spilled over into the public and was a precursor to the debate over Darwin's theory of evolution by natural selection that emerged some forty years later. Such ideas had been around for some time ever since medical science began to raise fundamental questions about the nature of life itself. Some began to wonder what exactly distinguished organic from inorganic matter. Was there some form of animating power in nature that gave life to organic matter? These questions gave rise to philosophical inquiry about the nature of mind and spirit and eventually to the traditional religious concept of the soul. How could these nonmaterial substances be explained in scientific terms, or could they simply be dismissed as nonsensical from a scientific perspective?[12]

In Germany the philosophy of Friedrich Schelling became popular for providing an answer to these questions. Schelling thought the entire natural world consisted of a system of invisible power and energies, something akin to a spiritual soul that made all physical objects aspire to higher states of evolution. This doctrine was best translated as "science mysticism." Carbon aspired to become diamonds, plants aspired to become sentient animals, and animals aspired to become humans which in turn aspired to become part of the world spirit. There was obviously some notion of evolution in these vitalistic ideas that had some attraction because of its optimism and reverence for the natural world.[13]

These ideas spilled over into England where there was a great deal of skepticism about the whole notion of vitalism that triggered quite a debate. One key question that was theological in nature was whether the "super-added" force, assuming it even existed, was the same idea as spirit or soul, which were theological concepts, or whether it was some intermediary element between body and soul such as some form of electrical fluid.[14] The whole notion of vitalism was attacked as being antiscientific, but scientific reductionism also came under attack and science was believed to be inevitably godless and maybe even blasphemous by fundamentalist Christians.[15]

Some tried to steer a metaphysical path between science and vitalism by trying to reconcile science with a sacred concept of life by arguing that something called the soul existed but had nothing to do with electricity. While denying that life was purely a physical organization the idea of some mystical life force was also rejected. While a "life principle" existed it had nothing to do with physiology. "It consisted in an inherent drive towards 'individuation' which moved up the chain of creation, and finally manifested itself in the unique form of human 'self-consciousness', which included the moral conscience and the spiritual identity or 'soul.' "[16]

The Vitalism debate also got tied up with the novel about Frankenstein written in 1818, in which a human life was physically reconstructed but the spirit or soul was irretrievably damaged. This creature was constructed from adult body parts as a fully developed human, but the mind of such a creature was that of a totally undeveloped infant. Frankenstein's monster had no memory, no language, and no conscience. He became a monster wreaking havoc wherever he went doomed to eternal solitude and destruction. The implication is that without a soul or spirit, some eternal spark that comes from beyond a mere scientific or materialistic approach to reality, humankind is doomed to a similar existence.[17]

Modern Approaches

Vitalism eventually died out as a movement or a philosophy to counter the rise of a scientific and materialistic approach to human consciousness. But the questions it was dealing with remain unanswered within the scientific and philosophical community. The nature of consciousness is a major challenge to modern neuroscience and remains one of life's abiding mysteries. In a book entitled *The Philosophy of Mind: The Metaphysics of Consciousness*, Dale Jacquette, who holds a senior professional chair at the University of Bern in Switzerland, presents the full range of choices that are currently available in addressing the mind–body problem. Instead of what he sees as the mainstream eliminativist and reductivist strategies to address this problem, he presents a defense of property dualism as an alternative solution to the mind–body problem.[18]

Eliminativism is the theory that there is no such thing as mind. This claim usually means that it is impossible to account for psychological properties by using observational techniques and experimental scientific method. One cannot look inside a person's mind to see what is going on there. The concept of mind can be done away with if cognitive phenomena are better explained by looking at behavior, brain events, or information processing.

Classical behaviorism, for example, tried to eliminate the importance of the mind by arguing that everything we need to know about psychological phenomena can be limited to the external bodily movements of human beings. The only thing of psychological interest is the external behavior of humans; therefore, the mind or mental states are of no importance to science.[19]

Reductivism is also an antimentalistic position that does not deny the existence of mental phenomena but holds that whatever truths are expressed in mentalistic terms can be expressed equivalently and more accurately and efficiently in a nonmentalistic vocabulary.[20] This view reflects the desire for a unity of the sciences that seeks to reduce all phenomena to a single set of underlying causes. These causes are ultimately reducible to physical causes and therefore all the other sciences are supposed to be reducible to physics and all properties of objects that are knowable to physical properties. According to Jacquette, "[t]here is an understandable urge to being mind and matter together in a single scientific synthesis in which mental properties are eliminated or reduced as unnecessary to psychological explanation."[21]

There are some other approaches to the mind–body problem that Jacquette mentions including materialism, which treats the mind as a physical entity that is completely explainable in terms of material properties alone. Materialism is the predominant metaphysics of contemporary science and is an ontology that has no place for immaterial minds or immortal body-independent souls or spirits. The mind is thus identical to the brain and its central and peripheral nervous system or its neurophysiological properties. Mental events are reducible to particular brain events that can be studied by neuroscience. Functionalism, on the other hand, rejects such materialistic theories as too restrictive on the basis that no particular kind of matter is essential to the functioning of the mind. This approach views the mind as an input–output information and control system that operates much like a computer program.[22] The mind is like a black box that is to be understood solely in terms of its inputs and outputs. The internal workings of this black box that make the transformation from inputs to outputs are obscure and hidden from being directly viewed and are therefore of no interest.[23]

Property dualism, on the other hand, holds that the mind has a dual nature as the name implies. According to Jacquette, the mind has "both behavioral-material-functional and behavioural-materially-functionally ineliminable and irreducible kinds of properties."[24] The hard psychological sciences can reveal the first three kinds of properties, but the mind has additional properties that science cannot adequately explain. The latter set of properties has an intrinsic intentionality or "aboutness," which involves the directness of thought toward intended objects.[25] The emergence of mind from matter is a natural phenomenon that is inexplicable in terms of the behavioral–material–functional properties of the entities from which it emerges.[26]

Property dualism avoids the causal interaction problem as it does not need to consider causal interactions between material and immaterial substances since it admits there are only material substances. It has no need to appeal to some divine abilities to account for mind-body interaction. It can absorb scientific findings about the functioning of the brain and nervous system without a commitment to the extrascientific ontology of eliminativism or reductivism. Property dualism maintains that there is an intuitive distinction between mind and body because of a difference in their properties. Without both types of properties there can be no satisfactory explanation of psychological phenomena.[27]

The explanatory adequacy of property dualism cannot be decided on scientific grounds but must be determined on the basis of its ability to provide a philosophically satisfactory metaphysics of the mind.[28] Intentionality is a key concept in this endeavor as it is said to explain the nonphysical properties of the mind that is postulated by property dualism and provides the basis for criticism of eliminative and reductive theories of the mind. Intentionality involves an abstract relationship between a mental state and the object that is thought about. It means that all thoughts are directed toward an intended object or objects. By virtue of its intentionality the mind is qualitatively different than purely materialistic or mechanical things. It gives the mind dignity, which we experience as freedom of the will and freedom of action. We are not robots but intentional actors in the world. "If the mind is intentional, and if intentionality is an ineliminable, irreducible and mechanically nonreplicable property of mind, then the mind is a new category or entity in the material world."[29] As Jacquette states,

> [i]f a property is such that our explanations are incomplete or incorrect when we try to get by without it, and such that we cannot replace it with any more conceptually more fundamental kind or category of property, then the property in question is indeed irreducible and as 'deep' as it is possible to go among the concepts needed to explain the world.[30]

The primacy of the intentional complements the theory of property dualism and supports it as a preferred ontology of the mind. The primacy of the intentional lies in the realm of metaphysics and conceptual analysis. It is not subject to observational or experimental investigation. It thus lies beyond the aims and methods of science. The mind requires a theory of its intrinsic intentionality, which distinguishes it from purely behavioral–material–mechanical things. The mind has intentional properties that are not part of the nonintentional entities from which it emerges. According to Jacquette, the mind is a new and metaphysically unique addition to the world whose qualities are not determined by its behavioral–material–functional properties.[31]

The intentionality of mind that marks its emergence from a materialistic universe distinguishes it from all other things in the universe. The mind develops from sentience to consciousness and finally to self-consciousness which adds to its dignity. The mind even in its most primitive condition is worthy of respect as a metaphysical entity that is special and distinguished from nonthinking entities. Intentionality is found in first-person experience, in the phenomenology of the mental life of the individual. As such it is a source of knowledge that is impenetrable to the public and scientific investigation. Thought is essentially nonpublic or private and accessible only in a first-person sense.[32]

According to Jacquette freedom of will begins with the mind's intending some state of affairs and producing action to bring it about. Agents initiate causal chains of events by an act of will and these causal chains cannot be completely reduced to what he calls "event causation antecedents" because they begin with an agent and not with an event. The act along with the agent is free in that sense and to that extent. If the basic action is intentional then it cannot be fully eliminatively or reductively explained in terms of event causation. Such action is free because when agents initiate causal chains, their casually free thought intrinsically intends an object or purpose. If such action is not free, then moral responsibility must be explained away as people cannot be held responsible if they were not free to do otherwise.[33]

In conclusion, Jacquette's main argument is that for a philosophy of mind to satisfactorily explain the nature of the mind it must include metaphysical considerations about the intentionality of the mind and what he calls the primacy of the intentional. This intrinsic intentionality is not accessible to science as the intentionality of the mind is an extrascientific, metaphysical property. Science has failed to provide a satisfactory account of the mind because it is adequate and appropriate for only the public behavioral–material–functional properties of nonthinking matter from which the mind emerges.[34] He says,

> By giving equal place to the metaphysics of intentionality in accounting for the mind's nonphysical properties, property dualism entails that the mind is something rather different, more special and important, than any pure physical thing with purely physical properties. If mind is other than the body, if it has properties that the living body and nonliving machines considered only as such do not have, then it need not be determined by laws discovered in the physical and hard psychological sciences. We can then be assured on the basis of a scientific metaphysics of mind that in a morally significant sense we are free in thought, causally undetermined in action, purpose and will.[35]

Jacquette thinks that in the final analysis traditional science needs to be supplemented by phenomenology in order to provide a complete and philosophically adequate explanation of the mind as a distinct entity that cannot be reduced to the brain and its activities. Such a phenomenological approach would have to include private first-person facts about the mind that can be known only by direct acquaintance. Such first-person accounts have to be considered as a valid source of knowledge about the mind and supplement the more objective methods of traditional science. A proper understanding of the mind cannot be purely scientific in nature and emerge from the hard psychological sciences alone. The intrinsic intentionality of thought is the proper subject of metaphysics while the brain's neurophysiological properties are the proper subject of the brain and information sciences. Both are necessary for an adequate understanding of the mind and its activities.[36]

In *Mind: A Brief Introduction*, John R. Searle, the Slusser Professor in the Department of Philosophy at the University of California, Berkeley, maps out the opposing camps in the debate about the mind and its reality. The dualist position includes those who cannot give up on the mental dimension and think of it as real and irreducible to anything else. In the other camp are the materialists who think that accepting such an irreducible mental component means giving up on the scientific worldview so that they deny the existence of any such mental reality and believe it all can be reduced to the material or eliminated altogether.[37] These are the same camps as the reductivistic and eliminativist strategies in Jacquette's book just reviewed. Searle thinks both of these approaches make the same mistake. However, the importance of this question about the reality of the mind cannot be overemphasized. Searle thinks that

> the central question in philosophy at the beginning of the twenty-first century is how to give an account of ourselves as apparently conscious, mindful, free, rational, speaking, social, and political agents in a world that science tells us consists entirely of mindless, meaningless, physical particles. Who are we, and how do we fit into the rest of the world? How does the human reality relate to the rest of reality?[38]

What does it mean to be human in a scientific world? The answer to this question as well as related questions begins with a discussion of the mind as mental phenomena are the bridge, so to speak, which makes it possible to connect with the rest of the world that we know through science. This connection is the central problem in a philosophy of the mind. For Descartes the solution was to separate the world into two kinds of substances, mental substances and physical substances. The essence of the mind for Descartes was consciousness, or what he called thinking and the essence of the body was extension meaning that bodies have spatial dimensions. Thus, Descartes solved the mind–body problem by assigning the material world to the scientists and the mental world to the theologians. Minds were not a proper subject for scientific investigation whereas bodies could be so investigated by the sciences.[39]

As modern physics began to explain more or the world we live in and became the accepted authority in matters related to how the world works, the dualism of Descartes could not only give an account of the causal relations between mind and body but had the additional problem that it was inconsistent with modern physics. Physics says the amount of matter/energy in the universe is constant; it can neither be created nor destroyed. But the dualism of mind and body implies that there is a mental energy or spiritual energy that is not fixed by physics. Thus, some of the most fundamental laws of physics, like the law of conservation of energy must be false. Attempts to make dualism consistent with physics proved to be futile.[40]

Furthermore, according to Searle, we know that consciousness cannot exist on its own without reference to some physical processes going on in the brain. The thought that consciousness can exist without any connection to something physical seems out of the question. These failures of dualism and the success of the physical sciences opened the door to the ascendancy of materialism, the idea that a complete account of the world and all there is to be said about it can be given in materialistic terms. The existence of some irreducible mental nonmaterialistic phenomena does not fit into this worldview. Different kinds of materialism developed but they all shared the same characteristic of rejecting any kind of dualism that postulated some nonmaterial realm that had a separate reality apart from the material world that can be examined by science.[41]

Materialists are convinced that they are right about their view of the mind–body problem, but Searle seems to think that they have never been able to formulate a version of it that they are completely satisfied with and that can be accepted by other materialists. The different versions of materialism leave out some essential features that we know to exist such as consciousness and intentionality. The materialists have a problem in giving a satisfactory account of the mind that incorporates the obvious fact that we all experience both conscious and intentional states and that these seem irreducible to physical elements that operate independently of conscious thought and intentional actions.[42]

Searle's method to deal with the mind-body problem is to put the history of the problem behind him as well as traditional ways of thinking about the problem. He first concentrates on the matter of consciousness and then deals with the problem of intentionality. Searle calls his approach to consciousness "biological naturalism" because, on one hand, it provides a naturalistic solution to the mind–body problem and, on the other hand, emphasizes the biological character of mental states and thus avoids both materialism and dualism.[43] Searle enunciates four theses related to this approach to consciousness:

1. Conscious states, with their subjective first-person ontology, are real phenomena in the real world. We cannot do an eliminative reduction of consciousness, showing that it is just an illusion. Nor can we reduce consciousness to its neurobiological basis, because such a third-person reduction would leave out the first-person ontology of consciousness.
2. Conscious states are entirely caused by lower level neurobiological processes in the brain. Conscious states are thus *causally reducible* to neurobiological processes. They have absolutely no life of their own, independent of the neurobiology. Causally speaking, they are not something "over and above" neurobiological processes.

3. Conscious states are realized in the brain as features of the brain system and thus exist at a level higher than that of neurons and synapses. Individual neurons are not conscious, but portions of the brain system composed of neurons are conscious.

4. Because conscious states are real features of the real world, they function causally. My conscious thirst causes me to drink water for example.[44]

Searle goes on to challenge the traditional distinction between the mental and the physical stating that "[t]here is no reason why a physical system such as a human or animal organism should not have states that are qualitative, subjective, and intentional." The distinction between quality and quantity is probably bogus, he says, pointing out that studies of perceptual and cognitive systems treat qualitativeness, subjectivity, and intentionality as within the domain of natural science and are thus considered to be part of the physical world. If the distinction between the mental and physical is going to be kept for whatever reason, the notion of the physical needs to be expanded to include a subjective, first-person, qualitative component.[45]

As for reductionism, while consciousness can be entirely causally explained by neurons firing in the brain, it cannot thereby be shown as nothing but such neuronal behavior. Searle makes a distinction between a causal reduction and an ontological reduction suggesting that the former is possible, but an ontological reduction cannot be made without losing the point of having the concept in the first place. Consciousness has a first-person ontology, and if it is redefined in third-person terms, the concept is lost and there its reality disappears. As a first-person ontology, if it consciously appears that I am conscious, then I am conscious, and that reality cannot be denied.[46]

Consciousness is part of the ordinary physical world and is not something over and above the materialist substrate. While consciousness has a first-person ontology neuronal processes have a third-person ontology that can be studied by science. The former cannot ontologically be reduced to the latter. Consciousness consists of ontologically subjective experiences that are part of the brain and not located in another realm as the dualists propose. There are not two metaphysical realms called the physical and the mental. There are just different processes going on in the brain some of which are conscious experiences.[47] When I raise my arm there are not two causes, one physical and one mental. When consciousness causes something like raising an arm it is a higher level of brain functioning than that of neurons and synapses.

Searle then turns to the problem of intentionality, which he considers to be second only to the problem of consciousness in terms of difficulty and importance when dealing with the mind in a philosophical sense. Demystifying the problem of intentionality means removing it from the abstract spiritual level down to the so-called concrete level of real animal biology. As with consciousness, intentionality is caused by the behavior of neurons in the brain system. Brain processes can cause feelings of thirst, for example, but thirst is an intentional phenomenon in that to be thirsty is to have a desire for a drink of water. Intentional states refer to objects and state of affairs in the world and have some sort of content that determines this reference. Intentions are not true or false the way beliefs are because they do not aim to match an independently existing reality.[48]

The key to understanding intentionality, according to Searle, is its conditions of satisfaction, as any intentional state can determine the conditions of its satisfaction. There is a connection between intentionality and conditions of satisfaction. Any intentional state is positioned in a network of intentional states and against a background of pre-intentional capabilities. The structure of intentionality is the structure of our conscious life as well as our mental life. When we make up our minds to engage in some course of action, when we intend to do something, this is a manifestation of the formal structure of intentionality. It should be noted that Seale does not intend any of this discussion of intentionality to be phenomenological as he does not think it is able to access the structure of intentionality.[49]

Regarding the question of how mental processes can ever have any physical effects in the real world, Searle questions the principle of causation, which says that every event has a cause. However, the existence of regularities in nature, that the thing we call cause is always followed by the thing we call effect, gives us the illusion of a necessary connection and this illusion gives us the conviction that every event has a cause. But the only reality is that of priority, contiguity, and constant conjunction. The connection we think exists in nature is an illusion as the only reality we see is that of regularity.[50]

Nonetheless, it is quite common to experience a causal connection between objects and states of affairs in the world. We experience our conscious intentions as causing certain bodily movements like raising our arm. And we experience things happening to us by objects and states of affairs in the world. Our difficulty in finding a job, for example, is caused by economic conditions that are beyond our control. The way out of the mental–physical causation problem is to abandon these traditional categories and see them as two different levels of one complete system. Consciousness does not have some separate causal role to play but it does have a first-person ontology that is not reducible to a third-person ontology, "even though there is no causal efficacy to consciousness that is not reducible to the causal efficacy of its neuronal basis."[51] According to Searle,

> [w]hen I say that my conscious decision to raise my arm causes my arm to go up, I am not saying that some cause occurred *in addition* to the behavior of neurons when they fire and produce all sorts of other neurobiological consequences, rather I am simply describing the whole neurological system at the level of the entire system and not at the level of particular microelements.[52] There is just the brain system, which has

one level of description where neuron firings are occurring and another level of description, the level of the system, where the system is conscious and indeed consciously trying to raise its arm. Once we abandon the traditional Cartesian categories of the mental and the physical, once we abandon the idea that there are two disconnected realms, then there really is no special problem about mental causation.[53]

The problem of free will, however, remains and results from two irreconcilable convictions, each of which seems to be correct and inescapable. The first conviction is that every event that occurs in the world, including our decisions and actions, are preceded by causally sufficient conditions that determine that those decisions and actions will occur. The second conviction is that we experience human freedom in making decisions and taking certain actions, a conviction, Searle says, that no matter how much we deny in theory cannot be denied in practice. We experience such freedom to act voluntarily every day of our lives. Such is the dilemma of free will.[54]

Searle believes the problem of free will cannot be satisfactorily resolved and will be with us for a long time. Various efforts that have been made in philosophy to explain or evade it only result in it resurfacing in another form. Even after having resolved the issues of mental causality and addressed the problem of intentionality the question as to whether we do actually have freedom of will remains. This is a case of human ignorance as we do not know how free will exists in the brain or how it could possibly work. We do not know how or why we have the unshakeable conviction of free will but we do know that it is inescapable. "We cannot act except under the presupposition of freedom."[55]

With regard to the self, Searle deals with the question of personal identity or what is it that makes a person the same person across time and change. What is it about a person that gives them a sense that they have a continuing identity through time which is in addition to the continuity of the body which is ever changing? The answer to this question according to Searle is to be found in the continuity of memory experiences that forms an essential part of one's being as a continual self through time and change. Someone else may have similar experiences that give him or her similar identity, yet each person retains a sense of themselves as a continuity that is somehow different.[56]

Finally, Seale discusses the underlying philosophical presuppositions he makes with regard to the scientific worldview. He explicitly states that science does not name an ontological domain as if there were a scientific reality that is different from the everyday reality or common sense. Science is rather a set of methods for finding out about those things that are subject to scientific investigation. There is no such thing as "scientific reality" or "scientific truth," there are just facts that we come to know by various methods. There is no such thing as a scientific world, a mental world, or a world of common sense; there is just the world, and we are simply trying to describe how it works and how we fit into this world.[57]

In a book titled *The Wonder of Consciousness*, Harold Langsam, a professor of Philosophy at the University of Virginia, claims that there are important facts that we can know about consciousness a priori, in other words before we experience them, and that the source of its wonder is its very intelligibility. We can discover things about consciousness through reflective thinking, thus making introspection a valid source of knowledge about consciousness. The function of reason is to understand intelligible relations between features of consciousness that make sense of the concrete world that we experience. Thus, the intelligibility of consciousness is wonderful because it helps to explain the presence of other wonderful things in human existence. It makes possible so many of the wonderful and worthwhile things that we experience. Through introspection we can obtain knowledge of some of the intrinsic properties of consciousness, and then through further reflection on these properties we can obtain a priori knowledge regarding the intelligible relations that hold among these properties.[58]

The Philosophy of Mind should focus its efforts on finding and articulating the intelligibility of the mind, but it has been distracted by reductive physicalism which solves the mind–body problem by reducing everything in the world including the mind to a physical or material phenomenon. Since it is difficult to relate a nonphysical mind to a physical body the solution is to reduce mental properties to physical properties. Those who oppose this view argue that there are nonreductive mental properties that are radically different from reductive physical properties and with their appearance something new appears in the world. This view ends up being dualist because these nonreductive mental properties are not physical. Langsam hopes to avoid this impasse by making the case that his particular view of nonreductionism is based on introspection rather than logical argument.[59]

Intelligibility in consciousness can only be discovered because the intrinsic nature of consciousness is fundamentally different from anything reductively physical and this intrinsic nature can ground consciousness.[60] Through introspection Langsam has learned that the mind has certain properties that are not reductive to physical properties and these properties are neither structural nor causal properties. "Our knowledge of nonreductive mental properties is based on empirical introspection, not a priori philosophical argument. Whether nonreductive mental properties exist in the world is something to be determined by investigating the world, not thinking about it."[61] Nonreductionism is an observational claim that is supported by introspection that informs one "that there are mental properties that are simple and categorical and thus nonreductive."[62]

Our observation of the world can take the form of perception or introspection, but in either case, these tell us something about the properties of certain objects. Through observation both sensory and phenomenal properties are related to the mind such that we can refer to them demonstratively and have propositional knowledge of their nature. The external world reveals itself to us in experience. Both experiences and thoughts represent things about the world, according to Langsam, but the world presents itself to us only through experience. Certain properties of experience are related to the properties of the world as we experience them and not merely to representational properties that may be in the mind.[63] When we experience the external world observable properties are not the only thing we experience, but we experience what appear to be independently existing objects.[64]

Langsam claims that some causal powers of conscious states are intelligible in that an intelligible explanatory connection exists between these causal powers and their underlying categorical properties. This connection is intelligible because it can be known a priori that certain categorical mental properties ground certain causal powers. Reflection on these mental properties can give us knowledge of the causal powers they intelligently support. "Our actions are often caused by the exercise of these intelligible causal powers, and we can thereby be said to act in intelligible ways," which suffuse our lives with intelligibility. According to Langsam there is such a thing as intelligible causation and he rejects the idea that all causation is brute causation.[65]

Experiences can intelligently produce knowledge. This is what it means to say that the world is known to us in experience. There is a connection between some intrinsic categorical property of experience and its causal power to produce knowledge. When the subject experiences an object, the subject can think and obtain knowledge about that object. An experiencing subject is conscious of the experienced object and its observable properties. Properties of the object are related to a subject such that the subject can focus his attention on them. The perceptual experience of a subject can intelligibly cause him or her to believe that there is indeed an external object that is present to his or her consciousness.[66]

Consciousness is required for rationality, and since only conscious states can be intelligible causes, it follows that conscious states are required to make attitudes toward propositions rational. A rational belief is one that is formed as a result of "sufficiently good" reasoning, and good reasoning is defined as reasoning that produces beliefs that are appropriately held meaning they are rational. If a subject is going to have reason for believing that some proposition is true, then that belief must be *intelligibly* connected to some relevant part of the external world. If a belief is to count as knowledge, it must be held for good reasons and, in this sense, is justified to constitute true knowledge. Such justification can make a belief rational. Beliefs must meet three standards to qualify as knowledge: (1) appropriateness, (2) correctness, and (3) correspondence, that is, the reason the belief is appropriate must also explain why the belief is correct.[67]

Desires are rational when we have reason to think they are desires for something that is valuable just as a belief is rational when there is reason to think that it is true. A desire is rational when the object of that desire is directed toward something that is good. If that desire is intelligibly caused it can provide reasons for action to satisfy that desire. Certain kinds of feeling have value as a value-laden world that is filled with good and bad things should be reacted to emotionally. As humans we are capable of being moved by things we encounter, and it is intelligible that we should react positively to good things and have negative feelings about bad things. Positive values ought to be celebrated, and the way value is celebrated is through our emotional responses. Pleasurable feelings give us perceptions of positive values and correspondingly painful feelings give us perceptions of negative values.[68]

In conclusion, Langsam argues that something new comes into being when consciousness appears in the world. "What is wonderful about consciousness is how it attaches itself to other properties in the world. It intelligibly relates us to the world and thereby enables the world to reveal itself to us."[69] It brings many new properties into the world and thus enriches our experience of the world around us that we relate to in various ways. Consciousness is different from everything else in the world. It does not separate us from the world but, rather, brings us into intimate relations with the world. The world is revealed to us through our experiences and feelings about the world. Through our beliefs and desires we form attitudes toward the world that give us an intimate stake in what the world is and what it could be under different circumstances.[70]

Owen Flanagan, the James B. Duke Professor of Philosophy at Duke University, identifies the "hard problem" within a science of the mind is to explain how mind is even possible in a material world. In other words, how can consciousness emerge out of neuronal activity? An even harder problem is to explain how meaning is possible in a material world. He states that "[m]eaning, if there is such a thing, is a matter of whether and how things add up in the greater scheme of things . . . Minimally it involves a truthful assessment of what living a finite human life adds up to." Consciousness exists, according to Flanagan, and it allows us to ask questions about the meaning of life, questions like "why and how, in the greater scheme of things, does any human life matter."[71]

The question of meaning requires more resources than the mind sciences and evolutionary biology can provide. The assumption or presupposition of these sciences is that we are finite biological organisms living in a material world. To answer the question of meaning in a material world requires philosophy, the history of religion, anthropology, sociology, and economics in addition to other fields of study. All of these disciplines are necessary to explain how we can make sense and find meaning for our lives given the fact that we are material beings living in a material world.[72]

Scientism is the doctrine that everything worth saying can be expressed in a scientific idiom. Scientism relies on the causal explanatory power of the scientific method and typically denies the truth of any theory that invokes nonnatural or supernatural causes or forces. Scientism takes the world that we live in and reduces it into a collection of mere objects. However, Flanagan makes the point that not everything worth expressing can or should be expressed scientifically. When it comes to art and music, for example, science comes up short in expressing what they are meant to convey. As Flanagan says,

> [t]he claim that not everything can be expressed scientifically is not a claim that art, music, poetry, literature, and religious experiences cannot in principle be accounted for scientifically, or that these productions involve magical or mysterious powers. Whatever they express, it is something perfectly human, but the appropriate idiom of expression is not a scientific one. The scientific idiom requires words and, often, mathematical formulas. Painting, sculpture, and music require neither. Indeed, they cannot in principle express what they express in words or mathematical formulas. Therefore, whatever they express is not expressible scientifically.[73]

Whether our lives have meaning depends in large part is how we participate in the spaces of art, science, technology, ethics, politics, and spirituality. Flanagan calls these six spaces the Spaces of Meaning. As social mammals we are required to find meaning in a culturally available Space of Meaning. Each of these spaces is a complex of theory and practice. "Whatever the spaces of meaning that make up some Space of Meaning are, they are the only locations available in which to locate meaning. But the nature, shape, and content of that Space of Meaning, and every other one that has ever existed, is a matter of historical contingency."[74] Flanagan defines what it is to live a meaningful life as follows:

> Meaningful human lives, we can now say, involve being moral, having true friends, and having opportunities to express our talents, to find meaningful work, to create and live among beautiful things, and to live cooperatively in social environments where we trust each other. If we have all these things, then we live meaningfully by any reasonable standard. If we have only some of them we live less meaningfully, and if we lack all these things, especially the first two, our life is meaningless.[75]

Obviously not everyone is able to attain all these things. Some might be motivated to discover their potential, but the social environment prevents them from getting the education and resources that might lead to a discovery of self. Or some may know what talents and interests they have, but there are no institutions in place for them to realize those talents and interests. If we believe that each person has intrinsic worth, says Flanagan, and each person deserves an equal chance to live a good life, then we should work to make the conditions that it takes to live a good life universally available. Certain socioeconomic conditions are needed for humans to flourish, which requires worldwide political reform.[76]

With regard to morals, Flanagan asks the question as to whether there can be a normative mind science. Can science tell us anything about what is good for us, and what is the right thing to do in a situation of moral conflict? Morals consist of habits of the heart, mind, and behavior and involve extraction of "good" practices from common practices that allow for smooth interpersonal relations, as well as for personal growth and fulfillment. Moral knowledge, however, is not a kind of "divine wisdom" that comes from God and involves the supernatural realm. Morality is a naturalistic phenomenon that can be studied naturalistically. Some kind of intuition is involved as feelings of approval and disapproval of certain practices just sort of emerge out of the situation, yet intuitions are not always reliable and need to be checked against a higher normative standard.

This leads Flanagan to deal with the issue of the coexistence of the scientific image of persons with spiritual and religious impulses, commitments, traditions, and institutions. Indeed he asks the question as to whether they can coexist at all. Spiritually and religion is usually interactive with art, poetry, music, and the visual arts, the aesthetic dimensions of life. These spaces evoke emotions of awe, solemnity, a sense of the holy, sacred, and precious. These emotions give meaning to life and keep it from becoming an objective and meaningless phenomena that only science can describe and understand. These spaces do not need a theistic foundation as naturalism, for Flanagan, is broad enough to make room for robust conceptions of the sacred, the spiritual, and the sublime and for moral excellence.[77] He describes naturalism as follows:

> [N]aturalism involves a commitment to a certain picture of the world and its operations—a metaphysic that is anti-supernaturalistic, and this is so because it considers certain epistemic approaches that warrant belief in supernatural posits—in this world, at least—to be discredited. It would be a mistake, however, to think that naturalism is derived solely from the scientific image. Science certainly played an important role in the ascendancy of naturalism. But so have the successes of certain methods of imagining and locating persons morally, spiritually, aesthetically, and politically that accept naturalism this far: They reject a common epistemic foe that involves grounding certain beliefs and practices on certain texts that are deemed to be the word of God.[78]

Many people who say that they are "spiritual" are not religious in any sense of the word. What they are saying is that they are trying to understand and develop a sense of connection to something that is transcendent, something that is greater and more comprehensive than their own selves. Meaning is sought in this manner and may be found and practiced in one's life, but these spiritual aspirations need not involve any theological beliefs. Spirituality involves "having coherent beliefs about the higher purpose and meaning of the universe; knowing where one fits within the larger scheme; having beliefs about the meaning of life that shape conduct and provide comfort."[79]

Every human being ought to have an equal opportunity to develop his or her talents and interests so as to live life in a fulfilling and meaningful manner. However, this development of talents and interests depends on the social context in which one is living. It depends on the recognition and on the availability of the means of advancing them. This includes the kinds of technological inventions that are available for the expression of one's talents and the kinds of things that are socially acceptable and are recognized as legitimate ways of expressing oneself within a given social context. Growth of the self does not take place in a vacuum but depends on the situation in which one is living.[80]

The most important question for Flanagan is whether humans can live in a manner that embodies universal love, compassion, and altruism not whether we can live up to unrealizable ideals. This kind of ethical conception, however, may be too demanding and psychologically or practically impossible. But the religious and ethical traditions Flanagan examines do not advocate any virtuous states of mind that are impossible to achieve. Happiness, flourishing, and meaning are ideals that go beyond one's own personal desires and are inclusive of all actual and future persons, as well as the Earth on which we live and our home in the larger cosmos. People can commit themselves to affirm this way of living and being, and according to Flanagan, that is "spirituality naturalized."[81]

The problem is still one of how an immaterial mind can cause the body to act and how the physical world can get information to such a mind. The dualist thesis remains alive and well as dualists insist an immaterial mind–body interaction somehow occurs and that there must be an explanation that accounts for this interaction between immaterial substances or properties and physical substances and properties. But dualism is not progressive in that no one has been able over the years to say anything intelligible about how this sort of interaction is possible. But the philosophical naturalist, who is equipped with (1) the Darwinian insight that we are fully embodied human beings, and (2) the neuropsychological insight that the brain keeps appearing as the most plausible site for "mind," has developed a progressive research program that Flanagan thinks has made "interaction" between a mind/brain and the rest of the body and the world intelligible.[82]

Mario Beauregard, an associate research professor at the Departments of Psychology and Radiology and the Neuroscience Research Center at the University of Montreal, believes vehemently that *the materialistic framework is not science*. He states that the paradigm of scientific materialism is based on a number of philosophical assumptions that come from classical physics. These are (1) the idea that only matter and energy exist in the universe what he calls *physicalism*; (2) the notion that complex things can be understood by reducing them to the interaction of their parts, or to simpler or more fundamental things what is known as *reductionism*; and (3) the thesis that scientists should investigate empirical facts in an objective manner or what is known as *objectivism*. Most scientists are not aware of

these assumptions and accept these ideas without question.[83]This materialistic outlook leads to what Beauregard calls a mind–brain identity theory,
which asserts that "mental events are created by, and are identical to, brain
events." Our sense of identity, beliefs and values, feelings, free will, and even
spiritual experiences are nothing more than electrical impulses and chemical
reactions in the brain.[84]

To counter this theory he cites numerous cases where the placebo effect,
which he defines as the ability to heal ourselves or alleviate pain by simply
believing in the treatment whether it is real or not, has clearly played a crucial role in treatments involving pills or injections. But it is also a factor in
surgical interventions where sham surgery has shown the power of the mind
over the body. The placebo effect is also evident in negative expectations
about one's own health as there is evidence to the effect that if one believes
that he or she is susceptible to heart attacks, this belief is itself a risk factor
for coronary death. The conclusion Beauregard draws from all these cases
is that what we believe in our minds "can significantly influence our experience of pain, the success of a surgery, even the outcome of a disease."[85]

He next discusses neurofeedback, which is a type of *biofeedback* where
real-time information is given to people about things like heart rhythm or
breathing so they can learn how to change certain aspects of the physical
functioning of their body to improve their health and performance. People
can actually use this information to produce at will certain desired physiological changes that persist even after the feedback is stopped. There are
many cases where neurofeedback has enabled the mind to control and
change certain aspects of the body.[86] The mind can also make changes in
the brain as the adult brain has been shown to be highly malleable and is
continually changing its structure and function by creating new neurons and
synaptic connections as well as reorganizing existing neuronal networks. He
presents evidence which shows that the brains of adults can be physically
changed by knowledge and that changes in thoughts, beliefs, and feelings
have the power to physically transform the brain as shown by neuroimaging
studies.[87]

With regard to hypnosis Beauregard believes that it can be a powerful tool
for harnessing the power of the mind to affect the way our brains and bodies function. Suggestions that are received by a person in a hypnotic state of
trance have been shown to reduce pain perception and even improve skin
conditions, allergies, and asthma. Such suggestions can alter the activity of
the brain, he claims, and lead to spectacular changes in the body and the
way it functions. These changes which seem to be produced by suggestions
from the hypnotist really depend on the mental activity of the patient.[88] He
goes on to say that

> [w]e are not, in fact, being controlled by hypnotic suggestion; rather,
> hypnosis can help us let down the normal barriers that prevent us from
> using the abilities that lay dormant within us. In the hypnotic state,

subjects seem to be able to access deeper levels of the mind. These deeper levels allow a connection with a larger intelligence hidden within us, which a much greater capacity than the normal waking mind to influence what is going on in the body.[89]

Beauregard then continues on to discuss psychic phenomena (psi for short) such as extrasensory perception (ESP) and psychokinesis (PK) and makes the claim that a growing number of scientists are accepting the reality of psi even though these phenomena are still considered to be "anomalies" because there are currently no theories in any science that can explain them convincingly.[90] Nonetheless, he claims that research suggests the existence of an interface between the objective *physical* world and the *subjective* psyche. He uses quantum theory as a possible explanation as it views the universe as fundamentally nonlocal: that particles and objects that appear to be isolated and separate are deeply intertwined or entangled regardless of their distance from each other. He refers to a researcher who thinks there is a possibility that the basic quantum fabric of reality connects everything including particles, organisms, minds, and brains into a single quantum system. Thus, the mind plays a fundamental role in nature, and the physical world and the psyche world are not radically separated.[91]

Near-death experiences and out-of-body experiences provide additional evidence for a nonmaterialistic perception of reality that does not depend on the senses of the physical body, that heightened mental functions can be experienced independently of the body, and thus, the mind transcends the bodily brain in some sense and operates independently of any material reality.[92] Finally Beauregard discusses mystical experiences and claims that studies show that such experiences can result in changes to a person's attitudes and behavior as well as worldviews, beliefs, values, relationships, and a sense of self. They are spiritual experiences that can provide a sense of purpose and meaning for the person who has such an experience. Mystical experiences have been reported throughout history and provide further evidence, claims Beauregard, that the mind and consciousness are fundamental features of existence and are closely interconnected with the physical world.[93]

In conclusion, what Beauregard is trying to do in this book is provide a scientific basis for the view that thoughts, beliefs, and emotions, things that are nonmaterial, can greatly influence what happens in our brains and bodies; that mental activity is not the same as brain activity; and that our minds and consciousness are a part of the reality we experience.[94] The materialistic worldview leads to a neglect of the subjective dimension of human experience and to a diminished importance given to the mind and consciousness creating a "severely distorted and impoverished understanding of humans and reality."[95] Stepping out of the materialist box enables scientists to explore new avenues of research related to psi phenomena, expanded and altered consciousness, and spiritual experiences. And most important, this new paradigm, as he calls it, emphasizes "a deep connection between our-selves and nature at large" and "promotes environmental awareness and the preservation of our biosphere."[96]

Finally, the role of minds and values in the quantum universe is discussed by Henry Stapp, who is a theoretical physicist at the University of Cali-fornia's Lawrence Berkeley Laboratory. Quantum mechanics according to Stapp, allows the consequences of decisions made by human subjects to enter into the laws governing the motion of matter. All observers and their acts of observation are parts of an evolving physically described universe. To leave mind and consciousness out of the causal loop and cling to the precepts of classical physics seems to be totally irrational. The physically described world is not a world of material substances but is rather a world of potentialities for future experiences.[97] According to Stapp,

> [t]he deepest human intuition is not the immediate grasping of the classical-physics-type character of the physical world. It is rather that one's own conscious subjective efforts can influence the experiences that follow. Any conception that makes this deep intuition an illusion is counterintuitive. Any conception of reality that cannot explain how our conscious efforts influence our bodily actions if problematic. What is actually deeply intuitive is the continually reconfirmed fact that our conscious efforts can influence certain kinds of experiential feedback. A putatively rational scientific theory needs at the very least to explain this connection in a rational way to be in line with our intuition.[98]

Heisenberg and the notion of probabilities that he introduced into the heart of observing nature argued that reality was not built out of matter, at least as matter was understood in classical physics. The probability function combines objective and subjective elements. It deals with statements about possibilities, although Stapp thinks *tendencies* would be a better word to use, and these statements are objective in that they do not depend on any observer. But the notion of probability also contains statements about our knowledge of the system, and these are subjective in that they are differ-ent for different observers. But perhaps "the most important change in the theory, vis-à-vis classical physics, was its injection of the thoughts and inten-tions of the human experimenter/observer into the physical dynamics."[99] As Stapp says,

> [i]n short, the quantum conceptualization is not *intrinsically* counterin-tuitive, problematic, or weird. It becomes these things only when viewed from a classical perspective that is *counterintuitive* because it, denies the causal efficacy of our intentional efforts, is *problematic* because it provides no logical foundations upon which a rational understanding of the occurrence of subjective experience could be built, and is *weird* because it leaves out the mental aspects of nature and chops the body of

nature into microscopic, ontologically separate parts that can communicate and interact only with immediate neighbours, thereby robbing both conglomerates and the whole of any possibility of fundamental wholeness or meaningfulness.[100]

A central feature of quantum mechanics is called the *observer effect*, which means that the observer, who is most likely a physicist, and the method used for observation are linked in that the results of the observation are influenced by the observer's intent. Thus, "the physical world cannot be fully understood without making reference to mind and consciousness . . . we must consider mind and consciousness if we are to reach a more adequate conception of nature and reality."[101]

Those with a materialistic view of reality do not, of course, agree that materialism has failed as an adequate conception of the universe and argue that eventually neuroscience will progress to the point where it can completely explain mind and consciousness. Belief in the materialist worldview allows scientists and philosophers to neglect the subjective dimension of human experience and downplay the importance of mind and consciousness. But and expanded view of nature allows for a deep interconnectedness between the mental world and the physical world. "This basic interconnectedness renders the mind capable of influencing various phenomena and events belonging to the physical world."[102]

Obviously, this problem of mind–body dualism is not going to be solved on these pages. But a sampling of how various philosophers and scientists have dealt with this problem can be instructive and help in understanding the scope of the problem.[103] Perhaps Descartes can be blamed for beginning this dualism between mind and body by starting with their separation at the outset of his philosophy. If we were to begin with a different ontological assumption, namely, that the body and mind are part of a whole entity we call the human being, and the separation is only necessary for analytical purposes then the whole dichotomy might disappear. But by giving ontological status to the parts, Descartes left us with this dualism. As stated by Philip Clayton, Ingraham Professor of Theology at Claremont School of Theology and professor of religion and Philosophy at Claremont Graduate University,

> Descartes could never solve the problem of the interaction of mind and body because he had defined them at the outset as two diametrically opposed substances with no common ground . . . Faced with this sort of ultimate dichotomy, all that remains is to center one's philosophical system on the one of the other. Descartes, still deeply influenced by the disembodied God of Western theism, made the (for him) obvious choice and placed all value upon he side of the mind, will, and rationality.[104]

If the mind–body problem cannot be resolved satisfactorily by an approach that reduces the mind to the brain by expanding on theories regarding operation of the brain and by new scientific methods of observation and experimentation, then science will have failed in its attempt to explain all of the world, in particular, how mental experience such as consciousness is created from the activities of what are apparently mindless nerve cells in interaction with each other in the brain. However, brain science is in its infancy and principles about how the brain processes information are not yet agreed upon. Thus, it is too early to say that the scientific approach to resolving the mind–body problem has failed. But it is as least uncertain whether such scientific progress will ultimately lead to a solution.[105] According to Andrew Bowie, professor of philosophy and German at Royal Holloway at the University of London,

> [t]he contemporary debate on, for example, whether the 'mind is the brain' seems to generate contradictory stances in such a way that adjudicating between claims does not lead anywhere which does not itself involve further contradictions . . . If the mind is just the brain and the brain is a 'machine' as it would appear to be from some versions of neuroscience, this gives us no purchase on the dimensions of mental life involving self-determination, deliberation, creative imagination, and so on. The question that generates the contradictions is how to see the world in terms of these two incompatible accounts.[106]

Thomas Nagel, University Professor of Philosophy and Law Emeritus at New York University, thinks it might be possible one day to understand how the brain causes consciousness, but it would require a total revolution in our way of thinking about reality and in our conception of scientific explanation because given our present apparatus we cannot conceive how subjective, qualitative inner experiences could arise from third-person neuronal phenomena.[107] Perhaps, then, a different understanding of science will aid in our ability to understand how something like consciousness can have a reality in our scientific world and how it is an important dimension of experience that cannot be ignored or cast aside as nonmaterial and nonobjective and thus having no standing as a real entity in our world.[108] According to Keith Ward, Emeritus Regius Professor of Divinity at Oxford University,

> [c]onsciousness is not just a new form of relationship between complex physical systems. Apprehension and understanding, and intelligent action for the sake of realizing some unvisaged but not yet existent goal, are properties, not of physically measurable entities, but of a distinctive sort of reality that is not material . . . such things as conscious intention and understanding have real existential statue. They are irreducible and distinctive forms of reality. They are kinds of "stuff" that are not reducible to the properties of physical elements such as electrons. Yet they come into existence at the end of a many-billion-year-long process of development from simple physical elements . . . it is consciousness that apprehends

and appreciates value. Only intelligent consciousness can have a reason for bringing about some state, and that reason would precisely be the actualization and appreciation of some as yet merely possible value . . . Consciousness, as we know it, is capable of conceiving possibilities as well as apprehending actualities, and of making possibilities actual for a reason.[109]

Consciousness needs material objects in order to operate, but the material stuff needs to be interpreted by consciousness to have meaning. Thus, mind and body seem to be integrated with each other, and consciousness could be seen as an emergent aspect or emergent property of an otherwise naturalistic system that cannot be reduced to brain functions. Even Descartes, who is usually blamed for mind–body dualism, is reported to have said, "I am not just lodged in my body like a pilot in his ship, but I am intimately united with it, and so confused and intermingled with it that I and my body compose, as it were, a single whole."[110]

Notes

1 Niels Henrik Gregersen, "God, Matter, and Information: Towards a Stoicizing Logos Christianity," in Paul Davies and Niels Henrik Gregersen, eds., *Information and the Nature of Reality: From Physics to Metaphysics* (New York: Cambridge University Press, 2010), 320.

2 Ibid., 159. Italics in original.

3 Ibid., 159–161. Descartes postulated that this connection took place in the pineal gland, a small organ located in the middle of the brain. This gland was supposedly well adapted to transfer movements from the body to the mind and from the mind to the body. This explanation proved to be unsatisfactory.

4 See Lucretius, "Does Neuroscience Refute Ethics?" *Mises Daily Article*, August 24, 2005, 1–7; Sharon Begley, "The Biology of Love—Not," *Newsweek*, February 18, 2008, 53; Jeffrey Kluger, "Why We Love," *Time*, January 28, 2008, 55–60; Carl Zimmer, "Romance Is an Illusion," *Time*, January 28, 2008, 98–99; Paul J. Zak, "The Neurobiology of Trust," *Scientific American*, June, 2008, 88–95; and Christof Koch and Susan Greenfield, "How Does Consciousness Happen?" *Scientific American*, October, 2007, 76–83.

5 Ibid., 36.

6 "[A] universe whose essential characteristic is fixed order and connection has no place for unique and individual existences, no place for novelty and genuine change and growth." John Dewey, *The Quest for Certainty* (New York: Capricorn Books, 1960), 209.

7 "The rise of new science in the seventeenth century laid hold upon the general culture in the next century. Its popular effect was not great, but its influence upon the intellectual elite, even upon those who were not themselves engaged in scientific inquiry, was prodigious. The enlightenment . . . testified to the widespread belief that at last light had dawned, that dissipation of the darkness of ignorance, superstition, and bigotry was at hand, and the triumph of reason was assured—for reason was the counterpart in man of the laws of nature science was disclosing." John Dewey, "Time and Individuality," in *The Later Works, 1925–1953*, Vol. 14, Jo Ann Boydston, ed. (Carbondale and Edwardsville, IL: Southern Illinois University Press, 1988), 100.

8 Matthew Fox and Rupert Sheldrake, *Natural Grace: Dialogues on Creation, Darkness, and the Soul in Spirituality and Science* (New York: Doubleday, 1997), 15–19.
9 Dale Jacquette, *The Philosophy of Mind: The Metaphysics of Consciousness* (New York: Continuum, 2009), 5–6.
10 Deepak Chopra and Leonard Mlodinow, *War of the Worldviews: Science vs. Spirituality* (New York: Harmony Books, 2011), 183.
11 Richard Holmes, *The Age of Wonder: How the Romantic Generation Discovered the Beauty and Terror of Science* (New York: Pantheon Books, 2008), 309.
12 Ibid., 313–314.
13 Ibid., 315.
14 Ibid., 317.
15 Ibid., 319–320.
16 Ibid., 321–322.
17 Ibid., 325–334.
18 Jacquette, *The Philosophy of Mind*.
19 Ibid., 49–52.
20 Ibid., 3.
21 Ibid., 79.
22 Ibid., 4.
23 Ibid., 65.
24 Ibid., 4.
25 Ibid.
26 Ibid., 23.
27 Ibid., 23–24.
28 Ibid., 35.
29 Ibid., 136.
30 Ibid., 144.
31 Ibid., 240.
32 Ibid., 241–246.
33 Ibid., 261–263.
34 Ibid., 270.
35 Ibid., 271–272.
36 Ibid., 271.
37 John R. Searle, *Mind: A Brief Introduction* (New York: Oxford University Press, 2004), 3.
38 Ibid., 7.
39 Ibid., 9–10.
40 Ibid., 29–30.
41 Ibid., 72.
42 Ibid., 34.
43 Ibid., 78–79.
44 Ibid., 79.
45 Ibid., 81–82.
46 Ibid., 83–86.
47 Ibid., 88–89.
48 Ibid., 115–118.
49 Ibid., 121–122.
50 Ibid., 140–141.
51 Ibid., 146–147.
52 Ibid., 146.
53 Ibid., 147. Searle, however, provides the following caveat: "There are, of course, very difficult problems about how it actually works in the neurobiology, and for the most part we do not yet know the solutions to these problems." Ibid., 147.

54 Ibid., 151–155.
55 Ibid., 164.
56 Ibid., 200.
57 Ibid., 208.
58 Harold Langsam, *The Wonder of Consciousness: Understanding the Mind through Philosophical Reflection* (Cambridge, MA: MIT Press, 2011), 3–5.
59 Ibid., 10–17.
60 Ibid., 14.
61 Ibid., 19.
62 Ibid., 21.
63 Ibid., 32–47.
64 Ibid., 65.
65 Ibid., 73–74.
66 Ibid., 79–95.
67 Ibid., 111–140.
68 Ibid., 146–176.
69 Ibid., 185.
70 Ibid., 188.
71 Owen Flanagan, *The Really Hard Problem: Meaning in a Material World* (Cambridge MA: The MIT Press, 2007), xi–xii.
72 Ibid., xii–xiii.
73 Ibid., 23.
74 Ibid., 37–39.
75 Ibid., 58.
76 Ibid., 58–59.
77 Ibid., 187–190.
78 Ibid., 194.
79 Ibid., 199–201.
80 Ibid., 201–202.
81 Ibid., 212–219.
82 Ibid., 221–222, n 3.
83 Mario Beauregard, *Brain Wars* (New York: HarperOne, 2012), 6.
84 Ibid., 12.
85 Ibid., 17–41.
86 Ibid., 43–64.
87 Ibid., 65–88.
88 Ibid., 109–132.
89 Ibid., 132.
90 Ibid., 137.
91 Ibid., 154–155.
92 Ibid., 157–182.
93 Ibid., 183–205.
94 Ibid., 207–209.
95 Ibid., 211–212.
96 Ibid., 214.
97 Henry Stapp, "Minds and Values in the Quantum Universe," in Paul Davies and Niels Henrik Gregersen, eds., *Information and the Nature of Reality: From Physics to Metaphysics* (New York: Cambridge University Press, 2010), 104–110.
98 Ibid., 112.
99 Ibid., 113.
100 Ibid., 116.
101 Beauregard, *Brain Wars*, 201–211.
102 Ibid., 211–213.

103   An article by Paul Bloom, a professor of psychology and cognitive science at Yale University, should also be mentioned. Bloom states that Aristotle's definition of man as a rational being has taken quite a beating from scholars who believe in the neural basis of mental life, where rational thinking and free choice are illusions. Thoughts and actions are the product of our brains, these scholars hold, and what goes on in our brains is determined by the laws of physics; there is no room for choice. But Bloom claims that this conception does not square with what we experience in our daily lives. "It certainly *feels* as though we make choices, as though we're responsible for our actions. The idea that we're entirely physical beings clashes with the age-old idea that the body and mind are distinct . . . Scientists have reached no consensus as to precisely how physical events give rise to conscious experience, but few doubt that our minds and brains are one and the same." See Paul Bloom, "The War on Reason," *The Atlantic*, March 2014, 64–70. See also Helmut Wautischer, ed., *Ontology of Consciousness: Percipient Action* (Cambridge MA: MIT Press, 2008), for a series of articles on the phenomenon of consciousness by various authors.

104   Philip Clayton, "Unsolved Dilemmas: The Concept of Matter in the History of Philosophy and in Contemporary Physics," in Paul Davies and Niels Henrik Gregersen, eds., *Information and the Nature of Reality: From Physics to Metaphysics* (New York: Cambridge University Press, 2010), 45.

105   John G. Taylor, "Mind-Body Problem: New Approaches." www.scholarpedia. org/article/Mind-body_problem:_New_approaches, accessed July 17, 2013.

106   Andrew Bowie, *Adorno and the Ends of Philosophy* (Cambridge, UK: Polity Press, 2013), 6.

107   Searle, *Mind*, 102. See Thomas Nagel, *The View from Nowhere* (Oxford: Oxford University Press, 1986); and Thomas Nagel, *Mind and Cosmos: Why the Materialist Neo-Darwinian Conception of Nature Is almost Certainly False* (New York: Oxford University Press, 2012).

108   By excluding the properties of mind—consciousness, intention—from the world it is studying, in order to be free of dogma and unverifiable speculation, hasn't science therefore excluded the mind as a possible object of study—no matter what is may discover about the brain?" See Jacob Needleman, *An Unknown World: Notes of the Meaning of the Earth* (New York: Tarcher/ Penguin, 2012), 130.

109   Keith Ward, "God as the Ultimate Informational Principle," in Paul Davies and Niels Henrik Gregersen, eds., *Information and the Nature of Reality: From Physics to Metaphysics* (New York: Cambridge University Press, 2010), 287–290.

110   Ibid., 295–297.

12 Science and Nature

There is no doubt that science has had an enormous impact on modern societies and that the technological applications of scientific discoveries have made our lives better. Science has enabled us to understand more and more aspects of our world and given us the ability to manipulate the world to deal with problems with which we are faced. We, by and large, turn to science for answers to questions about our natural world and increasingly for answers to questions about human behavior. While there are still elements of mythology operative in many cultures including our own, science has largely replaced the mythological worldview and influences how we think about all aspects of our world as a previous chapter attempted to illustrate. Science is, by and large, accepted as the way to get at the truth about our world through it rigorous methodologies and self-correcting process of inquiry.

Problems with Modern Science

Science has been a major contributor to the separation of humans from each other and in particular to the separation of humans from nature. With regard to the latter, science with its view of nature as something that can be completely objectified and is independent of human consciousness created a worldview that is embedded in all of us in that we grow up with a view of nature that is consistent with this worldview. Nature can be manipulated in our interests and brought under the control of science and technology to shape it and use it for purposes of continued economic growth. It is our manifest destiny to pave over every piece of land we can to build highways or develop every unused portion of our cities to build a building on. Nature needs developing, and this continued usage of land and growth of the economy is always considered to be a good thing that promotes human flourishing.

Many scientists have had a difficult time dealing with quantum mechanics and its view of human interaction with nature, the view that we are not just spectators observing an independent nature but that our efforts to measure and determine how nature works enters in to what we observe about nature. It was impossible for some to believe that nature was affected by our actions of observation and that we needed to take this into account with regard to what we accepted as true knowledge of nature. For example, in a book about Max Planck, the author Brandon R. Brown, professor of physics at the University of San Francisco, makes the following statement about Planck and his view of nature:

> But in that year [1926], he [Planck] publicly announced that, whatever came next from the new theory [quantum mechanics], physicists could rest assured that the bedrock foundation of physics stood firm. Namely, they could still rely on experiments that took a true measure of [the] natural world, without affecting it. That is, the exact wording of their laboratory questions would not affect the answers nature uttered in reply. Physics had long relied on the notion that particles were being observed discretely, like so many animals in an enormous nature preserve. With experiments functioning as silent telephoto lenses, we could count on observing a particle's natural state. But would the new brand of quantum theory render particle more like animals in a zoo, with behavior inseparable from the confines of the experiment? Could humans really trust what they observed as fundamental reality or were they looking at byproduct of their intrusions. 1926 Planck reassured everyone that physics rules out that worry, "from the very beginning." He couldn't have been more wrong, and his timing couldn't have been worse.[1]

Although Planck may have seen the writing on the wall, he was motivated to double down on his fundamental beliefs about science, humans, and the natural world and assured his audiences that no matter what quantum theory said, scientists would not have to worry subjects influencing experiments, meaning that scientists were, in fact, observing a nature that would behave as if nobody was watching. He made the claim that picturing a universe where data are collected without altering the system that was under study "is the basic presupposition of any sort of scientific knowledge." Brown goes on to say that Planck must have at times viewed Heisenberg and his gang as barbarians who threatened to ransack science back to darker times.[2] He claims that Planck and Einstein held the same view of science and causality:

> Planck and Einstein had both come to hold sacred reverence for the concept of causality. In Planck's words, causality is, "the fact that natural phenomena invariably occur according to the rigid sequence of cause and effect. This is an indispensable postulate of all scientific research." But some believed (and believe to varying degrees) that the probabilistic aspect of quantum mechanics deals a great blow to causality. Planck and Einstein trusted a universe where experiment A provided result B,

reliably and definitely. But Heisenberg rejected such outdated notions. "When one wishes to calculate the future from the present," he said, "one can only get statistical results." Planck saw the younger generation as resigning themselves to ignorance, and he must have heard in their statements echoes from Ernst Mach and the positivists.[3]

Scientists like Planck and even Einstein wanted to keep nature separate from humans, where nature had a completely independent reality and the laws that governed the universe were absolute and not probabilistic in their operation. Even the social sciences that dealt with human nature believed they were observing human nature in some objective manner, where the nature of their experiments or observations did not affect the outcome. Human nature itself could be objectified and observed as a spectator looking for regularities that could be used for predictive purposes. But this kind of view in challenged by quantum theory, which sees scientific findings as probabilistic rather than absolute, which leads to a different understanding of what scientists are doing. According to Stephen Shapin, a professor of sociology at the University of California at San Diego,

> [s]cience acquired its factual and explanatory power within a context that was "congruent" to those facts and explanations. It will be necessary, therefore, to look at science as a system of thought adequate to a certain historical epoch; try to separate ourselves from the common impression that it is an absolute, transcultural truth.[4]

The major problem of science in our contemporary world is when science becomes a metaphysical dogmatism that makes claims about absolute and complete knowledge and is considered to be the only true source of knowledge of the world in which we live. Such dogmatism holds that our lived experience in the world is of little or no value because what we observe in the world during the course of our daily lives is mere appearance. While we may observe color and smell something and sense how something feels to the touch, these are only appearances. The true reality behind these appearances is the waves and particles that make up these sensory illusions. While we may observe human behavior with its moods and emotions, these are only appearances and the realities behind these observations are the chemicals and neurons that go to make up our bodies and determine our behavior. It is when science becomes dogmatic and makes such metaphysical claims that it becomes a problem in contemporary society and is subject to philosophical inquiry as to whether such claims are valid. As stated by Maurice Merleau-Ponty, a French philosopher and phenomenologist, in *The World of Perception*,

> [t]he question which modern philosophy asks in relation to science is not intended to contest its right to exist or to close off any particular

avenue to its inquires. Rather, the question is whether science does, or ever could, present us with a picture of the world which is complete, self-sufficient and somehow closed in upon itself, such that there could be no longer any meaningful questions outside this picture. It is not a matter of denying or limiting the extent of scientific knowledge, but rather of establishing whether it is entitled to deny or rule out as illusory all forms of inquiry that do not start out from measurements and comparisons and, by connecting particular causes with particular consequences, and end up with laws such as those of classical physics.[5]

In the classical scientific worldview, our ordinary lived experience becomes disconnected from knowledge and is considered to be purely subjective in nature. Real knowledge is the building up of a storehouse of so-called objective facts gleaned from scientific studies based upon a spectator theory of knowledge where the researcher is only an observer of nature. We can't learn anything from our lived experience because it cannot be quantified and studied scientifically and is, therefore, useless for making predictions about future behavior or for learning anything significant about the world in which we live and move and have our being.

Science relegates ordinary experience to the subjective realm, where it can be ignored as having no relevance to our knowledge of the world. Yet the knowledge that most people have about the world comes through this lived experience. This experience teaches us things about the world in which we live and this knowledge helps us navigate our way through life's trials and tribulations. For most people, this knowledge is just as important as scientific knowledge is to the scientist. Science is but one type of experience that gives us a certain kind of knowledge that is extremely useful for certain things. Indeed, experience is the foundation for all scientific activity. But scientific experience is by no means the whole story about nature and human behavior, even though it may have a privileged position with respect to knowledge. It all depends on what kind of knowledge, as John Dewey, the American philosopher who taught at the University of Chicago states, is relevant to the task at hand:

> Thus "science," meaning physical knowledge, became a kind of sanctuary. A religious atmosphere, not to say an idolatrous one, was created. "Science" was set apart; its findings were supposed to have a privileged relation to the real. In fact, the painter may know colors as well as the physicist; the poet may know stars, rain and clouds as well as the meteorologist; the statesman, educator and dramatist may know human nature as truly as the professional psychologist; the farmer may know soils and plants as truly as the botanist and mineralogist. For the criterion of knowledge lies in the method used to secure consequences and not in metaphysical conceptions of the nature of the real.[6]

Thus, it is not going to help the painter do a better job if he or she knows something about physics and how it breaks down color into its component parts. This knowledge is not relevant to the job he or she is trying to accomplish and the consequences that are trying to be attained like, creating a pleasing effect in a particular room by choosing certain colors that will create this outcome. The same is true for the poet, the educator, or the farmer. What knowledge is important to them depends on the consequences they are trying to bring about. They are not interested in metaphysical claims about what is really real; what is real to them is what works to bring about the consequences they desire. They are interested in certain qualities of the things that they are dealing with that will help them to attain their goals and objectives. These qualities are as real to them as the qualities that are of interest to scientists even though scientists might consider them to be secondary qualities that are subjective in nature.

One of the most persistent problems created by modern science is what to do with qualities such as color, sound, smell, taste, and the like, qualities that we encounter every day in ordinary experience. Scientific definitions and descriptions leave no room for qualities as it is believed that the business of knowledge is to penetrate into the inner being of objects. Qualities were thus held to be subjective existing only in the consciousness of individuals and have no objective reality. However, the discovery that absolute space and time do not exist but are relative and relational showed that the primary qualities of solidity, mass, size, and so on are no more inherent properties of scientific objects than the secondary qualities of odors, sounds, and colors. Both are relational and changing.[7] As Steven Shapin writes,

> [p]rimary qualities were those that really belonged to the object in itself: its parts' shape, size, and motion. They were called primary (or sometimes "absolute") because no object, or its constituents, could be described without them. Secondary qualities—redness, sweetness, warmth, and so on—were derived from the state of an object's primary qualities. The primary caused (and was held to explain) the secondary . . . Only some of the ideas of our bodies might now be treated as objective—that is, corresponding to the nature of things themselves—and these would include our ideas of bodies as having certain shapes, sizes, and motions. However, other experiences and ideas would now have to be regarded as subjective—the result of how our sensory apparatus actively processes impressions deriving from the real, primary realm. Yet the rose of common experience is experienced not as an ordered aggregate of qualities but as itself: red, roughly circular, sweet smelling, three inches across, etc. The distinction between primary and secondary qualities, just like the Copernican view of the world, drove a wedge between the domain of philosophical legitimacy and that of common sense. Micromechanical reality took precedence over common experience, and subjective experience was severed from accounts

of what objectively existed. Our actual sensory experience, we were instructed, offered no reliable guide to how the world really was.[8]

This distinction took human experience of secondary qualities out of the realm of the real and primary, and ordinary human experience was not seen as a valid approach to reality. What was really real was what science discovered through its methods of inquiry which were believed to be free of any human or subjective influence and only thus could objective truth be ascertained. Ordinary human experience was thus considered to be a lower form of knowledge, or not knowledge at all, but merely subjective impressions that had no validity as far as real knowledge of the world was concerned. The split between primary and secondary qualities mirrors the split between the objective and subjective world, with the former treated as having an independent existence that could only be discovered through the methods of science and the latter considered to be conditional and dependent on the observer.

The difference between a scientific approach to reality and that of ordinary experience is to some extent a difference between theories of knowledge. Experiential knowledge is connected to the everyday affairs of humans and serves the purposes of the ordinary individual who is not interested in a specialized intellectual pursuit, but instead wants some kind of working connection with his or her immediate environment. This kind of knowledge is depreciated, if not despised, according to Dewey, and is considered to be purely utilitarian lacking in any scientific significance. Rational knowledge, on the other hand, is considered to be something that touches reality in an ultimate and intellectual fashion to terminate in theoretical insight into the workings of nature and not debased by application in behavior. Reason used in this manner is concerned with general principles and universals, which are above the welter of the concrete details involved with living in the world.[9]

Science gets hold of nature through a certain kind of method that involves reductionism and quantification along with the other characteristics mentioned in a previous chapter. But other experiences with nature may be equally important in certain circumstances to understand what the world is about and dealing with it in an appropriate manner. Despite its enormous success in the contemporary world, science does have limits to its ability to grasp and understand nature. It only understands that part of nature that can be fit into a scientific framework. What does not fit is left out of consideration as far as real knowledge is concerned. But in doing so science leaves behind a great deal of the richness that exists in nature and our experience with it and does not deal with any moral considerations regarding our responsibility to each other and for the world in which we live.

The scientific approach to nature splits it apart with its reductionistic method and its need to create discretes that can be measured and quantified so that nature can be manipulated. The problems that such a worldview poses for our understanding of the world in which we live can only be dealt with by a new philosophy that undercuts the dichotomies that science creates and presents alternative characteristics of science that leads to a different understanding of what science is doing. These problems cannot be addressed by the sciences themselves because every science is hopelessly trapped in its own worldview. They cannot be dealt with by a theory of everything that attempts to put the parts that science has created back together in some kind of overarching view that unifies the parts because the whole is more than the sum of the parts.[10] They cannot be solved by trying to find the basic building blocks of the universe because such a search assumes that reality is linear the same as did the medieval theologians who argued for the existence of God as first cause of everything.

What seems to be needed is some kind of a philosophy that is not based on the traditional reductionistic and atomistic assumptions of science but instead is a holistic philosophy that is relational in nature so as to capture relations between humans and nature in a nonmechanistic and noninstrumental manner. This philosophy must have a language structure that can get at a holistic relational view of nature and express it in a way that can be grasped by people rooted in atomic individualism. It must present a new way of looking at the world that is different from the scientific worldview and yet does not reject the knowledge that can be discovered by the scientific approach. It must treat ordinary experience as a form of knowledge that is useful for certain purposes. It must also bring the moral dimension into focus and show how morality is an essential part of all human experience and cannot be compartmentalized into a mere subjective experience that has no objective reality and therefore no validity.

Pragmatism and Science

Classical American Pragmatism is a uniquely American philosophy that attempts to do these things. It is not claimed that this philosophy is *the* answer to the problems of science but only that it offers a unique and different way of looking at science and what it is doing. It overcomes many of the self-defeating dichotomies that science has created and tries to preserve the unity that exists prior to any attempt by science to reduce the world to manageable categories that can be investigated by the scientific method. While it has some similarities to other philosophical movements such as existentialism and phenomenology, it is a more robust and comprehensive philosophy that encompasses the essential ideas of these philosophies and goes beyond them to open up new avenues of thinking.[11]

Pragmatism as a philosophical movement must not be confused with the popular use of the word to refer to the sort of practical approach to life's problems that is seen to be a critical part of the American character. Pragmatism as used here as nothing to do with this "pragmatic" approach that one often encounters in this country. The development of Pragmatism as a distinctive philosophy represents a historical period in American philosophy that spans the writings of Pragmatism's five major contributors:

Charles Peirce, William James, John Dewey, C. I. Lewis, and George Herbert Mead. These philosophers created what is called Classical American Pragmatism.

At the heart of American Pragmatism is a philosophic spirit, a philosophic pulse, enlivening a unique philosophic vision that, though brought to life in a particular period through diverse specific doctrines, is yet not confined within the limits of that period or those specific doctrines. Statements made about American Pragmatism in these pages may not always be found in the writings of the Classical American Pragmatists in the precise form in which they are stated though they are inspired by what is in these writings and are intended to capture and further the spirit of the Pragmatic approach. For this approach is more than just an interesting intellectual exercise but has vital importance for understanding ourselves and the world in which we live and offers guidance in our choices for the future we are creating.[12]

Classical American Pragmatism offers a way of understanding science and the scientific worldview that undercuts the fact-value distinction that poses a problem for ethics and the traditional dichotomies between subjective and objective and absolute and relative, dichotomies that reappear again and again in discussions of science and philosophy and appear to be irresolvable. It involves a different approach to understanding what science is doing and what it means to "think scientifically." While Pragmatism embraces science and focuses on scientific method, it rejects scientific dogmatism and the claim that science provides the only way to get at the truth of what is real about our world.

The philosophy of Pragmatism arose in part as a reaction to the modern worldview regarding the nature of science and the scientific object. Such an approach based largely on the presuppositions of a spectator theory of knowledge led to the view that scientific knowledge provided the literal description of objective fact and excluded our lived qualitative experience as providing access to the natural universe. This worldview resulted in a quantitatively characterized universe and the atomicity of discrete individual units that are related to each other through mechanistic laws or some mechanistic process. This, in turn, led to the alienation of humans from nature and a radical dehumanizing of nature. Nature as objectified justified nature as an object of value-free human manipulation.[13]

The human being was saved from being reduced to an atomistic object by being truncated into a dualism of mind and matter. The human body was a part of this atomistic and mechanistic nature but mind was considered to be "outside" of nature and beyond the realm of scientific study. Such a view, however, was not amenable to the emerging sciences of human behavior and eventually the human being as a whole, including the mind, became understood as part of this view of nature. As a result, humans, like atoms, were understood in terms of isolated, discrete entities that interact with each other through mechanistic relationships. Humans and their behavior were "reduced" to the mechanistic atomism of nature as characterized by Newtonian physics. The social and behavioral sciences as they developed thus became reductionistic in nature and shared these features of the physical sciences.[14]

A deep-seated philosophical tendency that is completely rejected by Pragmatism is the acceptance of this framework of Cartesian dualism. Humans are within nature, not outside of it, and inexplicably linked to nature. However, they are not reducible to nature and their behavior cannot be solely understood in a quantitative and atomistic manner that is no longer human but mechanistic and deterministic. The Pragmatic approach is naturalistic in that humans are within nature, but nature is not the atomistic and mechanistic universe of the traditional scientific worldview. What is involved is a more holistic understanding of nature where humans are an essential part of the naturalistic process and cannot be separated or abstracted out of this process. As Larry Hickman, a Dewey scholar who is director of the Center for Dewey Studies and professor of philosophy at Southern Illinois University at Carbondale writes,

> [f]or the bulk of philosophy in its modern period, nature was thought to be a vast machine. Living in the shadow of Darwin as he did, Dewey rejected the metaphor of the machine and replaced it with the organism. But even to those who have transcended the metaphor of world-as-machine there is still the fact of machine and the problem of how to relate to them. A machine can be contemplated as something finished and its workings discovered and admired. Further, it can be examined as something complete but in need of occasional repair. Or it can be treated as something ongoing, unstable, and provisional—as a tool to be used for enlarging transactions of self and society with environing conditions. It was Dewey's contention that the discussions of the nature of the world-as-machine in the seventeenth and eighteenth centuries were primarily focused on the first two of these attitudes. Of course each of these three possibilities involves some level of interaction with nature. But it is only with the third that there comes to be a genuine transaction with nature, awareness of such transaction, and inclusion of that awareness with the metatheories of science.[15]

Pragmatism is concerned with a philosophy of experience in attempting to broaden our conception of knowledge to include ordinary lived experience. Such experiential knowledge is practical rather than abstract; it does not deal with universal abstract laws and theories, even though these may underlie such experience. These laws and theories are implicit rather than explicit, and they are not necessarily available or relevant to practitioners. Ordinary experience is specialized and related to a particular time and place. It is contextual and exists for a particular purpose. It cannot be universalized to all time and places or generalized beyond the particular context in which the experience takes place.[16]

Abstractions, according to Pragmatism, do not belong to a metaphysical or ontological order that is superior to concrete experience. This view of experience goes against a long tradition of Western philosophy that began with Plato, who treated abstractions as metaphysical entities. For Dewey, abstractions are not ends in themselves but instead are tools for developing new meanings that can then be related to concrete experience. Abstraction is always involved in inquiry, as hypotheses are developed to guide inquiry. Experimentation maintains the relationship between the abstract and concrete, as it is through experimentation that the abstract is determined to have succeeded or failed and proves to be useful or not in the course of ongoing, concrete human experience.[17]

Experience must be free from constraints such as norms, ideals, theologies, prejudices, and other constraints that are used to regulate experience from "outside" of the experience itself and must be allowed to develop on its own account. Experience, then, in the pragmatic sense, does not have to conform to supernatural, ideological, or transcendental ideals or norms. Experience itself is capable of generating the norms and ideals that allow that experience to grow and develop.[18] Experience is not to be shaped and interpreted by anything outside experience itself, as experience must be allowed to develop as it will and be allowed to follow its own internal norms and ideals.

Pragmatism questions virtually all the assumptions governing what might be called the "mainstream" philosophical tradition and the kinds of alternatives to which they give rise. It offers novel solutions to the assumptions, alternatives, dilemmas, and impasses this tradition has reached. These solutions cannot be understood as an eclectic synthesizing of traditional alternatives but must be seen as an entirely new approach to philosophical problems. As Mead well warns in a statement that is echoed in various ways throughout the writings of the Classical American Pragmatists, "[t]here is an old quarrel between rationalism and empiricism which can never be healed as long as either sets out to tell the whole story of reality. Nor is it possible to divide the narrative between them"[19] What is needed is an entirely new approach that avoids these impasses.

The remainder of this chapter utilizes the vision offered by Classical American Pragmatism as a conceptual framework for rethinking science and the issues raised by the scientific worldview. The paradigmatic novelty of Pragmatism weaves its way through fundamental issues facing American society, undercutting old alternatives and offering constructive new ways of thinking about issues and advancing beyond traditional alternatives. Such a vision can best be brought to light not through the doctrines of any one of the Pragmatists but through the collective corpus of their writings. In what follows, then, the text roams freely through this collective corpus to clarify and makes use of its common conceptual framework.[20]

Pragmatism and the Scientific Method

The language of science is quantitative as even the social sciences, such as economics and political science, have become more quantitative in recent decades. However, what unifies the sciences is not a reduction of their content to a quantitative calculative language and mathematical laws, which underlie the subject area they are trying to understand. From the perspective of Pragmatism, what unifies the sciences is the method by which they gain an understanding of the subject matter with which each science is concerned. Scientific method is practiced by the scientist no matter what his or her field of endeavor. It is what the scientist does that is the focus of attention in Pragmatism, not what the scientist finds as a result of his or her activities.

While there is a great deal of debate about what exactly constitutes scientific method and most would probably agree that there is no one method that can be identified as "the" scientific method, pragmatism nevertheless holds that it is possible to identify a general method of inquiry that can be termed "scientific." This method involves repeatability, falsifiability, transparency, and objectivity. This general method is different from methods of authority or a priori reasoning and is a self-correcting process. This method of inquiry rejects the notion of "absolute" and "timeless" truths and treats ideals and hypotheses as tools that may be altered when confronted with concrete experience.[21] Thinking and beliefs should be experimental, not absolutistic.

A proper understanding of scientific method shows that the nature into which the human organism is placed contains the qualitative fullness revealed in lived experience and that a full grasp of nature is not a mere passive assimilation of data to fit a preconceived theory but is rather a creative activity within nature. The human being is embedded within nature, and neither human activity, in general, nor human knowledge can be separated from the fact that human beings are natural organisms dependent on a natural environment. The human organism and the nature within which it is located are both rich with the qualities, values, and meanings of our everyday experience.[22]

While Pragmatism is concerned with scientific method as a particular kind of human activity, this does not mean that it ignores the findings of science and their import for human existence. Pragmatism pays careful attention to these findings and is influenced in its philosophical claims by the findings of the various sciences. However, Pragmatism's concern with scientific method is one thing, and its attention to the findings of the various sciences achieved by the general method of science is something quite different. These two realms should not be confused as it is the method of science that provides the key to Pragmatic thinking. What, then, does a Pragmatist find when examining scientific methodology and focusing on the lived experience of scientists rather than on the objectivities they present as their findings?

Looking at the very first stage of scientific inquiry, Pragmatism holds that such inquiry requires human creativity.[23] Scientists are not mere passive spectators gathering brute data about the world but, rather, bring creative theories to the data that enter into the character and organization of the data that are gathered. The creation of theories goes beyond what is directly observed, and without such meaning structures there is no scientific world, and there are no scientific objects. This creativity implies a radical rejection of the passive spectator theory of knowledge and involves the introduction of an active agent who, through meanings, helps structure the objects of knowledge and thus cannot be separated from the world the agent is trying to understand. Both scientific perception and the context within which it occurs are shot through with an interactional unity between knower and that which he or she is attempting to know though scientific research.[24]

Dewey illustrates this creativity by discussing the significance of Heisenberg's principle of indeterminacy. As he states, "[w]hat is known is seen to be a product in which the act of observation plays a necessary role. Knowing is seen to be a participant in what is finally known."[25] Neither the position nor the velocity of the electron may be fixed and depends on the context in which research is conducted. Both perception of what is there and the meaningful context within which it occurs are shot through with the interactional unity between knower and known, and how the electron or any other particle is seen depends on the goal-driven activity of the scientist who utilizes one frame of reference rather than another.

Scientific creativity arises out of ordinary experience and refers back to this everyday, ordinary "lived" experience. The objects of scientific creativity gain their meaning from and fuse their own meaning into ordinary experience. Though the contents of an abstract scientific theory may be far removed from the qualitative aspects of primary experience, such contents are not some "ultimate reality" that has been discovered but are rather creative abstractions the very possibility of which require and are founded upon the lived qualitative experience of the scientist.[26] The return to everyday primary experience is approached through the systematic categories of scientific thought by which the richness of experience is infused with new meaning.

This creativity implies a radical rejection of the passive spectator view of knowledge and an introduction of the active, creative agent who, through meanings, helps structure the objects of knowledge. The creation of scientific meanings requires a free creative interplay that goes beyond that which is directly observed. Without such creativity, there is no scientific world, and there are no scientific objects. As William James notes in regard to scientific method, there is a big difference between verification as the cause of the preservation of scientific conceptions and the creativity that is the cause of their production.[27] As Linda Simon in writing about James states,

> [f]or James, science itself was grounded in faith: that one method of verification, involving repeated testing and gathering of large amounts of empirical data, would lead inevitably to a discovery of truth. The scientific investigator, he said, "has fallen so deeply in love with the method" that "truth as technically verified" has become the only goal of science. James was skeptical, though, about science's claim of objectivity.

Science should imply, he said, a "certain dispassionate method. To suppose that it means a certain set of results that one should pin one's faith upon and hug forever is sadly to mistake its genius, and degrades the scientific body to the status of a sect." As James saw it, the sect held a "certain fixed belief,—the belief that the hidden order of nature is mechanical exclusively, that non-mechanical categories are irrational ways of conceiving and explaining such things as human life." Other ways of thinking— religious, poetical, emotional—were based on "the personal view of life" rather than the mechanical, the "romantic view" rather than the rationalistic.[28]

In the second stage of scientific inquiry there is directed or goal-oriented activity dictated by theory. Theory requires that certain activities be carried out and certain changes be brought about in the data to see if anticipated results occur. These activities are guided by the possibilities that are contained within the meaning structures that have been created. The system of meanings sets both the context for certain activities and limits the directions which such activity takes. Thus, James remarks that scientific conceptions are "teleological weapons of the mind,"[29] or instruments developed for goal-oriented ends, while Peirce claims that a concept is the mark of a habit of response or general purpose.[30]

As a third general characteristic of scientific method, the adequacy of such meaning structures in grasping what is there or in allowing what is there to reveal itself in a significant way must be tested by consequences in experience. Only if the anticipated experiences occur can truth be claimed for the assertions than have been made in theory. The test for truth is in terms of consequences. Does the theory work in guiding us to a better understanding of that part of our world anticipated by its claims? Does it resolve a problematic situation in a meaningful manner and can the claims that have been made be appropriately defended in a scientific context?

Initial feelings of assurance, insights, and common assent or any other origins of a hypothesis do not determine its truth. To be counted as true a claim must stand the test of consequences in experience. Thus, Peirce stresses that scientific method is the only method of fixing belief, for it is the only method by which beliefs must be tested and corrected by what experience presents.[31] In brief, scientific method as representing a self-corrective rather than a building-block model of knowledge is the only way of determining the truth of a belief. Our creative meaning organizations are developed through our value-driven goals and purposes must be judged by the consequences they produce.[32]

Truth is thus not something passively attained either by the contemplation of absolutes or by the passive accumulation of data but by activity shot through with the theory that guides activity. The theory itself is constituted by looking at many possible ways of acting toward the data and the anticipated consequences of these different theoretical possibilities. That these roles of purposive activity in the development of theory must ultimately be justified by workability are key features of the scientific method. When a theory does not work well, when it cannot integrate the data in meaningful ways that lead to anticipated consequences, when some data just to not seem to fit with the theory, then new theories must be developed which provide a broadened context that can encompass the problem being investigated in a newly integrated whole. Thus, the process continues and in this way scientific method is self-corrective.

Humans know the world through the structures of meanings they have created by their responses to the environment. Pragmatism's concern with the method of science is not just with the application of knowledge but with the way knowledge is obtained. Theory and practical activity are interrelated, and knowledge is not contemplative or otherworldly as opposed to a lesser realm of practice. Knowledge incorporates an awareness of human activity and its consequences. Humans are active agents in the production of knowledge, and human activity is built into the very structure of meaningful awareness of the world and its workings. The gaining of knowledge is structured by possible purposive activity.

The method by which science inquires into the nature of the world in which we live is experimental in nature, and this experimental method is embedded in the very nature of experience in general. All experience involves an interpretive perspective that directs our activity and, in turn, is tested by its workability relative to the consequences it brings about and is revised when it does not work properly.[33] By focusing on the method of science rather than its contents, the proper understanding of human experience is not one that reduces it to mechanistic laws or attempts in any way to substitute a quantitative calculative focus for the full richness of that experience.

While scientific objects are highly sophisticated and intellectualized tools for dealing with experience at an abstract level, they are not the product of any isolated intellect. Rather, the total biological organism in its response to the world is involved in the ordering of any level of awareness of this world, and scientific knowledge involves even the most rudimentary aspect of organism–environment interaction. While the purpose of science is to understand and manipulate the environment and the use of scientific concepts is an instrument of such manipulative control, all human activity even at its most rudimentary level is guided by values and potentially transformative of its environment. Human activity and the concepts that guide such activity are permeated by a value-laden and value-driven dimension, and this dimension pervades the activity of the scientist just as it pervades all human activity. As such it is instrumental and the abstractly manipulative and instrumental purposes attributed to science have their roots in human experience.[34]

Dewey recommends giving up the word *object* to refer to the distinctive material of the physical and adopts the more neutral term *scientific subject-matter* and thinks that this would greatly clarify the subjective–objective problem that modern science introduced into the nature of reality.[35] In other words, rather than trying to relate both subject and object in a way that does justice to both the nature of an independent reality and a consciousness that is attempting to know and understand this reality, Dewey would change the terms of the endeavor and thus do away with the problem. The reality that science thus pursues would be called the subject matter of science as opposed to the subject matter of ordinary experience, both of which require a human consciousness to know and understand.

All experience is experimental, not in the sense that it is guided by sophisticated levels of thought as in scientific endeavors but in the sense that the very structure of human activities both as a way of knowing and as a way of being embodies the features revealed in the examination of scientific method. It is not that human experience in any of its facets is a lower or inferior form of scientific endeavor but, rather, that scientific endeavor as experimental inquiry is a more explicit embodiment of the dynamics operative at all levels of experience, and hence, the ingredients are more easily distinguished.[36]

In focusing on scientific methodology, Pragmatism is providing an experientially based description of the lived activity of scientists, which results in the emergence of scientific objects. In doing so, Pragmatism is focusing on the ways in which any object of awareness can emerge within experience from the most rudimentary contents of awareness within lived experience to the most sophisticated objects of scientific knowledge. In providing a description of the lived experience within which the objects of science emerge, Pragmatism is uncovering the essential aspects of the emergence of any object of awareness. In brief, an examination of scientific method provides the features for understanding the very possibility of its existence as emerging from rudimentary experience.

The commonsense world and the scientific world result from two diverse ways in which the richness of the natural universe is approached by us in our interpretive activity. They do not get hold of different realities, nor does one approach get hold of what is "really real" to the exclusion of the other. Rather, they arise as different ways of understanding the natural universe in which we live as different areas of interest serving different purposes. The nature onto which our everyday experience opens is not totally captured by the contents of science, for its richness overflows such abstractions. The perceived world of everyday experience grounds the abstract inferences and experimental developments of the physical sciences which leave behind through the use of mathematics the sense of ordinary experience which grounds its endeavors. The things and events within nature as they arise within the world of science cannot be confounded with the natural universe in its fullness. If the explanatory net of science is substituted for the temporally grounded features of an indefinitely rich universe or becomes in any way the absolute model for understanding that universe, science has overstepped in boundaries.

Nature can be understood in three senses. First, there is nature as a "thick" and dense independent reality that is the foundation of all that is and for all the ways of being including meaningful human activity. Second, there is nature as our worldly environment as it emerges as a network of relations of things used in everyday purposive activity. Finally, there is nature as an object of science that we theoretically abstract from our everyday natural environment as a higher-level reflection on the world. Neither the richness of nature as that from which all life springs nor the richness of nature as the human everyday worldly environment can be confounded with or reduced to the abstract character of the events and objects in the world of science.

The abstract worlds of the various scientific disciplines, each utilizing their specialized tools of abstraction, are diverse and limited approaches to the rich, intertwined relational webs within which humans function. Each area of interest is highlighting a dimension of a unified and rich complexity from which each area draws its ultimate intelligibility and vitality. The problem is not how to unite ultimately discrete facts that are studied by the different disciplines but to distinguish the various dimensions of the concrete relational webs in which human experience is enmeshed.

Distinguishing these dimensions is necessary for purposes of intellectual clarity and advancement of understanding and is accomplished through the dynamics of experimental method. If the problem being investigated and its solution are viewed in this manner, then there will be no temptation to view the resultant "products" in ways that distort both the infinitely rich natural universe they are intended to clarify and the creative process by which these products are obtained. If such distortion is allowed to happen, then these products can too easily be seen as either self-enclosed relativistic environments immune from criticism from "outside" or as a direct grasp of "what is" in its pristine purity.

This is especially the case when one operates within the universe of mathematical quantification and the "rigor" this allows. One tends to forget that this tool in the very process of quantifying the world leaves behind all of the richness of nature, which cannot be caught by a quantitative net. The use of quantification predetermines the type of content that is apprehended as being inherently mathematizable, while the exclusively mathematizable type of content apprehended, in turn, reinforces the belief that it alone provides the truth about nature.

Nature as described by science is the creative product of an abstract, reflective restructuring of the nature revealed in everyday experience. It is not a substitute for this experience. As Mead stresses in rejecting such a realistic interpretation of science and the reductionism to which it gives rise, "the ultimate touchstone of reality is a piece of experience found in an unanalyzed world . . . We can never retreat behind immediate experience to analyze elements that constitute the ultimate reality of all immediate experience, for whatever breath of reality these elements possess has been breathed into them by unanalyzed experience."[37] In Dewey's terms, the refined products of scientific inquiry "inherit their full content of meaning" within the context of everyday experience.[38] Lewis's agreement with such a position is shown in his claim that any "truth about nature" must refer back to "what is presented in sense." This position is most succinctly expressed in Peirce's claim that the foundationally "real world is the world of sensible experience."[39]

The notion that if our concepts are to relate to reality, they must be able to capture a series of independently existing fully structured facts and, if they cannot do so, they bear no relation to reality at all is itself a remnant of the alternatives offered by the spectator theory of knowledge and the atomism of classical science. For the Pragmatist the world enters experience within the interpretative net we have cast upon it for delineating facts, for breaking its continuities, and for rendering precise its vagueness. Pragmatism does not reject the linkage of concepts and the world but, rather, looks at the nature of this linkage in a different manner than classical science. It does not reject the idea of reality's constraints on our language structure but, rather, rethinks the nature of these constraints in a way that rejects correspondence.

Our creative meanings do not deny the presence of reality within experience nor do they mirror this reality, but rather, they open us onto reality's presence as mediated by meanings, for meanings are emergent from and intertwined with ongoing interaction in a "dense" universe. We do not think our way to a reality to which language or conceptual structures correspond, but rather, we live through a reality with which we are intertwined. Our primal interactive embeddedness in a complex and rich world is something which can never be adequately objectified. All knowledge claims are fallibilistic, perspectival, and temporal but, nonetheless, grounded in the richness of the natural universe.

The purpose of knowledge is to allow us to engage this reality which is not beyond the reach of experience but is eminently knowable through a perspectival net by which we render intelligible its indeterminate richness. Within such a context, Lewis compares facts to a landscape: "A landscape is a terrain, but a terrain as seeable by an eye. And a fact is a state of affairs, but a state of affairs as knowable by a mind."[40] Peirce notes that instead of being "a slice of nature," facts are abstracted from it, for "[a]ny fact is inseparably combined with an infinite swarm of circumstances, which make no part of the fact itself."[41]

We do not know the natural universe in its pristine purity independently of the interpretations we bring to it, but the natural universe is always that which we experience, providing the given dimension within experience. Our lived perceptual world and the independently real natural universe are not two spatially, temporally, or experientially different realities. Our everyday worldly environment is the result of the way the natural universe enters into our interpretive experience and into our everyday active engagement with that environment. Various abstract levels of reflection arise from within this concrete everyday world of lived perceptual experience as various explanatory nets are cast upon it in an attempt to understand and live within this world.

The scientific method works well in investigating certain types of problems, but it is applicable far beyond these problems and has implications for human experience, in general. Pragmatism extends the relevance of scientific method and its mode of inquiry to all of human experience. Inquiry begins with a feeling of unease about something or dissatisfaction with some aspect of experience. The one who is inquiring then uses whatever tools of inquiry are at his or her disposal and are relevant to the nature of the thing being examined. These tools can include laboratory equipment, mathematics, formal logic, interviews, review of literature, therapy, or whatever is useful to the inquiry and can bring it to a fruitful conclusion. The outcome desired is a feeling of satisfaction with the results of the inquiry. If this result is not obtained, either the inquiry needs to be continued until satisfaction is reached or abandoned if the inquiry cannot be continued or is considered to be fruitless.[42] As Hickman again writes,

> [i]nquiry is thus a technological enterprise because it involves techniques: the invention, development, and cognitive deployment of tools or other artifacts (such as rules of inference), brought to bear on raw materials (such as data) and intermediate stock parts (such as the results of previous inquiries), to resolve and reconstruct situations which are perceived as problematic.[43]

From this understanding of a nonpassive or nonspectator view of scientific method, humans and their environment, organic and inorganic, take on an inherently relational aspect. To speak of organism and environment in isolation from each other is never true to the situation, for no organism can exist in isolation from an environment, and an environment is what it is in relation to an organism. The properties attributed to the environment belong to it in the context of that interaction. What exists is interaction as an indivisible whole, and it is only within such an interactional context that experience and its qualities function.

Pragmatism thus emphasizes the relational nature of things in the world, even space and time itself, a position that is consistent with what some scientists themselves are saying. Classical Newtonian physics believed that everything in the world existed against an absolute preexisting framework of space that is eternal and goes on forever. Particles move around in this space and their properties are defined with respect to this space. Time was also believed to be absolute and flowed whether anything happened or not in the same manner. This view changed with Einstein, who discovered that there is no fixed background as space and time are dynamic and no more than relations between events that evolve within time itself. "So space has no meaning apart from a network of relationships, and time is nothing but change in that network of relationships."[44]

Such a relational view of humans and their environment has pluralistic dimensions for environments are contextually located and significant solutions to problematic situations emerge within such contextually situated environments. Diverse perspectives grasp the richness of reality in different ways and must be judged in terms of workability. And workability requires growth; resolution of conflicts by an enlargement of context in which adjustments or adjudicating of conflicting perspectival claims can take place. Growth cannot be reduced to material growth or mere accumulation of knowledge but, rather, is best understood as an increase in the moral richness of experience.

Extending scientific inquiry to all of human affairs would allow the benefit of such inquiry to be realized by the entire society. Science would then contribute to making a better society as a whole and bringing about better consequences and should not be limited to certain industrial endeavors. Science would thus become humanistic, not just physical and technical, and would be used to contribute to bettering the social and material conditions of life rather that making a profit for private business organizations. Science can be, according to Dewey, a tool for creating a "liberating spiritualization" in being used to control the social effects that new technologies produce and directing these technologies to produce better consequences for the society as a whole.[45]

Characteristics of the Pragmatic Approach to Science

Instead of the characteristics of reductionism, atomism, discreteness, quantitativeness, and determinism, Pragmatism deals with emergence, holism, continuity, the qualitative, and indeterminism. Thus, Pragmatism involves a different view of the characteristics that go to make up the traditional or classical view of science and the scientific worldview. This view involves a reinterpretation of science, a different way to understand science and what it is doing. Pragmatism does not reject science or its approach to knowledge but looks at the scientific enterprise from a different perspective, which, in some sense, constitutes a different worldview.

Instead of reductionism, the pragmatic view of science emphasizes *emergence*. While reductionism thinks of parts in isolation, emergence focuses on the relationship between the parts of a system and emergent properties that stem from this relationship. For example, scientific reductionism would think of water as composed of its constituent elements hydrogen and oxygen, that these are the fundamental parts that go to make up what we call water. Emergence, however, would focus on the property of wetness that arises from the relationship of hydrogen and oxygen, a property that emerges out of the relationship between the parts. It is the wetness that is of concern to us in our everyday lived experience while the constituent elements are of concern to scientists.

This is a much different way of looking at nature and leads to different conclusions. In particle physics scientists are looking for the fundamental building blocks of matter. This is a reductionist approach that is linear in nature in going back to the most fundamental particle that is the unmoved mover, so to speak. From the standpoint of emergence, however, what results from experiments using supercolliders are new and different particles, no one of which can necessarily be taken as the most fundamental. Thus, emergence is related to nonlinearity, in that what particle physics is doing is discovering more and more complexity in the structure of atoms and is not necessarily going to find the most fundamental particle from which all other matter stems. How these particles relate to each other is more important than is the search for some ultimate particle.

The limits of reductionism are evident at levels of organization with higher amounts of complexity such as culture, ecosystems, and other systems that are formed from large numbers of interacting components. Given this complexity, it is impossible to reduce a system to one or even a few fundamental components. The important thing to deal with in these cases is the relationship between the components of a system and the emergent properties that arise from these relationships. Some scientists themselves, including a Nobel Prize winner by the name of Robert Laughlin, believe that we have moved into an age of emergence which has important implications for our understanding of what science is doing. In further amplifying on this idea he states,

> Much as I dislike the idea of ages, I think a good case can be made that science has now moved from an Age of Reductionism to an Age of Emergence, a time when the search for the ultimate cause of things shifts from the behavior of parts to the behavior of the collective. It is difficult to identify a specific moment when this transition occurred because it was gradual and somewhat obscured by the persistence of myths, but there can be no doubt that the dominant paradigm now is organizational . . . Ironically the very success of reductionism has helped pave the way for its eclipse. Over time, careful quantitative study of microscopic parts has revealed that at the primitive level, at least, collective principles of organization are not just a quaint side show but *everything*—the true source of physical law, including perhaps the most fundamental laws we know. The precision of our measurements enables us to confidently declare the search for a single ultimate truth to have ended—but at the same time we have failed, since nature is now revealed to be an enormous tower of truths, each descending from its parent, and then transcending that parent, as the scale of measurement increases . . . The transition to the Age of Emergence brings an end to the myth of the absolute power of mathematics. This myth is still entrenched in our culture, unfortunately, a fact revealed routinely in the press and popular publications promoting the search for ultimate laws as the only scientific activity worth pursuing, notwithstanding massive and over whelming experimental evidence that exactly the opposite is

the case . . . The myth of collective behavior following from the law is, as a practical matter, exactly backward. Law instead follows from collective behavior, as do things that flow from it, such as logic and mathematics.[46]

Thus, Newton's laws of motion are not fundamental, according to Laughlin, but rather, they emerge from a collective organizational phenomenon. With the rise of quantum theory, the behavior of atoms, molecules, and subatomic particles has been described by the laws of quantum mechanics, and laws emerge from the aggregation of quantum matter.[47] Emergence is thus introduced in the heart of physics. It is also evident at the level of the universe itself as, with the rise of big bang theory, it is now believed that everything we see in the universe today emerged from a singularity as small as the tip of a pencil. And in biology with evolutionary theory it is believed that more complex life-forms emerged from simpler ones rather than being created directly by some supernatural entity. And new life forms are emerging all the time as viruses develop new strains, for example, to counter the effects of human efforts to eradicate them.

Emergence is also operative in the different sciences that have developed. To a strict reductionist, science is a straightforward hierarchy; biology is founded upon chemistry, for example; and chemistry is founded on physics; and physics leads to the most elementary particles of matter. When these are found, then we have completed the linear chain back to the first cause that can explain everything else.[48] But in an emergent view, one science is not just an applied version of the science that precedes it. Each of these sciences is a different approach to its own part of the world, it deals with different theories, and entirely new laws and concepts are necessary to explain the phenomena it is interested in understanding. No one of these sciences is necessarily more fundamental than the other. They are all necessary and equally valid in understanding the complexity of our world.

A second characteristic of the pragmatic view of science is that is a *holistic* approach to nature. What science does is to break the whole apart through reductionism which allows us to manipulate more and more aspects of our world. However, what science separates science cannot put back together. The whole cannot be created by putting the parts back together. The whole has to be grasped with a new kind of consciousness that does not start with reductionistic parts but that has a different starting point that can grasp the whole more immediately. Only then can we get a realistic understanding of what nature is worth and what qualities of nature are worth preserving.

Rather than assuming that nature is atomistic and thus focusing on the parts in isolation from each other, pragmatism considers the whole phenomenon and the interactions of the parts within this whole. These relationships are considered to be non-directional or nonlinear in nature, they do not lead back to some fundamental atomistic something.[49] While an atomistic view of nature has proved useful in the physical sciences, such a view is more problematic in the social sciences as it seems impossible to isolate a single cause for any social process that is the primary determinant of something in society. It is more realistic to look at the whole society and study how the various parts of interest interact with each other within a holistic perspective.

Reductionism has always been less appropriate to the biological and social sciences, where knowledge hardly ever resides in theories with distinctive laws that are determinate of organism and human behavior. What is sought in these sciences is most often a *model* of a complex system that shows how its components interact to produce the properties and behavior of the whole system. These models attempt to demonstrate that the behavior of the system is most often due to the distinctive way its parts are put together. The behavior of the parts is constrained by their incorporation into a system and can lead to the system as a whole behaving in ways that are unexpected and unpredictable.

These properties are *emergent* in that they were not anticipated by the knowledge we had of the parts. Explanations of phenomena in these sciences are inadequate if only the parts are considered rather than the whole system. With such emergence it is not component behavior but the interactive organization of the whole system that is the critical explanatory feature. Complex wholes make the parts behave is a manner that is different from the way they would behave if they were not part of a particular complex system. When this happens new causal powers and properties can properly be said to have emerged.[50] According to Arthur Peacocke, who was a biochemist and theologian at Oxford University,

> [i]nferring from the behavior of a whole to a quality of its parts expressed only when they are acting as parts of that whole is just the opposite of reduction, understood as explaining the behavior of a whole in terms of the properties of its parts when these parts are considered in isolation. The former inference might be better described as explaining the parts in terms of the whole. The whole in such a case might still be said to be nothing more in ontological terms than a collection of its parts, but only on condition that the 'parts' are defined in equally ontological terms by the role they play in the whole. Reductionism and holism point in different ways.[51]

This perspective thus asserts that the whole is more than the sum of its parts and that the parts do not give the entire meaning to the whole.[52] All the properties of a given system cannot be explained by its component parts alone. The wetness of water cannot be explained by breaking water into its component elements of hydrogen and oxygen. Nor can the behavior of the system be determined from an examination of how the parts of the system behave. Instead, the system as a whole and the way the parts are organized and relate to each other within the system determine the way the parts behave. The emergence of quantum mechanics introduces holism into particle physics itself. In an article on holism from the University of Oregon, the following claim is made:

> The emergence of a quantum entity's previously indeterminate properties in the context of a given experimental situation is another example of relational holism. We cannot say that a photon is a wave or a particle until it is measured, and how we measure it determines what we will see. The quantum entity acquires a certain new property—position, momentum, polarization—only in relation to its measuring apparatus. The property did not exist prior to this relationship. It was indeterminate.[53]

When we look at anything in our world, we experience it as a totality not as an individual, atomistic, isolated part. We may intend to focus on a part, but all the background related to that part comes into play, even if it is on the periphery. For example, I may want to focus on the capital building when I look out my window, but it is impossible to ignore all the other buildings, the sky, the trees, and everything else that is taken in by my vision. All these other things place the capital building in a certain context and how I see that building is affected by all these other things in a holistic perspective. It is not possible for me to focus solely on a certain part of the totality.

We live in the world as a whole and derive meaning from this relationship. The parts have no particular meaning in and of themselves, so that adding up these parts will give meaning to the whole. For example, any one part of an automobile engine is meaningless and, for that matter, useless, in and of itself. However, when all these parts are combined into an engine that can power our car, the parts become useful to us and are meaningful in enabling us to go places and do things we could not experience before the invention of the automobile. The combination of these parts has enhanced our lives and made life easier and more meaningful than it was before this technology was employed.

Many informational systems have a specific function within a totality that is integrated into an emergent totality that exists as a system. This emergent reality is not just reducible to the laws of interacting particles considered in isolation. Structure becomes important to understanding how nature functions. Some scientists thus speak of a holistic explanation where the parts can only adequately be explained in terms of a greater whole. Quantum physics even extends the idea of a holistic explanation to the whole universe, which is considered to be a total physical system.[54] According to Keith Ward, an Emeritus Regius Professor of Divinity at Oxford University:

> Recent hypotheses in quantum physics suggest that the whole physical universe is "entangled" in such a way that the parts of a system— even the behavior of elementary particles—cannot be fully understood

without seeing their role within a greater whole; ultimately the whole of space-time. There be no non-physical bits of "stuff," but there seem to be laws of their interaction that can be specified only from a grasp of whole systems, rather than atomistically. In quantum cosmology we are encouraged to see the whole universe as a complex system, and to think that knowledge of the total system may be needed to fully explain the behavior of its simple parts.[55]

The pragmatic view of science also views reality as *continuous* rather than discrete. While science has to divide reality into discrete entities for purposes of analysis and measurement so that nature can be better understood and manipulated, we actually experience nature as continuous. When we walk to the door we actually get there despite Zeno's paradox. While time is broken up into hours, minutes, and seconds and we are conscious of these divisions under certain circumstances, like when we have to get to a certain place on time for example, for our ordinary experience time is a continuous flow and is not discrete. The table we eat off of is experienced as a continuous whole; it is not experienced as a bunch of atomic particles that are held together by an unseen force. These continuums are as real to us in our everyday experience as are the discretes to the scientist who is studying a certain part of nature. According to Charis Anastopoulos, writing in *Particle or Wave*,

> [b]ut even if we rested at the present level of knowledge and assumed that quarks and leptons are themselves the ultimate building blocks of matter, it would still be difficult to make the case that matter consists of discrete objects. The fundamental theory for the micro world, quantum field theory, relies on a rather physical principle; the duality between particles and fields. Particles are genuinely discrete objects, but fields are supposed to be continuous up to the tiniest of scales, and both descriptions seem to hold simultaneously.[56]

Dewey speaks about a continuity of the life process, that life is a self-renewing process that interacts with the environment in which it exists. This process, however, is not dependent upon the continued existence of any one single individual. While individual lives come and go, reproduction of life in all its forms goes on in a continuous sequence. Some species may even become extinct, but the life process continues to evolve ever more complex forms of life that are better adapted to their environment. Life goes on in a continuous fashion, and new forms of life evolve in relation to environmental conditions. As Dewey says, "[c]ontinuity of life means continual readapation of the environment to the needs of living organisms."[57]

Humans are continuous with nature; they do not exist apart from nature and are not outside of nature. Nature cannot be dehumanized nor can humans be denaturalized. Science treats nature as an objective reality that can be manipulated to serve human interests. Nature becomes dehumanized. and human impacts on nature are ignored. Some religions hold that humans, or at least the human soul, can exist apart from nature in some supernatural realm. Neither approach does justice to the interactions between humans and nature and the fact that there is a continuous relationship between humans and nature where nature shapes humans and humans shape nature in an ever evolving universe.

Continuities exist in all of our life experiences. At the most basic level, we do not experience life as a series of discrete events or objects that we then have to put together somehow. We do not think of ourselves as subjects that exist in an objective world. We experience ourselves as continuous with that world, not as something standing against a world that is seen as something alien and foreign to our existence. We exist in the world and live our lives in interaction with all parts of that world. Our lives are social in that we grow up in a certain social context that shapes who we are and gives meaning and purpose to our lives. We are not individuals that grow up in isolation from other selves and the natural environment. While science has to break the world into discretes for its purposes, this is not what we experience at the most basic level in our everyday lives.

We divide space into inches, feet, yards, and miles in the United States while other countries use the metric system of measurement. What measurement is used is more or less arbitrary and as long as a society sticks with the same unit of measurement in all its transactions there should be no problem. In July 1959 the United States, the United Kingdom, and other Commonwealth nations agreed to define the yard as 0.914 meters, making the inch exactly 25.4 millimeters. This often called the international measure. These units allow us to define private property and fix the boundaries of nations and states so that we can manipulate space for our interests.

Land is divided up into parcels to be bought and sold on the marketplace so that those who want that land can buy it and use it for their purposes. The land belongs to us if we have legal title to it and have obtained the title appropriately. The Native Americans had no need to divide land in this manner as rather than the land belonging to them they had a philosophy where they believed they belonged to the land. The land provided them open space and there was no need to fence it off and fine people for trespassing. The great plains were open to all who wanted to live there and hunt buffalo. But as Americans took over, land became the private property of individuals and institutions to use for private purposes.

With respect to time, science has been looking for the most regular regularity it can find in the universe on which to base its determination of time so as to be the most accurate division of time possible. The rotation of the earth itself proved to be too variable as did the rotation of the earth around the sun as well as the movement of the planets. Eventually there was a split between civil time and astronomical time as the former moved to atomic clocks as a more reliable determination of time intervals. Currently the cesium clock is used to measure time as the vibration of the cesium atom is accurate to one second in 300,000 million seconds. There is thus an infinitesimal variation between the vibrations of this atom that make it a reliable base from which to determine civil time. The second is thus defined as 9,192,631,770 oscillations of Cesium 133 as it travels from one electronic state to another.

This clock is located at the National Institute of Standards and Technology (NIST) in Boulder, Colorado, where there are two such atomic clocks named NIST-F1 and NIST-F2 that are linked to computer clocks and other timekeeping devices across the country. This official time is disseminated to such timekeeping devices via the Internet about 7 billion times a day, and the NIST also regularly updates about 50 million devices by radio. This official time is also used to time-stamp hundreds of billions of dollars in financial transactions every business day. The NIST standards also underpin telecommunications systems, GPS positioning and navigation, electric power distribution, and TV and radio broadcasts.[58]

Science then creates time rather than discovering time and divides up what is in its most natural sense a continuum into hours, minutes, seconds, and split seconds in order for humans to organize time for their own purposes. We are able to set times for meetings with the expectation that everyone necessary will show up for the meeting on time. We are able to schedule flights with a reasonable expectation that they will leave at the stated time of departure so that we can arrange our schedule to be at the airport on time and get on the flight. We can engineer precision measurement of time into things that have to happen simultaneously or in a certain precise order to accomplish a goal such as putting a man on the moon.

Humans thus experience scientific created time that is a departure from a continuous view of time. The most basic reality of time that we are not necessarily conscious of in our scientific world is that time is continuous; it is a continuous process that flows in one direction, the so-called arrow of time. While scientists would like to base this arrow of time on the notion of entropy as stated in the Second Law of Thermodynamics, we experience time as flowing only in a forward direction. We cannot go back in time, and despite the wish we often have of wanting to relive the past to do things differently, we eventually realize that the past can't be changed and have to move forward and live with the consequences of decisions and actions that are part of the past.

Time cannot even be spilt up into past, present, and future as each present moment we experience contains some of the past and the future. It is all wrapped up together in a continuous flow. Even if we could relive the past and a broken cup would go back together, time would still move forward and only the physics would have to change as entropy would have to go from disorder to order. This, of course, is not going to happen in our present universe. In any event, science splits time into pieces so that we can organize our lives to accomplish our purposes and interests. We live in the context or box that science created for us, and many of us are constantly under pressure to be on time or to use our time wisely and not waste it engaging in frivolous activities. Scientific time dominates our lives such that the only time we may have a chance to get in touch with the underlying nature of time as continuous is when we are on vacation and hopefully can relax and let time flow as it will.

Instead of a quantitatively characterized universe, pragmatism emphasizes the *qualitative* aspects of our experience. While a quantitative approach tells us something about how much of something we have, it does not say anything about the quality of that something. Quality in this sense does not refer to the qualities that a particular object may have, like color, texture, and the like.[59] Quality is really a judgment we make about something as to what it does to enhance our life experience. When we are considering whether to buy a work of art, for example, we do not make the decision solely on the price of the work. We make the decision on the basis of whether the artwork pleases us and will enhance our life as it hangs on the wall, and then take into consideration the price and whether it is worth the quantity of money we will have to part with in order to buy it. The same holds true for clothes, furniture, and all of life's choices relative to particular objects. They all come with a price, but the qualitative value of these objects enters into our decision making about these objects along with the quantitative aspects.

Quality is a unitary concept unlike quantity where an object can be measured and expressed in units of something. We experience quality as a whole, the whole artwork enters into our judgment as does the whole house and its environment when we are making a decision about purchasing a home. The experience of quality is continuous, it is not broken up into discretes. While we may like certain aspects of a house more than others, like a kitchen, for example, or a family room, the final judgment has to take the whole house into consideration. And its environment is equally important, whether it is in a safe neighborhood, the quality of the schools if we have children, and other such factors. All of these aspects are important, and they all blend together in a final judgment about the quality of the experience. Everything depends on the quality of this experience and the expectations about the ability of the house of continue to provide this quality in the future.

Attempts to quantify nature are problematical, at best, and bound to fail, at worst. Where there is no discrete owner and nothing to exchange, it is difficult if not impossible to put a quantitative value on nature. What is the value of preserving wilderness so people can enjoy hiking and camping in it and get away from the hustle and bustle of city living? These are qualitative experiences, and it is difficult to put a price on them. They are worth everything and nothing. Perhaps people can be forced to quantify these experiences by making them pay for it, but the quality of the experience is the determining factor that then has to be translated into some quantitative measure so decisions can be made about how much wilderness to preserve.

Modern science changed our understanding and approach to nature. In ancient Greece and the Middle Ages, science understood the world as impregnated with aesthetic and moral values; it was not considered to be value neutral. According to John Dewey, nothing was less important in ancient science than quantity. With the rise of modern science, however, matter and motion were transformed, and the quantitative measurement of change in space and time became the foundations of natural science.[60] Thus, there was a change from a qualitative approach to a quantitative approach, where nature was devoid of value and was measured and manipulated in human interests. Nature only had an instrumental value as it proved useful for human purposes; it had no value in and of itself.

Qualitative thinking is involved in appraising a work of art, as it is the underlying quality of the art that defines the work "that circumscribes it externally and integrates it internally" and controls the work of the artist as he or she creates the work. The nature of good art is a genuine intellectual and logical whole, where the parts "hang" together and reinforce and expand the quality of each other. Such a work cannot be understood by a quantitative approach that measures its size and amount of time involved or its price. Properties such as symmetry, harmony, rhythm, and proportion are what matter in judging a work of art to be valuable and form the basis of any quantitative measurement.[61]

Finally, rather than holding to a deterministic universe, pragmatism involves *indeterminism*. Recall that in a deterministic universe, all the information about its structure is contained in the initial conditions. Everything that is going to happen in the future is implicit in the starting state which contains all the information necessary to reconstruct the past and predict the future. But the quantum aspects of reality make perfect knowledge of the initial conditions impossible, not only in practice but in principle as well. This means that we cannot make accurate predictions of the future based on present conditions, and the assumption of a deterministic universe has to be abandoned in favor of a more complex and indeterminate universe.[62] As John D. Barrow states in *New Theories of Everything*,

> [e]ven if we can overcome the problem of initial conditions to determine the most natural or uniquely consistent starting state, we may have to face the reality that there is inevitable uncertainty surrounding the prescription of the initial state which makes the prediction of the exact future state of the Universe impossible. Only statistical statements will be possible.[63]

Indeterminism is thus built into the structure of the universe, it is intrinsic, and we will never be able to predict future events with absolute certainty. The issue is not one of needing more information about the initial conditions, as these conditions are themselves indeterminate. We live in an indeterminate universe and uncertainty is part and parcel of our experience. It cannot be avoided by developing better techniques of scientific analysis or better ways of processing information. There are too many complexities and too many unknowns for us to deal with, making the universe unpredictable and full of surprises.

Every situation with which we are faced is unique; it is indivisible and cannot be duplicated.[64] A fully deterministic universe has no place for such uniqueness and novelty, no place for growth and genuine change.[65] It is a fixed and closed world that is mechanistic in nature. An indeterministic universe, on the other hand, is open to change and novelty; the unexpected becomes the expected, and there is disorder as well as order. Rather than being a detached observer that is outside of nature, humans are participants in changing nature through their interactions. The intelligibility of the universe, according to John Dewey, is not based upon the notion of fixed laws that make possible exact predictions but incorporates probabilities and uncertainty.[66] He goes on to say,

> In technical statement, laws on the new basis are *formulae for the prediction of the probability of an observable occurrence.* They are designations of relations sufficiently stable to allow the occurrence of forecasts of individualized situations—for every observed phenomenon is individual—within limits of specified probability, not a probability of error, but of probability of actual occurrence. Laws are inherently conceptual in character, as is shown in the fact that either position or velocity may be fixed at will. To call them conceptual is not to say that they are merely "mental" and arbitrary. It is to say that they are *relations* which are thought not observed. The subject-matter of the conceptions which constitute laws is not arbitrary, for it is determined by the interactions of what exists. But determination of them is very different from that denoted by conformity to fixed properties of unchanging substances.[67]

Laws are thus means of calculating the probabilities related to observing an event in nature. They are not based on properties immutably inhering in things and of such a nature as to be capable of exact mathematical statement.[68] Nature is not irrational, however, as there are regularities and uniformities that make nature intelligible and understandable and subject to being manipulated for human purposes.[69] Our knowledge of nature may be indeterminate, but that does not mean nature is arbitrary and completely unpredictable. We can predict what effects global warming will have on the earth's climate and on the polar ice caps with some degree of confidence, but that does mean that nature won't surprise us as it has with faster melting of polar ice caps than was predicted. We cannot know with certainty what will happen in the future but can make intelligent predictions based on what we do know about climate change and need not wait, in some cases, for greater certainty before taking action.

Observation of any natural system also involves acting on it in some fashion. When dealing with large systems such as the universe as a whole, our actions can be ignored as they do not have a measurable effect on the bodies we are observing. Particle physics, however, is another matter. The uncertainty principle, which could perhaps more accurately be called the indeterminacy principle, holds that it is impossible to get an accurate measurement of the velocity and position of any body because of the interaction between the observer and the body being measured. The position and velocity of a particle are not fixed but is changing all the time because of this interaction with the act of observing, or, as Dewey puts it, "with the conditions under which observation is possible." This principle is the final blow to the old spectator theory of knowledge:[70]

> The change for the underlying philosophy and logic of science is, however, very great. In relation to the metaphysics of the Newtonian system it is hardly less than revolutionary. What is known is seen to be a product in which the act of observation plays a necessary role. Knowing is seen to be a participant in what is finally known. Moreover the metaphysics of existence as something fixed and therefore capable of literally exact mathematical description and prediction is undermined. Knowing is, for philosophical theory, a case of specially directed activity instead of something isolated from practice. The quest for certainty by means of exact possession in mind of immutable reality is exchanged for search for security by means of active control of the changing course of events.[71]

In sum, Pragmatism is an antifoundational philosophy.[72] It rejects attempts to provide ultimate foundations for knowledge claims and is in this sense a postmodern philosophy. Likewise, Classical Pragmatism rejects a spectator theory of knowledge where true knowledge is constituted by an accurate internal representation of external facts that we can know objectively. Instead, Pragmatism is perspectival with regard to knowledge holding that we approach the world from a certain perspective that influences how we go about inquiring into something. Pragmatism also holds that knowledge is gained from experience and rejects sources of knowledge located outside of experience, such as religious supernaturalism and other transcendental accounts of knowledge. Finally, it rejects the view that humans can achieve absolute certainty, "opting instead for versions of fallibilism according to which working hypotheses, rules of thumb, and even well proven instruments are open to revision under appropriate circumstances."[73]

For Pragmatism, there is no objective nature that provides a firm foundation for knowledge. Nature is not a "thing" but is instead a complex matrix of objects and events that are constructed within the history of human inquiry. Pragmatism rejects the epistemological foundations of classical science—a faith in quantification, a vision of linear and inevitable progress, an acceptance of the physical sciences as paradigmatic of all rationality, and a conception of nature as a machine to be dominated and exploited. Pragmatism emphasizes that humans are situated within nature and holds that science is only one of the many productive areas of human experience. It views progress as fragile and attainable only in piecemeal fashion. Knowledge is perspectival and fallible, but some forms of knowledge are better than others for certain purposes. What works best is judged in terms of the consequences it produces. Finally, Pragmatism denies any absolute or final split between fact and value or between culture and nature.[74] It is a view of science in which humans can reconnect with nature as this chapter described and with each other, a subject to which I now turn.

Notes

1 Brandon R. Brown, *Planck: Driven by Vision, Broken By War* (New York: Oxford University Press, 2015), 166.
2 Ibid., 170–171.
3 Ibid., 175–176.
4 Morris Berman, *The Reenchantment of the World* (Ithaca, NY: Cornell University Press, 1981), 50.
5 Maurice Merleau-Ponty, *The World of Perception* Oliver Davis, trans. (New York: Routledge, 2008), 43.
6 John Dewey, *The Quest for Certainty* (New York: Capricorn Books, 1929), 221.
7 John Dewey, "Time and Individuality," in Jo Ann Boydston, ed., *The Later Works*, Vol. 14, 1939–1944 (Carbondale and Edwardsville, IL: Southern Illinois University Press, 1988), 105.
8 Steven Shapin, *The Scientific Revolution* (Chicago: University of Chicago Press, 1996), 53.
9 John Dewey, "Theories of Knowledge," in Jo Ann Boydston, ed., *The Middle Works*, Vol. 9, 1916 (Carbondale and Edwardsville, IL: Southern Illinois University Press, 1980), 344.
10 See Stephen Hawking and Leonard Mlodinow, "The (Elusive) Theory of Everything," *Scientific American*, October 2010, 69–71.
11 Larry Hickman, for example, argues that Dewey's thinking represents advances beyond the positions taken by some of the authors who are commonly identified as postmodernists. He identifies some of the problems postmodernism leaves unresolved and shows how Dewey had already dealt with them in his writings. In this sense Dewey is a post-postmodernist and will be waiting for them when they reach the end of the road they are traveling. See Larry Hickman, *Pragmatism as Post-Postmodernism* (New York: Fordham University Press, 2007), 13–14.
12 Sandra B. Rosenthal, *Speculative Pragmatism* (LaSalle, IL: Open Court, 1986), 2–5. Credit for the rest of this chapter must be given to my wife Sandra Rosenthal, who taught me everything I know about American Pragmatism.
13 Ibid., 8.
14 Social science research based on statistical analysis presents particular problems given the many choices that have to be made relevant to how the research is conducted. Given the different ways such research can be conducted, it is inevitable that the conclusions that are based on this research will be different on any given issue. There is no such thing as the "definitive" study in most of these areas because scientific procedures are so different in these instances. No one procedure can be defended as the "correct" one to use with respect to a given

study. Granted some procedures are better than others, but no single procedure can be taken as definitive so that its results are the last word in the matter. Thus, different scientists come to different conclusions with respect to the issue under investigation.

Researchers, in fact, may not want to have a definitive study because that would close off an area of research to further study and possible funding. In the area of management and its social and ethical responsibilities, for example, countless studies have been done trying to find some kind of link between the social performance of companies or their ethical behavior and some measure of economic performance. In performing these studies there is the problem of defining social or ethical performance and operationalizing this variable so it can be quantified and measured in some fashion. And choosing a measure of economic performance is not straightforward either, as stock market performance, profits, return on equity, or other measures can be used for this purpose.

Nonetheless, numerous studies have been done on this issue, and as might be expected, different conclusions have been reached. Some studies have shown a negative relationship between social or ethical performance and economic performance, some have shown no relationship, and others have shown a positive relationship. No single study can be taken as definitive, however, so the area remains open for further research. Thus, there will be more studies of this nature appearing in management journals, where the researcher will review the existing studies, which gets to be more and more of an arduous task, point out the deficiencies of these studies from the researchers point of view and then go on to perform a new study that the researcher will claim is superior to the others. If the study is well done and receives favorable reviews, it will get published in a journal to be referred to at some later time by another researcher interested in the same topic.

15 Hickman, *Pragmatism as Post-PostModernism*, 118–119.

16 Stephen A. Marglin, *The Dismal Science: How Thinking Like an Economist Undermines Community* (Cambridge, MA: Harvard University Press, 2008), 132–134. This last statement has implications for the case method of instruction. It is difficult to draw generalizations form a particular case that are relevant to other situations. One must be careful about doing this because other situations take place in a different context. Nonetheless, one can learn how to approach situations and analyze them that may be useful in other situations.

17 Hickman, *Pragmatism as Post-PostModernism*, 216.

18 Ibid., 193.

19 George Herbert Mead, *The Philosophy of the Present* (La Salle, IL: Open Court, 1959), 98.

20 It has been argued elsewhere that the positions of the five major American Pragmatists form a systematic and unified movement. See Sandra Rosenthal, *Speculative Pragmatism* (Amherst, MA: The University of Massachusetts Press, 1986); paperback ed. (Peru, IL: Open Court, 1990).

21 Hickman, *Pragmatism as Post-PostModernism*, 95–196, 257n7.

22 See George Herbert Mead, "The Definition of the Physical," in A. J. Reck, ed., *Mead: Selected Writings* (New York: Bobbs-Merrill Co., 1964); and John Dewey, "Experience and Nature," in Jo Ann Boydston, ed., *The Later Works*, Vol. 1 (Carbondale and Edwardsville, IL: Southern Illinois University Press, 1981).

23 See William James, "The Principles of Psychology," in Frederick Burkhardt, ed., *The Works of William James*, Vol. 2 (Cambridge, MA: Harvard University Press, 1981), 1232–1234; and John Dewey, "The Quest for Certainty," in Jo Ann Boydston, ed., *The Later Works*, Vol. 4 (Carbondale and Edwardsville, IL: The University of Southern Illinois Press, 1984), 163–165.

24 Rosenthal, *Speculative Pragmatism*, 12–13.

25 Dewey, "The Quest for Certainty," 163.

26 Rosenthal, *Speculative Pragmatism*, 11.

27 James, "The Principles of Psychology," 1232–1234.

28 Linda Simon, *Dark Light: Electricity and Anxiety from the Telegraph to the X-Ray* (New York: Harcourt, 2004), 199.

29 James, "The Principles of Psychology," 961.

30 Charles Peirce, *Collected Papers*, Vol. 7, Arthur Burks, ed. (Cambridge, MA: Harvard University Press, 1958), 7.498.

31 Charles Peirce, *Collected Papers*, Vol. 5, Charles Hartshorne and Paul Weiss, eds. (Cambridge: Belknap Press of Harvard University, 1931–1935), 5.384.

32 Rosenthal, *Speculative Pragmatism*, 14.

33 See John Dewey, "The Seat of Intellectual Authority," in Jo Ann Boydston, ed., *The Middle Works*, Vol. 4 (Carbondale and Edwardsville, IL: Southern Illinois University Press, 1984), 137–138; John Dewey, *Essays in Experimental Logic* (New York: Dover Publications, 1916), 86; George Herbert Mead, *Philosophy of the Act* (Chicago: University of Chicago Press, 1938), 251; and C.I. Lewis, *Mind and the World Order* (New York: Dover Publications, 1929), 395–397.

34 Rosenthal, *Speculative Pragmatism*, 15.

35 John Dewey, "The Objectivism-Subjectivism of Modern Philosophy," in Jo Ann Boydston, ed., *The Later Works*, Vol. 14, 1939–1941 (Carbondale and Edwardsville, IL: Southern Illinois University Press, 1988), 196.

36 Rosenthal, *Speculative Pragmatism*, 15.

37 George Herbert Mead, "The Definition of the Psychical," *Mead: Selected Writings*, A.J. Reck, ed. (New York: Bobbs-Merrill Co., 1964), 34; Herbert Mead, *Philosophy of the Act*, 32.

38 Dewey, "Experience and Nature,"

39 Peirce, *Collected Papers*, 3.527.

40 C.I. Lewis, "Replies to My Critics," in P.A. Schilpp, ed., *The Philosophy of C.I. Lewis*, Library of Living Philosophers Series (La Salle, IL: Open Court, 1968), 660.

41 Charles Peirce, Microfilm Edition of the Peirce Papers, Sect. 647, 8.

42 Hickman, *Pragmatism as Post-PostModernism*, 39.

43 Ibid., 159.

44 Lee Smolin, "Cosmological Evolution" and "Loop Quantum Gravity," in John Brockman, ed., *Science at the Edge* (New York: Sterling Publishing Co., 2008), 156–157, 426.

45 John Dewey, "The Crisis in Culture," in Jo Ann Boydston, ed., *The Later Works*, Vol. 5, 1929–1930 (Carbondale and Edwardsville, IL: Southern Illinois University Press, 1984), 107.

46 Robert B. Laughlin, *A Different Universe: Reinventing Physics from the Bottom Down* (New York: Basic Books, 2005), 208–209.

47 Ibid., 31.

48 John D. Barrow, *New Theories of Everything* (New York: Oxford University Press, 2007), 163.

49 The relationship of nonlinear thinking to holism is captured in the following quote: "Thus, if a situation is linear or dominated by influences that are linear, it will be possible to piece together a picture of its whole behavior by examining it in small pieces. The whole will be composed of the sum of its parts . . . The output of a linear operation varies steadily and smoothly with any change in its input. Non-linear problems are none of these things. They amplify errors so rapidly that an infinitesimal uncertainty in the present state of the system can render any future prediction of its state worthless after a very short period of time. Their outputs respond in discontinuous and unpredictable ways to very small changes in their inputs. Particular local behaviors cannot be added together to build up a

global one: a holistic approach is required in which the system is considered as a whole." See Ibid., 225.

50 Arthur Peacocke, "The Sciences of Complexity: A New Theological Resource," in Paul Davies and Niels Henrik Gregersen, eds., *Information and the Nature of Reality: From Physics to Metaphysics* (New York: Cambridge University Press, 2010), 252–254.

51 Ernan Mc Mullin, "From Matter to Materialism . . . and (almost) Back," in Paul Davies and Niels Henrik Gregersen, eds., *Information and the Nature of Reality: From Physics to Metaphysics* (New York: Cambridge University Press, 2010), 35.

52 "Reductionism virtually destroys the meaningful wholes associated with our traditional understanding of humans and the world in which they live. For example, religion is reducible to some nonreligious origin such as the human psyche, human drives, or brain constitution. Human action as purposive or goal-oriented activity by which we relate to the meaningful world in which we live is reduced to neurophysiological behavior, with humans becoming nothing more than the object as studied by various disciplines such as physiology, neurology, anatomy, behavioral psychology, and so forth. Human values that direct action and the course of cultural development become identified with physiological or psychological drives and needs. Mental activity is reduced to biological or computational functions; mental phenomena are nothing more that neurophysiological functions. Human freedom is but a myth, with human actions governed by the laws of physiology, and with enough information, human actions could be predicted. At its extreme, physical objects themselves become nothing more than experienced sensations in our brain. In sum, the concrete fullness of humans and the qualitatively rich, value-laden, goal-directed contexts in which they have their being are all ultimately identical with, or reducible to, the systems of mathematical physics and physiology . . ." Sandra Rosenthal, "Reductionism," in Robert W. Kolb, ed., *Encyclopedia of Business Ethics and Society*, Vol 4 (Thousand Oaks, CA: Sage, 2008), 1784–1785.

53 "Holism," http://abyss.uoregon.edu/~js/glossary/holism.html, accessed August 23, 2008.

54 Keith Ward, "God as the Ultimate Informational Principle," in Paul Davies and Niels Henrik Gregersen, eds., *Information and the Nature of Reality: From Physics to Metaphysics* (New York: Cambridge University Press, 2010), 284.

55 Ibid.

56 Charis Anastopoulos, *Particle or Wave: The Evolution of the Concept of Matter in Modern Physics* (Princeton, NJ: Princeton University Press, 2008), 341.

57 John Dewey, "Democracy and Education," in Jo Ann Boydston, ed., *The Middle Works* Vol. 9, 1916 (Carbondale and Edwardsville, IL: University of Southern Illinois Press, 1980), 4–5.

58 See NIST Boulder Laboratories: Precision Measurements to Support Innovation. http://www.nist.gov/public_affairs/factsheet/boulder-lavoratories.cfm, accessed March 12, 2015. Astronomical time as determined by the rotation of the earth is adjusted by leap seconds to keep this time within one second of atomic time which is the average of atomic time clocks around the world. The earth is slowing down irregularly but slowly thus the rate of atomic time kept by NIST was adjusted to the earth's rotation in 1967, but the civil time we use called Coordinated Universal Time (UTC) needs to be adjusted to match the changing earth's rotation so that midnight at Greenwich is always within a second of UTC's midnight.

59 The qualities of objects did pose a problem for the rise of modern science. Scientific descriptions and definitions are framed in terms that made the qualities of objects superfluous. Science penetrated into the inner being of objects and the existence of qualities like colors, sounds, and texture, among others, was a

problem. What status did these qualities have in a scientific view of nature? The usual way of dealing with them is to consider these qualities as merely subjective existing only in the consciousness of individuals. They thus have no objective status. See John Dewey, "Essays: I Believe," in Jo Ann Boydston, ed., *The Later Works*, Vol. 14, 1942–1948 (Carbondale and Edwardsville, IL: University of Southern Illinois Press, 1988), 105.

60 John Dewey, "Essays: Has Philosophy a Future?" in Jo Ann Boydston, ed., *The Later Works*, Vol. 16, 1949–1952 (Carbondale and Edwardsville, IL: Southern Illinois University Press, 1989), 370–371.

61 John Dewey, "Qualitative Thought," in Jo Ann Boydston, ed., *The Later Works*, Vol. 5, 1925–1930 (Carbondale and Edwardsville, IL: Southern Illinois University Press, 1984), 251.

62 Barrow, *New Theories of Everything*, 63–65.

63 Ibid., 66.

64 John Dewey, "Essays: Inquiry and Indeterminateness of Situations," in Jo Ann Boydston, ed., *The Later Works*, Vol. 15, 1942–1948 (Edwardsville and Carbondale, IL: Southern Illinois University Press, 1989), 39.

65 John Dewey, "The Naturalization of Intelligence," in Jo Ann Boydston, ed., *The Later Works*, Vol. 4, 1929 (Carbondale and Edwardsville, IL: Southern Illinois University Press, 1984), 167.

66 Ibid., 166.

67 Ibid., 165. Italics in original.

68 Ibid. Dewey has this to say about the idea of universal laws: "It displaced once for all the notion of a world in which the unaccountable and the mysterious have the first and last word, a world in which they constantly insert themselves. It established the ideal of regularity and uniformity in place of the casual and sporadic. It gave men inspiration and guidance in seeking for uniformities and constancies where only irregular diversity was experienced. The ideal extended itself from the inanimate world to the animate and then to social affairs. It became, it may fairly be said, the great article of faith in the creed of scientific men." Ibid., 166.

69 Ibid., 168.

70 Ibid., 162–163.

71 Ibid., 163.

72 Foundationalism is the view that knowledge is arranged hierarchically with the most certain beliefs serving as evidence for all the rest.

73 Hickman, *Pragmatism as Post-PostModernism*, 53.

74 Ibid., 140.

13 Ideology and Politics

Science contributes to the individualistic outlook that informs American society and provides a philosophical basis for modern capitalism as I argued in my first book.[1] Individualism has been a key idea in Western societies for many centuries and is one of those unexamined assumptions about the way the world is constituted. Individualism is the idea that people are individual selves that are quite distinguishable from other selves and can be defined apart from any social context. The individual is held to be the primary unit of reality and the ultimate standard of value. Every person is an end in him- or herself, and no person should be sacrificed for the sake of another in some utilitarian context, where the greater good would override individual interests. While societies and other collective entities such as business organizations exist, they are nothing more than a collection of the individuals in them, not something over and above them that affects how individuals relate to each other as part of a whole. Organizations thus derive their being from the individuals who choose to become part of them and compose their membership.

Individualism

Within an individualistic outlook we are thought to be like atoms that are traveling around the world bumping up against other atoms or individuals in the course of our existence. As individual selves we are, by and large, alone in the world and in competition with other selves for the resources of society. We enter into contracts with other people in order to survive and provide for our needs through some form of cooperative endeavor, such as a business organization. Society is no more than the individuals within it who make contracts, but these contractual relationships are instrumental in that we relate to other people because they can do something for us and provide us with something we need for our existence. We are not linked to people except through these external ties that can never lead to a true community.

In this philosophy of individualism there is nothing but these external links to bind people and institutions together. Self-interested individuals and institutions that have separate wills and desires are constantly colliding like atoms in space; hence this philosophy of individualism is sometimes called atomic individualism. To minimize collisions and reduce conflict, people and institutions may come together on occasion to work out these differences and establish some sort of relationship. But while peripheral ties may be established when antecedent individuals enter into contract with one another or come together to more readily secure their own individualistic goals, these kinds of bonds cannot root them in any ongoing endeavor that is more than the sum of their separate selves, separate wills, and separate egoistic desires. There is never any possibility of developing a true community or society based on a sense of responsibility for each other.

If the community is seen as nothing more than the sum of its parts, society bounces back and forth between an emphasis on individual rights and community needs, between a celebration of diversity and the need for common goals and interests. Once the individual is taken as an isolatable unit, the individual and the community become pitted against each other in an ultimately irreconcilable tension. This tension between the individual and community causes a great deal of difficulty in arriving at mutually satisfactory solutions to social and political problems. Nothing binds individuals and institutions together except self-interest, and if one starts with individual and separate atomic bits of this sort, there is no way to get to a true community. True community can arise only in a form of action and thinking that does not attempt to fragment the whole of reality.[2]

Consistent with this view of individualism is the notion that rights inhere in individuals who are born with certain inalienable rights that are part and parcel of their being. These rights do not come from outside or in any sense belong to a community but are inherent in each individual in some sense when they are born. Our Declaration of Independence is based on this notion of rights as is the Bill of Rights spelled out in the first ten amendments to our Constitution. The former states that certain truths are held to be self-evident and that men are endowed by their Creator with certain unalienable Rights. This notion of rights is more or less universal as nations all over the world insist they have a right to do whatever they deem appropriate for their survival.

With its atomistic outlook, science contributes to the view that society is nothing more than a collection of individuals who bump up against each other in a competitive process. The whole of society is nothing more than the sum of the individuals who compose it, and these individuals have rights that reside in themselves as individuals. When these rights clash they must be adjudicated by the political process in some fashion so that the factionalism involved in such clashes can be kept under control and society continue to function. Thus, science involves a way of thinking that shapes the way we view the world and understand ourselves and our place in this world. This kind of individualistic thinking is pervasive in our society and informs how we understand ourselves and the world in which we live. While this kind of thinking has made it possible to manipulate our world and has led to technologies that have made our lives easier and more fulfilling, it also has limited our options and has cut us off from a richer understanding of our world as well as causing problems that we have not as yet been able to resolve.

The United States has a problem with government that is related to this kind of excessive individualism. Government is seen as a necessary evil and not as something positive that has useful functions to perform in society. It is something the populace must put up with while resenting the seeming necessity of government. The best government is the government that governs least and lets the market function with minimum interference. Many believe that our liberty itself depends on a distrust of government and that any acceptance of government as something positive in the life of our country will lead to extension of its powers that eventually will enslave its citizens. Many years ago Henry David Thoreau stated this credo in the following manner:

> I heartily accept the motto, "That government is best which governs least"; and I should like to see it acted up to more rapidly and systematically. Carried out, it finally amounts to this, which I also believe, "That government is best which governs not at all."[3]

Our Constitution, with its separation of powers, was designed to prevent the government from the exercise of arbitrary power and is not concerned about promoting the efficiency of government. The system of checks and balances contained in the Constitution prevents any one branch of government from dominating the others and makes it necessary to get agreement from all three branches before any legislation can be passed and upheld. This makes government slow and deliberative but prevents, so it is hoped, any one branch of government from gaining power over the others and acting arbitrarily in the use of this power to dominate society and exercise its will over its citizens. The framers were concerned about the misuse of government power and thus separated that power into the various branches that could act as a check on each other.

Liberty is considered to be a zero-sum game: that any power given to the government is by necessity subtracted from the liberty of the governed. Thus, any attempt to pass a health care bill is seen as taking away the freedom of individuals to choose their own way of fulfilling their health care needs, which may mean no insurance coverage and visits to the emergency room when health problems arise. Nonetheless, many believe it is better to go without health insurance than be enslaved by big government. Government is always under the suspicion that it will take away more freedom from its citizens than its services are worth.[4] According to John Dewey, it is seen as something that exists apart from the citizens that can take away their liberty:

> Upon its face, the struggle for individual liberty was a struggle against the overbearing menace of despotic rulers. This fact has survived in an

attitude towards government which cripples its usefulness as an agency of the general will. Government, even in the most democratic countries, is still thought of as an external "ruler," operating from above, rather than as an organ by which people associated in pursuit of common ends can most effectively cooperate for the realization of their own aims. Distrust of government was one of the chief traits of the situation in which the American nation was born. It is embodied not only in popular tradition, and party creeds, but in our organic laws, which contain many provisions expressly calculated to prevent the corporate social body from affecting its ends freely and easily through government agencies.[5]

Democracy requires some sense of community in order to function effectively, a sense that people are bound together by something more than self-interested reasons and that they are part of a tradition in which there are certain core values that make a country distinctive and something to which people can give their allegiance. There has to be some sense of common interests that binds people together and creates a society that is more than the sum of individual interests. Democracy in our country, however, is undermined by a sense of individualism that is part and parcel of our economic system that is based on free markets and thus spills over into our understanding of government and its role in society.

There is no sense of community in economic theory based on the free market as people are considered to be individual units with preferences that can be exploited by producers in the interests of selling their products. Any social reality of this sort is nonexistent as scientific reductionism inherent in economic theory focuses on the individual. Any conception of society is thus reducible to the individuals who compose the society. Competition is assumed to be the essential way that people relate to each other and this competition leads to the efficient use of scarce resources. People act rationally on the basis of economic self-interest and when they do not act in their economic self-interest they are believed to be irrational. Thus, government, which may allocate resources on a different basis than economic self-interest to accomplish some more common good for the community as a whole, is considered to be an irrational interference with the workings of the free market. According to Stephen A. Marglin writing in *The Dismal Science: How Thinking Like an Economist Undermines Community*,

> [i]t is the importance of ties of necessity that puts community at odds with the fundamental assumptions of economics. Markets, based on voluntary, instrumental, opportunistic relationships are diametrically opposed to the long-term commitments and obligations that characterize community. By promoting market relationships, economics undermines reciprocity, altruism, and mutual obligation, and therewith the necessity of community. The very foundations of economics, by justifying the expansion of markets, lead inexorably to the weakening of

community.[6] Community is important to a good and meaningful life. The market undermines community because it replaces personal ties of economic necessity by impersonal market transactions. Economics aids and abets the market; its very foundations make community and its virtues invisible and legitimize the focus on efficiency as the normative standard by which to judge economic outcomes.[7]

Individualism plays an instrumental role in economics as individuals are assumed to be so constituted that by their self-interested actions they produce efficient production and distribution mediated by a market system even it this if not part of their intention. The good as far as society is concerned is an aggregation of these individual assessments of well-being and is not something that can be assessed apart from these individual judgments on the basis of some overarching theory as to what constitutes the good society. Thus, attempts by government to create the good society amount to coercion of these individual choices in an attempt to create some utilitarian conception of the good. As Marglin states,

> [t]he basic idea of individualism is that society can and should be understood as a collection of autonomous individuals, that groups . . . have no normative significance as groups, that all behavior, policy, and even ethical judgment should be reduced to their effects on individuals . . . Responsibility means that individuals have agency; their preferences—subject to constraints (like income) but not to coercion (like physical force)—determine their choices, actions, and behavior. The idea that preferences are beyond discussion implies a radical subjectivism; one set of preferences is as worthy as another. Self-interest precludes acting for the sake of others, particularly acting for others out of a sense of duty or obligation.[8]

There is no better example of this individualism than the Tea Party Movement that appeared in 2010 and received a great deal of media attention. This movement, according to Mark Lilla writing in the *New York Review of Books*, grew out of a populist mood inspired by a radical individualism that had been brewing in the society for decades. During the Clinton years the country moved left on issues of private autonomy, such as sex and divorce, which had begun in the sixties and continued a rightward movement on economic autonomy that had started during the Reagan years with an emphasis on free markets and deregulation.[9]

The Tea Party Movement, according to Lilla, appealed to individual opinion, individual choice, and individual autonomy. Its rallying cry was one of wanting to be left alone as its members were tired of being told how to think about global warming, which foods they can eat, when they have to wear seatbelts and helmets, whether to insure themselves, and a host of other political grievances. The movement appealed to people who were convinced that they could do everything themselves if only they were left alone and that other people, including politicians, bureaucrats, doctors, scientists, and even schoolteachers, were controlling their lives and preventing them being autonomous individuals.[10]

These new Jacobins, as Lilla calls them, have two classic American traits, which are blanket distrust of institutions particularly government and what he calls an astonishing and unwarranted confidence in the self. People in this movement believe that they can do everything for themselves and that institutions should get out of the way and let them do their thing. They are trying to remind those in power that they are in their positions to do one thing and one thing only: to protect the divine right for people to do whatever they damn well please. For half a century, according to Lilla, Americans have been rebelling in one form or another in the name of individual freedom. The Tea Party Movement wants even more freedom, to be a people without rules to do whatever they want without outside interference.[11] But as stated by William Falk writing in *The Week* with regard to this libertarian approach,

"I am the master of my own fate—and no one, including the government, can tell me what to do." That's libertarianism in a nutshell, and in the abstract, it's a seductively appealing philosophy. Embrace it, and it leads to a natural corollary: Parents should not be forced to vaccinate their kids against childhood diseases. "The state doesn't own your children," as sometimes-libertarian Sen. Rand Paul explained this week. "Parents own their children, and it is an issue of freedom." In California and 13 other states caught up in a measles outbreak, we are now seeing a demonstration that one person's freedom can inflict painful and potentially fatal consequences on an entire community. Childhood diseases that medicine defeated decades ago are making a comeback, thanks to parents who seek "philosophical" exemptions from vaccinating their kids. Libertarians are absolutely right that personal freedom is important—and easily eroded. Left unchecked, government does indeed presume too much control over our decisions, our money, and our privacy. But in a country or 320 million souls, what we do affects each other—sometimes profoundly. In a libertarian paradise, Americans would still be free to smoke in enclosed offices and restaurants, and 50 percent of the population would still be lighting up—sticking society with their health-care costs. No one would be required to wear a seat belt in the car. And yes, vaccinations would be strictly optional, and the nation's "herd immunity" would disappear. As an old adage points out, your right to swing your fist ends at the tip of another person's nose. So go ahead, swing your fist—but good luck finding a space that doesn't have a nose in it.[12]

Such an approach is completely unrealistic in today's world. Any given individual cannot even begin to provide for themselves in a rugged individualism kind of manner. We live in a highly interdependent world that is now global in nature. What happens in some far-off place in the world affects us in ways we do not even understand. Naturally this gives us a great deal of insecurity and a feeling that we have lost control of our lives. And indeed, in many ways we have, but there is no turning back to a simpler world where we can live in relative isolation from other people and do as we please.[13] Our actions affect other people and we are affected by theirs, and this must be taken into account in any realistic assessment of the responsibilities we have for each other in such an interdependent world. Zygmunt Bauman, an emeritus professor of sociology at the University of Leeds, thinks that

> [i]ndeed, globalization looks now inescapable and irreversible. The point of no return has been reached—and passed. There is no way back. Our interconnections and interdependencies are already global. Whatever happens in one place influences the lives and life chances of people in all other places. Calculation of steps to be taken in any one place must reckon with the responses of people everywhere else. No sovereign territory, however large, populous, and resourceful, can single—handedly protect its living conditions, its security, long-term prosperity, preferred form of life, or the safety of its inhabitants. Our mutual dependency is planetwide and so we are already, and will remain indefinitely, *objectively* responsible for one another. There are, however, few signs that we who share the planet are willing to take up in earnest the *subjective* responsibility for that objective responsibility of ours.[14]

Ever since Ronald Reagan declared government to be the problem and not the solution to our problems, a negative view of government has increasingly informed our political environment and made governing more and more difficult. We have been asked to love our country by hating our government as if the two were totally separable entities. Reagan denigrated a government career so that we are obliged to despise the people we vote into office.[15] Rather than attracting the best and brightest people in society to go into public service, what we have seen is more people in government who do not believe in governing or in serving the public. According to Jeffrey D. Sachs,

> [t]he main effect of the Reagan Revolution, however, was not the specific policies but a new antipathy to the role of government, a new disdain for the poor who depend on government for income support, and a new invitation for the rich to shed their moral responsibilities to the rest of society. Reagan helped plant the notion that society could benefit the most not by insisting on the civic virtue of the wealthy, but by cutting their tax rates and thereby unleashing their entrepreneurial zeal. Whether such entrepreneurial zeal was released is debatable, but there is little doubt that a lot of pent-up greed was released, greed that infected the political system and that still haunts America today.[16]

Government is broken, and while there are many reasons for this condition, this development is certainly a major reason. For people to function effectively in any organization they have to believe in what they are doing and do their best to fulfill the mission of the organization for which they are working. But it is not only politicians who have a negative view of government; it exists in the society at large or they wouldn't get elected. To some extent, the government we have is a self-fulfilling prophecy. We get the government we want by electing politicians who share our values with respect to government service, and if the society at large does not believe in government they will elect politicians that reflect this belief and will act accordingly in making government dysfunctional. As David Sprintzen, professor emeritus of philosophy at Long Island University, concludes,

> [b]y now one thing should be totally clear: individualism is a theoretically and socially destructive doctrine. It might be called the social disease of modernity, completely mangling any capacity to understand the process by which society produces and nurtures individuals into adulthood . . . At its worst, it is a disintegrative attack on the pedagogical value and emotional sustenance of every collectivity, denying personal and collective moral responsibility for the quality of life of its members. It thus serves as a justification for a narrow self-seeking (often profit-maximizing) egoism . . . It is simply the atomism of the social world: and effort to reduce a complexly webbed relational world to the purported fundamental units encountered in direct perception out of which that world is supposed to have been constructed. Reducing society to individuals is thus all of a piece with the program of metaphysical reductionism, which at least implicitly serves as its theoretical justification. What it totally misses in the not directly perceivable relational structure that literally gives birth and substance to, and thus sustains, the emerging individual—even providing those cultural interpretations that lead some to misconceive of themselves as "self-made men."[17]

We like to think we are a procedural republic where the only agreed-upon value is that every individual should be free to pursue his or her own conception of the good without undue government interference. Government's only role is to assure that everyone has an equal opportunity to pursue his or her own goals and objectives in the context of a competitive marketplace. Critics of this notion, like Michael Sandel, think the procedural republic is a figment of the imagination rather than a basis for any kind of social reality.[18] For any kind of social cohesion to exist there must be some consensus beyond the virtue of pursuing one's own conception of the good. Otherwise, there is no possibility of community or of ever reaching an agreement about things that individuals cannot provide for themselves.[19]

John Dewey thinks of government not so much as an institution but as a way of life that is "controlled by a working faith in the possibilities of human nature" that are exhibited by every human being irrespective of color, sex, race, birth and family, and material or cultural wealth. Democracy involves the belief that in spite of individual differences regarding ends and means, people can cooperate on common courses of action by giving the other a chance to express itself instead of having one party forcefully suppress the other. People can learn from each other if differences are given a chance to show themselves. This freedom of expression is not only a right but a means of enriching one's own life experience in the context of community.[20]

Reaching a true community requires a view of the self which is inherently communal rather than individualistic. This social view of the self involves seeing the self as embedded in a moral community that allows for progression toward a common good. This notion of inherently communal selves enmeshed in a common "telos" is supported by a substantive political theory that envisions deliberation among citizens that leads to legislation which promotes the common good or a common conception of the good. This is in contrast to the notion of independent selves that are free of encumbrance by any social or moral bonds that are not self-chosen and is supported by a political theory that advocates a procedural approach to politics that is devoid of any social or moral content.[21] According to Sprintzen again,

> [t]he individual is *both* a relatively autonomous center of activity and an immersed participant whose being is sustained by, as it sustains, the ecological field of which it is a part. The autonomous individual is a fiction. Individuality is always partial, embedded, historical, and transactional.[22] By asserting the ultimate social reality of the single self-determining free individual, it [individualism] seems to be celebrating the values of human self-realization and individual achievement. But it does this only by failing to consider the social preconditions that make human development possible, thus implicitly sanctifying whatever is the existing structure of social benefits and burdens, no matter their source and moral justification. It further solidifies a social order that implicitly justifies a competitive struggle among individuals, ensuring that the success of some will inevitably at the expense of the rest. Then it reflexively justifies that competitive order by appealing to the completely misconceived ontological foundation provided by the very doctrine itself. It thus constitutes a self-enclosed circle of self-fulfilling ideological justification for a destructive and unequal war of all against all in which those who are currently ahead are most likely to stay there, and can do so freed from any moral qualms concerning the fate of the less successful.[23]

Alternatives to Individualism

E. J. Dionne, a widely respected columnist, published a book in 2012 titled *Our Divided Political Heart* that dealt with the issue of individualism versus community.[24] The American tradition, he argues, is not based on radical self-reliance and self-interest but, rather, on a balance between individual freedom and devotion to community. Both these values have informed the consciousness of the country since its inception. As he states, "[w]e are a nation of individuals who care passionately about community. We are also a nation of communitarians who care passionately about individual freedom. We believe in limited government, but also in active and innovative government." While these values are indeed opposed to each other, it is a balance between them that must be recovered in order for the country to move forward.[25]

Recent years, he says, have witnessed the rise of a radical form of individualism that denigrates the role of government in our lives and the importance of the quest for community. During most of the twentieth century, the United States prospered under what Dionne calls the "Long Consensus," a period when there was a balance between individualism and community. During this period the government assumed many new roles and grew in size and influence, but at the same time individual opportunities expanded. The United States became the most powerful nation on earth, and its citizens enjoyed a shared prosperity. But this consensus, he claims, is now under a fierce assault from an individualistic right that has become the most energetic force in the conservative movement and the Republican Party.[26]

The current political struggle centers on the question of whether we should refashion the Long Consensus in some manner or give up on it entirely. This question involves what role government should play in society: whether we should have a minimalist government (the best government is the one that governs least) or whether government is a constructive institution that should be used to address major problems in society. Democrats by and large favor the Long Consensus while Republicans, especially the Tea Party, seek to replace it with an individualistic free-market orientation.[27]

Dionne spends a good bit of the book attempting to reclaim the history of the country which he states has been distorted by one-sided accounts that cast individualism as the nation's primary value and opposition to government as its overriding passion. Dionne claims that such a view is not only a disservice to the facts of history, but also provides what he calls "a stunted view of the meaning of liberty and a flawed understanding of the Constitution." There is far too much talk, he argues, that emphasizes our commitment to individualism to the exclusion of our communitarian impulses. References to "community" or the "common good" are cast as alien to our commitment to "rugged individualism" of the Ann Rand type.[28]

Dionne's basic argument is that it is only by restoring the proper balance between individualism and community that the country can deal effectively with its problems. Our nation will never be purely communitarian any more than it will be purely individualistic. Americans will always fear a collective such as society that may overwhelm the individual and destroy autonomy and individual freedom. Yet we also recognize that it is only in relation to society that individuals can fulfill themselves. Dionne's primary argument is not with the entire conservative tradition but only with the form of extreme individualism that conservatism is currently taking. We must acknowledge both sides of our national character to restore our greatness as a nation and to heal our political wounds.[29]

Another book on the same theme was written by Tom Allen, who is a former Democratic congressman from Maine and was president and CEO of the American Association of Publishers at the time the book was written.[30] Allen believes that below the surface of debates in Congress over health care, budgets, education, or whatever lies an enduring tension in American politics and culture between individualism and community. Republicans are determined to cut taxes and regulations and, in general, shrink the size of government in order to increase personal freedom because they believe government spending restricts such freedom and induces a "culture of dependency." Democrats, on the other hand, advocate a federal role in health care, education, environmental protection, climate change, and a host of other problems facing the nation and believe that government is necessary to increase individual opportunity and strengthen the economy. The two parties have become polarized opposites of each other and cannot compromise on most major issues.[31] According to Allen,

> I see no way to diminish our current political polarization without a sustained public dialogue about individualism and community in American life, because that is the primary source of congressional gridlock. Our businesses, our sports, our military, and even our political parties are focused on team building. But our politics and capacity to govern ourselves successfully have been immeasurably weakened by a fierce hostility to government rooted in a radical individualism that denigrates the idea—in the context of government—that helping others strengthens the country.[32]

The Republicans have not developed a plan for health care reform, for example, that would replace Obamacare, which they hate because they don't believe government should be involved in health care in the first place. The same is true for energy, climate change, and other issues that Democrats believe necessitate government leadership. The Republicans have no policies to address these challenges and thus are unable and unwilling to engage Democrats in constructive compromise on these issues. The only thing they continue to advocate is smaller government and lower taxes, a stance which provides no means to develop a national strategy to address these issues, according to Allen, and results in a dysfunctional government.[33]

With regard to the how Democrats perceive Republicans Allen lists the following: (1) they [Republicans] appear to pay less attention to evidence about the economic consequences of a proposal and instead appear to be guided by broad principles related to the ineffectiveness of government, faith in free markets, and the exercise of power in foreign affairs, (2) they have a much greater emotional distance from Americans struggling to get ahead and a closer affinity with the successful, and (3) Republicans are obstructionists without a serious programmatic agenda of their own and no coherent plan to deal with issues other than stopping Democratic initiatives.[34] Republicans, on the other hand, see Democrats

> as the party of big government and [believe that] government screws up almost everything it touches; it is inefficient, wasteful, and in an attempt to improve people's lives, almost inevitably compromises their personal freedom of action. Since "free markets" are the most effective allocators of resources, markets provide the best path to prosperity in almost all circumstances. Republicans also believe that Americans struggle every day with unnecessary government regulations, an ineffective bureaucracy, and burdensome taxation, all of which retard economic growth and diminish personal freedom.[35]

Again, Allen sees the partisan differences between Democrats and Republicans growing out of the enduring tension between individualism and community: what we should do together and what we should do alone, and of those things we should do together, which should be addressed by government and which by other institutions. Allen sees individualism as the first language of American culture as we tend to explain our success and others' failures in terms of what we as individuals have done or not done rather than think in terms of larger social and economic forces that constrain and shape our choices. Our sense of community is sort of a second language that is much weaker in that we often have great difficulty describing the ties that bind us to family, friends, neighbors, fellow workers, and to society at large.[36]

When government is always seen as the problem rather than the solution, which has been the case for most Republicans since former president Reagan made this theme a major part of his program, the ability of Congress to debate and decide on a course of action for public issues is severely crippled. Denying a role for the federal government in strategic planning for the country in a world that is increasingly interconnected weakens the country, according to Allen. Engaging in constructive debates and decision making with regard to federal taxes and expenditures is crucial to our future prosperity. But Allen states that this kind of engagement didn't happen while he was in Congress, and he thinks it is close to impossible in the current Congress:[37]

> The struggle of the widest consequence occurs on the ground defined by budget and tax policy . . . Americans, most of them, fail to understand the lifeline between the public and private sectors, the necessity of spending public dollars to invest in fairness today and opportunity tomorrow . . . Our children are educated, our streets protected, our elderly housed and kept from poverty, our sick and disabled cared for,

and our businessmen and women supported, among many others, by the public through public decisions.[38]

Allen accuses conservatives of clinging to an old conviction that tax cuts pay for themselves because it works politically and allows them to avoid making the difficult choices of either reducing spending or increasing other revenues to offset the tax cuts that mainly benefit the already wealthy. Any restriction of personal freedom on the part of government is resisted. This worldview, according to Allen, "is in stark contrast to the Democratic belief that government is a vehicle for creating individual opportunity and taking collective action for the common good." If politics in America continues to be a battle of these kinds of worldviews, a struggle between what Allen calls our archetypical individualism and our engagement with others, national politics in his view will likely remain dysfunctional:[39]

> Democrats see Republicans as inattentive to evidence and expertise, unconcerned about Americans struggling to get by, and reflexively opposed to government action to deal with our collective challenges. On the other hand, Republicans see Democrats as the party of a government that routinely infringes on personal freedom, as creators of a "culture of dependency" among people who should stand on their own, and as promoters of change from traditional values that will leave us weaker than before . . . Above all, the abiding clash between the view of government as a vehicle for the common good and the view of government as an obstacle to progress and personal freedom sits close to the center of our ideological gridlock.[40]

The positions of the other side in Congress appear so extreme and incomprehensible that they must be resisted. The battle that both sides are engaged in involves what it means to be an American and what the lives of people in the future will be like. Allen quotes Abraham Lincoln who in 1854 said, "The legitimate object of government is to do for a community of people whatever they need to have done but cannot do at all, or cannot so well do, for themselves, in the separate and individual capacities."[41] The problem is that Democrats and Republicans have incompatible worldviews about relations with other people, what individuals can do by themselves, and what we need to do together. Allen believes that the inability to compromise on a host of issues is primarily driven by the ideological rigidity of Republicans who have "become hostile to almost any form of government action across a wide range of disparate subjects."[42]

Allen describes the vision of the Republicans as involving personal freedom, faith in free markets, and hostility to government action, which results in a government that must be "smaller" and taxes "lower." Allen calls this a simple agenda uncomplicated by the multiple and often contradictory desires of the American people. Everybody wants lower taxes; thus, the

Republican vision has a built-in advantage in getting people's attention and support. But the American people also want good schools for their kids, clean air and water, affordable health care, Social Security, safe streets, a dependable infrastructure, fire protection, and an effective national defense, and none of these public goods are free for the asking.[43]

The differences between the world views of Republicans and Democrats are deeply rooted making it much more difficult to compromise than differences in just economic interests. These worldviews are reinforced by media coverage of politics and the increasing sophistication of appeals to the emotions and attitudes of the public. The convictions these worldviews involve limit imagination and the ability to act on public issues. The convictions of the Republican Party that tax cuts pay for themselves, that climate science isn't proved, and the government-run or -regulated health care doesn't work are dangerous, says Allen, "as they deny the weight of credible evidence and expertise and produce consequences adverse to any concept of the common good."[44]

Americans speak both the language of individualism and the language of community, according to Allen, but this yin and yang of the American psyche have been split apart by worldview politics. Allen sees no hope of getting beyond ideological polarization and congressional dysfunction until the Republican Party escapes the grip of the libertarian worldview and agrees with the Democrats that the government can address problems beyond the capacity of the private sector. There are four neglected virtues that Allen thinks are diminished by the ideology of radical individualism and neglected by the mainstream media: (1) respect for evidence, (2) tolerance of ambiguity, (3) caring about consequences, and (4) commitment to the common good. These four virtues need to be nourished in order to compete with their opposites: (1) elevating opinion over evidence, (2) interpreting the world in black and white, (3) keeping an emotional distance from other people, and (4) accepting interest group politics as an ideal.[45]

Ultimately, Allen believes that a balance between individualism and community must be recovered and that a discourse of these two worldviews must involve all American citizens. As the challenges to the country grow more complex, the dumbing down of our political discourse erodes our confidence and undermines our collective capacity to thrive. Is it possible that Congress can be made to act in service to both the ideals of individualism and community? Allen believes that by some not-yet-visible process the country will eventually find its way to a more pragmatic leadership that is inspired by a commitment to the common good of the nation. He is optimistic about the long run, but the short run, as he says, "is anyone's guess."[46]

The Problem

Most Republicans, including the libertarians and Tea Partiers, usually frame the battle they are fighting with the government as the individual versus the collective: that the lonely individual has to do battle with other such individuals to preserve their freedom against the big, bad government (the collective), whose only function, it seems, is to rob individuals of their individual freedoms that are guaranteed by the constitution.[47] Many of these people are followers of Ann Rand, claiming to have read all 1,200 pages of *Atlas Shrugged*, and identify with the hero John Galt, who fought the bureaucrats in Washington to install his new innovation in rail making that was more efficient and durable than other technology.[48]

This is a rather odd way of stating the problem, even though many who are not even identified with the Tea Party or libertarians would probably agree that this is a correct way to state things as antigovernment sentiment is strong throughout the country. The only problem is that in reality, we all are part of a collective from our birth until the day we die. The great majority of us are born in a hospital, a collective of doctors, nurses, administrators, and other medical professionals who bring us into this world and nurse us as long as necessary to become sustainable babies who can leave the hospital. We are born into a collective called a family that hopefully provides us with all the things we need to grow and develop and also nurtures us to become fully functioning human beings.

We eventually attend another collective called a school which is a collection of faculty, administrators, and other educational professionals so that we can learn knowledge and skills that enable us to sustain ourselves in society by getting a job and contributing something to society. Many join a collective called the church, where we join with other people of like mind to provide for our spiritual and social needs in that kind of institutional setting. Most of us join a collective organization called a business to earn money to support ourselves and our families; few of us work strictly alone without any coworkers. We are part of a collective called a society that has shared values and ways of doing things. And yes, if we truly believe in a government of, by, and for the people we are part of collective called the government that we support by paying taxes and that provides us with certain goods and services that can't be provided by the private sector. Even the Tea Partiers and libertarians themselves are part are part of a collective of like-minded people who share their values and outlook on government and society.

Our individual identities are a collective amalgam of influences from families, churches, schools, friends, institutions, society, and a host of other factors that shape our values and attitudes and when mixed with our own unique talents and ways of looking at things constitute who we are, something called the self. There is no such thing as a strictly individual identity that is not influence by these outside factors. And when we die we are hopefully surrounded by a collective of family and friends at the funeral and are buried in a collective called a cemetery. Very few of us, if any, are buried in some individual plot that is off by itself in some lonely corner of a field or whatever.

A collective is a number of individuals acting together as a group with common goals and interests that cannot necessarily be pursued individually. It is impossible to imagine any individual that could survive solely on their own without being part of a group. How long could any of us survive if we were suddenly thrown into a wilderness all by ourselves with no tools or matches or anything else to help us survive except what we can find in nature. We would have to use our own ingenuity and use sticks and stones to kill animals if we could for food and eat berries or whatever and rub sticks together to make a fire to keep warm and cook things. Even allowing for the clothes on our back and shoes on our feet, which were made by someone else, it is impossible to imagine that anyone could survive very long under these circumstances. We all need each other to survive and make a decent life for ourselves. Collectives are necessary for life itself.

Management is a collective even though we don't like to think of it in those terms. When individual employees bargain with management over wages, salaries, and working conditions, they have no power to exercise against the collective power of management and more or less have to take whatever is offered to them or quit and seek another job more to their liking, which may not be possible given the economic conditions and other circumstances that exist at the time. Unions were formed to collectively bargain with management that gave employees some bargaining power to look after their own interests. But unions are generally hated in our society and have declined in recent years, so they no longer are much of a force in this regard. Public-sector unions have been under direct attack by some states that took away their bargaining rights. This has left employees on their own again, and while management and administrators receive ever-increasing salaries and bonuses, employee wages have stagnated or even declined in recent decades. The collective power of management is unchecked.

This is true of academia as well, as it was always us versus them in a university setting, meaning the faculty versus the administration. The administration always had the best offices and the highest salaries for the most part, and while faculty had some power and were protected by tenure, they were still by and large subject to the decisions of the administration. Tenure could be circumvented by the elimination of whole programs or departments so that faculty in those programs or departments had to seek employment elsewhere despite tenure. Salaries were set by the administration, and unless the faculty was unionized they had no bargaining power to counter these decisions. Many of us were perpetually on the market and could use offers from other schools to try to bargain with the administration, but many faculty who were not in high demand could not use this tactic.

The free market beloved by libertarians and the Tea Party has a collective element. The market works so well because it allows millions of individuals to express their preferences for specific goods and services that are offered on the market. The market sweeps up more information than any other arrangement and is more efficient than some planned economy because it responds to these individual preferences meaning that things are produced that people want in the quantities desired. But these individual's preferences are aggregated into a *collective* demand schedule that faces the productive institutions of society, and they respond to this collective aggregation rather than individual preferences. As stated by Holmes Ralston, III, University Distinguished Professor and Professor Emeritus at Colorado State University,

> [t]here is a feedback loop from single persons to society at large. The "unselfish" act of any particular individual benefits not only the person immediately assisted but, since it sets up a larger climate, benefits unspecified beneficiaries; and this common good promoted redounds to the benefit of the individual self. That entwines the "self" with the community at large, and there is nothing problematic about finding that self-interest is sometimes interlocked with the common good. We might not want to call such concerns pure altruism, but it is certainly not pure selfishness. Why not say that in certain areas, like public safety, there are shared values? Notice also that an ethical dimension is beginning to emerge, for, although those entering into such a social contract stand to gain on average, they also acquire obligations to support this contract.[49]

The reason the world collective engenders such strong hostile emotions may have a lot to do with communism and the collective thrust involved in this arrangement as agriculture was collectivized along with productive organizations that were placed under bureaucratic control. But this arrangement did not work out very well, and some form of free enterprise has evolved in most countries around the world. While the political system in China, for example, remains under communist control, there is more freedom in the economy for entrepreneurship and individual initiative that has benefited China with high growth rates and decreasing poverty. With the breakup of the Soviet Union and changes in China, collectivization as known under Stalin and Mao is a dead issue, and we ought to get over these associations we have in our minds when the word collective is mentioned.

The bottom line is that if we are at war with the collective we are really at war with ourselves. There is no way we can escape being part of a group or collective, and there is no such thing as an individual who has developed solely by him- or herself and who does not have a collective identity. What might be going on here is that there is some inner conflict that is unresolved, and this conflict gets projected onto the collective we call the government that is seen as this dreaded something robbing us of our cherished freedoms. We forget that the government is us acting together to do things collectively that we can't do for ourselves, like provide for national defense or for roads and clean air. In a democracy such as ours, we are the government, and what the government as an institution does is subject to our direction and influence.

However, we see government as something over against us that has to be fought against. And so we elect people to represent us who do not believe in government and only want to reduce its functions and cut the benefits to those who are most vulnerable, while in most cases, at least in recent years, increase the share of the economic pie going to the already wealthy. No other organization that I know of would want people in it who do not believe in what the organization is doing and want to what it does better and more efficiently and make it work for the entire citizenry. But that does not seem to be the case in our country as we believe in rampant individualism with rights and freedoms that are inherent in the individual and are in no way a social product. Thus, we have to protect these rights and freedoms by constantly doing battle with the government, which we believe is out to take those rights away in the name of the collective.

Phil Parvin, a scholar at the University of Loughborough who wrote a book about the philosopher Karl Popper, believes that collectivism became the enemy of conservatives during the 1960s and 1970s when a broad social democratic consensus developed as the state took on more responsibilities in rebuilding the shattered European societies and economies after World War II. This involved a redistribution of wealth and the provision of welfare to an extent that had not been seen before, and there was a general sense among politicians and the wider society, according to Parvin, "that the politics of the time called for a strengthening of unity and solidarity over individualism and competition." The idea that it was the responsibility of government to provide jobs, rebuild industry, provide welfare, and, in general, promote social unity through state action and that it was possible for the state to engage in a planned reform of society became more and more dominant.[50]

This move toward collectivism was of major concern to traditional liberals committed to free markets, individualism, and limited politics and conservatives committed to pragmatism, tradition, and a profound antisocialism. They both feared that governments were engaging in what they saw as unrealistic social engineering and that politics was becoming too dominated by powerful groups in society like the trade unions. In the late 1970s both liberals and conservatives thought things has gone far enough and united under the banner of the "New Right" and advocated for a return to political pragmatism, limited politics, individualism, and the freeing of the individual from the burden of a meddlesome and intrusive state.[51] In the United States the election of Ronald Reagan represented a turning point in this battle against collectivism, and ever since government has been seen as the problem rather than the solution.

For theoretical support liberals and conservatives turned to Friedrich von Hayek, who in *The Road to Serfdom* argued against government planning and state control over the means of production and advocated a return to *laissez-faire* economics.[52] Both Hayek and Popper rejected long-term economic and social planning and instead favored piecemeal progress through trial and error. They believed that reason alone was unable to provide certainty, and thus, one could not predict with precision the future consequences of any particular action or decision on the part of government. Both of them believed that an important task for philosophy "was to discover the limits of reason and to determine the appropriate means of structuring and reforming society in circumstances of epistemological uncertainty."[53]

Thus, we have moved toward an increasing belief in individualism over the past several decades and toward an increasing suspicion of anything government does as it is a collective that is not to be trusted. Elizabeth Warren, a senator from the state of Massachusetts, is one of the few lawmakers who holds a positive theory of government and believes that government permits us to do things than none of us could do alone. She mentioned infrastructure as an example of why a federal government is necessary and stated that we create something more valuable by working through government. By working together we help to create the conditions for people to become more innovative, more competitive, and ultimately more successful.[54] During her campaign for the Democratic senatorial nomination in Massachusetts she said the following:

> There is nobody in this country who got rich on their own. Nobody. You build a factory out there—good for you. But I want to be clear. You moved your goods to market on the roads the rest of us paid for. You hired workers the rest of us paid to educate. You were safe in your factory because of police forces and fire forces that the rest of us paid for ... You build a factory and it turned into something terrific or a great idea—God bless, keep a big hunk of it. But part of the underlying social contract is [that] you take a hunk of that and pay forward for the next kid who comes along.[55]

That her statement should have been controversial shows how far we have departed from the reality in which we live and that the idea of the self-made man and rugged individualism is alive and well in American society. Nonetheless George Will saw the need to try to refute her argument. He admits that "everyone knows that all striving occurs in a social context, so all attainments are conditioned by their context." But this assumption, he goes on to say, does not entail a collectivist political agenda. Such an agenda, he argues, is premised on the idea "that any individual's achievements should be considered entirely derivative from society, so that the achievements need not be treated as belonging to the individual." He goes on to say that "Warren's statement is a footnote to modern liberalism's more comprehensive disparagement of individualism and the reality of individual autonomy."[56]

That this is an overreaction seems obvious, but such is the reality in today's world of conservative dominance that any mention that government is necessary and that we just might need some kind of a collectivist agenda that involves government formulating public policies to deal with a problem is pure anathema to be put down quickly lest it take root in the public's thinking. This kind of individualistic mentality has to be overcome if we are ever to recover some sense of spirituality that can revive our connection with nature and with each other. We are part of a collective whether we like it or not, and in this highly interdependent and technologically complex world we need each other and rely on each other more than ever. To say otherwise is pure fantasy.

Aristotle believed that human beings cannot live the best possible lives that are completely flourishing unless they live in the right kind of political community. He insisted on meaningful citizen participation in government in order to keep government in the hands of ordinary people and prevent the formation of elite groups who would use government to serve only their own interests. The community must provide citizens with a level of material resources that enables them to participate in the life of the community, but the promotion of ownership and accumulation of material goods for their own sake must be avoided. Rather material goods must be used to creatively develop one's own rational powers or the powers of others. The exercise of our powers is enjoyable, and as they are developed more fully more and more of the world becomes comprehensible. Each time we learn something, our life becomes more enjoyable, which gives us an internal strength to conquer sadness and despair.[57] Politics is, according to Aristotle,

> about learning to live a good life. The purpose of politics is nothing less than to enable people to develop their distinctive human experiences and virtues—to deliberate about the common good, to acquire practical judgment, to share in self-government, to care for the fate of the community as a whole.[58]

That we are a long way from attaining this ideal should be readily apparent, as the radical individualism that currently holds sway in our society does not believe in community or in anything like the common good so there is nothing to deliberate about or care about as far as community is concerned. However, those who adhere to a radical individualism would do well to read other books besides those authored by Ann Rand to get a better sense of community and the common good. Besides reading ancient political philosophers such as Aristotle, more modern thinkers have much to say regarding the role and function of government.[59] For example, Jean-Jacques Rousseau has the following to say about what he calls the general will or the common good:

> The first and foremost consequence of the principles established above is that the general will alone can direct the forces of the state in accordance with the end for which is was instituted, that is, the common good, for, if the opposition of private interests has made the establishment of societies necessary, the agreement of these same interests has

made it possible. It is what these different interests hold in common that forms the social bond, and if there were not some point of agreement among them, no society could exist. Indeed, it is solely on the basis of this common interest that society should be governed.[60]

Rousseau goes on to say that the general interest is the common ground of particular interests as each particular interest contains in it the general interest, each particular will the general will. The general will is indestructible, inalienable, and always correct, which means the general interest always exits whether or not it is declared or eluded.[61] Thus, the state's purpose is to find this common ground rather than adjudicate between particular interests in some kind of balancing act, as the idea of a general will goes beyond a balancing of interests and points toward those things that are good for all people that should be incorporated into the laws passed by the legislature. Individualism works against this general will, and as long as we think of ourselves as individuals with particular interests and goals, it is difficult to develop a sense of the common good and create a true community where the clash of individual interests does not lead to a dysfunctional state and a society that is polarized. We must have a sense of a spiritual connection with each other for the general will to emerge.[62]

Both Dionne and Allen think that a balance between individualism and community needs to be restored, that these two worldviews are always in tension, but that when one of these polar opposites becomes dominant as is currently the case, society and its political system cannot function effectively. But one has to wonder if there is a fundamental contradiction between individualism and community that has been masked throughout most of our history and that only now is becoming readily apparent. Is it really possible to attain a balance between individualism and community that is functional, or is it necessary to transcend this dichotomy to reach a point where we are united with each other in a common purpose?

Notes

1 Rogene A. Buchholz, *Rethinking Capitalism: Community and Responsibility in Business* (New York: Routledge, 2009).
2 See David Bohm, *Wholeness and the Implicate Order* (London: Routledge & Kegan Paul, 1980).
3 Henry David Thoreau, "Civil Disobedience," in Owen Thomas, ed., *Walden, and Civil Disobedience* (New York: Norton, 1996), 224, as quoted in Garry Wills, *A Necessary Evil: A History of American Distrust of Government* (New York: Simon & Schuster, 1999), 15.
4 Wills, *A Necessary Evil*, 300.
5 John Dewey, "Civil Society and the Political State," in Jo Ann Boydston, ed., *The Middle Works*, Vol. 5 1899–1924 (Carbondale and Edwardsville, IL: Southern Illinois University Press, 1978), 425.
6 Stephen A. Marglin, *The Dismal Science: How Thinking Like an Economist Undermines Community* (Cambridge, MA: Harvard University Press, 2008), 27.

7 Ibid., 56.
8 Ibid., 45–46.
9 Mark Lilla, "The Tea Party Jacobins," *The New York Review of Books*, May 27, 2010, 53.
10 Ibid.
11 Ibid., 56.
12 William Falk, "The Week." *The Week*, February 13, 2015, 3.
13 See Andrew Romano, "America's Holy Writ," *Newsweek*, October 25, 2010, 33–37. Also see Jacob Weisberg, "A Tea Party Taxonomy," *Newsweek*, September 27, 2010, 33.
14 Zygmunt Bauman, *Does Ethics Have a Chance in a World of Consumers?* (Cambridge, MA: Harvard University Press, 2008), 26. Italics in original.
15 Wills, *A Necessary Evil*, 320.
16 Jeffrey Sachs, *The Price of Civilization: Reawakening American Virtue and Prosperity* (New York: Random House, 2011), 31.
17 David Sprintzen, *Critique of Western Philosophy and Social Theory* (New York: Palgrave Macmillan, 2009), 132.
18 See Michael J. Sandel, *Justice: What's the Right Thing to Do?* (New York: Farrar, Strauss & Giroux, 2009), for an exposition of this same criticism in regards to notions of justice.
19 Marglin, *The Dismal Science*, 28.
20 John Dewey, "Creative Democracy—The Task Before Us," in Jo Ann Boydston, ed., *The Later Works*, Vol. 14, 1925–1953 (Carbondale and Edwardsville, IL: Southern Illinois University Press, 1988), 226–228.
21 Sandra B. Rosenthal and Rogene A. Buchholz, "Pragmatism as a Political Philosophy for Emerging Democracies," in Leszek Koczanowicz and Beth Singer, eds., *Democracy and the Post-Totalitarian Experience* (New York: Rodopi, 2005), 194.
22 Sprintzen, *Critique of Western Philosophy and Social Theory*, 113.
23 Ibid., 132.
24 E.J. Dionne Jr., *Our Divided Political Heart: The Battle for the American Idea in an Age of Discontent* (New York: Bloomsbury, 2012).
25 Ibid., 5.
26 Ibid., 7–8.
27 Ibid., 10–11.
28 Ibid., 12–14.
29 Ibid., 265.
30 Tom Allen, *Dangerous Convictions: What's Really Wrong with the U.S. Congress* (New York: Oxford University Press, 2013).
31 Ibid., 4.
32 Ibid., 4–5.
33 Ibid., 5.
34 Ibid., 26–27.
35 Ibid., 27.
36 Ibid., 32–33.
37 Ibid., 65.
38 Ibid., 66–67.
39 Ibid., 67.
40 Ibid., 158.
41 Ibid., 183.
42 Ibid., 160.
43 Ibid., 172.
44 Ibid., 180–181.
45 Ibid., 185–194.

46 Ibid., 210–214.

47 Ryan Lizza, "FUSSBUDGET: How Paul Ryan Captured the GOP," *The New Yorker*, August 6, 2012, 34–37.

48 Many professed believers in Ayn Rand may not even be aware that her books are based on a particular philosophy called Objectivism that provides the foundation for her writing. For an exposition of this philosophy see Michael S. Berliner, ed., *Understanding Objectivism: A Guide to Learning Ayn Rand's Philosophy* (New York: New American Library, 2012). This book is based on a series of lectures given in 1983 by Dr. Leonard Peikoff, who worked closely with Ayn Rand for thirty years and was designated by her as heir to her estate.

49 Holmes Rolston, III, "Care on Earth: Generating Informed Concern," in Paul Davies and Niels Henrik Gregersen, eds., *Information and the Nature of Reality: From Physics to Metaphysics* (New York: Cambridge University Press, 2010), 235–236.

50 Phil Parvin, *Karl Popper* (New York: Continuum, 2010), 121–122.

51 Ibid., 122.

52 See F. A. Hayek, *The Road to Serfdom: Text and Documents*, Bruce Caldwell, ed. (Chicago: University of Chicago Press, 2007).

53 Parvin, *Karl Popper*, 123. See Julie E. Cooper, *Secular Powers: Humility in Modern Political thought* (Chicago: University of Chicago Press, 2013), who makes the case for humility in politics and a recognition of the limits to our knowledge and power, a virtue that is obviously lacking in many political decisions, particularly attempts to change societies by the force of military power and in policies designed to promote reliance on the market and reduce government regulation.

54 "Elizabeth Warren: Government Permits Us to Do Things Together that None of Us Could Do Alone," December 19, 2015. http://www.cnsnews.com/print/402900, accessed December 19, 2016.

55 William Galston, "How George Will Misunderstands Both Elizabeth Warren and Liberalism," September 7, 2011. https://newrepublic.com/article/95926/Elizabeth-warren-george-will-liberalism, accessed December 19, 2015.

56 George Will, "Elizabeth Warren and Liberalism, Twisting the 'Social Contract,'" *The Washington Post*, October 5, 2011.

57 Marcia Homiak, "An Aristotelian Life," in Louise M. Anthony, ed., *Philosophers without Gods: Meditations on Atheism and the Secular Life* (New York: Oxford University Press, 2007), 133–149.

58 Sandel, *Justice*, 193–194.

59 See Perry Anderson, *Spectrum: From Right to Left in the World of Ideas* (New York: Verso, 2005), for a broad range of contemporary ideas about the state and society that run from conservative to liberal to radical conceptions of the relationship. The book covers theories of the major minds on the topic from the twentieth century.

60 Alan Ritter and Julia Conaway Bondanella, eds., *Rousseau's Political Writings* (New York: W. W. Norton, 1988), 98.

61 Louis Althusser, *Politics and History*, Ben Brewster, trans (New York: Verso, 2007), 151. Rousseau also has something to say about equality: "with regard to equality, the word should not be understood to mean that the degrees of power and wealth are absolutely the same, but that power should fall short of all violence and never be exercised except by virtue of rank and law, and that, with regard to wealth, no citizen should be rich enough to be able to buy another, and none poor enough to be forced to sell himself; which presupposes moderation in wealth and influence on the part of the upper classes, and moderation in avarice and covetousness on the part of the lower classes. Such equality, they say, is a chimera of speculation which cannot exist in practice. But if abuse is inevitable, does it not follow that it should not at least be regulated? Precisely because the

force of things always tends to destroy equality, the force of legislation should always tend to uphold it." Ritter and Bondanella, *Rousseau's Political Writings*, 116. The last sentence is particularly relevant for tax cuts that favor the wealthy.

62 For an extensive discussion of the common good and its relation to business see Alejo Jose G. Sison and Joan Fontrodona, "The Common Good of the Firm in the Aristotelian-Thomistic Tradition," *Business Ethics Quarterly*, Vol. 22, No. 2 (April, 2012), 211–246. See also Melanie Johnson-DeBaufre, Catherine Keller, and Elias Ortega-Aponte, eds., *Common Goods: Economy, Ecology, and Political Theology* (New York: Fordham University Press, 2015).

Part V
Restructuring Capitalism

14 The Power of Numbers

Numbers was the name of a TV series that ran for several years that involved the use of mathematical techniques to aid the Federal Bureau of Investigation (FBI) in apprehending criminals. The mathematical genius who used these techniques taught at a local university and was the brother of the head of the FBI office in Los Angeles. So he was called upon in every episode, of course, to use pattern analysis and other such techniques to track down the bad guys, by, in some cases, predicting where the next attack would happen so the criminal or criminals could be caught. It was a rather clever show and somewhat educational as well in learning how certain mathematical theories could be applied to real-world crime situations.

Numbers and the Economy

Numbers are pervasive in modern societies and provide us with confidence that we have control of the situation and understand what we are doing, both highly questionable assumptions. Numbers were part of the problem in the financial meltdown the nation and the world experienced in 2008 as government officials and financial executives alike came to believe in the quantitative models that were used by financial institutions and thought such models allowed these institutions to measure and control the risk they were taking on so that the system was deemed safe and beyond crashing. That this was a misplaced belief is now all too evident, but at the time it seemed a reasonable approach and was part and parcel of the quantitative approach that prevailed with respect to financial activities. Quantitative models gave investors and financial institutions a sense of certainty and confidence they knew what they were doing.

Yet these models were no better than the assumptions that went into their creation. With respect to the financial house of cards that had been built these assumptions included the belief that housing prices would continue to increase with no end in sight, that even if a downturn happened it would be limited to only one or a few regions of the country and would not be nationwide, and that the mortgages underlying collateral debt obligations (CDOs) were not correlated, that is, that while some of the mortgages within the tranch might go bad they would not all go bad at the same time and the good ones would keep the CDO a viable investment. All of these assumptions were wrong and came back to haunt those involved in the crisis, from the homeowner who saw housing prices decline to the point where the mortgage was greater than the value of the house, to the financial firms whose stockpile of CDOs became relatively worthless.

What do financial numbers really represent? Do they have a reality that is different from what we might think? With respect to the economy as a whole, numbers are far more than simply representations that are used in some mathematical process to arrive at a prediction. Numbers are the basic reality in a free-market society, or in any society for that matter that uses money as a medium of exchange. Numbers allow the system to work and are what we are all seeking in one way or another. While it is usually believed that money is what keeps the system going and is the ultimate measure of value, it is really numbers that are what money is all about. Money in itself is nothing but numbers of one dimension or another, and money has no reality in and of itself. It is numbers that determine the value of money and the value of everything else for that matter. Numbers reign supreme and are the ultimate reality.

A dollar bill has the number 1 printed on it, a five-dollar bill has the number 5 printed on it, and so on through the whole range of denominations. That number represents something and has a certain kind of value as long as it is a valid bill and not a counterfeit. Our bank account consists of nothing but numbers. Our credit card purchases are represented by numbers, and we receive a credit statement each month that has a number printed on it that represents what we owe the credit card company. The checks we receive have a number written on them that can then be deposited into our bank account to increase the numbers we have in our account.

We work for numbers and are given a certain amount of numbers for our efforts. We invest numbers to hopefully make more numbers. The more numbers we have at our disposal, the better. What these numbers represent in the final analysis is the ability we have to get other people to do things for us that we cannot or are unwilling to do for ourselves. If we have enough numbers available in one way or another we can, for example, get a doctor to take care of a medical condition. Somebody has to transfer some numbers to the doctor to get him or her to do this activity. These numbers can be transferred from our bank account, our insurance company if we have insurance, or from the government if we are on Medicare or Medicaid. But some numbers from somewhere have to be transferred to the doctor's account to motivate the doctor to take care of our medical condition. The doctor, in turn, will use these numbers to get things that he or she needs to do his or her job such as buying new medical equipment and use the rest to provide for themselves and their families or store them in a bank account or some kind of investment to hopefully increase them for future use.

When we acquire a product in a store, we most likely transfer numbers it takes to get the product to a credit card account that will eventually require a transfer of numbers from our bank account to the credit card company. The retailer we got the product from has these numbers available to transfer them somewhere else to buy more product or store them somewhere. For the retailer to get the product, he or she had to transfer some numbers to a wholesaler, most likely, who in turn transferred numbers to a factory, that, in turn, had to transfer numbers to get the labor, capital, and materials necessary to make the product. What it all boils down to is that all the along the chain people were motivated by the prospect of getting numbers to do things like make machines and operate them, to extract resources from the ground, to work in a factory at some job, and to do all the other myriad jobs to get the finished product to a retailer so it can be sold to a customer.

It is numbers that keep the system going and make it work, and the acceptance of these numbers is a critical part of the process. People have to believe that the numbers they have in their possession will be accepted by others when they want to transfer them to get something they want. There has to be a basic trust that the numbers are valid representations of something and will be accepted throughout the system. There has to be a trust that bills of exchange are not counterfeit and that the numbers we have in our possession are legitimate and were not illegally or inappropriately obtained. If this trust isn't present, the system would break down and come to a halt, and people would not be able to get things they need for themselves or their families.

It is said that companies and the people in them are motivated by the profit motive to do the things necessary to produce a product or service. Companies need to make a profit in order to stay in business. But what is profit but numbers? Most employees of a company do not work for the profit of the firm in any significant sense. They work for the numbers that the company will put in their bank account or on a check they get so they can provide for themselves and their families. Those top managers who are concerned about the profit of the firms in a real sense are really interested in increasing the numbers the firm has at its disposal. Profit is nothing but numbers that show on the company's books and are reported on the annual and quarterly statements to stockholders.[1]

Numbers and Wealth

Economic wealth is supposedly created when resources that have no economic value in themselves are combined in such a way that goods and services are produced that are of value to the society. Most natural resources, for example, have no utility or economic value in their natural state. They have to be mined and processed through several stages in order to be made into something useful that can be sold in the marketplace. Similarly, land in its natural state usually has no economic value in and of itself but must be plowed so that crops can be planted and eventually harvested to be processed into food products. Or the land can be reshaped so that it can be used for a housing development or for some commercial project. Humans have no economic value in and of themselves. It is only when they learn certain skills that they can get a job that is of value to employers or provide a service such as lawn care or household cleaning that can be sold on the marketplace.

When these resources are then made into useful products that can be sold on the marketplace, the economic wealth of the nation is increased. If companies have done things right in the sense of producing something people want to buy because it is useful to them, and has done so efficiently so that people can afford to buy the things that are produced, they are rewarded with profits that represent companies' share of the wealth that has been created. These profits are used to support the operations of the corporation and are paid out as dividends to shareholders who have risked their money by investing in the stock of the corporation.

Economic wealth, however, is an elusive concept and something of a fiction. Several trillions of numbers disappeared from the American economy during the bursting of the high-tech bubble in the early years of the twenty-first century. All the major stock exchanges plummeted from their highs reached only a year or so earlier. Nasdaq was once over the 5000 level but plunged below the 2000 level as high-tech and dot-com stocks took a beating. The Dow went below the 12,000 level and stayed there for many months. Companies such as Cisco Systems, which in March 2000 had the largest market capitalization of any company in the country, larger even that General Electric or Microsoft, saw its stock, which at one time had been close to $90 a share, plunge to less than $20 a share. What happened to all these numbers? Where did they go? Can these numbers ever be created again?

A major reason for this loss was the end of the high-tech revolution, in particular the dot.com companies that had been created to revolutionize retailing. Many of these companies such as E-Toys, which had one of the best websites in the business, did not make it and went out of business. Other such as Amazon.com struggled through this period but continued as viable companies. There was talk during the dot.com frenzy that economic realities such as profits were no longer relevant as many of these companies continued to increase in wealth as measured by their stock prices whether or not they made any profits. But economic realities eventually set in and profits again became relevant. Numbers mean something.

Even more so-called wealth disappeared during the financial crisis later in the decade. Large investment banks like Lehman Brothers went bankrupt, and others were saved only by merging with other companies. The Dow plunged below 8,000 and the S&P 500 went below 800 at one point. All told some 8 trillion numbers disappeared as the housing bubble burst that was based on the assumption that housing prices would continue to increase. Where did these numbers go? What happened to all the economic wealth these numbers supposedly represented? Was it all just fictional based on an assumption that proved to be false? Was there anything real and objective behind all these numbers?

Were the routers and other equipment Cisco Systems produced any less important to the future development of the internet than they were before its stock price plunged and it became worth a great deal less in economic terms? Were the houses that people had to get out of because of foreclosure of any less value as far as providing living space to people? What is the real worth of a company like General Motors or General Electric? Was Citigroup worth the high stock price it once had, or was it worth the near zero it plunged to in the financial crisis? Were the services it provided to the economy any less valuable? Economic wealth has a fictional quality; it is an abstraction that represents something, but that something is elusive and certainly something much less than an objective entity.

Who gets to decide what any company listed on the stock exchange is worth? The real worth of these companies, one could argue, lies in the goods and services they produce and whether these goods and services enhance the lives of people such that they are willing to buy them on the marketplace. But people change their minds about what is of value to them, and sometimes this change can take place quite rapidly. The point is that wealth is, more or less, whatever what the community says it is, wealth is not objective in nature. What something is worth does not reside in the product itself, nor does it lie in an individual consumer or investor but emerges from the interaction of millions of people who participate in the marketplace. Value is an emergent property that represents the judgments of millions of people who express their preferences through marketplace transactions. It is a community or common product rather than being an individualistic and objective quantity.

Value, then, is not something subjective housed either as a content of mind or in any other sense within the organism, but neither is it something "out there" in an independently ordered universe. When we interact with objects in our natural or cultural environment, this interaction gives rise to qualities such as alluring or repugnant, fulfilling or stultifying, appealing or unappealing, and so forth. These qualities are real emergent properties that arise in the context of our interactions with our natural and cultural environments. These qualities are immediately experienced, are not reducible to other qualities, and are as real in their emergence as the processes within which they emerge. Our value judgments make claims about the importance of promoting or not promoting the production of these qualities.

Values change, however, as our experience within nature and culture undergoes continual change and the numbers that represent that value change accordingly. Some aspects of this experience are relatively stable; other aspects are unstable. Values can become problematic in certain situations. Humans have a strong desire to hold onto some values as a permanent basis of security in an uncertain world, and it is all too easy to focus on certain value aspects of experience and then falsely project them into an absolute, unchanging reality. Modern science challenges this view of values as absolute and claims that value is merely subjective and relative and a highly individualistic affair, no more than a subjective feeling or matter of opinion.

However, as emergent properties values are neither subjective nor objective, neither absolute nor relative, they are emergent in the ongoing course of experience. The experience of value is both shared and unique. Values are not experienced by the individual in isolation from a community, nor are they to be put in conflict with or in opposition to community values. Yet community values are not merely the sum of individual values, nor are individual values merely a reflection of community values. Instead, value in its emergence with everyday experience is a dimension of social experience. The adjustment between the shared and unique features of value gives rise to new dimensions of social change, brings creative solutions to the resolution of conflicting and changing value claims, and restructures the behavior and practices of individuals and institutionalized ways of behaving.

Thus, the price of a stock represents the judgments of all the people who participate in the stock market as to the continued viability of a particular company. The price of a product represents the values of all the people who make a judgment about the usefulness of that product to themselves. This is the genius of market systems, as they allow for much more information to be exchanged and thus can come up with some level of economic value that represents the judgment of the community as a whole. Socialistic systems that did not allow this kind of information to be processed had trouble coming up with values that were workable such that the system could perform efficiently. This inefficiency eventually led to their downfall.

The invisible hand of Adam Smith, then, is not all that invisible. The interactions of millions of people on the marketplace give rise to values as to how much a company is worth or how much a given product is worth to consumers as a whole. These values represent wealth, economic wealth that we are able to quantify with numbers and count that gives it a certain objective status. But this status is illusory; wealth is constantly changing as people's values change relative to what is important in their lives. This value dimension of human experience is what is most important, and it is what companies try to tap into with their products and marketing programs that try to create new values and new experiences that are valuable to consumers.

Economics is about value and how this value is determined. It is not about quantitative measures that give the illusion of something objective and scientifically determinable. The goods and services that are exchanged are discrete units, or they could not be traded on the market. The value that emerges from these transactions is an exchange value; it is not a value that resides in the thing itself or in the holder of the thing. Value emerges out of the interactions of thousands of people in the market, and that value is expressed in economic terms as a price. No one person can dictate what that price is finally going to be based on his or her values, nor can anyone ascertain on a scientific or any other basis the intrinsic value of the things traded on the market.

Economic wealth, then, is a community product. But communities are interested in much more than just economic wealth, as the people in those communities live out their lives in multiple contexts with the economic system being but one of their concerns. The community is also concerned about the state of its human resources, the health and educational level of its population, among other things. It is also concerned about the state of its culture and whether there are enough cultural activities for its people to enjoy. Society is also concerned about the state of the environment, its natural capital, if you will, and whether this is being depleted or degraded significantly so that the long-term prospects of the community will be seriously affected. These are all aspects of a community's wealth, if you will, and notions about wealth need to be expanded beyond just economic wealth to take in more contexts and embrace the fullness and richness of human existence in its entirety.

But what is called wealth is really nothing more than numbers, numbers that are in our bank accounts or in the national accounts that the government keeps. These numbers represent something that we call wealth. Supposedly the numbers that show the capitalization of a company has some connection to the value of that company to society, the products it makes, its future potential, and the physical plant and equipment it has, as well as its workforce. But what these numbers really represent is the efforts of countless people who created that company and keeps it going as a viable entity. Physical plant didn't just magically appear; it was made by somebody. Likewise with the products the company produces and sells on the marketplace. They are made by somebody and sold by somebody. Raw materials are dug out of the ground by somebody else and combined into useful products by somebody. All these somebodies are working for numbers they can call their own and use for their own purposes.

Why do rich people want to accumulate more and more numbers to have at their disposal? On the surface it would seem silly to want more and more numbers in accounts stashed here and there. Dedicating one's life to accumulating more and more numbers would seem to be a waste of one's time here on earth. Numbers are not an end in themselves but are a means to something else and can enable those who hold a sufficient amount of numbers to enjoy life to the fullest, or so it would seem. The question is, "How many numbers does it take to live a fulfilling lifestyle and have all the material goods and services one could possibly want?" It would seem that rich people with a lot of numbers would eventually become satiated with material goods so that beyond a certain point more numbers would be useless to them. As stated by Robert and Edward Skidelsky, the former an emeritus professor of political economy at the University of Warwick and the latter a lecturer in philosophy at the University of Exeter,

[t]he old civilizations of Europe, India and China all shared a basically Aristotelian outlook, even if it was not drawn from Aristotle. All viewed commerce as properly subordinate to politics and contemplation, while

at the same time recognizing and fearing its capacity to subdue these other activities to its own end. All regarded the love of money for its own sake as an aberration. Such agreement between these great and largely independent cultures ought to give us pause. In matters concerning the human good, the opinion of the world cannot err entirely. We too are more Aristotelian than our official thinking allows us to admit. We know implicitly, whatever the votaries of growth may tell us, that money is essentially a means to the enjoyment of the good things of life, not an end in itself. After all, to sacrifice health, love and leisure to a mere bundle of paper or electrical impulses—what could be sillier than *that*?[2]

Indeed, what could be sillier than endlessly striving to accumulate more and more numbers under one's control? But what these authors fail to recognize is that numbers represent power, and the more numbers one has, the more one has control over other people's lives and control over the society in which one lives. People who have enough numbers can exercise an influence far and above what an individual without many numbers can influence. They can influence legislation that is passed by governments on all levels by donating to political campaigns of particular legislators and thus having access and the ability to influence the votes of those legislators. Institutions like corporations that have lots of numbers can hire lobbyists to pursue their interests in governmental circles. The accumulation of a great deal of numbers gives one a sense of power and influence that seems to be insatiable as one supposedly can never have enough power to control the environment in which one is embedded.

The distribution of numbers in a society is of critical importance. If numbers become concentrated in a small number of people at the top rungs of society, these people are going to be able to exercise undue influence in society and shape society according to their interests and ride roughshod over the interests of other people in the same society. They can influence how other people vote through political advertising and other means of manipulation. They can threaten the very core of a democratic society by these means, and the government becomes a government of the rich, by the rich, and for the rich. The rest of the people who do not have many numbers are shut out of having much, if any, influence in what gets done by their government.

Concentration of numbers at the top also has an economic impact. People who have an abundance of numbers cannot spend them all on the goods and services that are available in the marketplace. They can only buy so many houses, so many cars, or so many of whatever. The rest of their numbers are most likely invested to make more numbers, but if this investment is in entities that produce more products, someone has to have enough numbers to buy these products. Yet if most people in the society do not have enough numbers to buy products because the numbers are too concentrated at the top, there will be nothing to invest in that can be productive. Aside from the fairness argument, there is a good economic argument against the concentration of numbers at the top, as the market will not work unless numbers are widely distributed across society,

The financial crisis in the United States that took place in 2008 reflects another aspect of numbers. Financial numbers have to relate to something that is of value in a society as they have no value in and of themselves. They merely represent what people think something is worth and are the result of a community evaluation of something in particular. In the financial crisis that something was houses. As the demand for housing rose it took more numbers to purchase a house, and many people did not have enough numbers in their possession or could not qualify for a mortgage, where numbers would be transferred to the builder by a mortgage company or a bank in exchange for a monthly transfer of numbers by the purchaser back to the mortgage holder.

So the mortgage companies like Countrywide Financial invented all kinds of what were called subprime mortgages to allow people to purchase homes without a down payment of numbers and reduce their monthly transfer of numbers with things like adjustable rate mortgages. People got into these mortgages with the anticipation that housing prices would continue to go up and they would be able to refinance their homes to keep their monthly transfer of numbers lower before the rates adjusted to a higher level. Others bought homes for speculation and hoped to flip them in order to make a profit. During the run-up to the financial crises of 2008–2009, mortgages were pooled into different kinds of packages called collateralized debt obligations (CDOs), mortgage-backed securities that were then sold to investors all over the world. These mortgage pools were messy and unstructured, making it difficult to rate the risk on these securities.[3]

This problem was solved through a process called tranching, which involved dividing a pool of mortgages into different risk categories. Those in the top category would be the first to be paid off, and so were the most highly rated. Those in lower categories would get a lower rating, but they also carried a higher rate of interest because of the higher chance of default. Thus, an investor could match the risk they were willing to take with the return they wanted. Tranches could be created that were Triple-A rated, even though none of components themselves were rated that highly. Lower-rated tranches of other CDOs were also put in another pool and tranched, which became known as a CDO squared. These investment vehicles became so far removed from the underlying mortgages that no one knew what they actually included.[4]

The financial sector is in the business of dealing with numbers and has grown in size over the last decade relative to other sectors of the economy. Its job is to accumulate more and more numbers for its clients, but in recent years more and more numbers went to the people who work in finance, particularly at the top levels of the companies in the financial sector. They really don't make anything useful for society, and their job in society is to make numbers available to the people who want to make something useful. But with all the innovative mortgages all they did was to create fictional numbers that were not based on real value. They were largely based on people who could not afford a house, should never have been sold a house in the first place, and were bound to default on their loans because they could never get enough numbers in their possession to keep transferring numbers to pay off the mortgage. The whole thing collapsed, and people started defaulting on their loans, which made the CDOs worthless or certainly worth much less that the investment banks assumed.

At the same time, housing prices declined, which was inevitable once demand started to slacken and people began to realize that the numbers that represented the value of their homes were way out of line with reality. Once reality set in many of the numbers that represented the value of these homes just disappeared because they were fictional and not based on any realistic value that represented what these homes were worth to people. In some sense, this was a gigantic Ponzi scheme. As long as people kept buying houses and new numbers kept coming into the system, it could continue and all the actors thought the real value of houses would continue to climb. Everyone in the system was accumulating more and more numbers for themselves, except for the people who actually took out the subprime mortgages and were the basis of the whole scheme. When they had no more numbers to put into the system, the Ponzi scheme collapsed.

Capitalism and Numbers

In the final analysis, financial numbers represent power in that they can be used to get people to do things one wants done, and the more numbers one has, the more power one has over other people. There is no such thing as economic wealth. People with an abundance of numbers who are normally considered to be wealthy can buy more dwellings, purchase more furniture to fill these dwellings, travel more places, and so on, all of which involve other people doing things to make these things happen. Someone has to design and build the dwellings, make the furniture, and carry out the things to make travel possible. All these people work for numbers that they can transfer to someone else to get them to do things they want or need done. This is the way the economic system works as numbers get transferred around so that everyone can participate to some extent in the economy.

At some point, however, wealthy people have enough power and the accumulation of more and more numbers produces diminishing returns to the point where another number is worthless in terms of it eventually being used to get somebody do something for them. So people who have excess numbers invest them in something to earn more numbers. These numbers get put back into the system to finance what is hoped to be a productive investment. If they are used to buy existing stocks these numbers are used to participate in what some call a big casino as they do not then provide capital for a new enterprise. But they may find their way into providing capital for expansion of an existing enterprise or financing a new one and, in this case, add to the existing productive capacity of the society.

However, what is the point of amassing more numbers when people reach a level where they already have everything they could want or, in other words, has gotten others to do things for them to the point where they do not need any more numbers to maintain their lifestyle? These numbers should go back into the system not only to provide more numbers for productive enterprises to expand or start operations but also to people who need more numbers to live a decent life and would use these numbers to purchase more consumption goods. Thus, there is an economic let alone a moral reason for wealthy people to be taxed at a high enough level to give more numbers to those people at the bottom rungs of society who, through no fault, of their own don't have very many numbers and the prospects of getting more are bleak, if not nonexistent. Consumption and production are both needed to keep the system going, and the numbers any society has available in the aggregate need to be distributed in such a way that there is some kind of balance between these activities.

Financial numbers have to have some kind of physical reality behind them for them to be legitimate, but they do not have the kind of precise meaning that numbers have for an engineer or a physicist. They can be based on a fiction which was the case with the financial numbers that were involved in the financial meltdown of 2008, where investment banks went either belly-up or were merged into another institution. The fiction was that housing prices would go up forever and that people who could not afford a house would somehow not default on their loans when the adjustable rate mortgage adjusted to a higher rate. Another fiction was the ratings given to CDOs by the rating agencies that, in most cases, had no idea of the quality of the mortgages that were in these instruments. Everyone was conning each other that all was well, and the financial system was healthy and that there were more and more numbers to be generated by continuing to do what they had been doing.

Eventually the fiction was exposed for what it was, and the financial system crashed. Financial institutions had to be bailed out by the government, which gave them some numbers so they could continue operations. These numbers represented the full faith and credit of the United States and thus were accepted as legitimate and could be used by these institutions as they saw necessary to continue in business. The ultimate source of these numbers distributed by the government is, or course, the taxpayer who provides the government with its numbers through its taxing authority. The fictional part of the transactions these institutions were engaged in was called toxic assets and was in large part absorbed by the Federal Reserve System through its Quantitative Easing (QE) program.

So numbers make the world go round and motivate people to do things for each other. While people may give their own interests and those of their family's first priority, what some would call self-interest, in the course of providing for themselves and their families they have to produce something or provide a service for other people. Maybe this is what Adam Smith meant in his famous quote about self-interest serving the greater good, but in any event this is what happens. Capitalism is a system that encourages people to take care of themselves, but in the course of doing so, they also take care of other people's needs through their productive activities. They produce goods or provide services that other people are willing to pay numbers for and use them for their own purposes. Thus, it is use value that is the base of the whole process as something has to be useful for enough people in order for it to have an exchange value and be sold on the market.

The ultimate goal of all this economic activity is not to increase the wealth of the nation by increasing the goods and services that are available on the market but to enable people to live meaningful and enriching lives by having the ability to acquire material goods they need for a decent existence and by being able to get nonmaterial things like an education and health care in sufficient quantities. The wealth of the nation resides in the people that compose a society and the kind of lives they are able to lead. The capitalistic system is one vast organism that organizes the activities of people to help each other to lead these kinds of lives and find work that is meaningful and contributes to the welfare of society as a whole. Numbers are used to coordinate all of these activities, but the numbers themselves are not what are important; they are just means to the end of giving people the ability to care for themselves and others in a vast cooperative endeavor.

Numbers and Management

Years and years of quantitative education in business schools has convinced its graduates that good business judgments are based on quantitative measures and that this alone is enough to make sound business judgments. Things like intuition, imagination, emotion, experience, and all the other aspects that go into decisions are relegated to the sidelines as factors that are not important enough and too fuzzy to consider. Stephen Marglin, writing in a book called *The Dismal Science*, calls this algorithmic knowledge that, he claims, became the dominant way of thinking about economic issues in our society and in making business decisions. Yet he argues that the uncertainty inherent in most business decisions forces decision makers to rely on other forms of knowledge that do not involve rational calculation and maximizing behavior. He says that

> [c]ontrary to the economic conception of knowledge, my assertion is that under conditions of uncertainty, decision makers do not and cannot mobilize the apparatus of calculation and maximization. Without something to peg probabilities on, individuals necessarily fall back on quite different methods—on intuition, conventional behavior, authority—in

short, on a different *system of knowledge* from that which drives maximizing behavior. This is a system of knowledge that is embedded in community, in the nexus of relationships that bind people to one another.[5]

The author goes on to say that business knowledge is largely experiential knowledge that is necessarily embedded in community. While algorithmic knowledge is held to be universal and applicable to all times and places, experience is contextual and closely allied to time and place. It is by its very nature specialized, reveals itself only through practice, and exists for a particular purpose and is geared to creation and discovery rather than to falsification and verification. Within experiential knowledge "one knows with and through one's hand and heart as well as with one's head."[6] However, the notion that real knowledge resides in algorithmic knowledge and that knowledge of experience is trustworthy only insofar as it is validated by an algorithm, has undermined the knowledge of experience to the point that it has lost value with regard to business decision making as well as in society as a whole.[7]

The quantitative culture that dominates business schools seemed to have started in the 1950s in response to two studies that were sharply critical of business school education as it was practiced at that time. The publication of the Gordon and Howell and Pierson reports funded by Ford Foundation and Carnegie Foundations, respectively, motivated business schools to become more analytical and rigorous in their approach to management education.[8] Both of these reports criticized business school education as being too vocationally oriented and consequently lacking academic respectability. These reports argued that management had become more of a science with the development of decision-making tools during the war years and provided generous funding to promote reforms of teaching and research along these lines. These efforts vastly improved business school education and helped it attain academic respectability.

Business schools began to attract better faculty and students and train them in rigorous analytical techniques to be used in solving business problems and in managing business organizations. These changes benefited business organizations and society at large through more efficient management of resources. But eventually the scientific paradigm took on a life of its own in business schools and became the dominant way to think of business school education. The best schools with some exceptions came to have highly quantitative curriculums and their best faculty published in the leading management research journals. These efforts have created a numbers-oriented culture in business schools to which students are exposed. This culture shapes the way they think about business and its relationship to the society at large and is carried over into the business organizations in which they eventually work.

While this approach has given business schools increased respectability in the academic community, it has also led to criticisms regarding the

414 *Restructuring Capitalism*

relevance of this academic research to the actual practice of management. If one looks at the articles published in the leading management journals it seems that they meant to be read by other scholars rather than a practitioner, and despite calls for more relevance and a more professional approach to management, there has been no significant change in this orientation. Faculties continue to be judged primarily on their publications in scientific management journals, and a highly quantitative curriculum continues to exist at many of the leading business schools in the country.

In addition to gaining academic respectability, the are other reasons for this development, not the least of which is that business education has a home discipline in economics that prescribes the role business is to play in society and how the firm functions to create economic wealth. This makes business different from the traditional professions of law and medicine, which have no home discipline that provides them with the rationale and justification for their existence. They are strictly practical activities that need no other justification beyond their duty to serve their client's interests. While it could be argued that certain courses in business schools such as organizational behavior have their roots in sociology, this orientation is subservient to the larger economic purpose and role of the business enterprise as prescribed in economic theory.

Perhaps it is no accident that in the 1950s and 1960s as business schools began to adopt the scientific model to promote a more rigorous curriculum, economics began to change from a political-economy orientation to the highly mathematized discipline it is today. Such changes may reflect society's fascination with science as a whole, as during this period science and technology ushered in a new age of affluence with a proliferation of new devices that made people's lives better and more comfortable. And the atomic age contained promises of unlimited sources of energy before concerns about both cost and safety entered the equation. Science was on a roll, so to speak, and its reductionistic and quantitative orientation dominated our thinking.

Economics prescribes the role of business in our society in a scientific manner and provides a moral justification for its existence. Business is considered to be solely an economic institution whose purpose is to create more and more economic wealth. This purpose can be quantified and measured by the profits that a business generates and the price of its shares traded on the stock exchanges. The success of society as a whole is measured by an increase or decrease of gross national product, or gross domestic product as it is sometimes called. Our fascination with and belief in quantification is reflected in these measures of success and as long as society as a whole continues to experience success along these lines there is no reason to change such an orientation. Marglin says the following in this regard:

> Economists claim that their discipline is part and parcel of post-Baconian science, which is to say that economics, like physics, is based on algorithmic deduction of propositions that are in turn subject to rigorous

testing in a confrontation with bare empirical data. It doesn't matter for this purpose whether economic agents themselves are calculating and maximizing, but it is of signal importance that these agents are understood in terms of a rigorous, axiomatic system, and therefore that the conclusions of economics are entitled to the deference due science. Just as one would not wish the criteria for the safe capacity of a bridge to be the subject of politics, so with economic questions like inflation and unemployment: economic policymakers need not be—indeed, ought not to be—politically accountable.[9]

The scientific paradigm was adopted by economics in the 1970s as economists believed they belonged to a real science apart from psychology and sociology. Economics even had an annual Nobel Prize to call its own and place it in the same rank as the so-called hard sciences of physics and chemistry.[10] The core tenant of scientific economics was that people acted in their rational self-interest in making decisions, the so-called rational economic man. This became the foundation principle of economics as everything else followed from people acting in their self-interest and guiding the allocation of resources to produce what people wanted in a manner such that they could afford to buy what was produced.

Most early economists took a laissez-faire approach to economic policy and took their cue from a textbook published by Alfred Marshall of Cambridge University in 1890 titled *Principles of Economics* that became the bible of the economics profession. Marshall banished equations to an appendix and developed graphs to depict supply–demand relations, as well as other economic phenomena that became familiar to students for years thereafter. Scholars became enamored of Marshall, and his approach became popular. There were dissidents that became known as the institutionalists who emphasized the role of economic institutions, such as laws and customs over the role of individual decision makers, but this view was more or less marginalized.[11] Both of these approaches waned as economics became more scientific and quantitative in its approach.

The first serious attempt to use reason and science to understand the way the financial markets work came in the early decades of the twentieth century. Irving Fisher, an economics professor at Yale University, published *The Nature of Capital and Income* in 1906, in which he advocated a more rational and quantitative approach to the market. He recommended that stock market players adopt a more scientific approach, but his efforts were rendered to the ash heap of history after he missed the stock market crash of 1929 and asserted that stock prices had reached a "permanently high plateau," blowing his entire fortune in the process.[12]

Despite this setback, finance eventually became more scientific and quantitative in its approach. The corollary of the principle of the rational economic man in the financial world is that financial markets are rational rather than haphazard and unpredictable. Quantitative models began to be developed based on this assumption. The Capital Asset Pricing Model (CAPM), portfolio theory, and, in particular, the efficient market hypothesis became the core of the new quantitative approach to finance. The fundamental assumption was that market forces invariably pushed security prices toward their correct, fundamental values.[13] It was believed that there was some intrinsic value to all the entities traded in the financial system. As John Cassidy, a journalist for the *New Yorker* and the author of a book titled *How Markets Fail*, says,

> [t]he efficient market hypothesis, which Eugene Fama, a student of Friedman popularized, states that financial markets always generate the correct prices, taking into account all of the available information . . . For somebody lacking the benefit of a higher degree in economics or finance, it may be difficult to accept that the daily lurches of the Dow and the S&P 500 reflect a calm and rational processing of new information on the part of investors; that the tripling of home values in some parts of the country between 1996 and 2006 was nothing untoward; and that crude oil was correctly priced at roughly $50 a barrel in January 2007, was equally reasonably valued at $140 a barrel in June 2008, and was also accurately priced at $40 a barrel in February 2009. But such is the message of the efficient market hypothesis.[14]

Cassidy goes on to say that Alan Greenspan and other economists had argued that the development of complicated and little-understood financial products such as subprime mortgage-backed securities, collateralized debt obligations, and credit default swaps had actually made the financial system safer and more efficient. The idea that informed this view was that by putting a market price on risk and selling it to investors who were willing to take on this risk, these complex securities greatly reduced the chances of a systemic crisis.[15] That this was a false view is now a part of history, but the crisis that shouldn't have happened but did calls into question the scientific approach to financial markets, according to Scott Patterson, writing in *The Quants: How a New Breed of Math Wizzes Conquered Wall Street and Nearly Destroyed It*:

> Physics, because of its astonishing success at predicting the future behavior of material objects from their present state, has inspired most financial modeling. Physicists study the world by repeating the same experiments over and over again to discover forces and their almost magical mathematical laws . . . It's a different story with finance and economics, which are concerned with the mental world of monetary value. Financial theory has tried hard to emulate the style and elegance of physics in order to discover its own laws . . . The truth is that there are no fundamental laws in finance.[16]

What did happen was the best example of what one author calls rational irrationality that one could hope for.[17] It was perfectly rational from an economically self-interested point of view for a borrower to take advantage of the products that were offered by lenders to buy a house they really could not afford in the hopes of benefiting from continually rising housing prices. It was perfectly rational for lenders to develop these products and sell them to willing customers and make lots of money in the process. It was perfectly rational for Wall Street investment banks to trade in hot, new products, such as CDOs, because they were moneymakers. It was perfectly rational for rating agencies that were paid by the banks whose securities they were rating to give high ratings and make more money than they had ever made in the process. As Gillespie and Zweig describe the process of rating securities,

> [s]ince the agencies are paid by the bond issuers (who could essentially shop for the highest ratings) and the fees are higher based on the size and complexity of the transactions, the agencies have powerful incentives to produce those quality assurances. The issuers needed them because many of their institutional investor customers had high ratings-based requirements on what they could buy. The ratings agencies charged double of triple the fees for rating subprime mortgage-based debt than for plain vanilla corporate bonds . . . The rating agencies' analytical models were based on assumptions that were fundamentally flawed and historical data that proved inapplicable. Very few financial services CEOs and directors had any real understanding of how these unimaginable complicated securities worked, but as profits skyrocketed from selling and trading them, these same leaders didn't ask questions. Many now say they relied on the ratings to assess their risks.[18]

People made choices based on an assessment of their economic self-interest, and these choices were supposedly rational from an individual perspective. Managers of the investment banks on Wall Street would have been taken to task for not investing in CDOs and reaping the profits from the sale of these financial instruments. Executives at institutions like Countrywide Financial would have been amiss to their shareholders if they had not offered exotic mortgages to try to beat the competition. It is only in hindsight that some of these executives, like Michaelson, can see how crazy some of the things they were doing really were, but at the time they seemed like the perfectly rational thing to be doing. Michaelson says,

> Corporations' self-interest was to return value to shareholders as fast and as profitably as possible, by giving the marketplace what it wanted to buy. In Countrywide's case, they provided easy access to money and reaped the fees and revenue rewards of that service. But common sense says that to give anyone a loan with a "no documentation" review

process is madness. To allow people to pay *less than* their mortgage demands every month is lunacy. To give anyone a loan who has a substantial history of poor repayment and bad credit, is dumb—no matter how high the interest rate.[19]

From the standpoint of society, however, such rationality was a disaster from which the country has not yet fully recovered. An unregulated market made such an irrational outcome possible as it provided incentives that were perverse from society's perspective. The same thing happens in other areas such as health care. From the perspective of an individual insurer it is perfectly rational to refuse to insure someone with preexisting conditions and cancel policies for sick people. That's the way insurance has to work in order to remain profitable. But from the perspective of society such practices are inhumane and inefficient. Sick people without insurance who don't get treated when they should eventually get worse and end up in an emergency room, which is a much more expensive proposition. They then have to be treated and somebody has to pay for their care.[20] *Rational irrationality* is the term used to refer to situations in which the application of rational self-interest results in an inferior and socially irrational outcome.[21]

The *rational herd* is a term also used to refer to the way people act in such situations. The basic idea is that while you may be doing something dumb, if everybody else is doing the same dumb thing at the same time, people will not think of you as stupid and your reputation will not be harmed.[22] Investment banks continued to buy CDOs even as their value began to be questioned because everyone else was doing the same thing. Then when it became apparent that they might not be such a good investment, everyone tried to sell them at the same time, but there were no buyers, and their value crashed. There were no buyers because everyone was trying to sell having made the same stupid assumptions.

As pointed out by Justin Fox, a columnist for *Time* magazine and author of *The Myth of the Rational Market*, the development of the efficient market hypothesis, the Black-Scholes option-pricing model, and all the other major elements of the rational scientific approach to financial markets took place during the end of a long period of market stability that was characterized by tight government regulation. As this author states, "[t]hese theories' reliance on calmly rational markets was to some extent the artifact of a regulated, relatively conservative financial era—and it paved the way for deregulation and wild exuberance."[23] The idea of efficient and rational market was given far more credit than it deserved.

The Quest for Certainty

Numbers are used to provide *certainty* to business school students and managers of business organizations. Students want a formula they can use to crank out a number that will give them the "right" answer to a business problem. This then gives them a degree of certainty, and they do not have to think more deeply about the problem and see it in all its complexity. The problem can be simplified to fit into a formula which will then crank out a relatively easy answer to a quite complicated problem. They do not have to reflect on the assumptions behind the formula or think about its applicability to the particular problem at hand.

As a visiting professor in one of the better business schools in the Southwest that had a highly quantitative program I could see this process in action. The course I taught was ethics and social responsibility and was a first-year course that was usually required in the first semester of their experience as MBA students. When the course first began, I got a sense that the students had an ability to reflect on ethical issues and handle the ambiguity that ethical issues usually involve. As the semester progressed, however, this reflective ability was gradually squeezed out of them in their exposure to quantitative techniques in other courses, and they became less and less able to handle unstructured problems and became impatient with the lack of a "right" answer that could be cranked out rather quickly.

Even one of the finance professors who was also a visitor complained about this lack of reflection. All the students wanted, he said, was a formula that would give them a number, and they did not want to reflect on the assumptions embedded in the formula and question whether it was appropriate to use in a given situation. The quantitative program was like a crucible that molded the student's thinking. What they wanted was a hard number that they could then believe was the "right" answer, a number that gave them a sense of certainty. They had less and less tolerance for "fuzzy" stuff like ethics that could not be expressed in a number but that required more reflective thinking and analysis.

This same desire for simplicity and certainty holds true for business managers as can be seen in another personal example. While working for a *Fortune* 500 company, I helped develop an inventory control system to be used by distributors of the company's products. These distributors accounted for about 25 percent of the company's business and handled the products on consignment. The marketing manager in charge of these distributors wanted a report he could send to them on a monthly basis containing order quantities for all the products they handled. The inventory control model used for this report was a typical one in basing order quantities on past history of sales eliminating figures that fell outside of so-called normal range so as not to distort the averages.

This model obviously assumed the future would be like the past and did not allow for any changes in the general economic conditions affecting sales of products. If general economic conditions changed that would affect what people were buying or a substitute came along for some of the company's products, these would not be reflected immediately in the order quantities on the report. The manager did not care about any of this, however; all he wanted was a report he could send out every month with numbers on it, and he wanted the system to operate more or less on autopilot. He didn't want to think about assumptions embedded in the model, assumptions that may have proved false at some time in the future because of changes that called for management judgment as to whether the order quantities on the report were realistic.

This quest for the certainty that numbers supposedly give can have disastrous consequences. During the run-up to the financial crises of 2008–2009, mortgages were pooled into different kinds of packages called CDOs, mortgage-backed securities that were then sold to investors all over the world. These mortgage pools were messy and unstructured as there was no guaranteed interest rate since homeowners could refinance or go into default on their homes. There was also no fixed maturity date as most homeowners sold their homes before the mortgage was fully paid. Consequently, it was difficult to rate the risk on these securities and assign a single probability for the chance of default.[24]

Enter David X. Lee, a mathematician who grew up in rural China in the 1960s and, after several degrees, including a PhD in statistics from the University of Waterloo in Ontario, Canada, wound up at Barclays Capital, where he was responsible for rebuilding its quantitative analysis team.[25] Quantitative people were becoming more and more popular in financial institutions to create and price the ever more complex investment vehicles that were being developed. In 2000 Li had published a paper in which he developed a way to model default correlation without looking at historical data. Instead, he used market data about the prices of a financial vehicle know as a Credit Default Swap (CDS).[26]

CDSs were in effect insurance against a borrower defaulting so that the investor can either get interest payments by lending directly to the borrower or insurance payments. The CDS market grew rapidly as an unlimited number of swaps can be sold against each borrower. Instead of waiting to assemble enough historical data about actual defaults, Li's model was used the price of these swaps as a shortcut to rate the default risk assuming that the CDS market could price the default risk correctly. Li's formula, which was known as a Gaussian copula function because it was based on correlations between credit default risks, was seen in the financial world as a positive breakthrough that allowed complex risks to be modeled with ease and accuracy. His method was adopted by everybody including bond investors and Wall Street banks to rating agencies like Moody's and regulators themselves. Nobody knew or even cared what was actually in these securitization packages as they now had a number that told them what risk was involved.[27]

The market for CDSs and CDOs grew together and fed on each other. In just seven years, from 2001 to 2007, the dollar amount of credit default swaps outstanding grew from $920 billion to more than $62 trillion. The CDO market grew from $275 billion in 2000 to $4.7 trillion in 2006.[28]People were making so much money that no one worried about the limitations of the model or the assumptions on which it was based. Foreign investors bought up huge amounts of these instruments as they promised higher returns than Treasury securities and the risk seemed manageable. After all, the rating agencies were telling what risk was involved in the various tranches, and they could take on whatever risk they felt comfortable with and match that against the expected return.

Then, of course, the whole thing collapsed. Homeowners started defaulting in record numbers because they had gotten into homes they could not afford, and when their adjustable rate mortgages adjusted to a higher rate, they could not afford to continue making payments. Nor could they refinance at a lower rate because home prices declined at the same time, making the mortgage they had taken out greater than the market price of the house. No one believed that so many homeowners would default at the same time or that housing prices would decline across the entire country. Individual homeowners might default because of loss of a job or whatever, but these individual problems would not affect the mortgage pool as a whole. And home prices might decline in some regions of the country but not in the entire country as a whole. Pooling of mortgages was supposed to offset these setbacks so that the pool as a whole would still be viable.

Thus, the assumptions behind the model were exposed with disastrous results for world financial markets. Who is to blame for these consequences? Li just invented the model and went back to China, heading up the risk management department at China International Capital Corporation. The quantitative people who should have been aware of the model's weaknesses were not the ones making the asset-allocation decisions. So should we blame the bankers who misinterpreted the model and used it inappropriately? But which bankers? The problem was that everyone adopted the model, and when everybody does the same thing, it creates a classic opportunity for a financial bubble and eventual burst.[29] Numbers have a high degree of certainty in the modern world, a certainty that is perpetuated in business school education. Numbers generated by a formula come to have a reality all their own regardless of how they are generated, and managers have come to put their faith in these numbers. As Felix Salmon says in "A Formula for Disaster,"

> [t]heir managers, who made the actual calls, lacked the math skills to understand what the models were doing or how they worked. They could, however, understand something as simple as a single correlation number. That was the problem.[30]

The financial numbers that managers of business organizations deal with are of a different kind than the numbers of concern to engineers and scientists. There is something out there that financial numbers represent, but that something is uncertain and imprecise. These numbers should not give us confidence that we know the true value of the thing we are concerned about. Financial numbers represent a reality that is constantly changing and cannot be quantified as precisely as a number would lead us to believe.

Numbers for an engineer refer to a physical reality, and those numbers express a precision that often goes beyond what any of us can comprehend. This precision has to be adhered to in most cases for a technology to work properly. There are countless examples of problems that developed because of failure to meet precise measurements the most well known of which may be the primary mirror of the Hubble Space Telescope, which was faulty when the Hubble was first launched.

Financial numbers could also be said to represent a physical reality in that stock prices have some relation to physical plants and human resources. But stock prices are based more on the earning potential of a company, and represent the value of that potential expressed in financial terms. This value is not precise and changes all the time as it depends on the assessment of tens of thousands of people participating in the market. Value does not reside in the stock itself as if there was some intrinsic value to these entities, nor does value reside solely in the people buying and selling stocks. It emerges in the interaction of the thousands or in some cases millions of people who participate in the stock market.

If a company is large enough, assets can be undervalued or overvalued by hundreds of thousands of dollars in some cases and it will not lead to a catastrophe, whereas something can be off a fraction of an inch in a particular technology resulting in failure. So the whole point of this discussion is that we should not put too much confidence in financial numbers. They are uncertain and do not necessarily convey with accuracy the underlying reality on which they are based. They are not scientific in the true sense of the word. Yet capitalism itself conveys a false sense of certainty making it attractive to those who demand certainty in decision making. As stated by Roger Berkowitz, an associate professor of political studies, philosophy, and human rights at Bard College,

> [t]he irresistibility of capitalism is part and parcel of the demand for certainty. Capitalism offers the certainty of a balance ledger and the clarity of profit and loss. Capitalism thus offers objective criteria on which to rationally evaluate all decisions. In its promise of objective certainty, capitalism is a symptom of what Hannah Arendt calls the experience of homelessness. Our world, the world defined by the loss of the authority of religions and the decay of traditions, is also a world defined by the loss of a spiritual home. Capitalism—the social system that defines good and bad, winners and losers, status and power, by clear and certain criteria of salary and wealth—is one way that a homeless humanity sets itself on a certain and stable foundation, albeit one of its own making.[31]

Management involves judgment and business school education should not convey the idea that quantitative analysis will give the "right" answer to a business problem and that what is important is to have a number. Any number must be put into perspective and the assumptions on what that number is based must be examined. Not doing so can lead to all sorts of problems as the financial crisis of 2008 illustrates. While we all need some degree of certainty in order to function as human beings, management must resist the temptation to put their faith entirely in numbers and ignore other factors that impinge on the decision they are facing. The reality behind the numbers is too complex to be grasped by numbers alone, and this fact must be part and parcel of management's understanding of what they are doing.

Notes

1 "This is why the current stage of capitalism, which is hyper-industrial to the degree that it is hyper-computational, insofar as it is capable of transforming everything into numbers, is encountering its limit and entering into a zone of very great danger." See Bernard Stiegler, *The Decadence of Industrial Democracy* (Cambridge, UK: Polity Press, 2011), 46.
2 Robert Skidelsky and Edward Skidelsky, *How Much Is Enough? Money and the Good Life* (New York: Other Press, 2012), 86.
3 Felix Salmon, "A Formula for Disaster," *Wired*, March 2008, 77.
4 Ibid., 79.
5 Stephen A. Marglin, *The Dismal Science: How Thinking Like an Economist Undermines Community* (Cambridge, MA: Harvard University Press, 2008), 128.
6 Ibid., 132.
7 Ibid., 159–160.
8 R. Gordon and J. Howell, *Higher Education for Business* (New York: Columbia University Press, 1959); Frank C. Pierson, et al., *The Education of American Businessmen* (New York: McGraw-Hill, 1959).
9 Marglin, *The Dismal Science*, 169–170.
10 Justin Fox, *The Myth of the Rational Market: A History of Risk, reward, and Delusion on Wall Street* (New York: Harper Business, 2009), 107.
11 Ibid., 30.
12 Ibid., 3–5.
13 Paul Krugman states that "[t]he belief that financial markets always set the right price blinded many if not most economists to the emergence of the biggest financial bubble in history." See Paul Krugman, "How Did Economists Get It So Wrong?" *The New York Times Magazine*, September 6, 2009, 36–43.
14 John Cassidy, *How Markets Fail: The Logic of Economic Calamites* (New York: Farrar, Struss, and Giroux, 2009), 86–87.
15 Ibid., 13.
16 Scott Patterson, *The Quants: How a New Breed of Math Wizzes Conquered Wall Street and Nearly Destroyed It* (New York: Crown Business, 2009), 294.
17 See John Cassidy, "Rational Irrationality," *The New Yorker*, October 5, 2009, 30–35.
18 John Gillespie and David Zweig, *Money for Nothing: How the Failure of Corporate Boards Is Ruining American Business and Costing Us Trillions* (New York: Free Press, 2010), 210–211.
19 Adam Michaelson, *Foreclosure of America: Life Inside Countrywide Home Loans and the Selling of the American Dream* (New York: Berkley Books, 2010), 306.
20 Cassidy, *How Markets Fail*, 138.
21 Ibid., 142.
22 Ibid., 177.

23 Fox, *The Myth of the Rational Market*, 320.
24 Salmon, "A Formula for Disaster," 77.
25 See also Patterson, *The Quants*, 192.
26 Salmon, "A Formula for Disaster," 78.
27 Ibid., 78, 76.
28 Ibid., 79.
29 Ibid., 112.
30 Ibid.
31 Roger Berkowitz, "The Burden of Our Times," in Roger Berkowitz and Taun N. Toay, eds., *The Intellectual Origins of the Global Financial Crisis* (New York: Fordham University Press, 2012), 7.

15 The Market and Public Policy

The free market is constantly being defended by business leaders and politicians from intrusions by the big, bad government that are said to hamper the market's efficiency and ability to allocate resources to their best uses. The market is best if left alone, it is argued, and government is seen as an alien force that can do no good. We do not have a positive view of government in this society that sees it as having a legitimate role in society by formulating public policy to deal with problems the market can't handle. Our radical individualism gets in the way and government is seen as taking away the freedom of people to do as they want in the economic realm, and many conservatives want to reduce its size so it can be drowned in a bathtub as if the society could function without any government at all. It is important, then, to get beyond our individualistic straitjacket and understand how the market functions and what it can and can't do and what role public policy plays in society.

Free-Market Ideology

Marxist theory shares with free-market theory the same scientific mechanistic approach to the economic dimension of society. Behind every believer in the free market is the idea the market works best when left alone so that the economic laws embedded in the nature of things can allocate resources to their most efficient uses. Government regulations and government programs to address some of the problems such as poverty and pollution that capitalism fails to address are seen as unnecessary intrusions on the free market. The market is seen as another kind of algorithm that will grind along, producing the best outcome for society as a whole. Every argument that is made against government regulation or interference of any sort in the workings of the free market is predicated on this assumption. The scientific approach to the economy, where there are laws of supply and demand that allocate resources to their most efficient uses in society, is believed to be like that of the physical sciences where there are laws that govern the behavior of physical phenomena. As John Dewey says,

> [e]conomic "laws," that of labor springing from natural wants and leading to the creation of wealth, of present abstinence in behalf of

future enjoyment leading to the creation of capital effective in piling up still more wealth, the free play of competitive exchange, designated the law of supply and demand, were "natural" laws. They were set in opposition to political laws as artificial, man-made affairs. The inherited tradition which remained least questioned was a conception of Nature which made Nature something to conjure with. The older metaphysical conception of Natural Law was, however, changed into an economic conception; laws of nature, implanted in human nature, regulated the production and exchange of goods and services, and in such a way that when they were kept free from artificial, that is political, meddling, they resulted in the maximum possible social prosperity and progress.[1]

This view of economic laws is prevalent in the writings of Adam Smith, who saw the economy as some kind of machine that operated best when left alone. The doctrine of laissez-faire is based upon belief in beneficent natural laws that will bring about harmony of personal profit and social benefit. People are to be left free to pursue their self-interest, and the invisible hand will assure that resources are allocated to their most productive uses in increasing the wealth of nations through the production of more and more goods and services. Any interference with this system of natural laws will result in an inefficient allocation of resources and hence a reduction in the wealth of the nation. According to Bob Goudzwaard, professor or economic theory at the Free University in Amsterdam, writing in *Capitalism and Progress*,

> Adam Smith developed his economic system on the basis of this revised natural law concept. In his view also the correct natural price results from the operation of free competition on the market. Natural law becomes the law of free, unhampered competition. It is precisely this natural order which the government is called upon to guard and conserve. Its task lies first of all in the protection of the civil rights of property, contract, and free enterprise, for these rights constitute the natural order, the indispensable condition for a truly flourishing and prosperous society. If the government would go beyond that by interfering directly in the operation of the free market, it would place itself between man and his potential for self-realization according to the providential plan for this world . . . In short, for Adam Smith the concept of natural law became a suitable servant of the economy.[2]

The so-called classical school of economics arose from this need to understand and describe these developing relations. Smith was the most prominent of these early economists and in his book the *Wealth of Nations* defined wealth as the goods and services produced by a society, which was a much different conception of wealth than was true in a mercantilist view of economic relations. Smith was interested in describing how this wealth was created in a factory system based on the specialization of labor and the role played by capital and markets. He identified self-interest as the driving force of this capitalistic system and through the metaphor of the *invisible hand* showed how this self-interest is directed by a self-regulating market system to the good of society as a whole:

> As every individual, therefore, endeavours as much as he can both to employ his capital in the support of domestic industry, and so to direct that industry that its produce may be of the greatest value; every individual necessarily labours to render the annual revenue of the society as great as he can. He generally, indeed, neither intends to promote the public interest, nor knows how much he is promoting it. By preferring the support of domestic to that of foreign industry, he intends only his own security; and by directing that industry in such a manner as its produce may be of the greatest value, he intends only his own gain, and he is in this, as in many other cases, led by an invisible hand to promote an end which was no part of his intention. Nor is it always the worse for the society that it was no part of it. By pursuing his own interest he frequently promotes that of the society more effectually than when he really intends to promote it.[3]

Thus, it was Adam Smith who, whether it was intended or not, made this feature of capitalistic societies into a virtue with the claim that the pursuit of economic self-interest led to the public good by increasing the wealth of nations through the production of more and more goods and services. Smith, however, did not advocate the pursuit of self-interest in a moral vacuum. In *The Theory of Moral Sentiments*, he stressed the role of sympathy and benevolence in creating a cohesive society. It seems clear that Smith assumed that the free pursuit by individuals of their own self-interest would serve the public good only if it occurred in a society that was morally disciplined in this regard. In this moral context, social cooperation and cohesiveness would be further advanced by the pursuit of self-interest. Given the division of labor and the enhancement of productivity this division brought about it would be in everyone's self-interest to engage in mutually advantageous cooperative economic transactions. Thus, self-interest was viewed in the context of certain background moral conditions that would direct it in the interests of the whole.[4]

This image of the "invisible hand" is a metaphor for the socially positive unintended consequences of the market, through which the economic self-interest of individuals is channeled into collective benefits for the society as a whole. Over time, this view of the market as a mechanism for directing self-interest for the social good took precedence over his view of moral sentiments as necessary background conditions for this to take place.[5] When taken out of context, the market itself offered individuals a comforting view that their own self-interest expressed in a system of free and open competition would be sufficient to further the economic interests of society as a whole. The invisible hand of the free market could, on its own, ensure an outcome that exploited the benefits of market exchange to the mutual advantage of all the participants in the market.

This proved to be a morally attractive outcome that was brought about by individual freedom without the need for government intervention and the explicit need for moral concerns. Self-interest and competition were shown to be positively beneficial, and a system of natural liberty for individuals to pursue their own interests was shown to be compatible with the good of society as a whole. One did not need to worry about the outcome of these self-interested actions, nor did anyone need to concern themselves with the moral implications of these actions. This was indeed a system that captured the imagination of people and warranted their allegiance. While *The Theory of Moral Sentiments* emphasized the role of sympathy, imagination, and desire for approval and benevolence in forming socializing attitudes and creating a cohesive society, *The Wealth of Nations* stresses the importance of self-interest as the driving force behind the development of cooperation and mutual dependence in society.[6]

What lies behind this view of the economy is the idea that the economy is a machine, a view that comes directly from the classical scientific world-view. The unregulated market will lead to an efficient allocation of resources that will benefit society as a whole, and any interference with this mechanism will only lessen the creation of economic wealth. As Smith himself put it, "the extension of trade and manufactures, are noble and magnificent objects . . . We take pleasure in beholding the perfection of so beautiful and grand a system, and we are uneasy till we remove any obstructions that can in the least disturb or encumber the regularity of it motions"[7] These obstructions in modern parlance include government regulation, business taxes, restrictions on international trade, and similar measures, all of which create a drag on the creation of economic wealth.

Thus, we have the view of a system driven by self-interest that allocates resources to their most efficient uses. Competition assures that any one producer will not be able to create a monopoly that can control market outcomes to favor that producer. Manufacturers are driven by the profit motive to produce things people want in an efficient manner to beat the competition. Resources will be distributed according to people's preferences as expressed through the market mechanism. Perfectly functioning free markets will lead to an efficient outcome for society. There is no need for ethical considerations to enter into market deliberations as they are not applicable to a system that functions as a machine with laws that govern its behavior analogous to the laws that govern the physical world. People participating in this system need have no moral or social intentions such as social responsibility that would only gum up the works and lead to a less satisfactory outcome for society. According to Richard Bronk, who obtained a first-class honors degree in Classics and Philosophy at Merton College in Oxford University, writing in *Progress and the Invisible Hand*,

> [f]rom the time Adam Smith published The Wealth of Nations, which examined the origins of wealth creation, the liberal free market he espoused has been seen to deliver an indefinite augmentation of wealth and living standards. Such economic growth has succeeded in making belief in perpetual progress in welfare, if not happiness, the dominant faith of modern man. Moreover, the modern liberal economy has seemed not only to promise the morally attractive outcome of maximizing the welfare of society as a whole, but to do so without even requiring individuals to have consciously moral or social intentions. For the 'invisible hand' of the market is seen to lead to the most efficient satisfaction of the wants of different market participants, and in this sense to maximize the social good, merely by harnessing the selfish desires of individuals to further their own ends.[8]

Economics as an academic discipline reflects this view of the economy as a machine. It deals with the laws of supply and demand, the law of diminishing returns, and the like, describing these as inexorable laws that govern the workings of the economy. Modern economics has gone more and more quantitative in recent decades, using calculus and other mathematical methods to describe how these laws function in allocating resources to their most efficient uses. Thus, economics reflects all the characteristics of classical science and has no need for ethical considerations, according to Julie A. Nelson writing in *Economics for Humans*, as these are only subjective impressions of the mind that have no bearing on the mechanical working of the economy:

> The separation of economics from ethics now seems entirely natural to many people. To my mainstream economist colleagues, economics is a positive science that seeks to understand the mechanisms underlying economic systems. Ethics, to them, seems like a soft, subjective topic, necessarily encompassing value judgments and ambiguity. Ethics is not, in their perception, a "hard" field, like their own, which starts with objective, "value-free" premises and then logically derives clear, precise, and defensible results. Most economists believe that economic science can proceed just fine without attention to ethics.[9]

Economics reduces nature, in this case, human nature, to the self-interested individual who maximizes his or her return on their investments or maximizes their satisfaction in consumer purchases. This so-called rational economic man or woman is soulless and uncaring about other human beings in an endless quest for profit or for an ever-increasing variety and quantity of goods and services available on the market. Economics treats these humans as atomistic with no sense of belonging to a larger community, where the whole is more than the sum of the parts. It deals with discrete products that can be bought and sold on the market. Economics has become highly quantitative, with mathematics being the language employed to express the laws that govern economic behavior. And finally, it is deterministic in being able to predict human behavior and manipulate it to accomplish the goals of the organization or society.

Economics thus assumes that society is nothing but the aggregation of atomistic individuals so that there are no social objectives to individual decisions.[10] The economy and economic activity are envisioned as separate realms of human activity that can be studied outside of their social and political contexts and have an existence separate from the rest of people's existence. Thus, one of the important accomplishments of economics has been to distinguish the economy as a separate realm of human activity and then see it as managed by an automatic mechanism that is both self-adjusting and socially rational, even though no rational thought is involved in its operation. Conscious direction of the economy is not only unnecessary but inappropriate and destructive. Through the competition among self-interested parties, the narrow self-seeking that motivates these individuals is canceled out and an outcome intended by none of these participants emerges. This outcome is supposedly rational in the sense of minimizing costs and using scarce resources efficiently in satisfying the aggregate preferences of the population.

Just as with Marx's dialectical materialism, however, there are no inexorable economic laws that operate independently of human behavior, human intentions, and human actions. Behind the so-called laws of economics are human choices: choices of one good or service over another, one job over other alternatives, and one type of investment over all the other choices available. There is nothing automatic or deterministic about these choices. Humans are free to differing degrees to digress from predictable patterns and do something that is different from the norm and unexpected. These choices shape the nature of the facts that we observe that are not free from human interests and concerns. These choices are hidden in the mathematical formulas that are prevalent in economics and make it appear to be an objective science. Dewey states the problem as follows:

> The prestige of the mathematical and physical sciences is great, and properly so. But the difference between facts which are what they are independent of human desire and endeavor and facts which are to some extent what they are because of human interests and purpose, and which alter with alteration in the latter, cannot be gotten rid of by any methodology. The more sincerely we appeal to facts, the greater is the importance of the distinction between facts which condition human activity and facts which are conditioned by human activity. In the degree which we ignore this difference, social science becomes pseudo-science.[11]

The law of supply and demand says that if a good becomes scarce its price will increase to make it more costly, thus more producers will be motivated to supply the good and make a profit, thus increasing the supply and eventually bringing the price down and creating an equilibrium between supply and demand. This so-called law depends on people acting in a certain manner on the basis of certain materialistic values that are captured in the price mechanism. Economic theory assumes people to be rational self-interested creatures that are in competition with each other for the resources that are available in a given society and are expected to act in accordance with this value system. But these laws are only probabilities and are not written into the structure of the universe as are the laws of gravity or thermodynamics. Resources can be allocated on a different basis than supply and demand, and market outcomes can be altered to achieve other goals that society deems important.

There are no scientific laws that operate with respect to the economy apart from human activity. It is human choices based upon values that drive the economy and make it function in a certain manner. These choices can be made in the market or in the political arena, depending on the nature of the problem to be addressed and the power that the actors in the public and private sectors possess. These choices involve a normative dimension as questions of justice and fairness are always at the heart of economic decisions. They cannot be dismissed by some quasi-scientific approach to the way economies operate. There are always moral questions related to distribution of the benefits any economic system provides the members of society. Bernard E. Harcourt, the Julius Kreeger Professor of Law and professor of political science at the University of Chicago, has the following to say about a natural order to the market:

> First, the ideas of natural order and market efficiency have helped naturalize the market itself and thereby shield from normative assessment the massive wealth distributions that take place there. Those distributions come to be seen as the natural consequence of an orderly market, and as such are less open to normative evaluation. They become more normal, somewhat necessary, and assessing them becomes practically futile. And the result is that those very distributional consequences get shielded from political, social, and moral debates: the naturalness of the market depoliticizes distributional outcomes . . . It is only when we let go of the illusion of natural order that we truly open the door to a full and robust political assessment of those distributional consequences— as well as of the politically and socially produced norms and rules that regulate markets and shape those outcomes.[12]

In recent decades economics has become a highly mathematized discipline and has no need for any moral considerations related to the distribution of wealth in our society or to the adverse effects of economic growth. Such a scientific approach allows for the objectification of people so that they are seen as nothing more than cogs in a machine whose purpose is the production of more and more goods and services so private companies can make a profit. People are treated as objects in economic theory rather than living human beings with hopes and fears, dreams and disappointments. They are made to serve the capitalistic system that is interested in profit and economic growth for its own sake. They have no responsibilities to each other or to themselves other than to make as much money as possible and keep on participating in the system so it can continue to grow and create so-called economic wealth. Economics treats the self as a rational economic entity that is solely concerned with its economic well-being and thinks of society as solely concerned with the growth of economic wealth. Other aspects of the self and society are not considered to be part of the system and are abstracted out of consideration.[13] Again according to Goudzwaard,

> [o]bjectification of people can occur with reference to employees (who are accordingly plugged into the production process as mere suppliers of almost infinitely divisible units of labor), as well as with reference to consumers. Consumers are made into objects when they are manipulated by marketing techniques as just so may bundles of psychic impression and motivations. The mark of objectification is that people are no longer treated as bearers of responsibilities. A business enterprise, for example, treats a consumer as an object when it no longer appeals to his sense of responsibility, but instead attempts to overrule or manipulate his choice. Employees, similarly, can be reduced to objects by the minimization or destruction of the possibility of making responsible choices of their own. Morality is always a matter of the recognition of other people's responsibilities.[14]

When market societies came into existence, they replaced the traditional social systems that had been in place and had served to prescribe roles and functions for people in society. Economic activity had always been subordinated to the social system and was merely part of a larger social reality that gave people a sense of identity and belonging. But market systems and the market principle took over and became social systems as other aspects of social life became subordinated to market duties and roles. The market itself became the primary manner by which industrial societies organized themselves and the roles of producer and consumer, along with other economic roles, became the most important roles in society.[15] These roles became objectified within this economic worldview, and moral considerations were undermined. The market system has no moral grounding and operates quite apart from moral and ethical considerations. The economy has become an end in itself and takes on a life of its own isolated from its social and moral context and subject only to the "laws" of the market.

The economy, however, cannot be so neatly separated from or absorb the rest of society. The economic system is fully woven into the fabric of society as only one dimension, inseparable from other dimensions of the sociocultural matrix in which we act out our day-to-day existence. The economic dimension is but one aspect of our existence, and the economic system, far from being a reality engulfing the social aspect, is the result of giving a supposedly independent status to a discriminable dimension of our total existence, an existence that is inherently social in nature. The economic system ultimately cannot even stand on its own conceptually, and to isolate it for purposes of analysis and manipulation severs it from the very context that makes it intelligible as a discriminable and moral force in society.[16]

The argument about a free-market approach as opposed to government regulation is not really about efficiency or innovation or any of the other reasons usually given in support of free markets. It is more of an ideology that is an assertion of truth rather than a quest for truth. It is really about who is going to control the system and make the important decisions and about who is going to gain the benefits the system produces.[17] Is it going to be corporate bureaucrats who make the major decisions about resource allocation and can then allocate themselves a disproportionate share of the resources the system produces as payment for their services, or is going to be government bureaucrats who pursue goals that the market by itself cannot attain? Is the corporate largess going to be shared with all the workers who make what the corporation does possible or is it going to be the top 1 percent who continue to get a disproportionate share of the economic pie?

The Functioning of a Market System

The market refers to a system through which decisions are made about what goods and services to produce, in what quantities they are to be produced, and what prices can be charged and other decisions of this nature. In a market system these decisions are made by millions of individuals who participate in one way or another in the market, either as consumers, producers, investors, or other such roles that are critical to the operation of a market system. In a planned economy these decisions are made by some government bureaucracy, but in a market system they are made by individuals. The market then coordinates these individual decisions into a collective demand schedule of some sort that guides corporate activities and, in this sense, acts as a planning mechanism to guide corporate behavior.

At the heart of a market system is an *exchange* process, in which goods and services are traded between the parties to a particular transaction. In a situation in which bartering is involved and money is not used, goods and services are exchanged directly for other goods and services. When money is involved it serves as an intermediate store of value in that goods and services are sold for money, and this same money can then be used to purchase other goods and services immediately or at some time in the future. Money has little or no value in and of itself but is valued for what it represents and for what it can purchase. The use of money greatly facilitates exchange over a barter type of economy and greatly increases the possible number of exchange transactions.

Thus, in the market all kinds of exchanges between people and institutions are continually taking place. People exchange their labor for wages or salaries and, in turn, exchange this money for goods and services that are available on the market. Investors exchange money for new stock or bond issues in a corporation, which exchanges this money for purchases of raw materials or new plant and equipment. Farmers exchange their produce for money, which may be used to buy new farm machinery or seed for the next planting.

Decisions as to whether or not to exchange one thing for another are made by individuals and institutions acting in their own self-interest and based on what they think the entities being exchanged are worth to themselves. People decide whether the item they are considering is of sufficient value to them to warrant the sacrifice of something they already have like money that is also of value to them. Exchanges will not normally occur unless there is an increase in value for both parties to the exchange. The exchange process is usually a positive sum game as both parties to the exchange believe themselves to be better off as a result.

Based on these individual market decisions, resources are allocated according to individual preferences for one kind of merchandise over another, one job over another, the stock of one corporation over another, and so forth across the entire range of choices the market offers. The value of particular goods and services emerges from these decisions and resources are allocated for the production of these goods and services according to these decisions. Enough people have to demand a particular good or service in order for it to be produced on a large enough scale so that it is affordable.

What is accomplished through at a most basic level is that the value of all the things available on the market is determined. What is the worth of all this stuff that is available on the market? What is the worth of an automobile, a house, a suit of clothes, and a steak, whatever? What is the worth of a particular stock? The value of all this stuff is determined through the exchange process as people express what something is worth to them. All these individual expressions or worth or value are then aggregated into a demand schedule that is the result of all these individual decisions. Value does not reside in the things itself, an automobile, for example, has no intrinsic value in and of itself. Its value lies in the usefulness it has for particular people. Nor does value lie in the individuals themselves such that it is intrinsic to human beings. *The value of these things available on the market emerges through the interaction of humans and the material things on the market.*

The genius of the market is that it aggregates all these individual preferences into a demand schedule that represents the collective expressions of value of all the individuals participating in the market. The market gathers all this information and put its together, so to speak, into a useful form for companies to use in setting a price for their goods and services. They set prices for a new product based on what they think consumers will pay for the product. Consumers respond to this price which is adjusted if necessary to entice them buy the product. It should be apparent that planning systems such as existed in the former Soviet Union had a great deal of difficulty in setting prices and determining production schedules for its factories. These decisions were more or less arbitrary as a small group of people on the planning agencies made these decisions on the basis of their own values and their own view of what was good for the people in the countries involved.

It must be pointed out, however, that people are not just expressing their individual preferences through the exchange process as the market is more than just the sum of these preferences. People are also creating a way of life for themselves through their choices on the market; they are expressing who they are and who they want to become. They are, in some sense, creating a future that they find attractive and believe the goods and services they choose to purchase on the market can contribute to this future. Thus, there is a community aspect to these choices as they are synthesized by the market, as participation in the exchange process creates a certain kind of community where people have to conform to certain rules for the market to work but also change what the market offers them through their individual decisions.

The nature of the goods and services exchanged on the market, then, are *private* in the sense that they can be purchased and used by individuals or persons or institutions for their own purposes. They become the private property of the persons or institutions that attain them and are of such a nature that they do not have to be shared with anyone else. The goods and services exchanged in the market are thus divisible into individual units and can be totally consumed and enjoyed by the people or institutions that obtain the property rights to them.

Thus, one can buy a house, car, or a piece of furniture, and these items become one's property to use and enjoy for one's own purposes. People can also contract for or purchase certain services and expect these services to be provided. The legal system supports property rights and enables persons and institutions to enforce these rights if necessary to protect their property from unwanted encroachment by others. This social and legal arrangement provides a degree of security regarding property and forces individuals and institutions to respect the property rights of others. Thus, property rights can be assigned to the goods and services exchanged in the market because of their divisibility into individual units that can be privately owned and consumed.

Whatever value emerges from the exchange of goods and services in the market has to be expressed in common economic units or a *common economic value system* for exchanges to take place. The worth of an individual's labor, the worth of a particular product or service, and the worth of a share of stock has to be expressed in economic terms, dollars and cents in our society, pounds in another. This is not to suggest that the fundamental value of everything is economic in nature. One person may value a particular automobile because of the status it confers, another may value a particular work of art because of the aesthetic pleasure it provides. However, for exchange to occur where money is involved these other values must be translated into the economic units of value that are operative in that society. It is numbers that make the system work as these numbers are transferred around the system to purchase the goods and services available on the market.

An economic value system thus serves as a common denominator in that the worth of everything exchanged on the market can be expressed in a common unit of exchange. This facilitates exchanges and makes it possible for individuals to assess the worth of a good or service to them more easily than if such a common denominator were not present. People can make an informal benefit–cost analysis when making a decision in the marketplace by comparing the benefits a good or service will provide with the costs involved in acquiring the good or service. People enter a store, for example, with money they have earned or will earn and can assess the price of things they are interested in buying by comparing the benefits these goods will provide them with the real costs (the effort involved in earning the money to buy them) of attaining them. Because both sides of this benefit–cost equation are expressed in the same units this assessment can be made rather easily.

This common value system allows a society to allocate its resources according to the collective preferences of its members. The diverse values that emerge in the exchange process are aggregated through the market system into a collective demand schedule facing corporations. If a particular product is not valued very highly by many people, aggregate demand for that product will not be very high, and its price will have to be low for it to be sold if it can be sold at all. Thus, not many resources will be used for its production, and it may eventually disappear from the market altogether.

Depending on general economic conditions, if a particular job is valued very highly by society and if the people who can perform that job are scarce relative to demand, the wage or salary paid to perform the job will have to be high to attract people to it. Resources are thus allocated according to the values of society as they emerge through the exchange process. Resources will go where the price, wage or salary, or return on investment is highest, all other things being equal, and are thus allocated where they can be combined to produce the greatest economic wealth for society compared with other alternatives.

In a market economy people are free to buy and use property, to choose their occupation, and to strive for economic gain as they wish, subject to limitations that may be necessary to protect the rights of others to do the same thing. Society may also place limitations on the use or property and choice of occupation because of moral standards or other reasons considered important enough to override market forces. The selling of drugs, for example, is illegal in this country even though a huge market for them exists. One cannot legally contract for a hit man to kill somebody you wish were dead. The same is true of other uses of property for purposes that are not seen as contributing to the welfare of society.

The pursuit of *self-interest* is assumed to be a universal principle of human behavior that is a more powerful motivator than being altruistic in the pursuit of other interests. The pursuit of one's own interests is believed to elicit far more energy and creativity that would the pursuit of someone else's interests or the interest of the state, especially under coercive conditions. Not only is it difficult to ascertain the interests of others, it is often difficult to find a way to sustain a high level of motivation if much of the effort one expends benefits others. The maintenance of motivation was a problem in both the former Soviet Union with its collectivization of agriculture and in Mao's China with its Great Leap Forward program that collectivized industry into small backyard steelmaking processes. In both cases hundreds of thousands of people died because of lack of productivity.

The determination of what is in one's interest is not provided by government in a market economy but by each individual participating in the exchange process. If the self-interest of an individual were defined by someone else the concept would lose all meaning. Self-interest is an individual concept in one sense, yet within a market system the definition of self-interest is not entirely individualistic in nature nor is it completely arbitrary depending on the whims of each individual. The existence of a common underlying economic value system gives the definition of self-interest a certain economic rationality.

If one is engaged in the market system, economic rationality dictates that self-interest take a certain form that involves maximization of one's return on his or her investment. Corporations are expected to maximize profits, investors to maximize their return in the stock market and sellers of labor to obtain the most advantageous terms for themselves. Consumers are expected to maximize satisfaction to themselves through their purchases of goods and services in the marketplace. If people were to do otherwise it would not lead to the maximization of wealth for the society as a whole. Thus, self-interest is tied to community interest, as the community as a whole has an interest in using its scarce resources wisely and obtaining the maximum benefit it can from their usage. Society does not want to waste its resources by using them inefficiently, nor do the individuals who make up that society. Thus, in the final analysis these interests are a social product rather than being totally individualistic in nature.

Resources are allocated by an *"invisible hand,"* according to Adam Smith, which is something of a mythological concept. But the point of this metaphor is that government should not be making decisions for society about what goods and services get produced and in what quantities and allocate resources accordingly. These decisions are made by individuals who participate in the marketplace and express their preferences based on self-interest. These preferences are aggregated by the market and if strong enough relative to particular goods and services they elicit a response from the productive mechanism of society to supply the goods and services desired.

The invisible hand consists of the forces of supply and demand that result from the aggregation of individual decisions by producers and consumers in the marketplace. Resources are allocated to their most productive use as defined by these decisions collectively. From these decisions values emerge relative to the worth of particular goods and services that are available on the marketplace. Society as a whole benefits from this kind of resource allocation, as the pursuit of self-interest without outside interference is believed to result in the greatest good for the greatest number. Thus, from an ethical perspective, the system is given something of a utilitarian justification.

The most important role in a market system is arguably the role of consumer, because consumers are supposed to be sovereign over the system. What such *consumer sovereignty* means is that consumers, through their choices, guide the productive apparatus of society and collectively decide what kind of goods and services get produced an in what quantities. When enough demand exists for a product, resources will be allocated for its production. If there is not enough demand, the product will not be produced and resources will go elsewhere.

Consumer sovereignty is not to be confused with consumer choice. In any society, consumers have a choice to purchase or not purchase the products than are available in the marketplace. Consumer choice exists in a totally planned economy. Consumer sovereignty, however, implies that the array of goods and services with which consumers are confronted is also a function of their decisions and not the decisions of a central planning authority. Consumers are ultimately sovereign over the entire system.

Some would argue that consumer sovereignty in today's marketplace is a fiction and that consumers are manipulated by advertising, packaging, promotional campaigns, and other sales techniques to buy a particular product. Sometimes this manipulation is said to be so subtle that the consumer is unaware of the factors influencing his or her decision. Thus, the demand function itself, so it is maintained, has come under the control of corporations and consumer sovereignty is a myth. Producers are sovereign over the entire system and consumers are manipulated to respond to the producer's decisions about what to produce.[18]

Although these views may hold some truth, they do not tell the whole story. It is hard to believe that consumers are totally manipulated by these techniques such that their decision-making power is taken over by corporations. It would seem that consumers must still make choices among competing products, and the producers selling these products are each trying to manipulate the consumer. In the final analysis, the individual consumer remains responsible for his or her decision and undoubtedly many factors other than the particular sales techniques used by a producer influence the purchase decision. In the absence of a central authority to make production decisions for society, it is safe to assume that some degree of consumer sovereignty exists. As long as competing products or acceptable substitutes exist, some products may not sell well enough to justify continued production.

Thus, they disappear from the marketplace, not because producers desire to remove them, but because consumers have decided not to buy them in sufficient quantities.

The reason products disappear when they do not sell is that there is no profit to be made. Profits are the lifeblood of a business organization, and without sufficient profits a business organization normally cannot survive. Profits are a reward to the business organization for the risks that have been taken in bringing a good or service to the market. If the management of a business organization guesses wrong and produces something people do not want and cannot be persuaded to buy, the market is a stern taskmaster as no rewards will be received for this effort.

Profits are also a reward for combining resources efficiently to be able to meet or beat the competition in producing a product for which there is a demand. Some companies may be able to pay lower wages or employ a more efficient technology or have some other competitive advantage. Thus, a lower price can be charged and high-cost producers are driven from the market. This effort is rewarded with increased profits as society benefits from having its resources used more efficiently.

The *profit motive* is thus an important component of a market system. Producers are motivated to bring goods and services to the market in the hopes of reaping a profit for the organization. But making a profit is not necessarily what a business is all about. Profits are like breathing is to an organism. Breathing is necessary for the organism to continue in existence, but the organism does not exist solely to breathe. Thus, profits are necessary but not sufficient in terms of justification for an organization's existence. If a business organization has done something that benefits society profits will follow all other things being equal. If a manager focuses solely on making a profit and loses sight of the larger purpose of his or her organization, which is to enrich the community in which the organization is embedded, this can be a problem for both the organization and society.

Competition is obviously an important component of the market system and essential to its functioning. In a market system companies compete with each other, products compete with other products, and people compete for the jobs that are available. Competition keeps people on their toes, so to speak, as they need to be concerned about gaining a position they do not have or about losing the position they do have to a better competitor. Competition is also seen as something of a regulatory device that puts constraints on individual egos and prevents any one business organization from attaining a monopoly position that would give it undue power in the market system. Such a monopoly would give a company the ability to set its prices and output based on general economic conditions rather than market forces and would result in an inefficient allocation of resources. The company in such a position would have a strong tendency to sit on its laurels, so to speak, and not strive to introduce new and better products into the marketplace.

The ideal form of competition is pure competition where the industry is not concentrated, where there are insignificant barriers to entry, and where no product differentiation exists. In this kind of competition, the individual firm has no other choice but to meet the competition since buyers and sellers are so small that they have no influence over the market, thus ensuring that the forces of supply and demand alone determine market outcomes. In this kind of situation, competition will cause resources to be allocated in the most efficient manner, thus minimizing the cost of products and benefiting the consumer.

Markets are not perfectly competitive, however, as there are many problems with competition in the real world that have to be dealt with in order to keep the system going and make it function to the benefit of society as a whole. In practice, unregulated markets tend toward concentration as competition in any industry is never perfectly balanced. If the object of firms is to win out over competitors, the natural expectation is that eventually one or a few firms will come to dominate the industries in which they compete because they were better competitors or were lucky enough to be in the right place at the right time with the right products. Thus, most industries in today's economy are oligopolistic, containing a few large firms which recognize the impact of their actions on rivals and therefore on the market as a whole.

Modern large corporations are not simply passive responders to the impersonal forces of supply and demand over which they have no control. These large firms do have some degree of economic power and some influence over the marketplace. They have some ability to control markets by the reduction of competition through merging with other firms in the industry to attain a larger market share and thus come to dominate the industry. Markets may also fail if the dominant firms in an industry are allowed to engage in collusive actions to maintain prices or interfere with the workings of supply and demand and the price mechanism in some other fashion. For these reasons the society saw fit to establish antitrust laws to deal with these problems.

The purpose of these antitrust laws is to limit the economic power of large corporations that can control markets by reducing competition through concentration. The role of these laws is to maintain something called a "workable competition" on the theory that resources are allocated more efficiently and prices are lower in a competitive system than one dominated by large corporations. Workable competition refers to a system in which there is reasonably free entry into most markets, no more than moderate concentration, and an ample number of buyers and sellers in most markets. The government tries to accomplish this goal by enforcing policies that deal with the conduct of corporations and the structure of the industries in which they function.

The competitive process is not a natural process that maintains itself indefinitely through the forces of supply and demand. It is not some mechanistic process that automatically holds the economic power of corporations in check through forces that are beyond the control of any economic actor. Managers do not necessarily like competition and do everything they can to drive competitors out of business. This is the name of the game, and it seems obvious that some corporations are going to be more successful than others and attain an ever-increasing market share that gives them more power to dictate the terms of the trade. Competition is something society strives to maintain because it is a commonly held value that the society views as essential for the enhancement of its welfare. The realization of this value is an achievement of society not a naturally given fact embedded in a certain kind of economic system.

Another feature of competition is that competitive behavior tends to sink to the lowest common denominator in an unregulated market system. If the object is to win in terms of market share or profits or some other economic indicator, there is always likely to be one or more competitors that will engage in predatory or questionable practices in an effort to emerge as the sole victor. If these practices allow the perpetrator to succeed, they will have to be engaged in by all competitors if they are to stay in business and remain competitive. If this situation is allowed to continue, the competitive system may eventually be destroyed.

Perhaps a comparison with professional football would be useful in understanding this problem. If there were no rules and no one to enforce them on the field, some teams would most likely do anything they could to win games. They would hold defensive linemen to keep them from getting to the quarterback, defensive linemen would try to hit the quarterbacks long after the play was dead and hope to injure them, defensive backs would interfere with wide receivers anyway they could to prevent them from catching the football, and other such practices. If these tactics resulted in winning football games, other teams would have to engage in the same behavior to stay competitive even if they found some of these tactics offensive. The game would then degenerate into a free-for-all that nobody would want to watch. Thus, there are rules to keep the game "honest" and referees and line judges to enforce them. The rules are changed from time to time to plug loopholes that develop as the game changes and to keep the game interesting for customers.

Thus, the government has institutionalized a concern with the *structure* of certain industries by giving the government the power to file suit against monopolies or attempts to monopolize an industry and to block mergers that would reduce competition. Monopoly power gives a corporation the potential to abuse that power to maintain its dominant position and society does not trust this kind of power to be used in society's best interest. The government also passes laws that deal with corporate *conduct* and attempts to promote fair competition by making certain forms of what are considered to be anticompetitive practices illegal. Certain practices such as price fixing and tying arrangements would eventually destroy the system if allowed to continue and erode trust in the fairness of competition.

A system of checks and balances is necessary to keep the free market functioning effectively just as checks and balances are necessary to keep a democracy functioning effectively. The business community itself has a common interest in keeping the competitive system going. No matter how strongly various members of this community may object to specific legislative and regulatory requirements and decisions by the courts, they all hold the common value of maintaining a competitive system and doing what is necessary to keep the game going. They have no interest in letting the game degenerate into a free-for-all, where anything goes and the system eventually destroys itself. Determining what is necessary to keep the competitive system going is an ongoing enterprise involving the entire society.

Market Deficiencies

There are certain goods and services, however, where the market does not work so that decisions about these goods and services have to be made in some other manner. These are called public goods and services and are of a different nature than the goods and services traded on the market as described earlier. One example of a public good that is often mentioned is national defense, something that is provided by government for all its citizens that cannot be provided by the citizens themselves. National defense is not something that can be purchased on the market as it is not divisible into individual units that can then be exchanged on the market. People cannot buy their own little piece of national defense, if they want it, and use it for their own purposes. The government decides what amount of money to pay for this good or service and then taxes it citizens to pay for it, and thus, everyone is provided roughly the same amount of national defense.

Pollution is generally considered to be an externality in the economics literature, defined as either a beneficial or detrimental (pollution is detrimental) effect on third parties, like a homeowner who lives close to a polluting factory who is not involved in the transactions between the principals (customer and producer) who caused the pollution because of their activities in the marketplace. Yet the results of pollution control, such as clean air and water, are more appropriately called public goods as they are entities with beneficial characteristics for human health that are widely shared in different amounts by the citizens of a society.

Again clear air is not divisible, and for all practical purposes one cannot buy a certain amount of clean air on the marketplace to enjoy privately.[19] If a society deems clean air important enough to spend some money for its provision, government has to pass laws establishing standards relative to how much of a certain pollutant is legally allowable and then enforce those laws through some enforcement mechanism. Government decides how much clean air to provide for all its citizens, and each citizen then enjoys roughly the same amount depending on how close they may live to a freeway or an electric utility or factory that pollutes the air to the extent legally allowed. Citizens pay for this clean air either through increased taxes or through increased prices for products that reflect the additional expenses producers have to pay to comply with pollution standards.

Water is a bit different in this respect, particularly drinking water. There is a huge market for bottled water, and there are many millions of dollars in profit involved in providing this product for consumers. Individual consumers in advanced countries can decide whether or not they want to incur this additional expense to provide themselves with safe drinking water or whether they will rely on tap water from municipal water systems. Thus, drinking water is a private good that can be purchased on the market. But for most other uses, water is provided by local governments and standards have again been developed to assure that water is clean enough to drink and use safely. Most people do not put in their own filtration systems to clean the water they use for themselves but depend on government to provide this public good for most purposes.

Something like equal opportunity might be called a social value that is consistent with free-enterprise philosophy. The most efficient combination of resources should result if those with the best abilities and talents get the best economic opportunities. Society is better off because people will end up in positions where their talents will be utilized to the fullest and those who are unfit for these positions will have to find jobs elsewhere. The principle of equal opportunity ensures that the best performers in society, no matter where they were born, what they believe, or what race and sex they happen to be, have a chance to rise to the top based on their proven ability to use society's resources efficiently and effectively, to do things society wants done and is willing to reward commensurately.

People with superior abilities will thus be able to get the better paying positions in society and are morally justified in receiving a greater share of the rewards society offers if they use their abilities to the fullest in benefiting society as a whole. People should be free to compete for these positions on the basis of merit and be free to go as far as their abilities, interests, and ambition will take them. Equal opportunity means that everyone in our society should be able to compete honestly and fairly on the basis of merit, referring to the performance of that individual in some capacity.

Considerations such as race, sex, religion, creed, or national origin are not supposed to be a factor, as the rewards are supposed to go to those who perform the best and compete most effectively. Thus, the removal of these discriminatory barriers to employment and promotion is a good thing for society, and policies designed to promote equal opportunity produce a public good that benefits society. People cannot necessarily purchase this good themselves on the marketplace, and so government passes laws and regulations that mandate companies treat people equally when it comes to workplace decisions and take steps to eliminate discriminatory policies and practices that may pervade the workplace.

Thus, the concept of public goods and services is an all-inclusive concept that refers to various entities that cannot be provided through the market. This broader usage also includes the maintenance of competition mentioned earlier as this competition is a public good that assures an efficient combination of resources to meet consumer demands. These public goods and services have to be provided by means that are external to the market itself and decisions about what public goods and services to produce and in what quantities are made through some other process, most likely through government, which decides on the basis of political considerations what to do in this regard and how much money to spend for their provision.

In some cases the market may be able to be used for some of these determinations. A good example is the cap and trade system that is being advocated for control of carbon dioxide emissions that is said to be the major culprit in global warming or climate change.[20] If the climate can be stabilized at least to some extent this again is a good thing because climate change on the scale forecast will result in major expenses for societies all around the world as they cope with rising sea levels, drought conditions for much of the world, the collapse of some industries dependent on a stable climate, and other effects that have been predicted. Again this is not a public good that can be bought and sold on the market in an ordinary manner as climate change is not divisible into private property. But the market can be used for some of the decisions that have to be made about global warming.

This cap and trade program allows sources to select their own compliance strategy rather than having this dictated by the federal government with a command-and-control approach. They can use coal containing less sulfur, wash the coal, or use devices called scrubbers to chemically remove pollutants from the gases leaving smokestacks. They can also use a cleaner-burning fuel like natural gas or reassign some of their energy production from dirtier units to cleaner ones. Sources may also reduce their electricity generation by adopting conservation or efficiency measures or switch to alternative energy sources such as wind power or solar energy.

It is important to note, however, what the market does and does not do in these situations. The market does not make the decision to reduce emissions of sulfur dioxide or carbon dioxide. These decisions are made by the government; they are public policy decisions that are made by a public body accountable to the citizens. The government also decides what level or standard to set regarding the overall amount of these pollutants that are allowable in a certain time frame. Thus, the government makes the decisions about what to produce and the quantities involved, that is, how free the air should be of certain pollutants based on the best scientific evidence available. The government creates a market for pollution credits that it issues, and the market is only used to promote a more cost-efficient way to reduce these pollutants by allowing greater freedom for companies to develop their own way of meeting the standards.

In many, if not most, cases, the dividing line between public and private goods and services seems clear enough, as, in general, these public goods and services cannot be bought and sold on the market and private property rights to not apply. In other cases, however, the line is not so clear, and whether a particular good or service is public or private is debatable. The provision of electricity is a case in point. In an article appearing in the *Denver Post*, Marjorie Kelly and Richard Rosen criticize the nation's attempt to deregulate electricity, calling it a misguided experiment that has left consumers in many states paying electricity bills that are as much as 100 percent higher than was true in the immediate past.[21]

The main culprit, they claim, is the Federal Energy Regulatory Commission (FERC), which has been steadily undermining the consumer-friendly electricity regulatory framework for nearly two decades. As a result, in 2006 consumers in deregulated states paid 55 percent more for electric power that those in regulated states. Increased volatility hit some states hard as in California when in just one year the cost of power quadrupled from $7 billion to $28 billion. The cause was a runaway wholesale market for electricity. The FERC is supposed to see that electricity prices are "just and reasonable," but in stripping authority from state utility commissions and handing electricity price-setting over to markets, it eliminated any and all means of protecting consumers. Four states filed suit against the FERC, claiming that the switch to market-based pricing was illegal in that the agency violated its own mandate to protect consumers.[22]

Perhaps the most interesting comment in the article, however, is the following: "What we must remember is that public services like electricity are not commodities but public goods, necessities of life essential to the well-being of all, and thus must be subject to public oversight and not left to markets."[23] Is this the case, is electricity a public good or service? What are people buying when they purchase electricity? On one hand, it could be argued that people are buying a service provided by utilities, and electricity is not a good at all. When people hook into the local grid they are purchasing the right to a service. On the other hand, the product provided is able to be measured, so is what people are really purchasing the current that flows into their dwelling that is billed to them on a monthly basis?

Besides this complication, consumers cannot shop around among competing providers to find the lowest rate; they have to take whatever is charged by the local utility company. There is no market setting the price as far as consumers are concerned, and there is no competition at the retail level that keeps prices under control. Does this mean, then, that we have to have public service commissions at the state level to see that these prices are "just and reasonable"; is this the only way to protect consumers? While the government does not provide electricity and actually own the utilities, should it have the authority to regulate prices in the "public interest" on the supposition that even though electricity is provided by private utilities, it is a public good or service and prices need to be determined by some public body acting in the "public interest" rather than by the market?

Health care is another case as it had become privatized in recent years. The result has been one of the costliest health care systems in the world with 45 million people uninsured and 16 million or so underinsured. When a severe health problem hits these people they are wiped out economically. Is the problem that health care is a public good or service and that all people in this country have a right to some level of health care regardless of their economic resources? Should we have a single-payer system that guarantees the best care at the lowest cost to all citizens? Should Medicare, for example, which many have argued is an efficient system, be extended to all citizens of the country? Do we want people in running the health care system who are interested in making a profit rather than having the health of the populace foremost in their decisions?

There has been a trend to privatize more and more public services over the past several years on the assumption that these services can be provided more efficiently by the private sector. But the high cost of our health care system challenges this assumption. This privatization also extends into our national park system, where park employees have been eliminated in the interests of privatizing some of the services they provided. But do we want people in our national parks who are mainly interested in exploiting the parks to make a profit rather than dedicated public servants like the park rangers who are interested in preserving the parks for present and future generations to enjoy? These are questions that need to be asked in the rush to privatization.

The market is not always the best means to provide these goods and services, particularly if they have some of the characteristics of public goods and services. It is always assumed that the market is more efficient than the government despite evidence to the contrary. People do not necessarily take care of private property any better than do public servants paid by the government to look after public resources. We all know people who do not take care of their lawns or their cars and let their houses deteriorate. The efficient use of resource and their upkeep depends on many factors other than simply private property and the market. We need to get over this blind faith in the market and ask questions about the nature of the goods and services in question as to whether they are private or public and whether these goods and services are better provided by the market or the public policy process. Community interests need be kept in mind rather than the single-minded pursuit of profits for private entities.

Public Policy

Public policy refers to the course of action taken by a public body, usually the government, with respect to a particular problem society is experiencing. These are problems such as climate change, gun control, and immigration, just to mention three problems the government was dealing with as this book was written. These are problems that the market is not designed to deal with because they are truly public problems that affect the entire society and require some form of collective action to deal with effectively. The term *public policy process* refers to all the various ways in which public policy is made in our country. Public policy can be made through legislation passed by Congress, regulations issued by government agencies, executive orders issued by the president, or decisions handed down by the Supreme Court. The process of making public policy begins in the society as problems and issues are defined.[24]

The *public policy agenda* is that collection of topics and issues with respect to which public policy may be formulated. There are many problems and concerns that various people and groups in society would like to see some action on but only those that are important enough to receive serious attention from policy makers compose the public policy agenda. Such an agenda does not exist in concrete form but is found in the collective judgment of society, actions and concerns of interest groups, legislation introduced into Congress, cases being considered by the Supreme Court, and similar activities. The manner in which problems in our society get on the public policy agenda is complex and involves many different kinds of political participation.

Resources necessary to address certain problems on the public policy agenda are allocated through a *political process* rather than an exchange process, and in this political process, values emerge relative to common objectives and courses of action. The function of a political process is to organize individual effort to achieve some kind of social goal or objective that individuals or groups find it difficult, if not impossible, to achieve by themselves. Suppose some people in a community want to build a road that no one person in the community can or would want to build by themselves. To get the road built, enough people in the community have to agree they want a road and would contribute the necessary resources to getting it built. Even after this decision is made, these people are going to have different ideas as to what kind of road should be built, where it should be located, and other related matters. These differences have to be resolved through the political process in order for the road to be constructed.

The task of a political system is to adjudicate such conflicts by (1) establishing rules of the game for participants in the system, (2) arranging compromises and balancing the interests of the various participants, (3) enacting compromises in the form of public policy measures, and (4) enforcing these public policies.[25] The outcome of a political process depends on how much power and influence people have, how skillful they are at compromising and negotiating, and the variety and strength of the interests involved in making the decision. Decisions can be made by majority rule, by building a consensus, or by exercising raw power and coercing other members of a group to agree on a given course of action.

The reason public policy decisions have to be made through a political process is the nature of the goods and services that are provided through the public policy process. These goods and services can appropriately be referred to as *public goods and services* as distinguished from the private goods and services exchanged in the market system. Public goods and services are provided to meet the needs of people as expressed through a political system that deal with things that are held in common, such as clean air and water or the ideal of equal opportunity for all participants in the workplace.

These things held in common are indivisible in the sense that they cannot be divided into individual units to be purchased by people according to their individual preferences. For all practical purposes, for example, one cannot buy a piece of clean air to carry around and breathe wherever one goes. Nor can one buy a share of national defense over which one would have control. This indivisibility gives these goods and services their public character because if people are to have public goods and services at all, they must enjoy roughly the same amount.[26] No one owns these goods and services individually; they are collectively owned in a sense or held in common and private property rights to not apply. Thus, there is nothing to be exchanged on the market, and the values people have with regard to these goods and services, and decisions about them cannot be made through an exchange process.

There is also something of a perverse incentive system with regard to public goods and services. If one person were concerned about clean air such that he or she paid extra money to have pollution-control equipment installed on his or her car, this action would make no difference in the quality of the air that person lived in and he or she would be getting nothing for their money. If, on the other hand, enough people did make this decision to have an impact on air quality, one would be motivated to be a "free rider" and buy a car without pollution-control equipment and enjoy cleaner air without paying a cent for its provision.

Because of these characteristics of human behavior and the nature of public goods and services, the market system will not work to provide them for a society that wants them. When goods and services are indivisible among large numbers of people, an individual consumer's actions as expressed in the market will not lead to the provision of these goods and services.[27] Society must register its desire for public goods and services through a political process because the bilateral exchanges facilitated by the market are insufficiently inclusive.[28] Only through the political process can compromises be reached that will resolve the conflicts that are inevitable in relation to public goods and services.

Value conflicts are more pronounced in the public policy process because of the existence of *diverse value systems*. There is no underlying value system into which other values can be translated; there is no common denominator by which to assess trade-offs and make decisions about resource allocation to attain some common economic objective, such as improving one's financial situation or increasing the nation's gross national product. What is the overall objective, for example, of clean air and water, equal opportunity, occupational safety and health, and similar public goods and services? One could say that all these goods and services are meant to improve the quality of life for all members of society. But if this is the objective, what kind of common value measure underlies all these goods and services so that benefits of specific programs can be assessed in relation to costs and trade-offs analyzed in relation to this common objective of improving the quality of life?

The costs of pollution control equipment can be determined in economic terms. The benefits this equipment should be positive in improving health by reducing the amount of harmful pollutants people have to breathe and making the air look and smell better. The difficulty lies in translating or quantifying these benefits into economic terms so that a direct comparison with costs can be made. What is the price tag for the lives saved by avoiding future diseases that may be caused by certain pollutants? What is the value of reducing the probability that children will be born with abnormalities because of toxic substances in the environment? What is the value of preserving one's hearing because money has been spent to reduce the noise emitted by machinery in the workplace? What is the appropriate value of being able to see across the Grand Canyon and enjoy whatever benefits this view provides?[29]

An interesting attempt to quantify nature appeared in the effort of an international collection of economists, ecologists, and geographers from twelve prestigious universities and laboratories in three nations to place a dollar value on nature. In an article that appeared in the May 15, 1997 issue of *Nature*, these experts estimated that the economic value of the biosphere's essential "ecosystem services" such as climate regulation, soil formation, food production, flood control, and water supply averages about $33 trillion annually. To put this number in perspective, the value of the output of the total world economy each year is $18 trillion.[30]

The reactions to this effort were interesting. Some conservationists saw some positive value in this effort in that putting a dollar figure on what is likely to be destroyed over the next few years if we do not change our ways is a useful tactic to argue for greater conservation efforts. Some argued that it succeeds in speaking in a language that business might begin to hear regarding the value of what we collectively, and thoughtlessly, are destroying. Others, however, felt differently. When asked to comment on this nature-valuation effort, an ecologist by the name of David Ehrenfeld said, "I am afraid that I don't see much hope for a civilization so stupid that it demands a quantitative estimate of its own umbilical cord."[31]

Such quantification only further objectifies nature and leaves out our experience with nature and our so-called subjective relationship with the world. If nature has to be quantified for us to have a sense of its value, then we have lost any real connection with nature and see it, as well as ourselves, as nothing more than an object in a quantified universe. Our spiritual and emotional connection to the source and substance of our very being is no less real and no less important for the fact that it cannot be quantified. As stated in one comment on the subject of valuing the environment, "[p]ut me in a red rock canyon and let me watch a mule deer moving beneath the dappled shadow of a cottonwood grove, and I do not need to be told how much what I see and feel there is worth: it is worth nothing—and everything."[32]

The difficulty of expressing all these intangibles in economic terms so that people's individual preferences can be matched should be apparent. When people make individual choices about private goods and services offered on the market, diverse value systems present no problems. They are forced to translate these diverse values into economic terms and make choices accordingly. But making choices about public goods and services is another matter. There seems to be no way to force a translation of diversity into a common value system that is acceptable, realistic, and appropriate. Thus, the political process seems to be a reasonable way to respond to the diversity of people's values to make a decision about a common course of action. Values emerge for particular public goods and services from the interactions of the millions of people who participate in the political process.

The average person participates in the political process by voting for a representative of his or her choice, contributing money to a campaign, writing elected public officials on particular issues, and similar actions. Joining large social movements such as the civil rights movement is another way for the average person to exercise political influence. Widespread support for issues has an effect on the voting of elected public officials. People can join public interest groups or support them with contributions and fulfill a political role in this fashion. Most citizens, however, are probably content to simply elect others to engage in the business of governing the country and go about their daily tasks with a minimum of political participation.

The vote is the ultimate power that citizens have in a democratic system and gives them a degree of *sovereignty* over the public policy process. A public official can be voted out of office is he or she does not perform as the majority of citizens in his or her constituency would like. A major problem with such sovereignty, however, is the reputation that the average citizen has with regard to participation in the political system. Voter turnouts are low in many elections, and most of those who do vote probably know little about the candidates and the issues that are at stake in the election. Most people are not interested in public issues much of the time, particularly those that do not affect them directly.

Taking such an interest means spending time on political concerns that might be more profitably devoted to family or leisure activities. Most citizens do not derive primary satisfactions from political participation, and unlike the marketplace, they do not have to participate to fulfill their basic needs and wants. The cost of participation in public affairs seems greater than the return. People who do not participate thus sacrifice their sovereignty and power to the minority in society who do have a strong interest in political life and choose to actively participate in the formulation of public policy for the society as a whole.[33]

Through the public policy process, the self-interest of all the participants is aggregated into a collective whole that represents the public interest.[34] Something of a supply and demand process occurs here in that if enough citizens demand something, at least in a democratic society, the system will eventually respond. But the decisions about resource allocation are visible in that certain people in the public policy process, elected public officials and government bureaucrats, for example, can be held accountable for these decisions if they are not acceptable. The concept of the invisible hand is thus appropriate for a market system but not for the public policy process.

Markets and Public Policy

When it comes to thinking about public policy and its role in society, different levels of abstraction are often confounded. Public policy is not to be equated with government, even though government formulates and implements most public policies in our society. However, public policy must be considered at the same level as the market and must not be saddled with all the ideological baggage that is involved in discussing the role of government in our society. Government is an institution at the same level as business, while public policy and the market are at a different level of abstraction.

Government does not interfere with the market as the market works as it always has and operates with the same laws of supply and demand regardless of what government does or does not do with respect to problems in society. What government does do is interfere with business practices and prescribes through laws and regulations what business can and cannot do with respect to certain activities. Many, if not most managers, see the government as intruding on what are essentially private decisions made in the interests of promoting economic efficiency. Government intrusion in any form is seen as interfering in the workings of the free-market system and is best kept to a minimum. Managers think they are operating in something called the private sector that is judged by an efficient use of resources while government operates in the public sector that operates on different criteria for measuring success.

The free-market system, however, does not exist in a vacuum. It is instead embedded in a social system that can exercise control over corporate activities. The free market cannot stand alone, and no society can organize all its activities according to free-market principles. While our society makes many decisions through the market, it also makes many decisions through the public policy process. Society as a whole decides what to do with certain issues that are more public than private in nature.[35]

One important issue at this level is what problems can best be addressed by the market and which by the public policy process. This is a different question than asking whether business or government is the best institution to deal with a particular problem. When the market does not work in dealing with certain problems the society deems important, adjustments to corporate behavior must be made through some other process that is different from the market. These changes are simply implicit in the nature of corporations as social entities that are subject to change along with the society of which they are a part. In other words, corporations do not stand apart from society; they are embedded in society and subject to its changing values.

The issues that receive attention in the public policy process and the shape of policies with respect to these issues reflect the values of society at large. And if those values stem from an individualistic conception of rights, then clashes between rights will inevitability occur. The underlying issue with respect to most regulation is one of rights, civil and human rights versus property rights. Whose rights should take priority, the rights of workers to a safe workplace, the rights of minorities and women to be treated equally, the rights of consumers to safer products, the rights of all citizens to a clean environment, or the rights of shareholders to the highest return on their investment? Social regulations cost money, and they affect the property rights of shareholders as the corporation can no longer be operated solely in their interests. Social issues have to be taken into account, and the corporation can either comply with these regulations or be taken to court and sued for noncompliance.

> All democracies have championed the freedom to participate in government, and most have also sought to enshrine in law certain individual rights that seek to secure for individuals some inalienable areas of freedom of action and thought. Progress has, in part, been defined in the liberal tradition as the gradual extension of these individual freedoms and rights. The central problem for liberal democracy, however, is that one person's right to freedom of action may clash with another person's right not to be harmed . . . But in our increasingly interconnected and congested world, many people argue that surprisingly few actions by individuals are without important consequences for others. The crucial debate has centered around what role democratic government should have in trying to ensure greater harmony of interests between members of society, and what role government should have in forging the best social and environmental outcome for society as a whole.[36]

When rights are seen as stemming from an individualistic conception of the self, such clashes are inevitable. While the concept of public policy does contain some notion of community it is undermined by an individualistic approach where public policy represents nothing more than the aggregation of citizen preferences for public goods and services as expressed through the political process. This is the same way a market system works as it aggregates individual preferences for private goods and services. This view is reinforced by the notion of rights that inhere in individuals and are part and parcel of their nature. Thus, public policy reflects these ideas of individualism and rights that are part of the society at large and the process ends up being in irreconcilable conflict over which rights take priority as individuals and groups battle each other in pursuing their interests. What would help is a new framework for understanding these tensions that exist within society, one that undercuts the notions of isolatable individuals with absolute rights in favor of inherently social persons that are an integral part of a larger community.

Society can choose to allocate its resources any way it wants an on the basis of any criteria it deems relevant. If society wants to enhance the quality of air and water, it can choose to allocate resources for the production of these goods and put constraints on business in the form of standards or other incentives to shape business behavior. These nonmarket decisions are made by those who participate in the public policy process and represent their views of what is best for themselves and society as a whole. It is up to the body politic to determine which market outcomes are and are not appropriate. If market outcomes are not to be taken as normative, a form of regulation which requires public participation is the only alternative. When business acts contrary to the wishes of society only public policy can replace the dictates of the market.

Public policy theory, then, lays out the theoretical frame within which the insights of stakeholder theory, as well as other theories of the firm in society, can be implemented. Public policy is more than a political process required to keep the market functioning; it is a social process that helps infuse the market with moral vision, and it develops its own organs of adjudication for dealing with the cultural, environmental, and technological issues that are raised in society. Public policy cannot work, however, without a certain moral sensitivity in the business community, and public policy can never replace that sensitivity. One cannot operate morally just in terms of rewards in the marketplace and punishments from the public policy process; responding to rewards and punishments are generally considered to be the lowest stage of moral development. Public policy must be fed by moral perceptiveness, and public policy, in turn, should nurture moral sensitivity and the moral direction of market forces by providing a socioeconomic context in which morally attuned actions can flourish without undue economic penalty.

Market activities can be infused with moral vision, as managers can be sensitive to the moral dimensions of their decisions, and take into account interests of stakeholders affected by corporate actions. This was the purpose of those who advocated social responsibility, to convince managers to take into account the social impacts of their decisions. But some vague sense of social responsibility or a stakeholder model can never replace public policy, as these models cannot "speak" for society as a whole. It is only through the public policy process that society as a whole can decide what it wants done with respect to climate change other environmental issues, product safety, affirmative action, and a host of other issues that involve business organizations.

The relationship between business and society is inherently relational, for no business organization can exist in isolation from society or from its environment, and society is what it is in relation to its constituting institutions. Business is a social object, not an isolatable institution, and is an acting agent in society within the context of other acting agents. But no absolute line can be drawn business and society, for the origin and foundation of business is social in nature. Business has to consider its obligations to the surrounding community. But corporations, like individuals, are part and parcel of the communities that created them, and the responsibilities that they bear are not products of argument or implicit contracts but are intrinsic to their very existence as social entities.[37]

Corporations have to take the perspective of the society as a whole and incorporate the standards and authority of society, even as they remain a unique center of activity that has a creative dimension to add to the total social experience. The corporation thus incorporates both the conformity of society's perspective and creativity of its unique individual perspective. A society is constituted by the dynamics of adjustment between the corporation and the society as a whole as reflected in social expectations, which involves an accommodation in which each creatively affects and is affected by the other through accepted organs of adjudication.

And what are these accepted organs of adjudication? In the case of material goods and services, the accepted organ of adjudication is the market system, which coordinates the wishes and desires of millions of individuals in society into collective demands for certain kinds of goods and services that can be produced in sufficient quantities to earn a profit for corporations. This market system is not, however, a mechanistic process in which individuals merely express their individual desires as consumers to autonomous corporations that are limited in their power over consumers by competition. The market is a social process that expresses the collective wishes of society for a better life to which material goods and services produced by corporations can contribute. It is an interactive process in which corporations and consumers mutually influence each other to reach a satisfactory resolution of what goods and services should be produced.

What about social problems such as equal opportunity, safety and health in the workplace, pollution control, consumer protection, and other problems of this nature? What is the appropriate organ of adjudication for these issues? Is it the corporation itself that should adjudicate these issues out of a sense of social responsibility, responding to pressures from stakeholder groups, or to some abstract notions about a changing social contract? Can management discern the responsibilities of the corporation to society by responding to stakeholder concerns, getting serious about its social responsibilities or ethical obligations to society, or responding to the requirements of a new social contract? It would seem that there are many problems with these approaches and that the public policy process is the only legitimate way to deal with these kinds of social problems. The public policy process involves taking the perspective of society as a whole and discerning how society articulates its expectations regarding corporate behavior. Society is the entity in which corporations are embedded, and it is society that decides what corporations are to do with respect to social issues through the public policy process

Through the constant adjustment that goes on between the corporation and society through the market process, on one hand, and the public policy process, on the other, values emerge, values with respect to goods and services for sale on the market, and values with respect to public goods and services provided through the public policy process. These values are both shared and unique; they emerge in the ongoing course of experience. Neither individual corporations nor society as a whole are bearers of value, but they emerge in the interactions between different business and consumers in a marketplace context or between business and citizens in a public policy context.

While the corporation finds itself continually adjusting to community interests as expressed through the public policy process, such adjustment is not a passive process and corporations need not be merely passive respondents to public policy, merely meeting the requirements that society imposes on corporate behavior in the form of new public policies. There must be a dynamic, creative interaction between these two dimensions. Corporations must continually take on the responsibility of providing creative input into the society which leads to ongoing revision and improvement of public policy. Value conflicts are inevitable, but the resolution of these conflicts leads to growth of the corporation and the society of which it is a part. For growth to take place there must be openness to change and a willingness to reconstruct problematic situations.

When habitual modes of organizing the behavior of corporations in society do not work in resolving problematic situations involving conflicting values, new norms and ways of organizing behavior emerge that reconstruct the situation in an attempt at successful resolution of problems. When this adjustment happens, and when corporations are made to respond to social problems through new laws and regulations, this is not indicative of a new social contract between independent entities or the result of pressures from external stakeholder groups or the result of a new set of responsibilities called social responsibilities that business must now accept. These changes are simply implicit in the nature of corporations as social entities that are subject to change along with the society of which they are a part; in other words, corporations do not stand apart from society, they are embedded in society and subject to its changes of valuation and values.

The corporation and the public policy process are related to each other in a complex manner, and the actions taken by the corporation can have important effects on the public policy process while the actions of the corporation are themselves determined to some extent by events that take place in the public policy process. The public policy process affects the market and values expressed in the market affects public policy. The way issues are dealt with through the public policy process, for example, increases public awareness about certain kinds of problems and may result in a change in public expectations. These changes provide a further impetus to the public's changing experience of value, thus making it profitable to produce different kinds of goods and services for sale on the marketplace. The experience of the market also feeds back into public policy, however, as company's experience difficulty in responding to these expectations.

Over the past several decades, public policy has become an ever-more important determinant of corporate behavior, as market outcomes have been increasingly altered through the public policy process. What happens in the public policy process has become more and more important to corporations, and they have become more active in politics through lobbying, campaign contributions, and other activities of this sort. Most corporate social behavior is the result of responding to government regulations of one sort or another. These changes are making it increasingly clear that business functions in both the market system and public policy process, and both processes are necessary to encompass the broad range of decisions a society needs to make about the corporation and its role in society.

As stated so well by Lee E. Preston and James E. Post, public policy is, along with the market mechanism, the source of guidelines and criteria for managerial behavior. The public policy process is the means by which society as a whole articulates its goals and objectives and directs and stimulates individuals and organizations to contribute to and cooperate with them. Appropriate guidelines for managerial behavior are to be found in the larger society, not in the personal vision of a few individuals or in the special interest of groups. Thus, a business organization should analyze and evaluate pressures and stimuli coming from public policy in the same way it analyzes market experience and opportunity.[38]

Notes

1 John Dewey, "The Democratic State," in Jo Ann Bodyston, ed., *The Later Works*, Vol 2, 1925–1927 (Carbondale and Edwardsville, IL: Southern Illinois University Press, 1984), 291.

2 Bob Goudzwaard, *Capitalism and Progress: A Diagnosis of Western Society* (Toronto, ON: Wedge Publishing Foundation and Grand Rapids, MI: William B. Eerdmans, 1979), 26–27.

3 Adam Smith, *The Wealth of Nations* (New York: Modern Library, 1937), 423.

4 "For Smith, the promotion of national wealth through the market was a goal worthy of the attention of moral philosophers because of its place in his larger moral vision. Smith valued commercial society not only for the wealth it produced but also for the character it fostered. He valued the market in part because it promoted the development of cooperative modes of behavior, making men more gentle because more self-controlled, more likely to subordinate their potentially asocial passions to the needs of others. In his own way, *The Wealth of Nations*, like Smith's *The Theory of Moral Sentiments* (1759), was intended to

make men better, not just better off." Jerry Z. Mueller, *The Mind and the Market: Capitalism in Modern European thought* (New York: Knopf, 2002), 52.

5 Justin Fox writing in *Time* claims that the reason the invisible hand emerged as the one idea from Smith's work that everyone remembers is because it is too simple and powerful. "If the invisible hand of the market can be relied on at all time and in all places to deliver the most prosperous and just society possible, then we'd be idiots not to get out of the way and let it work its magic. Plus, the supply-meets-demand straightforwardness of the invisible-hand metaphor lends itself to mathematical treatment, and math is the language in which economists communicate with one another." Justin Fox, "What Would Adam Smith Say?" *Time*, April 5, 2010, 18.

6 Richard Bronk, *Progress and the Indivisible Hand* (London: Warner Books, 1998), 90.

7 Adam Smith, *The Theory of Moral Sentiments* (New Rochelle, NY: Arlington House, 1969), 265–266.

8 Richard Bronk, *Progress and the Invisible Hand* (London: Warner Books, 1998), 7.

9 Julie A. Nelson, *Economics for Humans* (Chicago: The University of Chicago Press, 2006), 22.

10 Thomas Michael Power, "Trapped in Consumption: Modern Social Structure and the Entrenchment of the Device," in Eric Higgs, Andrew Light, and David Strong, eds., *Technology and the Good Life* (Chicago: University of Chicago Press, 2000), 271–293.

11 John Dewey, "Search for the Public," in Jo Ann Bodyston, ed., *The Later Works*, Vol. 2, 1925–1927 (Carbondale and Edwardsville, IL: Southern Illinois University Press, 1984), 240.

12 Bernard E. Harcourt, *The Illusion of Free Markets* (Cambridge, MA: Harvard University Press, 2011), 32, 195.

13 William Deresiewicz, a former professor at Yale University, thinks that as university education shifts its focus from the humanities to more "practical" subjects like economics, students are losing the ability to think independently. See William Deresiewicz, *Excellent Sheep: The Miseducation of the American Elite* (New York: Free Press, 2014).

14 Goudzwaard, *Capitalism and Progress*, 214.

15 See Karl Polanyi, *The Great Transformation* (Boston: Beacon Press, 1944). Michael J. Sandel, a political philosopher at Harvard University, argues that we have become a market society where market values seep into every aspect of human endeavor and where social relations reflect the image of the market. The market mentality involves a certain kind of reason that empties public life of moral argument. See Michael J. Sandel, "What Isn't for Sale," *The Atlantic*, April, 2012, 62–66.

16 See Sandra B. Rosenthal and Rogene A. Buchholz, *Rethinking Business Ethics: A Pragmatic Approach* (New York: Oxford University Press, 2000), 120–122.

17 In an article appearing in *The American Prospect*, Jeff Madrick makes the claim that while free-market economics may be at odds with reality, it fits the needs of the rich and powerful. See Jeff Madrick, "Why Economists Cling to Discredited Ideas," *The American Prospect*, Winter 2015, 75–79. See also Jeff Madrick, "What's the Matter with Economics? An Exchange," *The New York Review*, January 8, 2015, 40, and Alan S. Binder, "What's the Matter with Economics," *The New York Review*, December 18, 2014, 55–57. In the latter article Binder admits being distressed by what he notes is a high correlation between economists' political views and their allegedly objective research findings. While in academia, I had a good friend who was a fervent believer in free markets and I could predict with 100 percent certainty what his conclusions would be with respect to government regulation. No matter what issue he researched, and he did excellent research that was always published in the best journals, markets

would always be shown to be more efficient and produce a better outcome for society than government regulation.

18 See, for example, John Kenneth Galbraith, *The New Industrial State* (Boston: Houghton Mifflin, 1967).

19 It seemed safe to use air as an example of a pure public good that is not divisible into individual units that can be bought and sold on the market. But then along comes a Canadian company called Vitality Air that bottles air from the Canadian Rocky Mountains and sells it to people in China who live in extremely polluted circumstances. Nothing is ever absolute. See "Beijing," *The Week*, December 25, 2015, 9.

20 The European Union created a market to control carbon dioxide emissions in 2005 by establishing a cap and issuing tradable allowances based on this cap. At the time of writing Congress was considering seven proposals to set up a similar program in this country. See Bret Schulte, "Putting a Price on Pollution," *U.S. News & World Report*, May 14, 2007, 37–39.

21 Marjorie Kelly and Richard Rosen, "The Failure of Electricity Deregulation," *The Denver Post*, May 6, 2007, 1E. For a counterargument see Nicholas G. Muller, "The Real Story on Electricity Deregulation," *The Denver Post*, May 17, 2007, 7B.

22 Ibid.

23 Ibid.

24 Private philanthropy is a special case. People like Bill Gates, Warren Buffet, and more recently Mark Zuckerman have donated most of their fortune to dealing with public problems such as AIDS and education through their private foundations. Since these individuals or their representatives are making the decisions about what problems they address based on their own preferences and how much money to allocate to these problems, this is obviously not a collective decision-making process and thus cannot really be called public policy.

25 Thomas R. Dye, *Understanding Public Policy*, 3rd ed. (Englewood Cliffs, NJ: Prentice Hall, 1978), 23.

26 John Rawls, *A Theory of Justice* (Cambridge, MA: Harvard University Press, 1971), 266.

27 Gerald Sirkin, *The Visible Hand: The Fundamentals of Economic Planning* (New York: McGraw-Hill, 1968), 45.

28 James Buchanan, *The Demand and Supply of Public Goods* (Chicago: Rand McNally, 1968), 8.

29 See Michael J. Mandel, "How Much Is a Sea Otter Worth?" *Business Week*, August 21, 1989, 59, 62.

30 See T. H. Watkins, "The Worth of the Earth," *Audubon*, Vol. 99, No. 5 (September–October 1997), 128; Donella H. Meadows, "How Much Is Nature Worth?" *Business Ethics*, Vol. 11, No. 4 (July/August, 1997), 7.

31 Watkins, "The Worth of the Earth," 128.

32 Ibid.

33 Aaron Wildavsky, *Speaking Truth to Power: The Art and Craft of Policy Analysis* (Boston: Little, Brown, 1979), 253–254.

34 There is a school of thought called public choice theory that looks at government decision makers as rational, self-interested people who view issues from their own perspective and in light of personal incentives. While voters, politicians, and bureaucrats may desire to reflect the "public interest" and often advocate it in support of their decisions, this desire is only one incentive among many with which they are faced and is likely to be outweighed by more powerful incentives related to self-interest of one sort or another. See Steven Kelman, "Public Choice and Public Spirit," *The Public Interest*, No. 87 (Spring, 1987), 80–94 for an interesting critique of the public choice school of thought.

35 See Robert Kuttner, "The Libertarian Delusion," *The American Prospect*, Winter 2015, 71–74. Kuttner claims that what he calls the free-market fantasy has been discredited by events such as the financial collapse of 2008 where a conservative administration had to bail out private business organizations in the interests or preventing a total economic breakdown. The challenge society faces now is to redeem effective and democratic government. The cure for market failure is not more market as some economists claim, but the cure for a lost faith in democratic government has to be a stronger democracy.

36 Bronk, *Progress and the Invisible Hand*, 59.

37 Robert C. Solomon, *Ethics and Excellence: Cooperation and Integrity in Business* (New York: Oxford, 1993), 149.

38 Lee E. Preston and James E. Post, *Private Management and Public Policy: The Principle of Public Responsibility* (Englewood Cliffs, NJ: Prentice Hall, 1975), 11.

16 The Spirit of Capitalism

The *spirit of capitalism* refers to a certain kind of attitude or set of characteristics that are deemed necessary if not crucial to the development and continued functioning of a capitalistic system. People have to be captured by some kind of moral admonition that enables them to commit themselves to the tasks that capitalism requires in order for it to operate. They have to be motivated to engage in all the activities that are on the production side of the equation and equally to be engaged as consumers on the other side of the equation so that products can be produced or services provided that people are willing and able to use in their daily lives. While materialistic values are a large part of this commitment in that people need to work in order to consume, a moral dimension is also important for this commitment to adequately motivate people to do the things necessary to keep capitalism going. In this chapter we will thus look at two major developments in this regard.

The Protestant Ethic

In the sixteenth century, feudalism proved to have inadequate answers to the social and economic problems created by the growth of towns, the expansion of trade, the development of technology, and the growth of banks and other large-scale enterprises. It no longer provided an institutional context in which the potentials of these emerging developments could be exploited. Economic forces had to be given their own course free from the domination of the church and the old feudal order. Eventually a new economic order emerged out of the Industrial Revolution that we now call capitalism with new power centers and new sources of wealth. As Michael Lerner, who holds PhD degrees in both philosophy and clinical psychology, writes, there developed a rebellion against old feudal order that led to a very different kind of economic order that came under the control of different classes in society:

> Leading the rebellion were the merchants, traders, shopkeepers, bankers, and independent professionals of the social middle class (collectively

referred to as "the bourgeoisie"), who felt most resentful of the older feudal order. These people resented the degree to which the church had set limits on their own economic activities. For example, the church often set a "fair price," a "fair profit," and a "fair wage," in ways that impeded the creation of a free market. The traders and shopkeepers did not want the larger society to limit the profits they could make or to demand that they be responsible for the well-being of their workers.[1]

A new moral dimension was provided by the Protestant Ethic that informed the development of the capitalist systems and provided a legitimacy for its existence. On one hand, it created a moral incentive for people to be productive and increase economic wealth. On the other hand, it provided a moral limit to consumption in the interests of building up a capital base for production. Max Weber provided us with the first comprehensive study of the significance of the Protestant ethic.[2] In his book *The Protestant Ethic and the Spirit of Capitalism*, he sought to provide an explanatory model based on religious beliefs for the growth of capitalistic activity in the sixteenth and seventeenth centuries.[3]

These religious beliefs, which Weber called the Protestant ethic, produced a certain type of personality with a high motivation to achieve success in worldly terms by accumulating wealth and working diligently to create more wealth. This ethic contained two major elements: (1) an emphasis on the importance of a person's calling, which involved a primary responsibility to do one's best at whatever worldly station one was assigned to by God, rather than to seek religious meaning in withdrawing from the world, and (2) the rationalization of all of life by Calvin's notion of predestination through which work became a means of dispersing religious doubt by demonstrating membership in the elect to oneself and others.[4]

The self-discipline and moral sense of duty and calling, which were at the heart of this ethic, were vital, according to Weber, to the kind of rational economic behavior that capitalism demanded, behaviors such as having a mentality that embraced calculation in order to keep account of wealth, the commitment to be punctual and be on time and show up for work at the appointed time, and the dedication to be productive in all of one's activities. The Protestant Ethic contributed to this spirit, a spirit that was supportive of individual human enterprise and accumulation of wealth necessary for the development of capitalism. Within this climate, people were motivated to behave in a manner that proved conducive to rapid economic growth of the capitalistic order and shared values that were consistent with this kind of development.[5]

Within this ethical system, work was understood to be something good in itself and was neither a curse nor something fit only for slaves. Rather, work itself, which in the period before the Reformation was, by and large, considered to be a morally neutral activity at best, was given a clear moral sanction. Every person's work was of equal value in the eyes of God and contributed to the creation of more and more economic wealth in society. This ethic thus motivated one to work hard to be productive and accumulate wealth, which was a sign that one was doing things right and earning God's favor.

But this wealth was not to be pursued for its own sake or enjoyed in lavish consumption. The world existed to serve the glorification of God and for that purpose alone. The more wealth one had, the greater was the obligation to be an obedient steward and hold these possessions undiminished for the glory of God by increasing them through relentless effort. The accumulation of material wealth was as sure a way as was available to disposing the fear of damnation. One was not to rest of his or her laurels or enjoy the fruits of his or own labor. Whatever wealth one was able to accumulate must be reinvested to accumulate more wealth in order to please God and as a further manifestation of one's own election. As described by Gerhard Ditz in an article in *Kyklos*,

> [t]he upshot of it all, was that for the first time in history the two capital producing prescriptions, maximization of production and minimization of consumption became components of the same ethical matrix. As different from medieval or communist culture these norms were not reserved for or restricted to specific individuals or groups. everyone hypothetically belonged to that universe from which the deity had drawn the salvation sample, without disclosing its size or composition. The sampling universe had no known restriction of biological or social background, aptitude, or occupational specialization. Nobody could opt out from the sampling process, indeed, everyone had to act as if indeed he had been selected. For the mortal sin was to mock the deity by contradicting through his behavior God's primeval sampling decision. Everybody not only could but had to presume potential sainthood and correspondingly optimize his performance both as producer and consumer. The more his performance excelled relative to his reference group's, the higher the probability that indeed he had been selected. The ethic then pressured equally towards effective production and efficient consumption, which, while sustaining maximum productivity also maximizes savings and potential investment capital.[6]

Not only did the ethic thus stress physical work on the part of every person, but also whatever money one had was also to be put to work in making more money. A worldly asceticism was at the heart of this ethic, which gave a religious sanction for the acquisition and rational use of wealth to create more wealth. This new understanding of acquisitiveness and the pursuit of wealth became something of a moral imperative as what formerly had been regarded as a personal inclination and choice had now become something of a moral duty.

The Protestant ethic was an ingenious social and moral invention that gave a moral sanction and justification to behavior that was of crucial importance in the early stages of capitalism. It emphasized both the human and capital sources of productivity and growth, by focusing on hard work and the aspect of the calling, and advocating that the money people earned should also be put to work in earning more money. Inequality was thus morally justified if the money earned on capital was reinvested in further capital accumulation that would benefit society as a whole by increasing production and creating more economic wealth.

The Protestant ethic proved to be consistent with the need for accumulation of capital that is necessary during the early stages of industrial development. Money was saved and reinvested to build up a capital base. Consumption was curtailed in the interests of creating capital wealth. People dedicated themselves to hard work at often disagreeable tasks and accepted the rationalization of life that capitalism required. Such attitudes and activities represented a major shift away from the behavior and attitudes that informed medieval agrarian society.

The Protestant ethic served to pattern behavior and for its adherents it helped to make sense of the new industrial order, where people had to learn new roles and occupations. The pursuit of gain was legitimized and made something of a moral duty. People were to work diligently at their ordained tasks and accumulate wealth for the glory of God and as an indication of their own salvation. The Protestant ethic was something of a road map that provided a guide for behavior in the midst of a terribly confused and disorganized cultural system. It gave meaning to people's lives in the form of a religious and moral system to a rapidly changing society and enabled its adherents to act purposively within the emerging capitalist economic system. It provided a moral foundation for productive activity and legitimized the pursuit of profit and accumulation of wealth on the part of those who worked hard and invested their money wisely.

While the Protestant ethic contained a moral limit on consumption in the interests of generating more economic wealth and building up a capital base to increase production for the entire society, it also made production of the wealth an end in itself and did not provide a moral purpose for production that was rooted in the fulfillment of human existence. It was tied to religious justifications that were abstractions from human existence and allowed for exploitation of both humans and nature in the interests of increasing production. Natural law in which the state confines itself to the protection of individual rights in the context of an emphatic respect for the free market became sanctioned along with a utilitarian ethics, which imposed only one moral demand on the new industrialists, that is, to strive for the greatest possible quantity of utilities for themselves and, so it was thought, for their fellowmen.[7]

During the Enlightenment, nature came to connote not divine ordinance, but human appetites, and natural rights were invoked by the individualism of the time as a reason why self-interest should be given free play. The conception that the church possesses of its own authority an independent standard of social values that it could apply to the practical affairs of the economic world grew weaker.[8] Economic life came to be grounded in a naturalistic conception of society in which the world of human affairs is regarded as self-contained and in need of no supernaturalistic explanation. The science of economics eventually emerged to explain how the capitalistic system worked and described the laws that governed economic behavior. As stated by Bob Goudzwaard, a professor of economic theory at the Free University in Amsterdam,

> [i]t was precisely in the spiritual climate provided by deism, which looked upon the social and economic life of man as a cosmos controlled by natural laws and completely accessible to human analysis, that the science of economics could gradually emerge. The character of this science of course presupposed a primarily mechanistic view of the world. The timepiece manufactured by the clockmaker could, so to speak, now be opened up by man, and the wheelwork inside could be analyzed as carefully as possible.[9]

This ethic was of particular importance in American society as capitalism developed and economic wealth was created. The country needed investment capital to expand industry and build railroads and canals to link the country together. People worked hard and saved their money to be invested in this expansion and share in the growth of the economy. The opportunities in this country seemed limitless and resources were considered to be infinite. One could become as wealthy as one wanted by taking advantage of these opportunities and pursuing the American dream. But this dream was never realized; it was always in the future and was thus something that continued to provide motivation and purpose.

The notion of the Protestant ethic eventually became secularized in American society and stripped of its religious trappings. Secularization refers to the process of de-emphasizing the religious elements of any particular notion or concept and increasingly referring to worldly or temporal elements as distinguished from the spiritual or eternal realm. Thus, a secular view of life or of any particular matter is based on the premise that religion or religious considerations should be ignored or purposely excluded. The Protestant ethic thus became known as simply the work ethic and is now almost exclusively discussed in secular terms with very little reference made to its religious origins except in certain scholarly and religious circles.

However, its basic assumptions about the importance of work and investment remained much the same and continued to inform American society. Embedded in the notion of the Protestant ethic is the moral imperative both for the maximization of production and for the minimization of consumption. This ethic thus pressured equally toward effective production and efficient consumption, which also maximized savings and potential investment capital. But of even deeper significance is the fact that while the Protestant ethic contained a moral limit on consumption in the interests of generating more economic wealth and building up a capital base to increase production, production of this wealth became an end in itself as the ethic became secularized. As stated by Christopher Lasch in a book titled *The Culture of Narcissism*,

> [u]ntil recently, the Protestant work ethic stood as one of the most important underpinnings of American culture. According to the myth of capitalist enterprise, thrift and industry held the key to material success and spiritual fulfillment. America's reputation as a land of opportunity rested on its claim that the destruction of hereditary obstacles to advancement had created conditions in which social mobility depended on individual initiative alone. The self-made man, archetypical embodiment of the American dream, owed his advancement to habits of industry, sobriety, moderation, self-discipline, and avoidance of debt. He lived for the future, shunning self-indulgence in favor of patient, painstaking accumulation; and so long as the collective prospect looked on the whole so bright, he found in the deferral of gratification not only its principal gratification, but an abundant source of profits. In an expanding economy, the value of investments could be expected to multiply with time, as the spokesman for self-help, for all their celebration of work as its own reward, seldom neglected to point out.[10]

For many years, then, the Protestant ethic was one of the most forceful shapers of American culture. In the 1970s, however, people began to take note of a gradual conceptual shift in values. One topic of interest and concern that appeared frequently in both popular and professional literature during this time was the weakening or disappearance of the Protestant ethic from American culture. There was a good deal of evidence to suggest that the traditional values regarding work and the acquisition of wealth as expressed in the Protestant ethic were changing in some fashion. Many articles indicated that young adults in particular had little interest in the grinding routine of the assembly line or in automated clerical tasks. They were turning away, it was suggested, from their parents' dedication to work for the sake of success and were more concerned about finding meaningful work, something that was satisfying and personally rewarding in terms other than money. Young people were seeking to change existing industrial arrangements to allow these intangible goals to be pursued.[11]

They also began to discard the notion of deferred gratification and the worldly asceticism that provided a limit to consumption began to be less effective in shaping behavior. There was more of a sense of immediacy in living life to the fullest rather than waiting for some future time. Young people were motivated to spend money on immediate consumption rather that save it for something they could purchase in the future. This was again consistent with the developing economy as a capital base was created that became more productive. Somebody had to buy the things that were being produced in order to keep the economy growing.

Change in values was already noted as early as 1957 by Clyde Kluckhohn, a sociologist who did an extensive survey of the then available professional literature to determine if there had been any discernible shifts in American values during the past generation. As a result of this survey, he discovered that one value change that could be supported by empirical data was a decline of the Protestant ethic as the core of the dominant middle-class value system.[12] Kluckhohn cited numerous studies to support this conclusion as indicated in the following quote:

> The most generally agreed upon, the best documented, and the most pervasive value shift is what Whyte has called "the decline of the Protestant Ethic." This a central theme of Whyte's book. It is a clear-cut finding of the Schneider-Dornbusch study of inspirational religious literature. It is noted by essentially all the serious publications on recent value changes and on the values of the younger generation.[13]

Related to this fundamental shift are a number of others mentioned that have the Protestant ethic as their central point of reference. These shifts are interconnected and mutually reinforcing and are a result of the weakening of the Protestant ethic but may also, in turn, contribute to this weakening. There has been a rise in value upon "being" or "being and becoming" as opposed to "doing," according to many studies cited by Kluckhohn. Another such shift is the trend toward "present time" in contrast to "future time" value orientation, which meant that the notion of deferred gratification was changing.[14]

Last, there was a trend toward an increase of aesthetic and recreational values as good in themselves, a development of "values which the Puritan Ethic never placed upon recreation (except as a means to the end of more effective work), pleasure, leisure, and aesthetic and expressive activities. American began to enjoy themselves more and with less guilt than ever before. Moreover, there has been a remarkable diversification and broadening of the base of leisure-time activities within the population."[15]

In 1976 Daniel Bell, a sociologist at the New School for Social Research in New York City, argued that the Protestant ethic has been replaced by hedonism in contemporary society; the idea of pleasure as a way of life. During the 1950s, according to Bell, the American culture had become primarily hedonistic, concerned with fun, play, display, and pleasure. The culture was no longer concerned with how to work and achieve but with how to spend and enjoy:[16]

> In the early development of capitalism, the unrestrained economic impulse was held in check by Puritan restraint and the Protestant Ethic. One worked because of one's calling, or to fulfill the covenant of the

community. But the Protestant Ethic was undermined not by modernism but by capitalism itself. The greatest single engine in the destruction of the Protestant Ethic was the invention of the installment plan, or instant credit. Previously one had to save in order to buy. But with credit cards one could indulge in instant gratification. The system was transformed by mass production and mass consumption, by the creation of new wants and new means of gratifying those wants.[17]

Thus, the cultural if not moral justification of capitalism had become hedonism. This cultural transformation was brought about by (1) demographic change that resulted in the growth of urban centers and shift in political weight, (2) the emergence of a consumption society with its emphasis on spending and material possessions rather than thrift and frugality, and (3) a technological revolution that through the automobile, the motion picture, and the radio broke down rural isolation and fused the country into a common culture and a national society.[18]

Bell argued that this abandonment of the Protestant ethic left capitalism with no moral or transcendental ethic and produced an extraordinary contradiction within the social structure of American society. The business corporation requires people who work hard, are dedicated to a career, and accept delayed gratification, all traditional Protestant Ethic virtues. Yet in its products and advertisements, the corporation promotes pleasure, instant joy, relaxing, and letting go, all hedonistic virtues. In Bell's words, "one is to be straight by day and a swinger by night."[19] Capitalism thus continued to demand a Protestant ethic in the area of production but needed to stimulate a demand for pleasure and play in the area of consumption.[20]

Finally, Christopher Lasch argued that a new ethic of self-preservation had taken hold in American society. The work ethic had been gradually transformed into an ethic of personal survival.[21] The Puritans believed that a godly man worked diligently at his calling not so much in order to accumulate personal wealth as to add to the wealth of the community.[22] The pursuit of self-interest was changing from the accumulation of wealth to a search for pleasure and psychic survival. The cult of consumption with its emphasis on immediate gratification created the narcissistic man of modern society. Such a culture lives for the present and does not save for the future because it believes there may not be a future to worry about.[23]

This alleged weakening of the Protestant ethic with its inherent restriction on consumption is consistent with behavioral changes in American society. Prior to the Second World War, people, by and large, were savings oriented and lived by the ethic of deferred gratification. They would not buy houses with large mortgages and run up huge credit card balances, as these options were not available to many people. Rather, they would save their money until they could buy things outright. Gratification of their desires was deferred until they could afford to satisfy them and then, and only then, was it appropriate to buy things to enjoy. In other words, people lived within their immediate means and did not borrow for purposes of increased consumption.

After the war this ethic changed into one of instant gratification as a consumer society was created where people were encouraged to satisfy their desires now rather than wait until they had the money in hand. Buying on credit was encouraged and long-term mortgages became the order of the day with respect to housing. Why defer gratification when one could buy things immediately and pay for them in the future? Companies helped to create this kind of society by making credit easy to obtain through the use of credit cards and by using more sophisticated forms of advertising to increase demand for their products.

The United States became a society where consumption was emphasized and money was made available so people could buy on credit and pay their debts sometime in the future. Television fed this change with sitcoms that portrayed the typical American family as one that lived in a nice house in the suburbs with two cars and all the latest kitchen appliances and electronic gear in the rest of the house. Advertising on television also became more sophisticated to stimulate demand for products. Companies fed this consumption binge with a proliferation of products that appealed to every taste that could be imagined, which encouraged people to go into debt to enjoy the pleasures these products could bring immediately rather than in some future period.

There were many factors behind this change in behavior, and no one factor in particular was responsible for this change. They all helped to create a new approach to consumption where instant gratification became a cultural trait in contrast to earlier times when saving for the future was emphasized. The implications of this change were profound for lifestyles and habits of people as society became more wealthy and prosperous. Many people lived more interesting lives and had more diversity available to them as never before. They traveled more miles, wore more and different clothes, drove more expensive and sophisticated cars, and in general enjoyed rising standards of living that involved consumption of the latest products.

Thus, the Protestant ethic failed to provide a moral framework for production and consumption activities as it apparently did during the early stages of industrial development. In the midst of affluence and advanced technology that made possible a high level of consumption, it has not enabled many people to act purposively in keeping the system going and in enjoying the benefits of technology. It has not provided the kind of information necessary to deal adequately with the present cultural and economic situation, nor did it provide a means of effectively responding to environmental problems. It became more and more irrelevant to the economic system as it emerged and changed to deal with new concerns. While the Protestant ethic served an important function in limiting consumption to build up a productive capital base, once that base was established people needed to consume more in order to keep the system going.

The demise of the Protestant ethic has left capitalism without a comprehensive ethical or moral system to provide legitimacy for the accumulation
of wealth and to root capitalism in a larger moral purpose beyond itself.
The system became self-justifying and any ethical concerns had to adapt
themselves to the requirements of the economic system. Perhaps this was
inevitable as during the Reformation the authority of the medieval Catholic
Church was broken and the unity of civilization it symbolized was destroyed
setting secular forces free to develop free from the church's overpowering
domination. Economic forces in particular were set free to develop without
being hampered by the notions of "just wage" or "just price" that were of
concern to medieval religion. Wages and prices were set by the laws of supply and demand rather than some moral principles stemming from religion,
and the capitalistic system came to operate according to its own "scientific"
principles born out of an enlightenment philosophy. While the Protestant
ethic may have played a role in the development of capitalism, it had to
shape itself to the capitalistic organization of production.

The New Spirit of Capitalism

This is the title of a book by two French authors, Luc Boltanski and Eve Chiapello, published in 2005 by Verso Press. This is another lengthy tome running some 600 pages in paperback and, for the most part, is very difficult to
understand. The idea for the book was born out of the perplexity shared by
numerous observers that was created by the deterioration in the economic
and social position of a growing number of people and by what they call a
profoundly restructured capitalism. Many people of working age became
impoverished, and there were regular increases in unemployment and job
insecurity as well as stagnation in incomes from work at a time when income
from profits were rising and inequalities growing. Capitalist restructuring
occurred around the freeing-up of financial markets and merger-acquisition
activities at a time when government policies with regard to taxation, wages,
and social security were favorable to capitalism. Companies also had more
labor flexibility for hiring on a temporary basis while experiencing a reduction in the cost of layoffs, which gradually whittled down the social security
systems that had been established by many countries.[24]

These trends produced an increased skepticism about the ability of capitalism, with respect to currently educated generations, to maintain the
living standards their parents enjoyed and in more general terms their lifestyle. Under these conditions, according to the authors, capitalism will face
increasing difficulties if it does not restore some measure of hope "to those
whose engagement is required for the functioning of the system as a whole."
It is obvious to the authors that a social, and I might add economic, system
that can no longer satisfy the classes it is designed to serve is menaced. The
demoralizing effect of this new order of things is fairly widespread throughout Western societies. The authors hope to strengthen the resistance to this

kind of fatalism without retreating into nostalgia for the past by provoking a change in the mindset of the readers by helping them to consider the problems of the period from an alternate perspective:[25]

> We have sought, on the one hand, to describe as unique conjuncture when capitalism was able to extricate itself from a number of fetters linked to is previous mode of accumulation and the demands for justice it prompted; and on the other, basing ourselves on this historical period, to establish a model of change in values on which both the success and the tolerability of capitalism depend—a model with more general claims to validity.[26]

The subject of their book, then, is the *"ideological changes that have accompanied recent transformations in capitalism."*[27] Use of the notion of *spirit of capitalism* became essential for the authors as it gave them the ability to articulate two central concepts on which their analyses are based, namely, *capitalism and critique*, in a dynamic relation to each other. They present what they call a minimal definition of capitalism that stresses an *imperative to unlimited accumulation of capital by formally peaceful means.* The constant reintroduction of capital into the economic system to make a profit—increasing capital that, in turn, will be reinvested—endows capitalism with a dynamic and transformative power that fascinates even the most hostile of observers. What really matters is the constant transformation of capital, plant, and various purchases like raw material and services into output, of output into money, and of money into new investments. There is no limit to this process, no possible point of satiation to this process, giving capitalism an insatiable character.[28]

The authors go on to define the spirit of capitalism as the *"ideology that justifies engagement in capitalism."*[29] They consider it to be the set of beliefs that are associated with the capitalist order to justify this order in the minds of people and sustain the kinds of actions and predispositions that are compatible with capitalism. These beliefs support the performance of more or less unpleasant tasks and in general commitment to a lifestyle conducive to the capitalist order. Enough people must adhere to the operation, benefits, and resources of the order in which they find themselves embedded to keep the system going. The arguments justifying capitalism must be strong enough to be accepted as self-evident by enough people to overcome the despair and nihilism, which capitalism induces in both those whom it oppresses and those who maintain it and transmit its values to future generations. Capitalism must be justified on both the individual level, where a person must find grounds for engaging in capitalist enterprise, and at a general level, where this engagement serves the common good.[30] Economic science is one candidate that can be of use to justify capitalism. As the authors state,

> the development of economic science, whether classical economics or Marxism, contributed to constructing a representation of the world

that is radically novel when compared with traditional thinking, marking the radical separation of the economic aspects of the social fabric and their constitution as an autonomous domain. This made it possible to impart substance to the belief that the economy is an autonomous sphere, independent of ideology and morality, which obeys positive laws, ignoring the fact that such a conviction was itself the product of an ideological endeavor, and that it could have been formed only by incorporating—and then partially masking it by scientific discourse—justifications whereby the positive laws of economics are in the service of the common good.[31]

The incorporation of utilitarianism into economics made it self-evident that whatever served the individual also served society. The passion for material gain and the establishment of an acquisitive society was offset by the quantifiable benefits of accumulating material goods. Within this perspective the sole criterion of the common good was increased wealth. This increase in wealth is exemplified on a daily basis by the profits of business organizations and their activity and growth which is the criterion for social well-being. The enormous amount of social labor that is involved in producing individual material advancement allowed capitalism to attain an unprecedented legitimacy.[32]

This spirit is in the midst of a significant crisis, according to the authors, as demonstrated by growing social confusion and skepticism which threatens the accumulation process as capitalism must guarantee people a certain minimum of security to have a place to live and provide for a family. Changes in the spirit of capitalism are consistent with changes in the living and working conditions and the expectations of workers who play a major role in the accumulation process without being its privileged beneficiaries. In today's world, retirement pensions are under threat, and careers are no longer guaranteed.[33] The capitalist is caught between its interest in measures that make it possible to maintain the commitment of the workers on whom profit creation depends and the need to keep wages low so as not to put the firm at a competitive disadvantage.[34] Any new spirit of capitalism must address the following three questions:

How is committed engagement in the processes of accumulation a source of enthusiasm, even for those who will not necessarily be the main beneficiaries of the profits that are made?

To what extend can those involved in the capitalist universe be assured of a minimum of security for themselves and their families?

How can participation in capitalist firms be justified in terms of the common good, and how, confronted with accusations of injustice, can the way that it is conducted and managed be defended?[35]

For capitalism to succeed it must engage the people who are indispensable to the accumulation process and incorporate a spirit that provides them with attractive and exciting life prospects while providing security and moral reasons for people to do what they do to keep capitalism going.[36] However, in capitalism the owners of capital are the dominant class, and history has shown that in the absence of legislative and regulatory requirements this class will tend to use their economic power to attain a dominant position in all spheres of activity, leaving workers with what the authors describe as "only the meanest share of the value added that has been created." Under capitalism it is the party of profit that invariably emerges victorious in these kinds of negotiations.[37] The historical forms of the critique of this kind of economic system have pretty much remained the same, say the authors, over the last two centuries. They are as follows:

1. Capitalism as a source of *disenchantment* and *inauthenticity* of objects, persons, emotions and, more generally, the kind of existence associated with it.
2. Capitalism as a source of *oppression*, inasmuch as it is opposed to the freedom, autonomy and creativity of the human beings who are subjects, under its sway, on one hand, to the domination of the market as an impersonal force fixing prices and designating desirable human beings and products/services, and rejecting others, and, on the other hand, to the forms of subordination involved in the condition of wage-labor (enterprise discipline, close monitoring by bosses, and supervision by means of regulations and procedures).
3. Capitalism as a source of *poverty* among workers and of *inequalities* on an unprecedented scale
4. Capitalism as a source of *opportunism* and *egoism* that, by exclusively encouraging private interests, prove destructive of social bonds and collective solidarity, especially of minimal solidarity between rich and poor.

The artistic critique of capitalism is a radical challenge to the basic values and options of capitalism as it involves a rejection of the disenchantment that results from the processes of rationalization and commodification of the world inherent in the capitalistic system. It presupposes an interruption or abolition of these features and thus involves a total abandonment of the capitalist regime. The social critique hopes to solve the problems of inequality and poverty by breaking up the power and operation of individual interests in the name of the common good. Critique of this sort obligates capitalism to justify itself and strengthen the mechanisms of justice it contains and refers to certain kinds of the common good in whose service it claims to be placed.[38]

The development of a new spirit of capitalism takes place in two stages: (1) "the sketching of a general interpretative schema of the new mechanisms and the establishment of a new cosmology, allowing people to get their bearings and deduce some elementary rules of behavior," and (2) refining this schema *in the direction of greater justice* with its organizing principles established and new tests that are stricter in nature regarding the performance of capitalism. One of the first tasks of critique is to identify the most important tests in a given society to clarify the principles underlying these tests and then to develop a critique that is corrective or radical, reformist, or revolutionary, depending on the available options and strategies.[39]

The authors then identify a second spirit of capitalism that appeared in the management literature in the second half of the twentieth century as the operation of large corporations was transferred to salaried managers when owners largely withdrew to the role of shareholder except when they became salaried senior management themselves. This literature had to be based on normative concerns and show how the making of a profit might be desirable, exciting, interesting, innovating, or commendable and show a general orientation toward the common good.[40] Management by objectives gave workers some autonomy by giving decision-making power to those concerned with the immediate tasks to be accomplished and monitored their performance on the basis of the overall outcome rather than of each individual decision. This mechanism enabled firms to profit from a motivated workforce.[41]

Managers became professionals, not small-scale owners, and their work was characterized more by networks rather than a domestic framework. Firms became decentralized with workers organized in teams that had real autonomy. Firms were given a prominent role with respect to the general well-being of society and were judged not only on the wealth they created but also by the way they organized work and the kind of opportunities they offered.[42] The qualities of this new spirit of capitalism included autonomy, spontaneity, multitasking, novelty, creativity, and receptiveness to a whole range of experiences.[43] People were expected give themselves to their work, which facilitated an instrumentalization of human beings in their most specifically human dimensions.[44] This second spirit of capitalism is summed up by the authors as follows:

> Thus the second spirit of capitalism . . . was constructed in response to critiques denouncing the egoism of private interests and the exploitation of workers. It evinced a modernist enthusiasm for integrated, planned organizations concerned with social justice. Shaped through contact with the social critique, in return it inspired the compromise between the civic virtues of the collective and industrial necessities that underlay the establishment of the welfare state.[45]

This period came to a close with a dismantling of the world of work as exemplified in the demise of unionism, which contributed significantly to changing the balance of power between employers and employees in favor of the former and facilitated the task of restructuring capitalism. The rise of individualism in contemporary society and a culture of everyone-for-themselves, the crisis of confidence in political action, and the fear of unemployment are connected with the dynamic of capitalism. Union representatives became ever more isolated, had less and less contact with wage earners, and no longer had time to develop membership and even concern themselves with members.[46]

The casualization of work status, according to the authors, coupled with the fear of unemployment weakened workers' fighting spirit and their propensity to even join a union. *Breaking up the work community* through employing people with different job statuses that belong to different firms on the same worksite also disarmed and disoriented collective action. Membership in one and the same work community is thus dismantled by new forms of organization that severely handicap the formation of collectives. These and other actions by management such as having wage earners appraise one another made it difficult for workers to form a common front against management.[47]

Maintaining a high degree of solidarity between managers and workers charged with tasks of execution, which seemed of crucial importance in large and integrated firms with heavy concentrations of workers and combative trade unions is no longer a priority. The determination of pay, for example, occurs largely through an unbalanced relation of forces on the market bringing an individualized wage earner who needs the work in order to live face-to-face with highly structured firms controlled by management that is capable of seizing all the opportunities in the changed situation.[48]

Society is fragmented, say the authors, between strong and prosperous people and little people in a miserable state who have limited mobility. There is no link between these groups as they live in completely different worlds thus the idea of exploitation has no meaning since they must at least share a common world for exploitation to take place.[49] Social bonds have disintegrated, creating a sense of anomie, which, according to the authors, refers to the fading of the tacit norms and conventions regulating expectations. One indicator of this anomie is that the substitution of *ad hoc* jobs for steady employment and the prospect of a career have gone hand-in-hand with the rise of *short-term commitments in private life* indicated by a reduction in the number of marriages and an increase in divorce but also by the growing fragility of relationships without legal status that are defined as "cohabitation."[50]

Mechanisms associated with the new spirit of capitalism include outsourcing, profit centers within firms, quality circles, or other forms of work organization that arose to meet the demands for autonomy and responsibility that were obtained at the price of a reduction in job security. Separating people from this security condemns workers to factory discipline and meager pay that no longer allows them a properly human existence. Since the capitalist system condemns the majority of people to have to work in order to survive, what appears to be liberation is in fact just a new form of slavery. Workers are subject to the demands of the workplace just as consumers are subject to the demands of the marketplace. Consumers are in the grip of production and what they believe to be their own desires are really the product of a manipulation by the sellers of goods who enslave their imagination. They desire what they are led to desire and this desire must be constantly stimulated by advertising so that it becomes insatiable.[51]

In the concluding chapter the authors reiterate their main hypothesis that capitalism needs a spirit so as to engage the people who are necessary for production and the functioning of business. People cannot be forced to work as the state possesses something of a monopoly on legitimate violence. Capitalism depends on free labor and does not have total sway over people so that capitalism must furnish acceptable reasons to engage in capitalist activities. There reasons are contained in their notion of the spirit of capitalism. Furthermore, this spirit must incorporate a moral dimension to be capable of mobilizing people. They require a moral justification to get involved in the process, but capitalism must borrow the legitimating principles from an order of justification external to itself.[52]

In order to survive capitalism must both stimulate and curb insatiability. It is a process of unlimited accumulation and must constantly activate different forms of desire for accumulation. This desire tends to exhaust itself as human beings are satiable by nature; thus, the spirit of capitalism activates insatiability in the form of excitement and liberation while at the same time restricting it in the name of the common good. The spirit of capitalism also cannot be reduced to an ideology in which it is an illusion that has no impact on the world. It must deliver on its promises and must constantly transform itself by overcoming the effects of market saturation by creating new products and services and commodifying spaces that have been outside of the commodity sphere. The spirit of capitalism itself is transformed by critique, and this critique, which derives its energy from sources of indignation, can itself become one of the factors precipitating a change in capitalism.[53]

A capitalism that has no constraints, say the authors, knows no criteria other than the private interests of the strongest element in the system has no reason to take account of the general or common interest. There is no "invisible hand" to guide capitalism when institutions and agreements without which the market cannot function collapse. Thus, capitalism has never been able to survive without the state to guarantee property rights, enforce legitimate contracts, and respect the rights of workers. Capitalism that no longer produces an increase in the standard of living particularly for the poorest loses its credibility. New mechanisms of justice and new test procedures require the force of the state to constrain capitalism to serve the common good and not just the interests of private parties.[54]

The authors cannot tell from their analyses of capitalism whether it will be induced to set limits on itself or whether its untrammeled expansion will continue to produce destructive effects. The rise of individualism has limited the ability of people to form collectives to pursue the common good and has produced a sense of impotence, abandonment, and isolation. For this to be adequately addressed, both artistic and social critique must be kept alive to confront the destruction caused by capitalism "while avoiding the excesses that each of them risks inducing when it is given exclusive expression and not tempered by the presence of the other."[55] Both of these critiques are necessary to enable the kind of changes in capitalism that are necessary for its continued success.[56]

By way of summary then, the authors see the first spirit of capitalism as contained in the work of Max Weber, who developed the notion that the emergence of capitalism involved the establishment of a new moral relationship between human beings and their work. Work was defined as a vocation such that people could devote themselves to it firmly and steadily regardless of its intrinsic interest and qualities. Workers were motivated to fulfill their calling being obedient and tireless in their work and perform this duty wherever Providence had placed them in the grand scheme of things and not question the situation in which they found themselves. This ethic also gave merchants and entrepreneurs moral support for devoting themselves to undertaking the pitiless rationalization of their affairs in pursuing maximum profit and pursuing material gain, which were signs of success in fulfilling their vocation. All of this was a break from traditional practices and involved the demise of moral condemnations of profit and support for the process of unlimited accumulation.

This all changed in the later years of the twentieth century with the development of what has been called the human potentials movement. As the religious motivation for doing the tasks that capitalism required and values changed, there was a need for a new spirit to provide motivation for work. There was a great deal of literature in the second half of the twentieth century devoted to the workplace and the jobs people were doing.[57] The subjects covered were job satisfaction, enrichment of the workplace, fulfillment of the self in the work one was doing, growth of the self and similar topics. Apparently workers began to see intrinsic value in their work, and rather than working for the glory of God, they wanted work that interested them and provided opportunities for personal growth and development. Workplaces were restructured to allow more autonomy and decision-making power for workers by forming teams that gave workers control over the immediate workplace. Programs to promote job enrichment and job enlargement were instituted and workers were given more opportunities to be creative and make suggestions for improvement to the work they were doing to give them more freedom and promote efficiency for the company. All of this constituted the second spirit of capitalism according to the authors.

Today's workplace has changed into something entirely different from this description. Employees and employers have developed new relationships that reflect global competition. which drives down wages and rapidly developing technology that has replaced workers altogether. Companies have downsized by laying off workers and eliminating layers of middle-management. They have outsourced many functions to overseas locations to take advantage of lower costs. They have also used temporary hires or considered employees to be independent contractors in order to escape providing benefits to their workforce. And where this can't be done they have cut health benefits for employees or abandoned health coverage entirely because of cost pressures. Many companies have changed their pension plans to defined contribution plans that are under the control of the employee.

These changes in the workplace have resulted in destroying any sense of community in the workplace as the implied contract between employees and the corporation as changed. By and large, the old contract held that employees had obligations related to satisfactory attendance at work, acceptable levels of effort and performance, and loyalty to the corporation and management. In return for these commitments, employers provided fair compensation for the work done, fringe benefits such as coverage for health care and defined benefit pension plans, the chance for advancement based on seniority and merit, and a great degree of job security.

As job security has evaporated because of restructuring, downsizing, outsourcing, and other changes in the workplace so have prospects for advancement and predictable wage and benefit increases. Management demands for individual commitment and responsibility have largely taken their place. They want people to buy into long-term visions of the company and be committed to corporate goals while at the same time expecting them to cope with an ever present threat of termination. Such expectations seem to be one-sided and certainly have implications for employee loyalty particularly since the effects of many of these changes are distributed bimodally. Top executives are well rewarded and are given generous job security provisions and retirement packages while middle managers, clerical workers, and production workers face much greater uncertainty and have actually seen their incomes decline over the past few decades.

Instead of lifelong employment, the emphasis is on lifelong employability. Employees have had to take charge of their own careers and can no longer rely on a secure place in the corporate organization. They must continually acquire new skills to keep up with the development of new technologies. Employees are expected to share responsibility for their employment and in many places are gaining greater control over what they do in the workplace. Loyalty to the company is said to be dead, however, and in its place is loyalty to one's profession or job function.[58] Individualism seems to be the order of the day as workers are forced to take more responsibility for their own employment and can no longer depend on companies to have their interests in mind.

Meanwhile, unions, which provided some degree of collective bargaining power for employees, have been in decline for several decades and have been openly attacked by some government actions at both the federal and state level. Unions arose as industrialization took hold in this country and workers found that many problems they were experiencing in the workplace such as long hours, poor working conditions, low wages, and arbitrary hiring and firing practices were not being addressed. To deal with these problems they began to form unions to counter the power of management with an organized labor movement. These unions became a force to be reckoned with and won major benefits for their members in confrontations with management. During a forty-year period, from 1935 to 1975, unions grew in number and bargaining power with employers.

However, in recent decades labor unions have declined as a dominant force in American society. Since about 1975 the balance of power in collective bargaining has been shifting back to management. Unions have been declining in numbers and power over this period. While there was some increase of union activity in 1994, the resurgence of management strength in collective bargaining is likely to continue, at least for the immediate future. Thus, unions are not as able to look after the rights of labor in a changing workplace and do not provide a sense of community for the labor force that they once did in our society.[59]

The forces driving changes in the workplace such as global competition and rapid technological change will probably continue for the foreseeable future, making further corporate adjustments necessary. The foundations of the old social contract will continue to erode, making it increasingly clear that the old social contract cannot be preserved or reestablished. The question then becomes what kind of a new contract will emerge that will be satisfactory to all parties concerned and yet deal with the new realities of the workplace? What moral issues do these changes raise with respect to the relationship between employees and employers? Do companies have a moral responsibility to provide at least some degree of job security for its employees? Can the system function effectively if employee trust and loyalty disappear and responsibility for the employee's well-being is no longer a corporate concern?[60]

There are some benefits to this emphasis on employment security rather than job security. What employees need in this kind of economy is opportunity rather than security, and they must have the skills to take advantage of the opportunities that come along. This calls for continual growth on the part of employees, a willingness to learn new skills, an emphasis on continual learning and creativity, and an openness to change. Security in a given job or company can lead to stultification and boredom and creation of a workforce that is resistant to change. On the other hand, an opportunity society can degenerate into a free-for-all, where it's every man for himself and the devil take the hindmost. In this kind of environment top management has all the security with more than adequate pension plans and severance packages and employees have all the risk and little opportunity for any kind of security.

Obviously there is a need for a third spirit of capitalism that relates to this kind of workplace and gives people reason to get up in the morning and go to work. But as far as I can tell, the authors do not provide any kind of ideas in this regard. Is the shear need to survive enough of a motivation to keep workers doing the things necessary to keep capitalism going? Are they going to continue to put up with a growing differential between the pay of top management and the lowest paid employees in the company? Will they continue to improve their productivity when all the gains from productivity go to the top 1 percent? These are hard questions, and it is difficult to envision any kind of a new spirit of capitalism that will motivate employees to support capitalism without a major restructuring of the system to provide a fair wage and benefits to those workers who are necessary to keep capitalism going. Without their commitment and dedication to their work the system will collapse.

Notes

1 Michael Lerner, *The Politics of Meaning: Restoring Hope and Possibility in an Age of Cynicism* (Reading, MA: Addison-Wesley, 1996), 35.
2 Max Weber, *The Protestant Ethic and the Spirit of Capitalism* (New York: Charles Scribner's Sons, 1958).
3 Ibid., 35–40.
4 David C. McCelland, *The Achieving Society* (New York: Free Press, 1961), 48.
5 Richard LaPiere, *The Freudian Ethic* (New York: Duell Sloan and Pearce, 1959), 16.
6 Gerhard W. Ditz, "The Protestant Ethic and the Market Economy," *Kyklos*, Vol. 33(1980), 626–627.
7 Bob Goudzwaard, *Capitalism & Progress: A Diagnosis of Western Society* (Toronto, ON: Wedge Publishing Foundation; Grand Rapids, MI: William B. Eerdmans Publishing Co., 1979), 61. In a related passage, Michael Lerner states that "[a] materialist worldview emerged that validated only that which could be experienced by the senses. And in place of any ethical concerns of the community, this new social order insisted that the ultimate reality was the pleasure and satisfaction of each individual. The lone individual became the center of the universe, and if we built families and communities, it was only because the lone individual had found it in his or her interest to do so. All connections between human beings hereafter would be based on contract: free individuals choosing to make a connection with others. The sole goal of the state, in this scheme, was to ensure that there was a realm of free contracts in which no one would interfere." Lerner, *The Politics of Meaning*, 37.
8 John Gilchrist, *The Church and Economic Activity in the Middle Ages* (London: Macmillan, 1969), 123. Protestantism, as an institution, could never exercise the kind of control and domination over secular forces as did the medieval Catholic Church. The nature of the Protestant principle did not allow for this kind of control. The nature of the revolution it introduced supported political and economic forces to establish their own ground and authority. The challenge the Protestant movement presented the Catholic Church in questioning its claim to universal and eternal truth, and the revolutionary philosophy that informed it, did not allow Protestantism to then turn around and exercise the same kind of domination and control in the nature of a universal authority. Protestantism as an institution and a movement could not exercise a universal constructive approach to the ordering of life and still be true to the critical principles that informed its emergence. Economic forces had to be given their own course and develop secular sources of meaning and purpose. See Richard Niebuhr, *The Kingdom of God in America* (New York: Harper and Row, 1937), 28–30.
9 Goudzwaard, *Capitalism & Progress*, 22.

10　Christopher Lasch, *The Culture of Narcissism: American Life in an Age of Diminishing Expectations* (New York: Norton, 1978), 52–53.

11　The University of Michigan Survey Research Center asked 1,533 working people to rank various aspects of work in order of importance. Good pay came in a distant fifth behind interesting work, enough help and equipment to get the job done, enough information to do the job, and enough authority to do the job. See "Work Ethic," *Time*, October 30, 1972, 97.

12　Clyde Kluckhohn, "Have There Been Discernible Shifts in American Values during the Past Generation," in Elting E. Morrison, ed., *The American Style: Essays in Value and Performance* (New York: Harper& Bros., 1958), 207.

13　Ibid., 184.

14　Ibid., 207.

15　Ibid., 192.

16　Daniel Bell, *The Cultural Contradictions of Capitalism* (New York: Basic Books, 1976), 70.

17　Ibid., 21.

18　Ibid., 64–65.

19　Ibid., 71–72.

20　Ibid., 75.

21　Christopher Lasch, *The Culture of Narcissism: American Life in an Age f Diminishing Expectations* (New York: W.W. Norton, 1978), 53.

22　Ibid.

23　Ibid., 68–69.

24　Luc Boltanski and Eve Chiapello, *The New Spirit of Capitalism* (New York: Verso, 2007), xxxvii–xxxix.

25　Ibid., xii–xiv.

26　Ibid, xiv.

27　Ibid., 3.

28　Ibid., 4–5.

29　Ibid., 8.

30　Ibid., 10–11.

31　Ibid., 12.

32　Ibid., 12–13.

33　Ibid., 24–25.

34　Ibid., 18–19.

35　Ibid., 16.

36　Ibid., 24–25.

37　Ibid., 34.

38　Ibid., 39, 42.

39　Ibid., 34–35.

40　Ibid., 58–59.

41　Ibid., 66.

42　Ibid., 85–86.

43　Ibid., 97.

44　Ibid., 98.

45　Ibid., 201.

46　Ibid., 275, 278.

47　Ibid., 281–284.

48　Ibid., 309, 314.

49　Ibid., 360.

50　Ibid., 423.

51　Ibid., 437–430.

52　Ibid., 486–487.

53　Ibid., 487–491.

54 Ibid., 510–513.

55 Ibid., 531–536.

56 For a critique of this book see Bernard Stiegler, *The Lost Spirit of Capitalism* (Cambridge, UK: Polity Press, 2014). Stiegler thinks that Boltanski and Chiapello did not pay enough attention to the effects of financialization on the transformations of capitalism.

57 See, for example, *Editorial Research Reports on the American Work Ethic* (Washington, DC: Congressional Quarterly, 1973); Harold L. Sheppard and Neal Q. Herrick, *Where Have All the Robots Gone* (New York: The Free Press, 1972); Special Task Force to the Secretary of Health, Education, and Welfare, *Work in America* (Cambridge, MA: MIT Press, 1973); and Judson Gooding, *The Job Revolution* (New York: Walker & Co., 1972).

58 Allan A. Kennedy, *The End of Shareholder Value: Corporations at the Crossroads* (Cambridge, MA: Perseus, 2000), 95. See also Laura Sveen, "How Free Agency Is Challenging How We Understand Loyalty," *The Denver Post*, June 5, 2016, 2K.

59 David Rolf, president of a local union and architect of Seattle's $15 minimum-wage victory, argues that the old model of collective bargaining can't be resurrected and presents some new models of how workers can wield power and pursue their interests. See David Rolf, "Toward a 21st-Century Labor Movement," *The American Prospect*, Spring 2016, 11–13. See also Tamara Draut, *Sleeping Giant: How the New Working Class Will Transform America* (New York: Doubleday, 2016).

60 See Robert Kuttner, "Why Work Is More and More Debased," *The New York Review*, October 23, 2014, 52–53.

17 The Future of Capitalism

Capitalism is in trouble. There is first of all a mounting national debt that seems out of control. As of April 11, 2016, the debt was over 19 trillion dollars which amounted to $59,585.05 for each citizen given an estimated population of 322,739,769 at that time.[1] *Time* magazine did a rather clever thing in the April 25, 2016, issue to try to make this figure real for its readers. The cover page consisted of the name of each subscriber under the title of the magazine, and then the words "You owe" followed by the figure $42,998.12, which it claimed was what every man, woman, and child would need to pay to erase the $13.9 trillion U.S. debt, which was the amount the government owed others excluding what it owed itself. This meant that the publisher printed 2,949,767 different covers making each issue something of a collector's item as they said.[2]

This debt has continued to increase by an average of $2.46 billion per day since September 30, 2012, and shows no sign of slowing.[3] The interest payments on this debt are currently around $200 billion a year in an era of low interest rates. The Congressional Budget Office believes that interest rates will rise and that interest on the debt will be nearly $800 billion a year by the end of the decade. By 2021 it is estimated that these interest costs will exceed what the country spends on national defense, and a year later this interest expense will exceed nondefense discretionary spending.[4] More than $13.6 trillion of this debt has been borrowed from Americans as well as foreign investors and other governments. The rest is money the government owes itself such as the IOUs the government has issued for borrowing from Social Security trust funds to help keep the deficit down.

The largest part of the government's budget is and is projected to remain mandatory spending related to Social Security, Medicare, and Medicaid, which is currently more than $2 trillion and is expected to double to $4 trillion by 2025. This spending will rise from 12.4 percent of GDP to about 14.5 percent by the end of this period. This mandatory spending, of course, was mentioned in Chapter 1 as entitlements, along with other expenditures, were presented as the cost of keeping capitalism going. These expenditures were related to keeping competition alive, dealing with the instability of capitalism, responding to social problems like pollution, bailouts of companies and entire industries, and responding to increasing inequality. The costs associated with capitalism and its impacts on society and nature have been increasing for decades.

In addition, capitalism is not working to provide a living wage for millions of workers. In 2016, some 42 percent of American workers earned less than $15 an hour while the national minimum wage remained at $7.25 an hour, which works out to an annual salary of $15,080 well below the official poverty line of $24,300 a year for a family of four people. California and New York raised their minimum wage to $15.00 an hour over a period of years with other states expected to do the same.[5] This amounts to an annual wage of $31,200, which is barely above the $30,375 cutoff point for federal assistance for those who are not on active duty in the U.S. Armed Forces. This is barely a living wage in today's economy. While one may be able to barely get by in a rural area it is next to impossible in a pricey urban or suburban area of the country.

The problem with raising the minimum wage is, as economists are quick to point out, that employers in many cases will lay off workers rather than pay a higher wage, which hurts the very people the increase is supposed to help. It has been pointed out, for example, that in less affluent small towns and cities convenience stores and fast-food outlets will not want to pay cashiers the $27,000 a year that store managers make.[6] But this begs the question about the inability of capitalism to provide a living wage for most workers. If the system can only present workers with the choice of working for less than $15 an hour, which is barely a subsistence wage, or losing their jobs then it is a system that might need major reform. If a reasonable profit can't be made without exploiting people who are the most vulnerable in our society while the already rich get richer at their expense, then one has to ask questions about the long-term viability of the system.[7]

Meanwhile child poverty in the United Sates is among the worst in the world. According to a UNICEF report the United States ranks thirty-sixth out of the forty-one wealthy countries included in the report. Some 24.2 million children are living in poverty, which is about 25 percent of all children in the country. According to the UNICEF report, which defines poverty as an income below 60 percent of the national median income, nearly one third or 32.2 percent of children are living in poverty. By way of contrast, only 5.3 percent of Norwegian children meet this definition of poverty.[8] And children raised in poverty are most likely to remain in poverty the rest of their lives and pass it on to another generation. For the richest country in the world to tolerate this level of child poverty is not only an embarrassment, it is a disgrace.

The American dream is in crisis.[9] Relative mobility, as well as absolute mobility, has declined in our society, and most Americans are destined to remain where they started out in this society. Equal opportunity no longer exists in America, according to some scholars, as children born into rich families have advantages that are large and growing. We tend to overestimate the amount of upward social mobility in our society. Children born into poverty do not grow up in a "land of opportunity" but in a kind of society where the success you experience and the resources at your disposal is largely determined by how and where your life began. In other words, American society is becoming more and more a land of rigid social hierarchies that are difficult, if not impossible, to overcome.[10]

Paul Craig Roberts, a former assistant secretary of the Treasury in the Reagan administration, thinks that American citizens have been economically, politically, and socially dispossessed as the United States is no longer a model of "freedom and democracy." Millions of middle-class jobs have been moved offshore while the burden of massive losses in the financial sector was placed on the taxpayer. Politically, citizens have been stripped of representative government and find that they are unable to bring about change with their vote at the ballot box and have lost their civil liberties that protected them from the growth of a police state. And socially, they have been dispossessed because of inequality, and the loss of homes and careers as the ladders of upward mobility have been dismantled. Roberts thinks a class war is raging between the political elites and the monied interests that control them and everyone else, as the elites who make the decisions keep most of the benefits for themselves and share the costs with the poor, the future, and other species.[11]

While in the spring of 2106 the unemployment rate was down to 5 percent and new jobless claims were at their lowest level since 1973 as the economy appeared to have recovered from the Great Recession of 2008, these numbers did not tell the whole story. The numbers are low because many people have given up even looking for work, while many other were in low-paying jobs. Some 44 percent of new jobs created between 2008 and 2012 were in low-paid service jobs while freelance and contract workers grew from 10.1 percent of workers to 15.8 percent in 2015. These latter workers who at one time may have had stable middle-class jobs now have jobs that are tenuous and unpredictable and yet are considered employed. To these people the economy has yet to recover.[12]

People are increasingly coming to resent corporate executives reaping huge rewards whether or not the company they head is a success or failure. As an example the former CEO of Volkswagen is mentioned, who received $67 million in a golden parachute despite the problems the company experienced with its automobile emissions under his watch. They are also very concerned by the digital technologies that allow companies to expand without physical assets or even employees. Blockbuster had 9,000 locations ten years ago that employed 83,000 people. Netflix, which largely replaced Blockbuster in the movie rental business, employs only 2,000 people. While 1,200 firms have gone public in the United States since 2000, they have each created fewer than 700 jobs on average.[13] This is only further evidence that contemporary capitalism is not working for the ordinary worker. According to James K. Galbraith, holder of the Lloyd M. Bentsen Jr. Chair in Government/Business Relations at the University of Texas at Austin, inequality is to blame for this situation:

> In recent decades in America, economic inequality has increased. This was, however, not some general social process, widely spread across the structures of pay and income. It was, mainly due to extravagant gains by those in finance and in the leading sectors of the day: information technology in the 1990s, and the military and mortgage booms of the 2000s. What is astonishing, however, is how few people actually enjoyed the income gains. At their peak of expansion, the winning sectors did not generate many jobs; at best their success facilitated job creation in the many sectors that did not, themselves, experience rising wages. What we can see, plainly, is that the American economy became leveraged, in such a way that its performance as a whole came to depend on the possibility of a small number of people becoming rich in very limited lines of work.[14]

Corporate executives themselves are worried about the plight of the middle class and have a concern that capitalism isn't working for a broad swath of society. If capitalism can't deliver a decent living for middle-class people executives worry that these people will eventually become advocates for extreme change that will produce significant social upheaval in the country at large.[15] Too many CEOs "focus on the short term, pump up stock prices, make a bundle, and leave the company before it all comes crashing down." In the 1950s and 1960s, business leaders came to believe that they were responsible to not just shareholders but to the community as a whole. Some executives think that this changed with Milton Freidman, who advocated maximizing shareholder value as the sole purpose of business, which led to a divorce of business from society. This sense of responsibility to the broader community in which business operates must be recovered.[16]

Pope Francis not only weighed in on climate change; he also had choice words to say about global capitalism comparing its excesses to the "ding of the devil" and called greed for money a "subtle dictatorship" that condemns and enslaves people. He called the inequities of capitalism an underlying cause of global injustice and working for a more just distribution of resources is not just philanthropy, he said, but is a moral obligation for everyone and for Christians it is a commandment.[17] The encyclical he issued called Laudato Si draws on the traditions of the Catholic Church with regard to social justice and argues that in global capitalism, priority is given to speculation and financial gain, which fails to take into account the effects of such activities on human dignity as well as the natural environment. People believe they are free as long as they are able to consume what they want, but the pope states that those who are really free are the minority in the world who wield economic and financial power.[18]

The pope was criticized for not recognizing the role markets can play in dealing with climate change and other environmental problems. Environmental degradation is not the result of unethical behavior or excessive profiteering, some argue, but is the result of distorted market signals that do not put an appropriate price on environmental effects. The solution, then, is to raise the price of carbon emissions such that the market will reduce these emissions as business organizations take this cost into account in their decisions. While he acknowledges the soundness of climate science and the reality of global warming, he does not endorse a market-based solution as a practical way to deal with the problem.[19]

I also used to think that this was the solution to our environmental problems; that the market could be used to protect the environment. The only problem was to find a way to put a realistic price on carbon usage and other pollutants so they would be reduced. However, I now wonder that even if all these pollutants and the services the environment provides for society were appropriately priced, whether capitalism could continue to exist as these costs would be too high for the system to absorb.[20] In other words, the question is whether capitalism exists because it exploits the environment as well as workers and cannot appropriately take these costs into account and continue to provide a profit making opportunity for business organizations.

Saving Capitalism

In any event, modern capitalism has serious problems, and one has to wonder whether capitalism has a future as it currently exists. There have been many analyses of the system and its problems and many suggestions for reform to keep the system going and benefit all citizens of the country. For example, Robert Kuttner, writing in The *American Prospect*, thinks that there are two big factors that have prevented the issue of inequality and stagnation of earnings for many Americans from taking center stage. First is the skepticism that exists regarding government's ability to make things better. This cynicism and sense of resignation stem from the ideology of Republicans regarding the role of government and their efforts to block any attempt by the Democrats to do something to address these issues.[21]

Second, according to Kuttner, are the persistent divisions of race as well as a negative view of immigrants both of which undermine efforts to uplift working Americans generally. There is a fear that government aid would only go to the undeserving poor, which sheds light on opposition to the Affordable Care Act and why victims of the financial meltdown of 2008 did not receive more public sympathy. Racial division, according to Kuttner, has been part of the Republican playbook since Nixon's Southern Strategy, which was intensified under Reagan and extended by the Tea Party. The right gains credibility by cutting benefits for working families and continuing to push for more tax breaks for the wealthy.[22]

Kuttner claims that we can learn from what he calls the Good War, World War II, which altered the economy and created a more equal society with more opportunity and security than we have in today's economy. First of all, there was a massive economic stimulus provided by the war that assured full employment as more new jobs were created and opportunities for job training were available. The war recapitalized industry and gave government a critical role in developing science and technology; witness the Manhattan program to develop the atomic bomb. The war also transformed labor markets as unions were accepted as full social partners when defense contractors were made to recognize unions and work with them to give workers better wages and working conditions.[23]

Second, the war altered incomes as there was a steeply progressive income tax as high as 94 percent, limits on the compensation corporate executives could receive, and controls on the bond market that resulted in a compression of the income distribution. The war also enhanced social solidarity in that there was a feeling throughout the country that we are all in this together which reinforced support for egalitarian policies. These changes did not end when the war ended but continued for at least another generation. Thus, the shared prosperity of the postwar world was a child of the war, as Kuttner sees it, but it is also important to remember that many of these favorable outcomes were the result of deliberate political choices.[24]

While there is no global war today such as World War II, Kuttner claims that climate change could serve as an existential emergency to stimulate public investment that could produce many of the same distributive benefits. A broad-based effort to deal with this issue could also restore a sense of a common fate and reclaim faith in democratic government. The challenges climate change presents to the nations and the world could "become the basis for restoring shared prosperity and more democratically accountable government." A strategy the links repairing climate change to a commitment to full employment with public investment and good jobs will enhance domestic production and employment. This challenge will take political leadership to define this common threat for the America people and mobilize public investment in technology to allow good living standards for workers at a lower cost to the planet.[25]

Robert Reich, the Chancellor's Professor of Public Policy at the Richard and Rhoda Goldman School of Public Policy at the University of California at Berkeley, has written a book titled *Saving Capitalism*, in which he argues that the current threat to capitalism is not some outside force such as communism but is an undermining of the trust the system needs for its survival.[26] When people stop believing they and their children have a fair chance to better themselves and attain a decent lifestyle, the social contract that capitalism relies on for continued cooperation with the system begins to unravel. All forms of corruption then increase and more resources are allocated for protection rather than production.[27]

Reich is concerned with how the market came to be organized in a different manner from what it was a half century ago when it delivered widely shared prosperity. Many proponents of the "free market" who have benefited from it in recent years have reorganized it to benefit themselves, claims Reich, and would like the public to believe this is because of the natural workings of the market. But the market depends on rules regarding uses of property, what degree of monopoly is acceptable, what kind of contracts can be made, and what happens when bankruptcy occurs. These rules do not exist in nature but must be decided in one way or another by human beings. In the past several decades large corporations, Wall Street, and wealthy individuals have gained considerable influence over the political institutions that make these rules and have organized the market to further enhance their wealth.[28]

Reich believes that the claim that people are paid what they are worth is a tautology that ignores the question of how the market is organized as income and wealth in his view increasingly depend on who has the power to make and enforce the rules of the game. The increase of the working poor and the nonworking rich have risen simultaneously, which provides evidence for Reich that earnings no longer correlate with effort. The only way to reverse this situation, he says, is for the vast majority who have little or no influence over the rules of the game to become organized and unified to reestablish the countervailing power that was responsible for the shared prosperity that existed several decades ago in this country.[29]

In elaborating on this thesis, Reich states that the prevailing view of the American economy is that there is a "free market" somewhere in the universe into which government "intrudes." Reich, however, believes this view is utterly false and argues that there can be no "free market" without the government which makes and enforces the rules under which markets operate. Decisions have to be made about five key factors: (1) property, (2) monopoly, (3) contract, (4) bankruptcy, and (5) enforcement. These decisions have to do with what can be owned, what degree of market power is permissible, what can be bought and sold and on what terms, what happens when purchasers can't pay up, and how to make sure no one cheats on any of these rules. Reich calls these the five building blocks of capitalism.[30]

Some people can come to have disproportionate influence over the making and enforcement of these rules and thus make the system enhance their wealth while keeping everyone else relatively poor and economically insecure. Those few at the top of the income and wealth ladder can have enough influence over politicians, regulators, and judges to ensure that the "free market" works mostly on their behalf. It is no accident that these very people who benefit most from the system are among the most vehement supporters of the so-called "free market" and strong advocates of the superiority of the market over government.[31] As Reich says,

[p]ower and influence are hidden inside the processes through which market rules are made, and the resulting economic gains and losses are

disguised as the "natural" outcomes of "impersonal market forces." Yet as long as we remain obsessed by the debate over the relative merits of the "free market" and "government" we have little hope of see through the camouflage.[32]

The invisible hand of the market, Reich argues, is connected to a wealthy and muscular arm where a few people quietly and secretly alter the rules that govern the market to their own advantage. They champion freedom and liberty while ignoring the imbalance of power in our society that has slowly eroded the freedoms of most people. The consequences of such an imbalance have been to give greater and greater rewards to the top executives of large corporations, major stockholders in these corporations, and Wall Street banks, and smaller slices of the pie to everyone else in society. Workers have had to give up their right to take the company they work for to court by having to agree to terms in their contract that mandate arbitration of all grievances before an arbiter chosen by the company.[33]

Regarding the five building blocks of capitalism, Reich argues that due to the political influence of large corporations, political decisions have been made about the definition and uses of property that tend to enlarge the wealth and power of these corporations. He mentions several examples of concentrated economic power in contemporary society and argues that the failure of antitrust laws to address these concentrations is related to the power that corporations can exercise in the political system. He also argues that corporations have disproportionate power over what can be sold on the market but also over the rules regarding contracts as to what is permissible and enforceable. Regarding bankruptcy, he points out that while Wall Street investment banks were not allowed to go bankrupt with the exception of Lehman Brothers because of the "too-big-to-fail" doctrine students with excessive loans that they cannot repay are not allowed to work out a settlement under bankruptcy protection. Finally, with respect to enforcement, Reich argues that several recent court rulings have severely reduced the ability of consumers and workers to band together in class actions to counter the power of large corporations.[34]

Ideally the decisions about the rule of the market should reflect the best judgments of people who are authorized in a democratic system to make them in response to the values and desires of a majority of the citizens. However, in recent years those who control an increasing share of the nation's wealth have gained growing influence over these rules by which the market functions. This creates something of a vicious circle as those people who gain more wealth and power because the market is organized to benefit them then have more wealth and power to exert more influence over market decisions in the future.[35]

Reich then gets into the relation of work and worth, and questions what he calls the meritocratic myth, the broadly held assumption that individuals are rewarded in our economy in direct proportion to their efforts and abilities. He mentions people who work in the financial sector such as high-frequency traders who profit by getting information about stocks a fraction of a second earlier than other traders. People in these kinds of professions do not generate discoveries that benefit society or create works of art that deepen human consciousness. They simply find ways to squeeze money out of a given set of assets, he asserts, and use up the time and energies of some of the most educated people in the country whose talents supposedly could be put to better uses for the benefit of society.[36]

CEO pay increased 937 percent between 1978 and 2013 while the pay of the typical worker rose just 10.2 percent. The share of corporate income that went to the five highest-paid executives of large public firms increased from an average of 5 percent in 1993 to more than 15 percent in 2013. This was money corporations could have used for research and development or for higher wages for workers. Reich points out that practically all of this compensation was deducted from corporate income taxes, meaning the rest of us had to pay more taxes to make up for the shortfall. He mentions studies that show there is no connection between the company's performance and the pay its highest executives receive and concludes that any objective assessment would show that CEOs are not worth the compensation they receive.[37]

Wall Street executives typically earn even more than top corporate executives, according to Reich, and received billions in bonuses not because they work harder or are more clever than other Americans but because they work in institutions that hold a privileged place in the economy. These institutions are even more too big to fail since the Great Recession and taxpayers, who paid for the bailout of these institutions, will pay for the next one that comes along. These institutions hold a privileged place because they account for such a large proportion of campaign donations going not only to the presidential candidates of both parties but also to major candidates for Congress. The $26.7 billion these bankers received in bonuses in 2103 would have more than doubled the pay going to minimum-wage workers that year. Reich concludes that much of the income they receive is an involuntary transfer from taxpayers and small investors and that while they have enough wealth to influence the rules governing the market, they are not worth the income they get in any meaningful sense of the term.[38]

Meanwhile the bargaining power of the middle class has declined as beginning in the early 1980s the median household's income stopped growing altogether when adjusted for inflation. In 2103 the typical middle-class household earned nearly $4,500 less than it did before the Great Recession, and median household income was less than it was in 1989, which was nearly a quarter of a century before. And average incomes of the bottom 90 percent has dropped even more during the first six years of a so-called recovery from the Great Recession. The standard explanation for this shift is that with the advent of globalization and automation American workers have priced themselves out the market and are not competitive.[39]

But Reich isn't buying this and for an explanation looks instead to changes in the rules of the market that allowed corporations and Wall

Street to become more profitable while reducing the bargaining power and political clout of the middle class. The link between productivity and the income of workers has also been severed as since 1979 productivity has risen 65 percent but during this same period the median compensation for workers increased by just 8 percent. Reich claims that almost all the gains from growth have gone to the top of the income scale. Finally, the decline of unions has also contributed to the weakening of middle-class influence in the political system and in the society as a whole.[40]

For all of these and perhaps other reasons the American society has seen a substantial increase in the working poor; people who are working full-time but do no earn a living wage. Their ranks grew to 47 million people by 2013, which amounted to one out of every seven Americans. Fully a quarter of all full-time workers in the country were stuck in jobs that paid below what they needed to support a family of four above the poverty line defined by the federal government. Many workers were pushed into low-paying jobs in service industries, which, Reich claims, are virulently antiunion and have been successful in fighting against any efforts to organize their workers. Meanwhile those people at the opposite end of the income scale have so much money that they can live comfortably without ever having to get a job. Much of their wealth was inherited as six out of ten of them are heirs to prominent fortunes. In 1978, 20 percent of business income went to the richest 1 percent; by 2007 this had increased to 49 percent. This 1 percent was also getting 75 percent of all capital gains.[41] Thus, the rich have gotten richer and the poor poorer, and capitalism is not working for the vast majority of Americans. Redistribution has taken place, but it has been upward, not downward. As Reich states,

> [i]n reality, most redistribution in recent years has been in the oppo-
> site direction—upward from consumers, workers, small businesses, and
> small investors to top corporate and financial executives, Wall Street
> traders and portfolio managers, and the major owners of capital assets.
> But this upward redistribution is invisible. The main conduits for it
> are hidden within the rules of the market—property, monopolization,
> contract, bankruptcy, and enforcement—rules that have been shaped by
> those with substantial wealth and political clout. It is, in this sense, a
> *pre*distribution upward that occurs inside the market mechanism itself,
> a small portion of which government later redistributes downward to
> the poor through taxes and transfer payments.[42]

The problem with contemporary capitalism as Reich sees it is that there is "no longer a significant *countervailing* power" in American society "to constrain or balance the growing political strength of large corporations, Wall Street, and the very wealthy." The middle class and the poor have little or no power or agency, as Reich puts it, to pursue their interests in the political system and have some say in what rules pertaining to the market get passed and implemented.[43] This constitutes a serious threat to capitalism in that the social fabric will start to unravel as more and more people feel the game is rigged against them. The losers in this game, says Reich, will eventually try to stop the game out of a sense of fairness and fear of power and privilege. When the system fails to deliver economic gains to the majority of people in American society, it eventually stops delivering them at all even to a wealthy minority.[44]

Throughout its history the country has managed to save capitalism from its own excesses, as described in the first chapter, and Reich thinks it is time to do so again. The wealthy would like the less wealthy to continue to occupy themselves with battles over the size of the government and other issues like same-sex marriage, abortion, guns, race, and religion, but Reich hopes that they can eventually discover they have a common economic interest and form an alliance or set of alliances that would constitute the new countervailing power in our society. This power, Reich hopes, would be able do the following: (1) press for reform of the system of campaign finance to get big money out of politics, (2) work for reform that would reduce or eliminate the revolving doors between government and Wall Street, large corporations, and lobbying firms; and (3) change the rules so that expert witnesses, academics, and people in think tanks would be required to disclose any and all outside funding of their efforts.[45]

This countervailing alliance could also seek to end the upward predistributions that Reich thinks are embedded in the market and return antitrust to its original purpose of preventing and breaking up monopolies. It could resurrect something like the Glass-Steagall Act to separate commercial from investment banking and raise the minimum wage to half the median wage of all workers and have it adjusted for inflation thereafter. It could also see that educational resources are allocated on a more equitable manner by making schools no longer dependent on local property taxes as the major source of revenue. This alliance could also reinvent the corporation by instituting something like stakeholder capitalism that would make the corporation accountable to a broader constituency of groups that have a stake in corporate operations rather than just stockholders alone.[46]

Reich also foresees the impact technological advances will make on workers and points out that the nation is faced with not only labor-replacing technologies but also knowledge-replacing technologies. When more of everything can be produced by fewer people the profits will increase for a small circle of executives and owner investors and the rest will have less money to buy to buy what can be produced. As he puts it "the model of the future seems likely to be unlimited production by a handful for consumption by whoever can afford it."[47] This creates a capitalism that is gets to be so top-heavy it cannot be sustained. To deal with this situation he mentions a basic minimum income that would enable people to be economically independent and self-sufficient as a way to guarantee all citizens of the country a share in the future growth of the economy. He argues that this is not as radical as it sounds as even F. A. Hayek and other conservatives and libertarians have endorsed such a system.[48]

In conclusion Reich states that the choice our society is not between the "free market" and government, but it is between a market that is organized for a broadly based prosperity that works for everyone, or a market that will continue to deliver almost all of the gains from economic growth to those at the top of the income ladder. The pertinent issue, he says, is not how much the wealthy are to be taxed with that money redistributed to those at the bottom through transfer payments, but redesigning the market so that the economy provides a fair distribution to all workers on its own without having to institute large redistributions after the fact in order to keep the system going. He seem to be optimistic that this can happen by the vast majority of the nation's citizens joining together and making the political and economic systems work for the many and not just the few as the subtitle of his book indicates.[49]

In a rather gloomy book, Satyajit Das, an internationally respected financial expert and commentator on financial markets who predicated the global financial crisis of 2008, thinks that our economy is entering an era of protracted stagnation similar to what Japan has experienced in recent decades. He questions the assumption that economic growth can be perpetual and doubts that the country's political leaders have the ability to enact the tough structural changes that are needed to restore economic, financial, and social sustainability. He thinks that ever since the early 1980s economic activity and growth have been driven by financialization, by which he means that industrial activity has been replaced with financial trading and increased levels of borrowing to finance consumption and investment. The world has become addicted to borrowing as debt levels have risen beyond the repayment capacity of borrowers and acts as a brake on growth.[50] He goes on to say that

> [t]hese financial problems are compounded by lower population growth and aging populations; slower increases in productivity and innovation; looming shortages of critical resources, such as water food, and energy; and man-made climate change and extreme weather conditions. Slower growth in international trade and capital flows is another retardant. Emerging markets that have benefited from and, in recent times, supported growth are slowing. Rising inequality has an impact on economic activity.[51]

Wages are static where they are not falling, and American families in the middle 20 percent of the income scale earn less money and have a lower net worth than before the Great Recession. In developed countries things that were taken for granted like education, houses, health services, and a comfortable retirement are increasingly unattainable for much of the population. Countries that were more severely affected by the financial meltdown like Greece are in even worse shape. The Greek economy has shrunk by a quarter and spending is down 40 percent because of reduced wages and pensions. As one person put it, "the government could save money on education, as it was unnecessary to prepare people for jobs that didn't exist."[52]

While lower growth may reduce environmental damage and conserve resources, it makes the task of managing high debt levels more difficult, and revenues are reduced for business and governments alike. There is widespread denial of these problems, according to Das, as governments preach and sometimes may actually practice austerity, while at the same time assuring the population that their living standards can be maintained. Politicians, and I might add particularly the Republicans, cannot seem to accept that popular demand for public services is not compatible with lower taxes. Ordinary people refuse to acknowledge that having it all may not be possible and yet feel uneasy about the present and fearful of the future.[53]

The period immediately following World War II was a time of unprecedented optimism and expectations, where good jobs were available, and there was increasing prosperity, social mobility, and relative equality throughout the society. "The postwar dream was a good job, marriage, children, a house in the suburbs, and a growing number of possessions."[54] Yet the 1950s, says Das, was a time of stultifying conformity, while the 1960s was a time of increasing violence and self-absorption along with disengagement from social responsibility that set the stage for the age of greed and speculation that would follow in later decades. The 1970s was the era of stagflation, which means a combination of high unemployment and high inflation. In the next decade inflation was brought under control but the financial economy started to grow with an expansion of financial instruments and services that eventually became a major contributor to growth of the economy. The 1990s was again a period of strong economic growth and low inflation, but there were also several crises, such as the collapse of the hedge fund Long-Term Capital Management in 1998 and the default of Russia in the same year.[55]

In 2007 the financial crises began in the United States and spread throughout the world. Some estimates of the wealth lost in what was called the Great Recession were as high as between $60 and $200 trillion dollars. This collapse was caused, according to Das, by the increasing reliance on borrowing to create economic activity, a global imbalance in consumption, investment, and savings; the rapid growth of the financial sector with a reliance on financial engineering to deal with economic problems; what Das calls financialization; and finally the buildup of future entitlements that were not adequately financed.[56]

Dealing with these problems, says Das, required reducing debt, correcting imbalances, reversing financialization of the economy, and a scaling back of welfare programs and covering future obligations. Instead of adopting these measures, no major economies and only five developing economies reduced the ratio of debt to GDP in the real economy while twenty countries increased their total debt-to-GDP ratios by more than 50 percent.[57] Das is hard on the economics profession as was Picketty calling it a religion where government professes to have faith in whatever economic prophet is in fashion and consistent with their ideology. He says that "[e]conomists and central bankers with little experience of business or markets move mainly in each other's company, confusing wisdom with knowledge, knowledge with data, and data with noise."[58]

In response to the financial crisis of 2008, policymakers contradicted the long-held view of conservatives that markets are self-regulating self-correcting by deploying all available measures including bailouts of banks, programs to stimulate the economy, and other such measures. The result is that the public finances of many countries are unstainable because of high levels of debt, structural budget deficits, low economic growth, and increased costs of borrowing. Countries like Japan borrow more each year than they raise in taxes and spend about a quarter of these tax revenues on interest payments. The country provides an example of how difficult it is to engineer a recovery from the collapse of a debt-fueled asset bubble.[59]

Das thinks that economic expansion is not a continuous process that can persist forever. He believes that economic growth and improvements in living standards will slow significantly in the future. Changing demographics such as an aging population and slower productivity improvements threaten growth, and an increasing scarcity of resources like water, food, and energy, as well as environmental problems such as climate change, also provide constraints on growth. Yet the current economic, political, and social systems are dependent on continued economic growth and improvement in living standards. Such growth is also needed for government and private entities to deal with high debt levels.[60]

Das criticizes Piketty claiming that he ignores why inequality matters and whether the cost of any reduction of inequality might outweigh any benefits it could provide for a society. Piketty proposed higher taxes as a solution of up to 80 percent on high incomes, overlooking the fact that such policies adopted in the past failed to correct inequality as taxpayers relocated to places that had lower taxes or found other ways to avoid paying them. But the book did challenge the "mythology central to liberal societies of an egalitarian meritocracy based on skill, hard work, entrepreneurship, and competition."[61]

What Das calls economic apartheid which takes the shape of inequality threatens economic growth as inclusive capitalism that mainly benefits the rich excludes significant proportions of the population from sharing in the benefits of economic expansion. Higher income households have a lower marginal propensity to consume, which means they don't spend as much money proportionality as lower-income households. The latter consume a much greater amount of each additional dollar they have available than do higher-income households. This has an impact on consumption such that growth of demand and hence production to meet this demand is limited by a concentration of income at the higher end of the economic ladder. Inequality also results in poor health, which reduces participation in the workforce and productivity while a less-educated and lower-skilled workforce that is also the result of inequality reduces competitiveness, innovation, and growth. These and other factors "mean that a consumption-based economic recovery is unlikely without income redistribution to households with a higher propensity to spend, or finding a new source of demand."[62]

Das believes that gross inequality damages social cohesion and democratic beliefs, producing a democracy deficit that is as much of a problem as budget and trade deficits. Voters have personal grievances such as lack of jobs, mortgage foreclosures, and student loans, but they also have broader concerns such as the widening economic social gap, allocation of responsibility and burden of the Great Recession, and disenfranchisement of voters. But people who are experiencing these problems don't see anything being done about them, leading to a lack of trust in our major institutions particularly government that fuels social disorder. When there is an increase in living standards and people have money to buy consumer goods and services, this tends to make them focus on material prosperity and forego the time and effort it takes to engage in activism that might challenge the existing political and economic order. But when a materialistic lifestyle is unattainable for many people, they want change and may engage in political activism to have some say in the way society is structured and governed.[63]

Das believes the shared prosperity that existed after World War II may have been a unique coincidence of factors that were a historical aberration. Different influences now exist that threaten to halt further increases in economic growth and living standards. He believes that the Great Financial Crisis demonstrated that perpetual growth and progress is an illusion. It exposed the high debt levels developed countries had accumulated, the credit-driven consumption that fueled growth, the excessive financialization of the economy, and the unfinanced social entitlements that underpinned an unstainable economic model. The crises came at a time when there was increasing evidence of climate change and an emerging shortage of resources such as food and water in many parts of the world.[64]

In conclusion, Das raises the alarming question of whether the existing and projected levels of public and private debt are too high for either growth or austerity to resolve as reduction of debt would require high economic growth that is quite unlikely, deep cuts in government spending or higher taxes which are politically implausible and very large sale of assets. High levels of debt are dealt with by lending more, keeping interest rates low, and extending maturities, all of which disguise the problem. But "societies and individuals cannot expect to maintain high living standards and survive without a radical transformation of practices and more frugal living." This seems to be the solution that Das thinks would enable us to survive in the future:[65]

> Frugal living addresses economic and financial problems as well as conserving resources and environmental health, preserving both for

future generations. Public finances become sustainable. The burden of health care and aged care is reduced due to extended working lives. With people forced to live together in larger family groupings or communities, they have to share to get by. Responsibility for the care of the sick and aged shifts back to households, reducing claims on public services. Housing becomes more affordable; the amount of debt needed to finance a home is lower. Reduced consumption allows preexisting debt to be written off or gradually reduced.[66]

Such frugal living most certainly would produce an immediate contraction in economic activity, but eventually the economy would stabilize at lower levels of activity. Das mentions Iceland as a possible example of what the future holds. Iceland made a better recovery from the financial crisis that most countries by, first of all, "allowing its banks to fail, refusing to use taxpayers' money to bail out insolvent institutions. It protected local depositors but refused to pay out foreign lenders who had lent unwisely. Where mortgages were greater than the value of the house, the loan was written down to a level that could be reasonable repaid. The currency was allowed to devalue. Restrictions on capital outflows were implemented."[67]

These measures were extremely painful as costs skyrocketed, living standards fell sharply, and wealth was lost in the process. But Icelanders understood the current situation was unstainable and set about to return the economy to its traditional base of agriculture, fishing, geothermal energy, and tourism. Grassroots protests forced the resignation of the government and the new parliament took measures to see that the costs of rebuilding the economy and society were shared equitably. Senior business executives, bankers, politicians, and policy makers were actually prosecuted and some convicted. The country has not fully recovered from it problems, but Das obviously thinks they are on the right track and have learned to work together with a strong sense of the common good, something that is lacking in the United States and other countries, I might add.[68]

For most societies the scale and complexity of the problems have outpaced the ability of existing institutions to deal with them effectively. Regarding the global economy, the factors that drive economic growth are in decline making them less responsive to traditional economic policies. Sustainable growth must come from the real economy, says Das, but current policies are largely financial in their focus and do not directly increase jobs, wages, or encourage investment to enhance the potential of the economy. Authorities that make the major decisions cannot defer reality forever, and postponing the inevitable means that the adjustment of changed conditions will be more painful as the problems will have gotten bigger. As the last sentence of the book states, "[s]ooner or later, everybody has to sit down to a banquet of consequences."[69]

Finally, David A. Stockman, the budget director in the Reagan administration who became a private equity investor, has written a tome of slightly over 700 pages titled *The Great Deformation*, in which he examines the corruption of capitalism that has taken place over the past several decades. He starts by mentioning the fiscal cliff the nation is facing which over the next decade could be close to $20 trillion, calling it permanent and insurmountable. He claims that this fiscal cliff is the result of the capture of the state and especially its central bank by what he calls crony capitalist forces that are deeply inimical to free markets and democracy. He is especially critical of what went on during the fiscal crisis of 2008 what with bank bailouts and stimulus programs, but he also criticizes the administration he worked for, stating that Reagan left the welfare state standing, as it was barely 0.5 and 1 percent smaller than the previous administration of Jimmy Carter and added a massive structural deficit for future administrations.[70]

Stockman is interested in exploring how we got to the point where fiscal responsibility had been abandoned so completely as evidenced by the TARP bailout program and the stimulus program Congress authorized. "How did it happen that the nation's central bank printed nearly twice as much money in thirteen weeks as it had during the entire century before." How did the top ten Wall Street Banks, which were valued at $1 trillion in mid-2007, "crash into a paroxysm of failure and bailouts twelve months later."[71] For Stockman the fiscal crisis of 2008 did not appear mysteriously on a comet from deep space, as he puts it, but grew out of decades of corruption of the nation's financial condition with unfinanced wars, tax cuts, expansion of the welfare state, the plundering of the public purse by special interests, and the running of a casino out of the headquarters of the Federal Reserve Bank in Washington.[72]

Wall Street had become a vast casino, according to Stockman, as leveraged speculation and rent seeking had displaced its vital function of price discovery and capital allocation. The investment banks on Wall Street had become dangerous and unstable gambling houses and needed to be deflated rather than propped up so they could continue their baleful effects. The bailouts were based on the proposition that the nation was faced with a chain reaction of financial failures that would end in cataclysm, a proposition that Stockman thinks if completely false and led to a suspension of the normal rules of free-market capitalism and fiscal prudence so that "unprecedented and unlimited public resources could be poured into the rescue of Wall Street's floundering behemoths."[73]

None of the bailouts were necessary, says Stockman, as the meltdown was strictly a matter confined to Wall Street and would have burned out on its own if the free market had been allowed to work. Insolvent institutions, such as Morgan Stanley, Goldman, and Citigroup, among others, needed to be taken out, as he puts it, and allowed to go bankrupt. At the time of the crisis, he says, AIG was 90 percent solvent and no danger to anyone, and its CDS liabilities which accounted for less than 10 percent of its consolidated liabilities could have been readily liquidated in bankruptcy. The $400 billion of busted CDS insurance was held by a small number of the world's largest financial institutions that could have absorbed the loss as it amounted to no more than a few months' bonus accrual. Thus, the bailout of AIG, says Stockman, "was all about protecting short-term earnings and current year executive and trader bonuses."[74]

The financial customers of AIG like Bank of America were wards of the state, says Stockman, products of cheap debt, moral hazard, and speculative bubbles fostered by the Fed and other central banks around the world. It is no wonder that they were desperate when AIG failed and petitioned the Treasury secretary to help collect what Stockman calls their gambling debts from the company. And Treasury Secretary Paulson responded by desecrating the rules of the free market to make the banking giants whole on their gambling claims, which had been incurred in carrying out an end run around regulatory standards in the first place.[75]

The Greenspan Fed during the 1990s, says Stockman, engaged in a subtle assault on free-market capitalism using monetary policy to become the nation's prosperity manager. The nations' employment level, GDP, income, and general prosperity was no longer the result of market interactions but instead flowed from the visible activities of the Federal Reserve, which became the omnipotent overlord of daily economic life by the end of the decade. The Fed accommodated Wall Street with unlimited liquidity and other interventions to prop up the stock market and keep it from falling in response to free-market outcomes. What had developed out of this was what he calls an ersatz capitalism, where "stock market averages reflect monetary juice from the central bank, not anticipated growth of profits from free market enterprises."[76] Thus, it seems Stockman was saying what we have is a planned economy, manipulated by the Feds monetary policies to keep the Wall Street game up and running, rather than a free-market economy responding to the interaction of millions of consumers, producers, and investors.

Stockman blames the GOP for the financial meltdown of 2008, as Republican administrations had turned the nation's central bank over to the money printers and coddlers of Wall Street in appointing Greenspan and Bernanke to head the Federal Reserve Bank and celebrated the phony prosperity fostered by them as evidence of triumphant GOP economics. Republicans had adopted the notion that "deficits don't matter" and had no problem with George W. Bush's two massive tax cuts and two underfunded wars thinking that the fiscal house was in order. Paul O'Neill was forced out as Bush's first secretary of the Treasury because he dared to suggest that tax cuts and unfinanced wars were a recipe for disaster.[77] The roots of this abandonment of fiscal responsibility and sound money along with an honest free-market economy, however, go back all the way to the New Deal of Franklin Delano Roosevelt and the decades that followed up to the fiscal crisis of 2008. As he says,

> [i]n the intervening decades, a leviathan was arising through a process of economic governance that was halting, piecemeal, and more often than not driven by fleeting emergencies that were of no lasting moment.

But the common thread was the proposition that modern industrial capitalism was unstable and prone to chronic cyclical fluctuations and shortfalls that could be ameliorated by the interventions and corrective actions of the state, and most especially its central banking branch. That was upside down. The far greater imperfections and threat to the people's welfare were embedded in the state itself, and its vulnerability to capture by special interests—the vast expanse of K Street lobbies and campaign-money-dispensing PACs. Trying to improve capitalism, modern economic policy has thus fatally overloaded the state with missions and mandates far beyond its capacity to fulfill. The result is crony capitalism—a freakish deformation that fatally corrupts free markets and democracy.[78]

The first spell of this false prosperity was the unacknowledged yet massive exercise in deficit financing carried out by the Reagan and George W. Bush administrations where the public debt tripled and Federal red ink came to nearly 70 percent of GDP growth during those twelve years of Republican governance. The Bush administration abandoned fiscal rectitude once and for all with its "guns and butter," as well as tax-giveaways approach. Federal spending increased by 50 percent under Bush's watch, and the final budget of his administration soared to 25 percent of GDP, a post–World War II record. After the turn of the century the unstainable bubbles fostered by the state went bust, providing evidence that the nation's economic fundamentals had deteriorated for more than a decade.[79] Much of the wealth gain of the past three decades, Stockman says, originated in from these bubbles generated by borrowing of the state and the money-printing spree of its central bank rather than being the fruit of the free market.[80]

The so-called Reagan revolution, says Stockman, who was a vital part of that administration as budget director, was nothing of the kind when it came to domestic spending as it was not even an era of meaningful reform. While a few programs were pruned and no new ones started, the great majority of federal programs carried on as before Reagan took office. But ever since Reagan, some version of supply-side economics has been embraced by Republicans, who argue that we can grow our way out of debt by increasing growth. Tax cuts pay for themselves as they provide incentives for new investment in productive activities that will bring in more revenue to federal and state governments that will help to reduce the debt. Stockman thinks this theory was invalid from the very beginning, and I gather would agree with George H. W. Bush, who called supply-side economics voodoo economics in his campaign for the presidential nomination in 1980. What has happened according to Stockman is that the job of Republicans has been transformed from managing the finances of the government to a sub-branch of statist pretension, namely, centrally managing the growth of the economy by chronic fiddling with fiscal policy.[81]

In the third part of the book, Stockman begins by criticizing the New Deal by stating that it did not address the causes of the Great Depression, did not cure or even relieve its effects on the American economy, and amounted to little more than a politically driven period of Washington activism. What survived from the New Deal is a destructive legacy of crony capitalist abuse of state power, as the New Dealers failed to recognize that the state has an inherent flaw in that policies that are undertaken in the name of the public good become captured by crony capitalists and special interests who allocate resources from society's commons to accomplish their own private ends, which are not necessarily good for the society as a whole.[82]

It was World War II that really pulled the country out of the depression as the economy operated at full capacity and unemployment virtually disappeared. About 80 percent of the cost of the war was paid for by people's savings, either coerced saving in the form of taxes or voluntary saving in the form of investment in savings bonds or other savings instruments. Thus, the country emerged from the war in sound financial shape as the private debt burden had been virtually eliminated and the nation's balance sheet had some "headroom" for federal debt to be absorbed by national savings. The Korean War was also financed on a pay-as-you-go basis, according to Stockman, which was the last war that was adequately financed. Lyndon Baines Johnson didn't ask for more taxes to finance the Vietnam War until the very end, opening the way for the Iraq War four decades later to be carried on entirely tax free.[83]

During the Eisenhower years, the federal budget actually shrank in real terms and expansion of the welfare state was tamed paving the way for the country to pay its bills out of current taxes for the better part of a decade.[84] The Democrats attacked what they called the "plodding" Eisenhower economy, promising to increase growth to 5 percent annually, and Kennedy's election promised more aggressive fiscal and monetary policies to get the economy moving forward again. It was Kennedy who first took the fateful step down the slippery slope of deficit-financed tax cuts, which did indeed stimulate growth, but they also meant that the idea of stimulating the economy with tax cuts that created a deficit was taking root. They ushered in the era where it became part of the conventional wisdom that economic progress and prosperity would depend on macromanagement by the state rather than from the interaction of business and consumers on the free market. This idea was embraced even by the capitalists, as "[t]hey believe that whatever happens, the Government will somehow keep the economy strong and rising."[85]

After Kennedy was killed, LBJ vastly extended the New Deal with programs, like Medicare and Medicaid, and squandered the fiscal headroom Eisenhower had created resulting in a 40 percent increase of welfare expenditures. He also tried to extend the notion of the Great Society to the Mekong Delta, as Stockman puts it, greatly increasing war expenditures as well.[86] It was during the subsequent Nixon era that the country was taken off the gold standard, a move that was advocated by Milton Friedman, the free-market guru from the University of Chicago. He gave conservative sanction to open market purchases of government debt by the Federal

Reserve, which allowed politicians to spend without taxing and gave his blessing to the "fundamental Keynesian proposition that Washington must continually manage and stimulate the national economy." He also believed that the government should focus its efforts on managing the money supply which would keep capitalism growing.[87] Stockman thinks taking the country off the gold standard was a great mistake and a lethal threat to sound money and free markets that Friedman and other free-market gurus never saw coming:

> Friedman was a committed anti-statist who had low regard for politicians and much disdain for their attempts at the economic betterment of society. And justifiably so. Yet in pushing the gold standard and fixed exchange rate system onto the scrap heap of history, the modern-day godfather of free markets helped foster the greatest projection of statist intervention and subvention ever conceived—that is, monetary central planning of the national and, indeed, world economy by the Federal Reserve.[88] Nixon's estimable free market advisors who gathered at the Camp David weekend were to an astonishing degree clueless as to the consequences of their recommendation to close the gold window and float the dollar. In their wildest imaginations they did not foresee that this would unhinge the monetary and financial nervous system of capitalism. They had no promotion at all that is would pave the way for a forty-year storm of financialization and a debt-besotted symbiosis between central bankers possessed by delusions of grandeur and private gamblers intoxicated with visions of delirious wealth.[89]

The true foundation of the post–Bretton Woods monetary system, Stockman says, was government debt, "which permitted Americans to consume far more than they produce, while enabling the development Asian economies to export vastly more goods than their customers could afford."[90] Money and capital markets centered on Wall Street eventually morphed into casinos that were focused on speculation with the development of new financial products and hedging instruments not on raising capital for the main street economy. These hedging casinos with the massive churning taking place in the financial markets Stockman thinks are a profound deformation of capitalism. They are a dead-weight loss to society as they consume vast resources without adding a thing to society's output or wealth and "flush income to the very top rungs of the economic ladder."[91]

The Fed eventually capitulated to Wall Street by embracing a speculative-friendly monetary policy. It became the Street's new concierge, as Stockman puts it, giving birth to the bubble financing of later years by becoming more focused on supporting the stock market than on enforcing monetary discipline. And it worked wonders for a while as after the 1991 recession the stock market gained momentum and never looked back. By the time the dot-com crash in 2000 finally materialized, "the *S&P 500 index accomplished in eighteen years what should actually take a half century."* The index had risen from a level of 110 in 1982 when the Fed cut interest rates to stimulate the market to a level of 1,485 when it finally stopped rising when the dot-com crash began. According to Stockman, that amounted to a gain of 13.5 times and a 15.5 percent rate of compound growth for nearly two decades. There had not been anything like it at any time anywhere in modern financial history and created a get-rich-quick culture throughout the country.[92]

Those of us in the academic world, who obviously do not enter that profession to make money, made money beyond our wildest dreams. If we were saving the maximum we could in our retirement plans and had them invested in the market, and then were lucky enough to get out before the dot-com bust, and then retired soon after the turn of the century and annuitized those gains at high rates of interest, are now living a very comfortable lifestyle with a monthly income that is greater than the great majority of Americans are currently making in the job market. It was a time when not only the deficit didn't matter; earnings also didn't matter, as dot-com companies that hadn't made a dime saw their stock prices continued to go up just because they were dot-com companies.

There was a kind of craziness to it all as even those companies that were making some money saw their current earnings drastically overvalued to say nothing of those that were way overvalued solely on their future earnings potential. Stockman calls this Greenspan's runaway bull market, in which the market was effectively stripped of its fundamentally economic function of rationally discounting future corporate profits. Those who got caught in the downturn viewed their losses as a matter of poor exit timing, says Greenspan, not as the result of a "mania-driven stampede that had overvalued the market.[93]

Cisco Systems had at one time the highest capitalization of any company in the country as it was worth more than even General Motors and General Electric. Such a company had nowhere near the physical assets as these old-line companies, yet it became the first company to reach $500 billion in market capitalization. This cap represented nearly 26 times is sales for 2000 and nearly 200 times its net income. About 90 percent of this capitalization or $400 billion was what Stockman calls bottled air as it is currently valued at around $100 billion. Microsoft's market cap reached $600 billion by January 2000, which meant it rose a hundredfold from its valuation of $6 billion in 1990, a rise that Stockman calls sheer lunacy. Since today Microsoft is valued at about $200 billion, this meant there was also $400 billion of bottled air in its share price.[94]

At the end of the dot-com bust, $2.7 trillion of market cap had vaporized and the market as a whole lost more than $7 trillion in value. Greenspan claimed that we can have no knowledge of a bubble until after the fact, yet the explosion in market value of the dot-com companies had no historic precedent. Stockman thinks that "[t]here is simply no plausible circumstance on the free market in which the true value of giant companies like these can increase sixfold in such a brief interval." The financial markets, he says, had become unhinged by the Fed's actions to print money and pander to the stock market. Under its new prosperity management regime, the buildup of wealth did not require sacrifice or deferred consumption, and having fostered a bull market culture in the 1990s the Fed subsequently broadened its casino's offerings to include housing, real estate, and derivatives.[95]

Bubble finance had replaced old-fashioned habit of saving and frugality as the loss of household wealth in the dot-com crash should have resulted in a revival of savings, but the fundamental problem of too much consumption and not enough savings was not addressed by the very central bank responsible for the collapse. Instead the savings function was outsourced to China, which purchased the majority of our debt and kept us afloat. As the housing bubble developed, households recovered all they had lost and then some in the dot-com bust as paper wealth continued to rise to record levels. The economy was considered to be in great shape as Americans were spending everything they earned and all they could borrow. But the bubble burst again, and another $5 trillion of wealth disappeared for the second time in less than a decade. The stock market plunged, and investment banks went either bankrupt or merged into other companies with incentives provided by the government. The bubble of 2003–2008 proved to be built on an even shakier foundation than the dot-com bubble.[96]

In another book I went into some detail as to the magnitude of the financial Armageddon of 2008, as I called it, and an analysis of possible reasons for the meltdown so there is no need to go into that here.[97] Needless to say, at the turn of the century the economy was whipsawing people all over the place and instability prevailed at a level never before witnessed by most Americans. Once again the Fed responded by expanding its balance sheet at a pace that Stockman believes future historians will describe as berserk. The Fed's balance sheet was at $906 billion as of the week ending September 3, 2008, but by December 10 the same year it was $2.25 trillion, an expansion of 2.25 times in the blink of a historical eye.[98]

The root of this monetary deformation, according to Stockman, was that over the previous decades the Fed had destroyed the free market in interest rates, as they had become a bureaucratically administered value emanating from the Federal Open Market Committee (FOMC) rather than a market-clearing price that represented supply and demand for money and capital. When the Fed lowered interest rates to 1 percent by June 2003, it ignited what he calls a "ferocious housing price escalation." Real estate holdings shot up by 75 percent in just five years and peaked at $23.2 trillion in 2006, a rise of $11.4 trillion in just seven years. How could anybody including the Fed, says Stockman, see this as anything other than a dangerous deformation and an accident waiting to happen.[99]

In a section cleverly titled "John Maynard Greenspan," Stockman says that at the most fundamental level the prosperity model of the Greenspan

Fed was nothing more than the revival of an old illusion, that is, "that a nation can borrow its way to prosperity."[100] The result was a lot of spending from borrowed money but very little actual growth in real investment and earned incomes. Except for the temporary insanity of the dot-com Initial Public Offerings (IPOs), "there were only trivial amounts of primary equity raised during the entire run of the two Greenspan stock market booms."[101]

The fifth and last part of the book is called "Sundown in America: The End of Free Markets and Democracy," a rather ominous-sounding title. In the first chapter of this part Stockman is extremely critical of Mitt Romney, the Republican presidential candidate in the 2012 election, and Bain Capital, the firm that he founded, which Stockman says made its money through leveraged speculation in the financial markets. Romney did not build enterprises the old-fashioned way by fostering a new product or service on the market, but was rather a master financial speculator who bought, sold, flipped, and stripped businesses to make his money, all of which did not provide evidence that he knew how to grow the economy and create jobs and get the economy moving forward again. Bubble finance had created opportunities for companies like Bain to engage in financial engineering games that systematically channeled income and wealth to those at the very top of the income ladder.[102]

He is also critical of the $800 billion stimulus of the Obama administration, calling it a reckless and unspeakable folly that was not a rational economic plan but rather was a helter-skelter process that welcomed aboard every single pet project of any organization in the nation's capital. This stimulus bill was not an "investment" in the future of the country that would jump-start a stalled economy that would eventually pay back the debt it entailed but rather simply added to the permanent federal debt which was already bloated.[103] After mentioning several projects that the stimulus bill supported, Stockman says,

> The real crime is that the economy had already bottomed before these projects and the rest of the stimulus programs hit the spending stream. The giant Obama stimulus, therefore, amounted to a naked exercise in borrowing from the future on Uncle Sam's credit card to artificially inflate spending and income. There was no permanent national wealth gain at all, just a higher mortgage of taxes on future generations.[104]

So in spite of the stimulus, there has been no recovery of the Main Street economy; no revival of earned incomes on the free market. What we have is again what Stockman calls faux prosperity, which essentially consists of deliberate and relentless reflation of financial asset prices. What he calls breadwinner jobs are the foundation of the economy in that they generate more than 55 percent of earned wage and salary income. Some 5.6 million of these jobs were lost during the Great Recession, but only 4 percent of that loss had been restored after 40 months of the so-called recovery. Yet by September 2012 the S&P 500 was up 115 percent from is low during the recession and had made up for all its losses from the peak of the housing bubble.[105]

The United States has become a failed state fiscally, according to Stockman, as we have now reached the point where deficits and debt are too large and have become too embedded in social, economic, and political realities to be resolved. There will be relentless tax increases and spending cuts as far as the eye can see, and this fiscal sword of Damocles will permanently hang over the economy cutting the consumer economy down to size. The asset bubbles in dot.com stocks and housing misled households about their true wealth also gave the nation confidence that its social insurance benefits could be sustained indefinitely at full payment levels. Stockman thus thinks that the nation has arrived at a crucial pivot point as these foundational assumptions are about to be invalidated.[106]

The national debt is so large that there is no headroom left for policy makers to gamble with play money in the form of a fiscal stimulus program that in reality is money stolen from future taxpayers. Thus, the American economy faces what Stockman calls "a long twilight of no growth, rising taxes, and brutally intensifying fiscal conflict. These are the wages of five decades of Keynesian sin—the price of abandoning the financial discipline achieved . . . during the mid-twentieth century's golden age."[107] It's not that the deficit didn't matter but that printing press money mattered even more as it permitted spending without earning and investment without saving and created an artificial prosperity that was based on a mountain of debt. But the public will to push the debt ceiling through $20 trillion and beyond is lacking so Washington will struggle to keep the debt ceiling on a short leash as the fiscal cliff cannot be finessed anymore with gimmicks, phony cuts, and short-term deferrals. Thus, a true fiscal contraction will have to occur as the restoration of fiscal solvency and free-market prosperity requires a drastic reduction of the state's bloated machinery of welfare and central banking.[108] There is also a need for a massive reform of the political system to make it more responsive to the public and less supportive of crony capitalism. Stockman thinks that

> [e]ighty years on from the New Deal, therefore, crony capitalism has reached an end-stage metastasis. There is no solution except to drastically deflate the realm of politics and abolish incumbency itself; the machinery of the state and the machinery of reelection have become coterminous. But prying them apart would entail sweeping constitutional surgery: a package of amendments to extend congressional and presidential terms to six years, ban incumbents from reelection, provide public financing of candidates, strictly limit duration of campaigns (say, eight weeks), and impose a lifetime ban on lobbying by anyone who has been on the legislative or executive payroll.[109]

These sweeping changes are necessary, says Stockman, to cope with the contamination of the economic and financial system by what he calls a money-driven 24/7 regime of electioneering and hyper-politics. The problem is not only that politicians are bought and paid for by special interests, it is also the fact that they are involved in debate and maneuvering, I think a better word would be managing, every nook and cranny of our $16 trillion national economy. In that respect, he says, "Karl Rove's American Crossroads is as problematic as the oilmen's American Petroleum Institute."[110]

> Indeed, suffocation of the free market in totally mobilized political struggle is the ultimate evil of the Keynesian predicate. It causes every tick of the unemployment rate and every tenth of the GDP report to trigger waves of political praise, blame, and maneuver. The resulting nonstop partisan sound bites about how "our" plans would make the outcomes better and how "their" policies have made them worse continuously reinforce the presumption of more state action to bolster the economy.[111]

The Fed has been turned into a destroyer of honest financial markets by Greenspan and Bernanke and has instead turned into "an enabler of financial speculation on a scale never before imagined, and a reallocator of society's income and wealth to the 1 percent."[112] It sits at the edge of a financial abyss facing a coming fiscal collapse it cannot prevent because it is hostage to its four-decade-old excursion of printing money and macroeconomic management and cannot stop buying government debt.[113] The world economy, says Stockman, sits on the far edge of a monetary bubble that has been four decades in the making. All the major consumer economies of the world, including the United States, Japan, and Europe are failing which results in a democratic politics that will turn increasingly ugly, strident, and nationalistic as countries try to cope with this situation. In the United States, growth will grind to halt exposing the $20 billion prospective debt not obscured in the CBO's rosy scenario. The fiscal cliff will loom ever more forbidding and unmovable, and politics will become more fractured and paralyzed as the Keynesian state sinks into insolvency and failure. Gangs of crony capitalists and the opulent 1 percent may benefit from the central bank's money printing machine for a while, but eventually the "sundown" will descend upon the entire nation, even the 1 percent."[114]

In the last chapter Stockman lists thirteen steps that could be taken even at this late date to avoid the sundown scenario he has just outlined. Crony capitalism would have to be put out of business by a constitutional amendment. Welfare states would have to be put in a constitutional charity belt, and the rule of no spending without equal taxation would have to become standard operating procedure for a smaller government. If these things were done eventually "the free market could regain it vigor and capacity for wealth creation and, under a regime of sound money and honest finance, the 1 percent could continue to enjoy their opulence the old-fashioned way; that is, by delivering society inventions and enterprise that expand the economic pie, rather than reallocate it."[115] His thirteen steps to a healthy economy and society are as follows:

1. Restore Banker's Bank and Sound Money
2. Abolish Deposit Insurance and Limit the Fed Discount Window to Narrow Depositories
3. Adopt Super Glass-Steagall II
4. Abolish Incumbency Through an Omnibus Amendment
5. Require Each Two-Year Congress to Balance the Budget
6. End Microeconomic Management and Separate the State and the Free Market
7. Abolish Social Insurance, Bailouts, and Economic Subsidies
8. Eliminate Ten Federal Agencies and Departments
9. Erect a Sturdy Cash-Based Means-Tested Safety Net and Abolish the Minimum Wage
10. Abolish Health "Insurance" in All Its Forms
11. Replace the Welfare State With Genuine National Defense
12. Impose a 30 Percent Wealth Tax; Pay Down the National Debt to 30 Percent of GDP
13. Repeal the Sixteenth Amendment; Feed the Beast With Universal Taxes on Consumption[116]

Stockman admits that these steps would never be adopted "in today's regime of money politics, fast money speculation, and Keynesian economics." But he says they at least can be listed and are compelling.[117] He claims that in they were adopted the fiscal cliff would be averted, democracy could function, and people would be free to pursue their ends in a free-market context, where they would be liberated from crony capitalism and unfair windfalls to the 1 percent, and the inefficiencies and waste that result from the Keynesian state and its central bank would be eliminated. A return to sound money is most important as is a return to the free market that is liberated from Fed interference. As he says,

> [a]t the end of the day, the cure for the Great Deformation is to return to sound money and fiscal rectitude, and to correct the great error initiated during the New Deal era; namely, that in pursuing humanitarian purposes the state cannot and need not attempt to manage the business cycle or goose the free market with stimulates for more growth and jobs; nor can it afford the universal entitlements of social insurance. Instead, its job is to be a trustee for citizens left behind, maintaining a sturdy, fair, and efficient safety net regardless of whether unemployment is high or low. And most especially, the work of a citizen government attending to and managing the safety net for fellow citizens would proceed apace without regard to the opinion of Professor Paul Krugman or Art Laffer as to whether the free market was achieving the "potential"

output decreed by their deeply flawed models and theories. The proof is in the pudding.[118]

Thus, the book ends with this quote. It was number 4 on the *New York Times* best-seller list when first published and stayed on the list for a month. The book was not without its critics, of course, including Professor Krugman, who denounced his work as "sad" and "cranky old man stuff." Krugman thinks his analysis and history are way off base and dismissed the book in the *New York Review* in a single paragraph, calling it "an immensely long rant against excesses of various kinds, all of which, in Stockman's vision, have culminated in our present crises . . . any policies aimed at alleviating the current slump will just make this worse."[119]

By his own admission, the book had been denounced by the Republicans and Democrats alike; the Keynesians, supply-siders, and monetarists; by Wall Street and Bay Street; by the military-industrial complex; and the neocons, the social-cons, and the just-cons, which he said means everybody else in Washington who doesn't fit the other categories.[120] Stockman is honest about the thrust of the book admitting it is a polemic "that does not pretend to marshal the pro and con arguments in an even-handed fashion." It is written in a revisionist framework, he says, and contains a great deal of original interpretation of financial and public policy events and trends of the last century.[121]

Hopefully my review of the book will be of interest to readers as it is obvious that I sort of got wrapped up in the book. Stockman makes a persuasive argument because he keeps so well focused on the Fed and what he calls crony capitalism and sees everything through these lenses. One comes away from the book with a definite impression that the economy in our country is managed by the Fed with its manipulation of interest rates, its printing of money, and its purchase of federal debt as well the toxic assets of Wall Street banks. Stockman makes a strong case for the demise of free enterprise and the rise of central planning, if you will, and advocates a return to sound money and an economy based on free enterprise principles without constant intervention of the Fed. I would imagine he regrets the development of macroeconomics, which gives a theoretical rationale for manipulation of the economy.

However, one wishes he had said more about his view of free enterprise and whether he agrees with Reich that the free enterprise system needs rules related to competition, the uses of property, and so on or whether he views the free-enterprise system as being able to function on its own without rules and intervention to fix problems. This is kind of a basic issue mentioned earlier in this chapter, that is, whether one views the system as having laws that operate for the automatic benefit of society and therefore is best if left completely alone or whether the system needs intervention at times to correct for its deficiencies. Is the market something of a scientific construct that operates according to its own laws like the law of supply and demand or the law of diminishing returns, among others, or is it a more of a social construct that emerged during the Industrial Revolution when more new technologies arose and more products were produced that needed to be sold to consumers? Bartering works if there are few products to exchange, but such a system is not equipped to handle the thousands and even millions of different products that a factory system makes available to consumers; thus, a different kind of market eventually arose that made it possible for all these products to find their way to consumers.

A completely free market with no rules would seem to be a system that would end up in complete chaos. If there were no rules or no-one to enforce them producers would do whatever was necessary to obtain a monopoly position, they would engage in fraudulent practices of all kinds, they would try and cheat consumers out of their money in more ways that can be counted, they would misrepresent their financial position to stockholders, and so on ad infinitum. Competition alone would not prevent these things from happening. The market would be so chaotic that no one in their right mind would want to participate in in and would go back to bartering if necessary to get what they needed at a fair price.

My view of all the things that Stockman deals with respect to the economy, as presented in the first chapter, is that government interventions of various kinds were necessary to keep the free enterprise system running. Government intervention was necessary to prevent monopolies from forming, to do something about getting the system up and running again in a depression and try to promote a more stable economy that would keep on growing, to regulate business to promote a safer workplace and a less polluted environment, to bail out individual businesses and entire industries when necessary to protect jobs and keep the economy from tanking, and to deal with gross inequalities that threaten to divide the society into the 1 percent versus the rest.

The question I raised at the end of this chapter is whether the country could continue to afford capitalism with some major reforms that would enable us to reduce our debt which mainly has been the result of trying to deal with these deficiencies of the market. We don't know where Stockman would stand on this kind of issue. Most everything is the fault of the Fed and its monetary policies. He does mention some fiscal measures that were adopted by Congress including the bailout bill of the last years of the second Bush administration and the stimulus bill of the Obama administration and thinks neither of these were necessary. But while he says all of this started with the New Deal of the Roosevelt administration, he fails to recognize that the New Deal consisted mainly of fiscal policies passed by Congress and the creation of new administrative agencies to implement these measures. Thus, in his zeal to pin everything on the Fed I think he does not recognize the role that fiscal policies play in affecting the economy for good or ill.

He does, however, bring the issue of debt financed growth front and center. When one thinks of where we were at the end of the Clinton administration and where we are now it boggles the mind. At the end of the Clinton administration we actually had a surplus in the federal budget and were beginning to pay down the debt. But for a few hundred butterfly ballots in Florida, Gore would have been our president, and I hope, at least, that things would have turned out differently and that we would have continued down the path that Clinton had put the country on toward getting our fiscal house in order. I seriously doubt that he would have favored two tax cuts that mainly benefited the wealthy. And while I hope he would have dealt with Afghanistan after 9/11, I can say with a great deal of certainty that he would not have invaded Iraq of any other countries under such false pretenses and thus would have avoided the cost of that war which by some estimates cost us in the trillions of dollars.

The growth the economy experienced during the 1990s was certainly in part because of a bubble that burst almost as soon as Bush took office. But it was also, in part, real growth based on the efficiencies introduced by increased use of computers in all business organizations and the development of the internet. When I personally experienced the ease of writing in using word processing programs and the ease of looking up articles and doing research with use of the Internet, I began to get some sense of the impact these made on the entire society in making many things much easier and more efficient. While there would have been a dot-com bust, this was not nearly as bad the financial meltdown. Granted the Glass–Steagall was repealed under the Clinton administration, I doubt a Gore administration would have given derivatives a green light and might have regulated them in some fashion.

All of this is speculation, but we certainly have become much more of a debt-financed economy during the Bush and Obama administrations. So the basic question remains as to how long this can continue. The growing federal debt was not much of an issue during the 2016 presidential campaign as personal attacks on each other's character were much more prevalent than in any campaign I can remember. And some of the proposals made to do this and that would only increase this debt. The question of capitalism's viability in the future is still on the table. Can it provide a livable wage for workers, absorb the full costs of environmental degradation, and provide sufficient incentives for management of large corporations to continue to do whatever it is that they do and for entrepreneurs to take the risks of introducing a new product or service into the market? The strong growth and widely shared prosperity during the period immediately following World War II when the American dream was alive and well may have been a great exception in the performance of capitalism that can never be repeated.

In any event, the solutions present in the one article and three books reviewed in this chapter leave something to be desired. Kuttner's proposes that dealing with climate change could bring the nation together and relieve the distribution problems the country is experiencing. Reich advocates a new countervailing alliance of the less wealthy that would be able to counter the power of the wealthy and address inequality and other issues facing

America. Das thinks frugal living on the part of Americans is necessary to bring the debt down to manageable levels and restore growth of the economy.[122] Stockman has his thirteen steps that he believes would create a healthy economy and society.

All of these proposals, however, would require a connection with each other and with nature that doesn't exist and with our excessive individualism has no chance of emerging in our society. To deal with climate change requires a connection with nature and with each other to unite around this issue and take the steps necessary to reduce carbon emissions. The formation of a countervailing alliance obviously takes a feeling of being connected to other people with common interests. Frugality takes a common commitment on the part of both the wealthy and less wealthy to make the sacrifices necessary to reduce debt and restore growth. And for any of Stockman's thirteen steps to be enacted requires a common interest in restoring sound money and reforming the political system. None of these is possible without an underlying spiritual dimension that would enable people to trust each other and trust their government to do what is necessary to restore growth and lessen the inequalities in our society.

There are several other proposals that could be mentioned,[123] but one in particular makes the point about the need for Americans to connect with each other and recognize their interdependence and their responsibility to others as a counter to the individualistic emphasis on rights that has taken place over the past several decades, what the author calls a "rights revolution." This emphasis on responsibility jibes with the focus of my first book where the subtitle was "Community and Responsibility in Business," a book in which I argued for a balance between community and individualism and between rights and responsibilities. It is worth quoting at length from this author, who is Michael Kazin, the editor of *Dissent*, who in response to the "rights revolution," says the following:

> This expansion of rights—of freedoms, both individual and collective— has been the greatest achievement of the American left since the Second World War. But perhaps it's time to advance the idea of responsibility as well as rights. Talk of freedom from unjust authorities and traditions cannot address some of the most serious problems that currently face the United States and much of the world: the exploitation of workers and the poor, the rigged casino that is finance capital, the accelerating degradation of the environment. Celebrants of the autonomous, profit-maximizing individual did much to create and aggravate these injustices. They claim that businesses have a right to operate free of unions and government regulation and that the EPA has no right to compel landowners to follow any rules that might restrain what they do on their property. A rhetoric of interdependence, of responsibility to others is essential to rebutting these claims and to mitigating and, eventually, abolishing the outages they dismiss or legitimate. Bosses should be responsible to the well-being of their workers; wage-earners

to the consumers they serve; professionals to their clients; banks to the communities and nations where they operate; parents to their children; the rich to the poor; and everyone to preserving the natural world and reversing the damage industrial civilization has done. Every religion preaches a version of this ethic, which come call the Golden Rule. Socialists traditionally prefer to talk about solidarity, recognizing the need to transform a society in which those who have the gold make the rules. But whatever one calls it, the alternative is barbaric disorder, the war of all against all. And that would be a world in which the only right that mattered would be the right to survive.[124]

Restructuring Capitalism

The spiritual dimension allows us to transcend the structures we live in and have a vision of how these structures could be changed to enable people to live a more fulfilling and enriched life. But transcendent experiences themselves are one of the things that make life worth living and can include experiences like being confronted with a beautiful vista in nature or reflecting on a great work of art or architecture. Such experiences have the property of transcendence when they take us beyond our ordinary lives and somehow draw us out of and beyond ourselves and exceed the ordinary realm of our contemporary existence. Experiences of transcendence that give meaning to our lives need not be experiences of something outside ourselves, but can be a kind of activity that results from our orientation to the world in which we live and how we relate to our environment and other people. While religion is often the source of transcendent experiences, God is not necessary, argues Anthony Simone Laden, for someone to be infused with transcendent experiences that give life value and meaning.[125]

Transcendent experiences can pull people out of ordinary experiences and enable them to see their ordinary life and its ordinary surroundings as extraordinary. Transcendence involves a broadening of our vision, a widening of the world of interest and attention so that the ordinary world around us lights up with extraordinary qualities. It also involves a broadening of our understanding of what it means to be a person, to see ourselves in a new light that can be radically different from what is defined as familiar by our society. Transcendence in a secular world focuses on ourselves and our fellow human beings to see a new kind of humanity that is hidden and invisible in our ordinary experiences and involves seeing the connections between us that make us part of a collective or community.[126]

There is no such thing as individualism, as collectives are everywhere. We grow up in a family and join various institutional collectives throughout our entire life. Corporations are collectives than have a reality that is more than just the sum of the people who work for it. The corporation has an identity and a culture that is above and beyond its constituent parts. Management is a collective and workers are at a great disadvantage if they try and bargain with this collective on their own. They need to be part of a collective in order to get a fair shake from management. When entrepreneurs hire a second person to help them develop their idea they create a collective. The Republican Party is a collective that is something beyond its individual membership. The individual is what he or she is not only because of genes but also because of the collectives they are part of where their identity is shaped as they develop relationships with other people and with the environment.

There is also a collective understanding of capitalism and how it works to provide for the material needs of people. The ability to transcend this understanding might help in realizing that there is no such thing as economic wealth as the numbers that supposedly represent such wealth are really nothing more than a measure of the power that one has to get someone to do something they want done as described in an earlier chapter. The numbers that people have at their disposal mean nothing in themselves. They are simply a potential to be used to make other people your bidding whether it is to make a product you want to buy on the market or a service you want done for yourself. This potential sits there in our bank accounts or wherever and earns more numbers if invested in something that returns what we call interest. But the numbers have no value in and of themselves and are worthless as numbers. They only mean something when they are used, and their potential power is actually unitized.

There is also no such thing as a private sector and a public sector; they are all one and the same when their institutional boundaries are transcended. Institutions in either sector have to generate more numbers than they use up in their operations or they cannot continue in existence. The source of numbers for a so-called private-sector institution come from either borrowing or what they are given in exchange for whatever it is that they produce. The numbers for a public-sector institution come from taxes or borrowing, but they also have to produce something people want and are willing to support or eventually they will go out of existence. They cannot continue to tax people at higher and higher levels unless they are providing a worthwhile service and cannot continue to borrow unless there is confidence they will pay off this debt at some time in the future. People who work for private-sector institutions are performing a public service by making or doing something the public wants the same as a public-sector employee.

With respect to science, the distinction between objective and subjective no longer makes any sense. In quantum mechanics, the subjective nature of the observer affects whatever is being observed and helps determine the outcome of the observation. Subjective and objective are all merged into one activity, and what we observe depends on what instrument or process we use for the observation and our particular way of approaching the entity we are attempting to describe. The use of these terms no longer makes any sense, and we need to come up with a new term based on a new concept of what is really going on in science when it claims to be measuring or observing something on a strictly objective basis. Physical reality is not completely independent of the one who is observing and is not there in some sense of a brute given that we can grasp in a solely objective manner.

Facts and values are inseparable as what we eventually decide is a fact is affected by what we value. Facts again are not something that are brute givens unaffected by human concerns and interests. What are the facts about climate change, for example, and what do we choose to believe about scientific observations? The climate change deniers have their own set of "facts" to prove the earth is really cooling while their opposites have another set of facts to prove they are wrong. Eventually the preponderance of evidence begins to favor one side or the other, but it may take a while as no one study or observation can be taken as the final truth about the matter. Things change as is most evident in the nutrition areas where conventional wisdom is often overturned by new studies on things like fat and salt and other things we consume.

With regard to materialism and spiritualism itself, the main subject of this book, there is a kind of inseparability. The material objects we have available offer the potential to enhance the quality of our lives and make us more spirited individuals, while the spirit we bring to our activities affect the outcome of those encounters that most often involve material objects. Whether nature provides us with an enhanced spiritual experience depends in part on what we bring to the encounter with nature as well as the quality of the nature with which we interact. It is not a one-way street. If we see nature as strictly an object to be exploited it is doubtful if nature can provide us with a spiritual experience as we do not feel any connection with nature. The same holds true with people. If they are seen as strictly factors of production to be exploited in the interests of increasing production, we will never develop a spiritual connection with them and will lose part of what it means to be human.

We probably need to invent new kinds of language and new words to transcend some of these dichotomies that we are stuck with largely because of our scientific orientation. We need to categorize things in science so that we can specify cause and effect relationships and conduct research so we can measure the effect of certain variables. These variables need to be more or less precisely defined so they can be distinguished from everything else in the universe. Science thus forces us to think in black-and-white terms so that research can be conducted. So we distinguish between facts and values, materialism and spiritualism, subjective and objective, and all the other dichotomies that are part of the way we think about the world. Our language reflects this way of thinking and it will take new language to transcend these dichotomies and express a new kind of reality. As stated by William Ophuls in *Plato's Revenge*, "[w]e tend to perceive only what we have words for, so what we have words for is what we habitually perceive . . . language frames our reality so completely that the limits of my language mean the limits of my world."[127]

Implementing an Ethic of Service

In my previous books on capitalism I ended up advocating a professional model for management of public corporations and argued that to be a profession in the true sense of the word, management must put profits in a broader context, and recognize that their major objective is to *serve* all the clients of the organization, not just the stockholders.[128] This broader perspective includes the people who consume their products, who work for it and who depend on it for various things in the community. Serving the client's interests also involves giving consideration to the moral, economic, political, cultural, and natural environments in which these clients live. To be part of a profession, managers must change their focus to one of putting service to the client foremost in their decisions. If they do this, produce products that truly enhance people's lives, provide good jobs for their employees with adequate wages, and are concerned about the environments in which people live, profits will follow in a society that is committed to its well-being.

Business, then, has multiple clients, which is actually no different from the traditional professions. Hospitals and doctors have patients to satisfy, as well as the many nurses and clerical personnel that work for them. Private hospitals also have stockholders to satisfy. Lawyers have clients to keep happy as well as staff. Every decision they make will affect all of these clients to some degree. Management must then be concerned with producing goods and services that are going to better the lives of consumers and provide them with enriching experiences, with providing its employees with meaningful experiences and the opportunity to grow and develop as human beings during the time they spend working for the corporation and in providing stockholders with an ample return on their investment. It is not a matter of balancing these various interests against each other, but of giving all of them attention at the same time. They are all part of the same holistic nexus, and these interests are tied together in seeking a better life with more enriching experiences. This is what an *ethic of service* is all about.

This emphasis on service, I argued, also had relevance for the education of managers in business schools as promoting a sense of professionalism in business school students involved a change of the way the relationship between business and society was viewed. According to Giacalone and Thompson, two management scholars teaching in business schools, "[w]e teach students to perpetuate business' importance and its centrality in society, to do so by increasing wealth, and to assume that by advancing organizational interests, they advance their own and society's overall best interests."[129] The corporation must be de-centered and placed in the context of society at large. Business exists to serve society and enhance the well-being of the members of that society; the society does not exist to serve business and its interests. This entails the adoption of a different worldview of the part of business schools that tend to think of the business organization as being at the core of the universe.[130]

This idea that society and all its elements exist to serve corporate interests would have to change in order for business to be seen as a profession. Managers of these organizations have to broaden their perspective to think of society in their decisions and how the corporation can enhance the well-being of society's members in ways that involve more considerations than just the creation of economic wealth. Economic wealth, as stated in an earlier chapter, is something of an illusion and a fiction and merely reflects the value society places on economic entities. Business must serve a wider spectrum of values and interests than just economic ones and this broader perspective must be considered when managers formulate business policies and practices. According to Matthew Stewart, a former management consultant,

> [b]ut the modern idea of management is right enough to be dangerously wrong and it has led us seriously astray. It has sent us on a mistaken quest to seek scientific answers to unscientific questions. It offers pretended technological solutions to what are, at bottom, moral and political problems. It conjures an illusion—easily exploited—about the nature and value of management expertise. It induces us to devote formative years to training in subjects that do not exist. It favors a naïve view of the sources of mismamagement, making it harder to check abuses of corporate power. Above all, it contributes to a misunderstanding about the sources of our prosperity, leading us to neglect the social, moral, and political infrastructure on which our well-being depends.[131]

This idea of an ethic of service, I now realize, is not enough as even if business schools could change to promote this kind of professionalism, the corporation is still structured in such a way that this ethic would be difficult to implement even if managers had the best of intentions to serve all the clients of the organization. The capitalist system needs to be restructured to promote this ethic and enable managers to legally focus their attention on the multiple stakeholders of the corporation. Capitalism needs to live up to its name, and our understanding of capitalism needs to be broadened to include other stakeholders in the very structure of the corporate organization.

There are many different kinds of capital besides the physical capital the organization needs to produce products and the financial capital it needs to expand its operations. The notion of human capital has been around for a long time as has the discussion of natural capital referring to the physical environment and the resources it provides. Even the notion of social capital has appeared in the literature. Thus, the expansion of the definition of what capital comprises is nothing new and has been discussed rather extensively in academia and other places. So my proposal for restructuring capitalism builds on these ideas and simply argues for the inclusion of these different notions of capital into the heart of corporate operations and its responsibilities to promote the well-being of these different kinds of capital.

Thus, the corporation needs to concern itself with the status of its *physical capital* understood as the machines, buildings, and other material things it needs to produce its products or services. This physical capital must be maintained at a high level of functioning so as to make the company as efficient as possible and keep it competitive. Likewise *financial capital* refers to the money or numbers it has available to expand its operations or update its physical capital and can involve retained earnings or debt it needs to incur when it borrows numbers from a financial institution. It can even involve the sale of additional stock to have more numbers at its disposal. *Human capital*, of course, refers to the workforce the corporation has available and involves not only the quantity of people it needs to carry out its operations, but their education and training, their health and safety, whether they are paid a living wage or salary, the impact the corporation makes on their families, treating all workers equally in terms of opportunities and promotions, and other aspects that relate to the workforce. Management, by the way, is part of this human capital.

Natural capital refers to the physical environment that may be degraded and polluted by the production process. It also refers to resource usage by the firm and in particular the impact the company has on resources in short supply. This notion of natural capital involves the proper disposal of toxic substances the company may produce, a provision for disposal of its product when its useful life is ended, and the mitigation of other such environmental impacts. The goal is for the corporation to promote a healthy environment and take account of the resources it is using that come from the physical environment.[132] Finally, *social capital* takes into account the social aspects of the corporation's environment, the state of the community in which corporate operations are located and even the state of the nation as a whole. It could involve the state of education in the local community, its infrastructure, the health of its inhabitants, and other such community aspects. At the national level, it involves concern with the state of democracy and whether its political and lobbying activities support or undermine democracy.

These different kinds of capital need to be built into the structural aspects of the capitalist system and the way the corporation operates. For this structure to have meaning the profits of the corporation would need to be split evenly between these different forms of capital. If there happened to be a surplus in one or more categories of capital, this surplus should be divided evenly between the remaining forms of capital. For example, perhaps the corporation is not a major polluter and does not degrade the environment in other ways; thus, it might have a surplus in this area that would be split evenly among the other forms of capital. Likewise, the company may not have major debts to pay off and therefore has a surplus in the area of financial capital that would be evenly shared with the remaining forms of capital.

The traditional board of directors would be done away with in this restructured corporation, and corporate governance would take on a radically different form from that currently in place. During my academic career, corporate governance was always a major topic, and the focus was on reforming or revitalizing the board of directors to function more efficiently and effectively in the interests of stockholders. There was a great emphasis on creating compensation committees to reign in the excessive pay going to top management. Yet none of these recommendations has had any effect on management compensation that continues to climb and on severance packages, which, in most cases, are outlandish. So I think it is time to abandon the traditional board of directors entirely along with the idea that property rights take precedence in corporate governance.[133]

Each area of capital would have its own governance structure to concern itself with issues relevant to that type of capital. For example, physical capital would have its own board, if you will, composed of management and stockholders who would make decisions about the replacement of physical stock with modern and more efficient models, about the issuance of new stock to raise needed money, and, most important, about how much of its allocation would go to stockholders in the form of dividends and returns on the stock itself. This board would make all decisions pertaining to the use and replacement of physical capital and returns on the stockholder's investment. Representatives of the stockholders themselves would be part of this board so that the stockholders would have involvement as real owners who have some say in the operations of the company they, in theory, own.

In the area of financial capital, the board would be composed management and representatives of the major creditors of the company. This board would make sure the company met its obligations to pay off principal and interest on its debt and whether to buy back some of its stock. It would also make decisions about the level of retained earnings and what they should be used for as well as whether the company needed to take on more debt in order to expand its operations. In this case, the board would negotiate with potential creditors to get the best deal for the company regarding the terms of the loan and decide on where the money would go regarding expansion of its physical plant or product line and other matters related to the proposed expansion.

Human capital refers to all the issues related to the workforce including working conditions such as the promotion of safety and health in the workplace, eliminating discriminatory practices, the level of training the company needs to do to have an efficient workforce, and other such matters. Of course, its major function would be to determine wages and salaries for everyone in the corporation including top management. This board would be composed of representatives from both management and labor in equal proportions, and in the case of a tie, the matter would be taken to arbitration with the arbitrators agreed to and chosen by both parties. There might even have to be a subcommittee that would deal with compensation matters and make recommendations for the board to approve or disapprove.

The board in the area of natural capital would be composed of management and representatives for some of the major environmental organizations that have an interest in corporate operations and their impact on the environment. Decisions would have to be made on the allocation of its portion of the company's profits to mitigate its impacts on global warming if it has such impacts, to cut back if not eliminate its pollution of air and water or other aspects of the environment, and, in general, to mitigate its negative effects on the natural environment. This board would also look at the company's resource usage, particularly in regard to resource shortages, and determine if substitutes that are more readily available could be used in its production process.

Finally, with respect to social capital, the board would be composed of representatives from the local communities in which the company operates as well as representatives from management. Perhaps a representative of the federal government would also be appropriate. This board would deal with the philanthropic activities of the company and where they should be directed to deal with community and national issues that need to be addressed to promote a healthy and prosperous social environment. It would make sure the company pay its taxes on all levels in a timely fashion and discourage attempts of the company to avoid paying taxes that have been fairly and appropriately determined by taxing authorities. This board would also examine the lobbing activities of the company and its campaign contributions to determine if they not only served the interests of the corporation, but in addition to being self-serving, also contribute toward making a better society and strengthen democracy rather than undermining it.

All these boards would be composed of an equal number of representatives from its respective constituents where majority rule would apply and, in the case of ties, the decision would be submitted to arbitration with the arbitrators to be chosen and agreed to by both parties to the decision. Each board would have to have a chairman to be chosen by the members of the board itself. The agenda for board meetings would be determined by each board where management could draw up the initial agenda but submit it to all board members well in advance of a meeting so that everyone on the board could have input as to the issues to be discussed. Management would have to make relevant information about each issue available to all board members well in advance of board meetings so that nonmanagement members could have time to ask for more information if necessary and to find additional sources for information they may deem necessary.

This, indeed, is a radical proposal but perhaps a radical approach to the problems of capitalism is necessary. This kind of structure could have a very positive effect on the operations of the corporation and make it more responsive to the needs of society. There is a distinct possibility that it would eliminate the need for many government regulations in the area of the environment, workplace health and safety, labor relations, and perhaps other areas as well, as such a broad representation on the respective boards should assure that the corporation responds to issues of concern to its respective constituents and mitigate its negative impacts on natural capital, human capital, and social capital in particular. At least one can hope this is the result.

One major stakeholder left out of this structure is, of course, the consumer. Perhaps the notion of social capital could be legitimately expanded to include a consideration of the impacts of its products and services on the social environment, and the board in this area could have some consumer representatives. Certainly issues like product safety, truth in advertising, warranties, and other consumer issues should be considered somewhere. But it is not clear to me at this point where such concerns would best fit into this structure so that government regulation may remain necessary to address some of these issues.

In any event, this structure would definitely help in implementing an ethic or service that I advocated in my earlier books on capitalism. This ethic would be built into the very structure of the corporation itself and is not something imposed from the outside as is the case with most ethical proposals. Obviously the entire legal apparatus regarding the corporation would have to be changed to de-emphasize property rights and incorporate the different kinds of capital into the legal structure itself. Property rights are of less importance anyhow as professional management replaced owners in running the corporation based on their technical expertise rather than ownership and most stockholders became merely investors who had little or no impact or interest in being a part of the governance structure of the corporation they theoretically owned. We have known about the separation of ownership and control for close to a century: isn't it time we recognized this reality in the way the corporation is governed and did away with the fiction of stockholder democracy?[134]

Perhaps this structure might even mitigate the casino-like operation the stock market has become. At least some of the stockholders would be involved in running the company and have some say in what the company does and become true owners in this sense. This might create a shared understanding of the market as less of a casino where investors are in effect engaging in a form of gambling and promote more of a sense that the market exists to determine the value of corporations and provide an assessment of the future prospects of companies with their stock price reflecting these aspects more realistically than the stock market does at present. There would surely be other effects of this structure that may not be foreseen, call them intended consequences, but one can hope that the positive benefits of this structure to capitalism and society would far outweigh any negative effects.

So that is it as far as this book is concerned. We have journeyed through many issues pertaining to society as regards its economic and political systems and many philosophical issues pertaining to materialism and spiritualism. In the final analysis it will take something of a spiritual awakening to rethink and reform capitalism, referring to the title of my other two books on capitalism, and restructuring it to provide for the material needs of the entire society rather than just a small segment who happened to accumulate most of the numbers that the system generates and thus have disproportionate power to make the system continue to serve their interests. As stated by David Harvey, Distinguished Professor of Anthropology at the Graduate Center of the City University of New York,

> *The resultant unbearable denial of the free development of human creative capacities and powers amounts to throwing away the cornucopia*

of possibilities that capital had bequeathed us and squandering the real wealth of human possibilities in the name of perpetual augmentation of monetary wealth and the satiation of narrow economic class interests. Faced with such a prospect, the only sensible politics is to seek to transcend capital and the restraints of an increasingly autocratic and oligarchical structure of capitalist class power and to rebuild the economy's imaginative possibilities into a new and far more egalitarian and democratic configuration.[135]

This power must be broken in the interests of saving capitalism and making society whole so that people who participate in the system can live enriched and fulfilled lives. After all, the ultimate purpose of any economic system is not just to produce more and more goods and services and increase GDP, but it is to enable people to live their lives to the fullest and realize their potential to the greatest extent possible.[136] We must work to keep the material and spiritual dimensions of existence in some kind of balance, as the material dimension without the spiritual is empty and meaningless, and the spiritual dimension without some material realization is an unfulfilled dream without substance.

Notes

1 "U.S. National Debt Clock," http://www.brillig.com/debt/clock/, accessed April 11, 2016.
2 James Grant, "Make American Solvent Again," *Time*, April 25, 2016.
3 "U.S. National Debt Clock." Some commentators have pointed out that the presidential candidates for both parties in 2016 seemed unconcerned about this debt and ignored the need for entitlement reform. Democrats were proposing more spending for social programs, clean energy, and infrastructure repair, while Republicans proposed tax breaks that would cost the treasury $9.5 trillion over a decade. See Robert Samuelson, "Both Parties Are Ignoring Deficits," *The Week*, February 12, 2016, 12.
4 Josh Zumfrun, "The Legacy of Debt," *The Wall Street Journal*, February 3, 2015, B1.
5 Katrina Vanden Heuvel, "How a $15 Minimum Is Taking Hold," *The Denver Post*, April 10, 2016, 5D.
6 See "Minimum Wage: The $15-an-Hour Experiment," *The Week*, April 15, 2016, 17.
7 Those states and cities that did pass minimum wage laws are finding it difficult to ensure that workers are actually paid accordingly. Governments don't have the data to check up on employers and usually have to wait until an employee complains, which is difficult to do in most situations for fear of being fired. Some studies show that roughly one in four businesses cheat workers out of minimum wages by underestimating worker's hours or requiring them to work without pay off-the-clock. See Donna Gordon Blankinship, "Governments Struggle to Enforce 'Living Wage,'" *The Denver Post*, May 1, 2016, 2K.
8 Christopher Ingraham, "Child Poverty in the U.S. Is among the Worst in the Developed World," Wonkblog, *The Washington Post*, October 29, 2014, 1–2.
9 See Donald L. Barlett and James B. Steele, *The Betrayal of the American Dream* (New York: Public Affairs, 2012).

10 See Ray Mark Rinaldi, "American Dream in Crisis," *The Denver Post*, July 5, 2015, 2A; Michael W. Kraus, Shai Davidai, and A. David Nussbaum, "American Dream? or Mirage?" *The New York Times*, May 3, 2015, SR9; Nicholas Lemann, "Unhappy Days for America," *The New York Review*, May 21, 2015, 25–27; Jason DeParle, "No Way Up," *The New York Times Book Review*, March 8, 2015, 14; Jeff Sommer, "The Great American Dream, Still Deferred," *The New York Times*, February 8, 2015, BU3; Charles Homans, "The End of the American Daydream," *New York Times Magazine*, May 1, 2016, 50–53; and Nicholas Kristof, "U.S.A., Land of Limitations?" *The New York Times*, August 9, 2015, SR 1. In the last article Kristof says the following: "I hear form people who say something like: *I grew up poor, but I worked hard and I made it. If other people tried, they could, too.* Bravo! Sure, there are people who have overcome mind-boggling hurdles. But they're like the N.B.A. centers with short parents." See also "The White Working Class: Who's to blame for its misery?" *The Week*, April 1, 2016, 16.

11 Paul Craig Roberts, *The Failure of Laissez Faire Capitalism* (Atlanta, GA: Clarity Press, 2013), 83–84.

12 Sarah Kendzior, "The Illusion of Full Employment," *The Week*, May 6, 2016, 38. See also Andrew Ross Sorkin, "The Obama Recovery," *The New York Times Magazine*, May 1, 2016, 54–80; "Obama: How Will History Judge His Economic Legacy?" *The Week*, May 13, 2016, 6; and "Issue of the Week: An Underwhelming Jobs Report," *The Week*, May 20, 2016, 34.

13 "Capitalism Is Losing Fans," *The Week*, October 16, 2015, 38.

14 James K. Galbraith, *Inequality and Instability* (New York: Oxford University Press, 2012), 148–149.

15 According to one poll, 51 percent of 18- to 29-year-olds say they do not support capitalism while 33 percent support socialism. See "Pool Watch," *The Week*, May 6, 2016, 17.

16 Chrystia Freeland, "Is Capitalism in Trouble?" *The Atlantic*, December, 2013, 26–29.

17 Jim Yardley and Binyamin Appelbaum, "In Fiery Speeches, Francis Excoriates Global Capitalism," *The New York Times International*, July 12, 2015, 12.

18 William Nordhaus, "The Pope & the Market," *The New York Review*, October 8, 2015, 26–27.

19 Ibid., 27.

20 At least one other author makes this point: "Capital's conception of nature as a mere objectified commodity does not pass unchallenged . . . Capital cannot, unfortunately, change the way it slices and dices nature up into commodity forms and private property rights. To challenge this would be to challenge the functioning of the economic engine of capitalism itself and to deny the applicability of capital's economic rationality to social life. This is why the environmental movement, when it goes beyond a merely cosmetic or ameliorative politics, must become anti-capital. The concept of nature that underpins various philosophies of environmentalism is radically at odds with that which capital has to impose in order to reproduce itself. The environmental movement could, in alliance with others, pose a serious threat to the reproduction of capital. But so far environmental politics has not, for a variety of reasons, moved very far in this direction. If often prefers to ignore entirely the ecology that capital is constructing and nibble at issues that are separable from the core dynamics of what capital is about. Contesting a waste dump here or rescuing an endangered species or a valued habitat there is in no way fatal to capital's reproduction." See David Harvey, *Seventeen Contradictions and the End of Capitalism* (New York: Oxford University Press, 2014), 252.

21 Robert Kuttner, "The Hidden History of Prosperity," *The American Prospect*, May/June 2014, 42.

22 Ibid.
23 Ibid.
24 Ibid., 42–43.
25 Ibid., 43, 48.
26 For a review of this book see Paul Krugman, "Challenging the Oligarchy," *The New York Review*, December 17, 2015, 16–20.
27 Robert B. Reich, *Saving Capitalism: For the Many, not the Few* (New York: Alfred A. Knopf, 2015), xii.
28 Ibid., xii–xiv.
29 Ibid., xiv–xv.
30 Ibid., 4–8.
31 Ibid., 6, 10.
32 Ibid., 10.
33 Ibid., 11–13. The Supreme Court upheld this practice and also upheld a clause in the contract prohibiting class-action remedies for grievances against employers. See Katherine V. W. Stone, "Will Workers and Consumers Get their Day in Court?" *The American Prospect*, Spring 2016, 84–99.
34 Ibid., 16–80.
35 Ibid., 81–86.
36 Ibid., 89–96.
37 Ibid., 97–107.
38 Ibid., 108–114.
39 Ibid., 115–117.
40 Ibid., 118–132.
41 Ibid., 133–150.
42 Ibid., 154.
43 Ibid., 157.
44 Ibid., 163–167.
45 Ibid., 183–192.
46 Ibid., 193–210.
47 Ibid., 208.
48 Ibid., 203–217.
49 Ibid., 219.
50 Satyajit Das, *The Age of Stagnation: Why Perpetual Growth Is Unattainable and the Global Economy Is in Peril* (Amherst, NY: Prometheus Books, 2016), 1–2.
51 Ibid., 2.
52 Ibid., 3.
53 Ibid., 5–6.
54 Ibid., 15.
55 Ibid., 16–26.
56 Ibid., 33–54.
57 Ibid., 54–55.
58 Ibid., 63.
59 Ibid., 62–89.
60 Ibid., 119–120.
61 Ibid., 205.
62 Ibid., 225–226.
63 Ibid., 231, 155.
64 Ibid., 283–284.
65 Ibid., 294–289.
66 Ibid., 291. See Josh Sanburm, "The Joy of Less," *Time*, March 23, 2015, 44–50; Zachary Karabell, "Learning to Love Stagnation," *Foreign Affairs*, Vol. 95, No. 2 (March/April 2016), 47–53; and Robert J. Samuelson, "The Withering of the Affluent Society," Vol. XXXVI. No. 3 (Summer 2012), 42–47.

67 Ibid., 291, 294.
68 Ibid., 294–295.
69 Ibid., 295–297.
70 David A. Stockman, *The Great Deformation: The Corruption of Capitalism in America* (New York: Public Affairs, 2013), xi–xii.
71 Ibid., xv.
72 Ibid., xvii.
73 Ibid., 5.
74 Ibid., 6–7.
75 Ibid., 10.
76 Ibid., 14–17.
77 Ibid., 50–51.
78 Ibid., 52.
79 Ibid., 58–59.
80 Ibid., 68.
81 Ibid., 104–106. "Even out-and-out welfare programs like food stamps, Medicaid, and Aid to Families With Dependent Children (AFDC) had been reduced from the Carter level by just 10 percent. There turned out to be fewer welfare queens and more arguably needy participants in these programs than Republican campaign rhetoric had implied." Ibid., 104.
82 Ibid., 168–169.
83 Ibid., 202–205.
84 Ibid., 213.
85 Ibid., 213, 235, 249–250.
86 Ibid., 258.
87 Ibid., 272.
88 Ibid., 285.
89 Ibid., 281.
90 Ibid., 275.
91 Ibid., 289.
92 Ibid., 354.
93 Ibid., 354–355.
94 Ibid., 356–357.
95 Ibid., 358–360.
96 Ibid., 361–364.
97 See Rogene A. Buchholz, *Reforming Capitalism: The Scientific Worldview and Business* (New York: Routledge, 2012), 246–281.
98 Stockman, *The Great Deformation*, 365–366.
99 Ibid., 365–370.
100 Ibid., 437.
101 Ibid., 449.
102 Ibid., 558–559.
103 Ibid., 588–589.
104 Ibid., 589.
105 Ibid., 631–634.
106 Ibid., 645–647.
107 Ibid., 649.
108 Ibid., 669.
109 Ibid., 673.
110 Ibid.
111 Ibid.
112 Ibid., 702.
113 Ibid.
114 Ibid., 705.

115 Ibid., 706.

116 Ibid., 706–711.

117 Ibid., 706.

118 Ibid., 712.

119 William D. Cohan, "David Stockman against the World," *Bloomberg Business Week*, June 27, 2013, 61. This seems to be a particularly apt title.

120 Ibid., 59.

121 Stockman, *The Great Deformation*, 713.

122 Some commentators are not too optimistic about people in the United States ever adopting a frugal lifestyle. America's excessive consumption is driven by several factors that are difficult to change. Consequently, the country's primary response to problems like climate change and obesity will be adaption rather than mitigation, but this will generate serious equity problems both at home and abroad. See Robert Paarlberg, *The United States of Excess: Gluttony and the Dark Side of American Exceptionalism* (New York: Oxford University Press, 2015).

123 See Michael Lewis, "A Simple Plan to Save the World," *Bloomberg Business Week*, May 9/May 15, 2016, 12–14, where the case is made to put the financial sector back into the market, where failure is possible as it is in the rest of the economy; Peter Coy, "The Curse of the Big Bad Rut," *Bloomberg Business Week*, May 16/May 22, 2016, 12–14, that reviews the argument of Larry Summers, the Harvard economist, who argues that monetary policy alone cannot revive growth and needs to be supplemented with a strong fiscal policy; Martin Feldstein, "The Fed's Unconventional Monetary Policy," *Foreign Affairs*, Vol. 95, No. 3 (May/June, 2016), 105–115, who argues that the Fed's unconventional policy of quantitative easing has done little to mitigate the growing risk of financial instability; Scott Summer, "The Fed and the Great Recession," *Foreign Affairs*, Vol. 95, No. 3 (May/June 2016), 116–125, who thinks that if the Fed had acted decisively back in 2008, the financial crisis would have been far less severe; Rana Foroohar, "Saving Capitalism," *Time*, May 23, 2016, who argues that financialization that has permeated much of American business is the problem as the financial system has stopped serving the real economy and now serves mainly itself; Niall Ferguson, *The Great Degeneration: How Institutions Decay and Economies Die* (New York: Penguin Press, 2012), who thinks of the Great Degeneration as public debt where the older generation lives at the expense of the young and unborn, dysfunctional regulation, parasitic lawyers, and a civil society that withers into a no-man's-land between corporate interests and big government; and Roberts, *The Failure of Laissez Faire Capitalism*, who argues that globalism and financial concentration have destroyed the justifications for market capitalism, that too-big-too fail corporations that are sustained by public subsidies have destroyed capitalism's claim to allocate resources efficiently and that profits are no longer a measure of social welfare when they are attained by creating unemployment and declining living standards. The books and articles on capitalism just keep on coming.

124 Michael Kazin, "Editor's Page," *Dissent*, Spring 2014, 1.

125 Anthony Simon Laden, "Transcendence without God: On Atheism and Invisibility," in Louise M. Antomy, ed., *Philosophers without Gods: Meditations on Atheism and the Secular Life* (New York: Oxford University Press, 2010), 121–129.

126 Ibid., 126–132.

127 Ophuls, 51–52.

128 This change of focus has legal implications as shareholders have the right to file lawsuits based on the duty of managers to seek the highest possible financial return for the shareholders of the corporation. But a new Maryland law allows

for the creation of a new kind of company called a "benefit corporation" and gives it greater protection from such lawsuits. This kind of company would be created to attract investors with a social agenda. The states of Vermont and California were considering similar measures. See John Tozzi, "Is There More to Business than Profits?" *The Week*, May 7, 2010, 42.

129 Robert A. Giacalone and Kenneth R. Thompson, "Business Ethics and Social Responsibility Education: Shifting the Worldview," *Learning and Education*, Vol. 5 (September, 2006), 267.

130 A similar view is expressed by Marcus et al., in an article in *Business and Society*, where they describe the embedded view of the business–society–nature interface, where business is seen to exist within society and society within the broader natural environment. The business and societal systems do not merely overlap, but the business system is completely enveloped within the societal sphere and is not considered to be equal to society but is rather a component nested within the larger social system. See Joel Marcus, Elizabeth C. Kurucz, and Barry A. Colbert, "Conceptions of the Business-Society-Nature Interface: Implications for Management Scholarship," *Business and Society*, Vol. 49 (September 2010), 402–438.

131 Matthew Stewart, *The Management Myth: Debunking Modern Business Philosophy* (New York: W.W. Norton & Company, 2009), 12.

132 Paul Craig Roberts, a former assistant secretary of the Treasury during the Reagan administration, states that natural capital is treated as a free good in contemporary economic theory, and the use of natural capital is not considered to be a cost but as an increase in output. "The ruthless exploitation of nature's capital sacrifices the long-run sustainability of life in order to raise the consumption levels for a few generations. The depletion of natural resources and the pollution of air, water, and soil bite back in the end, and the ability of the planet to sustain life collapses." See Roberts, *The Failure of Laissez Faire Capitalism*, 66–68.

133 Marjorie Kelly, the cofounder and publisher of *Business Ethics*, has this to say on the subject: "After more than a decade of advocating social responsibility and seeing its promise often thwarted, I've come to ask myself, *What is blocking change*? The answer is now obvious to me. It's the mandate to maximize return for shareholders, which means serving the interests of wealth before all other interests. It is a system wide mandate that cannot be overcome by individual companies. It is a legal mandate with which voluntary change can't compete. This mandate, quite simply, is a form of discrimination: wealth discrimination. It is rooted in an ancient, aristocratic worldview that says those who own the property or wealth are superior. It is a form of entitlement out of place in a market economy . . . The time has come to recognize that corporations are not just pieces of property but are something more complex and alive, requiring a more nuanced set of human rights. Shareholder property rights can remain in some measure, but they must take their place alongside property rights for employees and the community. Aristocratic privilege must give way to economic equality, in a new corporate order that recognizes a constellation of economic rights." See Marjorie Kelly, *The Divine Right of Capital: Dethroning the Corporate Aristocracy* (San Francisco, CA: Berrett-Koehler Publishers, 2001), xii–xiii, 96.

134 See Adolf A. Berle and Gardiner C. Means, *The Modern Corporation and Private Property* (New York: Macmillan, 1932).

135 Harvey, *Capitalism*, 220–221. Italics in original.

136 "While people need a just economy for their self-respect and national pride . . . justice is not everything people need from their economy. They need an economy that is good as well as just . . . the good life involves using one's

imagination, exercising one's creativity, taking fascinating journeys into the unknown, and acting on the world—an experience I call flourishing. These gains are gains in experience, not in material reward, though material gains may be a means to the nonmaterial ends . . . We will have to turn from the classical fixation on wealth accumulation and efficiency to a modern economics that places imagination and creativity at the center of economic life." See Edmund Phelps, "What Is Wrong with the West's Economies?" *The New York Review*, August 13, 2015, 54–56.

Selected Bibliography

Adorno, Theodor and Max Horkheimer. *Dialectic of Enlightenment*, trans. John Cumming. New York: Continuum, 1990.

Albert, Michael and Robin Hahnel. *Marxism and Socialist Theory*. New York: South End Press, 1981.

Albert, Michael and Robin Hahnel. *Socialism Today and Tomorrow*. New York: South End Press, 1999.

Allegretti, J.G. *Loving Your Job, Finding Your Passion: Work and the Spiritual Life*. New York: Paulist Press, 2000.

Allen, Tom. *Dangerous Convictions: What's Really Wrong with the U.S. Congress*. New York: Oxford University Press, 2013.

Althusser, Louis. *Politics and History*. New York: Verso, 2007.

Althusser, Louis and Etienne Balibar. *Reading Capital*. London: Verso, 2009.

Anastopoulos, Charis. *Particle or Wave: The Evolution of the Concept of Matter in Modern Physics*. Princeton, NJ: Princeton University Press, 2008.

Anderson, Perry. *Spectrum: From Right to Left in the World of Ideas*. New York: Verso, 2005.

Antony, Louise M., ed. *Philosophers without Gods: Meditations on Atheism and the Secular Life*. New York: Oxford University Press, 2007.

Barlett, Donald L. and James B. Steele. *The Betrayal of the American Dream*. New York: Public Affairs, 2012.

Barrett, Vincent. *Marx*. New York: Routledge, 2009.

Barrow, John D. *New Theories of Everything*. New York: Oxford University Press, 2007.

Bauman, Zygmunt. *Does Ethics Have a Chance in a World of Consumers?* Cambridge, MA: Harvard University Press, 2008.

Beauregard, Mario. *Brain Wars*. New York: HarperOne, 2012.

Beiser, Frederick C. *After Hegel: German Philosophy 1840–1900*. Princeton, NJ: Princeton University Press, 2014.

Bell, Daniel. *The Cultural Contradictions of Capitalism*. New York: Basic Books, 1976.

Bennett, Jeffry. *Beyond UFOs: The Search for Extraterrestrial Life and Its Astonishing Implications for Our Future*. Princeton, NJ: Princeton University Press, 2008.

Berkowitz, Roger and Taun N. Toay, eds. *The Intellectual Origins of the Global Financial Crisis*. New York: Fordham University Press, 2012.

Berle, Adolf A. and Gardiner C. Means. *The Modern Corporation and Private Property*. New York: Macmillan, 1932.

Berliner, Michael S., ed. *Understanding Objectivism: A Guide to Learning Ann Rand's Philosophy*. New York: New American Library, 2012.

Berman, Morris. *The Reenchantment of the World*. Ithaca, NY: Cornell University Press, 1981.

Blaker, Kimberly. *The Fundamentals of Extremism: The Christian Right in America*. New Boston, MI: New Boston Books, 2003.

Bohm, David. *Wholeness and the Implicate Order*. London: Routledge & Kegan Paul, 1980.

Boltanski, Luc and Eve Chiapello. *The New Spirit of Capitalism*. New York: Verso, 2007.

Bowie, Andres. *Adorno and the Ends of Philosophy*. Cambridge, UK: Polity Press, 2013.

Brockman, John, ed. *Science at the Edge: Conversations with the Leading Scientific Thinkers of Today*. New York: Union Square Press, 2008.

Brockway, George P. *The End of Economic Man: An Introduction to Humanistic Economics*. New York: W.W. Norton, 2001.

Bronk, Richard. *Progress and the Invisible Hand*. London: Warner Books, 1998.

Brown, Brandon. *Planck: Driven by Vision, Broken by War*. New York: Oxford University Press, 2015.

Brown, Joseph Epps. *The Spiritual Legacy of the American Indian*. Bloomington, IN: World Wisdom, 2007.

Buchan, James. *The Authentic Adam Smith: His Life and Ideas*. New York: W.W. Norton, 2006.

Buchanan, James. *The Demand and Supply of Public Goods*. Chicago, IL: Rand McNally, 1968.

Buchholz, Rogene A. *Rethinking Capitalism: Community and Responsibility in Business*. New York: Routledge, 2009.

Buchholz, Rogene A. *Reforming Capitalism: The Scientific Worldview and Business*. New York: Routledge, 2012.

Capra, Frank. *The Web of Life: A New Scientific Understanding of Living Systems*. New York: Anchor Doubleday, 1996.

Carroll, Sean. *From Eternity to Here: The Quest for the Ultimate Theory of Time*. New York: Dutton, 2010.

Cassidy, John. *How Markets Fail: The Logic of Economic Calamities*. New York: Farrar, Straus and Giroux, 2009.

Chopra, Deepak and Leonard Mlodinow. *War of the Worldviews: Science vs Spirituality*. New York: Harmony Books, 2011.

Clegg, Brian. *Final Frontier: The Pioneering Science and Technology of Exploring the Universe*. New York: St. Martin's Press, 2014.

Cohen, Marshall, Thomas Nagel, and Thomas Scanlon, eds. *Marx, Justice, and History*. Princeton NJ: Princeton Press, 1980.

Cooper, Julie E. *Secular Powers: Humility in Modern Political Thought*. Chicago, IL: University of Chicago Press, 2013.

Cortright, S.A. and Michael J. Naughton. *Rethinking the Purpose of Business*. Notre Dame, IN: University of Notre Dame Press, 2002.

Coyne, Jerry A. *Faith vs Fact: Why Science and Religion are Incompatible*. New York: Viking, 2015.

Das, Satyajit. *The Age of Stagnation: Why Perpetual Growth Is Unattainable and the Global Economy Is in Peril*. Amherst, NY: Prometheus Books, 2016.

Davies, Paul and Niels Henrik Gregersen, eds. *Information and the Nature of Reality: From Physics to Metaphysics*. New York: Cambridge University Press, 2010.

Dawkins, Richard. *The God Delusion*. New York: Houghton Mifflin, 2006.

Dawson, Christopher. *Progress and Religion: An Historical Inquiry*. London: Sheed & Ward, 1929.

Deloria, Vine Jr. *God Is Red: A Native View of Religion*. Golden, CO: Fulcrum Publishing, 1994.

Dennett, Daniel C. *Breaking the Spell: Religion as a Natural Phenomenon*. New York: Viking, 2006.

Deresiewicz, William. *Excellent Sheep: The Miseducation of the American Elite*. New York: Free Press, 2014.

Dewey, John. *Essays in Experimental Logic*. New York: Dover Publications, 1916.

Dewey, John. *A Common Faith*. New Haven, CT: Yale University Press, 1934.

Dewey, John. *The Quest for Certainty: A Study of the Relation between Knowledge and Action*. New York: Capricorn Books, 1960.

Dewey, John. "Ethics," in *The Middle Works, 1899–1924*, Vol. 5, Jo Ann Boydston, ed. Carbondale and Edwardsville, IL: University of Southern Illinois Press, 1978.

Dewey, John. "Theories of Knowledge," in *The Middle Works, 1916*, Vol. 9, Jo Ann Boydston, ed. Carbondale and Edwardsville, IL: University of Southern Illinois Press, 1980.

Dewey, John. "Experience and Nature," in *The Later Works, 1925–1953*, Vol. 1, Jo Ann Boydston, ed. Carbondale and Edwardsville, IL: University of Southern Illinois Press, 1981.

Dewey, John. "The Crisis in Culture," in *The Later Works, 1925–1953*, Vol. 5, Jo Ann Boydston, ed. Carbondale and Edwardsville, IL: University of Southern Illinois Press, 1984.

Dewey, John. "The Public and Its Problems," in *The Later Works, 1925–1953*, Vol. 2, Jo Ann Boydston, ed. Carbondale and Edwardsville, IL: University of Southern Illinois Press, 1984.

Dewey, John. "The Seat of Intellectual Authority," in *The Middle Works, 1899–1924*, Vol. 4, Jo Ann Boydston, ed. Carbondale and Edwardsville, IL: University of Southern Illinois Press, 1984.

Dewey, John. "Authority and Social Change," in *The Later Works, 1925–1953*, Vol. 11, Jo Ann Boydston, ed. Carbondale and Edwardsville, IL: University of Southern Illinois Press, 1987.

Dewey, John. "The Objectivism-Subjectivism of Modern Philosophy," in *The Later Works, 1925–1953*, Vol. 14, Jo Ann Boydston, ed. Carbondale and Edwardsville, IL: University of Southern Illinois Press, 1988.

Dewey, John. "Time and Individuality," in *The Later Works, 1925–1953*, Vol. 14, Jo Ann Boydston, ed. Carbondale and Edwardsville, IL: University of Southern Illinois Press, 1988.

Dionne, E. J. Jr. *Our Divided Political Heart: The Battle for the American Idea in an Age of Discontent*. New York: Bloomsbury, 2012.

Druat, Tamara. *Sleeping Giant: How the New Working Class Will Transform America*. New York: Doubleday, 2016.

Durning, Alan. *How Much Is Enough?* New York: Norton, 1992.

Eagleton, Terry. *Why Marx Was Right*. New Haven, CT: Yale University Press, 2011.

Etzioni, Amitai. *The Moral Dimension: Toward a New Economics*. New York: The Free Press, 1988.

Falwell, Jerry. *Listen America*. New York: Doubleday-Galilee, 1980.

Ferguson, Niall. *The Great Degeneration: How Institutions Decay and Economies Die*. New York: Penguin Press, 2012.

Ferris, Timothy, ed. *The World Treasury of Physics, Astronomy and Mathematics*. Boston, MA: Little Brown and Company, 1991.

Ferris, Timothy. *The Science of Liberty: Democracy, Reason, and the Laws of Nature*. New York: HarperCollins, 2010.

Filken, David. *Stephen Hawking's Universe: The Cosmos Explained*. New York: Basic Books, 1997.

Flanagan, Owen. *The Really Hard Problem: Meaning in a Material World*. Cambridge, MA: MIT Press, 2007.

Flowers, Charles A. *A Science Odyssey: 100 Years of Discovery*. New York: William Morrow & Company, 1998.

Folse, Henry J. *The Philosophy of Niels Bohr: The Framework of Complementarity*. Amsterdam: North-Holland, 1985.

Fox, Justin. *The Myth of the Rational Market: A History of Risk, Reward, and Delusion on Wall Street*. New York: HarperCollins, 2009.

Fox, Matthew and Rupert Sheldrake. *Natural Grace: Dialogues on Creation, Darkness, and the Soul in Spirituality and Science*. New York: Doubleday, 1997.

Frederick, William C. *Values, Nature and Culture in the American Corporation*. New York: Oxford University Press, 1995.

Frederick, William C. *Corporation Be Good!* Indianapolis, IN: Dog Ear Publishing, 2006.

Fukuyama, Francis. *The End of History and the Last Man*. New York: Free Press, 1992.

Galbraith, James K. *Inequality and Instability*. New York: Oxford University Press, 2012.

Galbraith, John Kenneth. *The New Industrial State:* Boston, MA: Houghton-Mifflin, 1967.

Gardner, Gary T. *Inspiring Progress: Religion's Contribution to Sustainable Development*. New York: W.W. Norton, 2006.

Gaustad, Edwin S., Philip L. Barlow, and Richard Dishno, eds. *New Historical Atlas of Religion in America*. New York: Oxford University Press, 2001.

Gewirth, Alan. *The Community of Rights*. Chicago, IL: University of Chicago Press, 1996.

Giacalone, Robert A. and Carole L. Jurkiewicz. *Handbook of Workplace Spirituality and Organizational Performance*. 2nd ed. New York: M.E. Sharpe, 2010.

Gilchrist, John. *The Church and Economic Activity in the Middle Ages*. London: Macmillan, 1969.

Gillespie, John and David Zweig. *Money for Nothing: How the Failure of Corporate Boards Is Ruining American Business and Costing Us Trillions*. New York: Free Press, 2010.

Gilpin, Robert. *The Political Economy of International Relations*. Princeton, NJ: Princeton University Press, 1987.

Goudzwaard, Bob. *Capitalism & Progress: A Diagnosis of Western Society*. Toronto: Wedge Publishing Foundation; Grand Rapids, MI: William B. Eerdmans, 1978.

Greenberg, Edward S. *Capitalism and the American Political Ideal*. New York: M.E. Sharpe. 1985.

Greider, William. *The Soul of Capitalism: Opening Paths to a Moral Economy*. New York: Simon & Schuster, 2003.

Griswold, Charles L. Jr. *Adam Smith and the Virtues of Enlightenment*. Cambridge, UK: Cambridge University Press, 1999.

Guillory W.A. *Spirituality in the Workplace*. Salt Lake City, UT: Innovations International, 2000.

Hacker, Jacob S. and Paul Pierson. *Winner-Take-All Politics: How Washington Made the Rich Richer—and Turned Its Back on the Middle Class*. New York: Simon & Schuster, 2010.

Handy, Robert T. *The Social Gospel in America 1870–1920*. New York: Oxford University Press, 1966.

Haque, Umair. *The New Capitalist Manifesto: Building a Disruptively Better Business*. Cambridge, MA: Harvard Business Press, 2011.

Harcourt, Bernard E. *The Illusion of Free Markets*. Cambridge, MA: Harvard University Press, 2011.

Harris, Sam. *The End of Faith: Religion, Terror, and the Future of Reason*. New York: W.W. Norton, 2004.

Harvey, David A. *A Companion to Mars's Capital*. London: Verso, 2010.

Harvey, David A. *The Enigma of Capital and the Crisis of Capitalism*. 2nd ed. New York: Oxford University Press, 2011.

Harvey, David A. *Seventeen Contradictions and the End of Capitalism*. New York: Oxford University Press, 2014.

Hassard, John and Martin Parker, eds. *Postmodernism and Organizations*. London: Sage, 1993.

Hausman, Daniel M. and Michael S. McPherson. *Economic Analysis, Moral Philosophy, and Public Policy*. 2nd ed. New York: Cambridge University Press, 2006.

Hayek, F.A. *The Road to Serfdom: Text and Documents*. Chicago, IL: University of Chicago Press, 2007.

Heisenberg, Werner. *Physics and Philosophy: The Revolution in Modern Science*. New York: Harper Perennial, 1958.

Hickman, Larry A. *John Dewey's Pragmatic Technology*. Bloomington, IN: Indiana University Press, 1992.

Hickman, Larry A. *Pragmatism as Post-Postmodernism*. New York: Fordham University Press, 2007.

Higgs, Eric, Light Andrew, and David Strong. *Technology and the Good Life*. Chicago, IL: University of Chicago Press, 2000.

Hitchens, Christopher. *God Is Not Great: How Religion Poisons Everything*. New York: Twelve Books, 2007.

Holmes, Richard. *The Age of Wonder: How the Romantic Generation Discovered the Beauty and Terror of Science*. New York: Pantheon Books, 2006.

Honneth, Axel. *The Critique of Power: Reflective Stages in a Critical Social Theory*. Cambridge, MA: MIT Press, 1991.

Hospers, John. *Libertarianism*. Los Angeles, CA: Nash, 1971.

Hume, David. *Essays Moral, Political, and Literary*. London: Longmans, Green & Co. 1875.

Hume, David. *A Treatise of Human Nature*. Oxford: Clarendon Press, 1896.

Ingram, David and Julia Simon-Ingram, eds. *Critical Theory: The Essential Readings*. St. Paul, MN: Paragon House, 1991.

Jacquette, Dale. *The Philosophy of Mind: The Metaphysics of Consciousness*. New York: Continuum, 2009.

James, William. *The Will to Believe and Other Essays: The Works of William James*. Frederick Burkhardt, ed. Cambridge, MA: Harvard University Press, 1979.

Johnson-DeBaufre, Melanie, Kathrine Keller, and Elais Ortega-Aponte, eds. *Common Goods: Economy, Ecology, and Political Theology*. New York: Fordham University Press, 2015.

Jordan, Stuart. *The Enlightenment Vision*. Amherst NY: Prometheus Books, 2012.

Judson, Bruce. *It Could Happen Here: America on the Brink*. New York: Harper-Collins, 2009.

Kaiser, Robert G. *So Damn Much Money: The Triumph of Lobbying and the Corrosion of American Government*. New York: Knopf, 2010.

Kant, Immanuel. *Foundations of the Metaphysics of Morals*, trans. L.W. Beck. Indianapolis, IN: Bobbs-Merrill, 1959.

Kaufman, Stuart A. *Reinventing the Sacred: A New View of Science, Reason, and Religion*. New York: Basic Books, 2008.

Kelley, Marjorie. *The Divine Right of Capital: Dethroning the Corporate Aristocracy*. San Francisco, CA: Berrett-Koehler Publishers, 2001.

Kennedy, Allan A. *The End of Shareholder Value: Corporations at the Crossroads*. Cambridge, MA: Perseus, 2000.

Kournay, Janet A., ed. *Scientific Knowledge*. 2nd ed. Belmont, CA: Wadsworth Publishing, 1998.

Krugman, Paul. *The Return of Depression Economics and the Crisis of 2008*. New York: W.W. Norton, 2009.

Kuhn, Thomas S. *The Copernican Revolution: Planetary Astronomy in the Development of Western Thought*. New York: MJF Books, 1985.

Kuhn, Thomas S. *The Structure of Scientific Revolutions*. 3rd ed. Chicago, IL: University of Chicago Press, 1996.

Kuttner, Robert. *The Squandering of America*. New York: Knopf, 2007.

Langsam, Harold. *The Wonder of Consciousness: Understanding the Mind through Philosophical Reflection*. Cambridge, MA: MIT Press, 2011.

LaPiere, Richard. *The Freudian Ethic*. New York: Duell Sloan and Pearce, 1959.

Lasch, Christopher. *The Culture of Narcissism: American Life in an Age of Diminishing Expectations*. New York: Norton, 1978.

Laughlin, Robert B. *A Different Universe: Reinventing Physics from the Bottom Down*. New York: Basic Books, 2005.

Llewellyn, Vaughan-Lee, ed. *Spiritual Ecology: The Cry of the Earth*. Point Reyes, CA: The Golden Sufi Center, 2013.

Lerner, Michael. *The Politics of Meaning: Restoring Hope and Possibility in an Age of Cynicism*. Reading, MA: Addison-Wesley, 1996.

Lewin, Roger. *Complexity: Life at the Edge of Chaos*. Chicago, IL: University of Chicago Press, 1999.

Lewis, C.I. *Mind and the World Order*. New York: Dover Publications, 1929.

Lewis, Michael. *The Big Short: Inside the Doomsday Machine*. New York: W.W. Norton, 2010.

Lewontin, Richard. *The Triple Helix: Gene, Organism and Environment*. Cambridge, MA: Harvard University Press, 2000.

Lincoln, Bruce. *Holy Terrors: Thinking about Religion after September 11*. Chicago, IL: University of Chicago Press, 2004.

Lind, Michael. *Land of Promise: An Economic History of the United States*. New York: HarperCollins, 2012.

Locke, John. *Two Treatises of Government*. Cambridge, UK: Cambridge University Press, 1988.

Lynch, Michael P. *In Praise of Reason*. Cambridge, MA: MIT Press, 2012.

Magdoff, Fred and John Bellamy Foster. *What Every Environmentalist Needs to Know about Capitalism*. New York: Monthly Review Press, 2011.

Marglin, Stephen A. *The Dismal Science: How Thinking Like an Economist Undermines Community*. Cambridge, MA: Harvard University Press, 2008.

Martinez, Mark A. *The Myth of the Free Market: The Role of the State in a Capitalist Economy*. Sterling, VA: Kumarian Press, 2009.

Mayer, Jane. *Dark Money: The Hidden History of the Billionaires Behind the Rise of the Radical Right*. New York: Doubleday, 2016.

McCelland, David C. *The Achieving Society*. New York: The Free Press, 1961.

McKeon, Richard, ed. *The Basic Works of Aristotle*. New York: The Modern Library, 2001.

McKibben, Bill. *The End of Nature*. New York: Random House, 1989.

Mead, George Herbert. *Movements of Thought in the Nineteenth Century*. Merritt Moore, ed. Chicago, IL: University of Chicago Press, 1936.

Mead, George Herbert. *Philosophy of the Act*. Chicago, IL: University of Chicago Press, 1938.

Mead, George Herbert. *The Philosophy of the Present*. La Salle, IL: Open Court, 1959.

Mead, George Herbert. *Mind, Self, and Society*. Charles Morris, ed. Chicago, IL: University of Chicago Press, 1994.

Measuring the Immeasurable: The Scientific Case for Spirituality. Boulder, CO: Sounds True, 2008.

Merleau-Ponty, Maurice. *The World of Perception*, trans. Oliver Davis. New York: Routledge, 2008.

Michaelson, Adam. *The Foreclosure of America: Life Inside Countrywide Home Loans and the Selling of the American Dream*. New York: Berkley Books, 2010.

Mill, John Stuart. *Utilitarianism*. Oskar Piest, ed. Indianapolis, IN: Bobbs-Merrill, 1957.

Mitchell, Lawrence E. *The Speculation Economy: How Finance Triumphed Over Industry*. San Francisco, CA: Berrett-Koehler Publishers, 2007.

Moore, G.E. *Principia Ethica*. Cambridge, UK: Cambridge University Press, 1903.

Morris, Charles R. *The Two Trillion Dollar Meltdown: Easy Money, High Rollers, and the Great Credit Crash*. New York: Public Affairs, 2008.

Muller, Jerry Z. *Adam Smith in His Time and Ours*. Princeton, NJ: Princeton University Press, 1993.

Muller, Jerry Z. *The Mind and the Market: Capitalism in Modern European Thought*. New York: Anchor, 2003.

Nagel, Thomas. *The View from Nowhere.* Oxford: Oxford University Press, 1986.

Nagel, Thomas. *Mind and Cosmos: Why the Materialistic Neo-Darwinian Conception of Nature Is Almost Certainly False.* New York: Oxford University Press, 2012.

Nasar, Sylvia. *Grand Pursuit: The Story of Economic Genius.* New York: Simon & Schuster, 2011.

Nash, Roderick Frazier. *The Rights of Nature: A History of Environmental Ethics.* Madison, WI: University of Wisconsin Press, 1989.

Needleman, Jacob. *An Unknown World: Notes of the Meaning of the Earth.* New York: Tarcher/Penguin, 2012.

Nelson, Julie A. *Economics for Humans.* Chicago, IL: University of Chicago Press, 2006.

Nussbaum, Martha C. *Not for Profit: Why Democracy Needs the Humanities.* Princeton, NJ: Princeton University Press, 2010.

Onfray, Michael. *Atheist Manifesto: The Case against Christianity, Judaism, and Islam.* New York: Arcade Publishing, 2011.

Ophuls, William. *Plato's Revenge: Politics in the Age of Ecology.* Cambridge, MA: MIT Press, 2011.

Paarlberg, Robert. *The United States of Excess: Gluttony and the Dark Side of American Exceptionalism.* New York: Oxford University Press, 2015.

Patterson, Scott. *The Quants: How a New Breed of Math Wizzes Conquered Wall Street and Nearly Destroyed It.* New York: Crown Business, 2009.

Phillips, Kevin. *Bad Money: Reckless Finance, Failed Politics, and the Global Crisis of American Capitalism.* New York: Viking, 2008.

Pickover, Clifford A. *Archimedes to Hawking: Laws of Science and the Great Minds Behind Them.* New York: Oxford University Press, 2008.

Piketty, Thomas. *Capital in the Twenty-First Century.* Cambridge, MA: Belknap Press, 2014.

Polanyi, Karl. *The Great Transformation.* Boston, MA: Beacon Press, 1944.

Posner, Richard A. *A Failure of Capitalism: The Crisis of '08 and the Descent into Depression.* Cambridge, MA: Harvard University Press, 2009.

Posner, Richard A. *The Crisis of Capitalist Democracy.* Cambridge, MA: Harvard University Press, 2010.

Preston, Lee E. and James E. Post. *Private Management and Public Policy: The Principle of Public Responsibility.* Englewood Cliffs, NJ: Prentice Hall, 1975.

Prins, Nomi. *All the Presidents' Bankers: The Hidden Alliances That Drive American Power.* New York: Nation Books, 2014.

Ralston, Holmes III. *Philosophy Gone Wild: Essays in Environmental Ethics.* Buffalo, NY: Prometheus Books, 1987.

Rawls, John. *A Theory of Justice.* Cambridge, MA: Harvard University Press, 1971.

Reich, Robert B. *After-Shock: The Next Economy and America's Future.* New York: Alfred A. Knopf, 2010.

Reich, Robert B. *Saving Capitalism: For the Many, Not the Few.* New York: Alfred A. Knopf, 2015.

Reid-Henry, Simon. *The Political Origins of Inequality: Why a More Equal World Is Better for Us All.* Chicago, IL: The University of Chicago Press, 2015.

Repcheck, Jack. *Copernicus' Secret: How the Scientific Revolution Began.* New York: Simon & Schuster, 2007.

Ritter, Alan and Julia Conaway Bondanella, eds. *Rousseau's Political Writings*. New York: W.W. Norton, 1988.

Roberts, Paul Craig. *The Failure of Laissez Faire Capitalism*. Atlanta, GA: Clarity Press, 2013.

Rosanvallon, Pierre. *The Society of Equals*. Cambridge, MA: Harvard University Press, 2013.

Rosenberg, Alex. *The Atheist's Guide to Reality: Enjoying Life Without Illusions*. New York: W.W. Norton, 2011.

Rosenthal, Sandra B. *Speculative Pragmatism*. LaSalle, IL: Open Court, 1986.

Sachs, Jeffrey D. *The Price of Civilization: Reawakening American Virtue and Prosperity*. New York: Random House, 2011.

Sandel, Michael J. *Democracy's Discontent: America in Search of a Public Philosophy*. Cambridge, MA: Belknap Press, 1996.

Sandel, Michael J. *Justice: What's the Right Thing to Do?* New York: Farrar, Strauss & Giroux, 2009.

Searle, John R. *Mind: A Brief Introduction*. New York: Oxford University Press, 2004.

Shapin, Steven. *The Scientific Revolution*. Chicago, IL: University of Chicago Press, 1996.

Shermer, Michael. *The Science of Good and Evil*. New York: Times Books, 2004.

Sirkin, Gerald. *The Visible Hand: The Fundamentals of Economic Planning*. New York: McGraw-Hill, 1968.

Skidelsky, Robert and Edward Skidelsky. *How Much Is Enough: Money and the Good Life*. New York: Other Press, 2012.

Smith, Adam. *The Theory of Moral Sentiments*. New York: Arlington House, 1969.

Smith, Adam. *The Wealth of Nations*. New York: Bantam Dell, 2003.

Sperber, Jonathan. *Karl Marx: A Nineteenth-Century Life*. New York: Liveright Publishing Corporation. 2013.

Sprintzen, David. *Critique of Western Philosophy and Social Theory*. New York: Palgrave Macmillan, 2009.

Standing Bear, Luther. *Land of the Spotted Eagle*. Boston, MA: Houghton-Mifflin, 1993.

Steigler, Bernard. *The Decadence of Industrial Democracy*. Cambridge, UK: Polity Press, 2011.

Steigler, Bernard. *The Lost Spirit of Capitalism*. Cambridge, UK: Polity Press, 2014.

Steigler, Bernard. *The Re-Enchantment of the World: The Value of Spirit against Industrial Populism*. London: Bloomsbury, 2014.

Steinberg, Paul F. *Who Rules the Earth? How Social Rules Shape Our Planet and Our Lives*. New York: Oxford University Press, 2015.

Stenger, Victor J. *God the Failed Hypothesis: How Science Shows That God Does not Exist*. Amherst, NY: Prometheus Books, 2007.

Stenger, Victor J. *The New Atheism: Taking a Stand for Science and Reason*. Amherst, NY: Prometheus Books, 2009.

Stewart, Matthew. *The Management Myth: Debunking Modern Business Philosophy*. New York: W.W. Norton, 2009.

Stewart, Matthew. *Nature's God: The Heretical Origins of the American Republic*. New York: W.W. Norton, 2014.

Stiglitz, Joseph E. *Free Fall: America, Free Markets, and the Sinking of the World Economy*. New York: W.W. Norton, 2010.

Stiglitz, Joseph E. *The Price of Inequality: How Today's Divided Society Endangers Our Future*. New York: W.W. Norton, 2012.

Stiglitz, Joseph E. *The Great Divide: Unequal Societies and What We Can Do about Them*. New York: W.W. Norton, 2015.

Stockman, David A. *The Great Deformation: The Corruption of Capitalism in America*. New York: Public Affairs, 2013.

Susskind, Leonard. *The Cosmic Landscape: String Theory and the Illusion of Intelligent Design*. New York: Little-Brown, 2006.

Tawney, Robert H. *Religion and the Rise of Capitalism*. Gloucester, MA: P. Smith, 1962.

Taylor, Charles. *The Ethics of Authenticity*. Cambridge, MA: Harvard University Press, 1991.

Tucker, Robert C., ed. *The Marx-Engels Reader*. 2nd ed. New York: W.W. Norton, 1978.

Wautischer, Helmut, ed. *Ontology of Consciousness: Percipient Action*. Cambridge, MA: MIT Press, 2008.

Weber, Max. *The Protestant Ethic and the Spirit of Capitalism*. New York: Scribner's Sons, 1958.

Wendling, Amy. *Karl Marx on Technology and Alienation*. New York: Palgrave Macmillan, 2009.

Wills, Garry. *A Necessary Evil: A History of American Distrust of Government*. New York: Simon & Schuster, 1999.

Index